College Choices

A National Bureau
of Economic Research
Conference Report

College Choices
The Economics of Where to Go, When to Go, and How to Pay for It

Edited by **Caroline M. Hoxby**

The University of Chicago Press

Chicago and London

CAROLINE M. HOXBY is professor of economics at Harvard University. She is also director of the Economics of Education Program for the National Bureau of Economic Research (NBER) as well as a distinguished visiting fellow of the Hoover Institution. She is the editor of *The Economics of School Choice,* also published by the University of Chicago Press.

The University of Chicago Press, Chicago 60637
The University of Chicago Press, Ltd., London
© 2004 by the National Bureau of Economic Research
All rights reserved. Published 2004
Printed in the United States of America
13 12 11 10 09 08 07 06 05 04   1 2 3 4 5
ISBN: 0-226-35535-7 (cloth)

Library of Congress Cataloging-in-Publication Data

College choices : the economics of where to go, when to go, and how to
    pay for it / edited by Caroline M. Hoxby.
        p. cm. — (A National Bureau of Economic Research conference
    report)
    Includes bibliographical references and index.
    ISBN 0-226-35535-7 (alk. paper)
    1. College choice—Economic aspects—United States—
Congresses. 2. Student aid—United States—Congresses. 3. College
attendance—United States—Congresses. I. Hoxby, Caroline
Minter. II. National Bureau of Economic Research. III. Series.

LB2350.5.C647 2004

                                                         2004048030

Relation of the Directors to the
Work and Publications of the
National Bureau of Economic Research

1. The object of the NBER is to ascertain and present to the economics profession, and to the public more generally, important economic facts and their interpretation in a scientific manner without policy recommendations. The Board of Directors is charged with the responsibility of ensuring that the work of the NBER is carried on in strict conformity with this object.

2. The President shall establish an internal review process to ensure that book manuscripts proposed for publication DO NOT contain policy recommendations. This shall apply both to the proceedings of conferences and to manuscripts by a single author or by one or more co-authors but shall not apply to authors of comments at NBER conferences who are not NBER affiliates.

3. No book manuscript reporting research shall be published by the NBER until the President has sent to each member of the Board a notice that a manuscript is recommended for publication and that in the President's opinion it is suitable for publication in accordance with the above principles of the NBER. Such notification will include a table of contents and an abstract or summary of the manuscript's content, a list of contributors if applicable, and a response form for use by Directors who desire a copy of the manuscript for review. Each manuscript shall contain a summary drawing attention to the nature and treatment of the problem studied and the main conclusions reached.

4. No volume shall be published until forty-five days have elapsed from the above notification of intention to publish it. During this period a copy shall be sent to any Director requesting it, and if any Director objects to publication on the grounds that the manuscript contains policy recommendations, the objection will be presented to the author(s) or editor(s). In case of dispute, all members of the Board shall be notified, and the President shall appoint an ad hoc committee of the Board to decide the matter; thirty days additional shall be granted for this purpose.

5. The President shall present annually to the Board a report describing the internal manuscript review process, any objections made by Directors before publication or by anyone after publication, any disputes about such matters, and how they were handled.

6. Publications of the NBER issued for informational purposes concerning the work of the Bureau, or issued to inform the public of the activities at the Bureau, including but not limited to the NBER Digest and Reporter, shall be consistent with the object stated in paragraph 1. They shall contain a specific disclaimer noting that they have not passed through the review procedures required in this resolution. The Executive Committee of the Board is charged with the review of all such publications from time to time.

7. NBER working papers and manuscripts distributed on the Bureau's web site are not deemed to be publications for the purpose of this resolution, but they shall be consistent with the object stated in paragraph 1. Working papers shall contain a specific disclaimer noting that they have not passed through the review procedures required in this resolution. The NBER's web site shall contain a similar disclaimer. The President shall establish an internal review process to ensure that the working papers and the web site do not contain policy recommendations, and shall report annually to the Board on this process and any concerns raised in connection with it.

8. Unless otherwise determined by the Board or exempted by the terms of paragraphs 6 and 7, a copy of this resolution shall be printed in each NBER publication as described in paragraph 2 above.

Contents

Acknowledgments

The idea for this book grew out of discussions about the most interesting policy questions in higher education. Some of these discussions were informal, but the Teachers Insurance and Annuity Association–College Retirement Equity Fund (TIAA-CREF) Institute was generous enough to sponsor a formal forum for discussion in the fall of 2000 in Cambridge, Massachusetts. The forum was, in part, the brain child of John Biggs, then chairman, president, and CEO of TIAA-CREF, and Mark Warshawsky, then director of research for the TIAA-CREF Institute (now assistant secretary for economic policy in the United States Department of the Treasury). To ensure that we were hearing about the latest policy issues, the forum included talks by several people who were in the process of leading important policy initiatives: Gary T. Barnes, vice president for program assessment and public service at the University of North Carolina; Pat Callan, president of the National Center for Higher Education Policy; Terry Hartle, senior vice president and director of the Division of Government and Public Affairs at the American Council on Education; Timothy Lane, vice president of client services at TIAA-CREF; Dan Madzelan of the Office of Postsecondary Education, United States Department of Education; Gretchen Rigol, vice president of the College Board; and Rae Lee Siporin, director of admissions at the University of California, Los Angeles. Higher education thinkers and researchers from across the country were grateful for their insights and the way they focused us on important problems of the day.

One goal in writing this book was to be current; the other was to be rigorous about evidence. The participants at the conference helped us with the first goal; the discussants for the papers in this volume helped us with the second. They have distilled their thoughts here into a few pages, but they generously gave the authors a wealth of constructive criticism and many important leads. Better discussants than Charles Clotfelter, Thomas Dee, Jon Guryan, Michael McPherson, Harvey Rosen, Michael Rothschild, Bruce Sacerdote, Christopher Taber, and Michelle White could not have been found. The authors also want to acknowledge the comments and advice of Julian Betts, David Breneman, Paul Courant, Jerry Davis, John Kain, Elizabeth Kent, Martin Kurzweil, Sarah Levin, Joseph Meisel, Cara Nakamura, Derek Neal, Abigail Payne, Derek Price, Roger Schonfeld, and Randolph Waterfield. If there is one thing I have learned as I age, it is that great papers are founded in the blast furnace of a barrage of questions and suggestions. The authors and I are truly grateful for all the input that others have put into this book.

The authors and I wish especially to acknowledge the contribution of Martin Feldstein, whose support for and interest in the economics of higher education have been the driving forces behind not just this book but the growth of a vigorous, creative body of economists who work on higher education issues. Martin Feldstein has been invaluable.

I want also to thank Charles Clotfelter, not just for being a superb discussant but also for so ably leading the higher education group at the National Bureau of Economic Research (NBER). He has fostered the community and kept it interactive, though always constructive.

Many people helped transform the manuscript into a book. At the NBER, Helena Fitz-Patrick in publications kept the manuscript on the rails. She is a wonderful ally for an editor, and I thank her for her care and persistence. Amy Tretheway, Carl Beck, and Autumn Bennet made the conferences run so smoothly that I have trouble recalling the organizational duties I had. At the University of Chicago Press, Catherine Beebe and Peter Cavagnaro have guided us swiftly and skillfully through the review process. It has been a real pleasure to work with them. Amanda DeWees at Graphic Composition, Inc., was a scrupulous and thoughtful copyeditor. The authors went to work on the latest issues; they are grateful to everyone who has helped to make the book arrive quickly.

Finally, the authors would like to thank their families, whose support is so essential.

Introduction

Caroline M. Hoxby

It Is Not Just About Attending College Anymore

I, like the other authors of this book and, indeed, most Americans, was brought up on the idea that attending college was a crucial decision. How often did we hear someone say, "If only she had gone to college" or "It would have made all the difference if he had enrolled in college" or "I would have pursued a different career if I had not gone to college"? Most people believed in the transforming role of college attendance. Some people even invested it with mythic importance that was more emotional than analytic (e.g., "all Americans are descended from immigrants"). Nevertheless, I have no doubt that many of the statements we heard were true. There *was* a sizeable group of people who were just on the margin of attending or not attending college and for whom college was transforming. We probably all know at least a few people for whom college opened "a new heaven and a new earth," yet who might easily not have gone to college at all, had circumstances been a little different.

If there is one theme of this book, it is that this group of people no longer exists. Put more bluntly, it is not about *attending* college anymore. The simple margin of whether to attend is not where the action is. This is not to say that college is not transforming: It is, for some people, but they are apparently people whose *attendance* decision is not easily swayed by circumstances. This is not to say that college decisions are not important: They are, but the important decisions are more complicated. The action is not in *whether* a student attends, but *which college* he attends (in-state or out-of-

Caroline M. Hoxby is professor of economics at Harvard University, and director of the Economics of Education program and a research associate of the National Bureau of Economic Research.

state, two-year or four-year, more or less selective) and *how* he attends (continuously or sporadically, full-time or part-time, immediately after high school graduation or delayed). Simply put, it is not college attendance that is interesting, but college choices—thus the book's title.

Often, writers of introductions to multiauthor volumes dread the task of finding a common theme among the chapters while also doing justice to their diversity and richness. I am fortunate. My theme (it is not just about attending college anymore) simply fell out of the chapters that follow, distinct as they are. We did not begin writing this book with the plan of demonstrating that the attendance margin was no longer interesting. We began with two ideas. First, we wanted to illustrate what researchers could do with the best methods and latest available data on colleges. Recent years have witnessed great improvements on both fronts, and the advent of massive data sets based on students' records has allowed us to use exemplary empirical techniques. Second, we wanted to explore the newest, most underinvestigated topics in higher education. Some were underinvestigated because they dealt with very recent policies: education savings accounts, higher education tax credits, and state merit scholarships. Other topics were underinvestigated because they dealt with problems that, while not new, have only recently risen to prominence: the lack of persistence among college students and the role of out-of-state students at public universities. Still other topics were underinvestigated because data have been unavailable until the authors of this book gathered it for themselves: whether high merit students are swayed by the scholarships offered them, whether college mentoring programs work, whether the Pell Grant helps prevent students from dropping out of college, and whether one's college peers matter.

This book has its roots in a conference where we authors (and many other researchers) listened instead of spoke. We heard from chief practitioners of higher education: deans and provosts, college advisors, college admissions chiefs, designers of financial aid, and leaders of advocacy groups. They told us which new policies needed analysis, which old questions needed new answers, and which were the up-and-coming trends.

None of the participants at that conference suggested that the attendance margin had given place to other college choices. On the contrary, the practitioners mainly advised us to analyze policies that they (and we) believed had substantial effects on attendance. Conference participants would typically phrase their questions in terms of attendance—for instance, "How do states' merit scholarship programs affect attendance?" Even at the very recent conference where we presented these chapters, participants hesitated to announce that the attendance margin was passé, despite the evidence piling up around them. Yet, rereading these chapters, the conclusion is unescapable. Again and again, we learn that a new or important policy has little effect on attendance but does significantly affect students' other college choices.

What does it mean and why does it matter that the college attendance margin is passé? What it means is that opportunities to attend college have sufficiently expanded so that almost every young person who is eligible and likely to benefit from college does try it at some point, in some form. The vast majority of seventeen-year-olds in the United States claim that they plan to attend college, and the vast majority do. *How* and *when* they attend are another matter. Put another way, college education has an extensive margin and an intensive margin. It appears that the extensive margin is now exhausted, while the intensive margin remains active.

A skeptic might say that we have always known that the intensive margin was important and that I am belaboring the point. While I could see where the skeptic was coming from, I would have to disagree. On the one hand, many families do believe that intensive-margin decisions, like where and how to attend college, are important. Indeed, the fact that policies affect these decisions *demonstrates* that families are thinking about them. On the other hand, families have very little evidence on which to base their intensive-margin decisions, such as "Does it matter whether I attend college right away?" and "Does it matter whether I begin at a two- or four-year college?" and so on. Families are also not being helped by policymakers, many of whom talk exclusively about "access," attendance, and "making the thirteenth year of education universal." News flash to policymakers: The vast majority of Americans *are* getting through the access door, so your policies are mainly affecting what they do once inside it. Mind you, policymakers may be more much more alert to the intensive margin than they let on: It is diplomatic and democratic to ignore the distinctions among colleges and different patterns of college attendance. Nevertheless, the evidence in this book suggests that we need to learn how to assess policies on the basis of their effects on college choice, timing of attendance, and so on.

Contributors and Contributions

The fact that I can make such pronouncements with confidence is owing to the authors of this book, whose work is up to date in every way. They not only analyze the newest policies and questions but use the latest, best methods. Every chapter illustrates high-quality analysis. In econometric terms, the results are all well identified. The data are so up-to-date that several authors took "just-on-time" data delivery and wrote chapters that they could not have written a few months before.

Lest the authors get all the credit for their good methods and contemporaneity, let me gratefully acknowledge the vital work of the discussants and the higher education practitioners who spoke at the seminal conference. Our discussants played two key roles. First, they scoured papers for weaknesses in methods, data, and exposition. Their constructive criticism enabled authors to make the revisions that underlie every really good piece of research. Second, the discussants put the research in context, reminding us how the results fit into the larger questions troubling the higher education community. In the comments published in this volume, the reader will mainly see the discussants in their second role because their detailed criticisms were largely absorbed by the authors. We are *very* grateful to our discussants: Charles Clotfelter, Thomas S. Dee, Jonathan Guryan, Michael McPherson, Harvey S. Rosen, Michael Rothschild, Bruce Sacerdote, Christopher Taber, and Michelle J. White. We are also grateful to Derek Neal and Doug Staiger, whose conference comments were important to several authors.

The higher education practitioners who gave us a window on the latest concerns in higher education deserve much of the credit for the up-to-dateness of the book. They are too many to list, but we want especially to acknowledge Gary Barnes (University of North Carolina), Pat Callan (National Center for Higher Education Policy), Timothy Lane (Teachers Insurance and Annuity Association–College Retirement Equity Fund [TIAA-CREF], Dan Madzelan (U.S. Department of Education, Office of Postsecondary Education), Gretchen Rigol (The College Board), and Rae Lee Saporin (University of California, Los Angeles [UCLA]).

College Choices: What We Learned

Sarah Turner sets up the book by showing the big picture on college-going over the last thirty years. She starts with the observation that policy-makers tend to focus exclusively on getting students to start college, neglecting the question of whether they *complete* college. She demonstrates that this emphasis is misplaced because, although the rate of college *attendance* has risen significantly, the rate of college completion has been falling. Thus, despite their much higher attendance, today's high school graduates are only slightly more likely to complete college by age twenty-three than their 1970 counterparts. Also, many of today's students who eventually complete college progress through college very slowly, with sporadic course-taking and transfers among colleges. All this has occurred during two decades of steady increases in the return to college completion, which suggests that the employers need more college graduates. Employers apparently want prompt completers too: Students who complete college in a sporadic fashion have much lower earnings than those who complete it by age twenty-three.

Having demonstrated that a lack of demand for on-time college graduates is surely *not* the explanation for falling college completion, Turner investigates other explanations. Because of the large number of possible explanations, Turner does not attempt a definitive study of each. However, she does exclude some explanations—for instance, changing U.S. socio-demographics do *not* account for falling completion. She finds empirical evidence for several explanations, which are not mutually exclusive. For instance, some of the decrease in completion is due to the marginal college enrollee having lower aptitude than his earlier counterpart. Some of the decrease is due to federal financial aid having been increasingly focused on marginal enrollees. Additional decreases are due to states having increasingly focused their resources on their inexpensive two-year colleges as opposed to their four-year colleges. Turner leaves us with a question that is still largely open.

Conference participants were willing to propose a variety of other actors for blame. Some suggested that secondary schools were at fault because they had allowed the quality of college preparation to decline (even if the aptitude of the marginal attendee has declined only slightly). Others suggested that colleges were to blame because they increasingly facilitate sporadic attendance patterns by allowing students to pay on a per-course (as opposed to a per-semester) basis, liberally granting transfer credits, and not penalizing students for lack of timely progress. Still other participants focused on students' lack of realism about the skills and effort required by college.

Susan Dynarski explores state merit aid programs, which have swept through state legislatures, fast becoming state governments' most important form of support for higher education. Although the Georgia Helping Outstanding Pupils Educationally (HOPE) Scholarship is the best known state merit scholarship, similar programs now exist in most Southern states, some Southwestern states, and a smattering of other states, including Michigan. The typical program grants scholarships to all students with a certain grade point average (such as a B) and/or a certain score on college admission tests. The scholarships are good only at in-state colleges and are frequently generous enough to cover tuition at the state's public colleges.

Dynarski's first question is whether state merit scholarships raise college attendance. Carefully exploiting changes in the timing of the programs to identify their effects, she demonstrates that the typical merit aid program raised the enrollment rate by only 1.4 percentage points, an amount that is not statistically significantly different from zero. This lack of an effect suggests that the vast majority of students who get merit scholarships would have attended college anyway. She goes on to show, however, that merit scholarships do alter students' matriculation decisions. For instance, the scholarships induce students to "upgrade" from two-year colleges to four-year colleges.

Dynarski examines the distributional consequences of the merit aid programs, demonstrating that the typical program is somewhat regressive (they primarily benefit middle- and upper-income families but are paid for by taxes and lotteries that affect lower-income families) and that Georgia's

Hope Scholarship is dramatically regressive because students cannot simultaneously take it and a Pell Grant (a federal grant for poor students).

Dynarski and conference participants enjoyed animated speculation about the political popularity of merit aid programs, especially in Southern states, which are eager to catch up to and surpass the traditional education-oriented states of the Northeast and Midwest. All states can see that jobs are gravitating towards concentrations of well-educated workers, and the South is perhaps using merit aid as a way to efficiently focus its educational resources on students who are likely to succeed. Conference participants also wondered what will happen when all states have merit programs and realize that the game of keeping the "best and brightest" at home is a zero-sum game (or worse, because it implies inflexible, and thus inefficient, allocation of resources).

Bridget Long shows us that the Hope Credit and the Lifetime Learning Tax Credit (LLTC), enacted in 1998, will almost certainly become by far the largest federal programs for higher education. When everyone eligible for the credits discovers them and takes them up, the federal government will spend more on the credits than it does on the next two largest higher education programs *combined*. This is both because the credits are reasonably generous ($1,500 to $2,000) and because eligibility for the credits is very broad (a person who merely takes a recreational college course can be eligible). Long finds that the tax credits suffer from the slow information dispersal that plagues other aid programs: Take up of the credits was far below projections during their first three years, but participation is climbing at double-digit rates.

Long's first question is whether the credits increased postsecondary enrollment among eligible students. She finds that they did not. She then investigates whether the credits altered students' college choices: They did, causing students to "upgrade" to colleges with greater resources and higher tuition.

William Bennett is usually credited with the hypothesis that colleges attempt to "capture" financial aid and scholarships by raising tuition when government grants and loans become more generous.[1] Long points out that the tax credits have distinctive features that make them less likely to be captured than other government aid. Families receive the tax credits several months after paying college tuition, and the recipient of the credit is typically the parent, not the student. Nevertheless, Long carefully works out which colleges are most likely to engage in capture behavior. These turn out to be public colleges because they can coordinate tuition increases, which would be risky if undertaken unilaterally in the competitive college market. Long then shows that some states did raise their public colleges'

---

1. The Bennett hypothesis remains a popular idea, despite a lack of evidence to support it.

tuition in order to capture the federal credits, especially the tuition of colleges with many eligible students.

Conference participants debated whether the tax code is a good vehicle for federal aid to higher education. What seems undebatable is that it is an increasingly important vehicle.

This point is underscored by Jennifer Ma's study of the newly enacted education savings accounts, which encourage families to save for college expenses by allowing their savings contributions to accumulate tax free. In fact, education savings accounts are very similar to the familiar Roth Individual Retirement Account (IRA) except that the savings are to be spent on college, not retirement. The federal education savings accounts (Coverdell Accounts) allow families to save up to $2,000 per child per year. The state-sponsored education savings accounts (529 Plans) have no annual limit on savings and have high overall savings limits as well. Some 529 Plans even make contributions tax deductible. In short, education savings accounts should be extremely attractive savings vehicles for many families who face future college costs.

Some commentators worry that families will not save more when offered the chance to use education savings accounts: Perhaps they will merely move existing savings from regular accounts to education savings accounts. Such behavior would defeat the purpose of the accounts. Readers familiar with the literature on retirement will recognize that the same concern haunts IRAs and 401(k)s. Using new data that appear to be the *only* data that can address this concern, Ma shows us the first empirical evidence on the savings effect of the education savings accounts. To control for families' preexisting propensity to save, she employs several alternative techniques, including recently developed propensity score methods. Part of her study focuses particularly on families who already have IRA accounts. Since they are habitual savers already familiar with tax-advantaged savings accounts, they are perhaps the most likely to move existing savings into education savings accounts. Ma does *not* find evidence that education savings incentives reduce other household savings; Education savings accounts apparently do raise savings.

Conference participants thought that education savings accounts will eventually be an important prong of government support for higher education. If parents start saving when their child is small, not only will they enjoy substantial benefits, but their child will also know that he should prepare for college during his key years of secondary school. Observers have long speculated that teenagers who are unsure about whether their families are prepared to support them in college are teenagers who do not prepare well for college.

Poor students in the United States are eligible for the Pell Grant, which is intended to help them pay for college education without undue financial hardship. That is, the Pell Grant is designed to help students stay in college. Yet most previous studies of the Pell Grant suggest that it has no effect on college completion. Some studies have even claimed to find that the Pell Grant *reduces* college completion, leading observers to speculate that the Pell Grant might induce students to enroll in college frivolously so that they soon drop out. Eric Bettinger starts with this puzzle and demonstrates that previous studies do not account sufficiently for the fact that Pell Grant recipients are more likely to drop out of college ex ante.

Using unparalleled administrative data on every student in Ohio who applies for financial aid, Bettinger provides convincing estimates of how Pell Grants affect a student's probability of staying in college. Because he has complete administrative data, he is able to identify those students for whom the Pell Grant changed exogenously between their freshman and sophomore years (this occurs largely because a students' family composition changes through a sibling being born or leaving home). He finds that students whose Pell Grant rose were slightly more likely to stay in college; students whose Pell Grant fell were slightly less likely to stay in college. That is, the Pell Grant does appear to work as designed: It helps students stay in college. Bettinger concludes by noting that even if the Pell Grant does not have a dramatic positive effect on college completion, it is surely important to know that previous studies were wrong when they concluded that the Pell Grant induced students to drop out.

Conference participants were excited by the possibilities of data like Bettinger's, which allowed him to use empirical techniques that demand a great deal of data: simulated instrumental variables and regression discontinuity. Readers may enjoy Bettinger's chapter as much for the display of methods and data as for the results.

Hoxby and Avery investigate how students respond to the packages of financial aid and scholarships they are offered. They focus on high-aptitude students because such students are offered the most complex and attractive packages of aid. Interestingly enough, Hoxby and Avery had to create a survey and gather data from more than 3,200 students to research this question. This is because even very large surveys, such as the U.S. Department of Education's surveys of over 50,000 students, contain tiny numbers of high-aptitude students and are not oriented toward gathering the details of the complicated scholarship packages they are offered.

Using econometric methods especially suited to studying college choice (conditional logit), Hoxby and Avery identify how each student responds to his menu of college options, each with its own financial package and college characteristics. Their first question is whether college students seem broadly rational when making college choices. The answer is yes: The typical high-aptitude student is sensitive to college characteristics like tuition (lower tuition is more attractive) and the aptitude of fellow students (higher peer aptitude is more attractive). Although students from different backgrounds exhibit slightly different college choice behavior, the differences are not dramatic; most college choice behavior is shared by the entire array of high-aptitude students.

Hoxby and Avery go on to ask how students respond to the various components of their financial aid packages. They find that about two-thirds of students do alter their college choices in response to more generous grants, loans, and work-study. The remaining third appear to be indifferent to aid packages, largely because they are well off enough to be swayed by other college characteristics, such as the peer group and resources it offers.

Among the two-thirds of high-aptitude students whose decisions can be swayed by aid packages, about half respond to aid like "rational" investors in their own human capital, and half do not. The rational investors accept only aid offers that are more than generous enough to offset the reductions in college resources that are associated with the aid. The remaining students do not look like rational investors because they are excessively attracted by loans and work-study—for instance, they like a dollar of loans as much as a dollar of grants. They also are attracted by superficial aspects of a grant, like its being called a "scholarship" and its being front-loaded. They care more about the share of comprehensive costs that a grant covers than the actual amount of the grant.

Hoxby and Avery speculate about what explains the irrational students: naïveté or a simple lack of cash. Open-ended responses to their survey suggest that naïveté may be the more important explanation. Conference participants were divided in interpreting the results. Some thought the glass was half full: Most students seem to understand financial aid offers and act accordingly. Some thought the glass was half empty because aid packages seemed to confuse a substantial minority of students—and high-aptitude students at that.

Rizzo and Ehrenberg begin by observing that different state universities pursue very different strategies with respect to nonresident enrollment and in-state and out-of-state tuition levels. Some state flagship universities charge high out-of-state tuition and allow nonresidents to make up a significant minority of their students. They may do this in order to raise revenue, but they may also be using nonresident students to raise peer quality. Other state flagship universities pursue entirely different policies. Some sharply limit the number of out-of-state students. Some charge out-of-state tuition that is similar to in-state tuition. Some even sign tuition reciprocity agreements so that out-of-state students pay in-state tuition. What explains these diverse strategies? Rizzo and Ehrenberg explore explanations based on politics, demographics, income, history, university governance, and the local availability of private colleges.

The challenge Rizzo and Ehrenberg face is that colleges make a lot of decisions simultaneously. For instance, they do not choose their in-state tuition and student body first and only then turn to setting out-of-state tuition and admitting nonresidents. They have to take their out-of-state policies into account when setting their in-state policies and vice versa. Thus Rizzo and Ehrenberg must jointly estimate a college's choice of in-state tuition, out-of-state tuition, in-state admissions, out-of-state admissions, and tuition reciprocity agreements. This is a difficult problem, and the authors meet it by using a long panel of data. This allows them to see how colleges change their policies in response to changing circumstances. They also conducted their own survey of tuition reciprocity agreements.

Rizzo and Ehrenberg find that most public flagship universities seem not to use nonresident enrollment primarily as a revenue-generating strategy. Instead, the institutions appear to enroll nonresident students in an effort to raise their peer quality. The authors also find that state universities enroll nonresidents in order to achieve economies of scale in programs that would be too small for cost efficiency with in-state students only. Rizzo and Ehrenberg show population pressure probably explains why certain states strictly limit out-of-state students who could be a potential source of revenue. California, for instance, finds it hard to build colleges fast enough to cope with its growing student population. Conversely, states like Vermont have no population pressure and welcome out-of-state students. Conference participants were intrigued by the political and historical factors that make otherwise similar states, like Ohio and Michigan, pursue different strategies.

Avery and Kane are motivated by two puzzles that emerge from previous studies. First, students react much more to changes in tuition than they do to equivalent changes in aid or in the wage gain associated with college. This suggests that students pay more attention to tuition, which is easy to observe, than to costs and benefits of college that are more difficult to decipher. Second, survey data have long shown that students from low-income and minority families display a sort of cognitive dissonance about their likelihood of attending and completing college. Even when they are not taking the steps necessary to get into college, many say that they expect to get baccalaureate degrees.

In a major effort that combined surveying and mentoring, Avery and Kane collected data from three inner-city Boston high schools and a public high school in a middle to upper-income Boston suburb. The suburban students were simply surveyed, but inner-city students who expressed an interest in college were assigned to mentors who guided them through the college application process. The mentors were Harvard undergraduates, who are about as skilled in the application process as anyone could be. In fact, between their own recent experience and their training, the mentors were probably significantly better informed about applying to college than were the parents of the suburban students.

Avery and Kane first asked whether the suburban students started with better information about the costs and benefits of college. If they did, it might explain why they were taking concrete steps to get into college while inner-city students were not. This first result surprised Avery and Kane: The suburban and inner-city students had *very* similar information about the costs and benefits of going to college. The two groups had strikingly similar estimates of college tuition and the wage gain associated with college. In short, the evidence suggested that a simple information gap was not the problem and that the mentors would need to do more than relay information if they were to alter the behavior of inner-city students.

Avery and Kane then investigated whether mentoring, which included help with scheduling college admission exams and completing applications, raises an inner-city student's probability of enrolling in college. They find that it does.

Even so, a substantial minority of the inner-city students continued to exhibit a sort of cognitive dissonance. Even when mentored, they simultaneously failed to take adequate steps to get into college and *still* expressed a high degree of confidence about getting a baccalaureate degree.

Conference participants were wondered about longer term outcomes among the inner-city students who received mentoring. Will the mentoring simply have boosted their probability of attending? Will they quickly drop out or, instead, be more likely to attain their goal of a baccalaureate degree? These are questions that Avery and Kane must answer later; they were some of the authors who took just-on-time delivery of their data.

Finally, Winston and Zimmerman study peer effects in college. I have consciously kept back their study for the end of the book (and the end of this summary) because peers are a theme of almost sublime importance in the economics of college education. Until one has studied the choices of students and college, it is hard to appreciate why it matters so much whether peer effects exist and what they are like. If the reader looks back over the chapters already described, however, he will see that peers bob up again and again. They help explain why students upgrade when given tax credits, why states create merit scholarships to encourage students to stay in-state, why high-aptitude students receive the array of aid they do, and why public universities enroll nonresident students. Most studies of college education implicitly assume that peer effects exist, not because the researchers believe in peers per se, but because the researchers just cannot make sense of what they see unless they attribute some role to peers. This is Winston and Zimmerman's first point: They explain, in an admirably clear way, why it is so important that we learn about peer effects. They also explain why peer effects need to be nonlinear. I will leave the details to them, but I will briefly state that the colleges we see do not make sense unless some arrangements of peers produce more learning than others. If rearranging peers did not make any difference on net (one student's loss of a good peer was exactly offset by another student's gain of that peer), then the peer arrangements that we see would not arise.

Winston and Zimmerman provide us with some of the best evidence on peer effects in college. They use a "natural experiment" that takes place at all colleges that randomly assign freshmen roommates. A randomly assigned roommate is a randomly assigned peer. If a high-achieving peer is good for a student's own achievement, then being assigned a roommate with higher incoming achievement should raise his achievement. Observe that the natural experiment avoids a fundamental problem that can plague studies of peer effects: Most peers are *not* assigned randomly. A person's own choices affect who ends up being his friends and fellow students. Thus, it is normally hard to tell whether two high-achieving students are friends because their similarity drew them together or because they were friends first and then influenced one another.

Winston and Zimmerman show us the results from three such natural experiments (three different colleges). They also carefully survey the evidence from similar natural experiments in a few other colleges. They conclude that peer effects do exist, in the expected direction: a higher achieving peer is better for a student's own achievement. They also find some evidence that peer effects are nonlinear. Roughly speaking, middle-achieving students are sensitive to low-achieving peers, but high-achieving students are not. Also, high-achieving students are especially sensitive to one another.

The conference participants emphasized that evidence like Winston and Zimmerman's is just the tip of the iceberg. This is because roommates at a selective college vary only so much and because a student's roommate is only one of many peers with whom he interacts. If we could observe the full range of possible peer matchups, we might find much larger peer effects.

Next on the Agenda for the Economics of College Education

Reviewing these chapters makes me eagerly anticipate the next decade of economic research on college education. I cannot regret the passing of the era in which all research was expected to end in the question, "Did attendance increase?" While we will not neglect attendance, we will expect to look at a richer set of questions: which college to attend, when to attend it, and how to pay for it. Our data will undoubtedly continue to improve, and we should be able to provide evidence that allows both families and policy-makers to make their college choices better.

1

Going to College and Finishing College
Explaining Different Educational Outcomes

Sarah E. Turner

More students are attending college than ever before and the labor market rewards to completing a college degree have increased appreciably over the last quarter century. Yet, the rise in the incentives for collegiate completion has not been accompanied by an increase in the share of students making the transition from college enrollment to college completion.[1] Among individuals aged twenty-three in 1970, 23 percent of high school graduates had completed a BA degree, while about 51 percent had enrolled in college for some period since high school graduation. For the same age group in 1999, the share of high school graduates who had enrolled in college at some point rose substantially, to 67 percent, while the share receiving a BA degree rose only slightly, to 24 percent of the cohort. Thus, for college participants measured in their early twenties, completion rates fell by more than 25 percent over this interval. Completion rates measured at older ages are closer to stagnant, implying an overall increase in the time to degree.

It is the combination of collegiate attainment and time to degree that determines the overall supply of workers with college-level skills. The time it takes to complete a degree is an important economic variable in its own

Sarah E. Turner is associate professor of education and economics at the University of Virginia, and a faculty research fellow of the National Bureau of Economic Research.

1. This analysis will concentrate on the link between college enrollment and BA degree attainment; this is not to suggest that attaining a BA degree is the only collegiate credential relevant in the labor market. Data from the Beginning Postsecondary Students longitudinal survey indicate that five years after initial enrollment at four-year institutions, 2.9 percent of students received certificates, 4.2 percent of students received the associate degree and 53.3 percent of students received the BA degree; among students beginning at community colleges, 13.8 percent of students received a vocational certificate, 18.6 percent of students received the associate degree, and 6.1 percent of students received the BA degree within this time frame.

right. Delay in degree attainment implicitly lowers the supply of skilled workers to the economy. Moreover, even if individuals receive some consumption benefit by extending their time in college beyond the four-year norm, the public cost is sizable given the high degree of subsidy from state and federal sources. Implicitly, the opportunity cost of extended time to degree (in the absence of perfect elasticity of supply in the collegiate market) is that other students may be denied college opportunities.

That a college education is more important now than ever is certainly cliché, though it is borne out by the overall increase in the college wage premium. The value of a college degree in the labor force has increased substantially, rising from a premium over a high school degree of about 40 percent in 1980 to over 65 percent two decades later.[2] Reduced growth in the supply of college-educated workers may hamper long-term increases in productivity while also increasing the degree of inequality in earnings. How the higher education market transforms student enrollment into collegiate attainment, including degrees conferred, is fundamental to understanding the determinants of the supply of college-educated workers.

It is surprising that collegiate attainment and time to degree have not received more attention. With few exceptions, recent discussions in policy circles have focused on questions related to *access,* loosely defined as the extent to which individuals from different circumstances enroll in college, to the near exclusion of questions of attainment. Emphasis on vaguely defined notions of "collegiate access and affordability" in public discourse has diverted attention from the monitoring of outcomes, such as courses completed and degrees awarded. Enrollment rates are, of course, an important measure of college entry, but they do not provide a measure of the degree to which students and colleges are able to transfer time and resources to completed courses, years of attainment, or degrees earned. These outcomes are measures of human capital acquired and, while necessarily somewhat inexact, they are indicators of the addition to the stock of skills available to the labor force. Degree and credit outcomes register that a student completed a certain path of study with proficiency, while enrollment measures indicate only transitory participation. That the economic return to a BA degree has risen more rapidly than the premium afforded to "some college" is but one indication of the importance of degree attainment.

It is important to ask why many education analysts (including economists) focus on the enrollment measure, which is an indicator of potential investment, rather than on degrees or credits, which measure additions to

2. Here, I am citing the raw percentage difference between earnings of college graduates and earnings of high school graduates. These earnings differences include not only the return to college education but also the return to unmeasured ability and skills associated with self-selection into college. If the return to unmeasured ability and skills has risen over the past few decades, as some evidence suggests it has, the change in the raw earnings difference overstates the change in the return to college education.

human capital stock.[3] One explanation is that enrollment is simply much easier to track than outcomes, such as credits earned.

Yet enrollment per se does not capture how individuals, along with colleges and universities, convert "participation" to outcomes such as BA degrees or course credits. That there may be substantial increases over time in the relative enrollment among individuals from poor families or racial minorities need not imply a narrowing in the difference between these groups in collegiate attainment. It is these differences in attainment, not in enrollment, that ultimately affect the distribution of earnings.

The objective of this analysis is to document the changing relationship between college enrollment and college completion, to assess the factors responsible for these shifts, and to consider their implications. In doing so, this analysis sets a new direction for higher education research by documenting the gap between enrollment rates and completions and identifying the universe of possible explanations. The first section considers the measurement of college enrollment and college completion, focusing on the intersection of results from a range of different data sources. The second section sets out a basic framework for analysis, starting with the human capital investment model, and outlines explanations for why individuals who begin college do not complete it or complete it in an extended period of time. In the third section, I provide empirical evidence distinguishing the explanatory role of these various factors. The concluding section summarizes the challenges for future research, as well as suggesting some implications for policy and data collection.

If there is one overriding policy conclusion, it is that the traditional focus of economists and policy analysts on the paired concepts of "enrollment" and "access" is insufficient to insure the supply of college-educated workers needed to meet demand, to reduce income inequality, and to narrow intergenerational differences in education and earnings.

Explaining why completion rates have decreased for those in their early twenties and why time to degree has increased rests on understanding the decisions of individuals to invest in college beyond their initial enrollment. Of particular concern is whether characteristics of today's marginal students, those who might not have started college in previous periods, are systematically different in terms of income or achievement from students beginning college in previous years. Changes over time in the academic preparedness of the marginal student may also reduce completion and in-

---

3. That "access to college" is more likely to be emphasized in the policy dialogue than attainment is more than an impressionistic claim. A search of *The Chronicle of Higher Education* identifies eighty-four stories since August 1998 with exact matches to the phrases "collegiate access" or "access to college" or "college access." Searching over the same time period for references to "collegiate attainment" or "college completion" or "degree attainment" resulted in only fourteen matches. In the legislative arena, a search of all federal bills in the 107th through the 105th congressional sessions produced forty-two references to "college access" or "access to college," relative to twelve references to "college completion" or "degree attainment."

crease time to degree. Financial constraints, combined with imperfect access to capital markets, are one demand-side force potentially reducing completion and extending time to degree. Because policy implications associated with credit constraints are dramatically different than those associated with selection effects, considerable care is warranted in distinguishing empirically between these two. Beyond demand-side factors, expansion on the supply-side of the market has been dominated by growth of community colleges and institutions with relatively low resources per student; as such, these institutions are able to contribute less to college completion than are institutions with greater resources per student or more upper-level courses. Public policies, including federal programs such as Pell grants and direct state appropriations to higher education, are not well-targeted and often do not increase opportunities for academically well-prepared students to complete four-year programs.

1.1 The Relationship Between College Enrollment and Collegiate Attainment

The measurement of college enrollment, college participation, and college completion is fundamental to this analysis, but the definition of these variables is often given too little attention. First, college enrollment is inherently a flow variable, representing the number of students participating at a given educational level at a single point in time. College enrollment can be measured from data tabulated by colleges and universities (in which case the age of the enrolled students is often unknown) or it can be tabulated through survey data, including the census, the Current Population Survey (CPS), or other sources, capturing what an individual is doing at a specific point in time. Collegiate attainment is, on the other hand, a stock variable—measuring the sum of education acquired by a given point in time. The metric for measuring collegiate attainment includes measures of credits, years completed, or degrees awarded; implicitly, the defining feature of these variables is that they are nonrevocable.[4] The most general stock measure is "college participation," indicating that an individual completed at least some college.[5]

---

4. Human capital or skills may depreciate, but measured educational attainment does not decrease for an individual with age. Implicitly, when using microdata, collegiate attainment is always truncated at a given age, as an individual can always receive more education, but the level will never decrease.

5. The measure of "some college" follows directly from the data available for the 1970 to 2000 period. Ideally, we would have more direct measures of attainment, such as the fraction of the population receiving three years of college. A coding change in large surveys, including the CPS and census, which shifts the educational attainment question from years of attainment to specified degree attainment, makes the comparison particularly difficult. The most ambiguous category in the new scheme is "Some college, no degree," which might include any level of attainment from dropping out in the first semester to completing three years at a four-year institution.

In this paper, college completion is used to denote the receipt of a four-year baccalaureate degree, though one might identify other types of completion in the undergraduate pipeline, such as receiving the associate degree. Linking initial college enrollment and degree receipt is time to degree. Following the rather considerable literature analyzing time to degree at the PhD level, total time to degree is the gross difference between data at BA completion and initial enrollment, while the net measured or elapsed time to degree captures the calendar period in which a student is enrolled. For any birth cohort, time to degree is an inherently truncated variable as students continue to receive degrees at late ages. Calculation of time to degree from microdata may follow two approaches. First, longitudinal data, such as the National Longitudinal Survey of Youth (NLSY), record the year of degree receipt. Alternatively, repeated cross sections, such as the CPS, afford the opportunity to examine how the educational attainment of a birth cohort changes over time.

In each year, recent high school graduates form the "basic" pool of potential college students, and the fraction of these students who enter college define the "traditional" college enrollment rate. Shown in figure 1.1, the enrollment rate of this group surged in the late 1960s (for men, partly

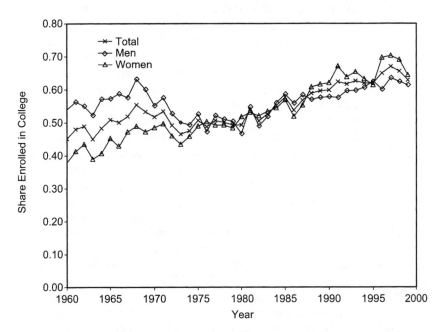

Fig. 1.1   College enrollment of recent high school graduates

Sources: U.S. Department of Labor (various years), with data tabulated from the October CPS.

Note: Includes individuals aged sixteen–twenty-four graduating from high school in the preceding twelve months.

in response to the Vietnam war), and it then stagnated in the 1970s.[6] Between the late 1960s and the mid-1970s, enrollment rates for men and women converged, with the relative decline in enrollment more muted for women than for men over this interval. Since 1980, the rise in the enrollment rate of recent high school graduates has been consistent, and the enrollment rate is now near 65 percent, relative to about 50 percent in 1980.

Collegiate attainment is a function of both initial enrollment rates and the transition of the cohort through the education pipeline. Collegiate attainment, measured for a cohort, is also inherently a truncated variable. A birth cohort measured at age thirty will have had more of an opportunity to acquire education than a birth cohort measured at age twenty-three. Yet the timing of educational attainment is also an economic variable, as individuals acquiring education at relatively young ages will have more years to accrue the returns to the skills they have acquired. By near tautology, increased college enrollment rates of recent high school graduates translate to increases in the fraction of a cohort attaining some college.

Figure 1.2 presents a snapshot of the educational attainment of young adults and shows the proportion completing college and the proportion with any collegiate participation at the age of twenty-three from 1968 to 2000. (The data are presented for birth cohorts from 1945 to 1977, which is analogous to the 1968 to 2000 years of observation.) While participation rises in much the same pattern visible in figure 1.1, the change in the proportion with a college degree is far more muted. There is little visible rise in the share completing college in the birth cohorts born after 1960, in spite of the quite visible increase in participation. Overall, the average annual increase in the college participation rate is 1.1 percent, while the increase in college completion is a more modest 0.7 percent. Beyond the aggregate picture, the data suggest three distinct regimes, with the latest period marking the most substantial divergence between enrollment rates and completion rates. First, for the early cohorts born between 1945 and 1952 (equivalently the children of the baby boom and the college students of the Vietnam era), college enrollment rates and college completion rates both increased sharply for cohorts measured at age twenty-three, with college completion increasing by about 35 percent and college enrollment by about 37 percent over this interval. A reversal followed, with absolute declines in enrollment and completion between the 1952 and 1958 cohorts (those cohorts aged twenty-three between 1975 and 1981), and the relative decline in college completion (about 13 percent) was somewhat larger than the relative decline in enrollment rates (about 18 percent). Then, from the 1958 cohort on, college enrollment increased markedly, surpassing the

6. Card and Lemieux (2001) find that educational deferments effectively raised college enrollment and completion for men likely to be at risk of conscription during the Vietnam War. Card and Lemieux (2001) find that draft avoidance raised college attendance rates 4–6 percentage points for men in the late 1960s.

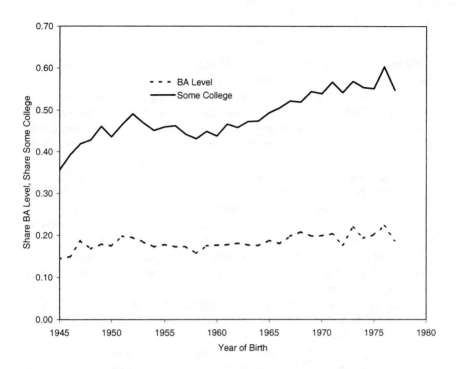

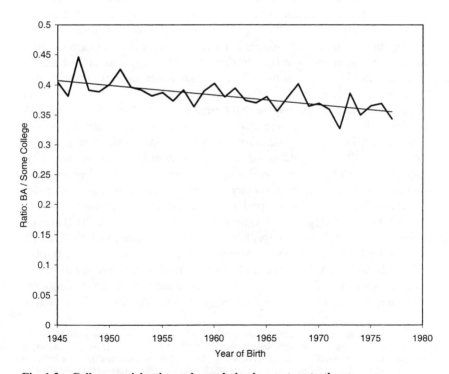

Fig. 1.2   College participation and completion by age twenty-three

Source: Author's tabulations from the October CPS.

Note: See appendix A for detail.

1952 local maximum by 10 percentage points by the time those born in the late 1970s reached the age of twenty-three.

Thinking about the difference between enrollment rates and completion rates as a difference in levels conveys much of the same information and also illustrates the widening gap between enrollment rates and completion in recent birth cohorts. Among those born in 1957 and aged twenty-three in 1980, the expected difference between enrollment and BA completion among high school graduates was about 27 percentage points; by 2000, the gap was 36 percentage points for the cohort aged twenty-three (born in 1977). It follows that the college completion rate (the share of those with some college receiving a degree) decreased from nearly 40 percent to about 34 percent, with this trend shown in the bottom panel of figure 1.2.[7]

Turning to the same trends in college participation and completion for demographic subgroups, figure 1.3 shows the trends for men and women and figure 1.4 shows the trends for blacks and whites. Gains in college participation are marked for blacks, rising at an average annual rate of 2.5 percent, though these gains are not replicated in the completion measure. Men and women display about the same modest overall decline in completion rates, but for men this is against a backdrop of stagnant college participation, while college participation has been rising for women. For each subgroup, completion rates decline over the entire interval, though the decent is strikingly larger for blacks than for those in other ethnic groups.

The observation of individuals at age twenty-three is a truncated picture of completion; changes in time to degree and the age structure of enrollment also need to be considered. To provide a firmer understanding of how these measures of collegiate attainment change over time, figure 1.5 shows college completion and college enrollment over time for different age levels. Most striking is the divergence between the top panel, showing participation, and the bottom panel, showing completion. For the most part, students who will participate in the collegiate system have had at least some college by age twenty-two, as the share recording *some college* for each birth cohort at this age is nearly identical to the share with *some college* for age thirty. It is in the bottom panel showing college completion where we see substantial divergence by time and by age. For all cohorts there are gains in BA completion by age, but these differences become particularly pronounced after the 1955 birth cohort, where the share of twenty-two-year-olds with a BA degree actually declines while degree receipt increases at older ages, particularly over twenty-five. That few of the students beyond age twenty-two are new participants provides an indication that

7. Define CG as the overall graduation rate (college graduates/population) and SC as the college participation rate (some college/population). The completion rate, or probability of graduation conditional on enrollment, is $CR = CG/SC$. It follows that the difference between the graduation rate and the participation rate is $SC - CG = SC(1 - CR)$ and thus widens with either an increase in college attendance or a decrease in the completion rate.

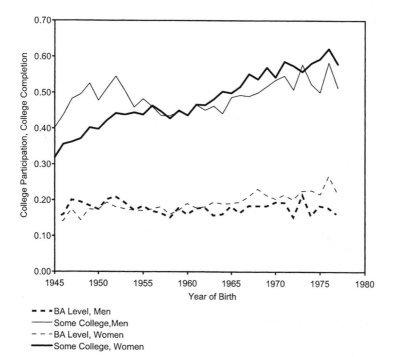

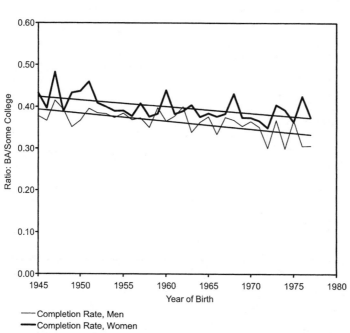

Fig. 1.3   College participation and completion by age twenty-three and sex, 1968–2000

Source: Author's tabulations from the October CPS.

Note: See appendix A for detail.

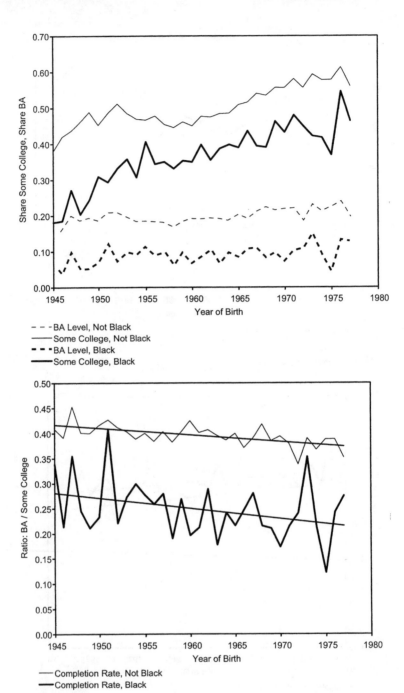

Fig. 1.4   College participation and completion by age twenty-three and race, 1968–2000

Source: Author's tabulations from the October CPS.

Note: See appendix A for detail.

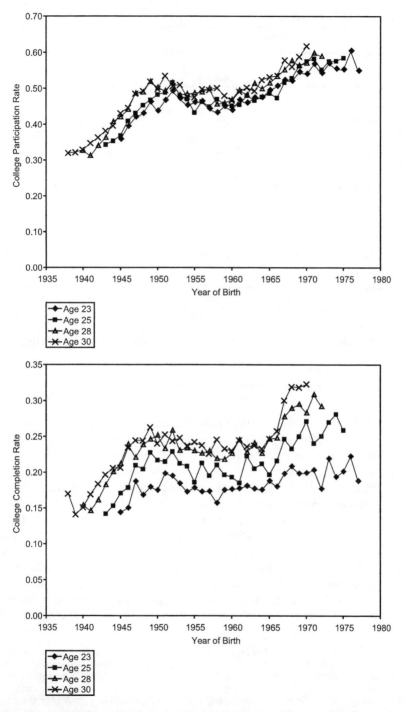

Fig. 1.5   College completion and enrollment by age

Source: Author's tabulations using the October CPS, 1968–2000.

Note: See appendix A for detail.

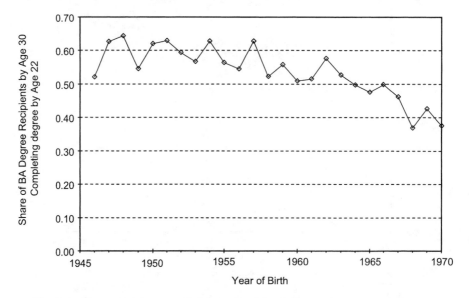

Fig. 1.6   Time to BA by year of birth, share of BA degree recipients completing by age twenty-two

Source: Author's tabulations using the October CPS, 1968–2000.

Notes: Individual weights are employed. See appendix A for detail.

either the duration of enrollment required to receive a BA has increased or more students complete their degrees after a series of spells of discontinuous study. Thus, for students receiving BA degrees between ages twenty-eight and thirty, the total time to degree likely exceeds ten years.

Unambiguously, the expected time to BA completion has increased in recent decades. Because the CPS enables us to trace birth cohorts and their educational attainment over an extended horizon, data on completion rates by age traces out the profile of time to degree. Figure 1.6 shows the trend in the proportion of degree recipients by age thirty receiving degrees by age twenty-two. While this trend is quite flat through the 1955 birth cohort, it declines in subsequent cohorts, reflecting the relatively high incidence of degrees awarded to individuals in their late twenties in the most recent years.[8]

Taking observed collegiate attainment by age at face value, table 1.1

---

8. A concern is that measured changes in degree completion may capture "education inflation" rather than degree attainment. One reader suggested that respondents might feel more self-conscious about not yet having completed by age twenty-eight than by age twenty-three. Tabulations from the NLSY showing year-to-year changes in educational attainment for those not enrolled in the prior period help to address this question. If recording errors were random, about the same share of people would report losing a year as the share reporting gaining a year. While about 0.004 of those aged thirty reported a year less of education attainment, more than 0.03 reported an increase in attainment without a corresponding record of enrollment. Still, to argue that the observed trend is tied to reporting issues requires a hypothesis about why this behavior has changed over time.

Table 1.1   **Average Annual Rates of Increase in College Completion and College Participation, 1968–2000**

	All			
	Share BA Degree (1)	Share Some College (2)	Ratio BA/Some College (3)	Difference Some College – BA (4)
Age 23	0.007	0.011	−0.004	0.013
	(0.002)	(0.001)	(0.001)	(0.001)
Age 25	0.012	0.012	0.000	0.011
	(0.002)	(0.001)	(0.001)	(0.001)
Age 28	0.014	0.014	0.001	0.013
	(0.002)	(0.002)	(0.001)	(0.002)
Age 30	0.016	0.015	0.001	0.014
	(0.002)	(0.002)	(0.001)	(0.002)

	White				Black			
	Share BA Degree (1)	Share Some College (2)	Ratio BA/Some College (3)	Difference Some College – BA (4)	Share BA Degree (5)	Share Some College (6)	Ratio BA/Some College (7)	Difference Some College – BA (8)
Age 23	0.007	0.011	−0.003	0.013	0.016	0.025	−0.008	0.027
	(0.002)	(0.001)	(0.001)	(0.001)	(0.006)	(0.003)	(0.004)	(0.003)
Age 25	0.013	0.011	0.002	0.010	0.019	0.030	−0.010	0.035
	(0.002)	(0.001)	(0.001)	(0.001)	(0.005)	(0.004)	(0.004)	(0.005)
Age 28	0.014	0.014	0.000	0.013	0.026	0.025	0.001	0.025
	(0.002)	(0.002)	(0.001)	(0.002)	(0.006)	(0.003)	(0.004)	(0.004)
Age 30	0.016	0.015	0.001	0.014	0.029	0.031	−0.002	0.033
	(0.002)	(0.002)	(0.001)	(0.002)	(0.003)	(0.004)	(0.003)	(0.004)

	Men				Women			
	Share BA Degree (1)	Share Some College (2)	Ratio BA/Some College (3)	Difference Some College – BA (4)	Share BA Degree (5)	Share Some College (6)	Ratio BA/Some College (7)	Difference Some College – BA (8)
Age 23	−0.001	0.005	−0.005	0.007	0.013	0.017	−0.004	0.019
	(0.002)	(0.001)	(0.001)	(0.002)	(0.002)	(0.001)	(0.001)	(0.001)
Age 25	0.004	0.005	0.000	0.005	0.020	0.019	0.001	0.018
	(0.002)	(0.002)	(0.001)	(0.002)	(0.002)	(0.002)	(0.001)	(0.002)
Age 28	0.005	0.005	0.000	0.005	0.025	0.023	0.002	0.022
	(0.003)	(0.002)	(0.001)	(0.002)	(0.002)	(0.002)	(0.001)	(0.002)
Age 30	0.006	0.007	−0.001	0.009	0.028	0.024	0.004	0.020
	(0.003)	(0.002)	(0.001)	(0.002)	(0.002)	(0.002)	(0.001)	(0.002)

Notes: Data are from author's tabulations using the October CPS, 1968–2000. In each equation, the dependent variable is the log of the variable indicated in the column heading, and the coefficient estimate corresponds to the year of observation. Individual weights are employed, and standard errors (in parentheses) are corrected for heteroskedasticity.

brings the trends over time together with the presentation of the average annual rates of change in college participation, BA completion, the ratio of BA completion to participation, and the absolute difference between participation and completion over the more than three decades between 1968 and 2000 for a range of ages and demographic classifications. Focusing first on the completion rate conditional on enrollment measured at age twenty-three produces the consistent result of a declining completion rate, with this decline somewhat larger for blacks than for other groups. The completion rate declined significantly, while the absolute difference between participation and completion rose appreciably.

This analysis demonstrates several related, yet distinct, changes in the pattern of collegiate participation and attainment. First, the rate at which college participation is transformed into degree completion (the completion rate) has decreased over time when outcomes for those in their early twenties are examined. This divergence is particularly large for black Americans. Second, when attainment is examined at somewhat older ages, the completion rate has been largely stagnant.

Ideally, we should be able to offer more evidence (even if just descriptive) about the link between family circumstances and the outcome of college completion; however, the absence of good measures of parental resources (and education) and precollegiate achievement in sources like the CPS and the census limits what we can do. Other longitudinal microdata sets such as High School and Beyond, NELS, and NLSY allow for tabulations of college going by family income and student achievement at different points in time, though differences among these surveys lead to something less than a true time series. Secondary tabulations (notably Ellwood and Kane [2000] and Carneiro, Heckman, and Manoli [2002]) illustrate a narrowing of the difference in college enrollment by family income for high-achieving students. For the high school class of 1980, high-income students in the top tertile of the achievement distribution were 26 percentage points, or 61 percent, more likely to attend college than their peers from the low-income quartile; for the high school class graduating in 1992, enrollment rates rose across the board, though disproportionately for low-income, high-achieving students, and the gap narrowed to 23 percentage points, or 31 percent. For low-achieving students, the difference in enrollment by family income rises in both absolute and relative terms over this interval.[9] Thus, it is plainly too simplistic to make sweeping statements about "collegiate access" changing by family income.[10]

9. In her congressional testimony, Hoxby (2000) makes similar calculations, with more narrowly defined achievement ranges (quintiles rather than tertiles), and finds that the narrowing of the gap is particularly pronounced at the top of the achievement distribution.

10. For example, the report *Access Denied* (Advisory Committee on Student Financial Assistance 2001, 12) makes the broad claim that "the current generation of low income young Americans today face diminished educational and economic opportunity as a result of lack

1.2   Explaining College Completion and Extended Time to Degree

Increases in the return to a college degree provide a prima facie motivation for the expectation that we would observe increases in college completion and reductions in time to degree. That such a response is not apparent—and, in fact, the data on completion rates and time to degree point in the opposite direction as demonstrated in the prior section—suggests the need for broad examination of the explanations for why individuals who begin college do not complete it or extend the time to degree completion well beyond the four-year norm. This section begins with a review of the college investment decision and then turns to the discussion of the reasons why this type of framework is likely to be inadequate.

1.2.1   Framework and Its Failure

In considering the potential explanations for college attrition and extended time to degree, we begin with the basic human capital investment problem. Key parameters include the expected wage-schooling locus and the expected costs of additional attainment at the individual level. In general, attending college bears many similarities to other investment decisions, like buying a car or a piece of machinery at a firm. Potential students weigh the benefits from collegiate choices with the costs. Benefits include higher earnings over the remaining working years and whatever consumption utility (or disutility!) is associated with the educational experience. Costs include the direct costs of college and foregone earnings. While tuition costs receive most of the attention in the popular press, it is the foregone earnings that typically form the largest share of college costs.

Typically—and in very general form—economists model the college choice as individuals (i) choosing among the range of collegiate options (both school quality [j] and attainment [s]) to maximize lifetime utility, with a numeraire reflecting the option of no college. Individuals are likely to differ in a number of dimensions including expected returns from particular collegiate options, the available set of choices, and earnings independent of further educational attainment. The choice set varies with both institutional admissions decisions and factors potentially unrelated to economic returns, such as distance to a college or state of residence.

Assuming full information about earnings and the nature of the college

of access to a college education." Similarly, an editorial in the *New York Times* (2002, 14) makes the sweeping statement, "The dearth of student aid for lower-income families is discouraging the neediest from applying to college at all and driving them toward low-paying jobs that keep them at the very margins of society. These are ominous developments at a time when a college diploma has become the ticket for admission into the new economy and a basic requirement for a middle-class life. The most alarming figures show that the college attendance gap between high-income and low-income Americans has widened and that about a quarter of high-achieving low-income students fail to go to college at all."

experience, individuals must choose the length of the program and the college or university to attend to maximize utility. To simplify, we can frame the question as a financial investment decision, with individuals choosing the length of enrollment (s) and the particular college program (j) in order to maximize the lifetime value of earnings.

$$\text{Choose } s, j \text{ to maximize} \sum_{t=s+1}^{T} \frac{Y_{sji}}{(1+r)^t} - \sum_{t=1}^{s} \frac{F_j}{(1+r)^t} - \sum_{t=1}^{T} \frac{Y_{0i}}{(1+r)^t},$$

where Y_{sji} is the annual earnings for individual i attending institution j for s years, Y_{0i} is the annual expected earnings with no further education, and F is the level of direct college costs.[11] Implicitly, this specification assumes no limitations in credit markets, with individuals able to borrow and lend at the market rate r.

Taken at face value, this simple formulation leads to a number of important predictions. First, increases in the return to education should lead to growth in both enrollment and attainment, though the relative magnitude of these changes will depend on the relative numbers at each margin.[12] Second, individuals who make collegiate investments will invest more in the initial periods rather than in later years. Early investment provides more years over which to accrue the benefits.[13] Further, individuals choosing to invest in college will generally choose immediate and continuous en-

11. Discrete time discounting, payments at the end of each period, and the assumption of fixed annual payments are assumed for expositional simplicity. Adding appropriate timing of payments (tuition at the start of the period) and growth of earnings of the life cycle does not change the substantive implications.

12. It is typical to focus on expected individual earnings as a function of schooling (S_i), ability (A_i), and a random error term (ε_i), such as $y_{it} = \beta_t S_i + \gamma_t A_i + \varepsilon_{it}$ (Griliches 1977; Taber 2001). In this case, β can be thought of as the return to education at time t, with increases in the demand for skilled workers in the labor force leading to increases in this parameter. Yet the fundamental concern (even in the cross section) is that because A is likely to be unobserved and omitted or poorly measured in this specification, estimates of the return to education are biased. This complicates the interpretation of the rise in the observed college–high school wage differential as an indicator of the expected return to college completion, as a clearly viable alternative hypothesis is that it is the return to ability (A) that has risen rather than the return to college completion (see, for example, Taber [2001] and Murnane, Willet, and Levy [1993]).

13. To illustrate, attending four years of college in the initial period is preferred to attending four years of college after a hiatus so long as

$$\sum_{t=5}^{T} \frac{Y_C}{(1+r)^t} - \sum_{t=1}^{4} \frac{F}{(1+r)^t} > \sum_{t=1}^{4} \frac{Y_H}{(1+r)^t} + \sum_{t=9}^{T} \frac{Y_C}{(1+r)^t} - \sum_{t=5}^{8} \frac{F}{(1+r)^t}.$$

It can be shown that this inequality holds so long as

$$\left(\frac{Y_C + F}{Y_H + F}\right)^{1/4} - 1 > r,$$

which must be the case because even with an infinite period over which to recoup returns.

rollment to a split of time between college attendance and employment at the noncollegiate wage.[14]

Evidence of extended time to degree and discontinuous spells of enrollment are in conflict with the predictions generated by this basic model. Important missing pieces from this analysis include the role of uncertainty in assessments of costs and benefits and the potential presence of credit constraints.

1.2.2   Violations of the Assumptions in the Basic Investment Analysis

This section briefly enumerates the potential violations of the assumptions in the basic investment analysis that would inhibit completion and extend time to degree. Note that to understand the empirical trends observed, it is necessary to explain why such explanations have taken greater significance over time.

Individual Constraints

The basic human capital model assumes that individuals are able to borrow at a market rate (r) in order to finance college. The violation of this assumption, owing to the reluctance of banks to make loans that they are unable to collateralize, will lead to an underinvestment in education at the collegiate level. Inability to borrow to finance education "up front" may explain why individuals may work before enrolling in college or pursue studies on a part-time basis. Moreover, even with some capital provided through government-sponsored student loan programs, students may exhaust borrowing capacity relatively quickly, forcing the termination or postponement of continued college study. Credit constraints are likely to be particularly significant for students from economically disadvantaged backgrounds. Providing clear identification of credit constraints in an empirical context is no easy task as economic disadvantage, including the inability of parents to contribute to the financing of college, is likely to be correlated with other factors determining collegiate outcomes, some of which may be difficult for researchers to observe.

Beyond the pecuniary costs of college and the capacity of individuals to

---

14. A simple demonstration is provided by the comparison of full-time attendance for four years to part-time attendance and employment for eight years:

$$\frac{1}{2}\sum_{t=1}^{8}\frac{Y_H}{(1+r)^t} + \sum_{t=9}^{T}\frac{Y_C}{(1+r)^t} - \frac{1}{2}\sum_{t=1}^{8}\frac{F}{(1+r)^t}.$$

It can be shown that full-time attendance is preferred so long as

$$\left(\frac{2Y_C+F}{Y_H+F}\right)^{1/4} - 1 > r,$$

which will again hold whenever any college has a positive net present value.

finance these investments, cognitive and noncognitive skills affect the costs and returns to collegiate investments.[15] Poor secondary performance plausibly explains some college attrition as students who have difficulty with subjects such as algebra or written expression may find that the costs associated with upper-level courses in which these skills are a prerequisite are prohibitive. Variations across local areas or over time in the effectiveness of elementary and secondary schooling could explain some of the observed changes in the level and timing of college completion. Moreover, people with General Education Development (GED) certificates rather than traditional high school diplomas may lack the task commitment and other noncognitive skills necessary to complete college. As such, changes in high school dropout rates and GED receipt may be a significant indicator of the potential for college completion. Because education is fundamentally iterative (unlike other investments, such as home ownership or owning a bond), costs at the collegiate level are related to outcomes in prior periods.

Supply-Side Constraints in Higher Education

Changes in tuition price and variations in the availability of collegiate options affect college completion and time to degree. Most colleges and universities (though not all) are either public institutions or private nonprofits, which receive substantial public subsidies. One implication of the mixed-market structure in higher education is that it is inappropriate to assume perfect elasticity of supply.

Increases in college price, particularly the difference between the tuition charged by two-year and four-year institutions, might have an adverse impact on attainment, though direct college charges are small, relative to opportunity costs. Ceteris paribus, increases in net college costs decrease attainment (weakening the link between enrollment and completion), while reduction in net cost increases attainment.[16]

Similarly, decreases in the quality of offerings or reductions in relative

15. In this chapter, individual cognitive and noncognitive skills are considered as part of the cost of collegiate attainment. Quite plainly, such characteristics affect both the costs and the returns to marginal investments in education. For a model illustrating individual heterogeneity in costs and returns, see Card (2001).

16. In considering the effects of public subsidies on collegiate participation and attainment, the characteristics of students at the margin will have a large effect on outcomes, particularly if the college preparedness of students receiving aid differs markedly from that of those likely to attend college without aid. Moreover, as the student at the enrollment margin changes in college preparedness, so too does the likelihood of college completion: that is, d BA/d Aid may well decrease as students further down the achievement distribution choose to enroll in college. It is particularly important to focus on "net price" rather than "sticker price" in evaluating how college costs affect enrollment and completion, as work by Hoxby (2000) and others demonstrates that changes in net price over the last two decades have been appreciably less than changes in the sticker price of college.

capacity at upper-level institutions would adversely affect persistence. It is well documented that institutional resources (some of which are very difficult to measure) affect both the economic benefits to college attainment as well as the likelihood of completion. Just as we would expect individuals with relatively strong elementary and secondary options to complete more years of education (Card and Krueger 1996), so too would we expect individuals with access to relatively high-quality collegiate options to complete more years of education. For this reason, policy makers at the state level may have significant impact on the supply-side of higher education through their role in setting tuition and determining the level and distribution of state appropriations to two-year and four-year institutions.

Uncertainty, Information, and College Persistence

It is typical to develop models of collegiate investment under the assumption that all of the parameters of the college investment problem are known to potential students at the time of college choice and that individuals do not make systematic mistakes in their assessment of the investment problem. Information available to potential college students and the ex ante uncertainty associated with different choices may have a substantial impact on the college investment problem and may explain behavior not well described in the traditional human capital investment formulation. Two types of information problems may contribute to the gap between enrollment and college completion: (1) individuals face considerable uncertainty about both the costs and the benefits of college investments; and (2) individuals make systematic mistakes by enrolling or persisting in college when it is perfectly predictable, given available information, that the costs of college completion will outweigh the benefits. Note that the first explanation is an economic argument involving uncertainty, while the second is inherently not an economic argument but a psychological argument.

Option Value

Collegiate attainment is really an investment under uncertainty.[17] As individuals consider college options they must form expectations about the true costs and returns, as well as assessing the likely variation in their forecasts of these variables. Variation in costs derives from uncertainty about one's own ability, the ability of classmates, and the characteristics of the college experience (the quality of faculty and so forth). Variation in the re-

---

17. Both Manski (1989) and Altonji (1993) present models where collegiate attainment is the product of sequential choice under uncertainty. While some individuals would not invest in college ex poste, the ex ante return is positive. In this regard, initial college attendance has an option value. Altonji (1993) provides a formal model of this decision process, with new information on individual ability and college characteristics affecting persistence from enrollment to college completion.

turns comes from uncertainty about future demand and supply conditions in the labor market. Taken together, these sources of variation imply that college is a risky investment, particularly since it cannot be bought and sold, and the risk cannot be separated from its owner through diversification.[18] An interesting question is whether one strategy individuals use to reduce the risk associated with collegiate investments is to combine school and work. Such a strategy would allow the accrual of both education and work experience, at the cost of somewhat longer time to completion in the collegiate program.

It is also likely that potential costs of college may vary systematically with individual characteristics, as potential students from the most advantaged backgrounds may have better information about different types of college options because they have more opportunities for campus visits and other types of information gathering. Research in progress by Avery and Kane (chap. 8 in this volume), studying the College Opportunity and Career Help program (COACH) intervention in financial aid guidance and college application at a number of schools in Boston, is likely to shed considerable light on the role of information available to high school students as they consider college options.[19]

Systematic Mistakes: Psychological Explanations

Youth predictions about success in college may be inconsistent with actual academic prospects and, as such, students may make mistakes in enrolling in college when it is predictable that the likelihood of a positive return is very low. Placed in the context of recent analysis at the intersection of economics and psychology, one might consider this to be "belief perseverance" or "overconfidence bias," capturing the reluctance of individuals to abandon college aspirations after receiving poor academic marks at the secondary level.

Much of the work exploring these psychological explanations for college attrition has fallen to sociologists, with one of the earliest assessments attributable to Burton Clark (1961), who hypothesized that open access institutions like community colleges may serve a "cooling out" function and thus have very high attrition rates. Rosenbaum (2001) suggests that one explanation for high college attrition is the mismatch between expectations formed in high schools which encourage a "college-for-all" norm and (un-

18. Levhari and Weiss (1974) present a model of the effect of risk on human capital investment. They make the further point that, under the circumstance where the variance in return increases with education, the average return (across individuals) will exceed the private marginal return, providing a rationale for a transfer of resources to human capital investment. In short, society is able to diversify the risk where individuals cannot.

19. In another example, Avery, Fairbanks, and Zeckhauser (2001) note that the early decision process may favor those from relatively affluent educational settings who are well informed about the "rules of the game," while others are effectively "informationally disadvantaged" in their college selection, which would ultimately affect college choice and persistence.

explained) realities related to the academic requirements for degree completion.[20]

1.3   Empirical Evidence on the Divergence

Understanding why college completion has not increased over time and why time to degree has increased depends on the determinants of college going, college choice, and college persistence. On one side of the market, changes in the characteristics of individuals—both financial and academic—affect collegiate attainment. On the other side of the higher education market, the structure of the production functions for colleges and universities and the level and form of state support for higher education affect the price, quality, and availability of undergraduate options and, in turn, affect the observed level of educational attainment.

The clear statistical identification of the impact of competing explanations is a difficult challenge that is largely unresolved in the empirical analysis that follows. Rather, the following section presents evidence that addresses the plausibility of competing explanations for the widening of the gap between participation and completion at young ages and the extension of time to degree. I begin with the assessment of underlying changes in demographics, family circumstances, and student achievement that may affect attainment at the collegiate level and BA attainment. Then I turn to the institutional and policy variables that are likely to affect college completion.

1.3.1   Demand Side: Individual Choices

Parental Financial Resources and Credit Constraints

The widely discussed changes in the structure of earnings have significant intergenerational effects, leading to increased inequality in parental income and, thus, the capacity to finance college. The top panel of figure 1.7 illustrates real family income in families with fifteen- to seventeen-year-olds by quartile and shows the widely known result that after 1980 there has been a substantial divergence between the top and bottom quartiles. What this implies is that in an environment of relatively constant or

20. The "college-for-all" norm is not just a coined phrase but an empirical observation—95 percent of high school seniors in the class of 1992 planned to attend college, despite the fact that nearly half of the twelfth-grade students' math and verbal skills were below the ninth-grade level. Rosenbaum's assessment of degree attainment a decade after high school for the 1982 cohort shows that aspirations are insufficient to guarantee degree attainment. Among those with BA aspirations, about 66 percent of those with As in high school had received a BA degree, while only 16.1 percent of those with Cs in high school had achieved the BA degree. At a more general level, Rosenbaum (2001) finds that those with low high school grades are the most likely to enter college and complete zero credit hours, with nearly 13 percent of C students with BA aspirations ending up with this outcome.

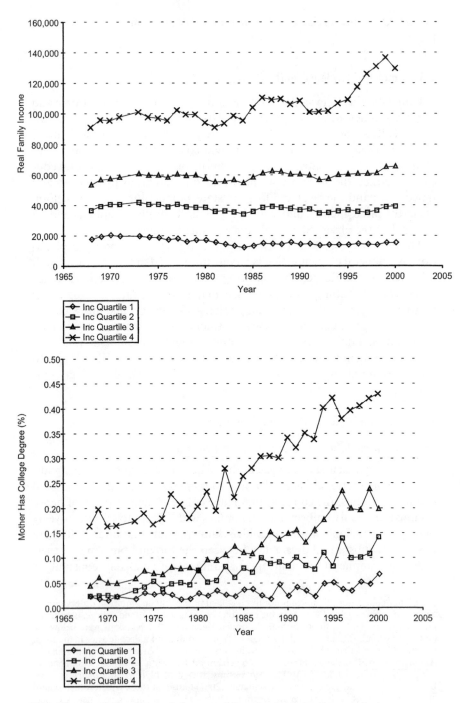

Fig. 1.7 Family background characteristics of potential college students
Source: Author's tabulations from the March CPS.

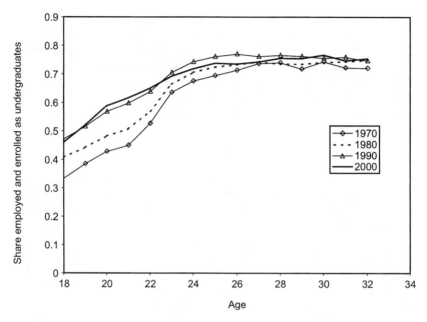

Fig. 1.8   Employment among undergraduate students by age, census years
Source: Author's calculations from 1970, 1980, 1990, and 2000 census microdata.
Notes: See appendix A for details. "Enrolled as undergraduates" includes those students enrolled with educational attainment greater than twelve and less than sixteen completed years before 1990 and attainment at least "Some College" and less than a BA degree in 1990 and 2000.

diminishing financial aid availability, those in the bottom quartiles of the income distribution are likely to face increasing difficulty paying for college in the absence of perfect credit markets or increased financial aid.

A second point, suggesting that recent high school graduates may find it increasingly difficult to finance full-time college study, is that the proportion of students working and enrolled in college has increased markedly over the last several decades (see figure 1.8). While employment rates have always been high among those students enrolled in their mid- to late twenties, a decided increase in employment among those in their late teens and early twenties took place between 1980 and 1990, persisting through 2000. This evidence of increased employment is consistent with the presence of credit constraints, though it does not prove that the young people who are dividing their time between school and work do so *because* they have exhausted credit markets.[21]

21. There is some research literature on the question of whether undergraduate employment reduces academic performance. Stinebrickner and Stinebrickner (2003) show that an additional hour of employment while in college substantially reduces academic performance.

Because it is inherently difficult to prove the existence and magnitude of credit constraints in higher education, this analysis goes no further than to assert their plausibility and to refer the reader to the related literature.[22] (See, for example, Heckman and Carneiro [2003] and Ellwood and Kane [2000].) What is imperative to the facts at hand is not just that credit constraints exist, but changes in economic circumstances and the pricing of higher education over the last two decades exacerbate the magnitude of these effects.

Demographics and Compositional Changes

Because the primary source of this divergence is the increased return to education, potential students in the top quartile of the income distribution are increasingly likely to come from a family with a college-educated parent. The bottom panel of figure 1.7 shows maternal educational attainment by income quartile over time. Among those teens in the top quartile of the income distribution in 1980, about one-fifth had a mother with a college degree. By the year 2000, this share had doubled to about 40 percent, while the change in the collegiate attainment of those in the bottom quartiles was much more modest. What is striking is the concentration in the rise in parental education in the top quartile of the income distribution. Thus, young people of college age in the top of the income distribution in the 1990s are better off than those in the same relative position in the income distribution in the 1970s for two reasons: their parents have more real financial resources and they are more likely to benefit from a college-educated parent. College participation and college completion are expected to rise with family income; at issue is the expected relative change in these outcomes.

What matters for this analysis is how changes in parental education and the level and distribution of parental income affect the link between college enrollment and college completion. One way to address this question is to estimate the change in college completion under the assumption of a known cross-sectional relationship between collegiate outcomes and

22. Two of the strongest pieces of evidence that potential college students would be better off with more access to credit markets are provided by examinations of federal loan programs. First, Kane (1999, figure 4.1) demonstrates a high degree of stacking in the distribution of student loans, with many students apparently constrained at the lower division limit of $2,625 and the upper division limit of $4,000. In addition, Dynarski (2002) finds significant changes in attendance behavior with the removal of home equity from the needs analysis formula in the early 1990s. Still, these observations do not demonstrate that increasing access to credit would increase collegiate attainment and completion. Using data from the NLSY, Cameron and Taber (2000) explore a number of different estimation strategies and fail to find evidence that borrowing constraints affect collegiate attainment. In a very different type of study, Stinebrickner and Stinebrickner (2001) examine the collegiate progression at Berea College, a school where all students receive full-tuition scholarships, and find that completion rates are persistently lower among the most economically disadvantaged, even when observable student characteristics such as test scores are held constant.

parental characteristics.[23] Taken as descriptive parameters, cross-sectional expressions show the very powerful relationship between maternal education and expected collegiate outcomes. The effects of parental income are also significant, but somewhat less robust, likely reflecting the presence of more measurement error in the reporting of income than education and the high correlation between parental education and income. Focusing on cross-sectional estimates from the NLSY, collegiate degree attainment by the respondent's mother corresponds with a 14 percentage point increase in the probability that the respondent will attain a BA and a 6 percentage point increase in the likelihood of college participation by age twenty-eight.[24] Thus, the dramatic increase in maternal education among potential college students, from 6.4 percent of mothers of those in their teens in 1970 to 21.2 percent of mothers of those in their teens in 2000, would have led to a *narrowing* in the difference between college participation and college completion for those entering college in the last three decades. Thus, changes in other factors—at the level of the individual college student or in the market for college education—must swamp the expected increase in college completion associated with the rise in maternal education.

Beyond parental economic circumstances, employment and family circumstances of students may have a significant effect on the level of collegiate attainment and time-to-degree attainment. With increased age comes a different set of responsibilities, including children and employment.[25] College enrollment among women with children has increased dramatically over the last two decades, and the presence of young children may limit attainment in several ways—reducing the time available to study and limiting course and institutional options, for example.[26] Tables 1.2 and 1.3 show the enrollment rate among women with and without children in cen-

23. This approach assumes constant parameters over time in the relationship between parental characteristics and collegiate outcomes, correct specification of the cross-sectional regression equation, and the absence of general equilibrium adjustments associated with changes in college-going.

24. All coefficients are statistically significant; other included covariates are dummy variables for maternal education at the some-college and high school degree levels, race, and sex. Estimates with the inclusion of respondent's Armed Forces Qualification Test (AFQT) score produce effects of maternal college education of 0.06 and 0.14 on college participation and college completion, respectively.

25. In discussing the relationship between nontraditional collegiate attributes and outcomes, the ambiguity of the causal arrows needs to be acknowledged. In particular, the changes in achievement and the demographic characteristics of potential college students may contribute to higher levels of participation among older, nontraditional students. At the same time, changes in federal and state policies may lead to institutional adjustments that favor the expansion of programs aimed at nontraditional students. To this end, an important further research agenda is the explanation of the rise of nontraditional student enrollment.

26. Causation seems nearly impossible to identify here. One hypothesis is that people who have children in their late teens or early twenties may lack some of the unobservable attributes contributing to college success, while another explanation is that children have a negative effect on educational attainment.

Table 1.2   **Undergraduate Enrollment Rate for Women With and Without Children,**
                       Decennial Census Data: Enrollment Rates

	No Children			With Children		
Age	1970	1980	1990	1970	1980	1990
18	0.32	0.31	0.22	0.01	0.03	0.04
19	0.43	0.45	0.44	0.02	0.04	0.07
20	0.37	0.41	0.48	0.02	0.04	0.07
21	0.31	0.36	0.43	0.02	0.04	0.07
22	0.14	0.20	0.28	0.02	0.03	0.07
23	0.06	0.10	0.17	0.01	0.03	0.06
24	0.04	0.08	0.12	0.01	0.03	0.06
25	0.03	0.07	0.10	0.01	0.03	0.06

Notes: Author's tabulations using census microdata files for 1970 (2 percent), 1980 (5 percent), and 1990 (5 percent). Undergraduate enrollment rate is defined as the number of individuals enrolled in school with at least a high school degree divided by the total number of women in the age group.

Table 1.3   **Undergraduate Enrollment Rate for Women With and Without Children,**
                       Decennial Census Data: Grade Attending

	No Children		With Children	
	1970	1980	1970	1980
1st	0.36	0.34	0.35	0.47
2nd	0.27	0.25	0.28	0.28
3rd	0.20	0.19	0.21	0.15
4th	0.16	0.22	0.16	0.11

Note: Author's tabulations using census microdata files for 1970 (2 percent) and 1980 (5 percent).

sus years. Women with children have always been appreciably less likely to enroll in college than those without children in their late teens and early twenties. Nevertheless, dramatic increases in college enrollment have occurred among women with children, and the share of young women with children enrolled in college has approximately doubled over each decennial census interval. Table 1.3 shows the year of college enrollment for these women. While about 1/3 of the women without children are in their first year of college, about one half of the women with children are in their first year of college. This relatively limited level of education suggests that women with children may be particularly likely to have interrupted spells of college participation and to end up with modest levels of college attainment and low levels of college completion.

More generally, recent policy reports highlight the rise in the number of nontraditional students and raise questions about the collegiate trajectories of the increasing share of nontraditional students.[27] Empirically, there is no question that nontraditional students are less likely than traditional students to attain a degree within five years of initial enrollment. Yet it is far from clear that this gap is caused by the conditions of nontraditional enrollment (type of programs available, jobs, and family constraints) rather than individual characteristics that determine nontraditional status.

Student Achievement

While parental educational attainment has risen over the last two decades, student achievement has not followed suit. Judging by standardized test scores, there has been a modest decrease over time in the college preparedness of high school students. For example, average National Assessment of Educational Progress (NAEP) math scores for seventeen-year-olds have decreased by about ten points since 1970. With a 9 percentage point increase in the college participation rate, this change implies that the student at the margin of college enrollment has declined about a quarter of a standard deviation in test performance, as illustrated in figure 1.9.[28] Combined with increasing rates of college-going, the implication is that the marginal college student may be less prepared to complete the college curriculum than students attending college in prior decades. Yet the completion rates for these marginal students would need to be unrealistically low—on the order of about 2 percent—for changes in students achievement to explain the observed change in college enrollment among those in their early twenties.

What is more, there are other potential changes in college preparedness to consider, including the observation that more and more college students are entering with a GED rather than a traditional diploma. Although high school graduation is often thought of as an important part of the educational pipeline through which students advance, a regular high school degree need not be a prerequisite for college enrollment, particularly at community colleges or other open-access institutions. Many institutions accept the GED as a substitute for a high school diploma, and a number of institutions allow older students to enroll without an equivalency certificate. While there is a long literature debating the returns to a high school

27. A recent report released by the U.S. Department of Education (2002) notes that nearly 73 percent of undergraduates in 1999–2000 were in some respect nontraditional, defined in terms of characteristics like the presence of dependents, the absence of a high school diploma, no parental financial support, and full-time employment.

28. Plainly, these calculations are oversimplified as they assume that college-going is perfectly correlated with test scores. Nevertheless, the calculations are illustrative, providing an upper bound on the extent to which achievement changes affect college completion. We can back out the effect of achievement on college persistence necessary for changes in test scores to accord with observed levels of college completion.

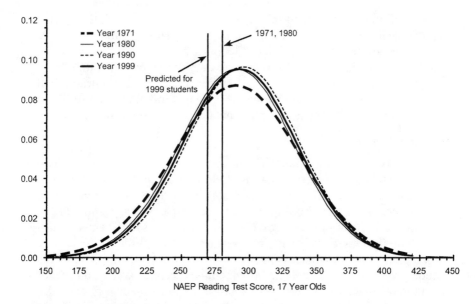

Fig. 1.9   Student achievement by cohort

Sources: Means and standard deviations of test performance in each year are from NCES tabulations. Computation of the normal distribution and predicted ability of marginal college students are author's calculations.

degree, it seems plausible that whatever characteristics of persistence are associated with high school completion may also affect college persistence—even if these "skills" are somewhat different than measured cognitive achievement. Recipients of the GED have increased dramatically as a fraction of the eighteen–twenty-four age group, rising from about 0.8 percent in 1989 to 1.3 percent of this age group in 2000 (U.S. Department of Education [2001] tables 15 and 106). Moreover, the rise in the share of test-takers who are nineteen years of age, from about 33 percent in 1975 to about 42 percent in the year 2000, suggests that an increasing number of young people may be substituting the GED for traditional high school completion. GED recipients are less likely to persist in the higher education pipeline than traditional high school graduates. On average, GED recipients complete fewer years of postsecondary education than high school graduates. An analysis by Garet, Jing, and Kutner (1996) shows that almost three-fourths of GED recipients enrolling in a higher education program completed one year or less of college, and the results shown in the tables presented in Cameron and Heckman (1997) are broadly similar. Thus, an increase in GED recipients in the collegiate pipeline implies an increase in the concentration of students who are least likely to persist in higher education, moving in the direction of explaining the gap between college participation and college completion as well as the increased time to degree.

1.3.2   Supply Determinants and Public Policy

Market Structure: Changes in Institutional Shares

The stratification in the market for higher education has increased over time, with substantial differences among colleges in resources and course offerings. Considering changes in the distribution of enrollment and degrees across types of institutions provides an empirical starting point (see figure 1.10). In 1967, about 1/5 of all undergraduates were enrolled at community colleges, about 51 percent were at public four-year institutions, and the remainder were at private institutions, with selective private liberal arts colleges and research universities accounting for the relatively modest share of 7 percent. A major shift occurred between 1967 and 1977, with both an increase in the level of undergraduate enrollment and a shift in the distribution of enrollment away from four-year institutions toward com-

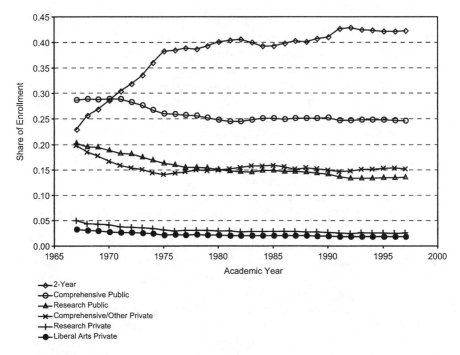

Fig. 1.10   Enrollment by type of institution
Source: Author's tabulations from HEGIS/IPEDS fall enrollment surveys.
Note: See appendix A for detail.

munity colleges—the two-year share rose from 21 percent to 34 percent. These results do not resolve the question of whether the change in the distribution of individuals across institutions reflects changes in the type of collegiate experiences demanded by students or shocks to the supply side of the market.

Not surprisingly, shifts in undergraduate enrollment across institutions are likely to affect BA output because persistence and the likelihood of degree completion differ across these institution types. Between 1967 and 1977, the ratio of full-time equivalent undergraduate enrollment to BA degrees increased from about 8 to 8.5. Enrollment growth at open-access institutions may not translate to growth in degree attainment if many of the courses of study are terminal certificate programs or if students find it difficult to get the courses they need in order to graduate. Many selective institutions, particularly in the private sector, are unlikely to respond to increases in enrollment demand with expansion in their residential undergraduate programs, as this would lead to dilution in per-student subsidies and reductions in quality.

Across states, there is considerable variation in the mix of different types of colleges and universities. A salient question is how these structural differences, as well as changes in the distribution of resources across institutions, affect degree completion within states. Over time, increased geographical integration in the marketplace has plainly led to a greater and greater concentration of the most able students at a relatively small number of institutions (Hoxby 1997). This stratification, in turn, raises quality at some institutions while reducing peer quality at other institutions. Institutional resources combined with peer quality are likely to have a real behavioral effect on college completion, and it is difficult to disentangle the effects of own ability, peer ability, and institutional resources in predicting completion. Yet, because more able students also attend the most selective schools, it is inherently difficult to disentangle the effects on outcomes of student characteristics versus institutional characteristics. To frame this point more concretely, consider the graduation rates from the National Collegiate Athletic Association (NCAA) Division I schools by Carnegie classification. Private research universities reported graduation rates of 84 percent, public research universities (which are generally somewhat larger) graduate about 60 percent of first-time students, while public institutions that do not award doctorates graduated only about 37 percent of entering students within six years. There are some distinctive examples at the bottom and top of the quality distribution. Among the institutions with six-year completion rates of less than 20 percent are Chicago State University, Texas Southern University, and McNeese State University (Louisiana). At the other extreme, institutions with completion rates over 90 percent include the University of Virginia, Georgetown University, and Northwestern University.

State Higher Education Policy

State-level politics may be a particularly important factor in the determination of the location, type, and number of institutions, as well as the relative support for research institutions, relative to comprehensive colleges or community colleges. To the extent that shifts in state support are driven by politics (e.g., the desire to reward the governor's alma matter or a move to reward a legislative leader with the opening of a community college in his home district) rather than student demand, shifts in state appropriations will operate like supply shocks. Shifts toward institutions with relatively low completion rates will likely lead to a reduction in the link between participation and completion.

One hypothesis to consider is that, in the last several decades, the political process has favored community colleges relative to four-year institutions, leading to a relative decrease in the supply of course offerings at upper-level institutions. Community colleges may advertise stronger direct links to local economic development than universities by providing job training for local employers. In addition, because community colleges are open to all local residents and are relatively widely dispersed across counties (while universities generally have much more limited locations), state legislators may receive much greater political rewards (in terms of reelection prospects) for increasing community college funding than increasing appropriations for the state flagship university, which may be hundreds of miles away and practically out of reach for many constituents. As an empirical matter, a regression of the share of state appropriations to higher education directed to four-year institutions on a time trend and state fixed effects for 1973 to 1996 shows a decidedly negative trend (–0.002 [0.0001], see table 1.4). For those states in which this trend is most pronounced, we would expect to see relative declines in the link between college enrollment and college completion, particularly among students in their early twenties. Our measures of state-specific completion rates are limited to crude indicators—either the ratio of BA degrees conferred to enrollment using the institutional data or the ratio of college completion to college participation for young people in the census.[29] Still, regression results that use variation across states in the change in the share of state appropriations as the key explanatory variable present a clear result (table 1.4). Increasing (decreasing) the share of state appropriations to four-year institutions has a strong positive (negative) effect on completion, with a 5 percentage point decrease in the share of appropriations directed to four-year institutions associated with a 1.7 percentage point decrease in college completion mea-

---

29. Note that these measures are fundamentally different. The institutional measure of degrees awarded relative to enrollment uses the ratio of two flows, while the census measure captures the age-specific stock of collegiate attainment.

Table 1.4   Within-State Changes in the Share of State Higher Education Appropriations and College Completion

Dependent Variable	Coefficient of Interest	Coefficient	Other
4-year share of state appropriation	Time trend	−0.002 (0.000)	State fixed effects
Ratio BA degrees conferred to undergraduate FTE enrollment	4-year share of state appropriation	0.049 (0.021)	State and year fixed effects
Decennial difference (90-80) in state completion rate (BA/any college)	Decennial difference (85-75) 4-year share of state appropriation	0.353 (0.125)	Age-specific dummy variables

Notes: Measures of the share of state appropriations to four-year institutions and two-year institutions are from the author's calculations using data from the HEGIS/IPEDS surveys of institutional financial characteristics. Data on degrees conferred and enrollments are also from the author's calculations using data from the HEGIS/IPEDS surveys. Census-based completion rates are calculated from the 1980 and 1990 census microdata. Share some college and share college completion is calculated at ages twenty-three–twenty-five and state reflects the place of residence five years prior in order to measure outcomes without the effects of migration. Calculations are based on forty-seven continental states, as South Dakota lacks a community college system. Standard errors in parentheses. FTE = full-time equivalent.

sured using outcomes from the census. Still, additional evidence on the exogeneity of state appropriations (demonstrating that shares are not adjusting to changes in local demand conditions) is necessary before claiming a causal relationship.

Tuition

It is well established that enrollment decisions are sensitive to tuition levels, yet there is very little evidence on how students at this enrollment margin progress in the collegiate pipeline (Kane 1995). Low-tuition strategies come at a substantial cost, as below-market tuition is essentially an across-the-board subsidy to all students, including those who would continue to enroll at higher tuition levels. Whether low-tuition policies have any affect on collegiate attainment is critical to determining whether public calls for continued reductions in tuition are sound policy recommendations.[30]

With the majority of undergraduate students attending public colleges

30. A significant trend in higher education finance in the last five years has been real declines in tuition costs in several major state systems (e.g., California, Michigan, New York). Governors and state legislators have found that low-tuition policies are particularly popular among their constituencies, and several governors instituted tuition rollbacks for in-state students. For example, in-state students in the 1998–1999 academic year at the University of Virginia paid $4,866 in tuition and required fees, followed by a rollback to $4,130 in the 1999–2000 academic year. California and Texas also reduced nominal tuition in the late 1990s. While reductions in state budgets have put upward pressure on tuition for the 2002–2003 academic year in many states, these increases come with reduced state appropriations and generally reduced resources per student. Efforts to freeze tuition at public colleges and universities are politically popular because they provide tangible near-term relief in an area of intense voter interest. Yet, without higher tuition, institutions of higher education may be forced to reduce quality or capacity.

Table 1.5   **Effect of Tuition and Resources on Enrollment and Completion**

Dependent Variable (in logs)	Coefficient on In-State University Tuition		
	(1)	(2)	(3)
FTE undergraduate enrollment	−0.21	−0.14	
	(0.06)	(0.04)	
BA degrees	−0.10	−0.02	0.05
	(0.02)	(0.04)	(0.04)
State effects	Y	Y	Y
Year effects	Y	Y	Y
Population 18–22	N	Y	Y
Undergraduate enrollment	N	N	Y

Notes: Author's tabulations from HEGIS/IPEDS "Degrees Conferred" and "Fall Enrollment" surveys. Tuition data are from Washington State Higher Education Control Board. Each set of estimates represents the effect of tuition (measured in lns) on full-time equivalent (FTE) enrollment or degrees as indicated (also measured in lns) using data from 1972–1996 at the state level with state and year fixed effects, with standard errors corrected for heteroskedasticity and clustering at the state level.

and universities in-state, direct tuition prices are often well below the cost of educational production. Indeed, about 43 percent of all students attend institutions with tuition prices less than $4,000 per year. Because tuition is only a fraction of total college costs, with foregone earnings of persistence in college likely to exceed direct college costs, it may be that changes in tuition levels do not have a significant effect on persistence decisions. At public colleges and universities, state policy makers have substantial influence in determining tuition levels and relative charges within state systems.[31] Ideally, the data would allow for the investigation of the extent to which the differentiated tuition policies within a state (e.g., the relative tuition at community colleges and flagship universities) affect attainment in addition to the effects of the levels on attainment. However, because there is only limited variation within states in relative tuition by institution type, it is very difficult to employ this source of variation, while variation across states may be related to other systematic differences between states.

Estimates in table 1.5 use within-state variation over time in regressions of enrollment and BA completion on tuition (producing coefficients in elasticity form). What is unambiguously clear from these specifications is that the behavioral effect is entirely concentrated at the enrollment margin as the BA degree elasticity is no larger than the enrollment elasticity. Inclusion of measures of cohort size (the population aged eighteen–twenty-

31. A survey of state higher education executive officers finds that in ten states legislatures explicitly set tuition in practice or in statute. In other states, tuition determination is generally the responsibility of governing boards or state higher education authorities, with these authorities often composed of political appointees (Kane, Orszag, and Gunter 2002).

two within the state) or undergraduate enrollment in regressions of BA degrees awarded on tuition produces effects that are consistently indistinguishable from zero. One explanation is that the demand for a BA may be quite inelastic among those students who are not at the enrollment margin.

Federal Policy

A final dimension to consider is the effect of federal policy on student enrollment and completion.[32] The primary instruments for federal policy designed to increase collegiate attainment over the last three decades have been the programs under Title IV of the Higher Education Act, notably Pell grants and Stafford student loans. More recently, beginning with the Tax Reform Act of 1997, tuition tax credits have provided another mechanism for the federal government to reduce the cost of college to students (the details of these programs are discussed elsewhere in this volume). A third type of aid funded at the federal level is the specially-directed aid aimed at specific populations to achieve objectives other than meeting financial need; these programs include G.I. benefits and the Social Security Student Benefit (SSSB) program.

Focusing first on Title IV, the primary programs are the Pell Grant program and the Stafford student loan program. Both programs are means tested, and eligibility is determined through the evaluation of a Free Application for Federal Student Aid (FAFSA) form that records student and parental assets and incomes. Applying a nonlinear benefit reduction formula yields an expected family contribution, and the difference between allowable college costs and expected family contribution is the aid eligibility.[33] Title IV financial aid is remarkable in the breadth of the programs covered and the range of potential students eligible to benefit. While early federal higher education programs such as the National Defense Education Act (NDEA) focused on selected degree programs, the only academic criteria for Title IV eligibility is "ability to benefit" from a postsecondary program, and the aid may be used at a range of postsecondary institutions, including nondegree granting institutions and proprietary institutions.[34]

32. For the most part, the federal role in financing higher education has historically been much more modest and considerably more targeted than the state role. Still, at particular times in history, federal support for institutions of higher education, including the Morrill legislation chartering many public institutions, has been decisive in determining the level and distribution of higher education services. Federal research funding no doubt has a significant effect on enrollment and completion in graduate programs, even though these resources are allocated largely at the institutional level (the Javitts and National Science Foundation [NSF] programs are exceptions).

33. In essence, a tax rate is applied to a measure of available resources, both income and assets, with fixed adjustments for family size and number of members of the family in college to determine the student's "ability to pay." If this amount is less than allowable college costs, the student is aid eligible.

34. The inaugural Higher Education Act passed in 1965 separated academic and vocational training in determining program eligibility. Most of the programs funded under the 1965

The Title IV financial aid programs are often described as the cornerstone of federal higher education policy; in academic year 2000–2001, Pell Grant aid totaled $7.9 billion in expenditures, while loan programs provided over $26 billion in capital, with about $12.6 billion of the amount provided through the subsidized Stafford loan program.

Despite the rhetoric (and almost sentimental attachment) surrounding the Title IV programs as the key dimensions of federal policy aimed at eliminating credit constraints, empirical evidence on the behavioral effects of these programs is mixed. Focusing first on the enrollment effects for traditional college-age students (defined as students who are recent high school graduates and still depend on their parents for financial support), evaluations consistently yield no evidence that the program changed enrollment (Hansen 1983; Kane 1994).[35] What is more, evidence presented by Manski (1992) indicates that low-income youth graduating from high school between 1972 and 1980 (after the introduction of the program) show no relative gain in college completion. One explanation for why the Pell Grant program has had such modest effects is that the complexity of the program and the difficulty in determining benefit eligibility may impose a high cost, inhibiting many potential students at the margin from applying. Another explanation is that factors beyond financial constraints, including academic achievement, are the factors limiting college enrollment and college attainment for the marginal low-income student.

While the Pell Grant program has not had a discernable effect on the collegiate attainment of traditional students, the effects on college participation for nontraditional students have been marked.[36] Despite restrictions

---

Higher Education Act were campus based (providing resources to institutions rather than portable aid to students). According to Gladieux (1995), Title IV of the Higher Education Act was the first explicit federal commitment to equalizing college opportunities for needy students, which was to be achieved through means-tested grant aid as well as student support programs (Upward Bound, Talent Search, and the programs now known as TRIO). The primary means-tested aid vehicle was the Student Educational Opportunity Grants (SEOG); award of aid under this program was administered by colleges and universities that were required to "make 'vigorous' efforts to identify and recruit students with 'exceptional financial need.'" (See Gladieux [1995] for additional history.) Under the 1972 reauthorization of the Higher Education Act, Congress substituted the term "postsecondary education" for "higher education," intending to broaden the range of options beyond traditional baccalaureate programs. In this regard, the Basic Educational Opportunity Grants (known now as the Pell Grant) included two- and four-year colleges and proprietary schools from the inception. Thus, in 1972, federal financial aid changed the choice set of students to include a wider range of short-term, nonbaccalaureate degree and vocational programs under Title IV.

35. In one of the initial assessments of the program using time series data, Lee Hansen examined the relative enrollment rates of more and less affluent students before and after the introduction of the Pell Grant program. Hansen's review of the evidence "suggests that expansion of federal financial aid programs and their targeting toward youth from lower-income and lower-status families did not alter to any appreciable degree the composition of postsecondary students or the college enrollment expectations of high school seniors over the 1970s" (Hansen 1984).

36. Under Title IV of the Higher Education Act, federal financial aid policy makes a statutory distinction between "dependent" and "independent" students in the determination of

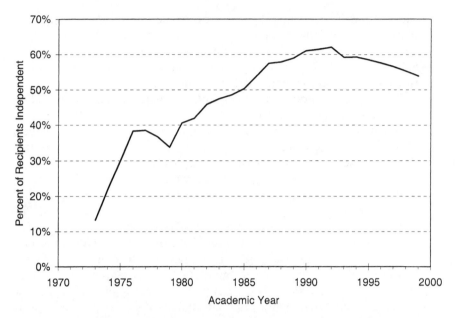

Fig. 1.11   Share of Pell Grants awarded to students classified as independent students
Source: College Board (2002), table 7.
Note: "Academic year" refers to the academic year beginning in the indicated year.

that potentially limit independent student eligibility, the share of Pell Grant recipients who are independent has risen steadily over the last three decades, from about 30 percent in 1975 to over 60 percent in the early 1990s (see figure 1.11). Research by Seftor and Turner (2002) finds that the introduction of the Pell Grant program, as well as changes in program eligibility, have a significant effect on the college enrollment decisions with college cost elasticities of about –0.26 for men and –0.67 for women. Overall, a review of changes in the determination of eligibility for Title IV aid, particularly the Pell Grant program, shows that many of the most significant changes in benefit determination have affected nontraditional students. To take but one example, Simmons and Turner (2003) examine the effects of the inclusion of child care expenses under allowable college costs

program eligibility. Eligibility for independent students rests only on the financial position of the applicant and his or her spouse, relative to direct college costs and other demands on resources including the number of children in the family. To be eligible for aid as an independent student, an individual must not be claimed as a dependent in the prior or current year for tax purposes and may only receive limited cash and in-kind contributions from parents. Eligibility for students claiming independent status has become more restrictive since the inception of the program. The 1986 amendments to the Higher Education Act required students to be at least twenty-four-years-old, married, or with children to qualify for aid as an independent student.

in aid determination and find that the addition of this benefit has a significant effect on enrollment for women with children. Expansion of the availability of federal financial aid for undergraduates to older students opens enrollment in higher education to many individuals who would not have been able to enroll in higher education in earlier decades. Yet such results raise three questions about the distribution of federal student aid. First, to what extent are older students able to convert enrollment to collegiate attainment and, in turn, earnings growth? Second, does the extended availability of federal financial aid through the life course encourage students to prolong or postpone studies? Finally, in the policy arena, does financial aid for nontraditional students come at the "expense" of higher levels of aid for younger postsecondary students?

Two programs targeting somewhat narrower groups of potential beneficiaries than Title IV aid are the SSSB program and the World War II G.I. Bill. Both initiatives had generally significant effects on both collegiate enrollment and completion (Dynarski 2003; Bound and Turner 2002).[37] The G.I. Bill and the SSSB program share several design features, including the transparency of eligibility determination, meaning that potential beneficiaries knew their eligibility and the level and duration of benefits without additional calculations or waiting for the results of a bureaucratic process, and the substantial size of the benefits, often covering the majority of college costs.

The evaluation of the effects of the SSSB program on enrollment and attainment yields results parallel in magnitude; Dynarski (2003) uses the death of a parent to estimate program eligibility and finds that college attendance dropped by about 4 percentage points per $1,000 of grant eligibility. A particularly striking feature of the SSSB program is that benefits expired at the end of the semester in which the recipient turned twenty-one, thereby creating a strong incentive to avoid extension of undergraduate degree programs beyond the four-year norm.

1.4   Implications for Future Research and Policy Tradeoffs

The economic consequences of the differences between college enrollment and college completion are near their historical maximum, as the

---

37. For veterans returning from World War II, Bound and Turner (2001) estimate that the effect of the G.I. Bill combined with the effect of World War II service on years of college completed was between 0.23 and 0.28 years of college (or 32 to 38 percent), and the effect on college completion rates was between 5 and 6 percentage points (or 39 to 46 percent). An exception to these results is the collegiate attainment of black men from the South eligible for the G.I. Bill who did not share the gains experienced by black men from non-Southern states or white men more generally (Turner and Bound 2003). Explanations for the divergence in these results include the limited supply of higher education opportunities for blacks in the segregated South as well as the potentially lower demand owing to the poor secondary school quality available to these men.

wage premium for a college degree, relative to a high school degree, remains near 60 percent (Murphy and Welch 1999). The divergence between college enrollment and college completion and the related extension in time to degree have a substantial impact on inequality as well as intergenerational opportunity. Hence, understanding the determinants of college completion and how public policies affect completion should be a fundamental concern for research at the intersection of economics and higher education.

An overriding conclusion from the data assembled for this analysis is that it is imperative to consider explanations (as well as policy interventions) beyond a myopic focus on "affordability" and student aid. Table 1.6 summarizes the empirical explanations discussed in the prior section, and what is clear is that there is no one factor that unambiguously explains the collegiate attainment behavior observed. Because many of the outcomes observed in higher education are affected by investments made in elementary and secondary education as well as family circumstances, it may be that students at the margin of college enrollment in recent years are less well prepared than those from prior decades. It is also possible that credit constraints, particularly for high-achieving students from poor families, may limit degree completion or extend the time it takes to complete a degree. On the other side of the market, colleges and universities—the institutions forming the supply side of the market—matter substantially in the process of transforming initial college participation to collegiate attainment and completion. Understanding how these institutions adjust to changes in demand and funding and how students are matched with institutions is critically important. Limited evidence points to soft supply constraints (Bound and Turner 2004) at four-year institutions as one factor limiting degree attainment.

However, what is known about the link between college enrollment and college completion is an insufficient basis for advocating direct policy interventions. Very broad-based programs such as tuition subsidies or across-the-board grants to low-income students are likely to have minimal effects on college completion while imposing large costs. A primary hurdle to the understanding of the enrollment–completion relationship is the absence of data for evaluation. One glaring failure is the absence of careful recording of collegiate experiences on the major surveys designed to measure economic well being, including the CPS and the census. "Some college" is the only measure of attainment available in the most recent census enumerations and the CPS in much of the decade of the 1990s for those who have not completed a degree. Unfortunately, this measure does not distinguish between the high school dropout attending college for less than a semester and a high school graduate completing three years of study. Distinguishing between these cases is critical for understanding the connection between enrollment and attainment. To this end, it is imperative to

Table 1.6   Summary of Evidence Potentially Explaining Reduction in Completion Rates and Extension of Time to Degree

	Evidence	Comment
	Individual Constraints	
Credit constraints	18-to-24-year-old students increasingly combine college enrollment and employment. For potential students with parents in the bottom quartile of the income distribution, capacity to pay for college has eroded in the last two decades.	Observation does not prove that credit markets are insufficient or that finances at the collegiate stage are the barriers to college enrollment.
Student characteristics		
Academic achievement	Combined with increases in college participation, the marginal student enrolling in college is likely to be less prepared academically than in prior decades.	Changes are unlikely to be sufficiently large to explain increased time to degree.
High school degree type	Increased GED attainment may indicate declines in affective skills of potential college students.	
Nontraditional status	There has been increased enrollment of women with children; increased employment of students, particularly in their early 20s; and increased college enrollment of older students.	These changes in enrollment may reflect other changes (in dimensions like achievement and capacity to pay for college) that have extended the time needed to complete the BA degree, rather than a direct effect of these characteristics on attainment.
Paternal education	Collegiate attainment of the mothers of students of college age has increased markedly over the last two decades. This variable is predicted to increase collegiate attainment.	Observed change goes in the "wrong direction" for explanation of overall trends in degrees conferred.
	Institutions and Policy	
Tuition policies	While increases in tuition prices at public institutions do have a significant negative effect on undergraduate enrollment, there is no additional effect on BA degree attainment.	It is not clear if this shift is caused by relatively exogenous political forces or is simply a response to student demand.
State appropriations	There has been a shift in the distribution of state support from four-year institutions to community colleges, potentially reducing the relative supply of upper-division courses and deterring college completion.	
Federal policy	Pell Grants and Title IV financial aid do not appear to have a substantial effect on enrollment or attainment of recent high school graduates. These programs do appear to have a substantial impact on the enrollment of older students. Programs like the Social Security Student Benefit Program (Dynarski 2003) have substantial effects on attainment. Such programs are generous, transparent, and relatively targeted.	

move beyond cumulative measures, recording only the last level of participation, and to add measures of the trajectory of educational experiences. For example, recording type (or presence) of high school credential and the duration and type of program for each spell of college participation would be particularly illuminating and not that costly.

Beyond traditional microdata, targeted policy experiments (such as the COACH program in Boston) provide one avenue for obtaining a sharper focus on how policy design affects behavior. From a different angle, the opening of detailed administrative data records (such as the institutional student records used by Bettinger and Long [2004] in Ohio), particularly when combined with employment and social service records, is likely to improve substantially the understanding of the economic, social, and institutional factors affecting college completion.

In addition to the need for additional empirical evidence, the observed growth in time to degree and the expansion of enrollment outside the late teens and early twenties suggest the need to revisit our traditional human capital investment theory with the objective of introducing a model that is more successful in capturing the observed pattern of collegiate attainment. The interpretation favored in this essay is that demand-side limitations in credit and information combined with supply-side constraints at four-year institutions contribute to the delay in degree completion. Alternatively, Taber (comment to this chapter) suggests a model in which individuals shift from investing in on-the-job training in the workplace to continuing education offered by postsecondary institutions, presumably resulting from either reductions in the relative cost of the former or increased complementarities between collegiate attainment and employment.

The primary contribution of this essay is in the clear documentation of the relationship between college participation and college completion. There are a number of developments, such as the rise in parental education and the growth in the return to college completion, that quite plainly go in the wrong direction to explain the relationship between college participation and college completion. It is more difficult to distinguish among other explanations—such as the relative importance of precollegiate achievement, limitations in the credit markets, and changes in the level and distribution of state and federal policy—in understanding the decline in the college completion rate among those in their early twenties and the stagnation in this rate for those at older ages.[38] These are not easy empirical questions

38. Starting with the unanswered questions in this paper, Bound and Turner (2003) take a closer look at the determinants of time to BA degree receipt. Employing data from multiple sources, including the annual October files of the CPS and the NLSY, this research will examine the extent to which BA degree recipients from more recent cohorts are less academically or financially prepared than those in prior decades. A competing explanation is that changes in the resources available to students at colleges and universities, particularly large public institutions, may limit the ability of students to complete their studies in a timely fashion.

to answer, but they are important to resolve if public investments in higher education are to contribute to economic productivity and to reduce intergenerational differences in opportunities.

Appendix A

The primary sources of data for this analysis are the CPS (March and October), institutional surveys of colleges and universities, and the decennial census files.

College Enrollment and BA Degree Outcomes

The nationally representative CPS is the primary source for information on collegiate enrollment and attainment by age (or birth cohort). As indicated, many tabulations in this analysis rely on the October questionnaire, which contains a module devoted to education. Additional tabulations use the March supplement, which focuses on income-related questions. The CPS records attainment in each year, but is not the ideal data set to the extent that information on prior educational experiences is somewhat limited. To this end, we do not observe individual time to degree directly, but must examine changes over time in the collegiate attainment of a birth cohort. In all tabulations, individual weights are employed, and observations are limited to those without allocated information.

The decennial census enumerations complement the CPS data by providing very large samples recording collegiate attainment to individuals by state of birth and age (or, implicitly, year of birth). All source data are from the Integrated Public Use Microdata Series (IPUMS; Ruggles and Sobek 2003) microdata, with a 3 percent (form 2) sample for 1970, 5 percent samples for 1980 and 1990, and the 1 percent sample available for 2000.

In using both the census and the CPS over an extended time horizon, changes in the structure of the education question leads to a relatively strong assumption about the correspondence between the degree-based enumeration (with direct indication of degree types) and the highest grade completed form of recording. When comparing across years where different questions were administered, it is assumed that sixteen years of completed education is equivalent to a BA degree. Jaeger (1997) provides an analysis of the empirical correspondence between these measures. For the CPS, surveys from 1992 to the present employ the degree-based question and early surveys use the attainment question. Census enumerations prior to 1990 used the years of completed education, while 1990 and 2000 have used the degree attainment question.

Beyond surveys of individuals, federal surveys of colleges and universities provide information on college enrollment and participation. The degree data are based on the annual "Earned Degrees Conferred" survey conducted by the National Center for Education Statistics (NCES), which records degrees awarded in the twelve-month academic year from July to June. The enrollment data are from the "Fall Enrollment" surveys, which record the number of students enrolled in classes in the fall. Through 1986, these surveys were part of the larger NCES Higher Education General Information Survey (HEGIS), which was subsequently redesigned as the Integrated Postsecondary Education Data System (IPEDS) collection. Machine-readable data are employed after 1966 (1967 for enrollment), which allows for the distinction of institutions by control (public/private) and Carnegie classification. These institution-based surveys are important for recording the "products" of the higher education system; however, because they record neither student ages nor track prior collegiate experiences, these data provide only indirect evidence on time-to-degree and completion rates.

Higher Education Finance Variables

Each year as part of the institutional reporting to the federal government, colleges and universities complete a survey of institutional finances in which they report basic income and expense items, including the sources of revenues and expenses. In years prior to 1977, all state-level financial data are from published tabulations as we have found the machine readable data for early years (through Webcaspar) to be unreliable, presumably due to problems with imputations. One of the primary variables from this source used in the analysis is state appropriations. Data on tuition and fees, measured as a price, are available from 1970 to the current year from the "Institution Characteristics" part of the HEGIS/IPEDS surveys. In addition, the Washington Higher Education Coordinating Board conducts an annual survey of tuition and fees at public institutions, which includes data from 1972–1973 to the present.

References

Advisory Committee on Student Financial Assistance. 2001. *Access denied: Restoring the nation's commitment to equal educational opportunity.* Washington, D.C.: Advisory Committee on Student Financial Assistance.

Altonji, J. 1993. The demand for and the return to education when education outcomes are uncertain. *Journal of Labor Economics* 11 (1): 48–83.

Avery, C., A. Fairbanks, and R. Zeckhauser. 2001. What worms for the early bird: Early admissions at elite colleges. KSG Faculty Research Working Papers Series no. RWP01-049. Cambridge, Mass.: Kennedy School of Government.

Bettinger, Eric, and Bridget Terry Long. 2004. Shape up or ship out: The effect of remediation on underprepared students at four-year colleges. Case Western Reserve University and Harvard University. Unpublished manuscript.

Bound, J., and S. Turner. 2002. Going to war and going to college: Did World War II and the G.I. Bill increase educational attainment for returning veterans? *Journal of Labor Economics* 20 (4): 784–815.

———. 2003. Understanding the increased time to the baccalaureate degree. University of Michigan and University of Virginia. Mimeograph.

———. 2004. Cohort crowding: How resources affect collegiate attainment. PSC Research Report 04-557 (April).

Cameron, S. V., and J. Heckman. 1997. The nonequivalence of high school equivalents. *Journal of Labor Economics* 11 (1): 1–47.

Cameron, S., and C. Taber. 2000. Borrowing constraints and the returns to schooling. NBER Working Paper no. 7761. Cambridge, Mass.: National Bureau of Economic Research, June.

Card, D. 2001. Estimating the return to schooling: Progress on some persistent econometric problems. *Econometrica* 69 (5): 1127.

Card, D., and A. Krueger. 1996. Labor market effects of school quality: Theory and evidence. In *Does Money Matter?* ed. Gary Burtless, 97–140. Washington, D.C.: Brookings Institution.

Card, D., and T. Lemieux. 2001. Draft avoidance and college attendance: The unintended legacy of the Vietnam War. *American Economic Review Papers and Proceedings* 91:97–102.

Carneiro, P., J. Heckman, and D. Manoli. 2002. Human capital policy. Harvard University, Alvin Hansen Lecture. Mimeograph.

Clark, Burton. 1961. The "colling-out" function in higher education. In *Education, economy, and society,* ed. A. H. Halsey, 513–521. New York: Free Press.

College Board. 2002. *Trends in student aid.* New York: College Board Publications.

Dynarski, S. 2002. Loans, liquidity, and schooling decisions. Harvard University, Kennedy School of Government. Mimeograph.

———. 2003. Does aid matter? Measuring the effect of student aid on college attendance and completion. *American Economic Review* 93 (1): 279–288.

Ellwood, D., and T. Kane. 2000. Who is getting a college education? Family background and the growing gaps in enrollment. In *Securing the future,* ed. S. Danziger and J. Waldfogel, 283–324. New York: Russell Sage.

Garet, M. S., Z. Jing, and M. Kutner. 1996. *The labor market effects of completing the GED: Asking the right questions.* Washington, D.C.: Pelavin Research Center, American Institutes for Research.

Gladieux, L. 1995. Federal Student Aid policy: A history and an assessment. Available at [http://www.ed.gov/offices/OPE/PPI/FinPostSecEd/gladieux.html].

Griliches, Z. 1977. Estimating the returns to schooling: Some econometric problems. *Econometrica* 45:1–22.

Hansen, W. L. 1983. Good intentions and mixed results: An update on the BEOG program eight years later. In *Public expenditure and public analysis,* ed. R. Haveman and J. Margolis, 493–512. New York: Rand McNally.

Heckman, J., and P. Carneiro. 2003. Human capital policy. NBER Working Paper no. 9495. Cambridge, Mass.: National Bureau of Economic Research, February.

Hoxby, C. 1997. How the changing market structure of U.S. higher education explains college tuition. NBER Working Paper no. 6323. Cambridge, Mass.: National Bureau of Economic Research, December.

———. 2000. Rising cost of college tuition and the effectiveness of government financial aid. Senate Hearing. 106-51.

Jaeger, David A. 1997. Reconciling the New Census Bureau Education Questions: Recommendations for researchers. *Journal of Business and Economic Statistics* 15 (4): 300–309.

Kane, T. 1994. College entry by blacks since 1970: The role of college costs, family background, and the returns to education. *Journal of Political Economy* 102 (5): 878–911.

———. 1995. Rising public college tuition and college entry: How well do public subsidies promote access to college? NBER Working Paper no. 5164. Cambridge, Mass.: National Bureau of Economic Research, July.

———. 1999. *The price of admission: Rethinking how Americans pay for college.* Washington, D.C.: Brookings Institution.

Kane, T., P. Orszag, and D. Gunter. 2002. State support for higher education, Medicaid, and the business cycle. Brookings Institution. Mimeograph.

Levhari, D., and Y. Weiss. 1974. The effect of risk on the investment in human capital. *American Economic Review* 64 (6): 950–963.

Manski, C. 1989. Schooling as experimentation: A reappraisal of the postsecondary dropout phenomenon. *Economics of Education Review* 8 (4): 305–312.

———. 1992. Income and higher education. *Focus* 14 (3): 14–19.

Murnane, R., J. B. Willett, and F. Levy. 1993. The growing importance of cognitive skills in wage determination. *Review of Economics and Statistics* 77:261–266.

Murphy, K., and F. Welch. 1999. Relative wages in the 1990s. University of Chicago, Graduate School of Business. Mimeograph. Available at [http://gsbwww.uchicago.edu/fac/kevin.murphy/research/aea99.pdf].

New York Times. 2002. Public colleges, broken promises. May 5, late edition, sec. 4.

Rosenbaum, J. 2001. *Beyond college for all: Career paths for the forgotten half.* New York: Russell Sage.

Ruggles, S., M. Sobek, et al. 2003. *Integrated public use microdata series: Version 3.0.* Minneapolis, Minn.: Historical Census Projects, University of Minnesota.

Seftor, N., and S. Turner. 2002. Federal Student Aid and adult college enrollment. *Journal of Human Resources* 37 (2): 336–352.

Simmons, S., and S. Turner. 2003. Taking classes and taking care of the kids: Do childcare benefits increase collegiate attainment. University of Virginia, Department of Economics. Mimeograph.

Stinebrickner, T., and R. Stinebrickner. 2001. Understanding educational outcomes of students from low income families: Evidence from a liberal arts college with a full tuition subsidy program. CIBC Working Paper no. 2001-4. London, Ontario: CIBC.

———. 2003. Working during school and academic performance. *Journal of Labor Economics,* 21 (2): 473–491.

Taber, C. 2001. The rising college premium in the eighties: Return to college or return to unobserved ability? *Review of Economic Studies* 68 (3): 665–692.

Turner, S., and J. Bound. 2003. Closing the gap or widening the divide: The effects of the G.I. Bill and World War II on the educational outcomes of black Americans. *Journal of Economic History* 63 (1): 145–177.

U.S. Department of Education. 2001. *Digest of education statistics, 2001.* Washington, D.C.: National Center for Education Statistics.

———. 2002. *The condition of education 2002.* Washington, D.C.: National Center for Education Statistics.

U.S. Department of Labor. Various years. *College enrollment of high school graduates.* Washington, D.C.: U.S. Department of Labor.

Comment   Christopher Taber

Sarah Turner has written a very nice paper on trends in college attendance and completion over the last thirty years. The most important point of the paper can be seen clearly in figure 1.2. College participation rates have increased considerably over time, but college completion has changed very little. Turner goes through a number of different explanations for this trend but finds no obvious explanation. We are left with a puzzle: w*hy has college completion changed very little while college enrollment has changed substantially?*

Turner documents another important, and in my view, even more puzzling trend. There has been a huge increase in the amount of time it takes students to complete their degrees. This can be seen clearly in the bottom panel of figure 1.5. The difference between completion rates at age twenty-three and completion rates at age thirty has increased substantially. Again, one can see no obvious explanation. We are left with a second puzzle: w*hy has the average amount of time that it takes students to complete their college degree increased?*

In this comment I will highlight and expand on a point that Turner made in her paper: economic theory can be a useful tool to understanding these puzzles. I will go through some schooling models that are useful in thinking about the two puzzles mentioned previously.

A Model of College Attendance and College Completion

The main point that I want to make in this section is that the difference in trends in college completion and in college attendance is not necessarily a puzzle with even a very simple schooling model. I develop a traditional Becker (1975) model whose solution is similar to Cameron and Heckman (1998) in that it resembles an ordered probit.

Assume that if individual i attended s years of school, he or she would receive log earnings of

$$\beta(s; \boldsymbol{\pi}) + \gamma(t - s) + \theta_i,$$

where $\beta(s; \boldsymbol{\pi})$ is the payoff to schooling level s and depends on parameter vector $\boldsymbol{\pi}$, t represents age so that $(t - s)$ is potential experience, and θ_i represents ability of the student. The student goes to school until age s and chooses schooling to maximize the present value of earnings

$$\int_f^T e^{\beta(s;\boldsymbol{\pi})+\gamma(t-s)+\theta_i}e^{-rt}\, dt = e^{\theta_i}\int_f^T e^{\beta(s;\boldsymbol{\pi})+\gamma(t-s)}e^{-rt}dt$$

$$\equiv e^{\theta_i}g(s; \boldsymbol{\pi}),$$

where r is the interest rate.

Christopher Taber is associate professor of economics at Northwestern University, and a faculty research fellow of the National Bureau of Economic Research.

Now suppose that students must incur some costs to attend school. To obtain commonly observed schooling patterns, assume that the cost of schooling differs for high school, college, and graduate school, so that the costs of schooling for individual i are

$$\mu_{1i} \quad \text{if} \quad s \leq 12$$

$$\mu_{2i} \quad \text{if} \quad 12 < s \leq 16$$

$$\mu_{3i} \quad \text{if} \quad s > 16.$$

Assume that g is increasing in s, differentiable, and concave and that $\mu_{1i} < \mu_{2i} < \mu_{3i}$. Solving the model leads to the following first-order conditions or inequalities:

$$e^{\theta_i} \frac{\partial g(s; \pi)}{\partial s} = \mu_{1i} \quad s < 12$$

$$\mu_{1i} \leq e^{\theta_i} \frac{\partial g(12; \pi)}{\partial s} \leq \mu_{2i} \quad s = 12$$

$$e^{\theta_i} \frac{\partial g(s; \pi)}{\partial s} = \mu_{12} \quad 12 < s < 16$$

$$\mu_{2i} \leq e^{\theta_i} \frac{\partial g(16; \pi)}{\partial s} \leq \mu_{3i} \quad s = 16$$

$$e^{\theta_i} \frac{\partial g(s; \pi)}{\partial s} = \mu_{3i} \quad s > 16$$

Now consider college attendance and college completion in this model. A student attends college if $e^{\theta_i}(\partial g[12; \pi])/\partial s > \mu_{12}$ and completes college if $e^{\theta_i}(\partial g[16; \pi])/\partial s > \mu_{12}$. Let F and f be the cumulative and probability distribution functions of μ_1/e^{θ_i}, then

$$\Pr(S_i > 12) = F\left[\frac{\partial g(12; \pi)}{\partial s} \right]$$

$$\Pr(S_i \geq 16) = F\left[\frac{\partial g(16; \pi)}{\partial s} \right].$$

My goal is to predict the manner in which college completion and college attendance adjust to parameter changes. Notice that

$$\frac{\partial \Pr(S_i > 12)}{\partial \pi} = f\left[\frac{\partial g(12; \pi)}{\partial s} \right] \frac{\partial^2 g(12; \pi)}{\partial s \partial \pi}$$

$$\frac{\partial \Pr(S_i \geq 16)}{\partial \pi} = f\left[\frac{\partial g(16; \pi)}{\partial s} \right] \frac{\partial^2 g(16; \pi)}{\partial s \partial \pi}.$$

One can see that the response of schooling to demand shocks at different levels of schooling depends on two things, the payment structure itself (e.g., $[\partial^2 g\{12; \pi\}]/\partial s \partial \pi$) and the density of individuals who are on the margin of whether to complete the schooling transition (e.g., $f[\{\partial g(12; \pi)\}/\partial s]$). One explanation of the difference in patterns is that the density of individuals that are close to indifferent about attending college is much larger than the density of individuals that are close to indifferent about completing college. There are a number of testable implications of this model that make this explanation straightforward to investigate.

A Model of Delayed Schooling

One objection to the previous model may be that I have assumed that students stay in school until a certain point and then leave. Turner clearly finds evidence to the contrary as she documents a large increase in part-time schooling (or fluctuating back and forth from schooling to work), leading to increased time to completion. In this section, I modify the previous model to allow for part-time schooling. In particular, assume that $I(t)$ is the fraction of time that an individual spends in school at the point in time t. The individual spends the rest of his or her time working. Schooling at time t, $s(t)$, is defined as the cumulative time spent in school:

$$s(\tau) = \int_0^\tau I(t)dt$$

I also extend the model to allow for utility maximization rather than just maximization of the present value of earnings. Let $c(t)$ be consumption at time t, let $u(.)$ denote the instantaneous utility from that consumption, and δ the discount rate. The student's problem is to maximize

$$\int_0^T u[(c(t)]e^{-\delta t}dt$$

subject to

$$\int_0^T c(t)e^{-rt}dt \leq \int_0^T [1 - I(t)]e^{\beta[s(t);\pi] + \gamma[t - s(t)] + \theta_i}e^{-rt}dt - \int_0^T I(t)\mu_i[s(t)]e^{-rt}dt,$$

where $\mu_i(s[t])$ is just defined as the marginal cost of schooling level s in a similar manner as the previous section.

It is straightforward to show that this model collapses to one analogous to the previous section.[1] First, notice that schooling only shows up on the right-hand side of the budget constraint. Thus, students make schooling decisions to maximize the present value of earnings. The second point that

---

1. It is not exactly identical due to the discounting of the costs of college. In the previous model if the marginal cost of a year of college is constant across years, but in present value terms that would mean that the marginal cost of a year of college is falling with years of schooling.

students will not choose part-time schooling is somewhat less obvious. The marginal benefit of investment falls over time because the horizon to reap the benefits falls, while the marginal cost in terms of forgone earnings rises because earnings increase with schooling. Thus, this model does not predict that students would participate in part-time schooling.

As Turner points out, borrowing constraints represent a reason why schooling may be delayed. To see why, consider an extreme example in which a student is completely excluded from credit markets so that they can neither borrow nor save. In this case they must just consume their income in each period. Thus, the student makes schooling decisions to maximize

$$\int_0^T u\{[1 - I(t)]e^{\beta[s(t);\pi]+\gamma[t-s(t)]+\theta_i} - \mu_i[s(t)]I(t)\}e^{-\delta t}dt.$$

As long as u has the property that $u(0) = -\infty$ and costs of schooling are nonnegative, it is clearly the case that students cannot be in school full-time, so $I(t)$ must be less than 1. In general, students will still invest in schooling so that at the beginning of their life $I(t) > 0$. Thus, borrowing constraints can explain why students participate less than full-time in school.

If it is indeed borrowing constraints that lead to partial schooling, there is potential for policymakers to act. The increase over time could be due either to worsening of the constraints or due to increases in the costs of schooling.

However, there is another standard human capital model that gives a quite different prediction. Consider the classic model of Ben Porath (1967). I keep the notation the same, but interpret $s(t)$ as human capital gained in school rather than years of schooling. Schooling now is produced according to the human capital production function

$$S(t) = A[S(t)I(t)]^\beta - \sigma S(t),$$

where A, β, and σ are parameters. People now choose time in school ($I[t]$) to maximize the present value of earnings. The solution to this problem is well known. Under many parameterizations, students first specialize in full-time schooling ($I[t] = 1$), and then investment gradually falls to zero.

In the classic Ben Porath (1967) model, the period with $I(t) = 1$ is interpreted as schooling. After the period of specialization, $I(t)$ is interpreted as in invested in training on the job. In this model, workers would be indifferent between investing in human capital on the job or in school. From that perspective, there is nothing puzzling about the increase in time to completion.

More generally, one might expect that colleges have a comparative advantage over firms in producing general human capital. If this is the case, it is puzzling why we don't observe more part-time schooling. The most obvious explanation is fixed costs of school attendance. It is straightforward to include fixed costs of school attendance in the previous model that could eliminate part-time schooling.

This model gives a quite different perspective on the increase in time to completion; it may be due to a fall in fixed costs of schooling. If this were the case, the fall in time to completion is actually welfare improving, and one can see no obvious reason why policymakers may want to intervene.

Whether the increase in time to completion is due to credit constraints or decreases in the fixed costs of schooling is ultimately an empirical question.

Conclusion

Turner does a very good job in documenting two important changes in schooling patterns over time—a divergence between college completion and college attendance and an increase in time to completion. There is much work to be done using both theory and empirical work to uncover these puzzles.

References

Becker, G. 1975. *Human capital: A theoretical and empirical analysis, with special reference to education.* Chicago: University of Chicago Press.

Ben Porath, Y. 1967. The production of human capital and the life cycle of earnings. *Journal of Political Economy* 75 (4, pt. 1): 352–365.

Cameron, S., and J. Heckman. 1998. Life cycle schooling and educational selectivity: Models and choice. *Journal of Political Economy* 106 (2): 262–333.

The New Merit Aid

Susan Dynarski

2.1 Introduction

Merit aid, a discount to college costs contingent upon academic performance, is nothing new. Colleges and private organizations have long rewarded high-achieving, college-bound high school students with scholarships. For example, the privately funded National Merit Scholarship program, established in 1955, annually awards grants to 8,000 entering college freshmen who perform exceptionally on a standardized test. Private colleges have long used merit scholarships to lure students with strong academic credentials.

While merit aid has a long history in the private sector, it has not played a major role in the public sector. Historically, government subsidies to college students have not been merit based. At the federal level, aid has been need based and strongly focused on low-income students. Eligibility for the two largest federal aid programs, the Pell Grant and Stafford Loan, is determined by a complex formula that defines financial need on the basis of income, assets, and family size. The formula is quite progressive: 90 percent of dependent students who receive federal grants grew up in families with incomes less than $40,000.[1]

At the state level, subsidies for college students have historically taken the form of low tuition at public college and universities. Most states have

Susan Dynarski is Assistant Professor of Public Policy at the John F. Kennedy School of Government, Harvard University, and a faculty research fellow of the National Bureau of Economic Research.

Andrea Corso, Vanessa Lacoss-Hurd, Maya Smith, and especially Betsy Kent provided excellent research assistance. Support from the Kennedy School of Government, the Milton Fund, and the NBER Non-Profit Fellowship is gratefully acknowledged.

1. Calculated from data in National Center for Education Statistics (1998a, table 314).

long had *some* form of merit aid, but these programs have traditionally been small and limited to the most elite students. For example, New York rewards each high school's top scorer on the Regents exam with a scholarship. While such small merit programs abound, the vast bulk of state spending on higher education takes the form of low tuition, made possible by the $50 billion in subsidies that states annually provide their postsecondary institutions. These institutional subsidies are highest at the flagship universities, which draw the highest-achieving students. In this sense, these institutional subsidies are, by far, the largest "merit aid" program in the United States. Access to this state subsidy has traditionally been controlled not by state governments but by the schools, who decide which students are sufficiently meritorious to gain admission.

Recently, however, state legislatures have gotten into the business of defining academic merit and awarding merit aid to hundreds of thousands of students. Since the early 1990s, more than a dozen states have established broad-based merit aid programs. The typical program awards tuition and fees to young residents who have maintained a modest grade point average in high school. Many require a high school grade point average (GPA) of 3.0 or above, not a particularly high threshold: In 1999, 40 percent of high school seniors met this standard.[2] Georgia, for example, gives a free ride at its public colleges and universities to residents who have a GPA of 3.0 in high school.[3] In Arkansas, the GPA cutoff is 2.5, exceeded by 60 percent of high school students.

This new breed of merit aid differs from the old style in both its breadth and, plausibly, its effect on students' decisions. The old style of merit aid was aimed at top students, whose decision to attend college is not likely to be contingent upon the receipt of a scholarship. By design, if not by intent, this elite form of merit aid goes to students whose operative decision is not whether to attend college, but which high-quality, four-year college to choose. By contrast, the new, broad-based merit aid programs are open to students with solid although not necessarily exemplary academic records. Such students may be uncertain about whether to go to college at all. When offered a well-publicized, generous scholarship, some of these students may decide to give college a try. Even among students who would have gone to college without the scholarship, the incentives of merit aid may have an effect on schooling decisions. For example, some may choose a four-year school over a two-year school, or a private school over a public

2. As I will discuss later in the paper, this figure varies quite dramatically by race and ethnicity. Source: Author's calculations from the 1997 National Longitudinal Survey of Youth (NLSY). This is the share of students with a *senior year* GPA of at least 3.0 and so is probably an upper bound on the share of students who achieve this GPA for their entire high school career. Unfortunately, NLSY does not contain GPA data for the entire high school career.

3. As the paper will discuss, the merit programs require that a high level of academic performance be maintained in college. In Georgia, a GPA of 3.0 must be maintained in college, a considerably higher hurdle than a 3.0 in high school.

school.[4] Those students planning to go to college out of state may instead decide to stay closer to home in order to take advantage of a merit scholarship.

This chapter will examine how merit aid affects this array of schooling decisions, using household survey data to measure the impact of the new state programs. I start with a case study of the Georgia Helping Outstanding Pupils Educationally (HOPE) Scholarship, the namesake and inspiration of many of the new state programs. I then extend the analysis to other states that now have broad-based, HOPE-like programs. In the empirical analysis, I pay particular attention to how the effect of merit aid has varied by race and ethnicity.

Merit aid might affect the decisions not only of students but also of institutions. Do colleges increase their tuition prices, in order to capture some of the subsidy? Do they reduce other forms of aid? Does the linkage of scholarships to grades lead to grade inflation at high schools and colleges? A number of studies have addressed these questions, and I will review the evidence on these topics. Finally, I will briefly discuss the political economy of merit aid. Why has it arisen where it has and when it has? What are the prospects for its continuation and growth, given the current, poor fiscal prospects of the states?

2.2   State Merit Aid: A Primer

Broad-based state merit aid became common in a very short span of time. In 1993, just two states, Arkansas and Georgia, had programs in place. By 2002, thirteen states had introduced large merit aid programs. Most of this growth has occurred quite recently, with seven programs starting up since 1999. As is clear from the map in figure 2.1, merit aid is heavily concentrated in the southern region of the United States. Of the thirteen states with broad-based merit aid programs, nine are in the South. Table 2.1 summarizes the characteristics of the thirteen broad-based merit programs. As was discussed earlier, dozens of states have some form of merit aid in place. The state programs detailed in table 2.1 were chosen because they have particularly lenient eligibility criteria, with at least 30 percent of high school students having grades and test scores high enough to qualify for a scholarship.[5]

4. Two-year colleges are generally cheaper than four-year colleges. Most merit aid programs make them both free.
5. The eligibility estimates are based on national data from the NLSY97. Many of the states listed in table 2.1 do not have enough observations in the NLSY97 to allow state-specific estimates of the share of students whose GPA qualifies them for their state's merit program. For all states, therefore, I use the national grade distribution to impute the share in a state that meets the eligibility criteria. When available, state-level data on the ACT and SAT are used to measure the share of students who meet these criteria. Note that these estimates are used only to choose the merit programs to be analyzed; they are not used in the paper's regression analyses.

1993

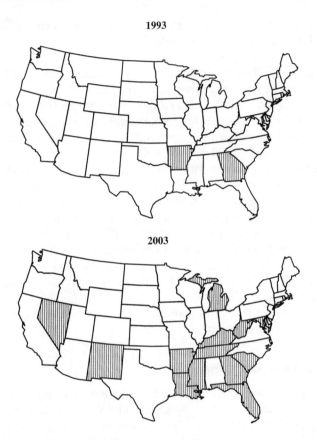

2003

Fig. 2.1   States with broad-based merit aid programs

For example, the Arkansas award requires a GPA of 2.5, a standard met by 60 percent of high school students nationwide. The state also requires a minimum on the American College Test (ACT) of 19, a score exceeded by 60 percent of test takers nationwide and well below the Arkansas state average of 20.4. Five other states, like Arkansas, condition eligibility on a minimum GPA and test score. Six states use only GPA to determine eligibility. Of the states that require a minimum GPA, four require a GPA of 3.0, while two make awards to those with a GPA of 2.5.

Only one state—Michigan—bases eligibility solely on standardized test performance. For the class of 2000, 31 percent of Michigan students had test scores sufficiently high to merit an award. However, this overall eligibility rate masks substantial heterogeneity: Just 7.9 percent of African American students met the Michigan requirement. Civil rights groups have protested that this wide gap in eligibility indicates that Michigan's achievement test is an inappropriate instrument with which to determine

Table 2.1   Merit Aid Program Characteristics, 2003

State	Start	Eligibility	Award (in-state attendance only, exceptions noted)
Arkansas	1991	initial: 2.5 GPA in HS core and 19 ACT renew: 2.75 college GPA	public: $2,500 private: same
Florida	1997	initial: 3.0–3.5 HS GPA and 970–1270 SAT/20–28 ACT renew: 2.75–3.0 college GPA	public: 75–100% tuition/fees[a] private: 75–100% average public tuition/fees[a]
Georgia	1993	initial: 3.0 HS GPA renew: 3.0 college GPA	public: tuition/fees private: $3,000
Kentucky	1999	initial: 2.5 HS GPA renew: 2.5–3.0 college GPA	public: $500–3,000[a] private: same
Louisiana	1998	initial: 2.5–3.5 HS GPA and ACT > state mean renew: 2.3 college GPA	public: tuition/fees + $400–800[a] private: average public tuition/fees[a]
Maryland	2002	initial: 3.0 HS GPA in core renew: 3.0 college GPA	2-year school: $1,000 4-year school: $3,000
Michigan	2000	initial: level 2 of MEAP or 75th percentile of SAT/ACT renew: NA	in-state: $2,500 once out-of-state: $1,000 once
Mississippi	1996	initial: 2.5 GPA and 15 ACT renew: 2.5 college GPA	public freshman/sophomore: $500 public junior/senior: $1,000 private: same
Nevada	2000	initial: 3.0 GPA and pass Nevada HS exam renew: 2.0 college GPA	public 4-year: tuition/fees (max $2,500) public 2-year: tuition/fees (max $1,900) private: none
New Mexico	1997	initial: 2.5 GPA 1st semester of college renew: 2.5 college GPA	public: tuition/fees private: none
South Carolina	1998	initial: 3.0 GPA and 1100 SAT/24 ACT renew: 3.0 college GPA	2-year school: $1,000 4-year school: $2,000
Tennessee	2003	initial: 3.0–3.75 GPA and 890–1280 SAT/19–29 ACT renew: 3.0 college GPA	2-year school: tuition/fees ($1,500–2,500)[a] 4-year school: tuition/fees ($3,000–4,000)[a]
West Virginia	2002	initial: 3.0 HS GPA in core and 1000 SAT/21 ACT renew: 2.75–3.0 college GPA	public: tuition/fees private: average public tuition/fees

Note: **HS** = high school.

[a]Amount of award rises with GPA and/or test score.

eligibility for a state-funded scholarship. Similar objections were raised in Arkansas, which initially based eligibility for its program only on performance on standardized tests but later broadened the criteria to include academic performance in high school.

These controversies point to a shared characteristic of merit programs: their scholarships flow disproportionately to white, non-Hispanic, upper-income students. One reason is that blacks, Hispanics, and low-income youths are relatively unlikely to attend college, so *any* subsidy to college students will flow disproportionately to white, upper-income youth. But even among those nonwhite, Hispanic, and low-income youths who do attend college, academic performance is a barrier to merit aid eligibility.

For merit programs that are based on standardized tests, it is unsurprising to see (as in Michigan) a large gap in the eligibility rates of whites and African Americans, as the correlation between standardized test performance and race is well documented. However, even those programs with only a GPA cutoff will experience large racial differences in eligibility, since academic performance in the classroom varies considerably by race and ethnicity. Forty percent of high school seniors have a 3.0 GPA or higher, while only 15 percent of African Americans and Hispanics meet this standard. Further, blacks and Hispanics receive relatively low grades in college, which threatens their ability to keep any merit scholarship they are able to win with their high school grades.

Since nonwhite youths are less likely to qualify, it is plausible that merit aid programs will have little positive impact upon their college attendance. Further, if the new merit aid crowds out state spending on need-based aid or leads to higher tuition prices, the programs may actually *decrease* low-income, nonwhite college attendance, since these populations will face the resulting cost increases but will be disproportionately ineligible for the new merit scholarships. Merit aid would therefore tend to widen existing gaps in college attendance, as it flows to those who already attend college at the highest rates. A countervailing force is that blacks and Hispanics may be relatively sensitive to college costs. Among those blacks and Hispanics who are eligible, a merit program could have a relatively large impact on schooling decisions. It is therefore an empirical question, to be investigated by this chapter, whether merit programs narrow or widen existing racial and ethnic gaps in postsecondary schooling.

2.3   Case Study: The Georgia HOPE Scholarship

In 1991, Georgia Governor Zell Miller requested that the state's General Assembly consider the establishment of a state-run lottery, with the proceeds to be devoted to education. The Georgia General Assembly passed lottery-enabling legislation during its 1992 session and forwarded the issue to voters, who approved the required amendment to the state's constitution in November of 1992. The first lottery tickets were sold in June of 1993. $2.5 billion in lottery revenue has flowed into Georgia's educational institutions since 1993. The legislation and amendment enabling the lottery specified that the new funds were not to crowd out spending from traditional sources. While it is not possible to establish conclusively that such crowdout has not occurred, spending on education has risen substantially since the lottery was initiated, both in absolute dollars and as a share of total state spending. Roughly equal shares of lottery funds have gone to four programs: the HOPE Scholarship, educational technology for primary and secondary schools, a new pre-kindergarten program, and school construction.

Residents who have graduated since 1993 from Georgia high schools with at least a 3.0 GPA are eligible for HOPE.[6] Public college students must maintain a GPA of 3.0 to keep the scholarship; a similar requirement was introduced for private school students in 1996. The HOPE Scholarship pays for tuition and required fees at Georgia's public colleges and universities. Those attending private colleges are eligible for an annual grant, which was $500 in 1993 and had increased to $3,000 by 1996. A $500 education voucher is available to those who complete a General Education Diploma (GED). The first scholarships were disbursed in the fall of 1993. Participation in HOPE during its first year was limited to those with family incomes below $66,000; the income cap was raised to $100,000 in 1994 and eliminated in 1995.

Two administrative aspects of HOPE differentially affected low- and upper-income youths. Since income is highly correlated with race and ethnicity, these administrative quirks may explain any racial and ethnic heterogeneity we observe in HOPE's effect. First, until 2001, HOPE awards were offset by other sources of aid. A student who received the maximum Pell Grant got no HOPE Scholarship except for a yearly book allowance of $400.[7] Insofar as blacks and Hispanics are disproportionately represented in the ranks of those who receive need-based aid, their HOPE awards would have been reduced more frequently than those of their white, non-Hispanic peers. Second, also until 2001, students from families with low incomes faced a more arduous application process for HOPE than did other students. Georgia education officials, concerned that students would forgo applying for federal aid once the HOPE Scholarship was available,

6. The high school GPA requirement is waived for those enrolled in certificate programs at technical institutes. For high school seniors graduating after 2000, only courses in English, math, social studies, science, and foreign languages count toward the GPA requirement.

7. As a result of this provision and the scaling back of the state's need-based State Student Incentive Grants (SSIGs), some low-income students have actually seen their state aid reduced since HOPE was introduced (Jaffe 1997). This contemporaneous shift in SSIG spending has the potential to contaminate the paper's estimates. However, SSIG spending was so miniscule—$5.2 million in 1995, before the program was scaled back—that the impact of its elimination on the estimates is likely to be inconsequential.

mandated that applicants from families with incomes lower than $50,000 complete the Free Application for Federal Student Aid (FAFSA). The rationale for the $50,000 income threshold was that few students above that cutoff were eligible for need-based, federal grant aid.[8] The four-page FAFSA requests detailed income, expense, asset, and tax data from the family. By contrast, those with family incomes above $50,000 filled out a simple, one-page form that required no information about finances other than a confirmation that family income was indeed above the cutoff. As a consequence of the two provisions just discussed, low-income students faced higher transaction costs and lower average scholarships than did upper-income students.

In 2000–2001, 75,000 students received $277 million in HOPE Scholarships. Georgia politicians have deemed HOPE a great success, pointing to the steady rise in the number of college students receiving HOPE. The key question is whether the program actually changes schooling decisions or simply subsidizes inframarginal students. In the next section, I discuss the data and empirical strategy I will use to answer this question.

2.4 Data

Any empirical analysis of state financial aid policy quickly comes face to face with frustrating data limitations. The data requirements appear minor, since eligibility for merit aid is determined by a very short list of characteristics: state of residence at the time of high school graduation, high school GPA, standardized test score, and, in some states, parental income. In order to use this information in an evaluation of the effect of merit aid, we would want these characteristics for repeated cohorts of high school students, both before and after merit aid is introduced in their state, so that schooling decisions of eligible and ineligible cohorts could be compared.[9] Finally, we need a data set with state-level samples large enough to allow for informative analysis.

No publicly available data set meets all of these requirements. Surveys that are limited to college students do not, by their nature, allow us to examine the college attendance margin. For example, the National Postsecondary Student Aid Survey (NPSAS) surveys college students about their aid packages and contains detailed information from students' aid appli-

8. In 1995, only 3.7 percent of dependent students from families with incomes over $40,000 received federal grant aid, while 57 percent of those from families with income under $20,000 did so (National Center for Education Statistics 1998a).

9. Alternatively, we could make use of the sharp discontinuities in the eligibility requirements to estimate the effect of merit aid from a single cohort. Kane (2003) uses this approach in an evaluation of California's CalGrant program, comparing the college attendance of those very slightly above and very slightly below the grade point cutoff. This approach requires very large samples; Kane uses an administrative data set that is a near-census of potential college entrants.

cations. By design, this data set cannot inform us about those students who decided *not* to go to college. Without making strong assumptions about how those who do not go to college differ from those who do, we cannot use the NPSAS to examine how aid affects the college attendance rate.

The NPSAS can be used to answer other questions of interest, however. For example, we might be interested in whether merit aid leads to higher tuition prices, or more or less government spending on other forms of aid. Or we might be interested in how the racial composition of a state's schools changes, if at all, after the introduction of a merit aid program. The NPSAS, as well as data that institutions gather about their students and report to the government through the Integrated Postsecondary Education Data System (IPEDS), can answer questions of this type.[10]

The National Longitudinal Surveys (NLSs) of Youth of 1979 and 1997 are particularly rich sources of data, containing information about academic performance on standardized tests, grades, parental income, and schooling decisions.[11] In a few years, the NLSY97 will be a useful resource for evaluating the newer merit aid programs, in particular those introduced in the late 1990s. The only weakness of the NLSY97 is that it is unlikely to interview enough youths in any one state to allow for detailed examination of a single merit aid program. Observations from multiple merit states could be pooled, however, as is done with the Current Population Survey in this paper.

Another potentially fruitful option for research in this area is data from administrative sources. Kane (2003) and Henry and Rubinstein (2002) take this approach in evaluations of programs in California and Georgia, respectively.[12] Kane matches enrollment data from California's public universities and colleges to federal aid applications and high school transcripts. He then uses regression-discontinuity methodology to estimate the effect of California's merit program on schooling decisions. Henry and Rubinstein use data from the College Board on high school grades and SAT scores in order to examine whether the Georgia HOPE Scholarship has led to grade inflation in high schools.

2.4.1   The Current Population Survey and the Analysis of State Aid Policy

The bulk of the analysis in this paper is based on a publicly available survey data set, the Current Population Survey (CPS). The CPS is a national

10. Papers that use college-based surveys in this way include Long (2002) and Cornwell, Mustard, and Sridhar (2003), both of which evaluate the Georgia HOPE Scholarship.

11. The U.S. Department of Education's longitudinal surveys of the high school cohorts of 1972, 1982, and 1992 contain similarly rich data. But because each survey contains a single cohort, we cannot use these data to observe schooling decisions in a given state both before and after merit aid is introduced.

12. California's program is not among the programs discussed in this chapter, as it is relatively narrow in its scope due to income provisions that exclude many middle- and upper-income youth.

household survey that each October gathers detailed information about schooling enrollment. Data on type of school attended, as well as basic demographics such as age, race, and ethnicity, are included in the CPS. While the CPS is the world's premier labor force survey, from the perspective of this chapter it has some key limitations.

First, the CPS lacks information about academic performance. We therefore cannot narrow the analysis to those whose academic performance makes them eligible for merit aid, and thereby measure the effect on schooling decisions of offering a merit scholarship among those who qualify (an effect I will denote π). From a policy perspective, the question we *can* answer is quite relevant: How does the existence of a merit aid program affect the schooling decisions of a state's youths? To answer this question, I will estimate a program effect (denoted β) that is the product of two interesting parameters: (1) π, the behavioral response to the offer of aid of youths eligible for the scholarship and (2) δ, the share of youths eligible for the scholarship:[13]

$$\beta = \pi\delta$$

When considering the effect of a financial aid program such as the Pell Grant, we generally are interested only in π. We assume that the parameters that determine Pell eligibility, such as family size and income, cannot easily be manipulated by those eager to obtain the grant. By contrast, merit aid is a program that *intends* to induce behavior that will increase the share that is aid-eligible. Policymakers consistently cite their desire to give students a financial incentive to work hard in high school and college as their motivation for establishing merit aid programs. Estimating π while ignoring δ would therefore miss half the story. Fortunately, data constraints prevent us from making this mistake!

A more serious weakness of the CPS is that it provides family background data for only a subset of youths. Highly relevant variables such as parental income, parental education, and other measures of socioeconomic status are available only for those youths who live with their families or who are temporarily away at college.[14] The probability that a youth has family background information available is therefore a function of his or her propensity to attend college. Under these circumstances, we cannot limit the analysis to those who have family background data without inducing bias in analyses in which college attendance is an outcome of interest.[15] In

---

13. This formulation ignores any heterogeneity in π, the effect of the offer of aid on those who are eligible. It is almost certain that this effect is not homogeneous. For example, the offer of aid will probably have a different effect on those whose grades place them just on the margin of eligibility and those whose grades are so strong that they are well within this margin.

14. These youths appear on their parents' CPS record and so can be linked to parental data. Other youths will show up in the CPS as members of their own households.

15. Cameron and Heckman (1999) discuss this point.

the analysis, therefore, I will make use only of background variables that are available for all youths.

2.4.2   Is State of Residence of Youth Systematically Mismeasured in the CPS?

A final weakness of the CPS is that it explicitly identifies neither the state in which a person attended high school nor the state in which he or she attends college. In this paper, I proxy for the state in which a person attended high school with current state of residence. This is a reasonable proxy, for two reasons. First, among eighteen-to-nineteen-year-olds, the group studied in this chapter, migration across state lines for reasons other than college is minimal. Second, when youths *do* go out of state to college, according to CPS coding standards they are recorded as residents of the state of origin, rather than the state in which they attend college.

The key question is whether these standards are followed in practice. We are confident that this protocol has been followed for those youths (78 percent of the sample) who appear on their parents' record.[16] Whether the CPS correctly captures the state of residence for the other 22 percent is an important question, as error in the collection of these data will bias the chapter's estimates.

If state of residence is simply a noisy measure of state of origin for this 22 percent, then the paper's estimates will be biased toward zero. But consider the following scenario, in which we will be biased toward finding a *positive* effect of merit aid on the probability of college attendance. Say that HOPE has no effect on the college entry margin but does affect whether students go to college in state. If the CPS incorrectly codes the state of residence as the state in which one is attending college, then any drop in the outward migration of Georgia college students induced by HOPE will mechanically induce an increase in the observed share of Georgia youths attending college.

A few simple tabulations can give us a sense of whether this is a problem. If the scenario laid out in the previous paragraph holds, then we should observe relative growth in the *size* of the college-age population in Georgia after HOPE is introduced. To test this hypothesis, I predicted the size of Georgia's college-age population by aging forward the high school–age population. Specifically, I compared the population of eighteen-to-nineteen-year-olds in a given state to the population of sixteen-to-seventeen-year-olds in the same state two years earlier. This is an admittedly crude prediction of cohort size. It will be wrong for any number of reasons, among them immigration and incarceration of teenagers (prisons are not in the

---

16. We cannot restrict the analytical sample to this subset because, as discussed earlier, whether a youth is on his or her parents' record is correlated with whether he or she is in college.

CPS sampling frame). However, the relevant issue is not how error-ridden this prediction is, but whether the sign and magnitude of its error *change systematically* when a merit program is introduced in a state. In particular, does the population of college-age youths expand unexpectedly when a state introduces a merit program?

Figure 2.2 plots the difference between the predicted and actual cohort sizes, with the difference normed by the predicted size. I plot the normed error for Georgia and the average normed error for the other states in the Southeast and the United States.[17] For measurement error to be inducing positive bias in the paper's estimates, the errors should grow relatively more negative in Georgia after HOPE is introduced. There is no such clear trend. The large negative errors in Georgia in 1993 through 1995 are somewhat disturbing, even though a muted version of this pattern also appears in the U.S. and Southeastern series. In figure 2.3, I show the same series for West Virginia, a southern state that had no merit program during this period. This state's pattern is almost identical to that of Georgia, suggesting that Georgia's shifts in cohort size are random noise and that the paper's estimates will not be contaminated by this source of bias.

2.5   Georgia HOPE Analysis

I begin by examining how the college attendance rate has changed in Georgia since HOPE was introduced, compared to how it has evolved in the other Southern states that have not introduced merit programs. The outcome of interest is whether an eighteen-to-nineteen-year-old is currently enrolled in college. I start with a parsimonious specification, in which an indicator variable for being enrolled in college is regressed against a set of state, year, and age effects, along with a variable, HOPE, that is set to 1 in survey years 1993 through 2000 for those who are from Georgia. In this equation, the HOPE variable therefore indicates that a young person of college age resides in Georgia after HOPE is in operation.

The estimating equation is as follows:

(1) $y_{iast} = \beta_0 + \beta_1 \text{HOPE}_{st} + \delta_s + \delta_t + \delta_a + \varepsilon_{iast},$

where y_{iast} is an indicator of whether person i of age a living in state s in year t is enrolled in college; δ_s, δ_t, and δ_a denote state, year, and age fixed effects, respectively; and ε_{iast} is an idiosyncratic error term. I use ordinary least

17. That is, I calculate the prediction error for each state-year and divide it by the predicted value for that state-year. I take the average of these normed, state-year errors separately for the Southeastern United States and the entire United States, in both cases excluding Georgia. Each state-year is treated as a single observation; I have not weighted by population.

The Georgia series is substantially more volatile than those of the Southeast and United States; however, any state's error will look volatile compared to averages for the region and country. See figure 2.3 for an example of an equally volatile state.

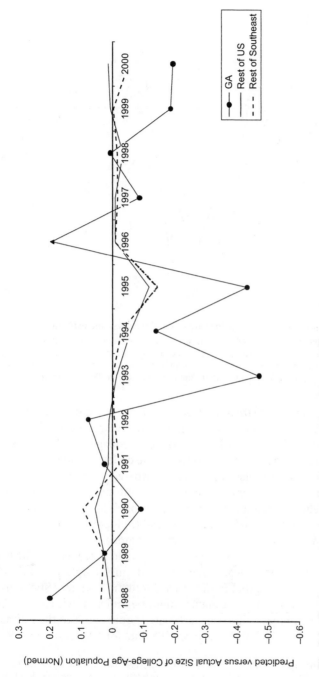

Fig. 2.2   Does measurement error in state of residence bias the estimates?

Note: The figure plots the difference between the predicted and actual population of college-age youth, with the difference normed by the predicted population. The predicted population of eighteen-to-nineteen-year-olds in a state is the number of sixteen-to-seventeen-year-olds in that state two years earlier. The data used are the October Current Population Surveys.

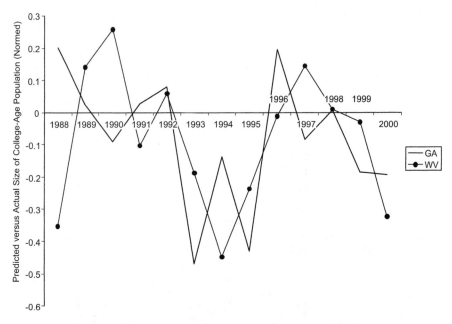

Fig. 2.3   Does measurement error in state of residence bias the estimates?

Note: The figure plots the difference between the predicted and actual population of college-age youth, with the difference normed by the predicted population. The predicted population of eighteen-to-nineteen-year-olds in a state is the number of sixteen-to-seventeen-year-olds in that state two years earlier. The data used are the October Current Population Surveys.

squares (OLS) to estimate this equation, correcting standard errors for heteroskedasticity and correlation of the error terms within state cells.

Recall that HOPE (1) decreases the price of college, (2) decreases the price of in-state colleges relative to out-of-state colleges, and (3) decreases the price of four-year colleges relative to two-year colleges. The corresponding predicted behaviors for Georgia residents are (1) increased probability of college attendance, (2) increased probability of in-state attendance relative to out-of-state attendance, and (3) increased probability of four-year attendance relative to two-year attendance.

Column (1) of table 2.2 shows the college attendance results. The estimates indicate that the college attendance rate in Georgia rose 8.6 percentage points relative to that in the other Southern, nonmerit states after HOPE was introduced. The estimate is highly significant, with a standard error of 0.8 percentage points. This estimate is quite close to the estimate in Dynarski (2000), which was based on CPS data for 1989 through 1997.[18]

18. The standard error is substantially smaller, however, than that in Dynarski (2000), which conservatively corrected standard errors for correlation at the state-year level. Bertrand, Duflo, and Mullainathan (2002) conclude that, in this type of application, the appropriate correction is for correlation at the state level.

Table 2.2   **Estimated Effect of Georgia HOPE Scholarship on College Attendance of Eighteen-to-Nineteen-Year-Olds (Southern Census region)**

	(1)	(2)	(3)	(4)
HOPE Scholarship	.086	.085	.085	.069
	(.008)	(.013)	(.013)	(.019)
Merit program in border state			−.005	−.006
			(.013)	(.013)
State and year effects	Y	Y	Y	Y
Median family income		Y	Y	Y
Unemployment rate		Y	Y	Y
Interactions of year effects with				
black, metro, Hispanic		Y	Y	Y
Time trends				Y
R^2	.020	.059	.059	.056
No. of observations	8,999	8,999	8,999	8,999

Notes: Regressions are weighted by CPS sample weights. Standard errors (in parentheses) are adjusted for heteroskedasticity and correlation within state cells. Sample consists of eighteen-to-nineteen-year-olds in Southern Census region, excluding states (other than Georgia) that introduce merit programs by 2000. See table 2.1 for a list of these states.

The result suggests that HOPE did, as predicted, increase the share of youths attending college.

I next probe the robustness of this result by adding a set of covariates to this regression. For reasons discussed earlier, I limit myself to covariates that are available for the entire sample and exclude any that require that a youth and his or her parents appear on the same survey record, such as parental education and income. Control variables indicate whether a youth lives in a metropolitan area, is African American, or is Hispanic. These three variables are each interacted with a full set of year effects, so that the effect of these attributes on schooling decisions is allowed to vary flexibly over time. I also include the state's unemployment rate and the median income of families with children who are near college age. These two variables are intended to capture any Georgia-specific economic shocks that may have affected college attendance decisions. Results are in column (2). The coefficient does not change, although the standard error increases to 1.3 percentage points.

I next examine whether the effect of merit aid extends across state borders. Since students travel across state lines for college, changes in postsecondary education policy in one state will reverberate in neighboring states. If more Georgians want to go to college, and the supply of colleges is inelastic, students from Florida, for example, will be pushed out of school when HOPE is introduced. The estimating equation is as follows:

$$(2) \quad y_{iast} = \beta_0 + \beta_1 HOPE_{st} + \beta_2 border\_merit_{st} + \beta_3 X_{st} + \beta_4 X_i + \delta_s + \delta_t$$
$$+ \delta_a + \varepsilon_{iast}$$

β_2 captures the effect of having a merit program in a neighboring state. X_{st} and X_i are the state-year and individual covariates discussed in the previous paragraph and used in column (2). Results are in column (3). The results weakly suggest that having a merit program on one's border has a small, negative effect on college attendance, indicating the presence of supply constraints. The point estimate is fairly imprecise, however: -0.5 percentage points, with a standard error of 1.3 percentage points.[19]

An identifying assumption of the preceding analysis is that Georgia and the control states were on similar trends in their college attendance rates before HOPE was introduced. If they were instead on divergent trends the estimates will be biased. In particular, if attendance was rising in Georgia relative to the other states before 1993, then we will falsely attribute to HOPE the continuation of this trend. The inclusion of these preexisting trends in the equation will eliminate this source of bias. In column (4), I add to the regression separate time trends for Georgia and the nonmerit states.[20] The point estimate drops moderately, to 6.9 percentage points, indicating that Georgia was trending away from the rest of the South before HOPE. However, there is still a substantial relative increase in attendance in Georgia that cannot be explained by this trend.

2.5.1   The Effect of HOPE on School Choice

I next examine whether HOPE has affected decisions other than college entry. In particular, I examine the type of college that a student chooses to attend. The October CPS contains information about whether a student attends a public or private college and whether it is a two- or four-year institution. I use this information to construct four variables that indicate whether a person attends a two-year private school, a two-year public school, a four-year private school, or a four-year public school. I then run a series of four regressions in which these are the outcomes, including the same covariates as in the richest specification of table 2.2. I show results that both do and do not include time trends. The results are shown in table 2.3. The attendance results of the previous table are included for ease of comparison.

The HOPE Scholarship appears to increase the probability of attendance at four-year public institutions substantially, by 4.5 percentage points (no time trends) to 8.4 percentage points (time trends included). Attendance at four-year private schools also rises, although the estimates are smaller than those (2.2 to 2.8 percentage points). There is a somewhat smaller rise in the probability of attendance at two-year private schools (about 1.5 percentage points) and a drop at two-year public schools (of 1.7

19. I have also tested the inclusion of the interaction of having a merit program in one's own state and having a merit program in a neighboring state. The interaction is never large or significant, and its inclusion does not affect the paper's estimates.

20. The time trends are estimated using pre-1993 data.

Table 2.3   Effect of Georgia HOPE Scholarship on Schooling Decisions (October CPS, 1988–2000; Southern Census region)

	College Attendance (1)	2-Year Public (2)	2-Year Private (3)	4-Year Public (4)	4-Year Private (5)
No time trends					
Hope Scholarship	.085	−.018	.015	.045	.022
	(.013)	(.010)	(.002)	(.015)	(.007)
R^2	.059	.026	.010	.039	.026
Add time trends					
Hope Scholarship	.069	−.055	.014	.084	.028
	(.019)	(.013)	(.004)	(.023)	(.016)
R^2	.056	.026	.010	.029	.026
Mean of dependent variable	.407	.122	.008	.212	.061

Notes: Specification in "No time trends" is that of column (3) in table 2.2. Specification in "Add time trends" adds trends estimated on pretreatment data. In each column, two separate trends are included, one for Georgia and one for the rest of the states. Sample consists of eighteen-to-nineteen-year-olds in Southern Census region, excluding states (other than Georgia) that introduce a merit program by 2000. No. of observations = 8,999. Standard errors in parentheses.

to 5.5 percentage points). All but two of the eight estimates are significant at conventional levels.

These shifts in schooling decisions are in the expected direction. Any subsidy to college will both pull students *into* two-year public schools (from not going to college at all) and push them *out of* two-year public schools (into four-year colleges). The HOPE Scholarship appears to push more students out of two-year, public institutions than it pulls in, producing a net drop at these schools. Most of these students appear to shift toward four-year public institutions, although some also shift into the private sector.[21]

2.5.2   The Effect of HOPE on Migration to College

We might expect that HOPE would also affect whether students choose to attend college in their home state. Data from both the University System of Georgia (USG) and the Department of Education's Residence and Migration Survey suggest that HOPE has had the effect of encouraging Georgia residents who would have attended a four-year college out of state to stay in Georgia instead. Data from the Residence and Migration Survey indicate that in 1992 about 5,000 Georgians were freshmen at two- and four-year colleges in the states that border Georgia. This represented an average of 3.4 percent of the border states' freshman enrollment. By 1998, just 4,500

21. Note that the coefficients for the four schooling options do not sum to the overall attendance effect. This is because the type of school is unknown for some students, who appear as college attenders but not as attending a specific type of school.

Georgians crossed state lines to enter college in the border states, account-ing for an average of 2.9 percent of freshman enrollment in those states. This drop in migration was concentrated in a group of border schools that have traditionally drawn large numbers of Georgians. At the ten border schools drawing the most Georgia freshmen in 1992, students from Georgia num-bered 1,900 and averaged 17 percent of the freshman class. By 1998, the ten top destinations enrolled 1,700 Georgians, who represented 9 percent of freshman enrollment. Jacksonville State College in Florida, for example, drew 189 Georgian freshmen in 1992 and only 89 in 1998; the share of the freshman class from Georgia dropped from 17 to 11 percent.

Further supporting the conclusion that Georgia's four-year college stu-dents are now more likely to attend college in state is a shift in the compo-sition of Georgia's four-year colleges. Figure 2.4 shows data from the USG on the share of freshman enrollees that are Georgia residents at Georgia's two- and four-year public colleges. The data are separately plotted for the two-year, four-year, and elite four-year colleges in the state. Here we see a definite shift toward Georgia residents since HOPE was introduced, with the effect most pronounced at four-year colleges (especially the top schools) and least evident at the two-year schools. This pattern fits with our understanding that four-year students are most mobile when making col-lege attendance decisions.

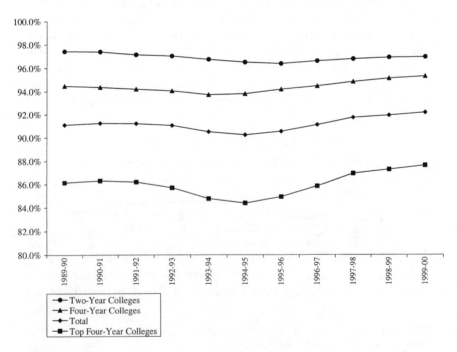

Fig. 2.4   University System of Georgia students, Georgia residents as share of total enrollment

2.5.3   The Differential Impact of HOPE by Race and Ethnicity

The effect of merit programs may vary across racial and ethnic groups for a number of reasons. First, as was discussed earlier, academic performance in high school is strongly correlated with race and ethnicity. Second, the rules of the programs are sometimes such that they are likely to have a lesser impact on low-income youths. Until recently, Georgia did not offer the grant to those youths who had substantial Pell Grants and low college costs. Mechanically, then, the program would have had a lower impact on African Americans and Hispanics, who tend to have lower incomes: in Georgia, 94 percent of African American but just 62 percent of white sixteen-to-seventeen-year-olds live in families with incomes less than \$50,000.[22] The numbers for the rest of the United States are similar.[23] Third, states that have merit programs may reduce need-based aid or appropriations to colleges. Both of these effects would tend to make college more expensive for those who don't qualify for the merit programs to which the money is being channeled. Finally, the elasticity of schooling with respect to a given grant may differ across demographic groups. A priori, it is not clear whether blacks and Hispanics would be more or less elastic than other students in their schooling decisions.[24]

To explore how the effect of merit aid programs varies by race and ethnicity, I repeat the analysis of the preceding section but allow the effect of HOPE to differ across racial and ethnic groups. I divide the population into two mutually exclusive categories: (1) white non-Hispanics and (2) Hispanics of any race plus blacks.[25] I then estimate the effect of merit aid separately for each group. The estimating equation is

$$(3) \quad y_{iast} = \beta_0 + \beta_1 \text{Merit}_{st} + \beta_2 \text{Merit}_{st} \times \text{black\_hisp}_i + \beta_3 \text{border\_Merit}_{st}$$
$$+ \beta_4 X_{st} + \beta_5 X_i + \delta_s + \delta_t + \delta_a + \varepsilon_{iast}.$$

Results for Georgia are in table 2.4, for specifications that do and do not include preexisting time trends.[26] The point estimates are somewhat un-

22. Author's estimates from the CPS. Note that this refers to the nominal income distribution. This is appropriate, since the Georgia rules were written in nominal rather than real terms.

23. These figures for the share with income below \$50,000 may appear high. This is because the unit of observation is not the family but the child. Since lower-income families have more children, the distribution of family income within a sample of children has a lower mean and median than the distribution of family income within a sample of families.

24. Dynarski (2000) develops a model of schooling choice that demonstrates this ambiguity. Dynarski (2002) reviews the evidence on the relative price elasticities of the schooling of low- and upper-income youths.

25. I would prefer to separately examine effects on blacks and Hispanics. I have attempted to do so, but the Hispanic results are too imprecisely estimated to be informative.

26. When time trends are included, they are estimated separately by state and race/ethnicity. Trends are estimated for four separate groups: (1) non-Hispanic whites in Georgia; (2) non-Hispanic whites in the rest of the Southern nonmerit states; (3) blacks and Hispanics in Georgia; and (4) blacks and Hispanics in the rest of the nonmerit Southern states.

Table 2.4   Effect of Georgia HOPE Scholarship on College Attendance Analysis by
                   Race and Ethnicity (October CPS, 1988–2000; Southern Census region)

	No Time Trends	Time Trends
Merit Program	.096	.140
	(.014)	(.013)
Merit · black/Hispanic	−.030	−.147
	(.023)	(.039)
R^2	.059	.056

Notes: Specification in first column is that of column (3) in table 2.2. Specification in second column adds trends estimated on pretreatment data. Separate trends are included for four groups: white-control, white-treat, nonwhite-control and nonwhite-treat. Sample consists of eighteen-to-nineteen-year-olds in Southern Census region, excluding states other than Georgia that introduce a merit program by 2000. Standard errors in parentheses.

stable, changing substantially when time trends are included. But the two sets of estimates agree that HOPE had a substantially greater effect on white attendance than black and Hispanic attendance. The estimated effect of HOPE on the white attendance rate is 9.6 to 14.0 percentage points, while that on blacks and Hispanics is –0.7 to 6.6 percentage points. The results indicate that HOPE has increased racial and ethnic gaps in college attendance in Georgia.

2.6   The Effect of Broad-Based Merit Aid in Other States

The Georgia program was one of the first, largest, and best-publicized merit aid programs. It has also been, by far, the best-studied program; at this point, dozens of papers have analyzed its impact. In the absence of sound empirical research on the effect of the other merit programs, the Georgia experience has been extrapolated in predicting their effects.[27] However, as is shown in table 2.1, there is heterogeneity in program rules, which may well lead to heterogeneity in the programs' effects. Further, initial college attendance rates and the supply of postsecondary schools vary across the merit aid states, which may affect the impact of the merit programs on schooling decisions. For all these reasons, results from one state may not provide a good prediction of the effect of another state's merit program.

Fortunately, many of the merit aid programs in table 2.1 have now been in existence sufficiently long to allow us to separately estimate program effects for each state. I will limit my analysis to the South, where all but three of the programs in table 2.1 are located. A benefit of focusing on the Southern merit states is that they have a natural control group: the non-

27. An exception is the study by Binder and Ganderton (2002), which examined the effect of New Mexico's merit program. They conclude that New Mexico Success has not affected the college attendance rate but, like HOPE, has shifted students toward four-year schools.

merit Southern states. The programs of three Southern states (Maryland, Tennessee, and West Virginia) are excluded, as they were introduced after 2000, the last year of the sample. That leaves seven merit programs, located in Arkansas, Florida, Georgia, Kentucky, Louisiana, Mississippi, and South Carolina.

I follow the approach used in the analysis of HOPE, creating a variable that indicates a year and state in which a merit program is in place. I estimate the following equation:

$$(4) \quad y_{iast} = \beta_0 + \beta_1 merit_{st} + \beta_2 border\_merit_{st} + \beta_3 X_{st} + \beta_4 X_i + \delta_s + \delta_t$$
$$+ \delta_a + \varepsilon_{iast}$$

Results are in table 2.5. The estimated overall effect of the seven merit programs is 4.7 percentage points. The estimate is highly significant, with a

Table 2.5   **Effect of All Southern Merit Programs on College Attendance of Eighteen-to-Nineteen-Year-Olds**

	All Southern States (N = 13,965)			Southern Merit States Only (N = 5,640)		
	(1)	(2)	(3)	(4)	(5)	(6)
Merit program	.047			.052		
	(.011)			(.018)		
Merit program, Arkansas		.048			.016	
		(.015)			(.014)	
Merit program, Florida		.030			.063	
		(.014)			(.031)	
Merit program, Georgia		.074			.068	
		(.010)			(.014)	
Merit program, Kentucky		.073			.063	
		(.025)			(.047)	
Merit program, Louisiana		.060			.058	
		(.012)			(.022)	
Merit program, Mississippi		.049			.022	
		(.014)			(.018)	
Merit program, South Carolina		.044			.014	
		(.013)			(.023)	
Merit program, year 1			.024			.051
			(.019)			(.027)
Merit program, year 2			.010			.043
			(.032)			(.024)
Merit program, year 3 and after			.060			.098
			(.030)			(.039)
State time trends			Y			Y
R^2	.046	.046	.047	.035	.036	.036

Notes: Specification is that of column (3) in table 2.2, with the addition of state time trends where noted. Sample consists of eighteen-to-nineteen-year-olds in Southern Census region, with the last three columns excluding states that have not introduced a merit program by 2000. Standard errors in parentheses.

standard error of 1.1 percentage points. In column (2), I allow this affect to vary across the seven states, by replacing the single merit dummy with a set of seven dummies, one for each state's program. The specification of column (2) is otherwise identical to that of column (1), and so the appropriately weighted average of the seven coefficients is the 4.7 percentage points of column (1). Six of the estimates are highly significant. Five are clustered between 4.9 (Mississippi) and 7.4 (Georgia). Well below Mississippi are Florida and South Carolina, with estimated effects of 3.0 and 0.2 percentage points, respectively.

We might suspect that the merit states are somehow different from the nonmerit states and that the nonmerit states therefore form a poor control group for these purposes. We can test the sensitivity of our results to the choice of control group by dropping the nonmerit states from the sample and estimating the effect of merit aid purely from the staggered timing of its rollout across the states. In this approach, the merit states form their own control group. Figure 2.5 graphically illustrates the identification strategy. During the first years of the sample (1988–1990), before the first merit program is introduced, all of the states are in the control group. In 1991, Arkansas moves into the treatment group, followed in 1993 by Georgia. By 2000, all of the states are in the treatment group. This approach assumes that the states that eventually have a merit program are on similar trends in the schooling outcomes of young people. The assumption is that the year in which a state's merit program begins is quasi-random, uncorrelated with any state-specific trends in or shocks to schooling decisions.

Results are in columns (4) and (5) of table 2.5. The estimated overall effect is insensitive to the choice of control group, with the estimate rising only slightly from 4.7 to 5.2 percentage points. The state-specific coefficients are somewhat more sensitive to the choice of control group. For five of the states, the two approaches yield similar results. The two exceptions are Arkansas and Florida, for whom the estimates vary substantially between column (2) and column (4). Arkansas's estimate drops from 4.8 to 1.6, while Florida's rises from 3.0 to 6.3.

Only South Carolina has a consistently small and insignificant effect,

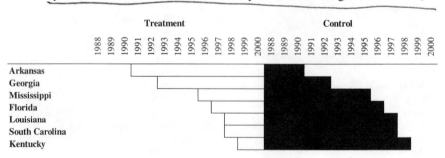

Fig. 2.5   Timing of introduction of state merit programs

which may be explained by its requirement that students score at least 24 on the ACT. Nationally, just 30 percent of test takers scored above South Carolina's ACT cutoff in 2000, while 88 percent met Missouri's requirement and about 60 percent met the requirements of Arkansas (19), Florida (20), and Louisiana (19.6).[28] The South Carolina legislature has come under pressure to loosen the scholarship requirements and has responded by adding another route to eligibility. As of 2002, students can qualify for a scholarship by meeting two of three criteria: 24 on the ACT, a GPA of 3.0, and graduating in the top 30 percent of one's high school class (Bichevia Green of the South Carolina Commission on Higher Education, personal communication, June 14, 2002). Further, the ACT requirement has been dropped completely for those attending two-year institutions. It will be of interest to see if the effect of South Carolina's program on college attendance rises with this shift in policy.

Next, I examine whether the inclusion of preexisting time trends affects the results. Preexisting trends could contaminate the results for both control groups. The merit states may be on different time trends from the nonmerit states, and they may be on different trends from each other. I estimate a trend for the entire 1988–2000 period for each state. Deviations from these trends after a state introduces merit aid are then attributed to the new program.[29]

Results are in columns (3) and (6). As was true in the specification without time trends, the merit-only control group produces somewhat larger estimates. Both approaches indicate that the effect of merit aid evolves over time, with the effect rising from 2.4 percentage points in the first year a program is in effect to 6.0 percentage points in year three and beyond. When the merit states are used as their own control group, the effect rises from 5.1 percentage points in year one to 9.8 percentage points in the third year. Note that these are not cumulative effects but period-specific program effects.

The effect of merit aid may rise during the first years of a program for several reasons. It may take time for information about the new programs to diffuse. It also takes time for high school students who are inspired to work harder to increase their overall GPAs. Those who are high school seniors when a program is first introduced can do little to increase their cu-

---

28. These figures refer to the national ACT distribution, which has a mean of 21. The black and Hispanic distributions have lower means, of 16.9 and 19, respectively. Fewer members of these groups will meet the state ACT cutoffs.

29. In this specification, a simple merit dummy will not properly identify the effect of the merit aid program, as such an approach would inappropriately attribute part of the aid-induced change to the trend. We can solve this problem by replacing the merit dummy with either a separate time trend or year effects after merit aid is introduced in a state. Wolfers and Stevenson (forthcoming) use this approach to estimate the effect of divorce law reform, which occurred in different states in different years.

mulative GPAs, while those who are freshmen have four years to increase their effort. The pool of eligible youths may thereby expand over time.

The effect could also *diminish* over time, if many college students fail to qualify for scholarship renewals and their younger peers are discouraged from taking up the scholarship. Further, in the presence of supply constraints, the effect of latecomer programs would be smaller than that of earlier programs, as attendance grows and the supply grows tighter. The results in table 2.5 indicate that, across the merit states, the incentive and information effects dominate the discouragement effect.

2.6.1 The Effect of Merit Aid on College Choice

The analysis of the previous section indicates that the state merit aid programs have increased college attendance. I next examine whether these programs have also affected the choice of college, as was true in Georgia. I use the analytical framework of the previous section, although I will only show results that pool the merit states in order to gain precision. All of the Southern states are included in the sample; results are similar, but less precise, when the sample is limited to the Southern merit states. I show results that do and do not include time trends.

Table 2.6 indicates that, overall, the Southern merit programs have had a strong effect on the choice of college, with a considerable shift toward four-year public schools of 4.4 percentage points, which is about the same

Table 2.6	Effect of All Southern Merit Programs on Schooling Decisions of Eighteen-to-Nineteen-Year-Olds (all Southern states; $N = 13{,}965$)				
	College Attendance (1)	2-Year Public (2)	2-Year Private (3)	4-Year Public (4)	4-Year Private (5)
No time trends					
Merit program	.047	−.010	.004	.044	.005
	(.011)	(.008)	(.004)	(.014)	(.009)
R^2	.046	.030	.007	.030	.020
State time trends					
Merit program, year 1	.024	−.025	.009	.034	.010
	(.019)	(.012)	(.005)	(.012)	(.007)
Merit program, year 2	.010	−.015	.002	.028	−.001
	(.032)	(.018)	(.003)	(.035)	(.011)
Merit program, year 3	.060	−.037	.005	.065	.022
and after	(.030)	(.013)	(.003)	(.024)	(.010)
R^2	.047	.031	.009	.032	.022

Notes: Specification is that of column (3) in table 2.2, with the addition of state time trends where noted. Sample consists of eighteen-to-nineteen-year-olds in Southern Census region. Estimates are similar but less precise when sample is limited to Southern merit states. Standard errors in parentheses.

as the overall attendance effect. There are no effects on other choices of college. As was discussed earlier, this is probably the result of equal-sized shifts toward and away from two-year public schools, by students on the margin of college entry and four-year-college attendance, respectively. The time trend specification gives similar results, although here there is more indication of a net drop in the probability of attendance at two-year public colleges.

2.6.2 Do All Merit Aid Programs Have the Distributional Impact of HOPE?

Many of the merit programs are quite new. Of the seven programs examined in table 2.5, three had been operative for fewer than four years by 2000. In this section, I examine the four more mature programs—those of Georgia, Florida, Arkansas, and Mississippi—in greater depth. An advantage of focusing on the older programs is that these states have sufficient postprogram observations to allow for the finer cuts of the data needed to examine heterogeneity in the effect of aid across demographic groups. Given the strong impact of HOPE on the racial/ethnic gap in schooling, it is of interest to examine whether the other programs have had a similar impact.

In table 2.7, I examine how the effect of the four programs varies by race

Table 2.7 **Effect of Merit Aid on College Attendance Analysis by Race and Ethnicity (October CPS, 1988–2000; Southern Census region)**

	Georgia ($N = 8,999$) (1)	Florida ($N = 10,213$) (2)	Arkansas ($N = 8,949$) (3)	Mississippi ($N = 8,969$) (4)
No time trends				
Merit program	.096	.001	.054	.002
	(.014)	(.022)	(.023)	(.011)
Merit · black/Hispanic	−.030	.077	.045	.120
	(.020)	(.021)	(.026)	(.032)
R^2	.059	.055	.061	.058
Time trends				
Merit program	.140	.030	.060	.016
	(.013)	(.021)	(.024)	(.015)
Merit · black/Hispanic	−.147	.000	.043	.083
	(.039)	(.030)	(.043)	(.033)
R^2	.056	.052	.059	.055

Notes: Specification in "No time trends" is that of column (3) in table 2.2. Specification in "Time trends" adds trends estimated on pretreatment data. In each column, separate trends are included for four groups: white-control, white-treat, nonwhite-control and nonwhite-treat. In each column, sample consists of eighteen-to-nineteen-year-olds in Southern Census region, excluding states (other than the treatment state) that introduce a merit program by 2000. Standard errors in parentheses.

and ethnicity. The control group is the nonmerit states. I show the results of specifications that do and do not include preprogram time trends.[30] While the estimates do change when time trends are included, and some are quite imprecisely estimated, a consistent story emerges from the table. The estimates are in concord with those of table 2.5, which showed that each of these four programs had a strong impact on the college attendance rate. However, table 2.7 shows that the *relative* effects on blacks and Hispanics differ substantially across programs. In particular, Georgia is an outlier in its relatively low effect on blacks and Hispanics, as compared to its effect on whites.

Georgia's HOPE has had the largest impact of all the state programs on the college attendance of whites, with the estimated effect ranging from 9.6 to 14.0 percentage points (without and with time trends, respectively). Analogous effects in the other states are substantially smaller, with no state's estimates for white non-Hispanics larger than 6 percentage points. Further, the effect of Georgia HOPE on blacks and Hispanics is 3.0 to 14.7 points *lower* than the effect on whites. In the other three states, the estimated effect of merit aid on blacks and Hispanics is consistently *more positive* than its effect on white non-Hispanics.

This is an important finding, as Georgia's is the only program whose distributional effect has been examined in depth, and the assumption has been that, in other states, merit aid would similarly widen the racial gap in college attendance (see, e.g., Cornwell, Mustard, and Sridhar 2003 and Dynarski 2000). The results in table 2.7 indicate that the other mature merit aid programs have not had this effect, with nearly all of the estimates suggesting that merit aid has actually *narrowed* the gap.

Why is Georgia different? Its HOPE Scholarship diverges from the other three programs in two key dimensions. First, of the four programs analyzed in table 2.7, Georgia's has the most stringent GPA requirements. Georgia requires a high school GPA of 3.0, while Arkansas and Mississippi require a GPA of only 2.5. Florida's high school GPA requirement is similar to Georgia's, but its renewal requirements are less stringent. While Georgia requires that a HOPE scholar maintain a GPA of 3.0 in college, in Florida a college GPA of 2.75 allows a student to keep the scholarship. A college GPA of 2.75 also qualifies a student for renewal in Arkansas, and only a 2.5 is required in Mississippi.

Scholarship renewal rates for blacks are substantially lower than those of whites in Georgia, indicating that the college GPA requirement hits them particularly hard. Blacks at the University of Georgia are twice as likely as whites to lose their scholarship after the freshman year (Healy

---

30. In the analysis of each program, four preprogram trends are estimated: two for white non-Hispanics (one for the treatment state and one for the control states) and two for blacks/Hispanics (one for the treatment state and one for the control states).

1997). A study at the Georgia Institute of Technology also found that blacks were substantially more likely than whites to lose their scholarships. This differential disappeared after accounting for differences in ability (as measured by SAT scores; Dee and Jackson 1999). More generally, since blacks and Hispanics have relatively low high school and college grades, less stringent GPA requirements will disproportionately benefit this group.

A second key difference between HOPE and the other state programs is its treatment of other sources of aid and associated paperwork requirements for students potentially eligible for aid. During the period under analysis, HOPE was reduced dollar for dollar by a student's other aid, and low-income students were required to fill out extensive paperwork in order to establish their eligibility for other aid. The net impact of these requirements was that lower-income students had to work harder for less aid than their well-off counterparts.[31] In stark contrast, Arkansas gives *larger* awards to low-income students, by allowing students who receive the Pell to keep their Academic Challenge Scholarships and by excluding from eligibility students from families with incomes above $55,000.[32]

2.7   Additional Effects of Merit Aid on Individuals and Institutions

The analysis in this paper has focused on the effect of merit aid on two critical margins: the decision to attend college and the type of college chosen. I have touched on another outcome that is quite important, at least to legislators: the decision to attend college within one's home state. I have found that merit aid moderately increases college attendance and shifts students from two-year schools toward four-year schools. The data also suggest that Georgia's merit aid program has increased the probability that a student will attend college in his or her home state. It remains to be determined whether merit aid keeps those students in state after they have completed their education, which is the ultimate goal of legislators who hope to use merit aid to staunch a perceived "brain drain." It also remains to be settled whether the merit programs have increased completed schooling, as opposed to attempted schooling.[33]

There are many other margins of behavior that merit aid may affect.

---

31. Georgia recently eliminated this aspect of its program. As more data become available, it will be of interest to examine whether this change has altered the distributional impact of HOPE.

32. This is the income cutoff for a family of four. Median income for a family of four in Arkansas is $45,000, so a large share of students falls under these income guidelines.

33. Data limitations, rather than conceptual difficulties, hamper the analysis of this particular margin of behavior. At a minimum, we require data on the completed schooling of adults, along with information about the state in which they graduated high school. As of 2002, these data are not available in any survey large enough for informative analysis of the existing merit programs. The 2000 Census microdata may prove useful in this context, and I am currently examining this question using these data.

Thoroughly addressing all of these potential effects would expand this lengthy chapter into a book. Here I will provide a necessarily brief discussion of these issues.

2.7.1   Additional Effects of Merit Aid on Individuals

A goal of merit aid is to increase academic effort in high school and college. The carrot of merit aid may cause students to work harder in high school and college in order to qualify for and then maintain their scholarships. This increased effort would be reflected in higher grades, test scores, and college attendance rates. However, observed academic performance may also improve for unintended reasons, in that pressure from students and parents on teachers may lead to grade inflation at both the high school and college level.

A small literature has examined the effect of merit aid on academic effort. Henry and Rubenstein (2002) show that the average high school GPA of freshmen entering the Georgia public universities rose from 2.73 in 1992 to 2.98 in 1999. In order to test whether this increase reflects greater effort or grade inflation, they examine SAT scores of entering freshmen, which are not subject to the same parental and student pressures as high school grades. The authors find that the average SAT score of entering freshmen in Georgia rose along with grades after HOPE was introduced, from 968 to 1010. While these results are suggestive, they are not conclusive, since this study examines only students in Georgia. It is quite possible that the increases in grades and SAT scores in Georgia are part of a broader secular trend rather than a consequence of HOPE.

Grades at the college level may also be affected by merit aid. First, students may work harder in their courses in order to keep their scholarships. This is an intended effect of the merit programs. Two unintended effects may also increase college grades. Professors may feel pressured to give higher grades so as not to threaten their students' continued eligibility for HOPE, and students may choose less demanding course loads for the same reason. Note that determining whether merit aid increases effort in college is inherently difficult. While the SAT is a well-accepted metric of the preparation of high school students, there is no equivalent instrument used to measure the achievement of college students.

Whether due to increased effort, less demanding course loads, or grade inflation, college grades at the University of Georgia are on the rise, with the proportion of freshman grades below a B dropping from 40 percent in 1993 to 27 percent in 1996 (Healy 1997). In New Mexico, Binder and Ganderton (2002) found support for the hypothesis that this is due, in part, to students taking fewer courses per semester, and therefore concentrating more effort on each course. They found support for the hypothesis that students respond to a merit program by taking on less-demanding course loads. They found that credit hours per semester dropped after the Success program was introduced. This work on New Mexico is the only conclusive empirical research regarding the question of effect of merit programs on academic effort in college.

Even the largest estimates of the effect of merit aid on schooling decisions suggest that the great majority of aid goes to inframarginal families—that is, to families whose schooling decisions are unaffected by their receipt of aid.[34] For these families, of interest is which margins of behavior *are* affected by the windfall receipt of scholarship funds. Do students use these funds to reduce the number of hours they work while in school? Do they increase their spending on leisure activities? Do families save the money, for retirement or later bequests to their children? One study suggests that at least part of the money is used for increased current consumption. Cornwell and Mustard (2002) examine new car registrations in Georgia and comparison states and find that car purchases rose faster in Georgia after the introduction of HOPE than before. They reach similar conclusions by examining the correlation between car registrations and the number of HOPE recipients at the county level within Georgia, finding an elasticity of new car registrations with respect to HOPE recipients of about 2 percent.

2.7.2 Impact of Merit Aid on Institutions

Dynarski (2000) compares the cost of attendance (room, board, tuition, and fees) at four-year schools in Georgia to that in the rest of the Southeast. She concludes that prices rose faster at public schools in Georgia than in comparable states after HOPE was introduced. Long (2002) subjects this question to a more thorough analysis, controlling for college selectivity and state characteristics. She separately examines the various components of the cost of attendance: tuition, room and board, and institutional financial aid. She finds that the increase in posted schooling prices in Georgia is fully explained by increases in room and board, which are not covered by HOPE. Further, she finds that institutional financial aid dropped as a result of the introduction of HOPE. Long hypothesizes that schools may have been under pressure from the state not to raise tuition, since any increases here would have to be met by increased HOPE outlays. Increases in room and board and drops in aid, however, could slip by with less attention. Private schools faced no such incentives to manipulate the form taken by their price increases, and accordingly their price increases are more evenly divided between tuition and room and board after HOPE.

Cornwell, Mustard, and Sridhar (2003) provide insight into how a merit

---

34. It is important to note that merit aid is not unique in this way. Estimates of the effects of other forms of student aid also indicate that aid largely goes to those whose observable schooling decisions are unaffected by the receipt of aid. Targeting of subsidies is a classic topic of public economics; there is no transfer program that is 100 percent effective in limiting its subsidy to those whose decisions are contingent on the receipt of the subsidy.

aid program affects the composition of institutions of higher education. They examine enrollment data for two- and four-year colleges in Georgia and the rest of the Southeast. Their empirical results show how the changing schooling choices of Georgia's young people translated into major shifts in the demographic composition of Georgia's schools. They find that enrollment expanded after the introduction of HOPE, relative to enrollment in comparable states. They also find a sharp rise in the enrollment of black students at Georgia's four-year colleges. Given the relatively small increase in the college attendance rate of blacks found in the present analysis, their increased presence at Georgia's four-year colleges probably reflects a shifting of black students from out-of-state colleges to Georgia schools.

2.8   The Politics and Finance of Merit Aid

State merit aid programs grew during the 1990s, a period characterized by strong economic growth and overflowing state coffers. Recently, merit programs have begun to feel the pinch of the recent economic downturn. As state legislators struggle to balance their budgets, merit aid programs dependent upon legislative appropriations (Arkansas, California, Louisiana, Maryland, and Mississippi) find themselves in direct competition with other state priorities such as elementary and secondary education and health care. Arkansas, the first state to introduce a broad-based merit aid program, has temporarily closed the program to new enrollees. Although current scholarship recipients can renew their awards, no new students are being admitted to the program. Funding for Louisiana's program barely avoided the chopping block during the state's last legislative session.

Those merit programs with committed revenue streams have been relatively buffered from the economic and political effects of the recession. Six states (Florida, Georgia, New Mexico, West Virginia, South Carolina, and Kentucky) fund their programs with revenues from a state lottery, while two (Nevada and Michigan) use funds from the tobacco litigation settlement. With their dedicated funding sources, merit aid in these states is not vulnerable to legislators seeking to cut spending in the face of sinking tax revenues. This puts merit aid in a unique position, since other sources of funding for higher education at the state level are not protected in the same way. For example, public universities are experiencing leaner times this fiscal year as their state appropriations are reduced. Aid for low-income students is also vulnerable. West Virginia's need-based aid program could not deliver scholarships to all those low-income students who were eligible during the 2002–2003 academic year. The same year, the state's new merit program, which has no income cap, was launched with full funding.

A similar dynamic has emerged at the federal level. The fastest-growing subsidies for college students—tax credits, savings tax incentives, and loans—are programs whose funding is not contingent upon legislative appropriation. By contrast, spending on the Pell Grant program, which funds the most needy students, is determined by annual legislative appropriation.

While lottery funding protects merit aid funding from downturns in tax revenue and associated drops in appropriations, using lotteries to fund merit scholarship is a particularly regressive form of redistribution. The high-achieving college students who receive merit funds are relatively likely to be white and from upper-income families. Lottery spenders, by contrast, tend to be disproportionately concentrated in the bottom of the income distribution. Through both the revenue and spending channels, then, lottery-funded merit programs are regressive in their impact.

Why have merit aid programs spread so rapidly and maintained such strong political support? One possibility is that merit aid is a politically astute way to build support for spending on postsecondary education. Consider three alternatives for subsidizing college: merit aid, subsidized public tuition, and need-based aid. Merit aid has a political advantage over low tuition in that it has a high profile. Parents (voters) generally do not understand that the public university tuition they pay is kept artificially low by state appropriations to the schools. As a result, they may be unsympathetic to legislative efforts to increase funding through this route. If, instead, their child receives a "scholarship" that pays for tuition, the perceived benefit is personal and immediate, inducing political support for the spending. This gives merit- and need-based aid a political edge over tuition subsidies as politically viable methods of subsidizing college costs.

A second dynamic gives merit aid an edge over the other subsidy options. Since students "earn" merit aid, families may feel a more personal connection to the program and fight for its continuation. In this way, a merit program is akin to Social Security: In both cases, voters are fiercely supportive of transfers that they perceive as earned rewards rather than unconditional entitlements.

A third political advantage of merit aid, again held in common with Social Security, is that it is broad based in its constituency. In most states, students of any income level qualify for a merit scholarship as long as they earn the required grades. All families are therefore potential recipients of, and political supporters of, merit aid scholarships. By contrast, the bulk of need-based aid flows to a relatively narrow slice of the population. The price of this highly progressive spending on need-based aid is that many voters do not perceive themselves as its potential beneficiaries. William Julius Wilson (1987) and Theda Skocpol (1991) have argued that robust welfare states are characterized by benefits that are widely available and, therefore, widely supported. They argue that means-tested antipoverty programs are politically weak because their scope is narrow. A similar dynamic could explain strong political support for merit-based aid paired with weak political support for need-based aid.

Do these political realities indicate that a progressive aid system is politically unviable? Skocpol and Wilson point out that politically popular "universal" programs can provide political cover for redistributive transfers. As Social Security shows, a universal program can be layered with transfers that channel extra dollars toward those with greater need. This does not necessarily require new spending, as existing need-based programs could simply be relabeled in a way that enhances their political viability. For example, federal need-based grants could be delivered to needy students through the tax system by making the Hope and Lifetime Learning tax credits refundable.[35] This would eliminate one layer of paperwork (the FAFSA) yet allow aid eligibility to still be determined with the detailed financial information that is provided in tax filings. More important, funding for low-income students would be shifted into a program with broad-based political appeal and a guaranteed funding stream.

2.9   Conclusion

This paper has examined how merit aid programs in seven states have affected an array of schooling decisions, with particular attention to how the effects have varied by race and ethnicity. I find that merit aid programs typically increase the attendance probability of college-age youths by 5 to 7 percentage points. The programs are therefore effective at getting more students into college. In fact, as I discuss presently, the merit programs appear to be *more* effective than need-based aid at achieving this goal.

The merit programs also shift students toward four-year schools and away from two-year schools. Why? Four-year colleges are far more expensive than two-year colleges, but merit aid programs generally reduce the direct cost (tuition and required fees) of each option to zero. It is therefore expected that a greater proportion of students would choose the four-year option than they would in the absence of merit aid. An open question is whether this shift toward four-year colleges is socially beneficial. Four-year colleges are more expensive to run than two-year colleges, so a shift toward these schools will increase the total cost of educating college students. Further, marginal students who cannot handle the rigors of a four-year college may drop out of school altogether, whereas at a two-year institution they may have received the support they needed to persist. A countervailing factor is that some students who would not have considered going on for a BA will do so once they are enrolled in a four-year school.[36]

---

35. Those who assail the need-based aid system for its complex application process will probably be horrified by this suggestion, as the federal tax system is also notoriously complex. But the Earned Income Tax Credit has proved to be an effective mechanism for transferring money to low-income families, and a refundable education tax credit has the potential to do the same for low-income students.

36. Rouse (1995) addresses the effect of community colleges on college entry and completion.

The current analysis does not allow us to address which of these effects dominates.

The merit programs also appear to close racial and ethnic gaps in schooling, at least in three of the four states whose programs are old enough to allow analysis by race. Merit aid programs in Arkansas, Florida, and Mississippi have closed gaps, with Georgia's the only program to widen them. I attribute the Georgia program's unique distributional effect to its relatively stringent academic requirements and a recently eliminated provision that channeled the most generous scholarships to higher-income students. This leaves open the question, however, of why merit aid does not simply have a race-*neutral* effect on schooling in states that do not have Georgia's unusual provisions.

One possible explanation for the role of merit aid in closing gaps in schooling is the simplicity and transparency of these programs. First, these programs are well publicized, and knowledge among potential recipients is unusually high; one survey found that 70 percent of Georgia high school freshmen could name the HOPE program without prompting, while 59 percent could identify its eligibility requirements (Henry, Harkreader, Hutcheson, and Gordon 1998). Second, unlike need-based aid, merit aid programs have minimal application procedures, and the applicant knows at the time of application both whether he is eligible and the amount of the award. By contrast, need-based aid requires that the applicant complete a complicated set of forms and wait for months to find out the actual award amount, which is a complicated function of family finances.

Collecting information about college costs and completing application forms may be particularly challenging to parents for whom English is a second language or who have not gone to college themselves. A program with low transaction and information costs may therefore find a particularly large response among nonwhite, low-income populations. This strong response among the eligible may more than compensate for the fact that a smaller proportion of nonwhites meet the academic requirements of merit aid.

This interpretation of the present results is consistent with a set of studies that have shown little effect of the need-based Pell Grant on schooling decisions (e.g., Kane 1995; Hansen 1983) but a large effect of simpler, more transparent subsidy programs (e.g., Dynarski [2003] on the Social Security student benefit program and Kane [1994] on tuition prices). Kane and Hansen both find no impact of the need-based Pell Grant on college attendance. By contrast, Kane, in his 1994 study, finds that tuition prices have a substantial impact on college attendance. Dynarski finds that the Social Security student benefit program, which had minimal application requirements, had a large impact on college attendance and completed schooling.

Whereas a benefit of a program with few paperwork requirements is that it may move more youths into school, a cost is the loss of targeting. Unlike the Pell Grant, a merit aid program subsidizes many middle- and upper-income students. A merit aid program is therefore relatively more costly to run than need-based aid. However, a merit aid program is no more costly than subsidized public tuition prices, which also benefit students regardless of income. Further, as was discussed earlier in this chapter, merit aid has a substantial advantage over both need-based aid and subsidized tuition in that it has a broad and loyal base of political support in states that have introduced the programs.

References

Bertrand, Marianne, Esther Duflo, and Sendil Mullainathan. 2002. How much should we trust differences-in-differences estimates? NBER Working Paper no. 8841. Cambridge, Mass.: National Bureau of Economic Research.

Binder, Melissa, and Philip Ganderton. 2002. Incentive effects of New Mexico's merit-based state scholarship program: Who responds and how? In *Who should we help? The negative social consequences of merit scholarships* (report by the Civil Rights Project), ed. Donald Heller and Patricia Marin, 41–56. Cambridge, Mass.: Harvard University Civil Rights Project.

Cameron, Stephen, and James Heckman. 1999. Can tuition policy combat rising wage inequality? In *Financing college tuition: Government politics and educational priorities,* ed. Marvin Kosters, 76–124. Washington, D.C.: American Enterprise Institute.

Cornwell, Christopher, and David Mustard. 2002. Merit-based college scholarships and car sales. University of Georgia, Department of Economics. Manuscript.

Cornwell, Christopher, David Mustard, and Deepa Sridhar. 2003. The enrollment effects of merit-based financial aid: Evidence from Georgia's HOPE Scholarship program. University of Georgia, Department of Economics. Manuscript.

Dee, Thomas, and Linda Jackson. 1999. Who loses HOPE? Attrition from Georgia's college scholarship program. *Southern Economic Journal* 66 (2): 379–390.

Dynarski, Susan. 2000. HOPE for whom? Financial aid for the middle class and its impact on college attendance. *National Tax Journal* 53 (3): 629–661.

———. 2002. The behavioral and distributional consequences of aid for college. *American Economic Review* 82 (2): 279–285.

———. 2003. Does aid matter? Measuring the effect of student aid on college attendance and completion. *American Economic Review* 93 (1): 279–288.

Hansen, W. Lee. 1983. The impact of student financial aid on access. In *The crisis in higher education,* ed. Joseph Froomkin, 84–96. New York: Academy of Political Science.

Healy, Patrick. 1997. HOPE scholarships transform the University of Georgia. *The chronicle of higher education,* November 7, 1997, A32.

Henry, Gary, Steve Harkreader, Philo A. Hutcheson, and Craig S. Gordon. 1998. Hope longitudinal study, first-year results. Georgia State University, Council for School Performance. Unpublished manuscript.

Henry, Gary, and Ross Rubenstein. 2002. Paying for grades: Impact of merit-based financial aid on educational quality. *Journal of Policy Analysis and Management* 21 (1): 93–109.

Jaffe, Greg. 1997. Free for all: Georgia's scholarships are open to everyone, and that's a problem. *Wall Street Journal,* June 2, 1.

Kane, Thomas. 1994. College entry by blacks since 1970: The role of college costs, family background, and the returns to education. *Journal of Political Economy* 102 (5): 878–911.

———. 1995. Rising public college tuition and college entry: How well do public subsidies promote access to college? NBER Working Paper no. 5164. Cambridge, Mass.: National Bureau of Economic Research.

———. 2003. A quasi-experimental estimate of the impact of financial aid on college-going. NBER Working Paper no. 9703. Cambridge, Mass.: National Bureau of Economic Research.

Long, Bridget Terry. 2002. Merit-based financial aid and college tuition: The case of Georgia's HOPE scholarship. Harvard University, Graduate School of Education. Unpublished manuscript.

National Center for Education Statistics, U.S. Department of Education. 1998a. *Digest of education statistics.* Washington, D.C.: Government Printing Office.

———. 1998b. *State comparisons of education statistics: 1969–70 to 1996–97.* Washington, D.C.: Government Printing Office.

Rouse, Cecilia. 1995. Democratization or diversion? The effect of community colleges on educational attainment. *Journal of Business and Economic Statistics* 13 (2): 217–224.

Skocpol, Theda. 1991. Targeting within universalism: Politically viable policies to combat poverty in the United States. In *The urban underclass,* ed. Christopher Jencks and Paul Peterson, 411–436. Washington, D.C.: Brookings Institution.

Wilson, William Julius. 1987. *The truly disadvantaged.* Chicago: University of Chicago Press.

Wolfers, Justin, and Betty Stevenson. Forthcoming. 'Til death do us part: The effect of divorce laws on suicide, domestic violence and intimate homicide. *Journal of Political Economy.*

Comment   Charles Clotfelter

Susan Dynarski has written a well-crafted analysis of the effect of state merit aid programs on college attendance. She has employed variation over time and across states in the utilization of merit aid programs to provide very credible estimates of their enrollment effects. Rather than pursue points already well developed in her paper, I will note two aspects of the general topic that I suspect were not really part of Dynarski's charge in writing her chapter but that nonetheless warrant further reflection by policy analysts and researchers. One is the distributional impact of these programs, and the other concerns the wider array of effects emanating from them and programs like them.

Before the introduction of the "new breed of merit aid," states offered fi-

Charles Clotfelter is Z. Smith Reynolds Professor of Public Policy Studies and professor of economics and law at Duke University, and a research associate of the National Bureau of Economic Research.

nancial aid largely in the form of low tuition levels and easy geographic accessibility. Rather than devise means-tested financial aid of the form used in federal aid programs or by private institutions using the federally endorsed "uniform methodology," most states have eschewed individually tailored aid in favor of low tuitions across the board. As Hansen and Weisbrod (1969) showed, however, this seemingly populist policy—combined with a pattern of subsidies that favored elite public universities and admissions standards that caused eligibility to be correlated with parental income—has the effect of aiding the affluent rather than the poor. This was the dominant policy of states until Arkansas, and then, most prominently, Georgia, introduced a new form of state financial aid, the Helping Outstanding Pupils Educationally (HOPE) Scholarship. Fully consistent with the nation's (and especially the South's) infatuation with using tangible rewards for spurring educational achievement and enabled by the revenues produced by its new state lottery, Georgia offered a striking new carrot to its high school students: achieve a B average and receive in return a full-tuition scholarship to any state college or university. (Those enrolling in private institutions in the state received a stipend to cover a limited amount of tuition.) As Dynarski makes clear, the program's required grade point average meant that a higher percentage of whites than blacks were eligible to receive support. Though data on the incomes of students were not available, it was clear that this program also had a pro-middle-income impact reminiscent of the California low-tuition policy studied by Hansen and Weisbrod (1969). Two other features increased this tendency: the Pell Grant recipients had their state awards reduced by the amount of these grants, and the income ceiling on eligibility for the HOPE Scholarship Program was eliminated in the program's second year. Add to these pro-affluent aspects of the expenditure side of the program the regressivity of the implicit tax on the revenue side, and you have a rather stunning distributional impact. Putting aside whatever pro-poor effect there might be in legalizing the lottery, the policy choice to finance this merit aid program with a heavy implicit tax paid disproportionately out of lower incomes is quite remarkable. To be sure, Georgia appears to be an outlier in the way it financed and designed its merit aid program. But it is probably safe to say that one effect of the new breed of merit aid is a small but real redistribution of income.

A second point that Dynarski's paper moves me to mention is the rather uncontroversial assertion that enrollment effects, as important as they may be, are only one of a number of effects likely to emanate from these new state aid programs. In fact, Dynarski mentions several types of effects. She notes, for example, that the programs are likely to affect not only the propensity to enroll in college (and, more specifically, the propensity to go to four-year institutions) but also students' choices among institutions.

With several thousand new dollars in pocket (dollars that cannot not be spent just anywhere, however), aspiring college students might well be expected to make different choices than they would have in the absence of the program. She notes as well that merit programs, as a result of new patterns of enrollment, might influence the racial composition of institutions. And, she notes, merit aid programs could impact other forms of aid provided by states or, indeed, other state policies. A final effect that she mentions, one in line with the so-called Bennett hypothesis that "greedy colleges" would respond to increases in aid simply by raising tuition, is the possibility that a generous new merit aid program might inspire institutions, both public and private, to raise their tuitions.

This said, I would argue that there are yet other effects that might result from the introduction of this new breed of merit program. Because eligibility for these scholarships is contingent on a high level of academic performance in high school, one might surely expect such a program to influence the effort expended by students in high school. In light of the financial rewards available, we might also expect parents to offer encouragement to their high school children beyond the normal level of parental hectoring. Once in college, successful scholarship holders must confront the prospect of further academic performance requirements for them to retain their scholarships. Thus one would reasonably expect another set of effects, including those on the amount of effort devoted to study and on the choice of a major. Average grades awarded in various departments can differ significantly within a single college, and it should not be surprising that undergraduates pay attention to such differences, especially when financial repercussions are added to the other consequences of making low grades. For their part, institutions might respond to these pressures by allowing grades to inflate. Effects on the choice of major and on grades suggest another effect—the likelihood that students will stay on to graduate.

Another set of effects would arise out of the altered composition of student bodies. If, as appears to be the case, these programs raise the average academic qualification of students at some state schools, the learning environments there could be altered, depending on what kinds of peer effects are at work. The changes in composition might also affect the institutions' ability to recruit and retain talented faculty. One might also imagine that the surge in demand by qualified students might cause some institutions to confront questions such as whether to establish new or revise existing enrollment caps.

Susan Dynarski's chapter represents a useful and insightful contribution to a volume focusing on decisions about college. She shows that one new form of state aid program, one based on measured achievement rather than financial need, has affected the decisions of many college applicants about whether and where to attend college. My comments have touched on two related sets of questions that I view as interesting extensions, not important omissions.

References

Hansen, L., and B. Weisbrod. 1969. The distribution of costs and direct benefits of public higher education: The case of California. *Journal of Human Resources* 4 (Summer): 176–191.

The Impact of Federal Tax Credits for Higher Education Expenses

Bridget Terry Long

3.1 Introduction

During the past several decades, changes in the American economy have favored college graduates, and a postsecondary degree has become increasingly important in labor market outcomes (Murphy and Welch 1993; Juhn, Murphy, and Pierce 1993). After accounting for inflation, the incomes of those with a bachelor's degree grew 14.6 percent from 1975 to 1998, while those with only a high school degree experienced a 2.1 percent decrease.[1] As a result, access to higher education has become an important national issue, with the federal government focusing its efforts on financial aid policies designed to help students afford college expenses. Programs have included grants, such as the Pell Grant, subsidies for working students, and loans like the Perkins and Stafford Loans. However, with the Tax Relief Act of 1997, the government introduced a new form of aid to college students—federal tax credits for higher education expenses. The passage of the Hope Learning Credit (hereafter referred to as HTC) and Lifetime Learning Tax Credit (LLTC) marked a shift in the way that governmental support would be distributed to postsecondary students and their families.

When first introduced by former President Clinton during a June 1996 commencement speech at Princeton University, the tax credits were touted as a step toward making "the 13th and 14th years of education as univer-

Bridget Terry Long is an assistant professor at the Harvard Graduate School of Education and faculty research fellow of the National Bureau of Economic Research. The author gratefully acknowledges valuable comments and suggestions from Caroline Hoxby, Michael McPherson, Susan Dynarski, and Sarah Turner. Baoyan Cheng, Michal Kurlaender, Joie Jager-Hyman, and Bomy Hong provided excellent research assistance.

1. According to the U.S. Census Bureau, March Current Population Survey.

sal to all Americans as the first 12 are today" (Greenwood 1996). However, the proposal also reflected Clinton's intention to provide targeted tax relief to the middle class (Purdum 1996). As a model for the proposal, Clinton used the Georgia Helping Outstanding Pupils Educationally (HOPE) Scholarship. This politically popular program had been instrumental in getting Governor Zell Miller reelected by appealing to the concerns of middle class voters (Applebome 1996).[2] In a similar fashion, Clinton set program earnings limits that targeted middle-income families and promoted the credits as a reward to students who worked hard in school. Furthermore, as a credit, the proposal was viewed as being more helpful to the typical middle-class family than a tax deduction (Purdum 1996).[3] To justify the middle-income target, government officials assert that the tax credits serve a need since the middle class makes up a large proportion of college participants but is excluded from other federal grant programs (Stoll and Stedman 2001).

As with any other financial aid program, tax expenditures for higher education are considered a human capital investment and expected to yield both private and social benefits, including higher individual incomes, greater productivity, and lower crime rates and government dependency. However, the particular attraction of using tax credits rather than traditional grants or loans to promote college participation develops at least partly from the fact that federal budget rules favor tax expenditures over discretionary spending programs (Kane 1999b). Consequently, this was not the first time tax credits had been considered to support college costs. During the mid-1960s and early 1970s, Congress had considered a couple of proposals.[4] However, tax credits for higher education were finally passed during a time when the government sought to reduce taxes: The creation of the HTC and LLTC were part of the largest American tax cut in fifteen years (Gray 1997). After years of debate over incremental changes to other federal financial aid programs, the tax side of the budget served to dramatically increase support for postsecondary education.

According to the U.S. Department of Education (DOE), the credits are projected to eventually benefit 13.1 million students (5.9 million from HTC

2. The Georgia HOPE Scholarship provides full tuition, fees, and a book allowance to Georgia residents with a B average who attend an in-state public college. Those students choosing to attend an in-state private college are given compensation of comparable value. Benefits were limited to families with less than $66,000 of income during the first year and $100,000 during the second year. Although the original tax credit proposal also included a grade point average requirement, this criterion was eliminated before the policy was signed into law.

3. Deductions tend to disproportionately favor upper-income families since they are more likely to itemize their taxes.

4. Former President Johnson defeated the tax credits proposal by creating the Guaranteed Student Loan program in 1965, and former President Carter counteracted with the Middle Income Student Assistance Act in 1978 (Hauptman and Rice 1997).

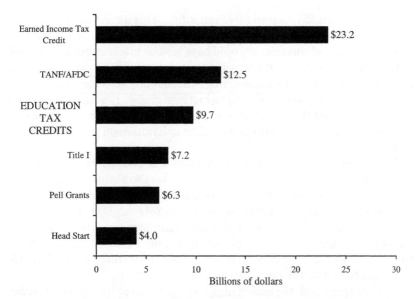

Fig. 3.1   Federal expenditure programs, 1997 (year of tax credit passage)

Sources: The expenditure on higher education tax credits is a projection by the Department of Education based on state-level enrollment, Pell Grant recipient data, and the president's fiscal year 2000 budget policy. Information on the other programs is from the College Board (2001b), NCES (1998), and U.S. Census Bureau (2000).

and 7.2 million from LLTC) at a cost of $9.7 billion (DOE 2000).[5] As shown in figure 3.1, this estimate is over 50 percent greater than the total amount spent at the time on the Pell Grant, the primary federal grant program. It also exceeds the amount spent on each of the three largest primary and secondary education programs (Title I, Head Start, and the School Lunch Program). Furthermore, the expected size of the program is only 20 percent less than expenditures on welfare (Temporary Assistance for Needy Families [TANF] or Aid to Families with Dependent Children [AFDC]). Although participation during the first three years of the program have not met the projections of the DOE, the total amount of tax credits has increased steadily each year, from $3.4 billion in 1998, the first year of the program, to $4.9 billion in 2000, an increase of 44 percent.[6]

The distribution of financial aid through the tax code is different from other forms of college assistance in several important ways. First, credits for tuition expenses in the current year do not accrue until the following year. Due to this timing, the delay between tuition payment and receipt of

5. According to Department of Education estimates based on state-level enrollment, Pell Grant recipient data, and the President's fiscal year 2000 budget policy.

6. According to calculations by author using data from the Internal Revenue Service, Information Services, Martinsburg Computing Center, Master File Service Support Branch.

the tax credit could be up to fifteen months.[7] This aspect of the program differs greatly from most other forms of aid, which are realized at the time of attendance, and this feature could have serious implications for how the aid affects college access. If the primary reason individuals do not enroll in college is due to liquidity constraints—the inability to secure present-day funding—then this aid is unlikely to increase access. For this reason, critics have suggested that the credits would only benefit students expected to attend college regardless of aid rather than individuals on the margin of enrolling.

The timing of the tax credits also creates a disconnect between the aid and activity (college enrollment). This increases the likelihood that the tax credits will not be used for postsecondary expenses. If students do not internalize the future payment as aid for present-day college expenses, then when they receive the support a year later, they may view the tax credit as income to be spent on other expenses. In a similar fashion, the support is too late to influence the educational investments of students who have already graduated by the time they receive the credit.

On the other hand, the timing of the aid may also be a beneficial feature. Other forms of aid, particularly grants, might encourage individuals not well suited for college to enroll since they are not fully responsible for the expenses incurred. This is an adverse selection problem. The tax credits, however, are unlikely to encourage frivolous investments in higher education due to the delay in receiving the support. Furthermore, the disconnect between the aid and college enrollment might also prevent postsecondary institutions from responding in ways detrimental to students. Critics suggest that postsecondary institutions may respond to the increase in financial aid by raising their prices. Due to the timing of the credits, colleges may be less likely to do this since students' present-day ability to pay has not increased.

A second important feature of tax credits is that there is no cap on the cost of the credits in terms of forgone tax revenue. Changes in individual behavior and/or state or institutional policy could quickly increase the estimated costs. For example, if a behavioral response to the program increased college enrollment significantly, there would be no limit to the amount of credits that could be claimed. Other governmental aid programs have experienced exceptional cost increases due to an unexpected response. For example, in New Mexico, the number of beneficiaries for the Lottery Success Scholarship so exceeded initial projections that the state was unable to meet the demand of students and benefits had to be reduced due to insufficient funds (Selingo 1999; Binder and Ganderton 2001).[8]

7. This assumes that tuition is paid in January of one year and taxes are filed in April of the following year (Conklin and Finney 1999).

8. While the scholarship had 8,000 recipients in 1998–1999, the total rose to 12,000 in 1999–2000 and was expected to be 16,000 the following year. In 2000–2001 the $16 million in lottery revenue available to fund the scholarship was insufficient to cover the $21.6 million in costs.

There is no similar budget constraint in terms of the higher education tax credits to limit the amount of benefits. Finally, since the higher education credits are tax expenditures, they are not subject to review in the annual federal appropriations process or the periodic reauthorization most federal programs undergo. Therefore, the regular examination of federal financial aid programs by the government will not include this very large program (Conklin and Finney 1999).

This paper examines the distribution and impact of the HTC and LLTC on taxpayers, students, and institutions. By reviewing the literature and analyzing several data sets on tax returns, individual behavior, and institutional activities, I examine three major questions. First, how have the tax credits been distributed by income? Have they really been a transfer to the middle class? Moreover, do a significant proportion of eligible families claim the credit, or are the information and transaction costs of distributing aid through tax credits exceedingly high? Although no program is likely to reach all eligible students, the higher education tax credits provide a new opportunity to test how effective it is to deliver college aid through the tax system. Second, how have the credits affected the college decisions of individuals? Have they prompted individuals to attend college who would not have otherwise? Have the credits encouraged students to choose more expensive colleges? Finally, how have postsecondary institutions responded to the tax credits? Have they altered their pricing policies in reaction to the introduction of the federal aid? What role have state governments had in the actions of their public colleges and universities? While many studies have tried to predict the likely impact of these higher education credits, this will be among the first to use data since enactment to estimate the actual results.

The paper is organized in the following way. Section 3.2 describes the tax credits with information on recipient eligibility, the expenses covered, and other details. Section 3.3 examines how the benefits of the HTC and LLTC were distributed and whether most eligible families claimed a credit. Section 3.4 considers the effect the tax credits have had on student enrollment decisions. Section 3.5 analyzes the impact on postsecondary institutions and state policies. Section 3.6 summarizes the results and concludes.

3.2 A Description of the Tax Credits

Before 1997, subsidies for higher education through the tax system were limited to postsecondary expenses for employment-related training (Cronin 1997). These expenses counted as an itemized deduction but did not cover training for the preparation of a new career. Additionally, the tax code allowed parents to claim exemptions for children up to the age of twenty-four if they were full-time college students and excluded interest on U.S. savings bonds redeemed to pay for tuition expenses. The only other special consideration given to higher education by the tax code was the exclusion of financial aid as income. This included scholarship and fellow-ship income, veteran's education benefits, and employer-provided educational assistance. However, the Taxpayer Relief Act of 1997 broadly expanded the treatment of higher education expenses with the HTC and LLTC. Table 3.1 summarizes the details of each credit.

The two tax credits complement each other by targeting different groups of students. While the HTC may only be used for a student's first two years of postsecondary education, the LLTC is available for unlimited years to those taking classes beyond their first two years of college, including college juniors and seniors, graduate students, and working adults pursuing lifelong learning.[9] For each credit, the expenses covered are tuition and required fees at an educational institution eligible for aid administered by the DOE. This amount is net grants, scholarships, and other tax-free educational assistance including Pell Grants, employer-provided education assistance, and veteran's educational assistance. The HTC provides a credit equal to 100 percent of the first $1,000 plus 50 percent of the next $1,000 of tuition paid during the tax year (a maximum credit of $1,500). The student must be enrolled at least half-time and pursue a degree or other recognized educational credential in order to be eligible for the HTC. In contrast, individuals do not need to be enrolled at least half time or pursue an educational credential in order to be eligible for the LLTC, thereby making the credit available to adults taking an occasional college course. The credit was equal to 20 percent on the first $5,000 of out-of-pocket tuition expenses (a maximum credit of $1,000), and since 2003 the LLTC has been based on expenses up to $10,000 (a maximum credit of $2,000).[10]

Figure 3.2 displays how the benefits for each tax credit compare to college expenses. For each amount of qualified tuition expenses noted on the x-axis, the solid lines trace to the amount of the tax credit on the y-axis. The dashed lines denote the mean costs of different types of colleges to highlight the amount of credit that would be received at that type of school. The average cost of a public, two-year college during the 1997–1998 school year would yield a $1,284 HTC or $313 LLTC benefit. The average costs of other types of schools would yield the maximum credit.[11] The HTC may be claimed on payments made after December 31, 1997, for college enroll-

9. To be eligible for HOPE, an individual must not have completed the first two years of college before the beginning of the tax year in question. Regardless of whether a student is full- or part-time, he or she may only take HOPE for two years. HOPE also requires that the student not have a felony drug conviction.

10. Several criteria originally included in the proposal were eliminated before enactment (Cronin 1997), including indexing the credit to inflation and requiring students to maintain a B-minus average in order to receive the HOPE. Additionally, the original proposal also allowed adults to deduct up to $10,000 per year ($5,000 in 1997 and 1998) for those enrolled at least half-time or for courses to improve job skills.

11. For the 1997–1998 school year, the mean tuition cost (enrollment weighted) for a public two-year college was $1,567, $3,111 for a public four-year college, $7,079 for a private two-year college, and $13,785 for a private four-year college (College Board 2001a).

Table 3.1   **Summary of the Federal Tax Credits**

	Hope Tax Credit (HTC)	Lifetime Learning Tax Credit (LLTC)
Targeted group	• Students in their first two years of postsecondary education	• College juniors and seniors • Graduate and professional degree students • Adults upgrading skills or changing careers
Recipient eligibility	• Available for the first two years of postsecondary education • Recipients must pursue a recognized credential • Recipients must be enrolled at least half-time • Recipients must not have a felony drug conviction	• Available for any postsecondary education • Available for an unlimited number of years • Recipients do not need to pursue a recognized credential • Available for one or more courses • Felony drug conviction rule does not apply
Amount	• 100% of the first $1,000 of qualified expenses; 50% of the second $1,000 (up to $1,500 credit *per eligible student*)	• 20% of the first $5,000 of qualified expenses through 2002 (up to $1,000 credit *per return*) • Starting in 2003 credit covers up to $10,000 of expenses (maximum of $2,000 credit)
Claimant	• Taxpayers may claim a credit for their own tuition expenses or those of their spouse or dependent children	• Maximum credit is determined on a per-taxpayer (family) basis, regardless of the number of post-secondary students in the family
Timeline	• Available for payments made after December 31, 1997, for enroll-ment after that date	• May claim the credit for amounts paid on or after July 1, 1998, for enrollment beginning on or after July 1, 1998
Expenses covered	• Tuition and required fees at an educational institution eligible for aid administered by the DOE minus grants, scholarships, and other tax-free educational assistance (including Pell Grants, employer-provided education assistance, and veteran's educational assistance) • Note: The expenses covered do not include the cost of insurance, medical expenses (including student health fees), room and board, transportation, or living expenses	
Income eligibility	• Phased out for joint filers with $80,000 to $100,000 of modified AGI ($40,000 to $50,000 for single filers) • Married couples must file a joint return to claim a benefit • Phased out for single filers with $40,000 to $50,000 modified AGI • Individuals must modify their AGI to include income earned abroad	
Other details	• Families are able to claim the LLTC for some members and HTC for others in the same year. However, the same student cannot take both credits.	

Source: Summarized from Internal Revenue Service (1998c) and Office of Postsecondary Education (1997).

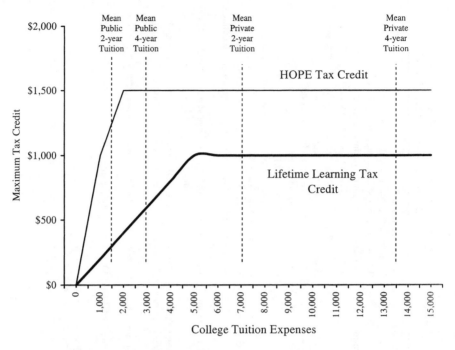

Fig. 3.2   Tax credit by college expense

Source: Tax credit information from Internal Revenue Service (1998c).

Notes: In 2003, the maximum LLTC will increase to $2,000. For the 1997–1998 school year, the mean tuition cost (enrollment weighted) for a public two-year college was $1,567, $3,111 for a public four-year college, $7,079 for a private two-year college, and $13,785 for a private four-year college (College Board 2001a).

ment after that date, while the LLTC can be claimed on expenses incurred as early as July 1, 1998, for college or vocational school enrollment beginning on or after July 1, 1998. Families are able to claim the LLTC for some members and the HTC for others in the same year. However, the same student cannot take both credits.

The benefits of the tax credits phase out for higher-income taxpayers. The phaseout begins at an adjusted gross income (AGI) of $80,000 for a joint return ($40,000 for single filers) with no benefit for families with incomes above $100,000 ($50,000 for single filers).[12] With these relatively high thresholds, tax credits for higher education expenses have the most extensive eligibility of any federal program. Data on tax returns from 1997 suggest that two-thirds of returns during that tax year would have been eligible based on filing status (joint or single) and AGI ($10,000 to $100,000

---

12. The AGI is total income minus deductions for items such as alimony, student loans, individual retirement accounts, and medical savings accounts. For most taxpayers, AGI is equal to total income. In 1998, only 17.6 percent of returns had any of the aforementioned deductions. The average deduction adjusted AGI calculation by $2,343 (Campbell, Parisi, and Balkovic 2000).

for joint filers, $10,000 to $50,000 for single filers).[13] In comparison, Pell Grants are strictly limited to families with incomes below $40,000. Nearly 90 percent of Pell Grant funds are awarded to families with incomes under $30,000, and 54 percent of those families have incomes under $10,000 (Kane 1999a).[14]

3.3   The Distribution of the Tax Credits

The first major questions that need to be answered to understand the effect of the HTC and LLTC are these: How have the benefits been distributed? Which groups have benefited the most from the credits? Is the policy progressive or regressive? As intended by Clinton, have middle-income families been the largest beneficiaries of the tax credits? This section examines these issues using data from the Internal Revenue Service for 1998, 1999, and 2000, the first three years of the tax credits. Furthermore, I investigate the extent to which eligible families have claimed a benefit.

3.3.1   Factors That Influence the Distribution of Benefits

From the first announcement of the tax credit proposal, many have hypothesized about the potential distribution of benefits based on the policy's criteria. One important feature of the tax credits is that they are not refundable. To receive a benefit, individuals must have income sufficient to produce positive federal income tax liability. Furthermore, if a family claims other tax credits or deductions, this will reduce its ability to benefit from the HTC or the LLTC.[15] Therefore, many lower-income groups are ineligible to receive a tax benefit (Kane 1997; McPherson and Schapiro 1997; Hoxby 1998). This fact, coupled with the income caps that prevent individuals from the most affluent backgrounds from collecting the credit, suggests that the tax credits primarily benefit students from middle- and upper-income families.

The middle-class nature of the tax credit is confirmed when one consults the federal tax forms (Internal Revenue Service 1998a,b). A dependent student from a married family of four needs at least $17,900 in family income to overcome the standard deductions and exemptions necessary to have tax liability.[16] To receive the maximum LLTC ($1,000), this student's fam-

13. According to the Internal Revenue Service, Information Services, Martinsburg Computing Center. The proportion of the eligible population based on AGI might be higher since presumably some married persons filed separately when they might have been eligible had they filed jointly.

14. Eligibility for Pell depends on an individual's Expected Family Contribution, which is a function of income and expected college costs.

15. Other tax credits reduce a family's tax liability dollar for dollar. Likewise, tax deductions reduce a family's AGI, the basis on which tax liability is calculated.

16. This calculation is for the minimum income possible using the 1998 standard deduction for a "married filing jointly" return ($7,100) and the exemption amount ($2,700 multiplied by the number of exemptions for incomes below $93,000). The minimum will be higher if a fam-

ily income must be at least $24,550, or $27,900 to receive a maximum HTC ($1,500). This suggests that the bottom 30 percent of the 1997 income distribution was ineligible to take the full HTC benefit due to insufficient tax liability based on the benchmarks of a dependent student.[17] Beginning in 2003, the maximum LLTC increased to $2,000 and dictated that families must make at least $31,250 to receive the full credit.[18] The bottom thresholds are lower for independent students due to a smaller standard deduction and fewer exemptions.[19] Independent students must have an income of at least $6,950 to have some tax liability, $13,600 to be eligible for the full LLTC, and $16,950 for the full HTC. Due to the income phaseout of eligibility, the top 20 percent of the 1997 income distribution would have been ineligible to take either the full or any credit. For single filers, the cutoff is even lower, making an even larger portion of the distribution ineligible.

Due to other features of the tax code, even eligible middle-income families may not be able to reap the full benefit of the tax credits. Claiming the HTC could subject many middle-income families to the alternative minimum tax (AMT). Although it was designed to ensure that wealthy taxpayers who shelter their incomes from taxation pay a minimum amount, Knight (1997) suggests that families with incomes as low as $41,350 might be penalized and not receive the full benefit of the credit. In an article for the *Washington Post,* Crenshaw (1997) calculated that a family earning $64,100 per year with two children in college would normally pay $6,743 in taxes if filing jointly. If the family claims HTC for one and LLTC for the other (total $2,500), the tax liability would be reduced to $4,243. However, under the AMT calculation, the family's tax liability is $4,966, a $723 reduction in the value of the tax credits.

A second important determinant of the distribution of benefits is the amount of tuition expenses incurred by different groups. Therefore, the distribution of benefits is affected by where individuals attend college. Because low-income students tend to be concentrated at lower-priced colleges, such as public two-year and four-year schools, their likelihood of receiving the full tax benefit is further reduced. In addition, since the credit is based on tuition expenses net of grants, the HTC and LLTC interact with

ily itemizes deductions or takes a credit for dependent care expenses (line 41), elderly or disabled (line 42), children under age seventeen (line 43), adoption (line 45), or foreign taxes (line 46). See Form 1040 for 1998 for more details.

17. The income distribution calculations were made using data on the U.S. income quintiles and median from the U.S. Census Bureau (1999).

18. A return's taxable income must be at least $6,650 for a tax of $1,000, $10,000 for a tax of $1,500, and $13,350 for a tax of $2,000. See the 1998 Internal Revenue Service Tax Table.

19. A student is defined as "independent" if he or she meets one of the following criteria: is over the age of 24; a veteran; an orphan or ward of the court; a person with legal dependents other than a spouse; married and not claimed by his or her parents; or a graduate student and not claimed by his or her parents. A single undergraduate student may be designated as independent if he or she is not claimed as a dependent by his or her parents and has been self-sufficient for at least two years.

other forms of financial aid. Most notably, this includes the Pell Grant, a means-tested federal aid program for students without a baccalaureate degree. Using the mean tuition levels of different types of colleges, Hauptman and Rice (1997) estimate that families with incomes below $20,000 will be eligible for the Pell Grant but not the tax credits.[20] Therefore, the interaction between the Pell Grant and higher education tax credits further raises the income benchmarks necessary for many individuals to claim the HTC or LLTC. According to figures from the U.S. Census Bureau, this benchmark makes the bottom 20 percent of the income distribution ineligible. Among female-headed households, half would not qualify for a tax credit.[21] In contrast, families with incomes of at least $50,000 would only be able to receive tax credits. Families between these benchmarks receive a combination of the two types of aid depending on the Pell Grant award and college price.

The most important criterion is, of course, college attendance. Since attendance rates differ by income and race, it is clear that the distribution of benefits is unlikely to be equal across groups even without the importance of the factors just discussed. Among dependent students aged eighteen to twenty-four, only 38.3 percent with family incomes in the bottom quartile participated in college in 1997. In contrast, 78.5 percent of dependent students in the top quartile attended college (Jamieson, Curry, and Martinez 2001). However, since one goal of the credits is to encourage participation in higher education, the incidence of the HTC and LLTC depends on their impact on college enrollment. If they encourage postsecondary attendance for certain individuals or groups, the relative benefits by income group or state could change. This possible effect is investigated in section 3.4.

Based on these criteria, table 3.2 displays the proportion of college students that are eligible for a higher education tax credit using data from the 1999–2000 National Postsecondary Student Aid Survey (NPSAS), a nationally representative survey of students. Eligibility for a credit was determined using information on family income, attendance intensity (full-time, part-time, or less than part-time), tuition expenses, and year in college. Assuming that the 1999–2000 school year is representative of any tax year, 43 percent of undergraduates are eligible for either the HTC or the LLTC.[22] Over half of master's and doctoral students are eligible. By college type, the greatest proportions of eligible students are at four-year colleges and proprietary schools (for-profit two- and four-year institutions). When the sample is limited to full-time students, the proportion eligible increases. Nearly 56 percent of full-time undergraduates are eligible for a tax credit. Further analysis shows that removing the requirement for net tuition ex-

20. This assumes full-time enrollment by a college freshman from a married family of four.
21. The median income of a female-headed household in 1997 was $21,023 (U.S. Census Bureau 1999).
22. Eligibility is measured with some error because it is defined by income rather than AGI.

Table 3.2   **Percentage Eligible for the Higher Education Tax Credits**

| | All Students (full-time and part-time) | | | |
	Hope	Lifetime Learning	Either Tax Credit	Full-Time Students: Either Tax Credit
Student level				
Undergraduate	22.33	20.80	43.13	55.94
Master's	n.a.	53.33	53.33	57.27
Doctoral	n.a.	52.82	52.82	50.83
Professional	n.a.	42.73	42.73	42.91
Other graduate degree	n.a.	45.68	45.68	62.09
College type				
Public two-year	24.45	10.62	35.06	52.98
Private two-year	35.61	7.68	43.28	55.97
Public four-year	14.58	34.96	49.54	54.42
Private four-year	15.05	37.80	52.85	58.18
Proprietary (for-profit)	32.81	21.01	53.83	70.92
Less than two-year	21.15	12.25	33.40	56.96

Notes: Calculations by author using the 1999–2000 National Postsecondary Student Aid Survey. Assumes that the 1999–2000 school year is representative of a tax year (January–December). Eligibility is based on income, year in school, intensity, and having net tuition expenses greater than zero (tuition minus all grants). To make nationally representative, weights supplied by the survey were used. n.a. = not applicable.

penses would increase the percent eligible for a credit by nearly a third.[23] Although students who have no tuition net of aid may still have living expenses, they do not qualify for a tax benefit.

Although there are a myriad of criteria that need to be satisfied in order to qualify for a tax credit including income benchmarks, college attendance, and positive net tuition expenses, a very large share of students are still eligible for a benefit. This is especially true in comparison to other financial aid programs. For example, only approximately one-fifth of students in the NPSAS were eligible for the Pell Grant.

3.3.2   Credit Beneficiaries by Income: The Internal Revenue Service Data

Due to the time delay associated with data, little analysis has been done nationally on the actual beneficiaries of the tax credits. The few studies that use actual data on credit usage (rather than assumed usage) focus on the University of California (UC) system. Hoblitzell and Smith (2001) examine usage of the credits by evaluating data collected on nearly 3,500 students. They find that more than 45 percent of families that claimed a tax

23. Without the requirement of positive net tuition expenses, 66.5 percent of undergraduates and 77.0 percent of master's and doctoral students would be eligible for a credit.

credit earned less than $50,000 per year, and 22 percent earned less than $20,000 annually. The estimated aggregate amount in tax credits ($80 million) was about 85 percent of the $95 million UC students receive in Pell Grants, the largest federal grant program. Among the 1,282 undergraduate students, 13 percent claimed the HTC (with a mean of $1,119 and 52 percent claiming the maximum) and 14 percent claimed the LLTC (with a mean of $661 and 28 percent claiming the maximum). Of the 543 graduate students in the survey, 32 percent claimed the LLTC (with a mean of $743 and 43 percent claiming the maximum). However, students in the UC system tend to be more affluent than the general population of college students. While the median income of respondents to the UC survey was $48,670 in 1999, the median U.S. income was $41,994 (U.S. Bureau of the Census 2000). Furthermore, Hoblitzell and Smith estimate that only 37 percent of UC students were eligible for the credits in 1999. These differences make the Hoblitzell and Smith study difficult to generalize for the nation as a whole and for the population of college students.

To give a national picture of the number of families benefiting from the higher education tax credits, this study uses data on tax returns from the Internal Revenue Service. The number and amount of credits taken are shown for the first three years of the program in table 3.3.[24] During tax year 2000, nearly 6.7 million credits were claimed amounting to almost $4.9 billion. Over 5 percent of returns claimed either the HTC or LLTC, and the mean tax credit was $731. When these figures are compared to those from the two previous tax years, it is evident that usage of the credits has grown. While the mean has remained stable ($726 to $731), the number and total amount of credits grew 44 and 45 percent, respectively, from 1998 to 2000. Most of this growth occurred between the first and second year of the credits (1998 to 1999). Experience with other federal benefit programs suggests take-up rates will continue to increase. Participation in the Earned Income Tax Credit, another benefit program that is distributed through the tax system, continued to grow from 70 percent in 1984 to an estimated 80 to 86 percent in 1990 even after a number of policy changes (Scholz 1994).

While many families claimed a higher education tax credit, not all were able to take the full credit for which they were eligible due to insufficient tax liability. This happened when families did not have enough income, minus tax deductions, to generate enough tax liability, net other credits. These returns are defined as nontaxable. Unless a family's tax liability is exactly equal to the amount they claimed in education tax credits, these nontaxable returns indicate the number of returns that were unable to take the entire education credit due to insufficient tax liability, perhaps in conjunction with the use of other credits. In general, 44 percent of all returns with AGIs between $5,000 and $100,000 were designated as nontaxable due to taking

---

24. Note that these figures are before returns have been audited.

Table 3.3   Higher Education Tax Credits

	All Returns	Size of Adjusted Gross Income					
		Below $10,000	$10,000 to $19,999	$20,000 to $29,999	$30,000 to $49,999	$50,000 to $74,999	$75,000 to $99,999
		A. Higher Education Tax Credits, 2000					
Number of returns	130,122,204	25,947,174	23,678,120	18,533,555	23,878,431	17,263,552	8,547,241
Higher education tax credits							
Number of credits	6,698,163	258,220	1,110,604	1,054,598	1,736,226	1,472,598	1,062,644
Amount of credits ($000s)	4,896,215	59,744	689,679	772,886	1,300,231	1,328,260	718,376
% of group that claimed a credit	5.15	1.00	4.69	5.69	7.27	8.53	12.43
Higher education tax credits beneficiaries							
Mean education credit ($)	731	231	621	733	749	902	676
% of education credits claimed	n.a.	3.86	16.58	15.74	25.92	21.99	15.86
Share of benefits compared to share of costs							
Share of credits (#) ÷ share of returns (#)	n.a.	0.18	0.83	1.00	1.28	1.50	2.19
Share of credits ($) ÷ share of returns ($)	n.a.	3.42	3.41	1.72	1.06	0.67	0.57
		B. Higher Education Tax Credits, 1999					
Number of returns	127,667,890	26,559,779	24,104,823	18,392,185	23,356,750	16,585,331	7,840,255
Higher education tax credits							
Number of credits	6,293,257	256,435	1,012,410	942,949	1,613,629	1,461,293	1,003,858
Amount of credits ($000s)	4,582,262	57,539	602,818	658,305	1,200,017	1,355,245	705,623
% of group that claimed a credit	4.93	0.97	4.20	5.13	6.91	8.81	12.80
Higher education tax credits beneficiaries							
Mean education credit ($)	728	224	595	698	744	927	703
% of education credits claimed	n.a.	4.08	16.09	14.99	25.65	23.23	15.96
		C. Higher Education Tax Credits, 1998					
Number of returns	124,770,662	26,289,293	24,625,806	18,292,760	23,108,693	15,886,502	7,221,303
Higher education tax credits							
Number of credits	4,652,596	185,999	675,633	647,673	1,203,273	1,186,887	753,125
Amount of credits ($000s)	3,376,047	40,045	411,495	430,119	843,528	1,092,185	559,273
% of group that claimed a credit	3.73	0.71	2.74	3.54	5.21	7.47	10.43
Higher education tax credits beneficiaries							
Mean education credit ($)	726	215	609	664	701	920	743
% of education credits claimed	n.a.	4.00	14.52	13.92	25.86	25.51	16.19

Source: Internal Revenue Service, Information Services, Martinsburg Computing Center, Master File Service Support branch.

Notes: Figures for 2000 represent all returns filed and processed through the Individual Master File (IMF) system during 2000. n.a. = not applicable.

some tax credit in 1999. The mean is slightly larger for returns that claim education credits (46 percent).[25] This means that half of the higher education tax credit beneficiaries were not able to take the full credit for which they were otherwise eligible.

Use of the HTC and LLTC varied considerably by AGI. As discussed, almost no individual below $10,000 claimed a credit (1 percent) due to insufficient tax liability and the interaction of the tax credit with other forms of aid. In contrast, 7.3 percent of returns with an income between $30,000 and $50,000 claimed an education credit, while 8.5 percent of families with incomes between $50,000 and $75,000 received a benefit. This pattern is also likely to be a function of the different types of families in each AGI group (single adults versus parents with children old enough to be in college). Individuals with incomes between $50,000 and $75,000 claimed the largest average credit ($902).

Not all taxpayers correctly claimed an education tax credit. Although they are not eligible for the higher education tax credits, in tax year 2000, 2,965 credits were claimed by returns with over $100,000 in income.[26] Experience from the Earned Income Tax Credit (EITC) suggests that possibly many more families improperly claimed the credit. Holtzblatt (1991) and McCubbin (1999) found that a significant fraction of taxpayers received the EITC when not technically eligible. Taxpayers will adopt a strategy by weighing the tradeoff between the benefit to misreporting income or expenses and the corresponding risk of detection and penalty (Allingham and Sandmo 1972). However, since the higher education tax credits are not refundable like the EITC, the number of improper claims will be limited to those with sufficient tax liability.

To get a sense of the distribution of costs (tax liability) and benefits (tax credits) by income, the bottom two rows in panel A of table 3.3 display the proportion of credits an AGI group claimed divided by the proportion of returns under $100,000 submitted by that group. Stated another way, this is an AGI group's share of benefits divided by its share of the tax burden. Using the number of returns and credits, families with an AGI between $20,000 and $29,999 had the same proportion of the education credits as they did returns. Families with incomes below this amount claimed relatively fewer credits, while returns with higher AGIs claimed a larger share of credits than their proportion of the tax returns. This suggests that usage of the credits is skewed toward higher incomes. However, when we compare the total monetary amount of credits claimed to the tax liability for the group, the result reverses. Families with AGIs below $50,000 claim relatively more in higher education credits than they pay in taxes.

Instead of comparing across incomes, tables 3.4 and 3.5 compare the

---

25. Calculations by author using Internal Revenue Service data in Campbell and Parisi (2001). Nontaxable returns are defined as having no tax liability after all credits and the alternative minimum tax are applied.

26. These returns are not included in the subsequent analysis.

Table 3.4 Total Tax Liability Relative to Total Higher Education Tax Credits by Income Group, 2000 (amounts in thousands)

	All Returns	Below $10,000	$10,000 to $19,999	$20,000 to $29,999	$30,000 to $49,999	$50,000 to $74,999	$75,000 to $99,999
				Size of Adjusted Gross Income			
Total taxable income ($)	4,510,367,610	15,797,752	114,306,435	238,991,172	593,307,519	734,353,450	535,083,911
Total federal tax liability ($)	1,019,928,541	4,236,231	18,264,729	34,275,965	91,388,580	123,438,299	103,771,900
Total education tax credits ($)	4,896,215	59,744	689,679	772,886	1,300,231	1,328,260	718,376
% of liability covered by credits (%)	0.5	1.4	3.8	2.3	1.4	1.1	0.7

Source: Internal Revenue Service.

Notes: Figures represent all returns filed and processed through 2000. Total taxable income is income minus deductions.

Table 3.5   Tax Liability Relative to Higher Education Tax Credits Calculated at the Means of Each Income Group, 2000

	All Returns			Size of Adjusted Gross Income			
		Below $10,000	$10,000 to $19,999	$20,000 to $29,999	$30,000 to $49,999	$50,000 to $74,999	$75,000 to $99,999
Mean taxable income ($)	42,719	1,846	6,113	13,243	25,014	42,629	62,680
Mean federal tax liability ($)	9,724	401	1,056	2,031	3,913	7,176	12,154
Total education tax credits ($)	731	231	621	733	749	902	676
% of federal liability covered by education credits	7.5	57.7	58.8	36.1	19.1	12.6	5.6
Lifetime federal tax liability ($)	320,892	13,233	34,848	67,023	129,129	236,808	401,082
Lifetime education credits taken ($)	5,848	1,848	4,968	5,864	5,992	7,216	5,408
% of lifetime liability covered by lifetime credits	1.8	14.0	14.3	8.78	4.6	3.1	1.4

Source: Internal Revenue Service.

Notes: Figures represent all returns filed and processed through 2000. Total taxable income is income minus deductions. To determine the lifetime credits taken, the mean amount is multiplied by 8 (assuming a family with two children who each attend college for four years). To determine the lifetime tax liability, the amount is multiplied by 33 as suggested by Murphy and Welch (1990) in their examination of earnings profiles.

benefits of the tax credits to federal tax liability within an AGI group. The last row in table 3.4 compares the total amount in tax credits claimed by a group to its total federal tax liability. For example, for all returns, the total monetary amount in higher education tax credits was 0.5 percent of the total federal tax liability of returns for the 2000 tax year. The percentage ranges from 0.7 to 3.8 for groups eligible for the tax credit, suggesting that the national mean (0.5 percent) is heavily skewed by individuals with over $100,000 in income. The amount of tax credits claimed when compared to tax liability is largest for individuals with an AGI between $10,000 and $19,999. The benefits were nearly 4 percent as large as the group's total tax liability. Likewise, the total amount in credits was 2.3 percent of the total tax burden for returns between $20,000 and $29,999. This ratio is smallest for families with incomes above $50,000.

Table 3.5 makes the same comparison but instead uses the mean credit (for returns with a credit greater than zero) and tax liability. For example, returns between $10,000 and $19,999 had on average $1,056 in federal tax liability. Moreover, those that claimed a credit in that group received an average benefit of $621. This suggests that the mean amount of tax benefits from the HTC and LLTC covered 58.8 percent of the tax liability for members of this group that claimed a credit.[27] This ratio is lower for groups with higher AGI. In summary, the credit covers more of the tax liability of low-income claimants than that of individuals with higher incomes.

In order to fully understand the incidence of the tax credit, it is necessary to consider the federal tax liability of a family over time. Using the earnings profiles estimated with CPS data by Murphy and Welch (1990), I approximate that individuals with twenty years of work experience (about the age to have college-age children) earn about 33 times that amount over the course of their working life.[28] Therefore, federal tax liability was multiplied by this number to get a return's lifetime tax burden. Furthermore, families are likely to receive the education credit for multiple years and perhaps for multiple children. Assuming a family has two children that attend college for four years each, the mean education credit was multiplied by eight. The results of these calculations are shown in the last several rows of table 3.5. For families that earn less than $20,000, the tax credits (under the assumptions given) make up about 14 percent of their lifetime tax liability. The percentage is less than one-third of that for returns with incomes above $30,000. For example, the total amount of education credits taken by a family with an AGI between $50,000 to $74,999 would only amount to 3 percent of its lifetime tax liability. However, this rough calculation is not a

27. This calculation implicitly assumes that returns that claim education credits have the mean characteristics of their AGI group.

28. This assumes that individuals work for forty years. See the diagrams in Murphy and Welch (1990).

good approximation for low-AGI returns if the taxpayer is actually a student. In this case, the incomes and tax liabilities are extremely likely to grow over time, and the assumption of multiplying by 33 will not be accurate.

3.3.3 The Distribution of Credits across States

The distribution of education credits does not vary only across income groups. States also varied in the amount by which they benefited from the tax credits. To determine which states have reaped the most in credits, the 2000 data were analyzed by state. Table 3.6 displays the number and amount of credits claimed by state. While the mean credit claimed by state is similar to the national mean, there was incredible variation between states. The mean credit for a state ranged from $552 (New Mexico) to $899 (Pennsylvania). When this is compared to the DOE projections, further dissimilarities become evident. States like New Jersey claimed 83 percent of the expected amount in tax credits during the third year of the program. Meanwhile, the District of Columbia had less than a quarter of the expected credits.

A number of state characteristics are likely to affect the degree to which it benefited from the introduction of the higher education tax credits. The earnings distribution of its residents will determine the proportion eligible by income. The relative size of its population of college-age individuals and the rate of postsecondary attendance will also affect usage of the credits. Finally, because the HTC and LLTC are awarded based on net tuition expenses, the cost of the colleges that a state's residents attend will be influential.[29] When the rankings of the states are compared, states with a larger proportion of returns claiming higher education tax credits did on average have a larger proportion of their population in college and higher mean public two-year tuition levels. States with the smallest percentage of returns with a credit had the largest mean proportion of eligible returns as determined by AGI but a smaller proportion of residents enrolled in college and a lower average tuition price at community colleges. The efforts of state governments and colleges to inform their students of the tax credits could also help explain differences in usage. For example, as discussed by Hoblitzell and Smith (2001), the UC system has actively tried to inform students and parents about the availability of the credit.

---

29. For most students, this will be the cost of an in-state college. Eighty-one percent of first-time freshmen in 1996 attended an in-state college. The proportion is higher for older students, including undergraduate upperclassmen, graduate students, and nontraditional students (U.S. Department of Education, National Center for Education Statistics, Integrated Postsecondary Education Data System [IPEDS], "Residence of First-Time Students" survey, 1996).

Table 3.6   Tax Credit Beneficiaries by State, 2000

Higher Education Tax Credit Beneficiaries

	Number of Returns	Total Credits ($000s)	Mean Credit per Return	Percent of Returns	Expected Number of Beneficiaries (government projection)	Actual ÷ Expected Number of Credits
State mean	130,771	95,243	725	5.24	256,843	—
(Standard deviation)	(147,077)	(104,425)	(85)	(1.00)	(326,552)	—
State median	80,855	57,854	718	5.29	165,000	
Alabama	88,196	64,806	735	4.63	197,000	44.77
Alaska	18,884	12,300	651	5.74	36,000	52.46
Arizona	117,874	71,328	605	5.48	307,000	38.40
Arkansas	47,480	30,473	642	4.25	91,000	52.18
California	824,789	502,925	610	5.55	2,073,000	39.79
Colorado	122,060	80,653	661	5.82	238,000	51.29
Connecticut	78,960	63,572	805	4.72	126,000	62.67
Delaware	18,110	13,780	761	4.79	32,000	56.59
District of Columbia	14,813	12,579	849	5.30	68,000	21.78
Florida	322,736	223,863	694	4.30	667,000	48.39
Georgia	141,427	101,535	718	3.89	284,000	49.80
Hawaii	34,234	24,680	721	5.98	58,000	59.02
Idaho	31,905	21,594	677	5.70	51,000	62.56
Illinois	319,085	247,883	777	5.51	659,000	48.42
Indiana	130,909	103,779	793	4.61	260,000	50.35
Iowa	93,110	70,529	757	6.89	150,000	62.07
Kansas	77,440	46,874	605	6.33	177,000	43.75
Kentucky	77,188	54,628	708	4.42	128,000	60.30
Louisiana	80,855	57,854	716	4.31	153,000	52.85
Maine	28,401	25,193	887	4.69	47,000	60.43
Maryland	144,925	113,372	782	5.65	272,000	53.28
Massachusetts	165,460	132,623	802	5.32	359,000	46.09
Michigan	244,532	182,154	745	5.29	503,000	48.61

Minnesota	151,921	118,549	780	6.37	257,000	59.11
Mississippi	41,742	28,763	689	3.56	100,000	41.74
Missouri	136,227	91,796	674	5.31	276,000	49.36
Montana	23,645	17,410	736	5.57	35,000	67.56
Nebraska	55,529	36,446	656	6.86	122,000	45.52
Nevada	43,342	25,714	593	4.54	78,000	55.57
New Hampshire	34,009	28,410	835	5.41	52,000	65.40
New Jersey	221,033	193,465	875	5.43	266,000	83.10
New Mexico	32,541	17,973	552	4.47	97,000	33.55
New York	498,887	424,878	852	5.82	757,000	65.90
North Carolina	174,416	109,906	630	4.80	351,000	49.69
North Dakota	22,405	16,294	727	7.40	30,000	74.68
Ohio	256,297	210,750	822	4.60	478,000	53.62
Oklahoma	73,057	44,005	602	4.99	165,000	44.28
Oregon	83,056	53,874	649	5.32	183,000	45.39
Pennsylvania	292,685	263,167	899	5.04	472,000	62.01
Rhode Island	28,549	21,382	749	5.77	65,000	43.92
South Carolina	77,692	54,186	697	4.31	152,000	51.11
South Dakota	24,884	20,148	810	7.01	34,000	73.19
Tennessee	112,161	81,360	725	4.37	211,000	53.16
Texas	444,974	309,031	694	4.92	893,000	49.83
Utah	75,800	53,309	703	8.05	118,000	64.24
Vermont	14,168	12,625	891	4.73	35,000	40.48
Virginia	171,398	115,641	675	5.13	325,000	52.74
Washington	144,792	100,558	694	5.22	243,000	59.59
West Virginia	33,311	23,992	720	4.44	71,000	46.92
Wisconsin	164,466	116,656	709	6.33	265,000	62.06
Wyoming	12,951	8,133	628	5.51	32,000	40.47

Sources: Beneficiaries data from IRS, Information Services, Martinsburg Computing Center, Master File Service Support Branch. Projections data from Education Department estimates based on state-level enrollment, Pell Grant recipient data, and the president's fiscal year 2000 budget policy.

Note: Classification by state is usually based on the taxpayer's home address. However, some taxpayers may have used the address of a tax lawyer or accountant or the address of a place of business.

3.3.4 Are Eligible Families Taking the Credit?
The NHES and NPSAS Data

Although many families are eligible for the aid, this does not necessarily mean that they will claim the tax credit. This may be due to a lack of information about the benefit or a complicated claiming procedure. It is clear from the results in the previous section that usage of the credits is well below DOE projections. The Federal Office of Management and Budget provides additional support for this notion that many eligible families did not claim the HTC or LLTC. During tax year 1998, they found that only 36 percent of families with eligible college students claimed the credit. That yielded 49 percent of the eligible amount to be claimed (Riley 2000).

Since there has been considerable growth in the number and amount of credits claimed since inception, part of this gap could be due to families slowly learning about the aid. However, during tax year 2000, the third year of the policy, of the 13.1 million projected recipients, only 6.7 million returns claimed a credit. Since one return can claim multiple credits (e.g., a HTC for one child and a LLTC for another), it is better to compare the projected and actual amount of credits claimed. Although the DOE expected that $9.7 billion in credits would be awarded, returns only claimed $4.9 billion in credits, 50.5 percent of the projected amount. Previous studies have found that individuals eligible for other types of financial aid programs do not necessarily apply to them (Orfield 1992). As with any financial aid policy, awareness of the subsidy is essential to having the desired impact. Moreover, differing take-up rates by background affects the relative distribution of its benefits.

To further reveal the general level of awareness about the credits and the proportion and characteristics of eligible families that claimed a benefit, I consulted two national data sets. The first, the National Household Education Survey (NHES), asked 8,552 parents in 1999 if they had ever heard about the HTC or LLTC.[30] As shown in table 3.7, most parents were not aware of the credits. While one-third had heard of one of the credits, only 21.5 and 18.7 percent had heard of the HTC and LLTC, respectively. The responses by demographic characteristics allow one to draw some inferences about how awareness of the tax credits differed by background.[31] In general, parents from racial minority groups were less likely to know about the credits than white parents, particularly in the case of the LLTC. Addi-

---

30. The NHES is a random-digit-dialed, computer-assisted telephone survey covering all fifty states and the District of Columbia. It was conducted in January through April of 1999 by the National Center for Education Statistics (see http://nces.ed.gov/nhes/Main/design .asp).

31. To produce reliable estimates for racial groups, the NHES oversamples black and Hispanic individuals. While the data set provides weights to make the sample nationally representative, because the tax questions were only asked for a subset of the sample, they are not used in this analysis.

Table 3.7   **Percent of Parents Who Have Heard of the Tax Credits, 1999**

	Either Tax Credit	Hope Tax Credit	Lifetime Learning Tax Credit	Number of Observations
Mean	33.3	21.5	18.7	8,552
Race				
White	32.8	22.5	21.4	5,355
Black	28.3	22.9	12.9	1,326
Hispanic	22.5	16.2	13.7	1,392
All other races	30.9	23.2	17.8	479
Household income				
$10,000 or less	19.3	14.6	10.4	540
$10,001–20,000	22.7	17.2	11.3	851
$20,001–30,000	24.6	18.5	12.2	1,202
$30,001–40,000	27.9	20.5	14.9	1,253
$40,001–50,000	29.0	20.6	18.5	1,023
$50,001–75,000	33.2	23.1	21.6	1,704
More than $75,000	39.9	26.9	27.9	1,979
Parent's education				
Less than high school	20.8	15.6	11.1	665
High school degree	22.7	17.5	10.7	2,105
Vocational or some college	30.0	20.9	17.0	2,657
College degree	37.4	26.1	25.0	1,465
Graduate degree	38.6	26.0	28.8	1,660
Child's level of schooling				
Elementary school	25.4	18.3	14.8	818
Middle school	28.7	19.0	17.0	2,639
High school	32.2	23.6	20.2	4,055
Combined school	31.3	22.7	20.2	922

Source: National Household Education Survey, parent interview, 1999.

tionally, awareness of the tax credits increased by household income and parent's level of education. Finally, parents with children closer to college age were more aware of the existence of the tax credits than parents with younger children. While differences existed between groups, in no case were over 40 percent of the parents cognizant of the availability of the tax credits.

The 1999–2000 NPSAS allows for a more detailed analysis of the characteristics of eligible students and families that did and did not claim a credit. It provides information on whether a student (or his or her family if the student was a dependent) claimed a higher education tax credit in 1999. Students were asked in a computer-assisted telephone interview if they or their parents had claimed a tax credit. Students who answered "don't know" were dropped from the sample. If the usage of the tax credits varies by the characteristics of eligible families, this could explain why some groups did not benefit as much as projected. Furthermore, differences could foreshadow how the distribution of the credits would change if efforts were made to increase awareness about the credits for certain groups.

Table 3.8 examines the usage of tax credits among eligible students. Unfortunately, the NPSAS does not allow one to perfectly determine tax credit eligibility, because income and net tuition information are provided for a school year (1999–2000) while eligibility for a credit is determined by a tax year (January to December). Given the way the variables are defined, I do not know how much of a student's tuition expenses were actually incurred during 1999 as opposed to the year 2000. Furthermore, I have no information about expenses incurred during spring 1999. To set a bound on this problem, two definitions of eligibility are utilized. The first uses information on family income, attendance intensity (full-time, part-time, or less than part-time), enrollment during fall 1999, and year in college. However, it does not exclude students according to their net tuition expenses. Therefore, the first definition may include students who did not have expenses that qualified for a higher education credit during 1999, and thus the calculations may overestimate the number of students eligible for a benefit. On the other hand, while some students may not have had net tuition expenses during the fall 1999, it is possible that, unbeknownst in the data, they did have expenses during spring 1999 and so did qualify for a credit. The second definition drops individuals with zero net tuition expenses, but as stated, this definition may exclude students who did have qualified expenses during spring 1999.[32]

Table 3.8 displays credit usage by demographic and college group. In general, less than one-third of eligible college students claimed either credit during the second year of the program. There were differences in the proportion that claimed a credit by background. A much larger percentage of independent students than dependent students claimed a credit. Relatively more female students claimed a benefit than their male counterparts, and more white students claimed credits than black, Hispanic, or Asian students. In terms of college level, the highest take-up rates were at four-year public or private institutions, but the percentage that claimed a credit was still quite low.

Table 3.9 examines differences in the use of the credits using regression analysis. Logistic models were run on different sample of students.[33] Odds

32. The percentage of the student population eligible for a credit using the second definition (excluding students with zero net tuition costs) is shown in table 3.2. While 43 percent of undergraduates were found to be eligible for a credit under this definition, when students with zero net tuition expenses are included, two-thirds of undergraduate students would be eligible. Likewise, including students with zero net tuition expenses increases the percentage eligible by about 23 percentage points for master's, doctoral, and other graduate students and 5 percentage points for graduate students in professional fields.

33. The analysis does not use the weights provided by the sample because it has been altered by dropping the following: international students, students who did not know if they used the credit, students not enrolled in fall 1999 (it is unclear whether they were enrolled at all during 1999 to be eligible for a credit), and those who are not eligible according to their income or attendance pattern.

Table 3.8   **Percentage That Claimed a Higher Education Tax Credit**

	All Students	Dependent (Traditional) Undergraduates	Independent (Nontraditional) Undergraduates	Graduate and Professional Students
Definition 1: Eligible by Income and Attendance (14,930 observations)				
Whole sample	27.27	19.63	31.79	34.83
Male students	25.66	17.73	31.40	32.68
Female students	28.35	20.97	32.00	36.49
White students	28.86	21.05	34.43	35.71
Black students	21.00	12.86	23.66	30.30
Hispanic students	21.97	15.24	25.26	32.39
Asian students	23.51	15.61	29.82	30.36
Not born in the United States	23.58	17.05	24.21	28.43
Parents: high school degree	27.01	18.63	31.68	32.16
Parents: some college	27.94	21.58	32.41	38.71
Parents: college degree	27.23	18.92	33.96	35.35
Full-time students	26.22	19.50	33.38	37.36
Part-time students	31.08	20.56	30.63	36.64
Public two-year	20.83	15.68	25.12	—
Public four-year	28.51	20.63	34.12	35.69
Private four-year	28.87	20.10	36.79	34.09
Proprietary college	23.82	18.99	25.41	26.83
Definition 2: Eligible by Income, Attendance, and Positive Net Tuition (11,742 observations)				
Whole sample	29.43	21.08	34.47	37.90
Male students	27.67	19.04	33.21	36.66
Female students	30.63	22.54	35.23	38.81
White students	30.73	22.18	36.77	39.01
Black students	23.81	14.29	27.12	32.21
Hispanic students	24.98	18.35	28.49	32.99
Asian students	25.77	16.67	31.00	34.31
Not born in the United States	25.36	17.93	24.91	31.43
Parents: high school degree	29.52	20.98	34.25	34.64
Parents: some college	30.43	23.53	34.84	43.59
Parents: college degree	28.95	19.46	36.37	38.96
Full-time students	28.48	20.95	36.68	41.87
Part-time students	32.71	21.78	32.36	38.47
Public two-year	23.19	17.57	28.52	—
Public four-year	30.91	22.46	37.16	38.44
Private four-year	30.76	20.82	38.85	37.75
Proprietary college	24.56	18.97	26.39	29.00

Source: 1999–2000 National Postsecondary Student Aid Survey, CATI respondents.

Notes: Sample limited to students who are eligible for a tax credit based on 1999 family income and attendance. Due to incomplete information on net tuition expenses for the 1999 tax year, the proportions were calculated with and without the restriction of positive net tuition for the 1999–2000 school year.

Table 3.9   Likelihood Eligible Students Claimed a Credit: Logistic Regression Models (dependent variable: claimed a tax credit in 1999; odds ratios reported)

	Eligible by Income and Attendance			Eligible by Income, Attendance, and Net Tuition		
	Dependent Undergrads (1)	Independent Undergrads (2)	Graduate Students (3)	Dependent Undergrads (4)	Independent Undergrads (5)	Graduate Students (6)
Demographics						
Female	1.2848**	1.1081	1.2899**	1.2940**	1.1733**	1.1971**
	(3.80)	(1.51)	(3.63)	(3.61)	(2.12)	(2.32)
Black	.6347**	.7019**	.8036*	.6400**	.7628**	.7715*
	(3.34)	(3.39)	(1.72)	(2.79)	(2.29)	(1.87)
Hispanic	.7048**	.6698**	.8615	.8274	.7168**	.7586*
	(2.72)	(3.21)	(1.00)	(1.32)	(2.38)	(1.67)
Asian	.6654*	.9986	.7480	.6688*	1.0575	.7663
	(1.88)	(0.01)	(1.45)	(1.66)	(0.21)	(1.23)
Immigrant	1.0069	.7142**	.7319**	.9873	.6450**	.7682
	(0.04)	(2.08)	(2.06)	(0.06)	(2.51)	(1.59)
Age	1.1808**	.9928**	.9846**	1.1674**	.9910**	.9844**
	(5.57)	(1.81)	(3.68)	(4.80)	(2.04)	(3.45)
Family characteristics						
Parents married	1.2847**			1.213**		
	(2.94)			(2.04)		
Parents: high school education or below	Baseline			Baseline		
Parents: some college education	1.2092**			1.1652		
	(2.17)			(1.62)		

	(1)	(2)	(3)	(4)	(5)	(6)
Parents: college degree	.9793			.8975		
	(0.25)			(1.21)		
Student married		1.2914**	1.2513**		1.3709**	1.1477
		(3.62)	(2.85)		(4.01)	(1.60)
EFC (000s)	1.0014	.9988	.9832**	.9963	.9938	.9859**
	(0.26)	(0.28)	(4.61)	(0.65)	(1.35)	(3.61)
College attendance characteristics						
Freshman or sophomore	.9605	.6585**		.9001	.6566**	
	(0.41)	(4.35)		(0.99)	(3.96)	
Part-time	1.0360	.9751	1.1227	.9593	.8742	.9809
	(0.26)	(0.33)	(1.26)	(0.29)	(1.60)	(0.19)
Less than part-time	1.5889	.6328**	.8037**	1.4891	.6153**	.7011**
	(1.43)	(3.42)	(2.31)	(1.17)	(3.31)	(3.39)
Net tuition (000s)	1.0070	1.0611**	1.0371**	.9928	1.0227	1.0075
	(0.83)	(4.57)	(4.90)	(0.76)	(1.56)	(0.88)
No. of observations	6,362	4,558	4,010	5,048	3,524	3,170
R^2	.0235	.0343	.0310	.0218	.0335	.0256

Source: 1999–2000 National Postsecondary Student Aid Survey, Computer-Assisted Telephone Interview respondents.

Notes: Sample limited to students who are eligible for a tax credit based on 1999 family income and attendance pattern. Due to incomplete information on expenses for the 1999 tax year, the proportions were calculated with and without the restriction of positive net tuition. Each regression also includes controls for the type of college attended and academic program for graduate students (master's, doctoral, professional, or other graduate program). EFC = expected family contribution. Standard deviations are reported in parentheses.

**Statistically significant at the 5 percent level.

*Statistically significant at the 10 percent level.

ratios are displayed and should be interpreted as the multiple by which that group was likely to claim a credit in comparison to the baseline group. Values less than 1 suggest the group was less likely to claim a credit. Specifications 1 through 3 use eligibility definition 1, while specifications 4 through 6 use definition 2.

As suggested by the descriptive results, all else being equal, eligible female students and white students were more likely to claim a credit than men or other racial groups. Usage of the credits was also higher among families in which the heads of the household were married (the parents for dependent students and the students themselves if they were independent). Although results from the NHES suggest that awareness of the tax credits increased with income and parents' education, there is little evidence to support this notion with the NPSAS. Dependent students with a parent who had some college were more likely to claim the credit than those with a parent who had a high school degree or less. However, a similar effect was not found for students who had a parent with a college degree. Likewise, the families of undergraduate students with greater expected family contributions were not more likely to claim a credit, and the families of graduate students with greater expected family contributions were *less* likely to claim a credit.

Given the differences that exist in who used the credit by background, increases in awareness of the tax credits could affect the relative distribution of benefits. For example, if minority groups who tend to be from lower-income backgrounds were to increase their rates of usage, the overall distribution picture would shift toward lower-income families. However, many upper-income families appear not to have claimed credits they were eligible for, and so if their awareness increases, the distribution of the credits could relatively favor middle- and upper-income families even more in the future.

3.3.5 Summary of the Distribution of Benefits

As suspected by many researchers, primarily middle-income individuals and families claimed the education tax credits. Nearly half of the credits claimed in 2000 were by returns with an AGI between $30,000 and $75,000, although this group makes up only 35 percent of the eligible returns. A report from the Congressional Research Service acknowledges that the credits were enacted to "preserve and enhance" access for middle- and upper-middle-income families (Stoll and Stedman 2001). Nonetheless, when the amount in credits is compared to federal tax liability, the greatest beneficiaries are those with incomes between $10,000 and $30,000. From the number of nontaxable returns, it is also clear that many families did not have sufficient tax liability to claim the full credit for which they were eligible. It is important to note, however, that the tax credits may become more progressive with time. The income phaseout levels are defined in nominal dollars, and there is no provision to index the benchmarks to inflation or changes in income. Therefore, greater numbers of upper-income families will become ineligible for a tax credit with each year. Moreover, the relative distribution may change as families from different backgrounds become more aware of the benefit.

With the intended goal of preserving and increasing access to college in the midst of rising costs, it is important to evaluate the effects of the HTC and LLTC on student college behavior. The next section considers whether the tax credits had any affect on college enrollment or whether the aid was just a transfer to the middle class without an effect on attendance.

3.4   Effects of Tax Credits on Student Behavior

With the introduction of the HTC and LLTC, government officials expressed a desire to increase access to higher education, especially for the first two years. While it has been found that the tax credits help to subsidize the educational costs of families in the middle-income brackets, the next question is whether this support increased college attendance as intended. The credits could affect postsecondary enrollment in several ways. First, they may encourage individuals to attend college who would not have otherwise thereby increasing total enrollment. Additionally, the credits could induce inframarginal students, those who would have attended college regardless, to increase their expenditures on postsecondary education. This could come in the form of attending a more expensive college, enrolling full-time rather than part-time, or completing more years of education. However, these possible effects are mitigated by the findings in the previous section that few parents are aware of the credits and that many eligible students do not claim a benefit.

Although numerous studies have examined the effect of changes in financial aid policies, none of the existing literature is based on tax credits for higher education or anything similar. Consequently, this study is among the first to analyze how tax credits for higher education expenditures affected the college enrollment decisions of individuals. This section begins by reviewing the literature on the effects of financial aid on enrollment and discussing the possible effects of the tax credits on enrollment. Then it examines some of these issues using data from the Current Population Surveys.

3.4.1   How Do Students Respond to Financial Aid Programs?

Much of the economic literature on the determinants of college attendance focuses on how price affects enrollment. While theory predicts that college demand is negatively related to the cost of education, many studies have tested for the sign and magnitude of the effect of tuition price. Leslie and Brinkman (1989) review studies from the 1970s and 1980s and conclude that a $1,000 (2001 dollars) change in college costs is associated with a 4 percentage point difference in college enrollment rates. More recent studies have found similar results. Several exploit state cross-sectional differences to estimate the effect of price. Kane (1995) uses the October Current Population Survey (CPS) to link individual enrollment decisions to the mean tuition costs of a state. He finds that states with higher public tuition levels had lower college entry rates and estimates a price effect similar in magnitude to that found by Leslie and Brinkman. Cameron and Heckman (1999) find a slightly larger effect of 6 percentage points using the 1979 National Longitudinal Survey of Youth (NLSY).

College price studies based upon cross-sectional variation in state-level tuition data are primarily identified by fixed differences between states. These estimates could be misleading because it is difficult to distinguish the impact of tuition from any other characteristic of the state that has remained constant over time. Therefore, other work exploits changes in financial aid policy to examine the effect of college costs on enrollment. Dynarski (2003) investigates how the elimination of the Social Security Student Benefit Program in 1982 affected attendance. She finds that the enrollment of the affected group dropped by more than a third, with the loss of $1,000 in aid translating into a decreased probability of attending college by 3.6 percentage points. This increase in price was also found to reduce the years of completed schooling by a tenth of a year.

The introduction of the Georgia HOPE Scholarship provides further opportunity to exploit a natural experiment. Dynarski (2000) examines the impact of the program on college entry for eighteen-to-nineteen-year-olds using 1989 to 1997 data from the October CPS. She finds that the HTC program raised college attendance rates between 7 and 8 percentage points. This translates into a 3 percentage point impact on college enrollment for every $1,000 (2001 dollars). Using institutional data on enrollment, Cornwell, Mustard, and Sridhar (2001) find slightly smaller estimates of an enrollment effect. Likewise, Kane (2003) analyzes the effect of the Cal Grant program and finds large enrollment impacts from eligibility (4 to 6 percentage points). While most studies have focused on recent high school graduates, Seftor and Turner (2002) examine the impact of college costs on nontraditional students with the introduction of the Pell Grant in 1972. They conclude that older individuals are more responsive to price after finding elasticities larger than those estimated for younger students (between –0.14 and –0.34).

College prices have also been found to affect choices between institutions. Long (forthcoming-a) exploits extensive match-specific information between individuals and colleges and approximates the nearly 2,800 alternatives available to potential students. Using the conditional logistic choice model and controls for college expenditures, student body characteristics, and distance, she estimates that an individual is 41 percent less likely to attend a college that costs $1,000 more (2001 dollars), all else being equal. For her sample of students from the National Education Longitudinal Study (NELS), this magnitude is enough to move the most preferred college to the fifth position for the average individual. For a simulation that cut the price difference between public and private colleges by half, Long finds that up to 29 percent fewer students are predicted to attend public, four-year colleges.

3.4.2 How Might the Tax Credits Affect College Enrollment Behavior?

Although the estimates from the literature are helpful in understanding the importance of price in college decisions, none are based on policies similar to the higher education tax credits. The manner of disbursement (through the tax code), the timing of the benefits (up to fifteen months later), and the eligibility constraints of the HTC and LLTC make them entirely unique. However, researchers have theorized about their possible effects on postsecondary investments.

The first major issue is whether the tax credits increased college enrollment. College access is of the greatest concern among low-income individuals. In 1997, while 89 percent of high school graduates aged eighteen to twenty-four from the top quartile of the income distribution participated in college, only 53 percent from the bottom quartile did so (Mortenson 1999). However, since the tax credits are nonrefundable and many low-income individuals are not eligible for the credits, many do not expect enrollment to increase for this group (Kane 1997, 1998, 1999b; Wolanin 2001). However, the elasticity of college attendance is likely to be reasonably high for the middle class since they are less likely to be liquidity constrained and have a high overall propensity to attend college. In her analysis of the Georgia HOPE Scholarship, Dynarski (2000) found middle- and upper-income students had the largest enrollment responses. Likewise, if nontraditional students are especially responsive to college costs, as found by Seftor and Turner (2002), the tax credits may increase the enrollment of older students.

While commentators do not expect a substantial enrollment response, some suggest that students may be induced to choose more costly colleges. The reason stems from the potential price and income effects created by the tax credits. The HTC and LLTC not only reduce the price of college for recipients; they also alter the marginal cost for students to increase their expenditures. Before the creation of the tax credits, each additional dollar of tuition cost the student an additional dollar. However, with the credits, an additional dollar of expense may not cost the student anything. For example, the marginal cost to a HTC recipient for increases in college tuition is zero for those who pay less than $1,000. To illustrate this point, suppose a school charged $500 in tuition. Its students would be eligible for $500 in HTC aid and therefore would be able to attend for free. However, the same would be true if the school increased its price to $1,000 and the cost of college net the HTC is zero until $1,000. Another way to state this is that the marginal subsidy for colleges that cost less than or equal to $1,000 is 100 percent. The marginal tuition subsidy for HTC recipients rises to 50 percent for those paying between $1,000 and $2,000. For recipients of the LLTC, the marginal subsidy is 20 percent up to $5,000, meaning the individual is only responsible for 80 cents for each additional dollar charged. Because of these price effects, individuals have clear incentives to attend more expensive schools or spend more on college courses.

Additionally, the tax credits effectively increase an eligible family's college budget. As a result, those eligible for the full HTC are now able to afford $1,500 more in college expenditures, while those with the LLTC receive $1,000 more in aid. This is the income effect generated by the tax credits. Depending on the preferences of the individuals, all or only part of this income gain may be spent on a more expensive school. If they are not spent on postsecondary education, the HTC and LLTC could have a consumption effect. Since the tax credits do not affect the marginal cost of tuition above $5,000 for recipients of the LLTC and $2,000 for recipients of the HTC, they may not lead to sizable increases in college expenditures by families already spending more than $5,000 (Kane 1998). Finally, the tax credits could prompt individuals to substitute them for other types of financial aid. For example, since the tax credits do not have to be repaid, they may be preferred over loans.

While the tax credits could encourage enrollment, the delay between the activity and receipt of the aid may reduce the likelihood of any effect. Assuming tuition is paid in January of one year and taxes are filed in April of the following year, it could take up to fifteen months to receive a tax credit (Conklin and Finney 1999). This makes the tax credits a distinctive form of financial aid, as most other programs provide support at the time of attendance. Because of this disconnect, the tax credits are more likely to be used for noneducational expenses than are other types of aid. Furthermore, credits do not help individuals whose reason for not attending college is liquidity.

3.4.3   Predictions from the Price Sensitivity Literature

Given the known responses of students to other financial aid policies, one may estimate the possible enrollment effects of the tax credits. Using the 1992–1993 NPSAS, Cronin (1997) calculates that the enrollment response by 2002 could be expected to be between 150,000 and 1.4 million additional students, with the likely response closer to the low end of the range. However, these calculations are based on the earlier version of the tax credit proposal, which included a tax deduction of up to $10,000 for older students, rather than the LLTC that eventually passed.

To get an approximation of the expected effect of the tax credits on attendance, I use estimates found in the literature on the effect of college costs. Assuming the 4 percentage point impact per $1,000 in cost, the mean education credit claimed during tax year 2000 ($731) translates to into a 2.9 percentage point effect. Before the enactment of the policy (fall 1997), 15.4 million students were enrolled in college (Martinez and Day 1999). This constitutes approximately 36.9 percent of traditional-aged students (aged 18 to 24), 11.8 percent of those aged 25 to 29, and 5.7 percent aged 30 to 34. Applying the estimated impact of a $731 credit, an additional 1.1, 0.34, and 0.17 percent of individuals aged 18 to 24, 25 to 29, and 30 to 35, respectively, should enroll in college. This translates into 101,244 additional students aged 18 to 24, 7,500 aged 25 to 29, and 1,897 aged 30 to 34, for a total of 110,641. Next one must take into account that not everyone is eligible for the aid. Given that approximately two-thirds of individuals are eligible for the credit based on 1997 tax returns, the estimated impact is approximately 74,000 new students aged 18 to 34. The policy could have an additional effect on older students by subsidizing occasional courses.

The tax credits could also affect individual choices between colleges. Because of the incentives created by the tax credits, this may especially be true for individuals who would have attended other colleges that cost less than $2,000 (for potential recipients of the HTC) or less than $5,000 (for potential LLTC recipients). For example, a person previously spending $500 might choose to take additional courses or attend a college that charged $1,000. In some instances, the credits reduce the cost gap between competing colleges. For example, before the credits, a $1,000 college and $3,000 college cost a difference of $2,000. However, if the person received a HTC, then the difference would be only $1,500 (the new prices would be $0 and $1,500, respectively). This decline in the price gap between colleges is an additional reason some individuals choose institutions that are more expensive than they would otherwise. The College Board (2001a) estimates that 21 percent of full-time undergraduates at four-year colleges paid less than $2,000 in 2000–2001. This translates into approximately 1.6 million students (NCES 2000). Applying the estimates from Long (forthcoming-a), the reduction in the price gap between two colleges due to the tax credits could cause up to 29 percent, or 464,000 students, to switch to more expensive schools. The total number is likely to be higher for part-time students since a larger proportion of these students spend less than $2,000.

These rough calculations are based on estimates from traditional financial aid programs. However, there are important distinctions between tax credits and other types of aid that could cause these estimates to inaccurately depict the possible impact on the behavior of students. To test for actual enrollment effects, the next section begins to analyze microdata from the period.

3.4.4 Empirical Strategy

To evaluate the enrollment effects of the HTC and LLTC, I use the 1990–2000 October supplement of the CPS. The CPS is a national household survey that gathers school enrollment information each October. Using the information available on family background, I identify the individuals likely to be eligible for a HTC or LLTC and link this to their enrollment decisions. In order to test for a possible effect, I compare how the attendance decisions of those eligible for the credits changed after the policy change. For a control group, I use individuals not eligible for the aid. This differences-in-differences analysis technique has been employed to study other financial aid programs, in particular with these data (see Dynarski 2000 and Kane 1995). Using logistic regression models, I estimate the following equation:

(1) $\text{Enroll}_i = \alpha + \beta_1(\text{TaxCredit}_i \cdot \text{After}_i) + \beta_2\text{TaxCredit}_i + \beta_3\text{After}_i + \varepsilon,$

where i is the ith individual. The parameter β_1 is the reduced-form enrollment effect of the tax credits. It measures whether individuals eligible for the credit acted differently from others after the enactment of the aid policy. The variables "TaxCredit" and "After" are dummy variables equal to 1 if the person qualifies to take either the HTC or LLTC or if the year is 1998 or after; otherwise the variables are equal to zero. Due to the fact that this paper relies on serially correlated outcomes, the standard errors are adjusted using clustering methods.[34] Because enrollment patterns differ by race, gender, age, and other demographics, these background characteristics are controlled for in the analysis. Additionally, I use state-level information about annual unemployment rates, per capita income, and the percentage of the population with a baccalaureate degree to account for differences in economic conditions, levels of wealth, and preferences for education across the country.

Table 3.10 displays summary statistics for the CPS sample. Means are calculated for traditional-aged (aged eighteen to twenty-four) and nontraditional-aged (aged twenty-five to forty) college students and broken down by eligibility status. The summary statistics highlight how the eligibility criteria favor families with higher income levels (but below the eligibility ceiling). Moreover, individuals eligible for the credit are more likely to come from families with married or joint tax return filers.

While the CPS provides a large, annual sample of individuals, there are several important limitations to this data set. First, information about family income is categorical, making it difficult to define the eligibility benchmarks exactly. This grouping also makes it impossible to put family income in constant dollars over time. Second, the income variable is capped at $75,000, which makes defining eligibility for joint returns difficult.[35] For

34. See Bertrand, Duflo, and Mullainathan (2001) for a discussion of how serial correlation affects the standard errors of differences-in-differences estimation.

35. To account for this, I summed the weekly earnings of everyone in a household. If this amount was greater than $100,000 as an annual income, the household was designated ineligible. While weekly earnings information was not available for the entire sample, when compared to the categorical family income variable, the amounts were similar for the upper income groups.

Table 3.10   **Summary Statistics of the 1990–2000 October Current Population Survey**

	Age 18–24 (traditional college age)		Age 25–40	
	Not Eligible for Any Credit	Eligible for a Higher Education Tax Credit	Not Eligible for Any Credit	Eligible for a Higher Education Tax Credit
Percentage	41.9	58.1	24.9	75.1
Demographic characteristics				
Age	21.2	21.1	32.0	33.1
	(1.8)	(2.0)	(4.6)	(4.5)
Female	53.8	51.2	53.1	51.9
Black	15.0	7.8	17.2	7.3
Asian	4.4	4.4	4.0	3.8
Hispanic	6.6	4.3	5.6	3.8
Married	18.9	17.1	31.6	75.2
Educational attainment				
High school degree	46.7	35.9	48.9	35.1
Some college	42.6	51.1	29.3	31.7
Bachelor's degree	9.3	11.7	14.8	23.5
Graduate degree	1.1	1.2	6.7	9.6
College attendance behavior				
Enrolled in college	35.7	46.3	9.5	6.7
Four-year college	73.9	75.5	70.0	70.4
	[14,720]	[26,453]	[7,048]	[15,044]
Full-time	83.7	85.1	60.0	33.2
	[14,720]	[26,453]	[7,048]	[15,044]
Income and labor market status				
Family income	4.52	10.53	5.26	10.20
(categorical)	(3.37)	(2.36)	(4.04)	(2.39)
Joint return (for parents if a dependent)	30.8	79.5	32.1	80.7
Single return	69.2	20.5	67.9	19.3
Employed	66.8	69.4	73.1	85.4
Unemployed	7.9	4.8	6.6	2.1
Out of labor force	24.2	25.1	19.7	11.3
Potential education tax credit benefit				
Maximum higher education credit	0	914	0	851
		(333)		(229)
Credit at a state public two-year	0	796	0	781
		(333)		(273)
No. of observations	41,220	57,074	73,952	222,889

Source: October CPS data 1990–2000.

Notes: Standard deviations are reported in parentheses. If the full sample was not used in calculating a mean, the number of observations is noted in brackets. The percentages of the sample that are attending four-year colleges or are full-time were calculated conditional on enrollment in college.

these reasons, some families are incorrectly being counted as eligible for a tax credit when their exact income would disqualify them. This measurement error is likely to attenuate the results. In addition, as shown in table 3.10, among the individuals who are enrolled in college, a greater proportion are in four-year colleges (as opposed to two-year colleges) and attend full-time (rather than part-time) than is found in the nation. This suggests that the college-going sample is not nationally representative. More important, this may imply that the data set does not accurately capture all students in the two-year college system and those that attend part-time. As a result, the analysis may not detect changes in enrollment at these types of schools or part-time attendance. Finally, parental income is only available for young adults that appear on their parents' CPS record. This will occur if the individual lives at home or is away at college. Therefore, the probability that a young person will have accurate family income information is a function of his or her propensity to attend college.

3.4.5   Analysis of the Enrollment Effects

To discern whether the tax credits had an effect on college enrollment, I test for three possible responses. First, did the likelihood of attending college increase for individuals eligible for a credit? This is a test of the credits' impact on general postsecondary access. Second, did the proportion of college students who were enrolled at four-year colleges increase? This is a way to examine whether students were induced to spend more on higher education after the creation of the credits. And third, did the percentage of college attendants that were full-time rather than part-time students increase? To measure eligibility, I alternate between three different measures: (1) eligibility for any credit; (2) the monetary amount of the maximum credit for which a person qualifies; and (3) the amount of the credit available if the person paid the mean cost of his or her state's public two-year colleges. The third definition is an approximation of what a marginal student who decides to attend a community college would receive. Since the credits differ in their target groups and generosity, I examine the behavior of several age groups. Younger students (aged eighteen and nineteen) are more likely to be affected by the HTC while older students are eligible for the LLTC.

The following analysis reports the results as odds ratios so that values less than 1 should be interpreted as having a negative relationship with the dependent variable. The coefficient of interest is β_1, which measures whether enrollment behavior changed for the group eligible for the credit after the introduction of the program ($\text{TaxCredit}_i \cdot \text{After}_i$). Several of the models exclude from the sample three states with large financial aid programs that preclude many students from receiving the tax credit (Georgia, Florida, and New Mexico). Each state has a scholarship program that covers full tuition at public colleges within the state for many students. In this circumstance, students would not be eligible to receive any additional aid from the federal government.

Table 3.11 displays estimates of the tax credit effect on the propensity to enroll in college. For panel A, I use whether an individual qualifies for any credit as the measure of eligibility. Overall, I estimate that individuals eligible for the credit are more likely to attend college, but generally, there is no differential increase in enrollment after the introduction of the tax credits. Panel B investigates if there is any effect on the enrollment decisions of individuals using the maximum monetary amount a student is eligible for based on credit criteria (in thousands of dollars). Similar to above results the estimates are statistically insignificant. The results are the same when defining eligibility using the mean tuition cost of public two-year colleges in the state of residence (panel C).

These results are robust to different definitions of college-going behavior (the inclusion or exclusion of those taking vocational courses; using respondents who answered college-related questions but signified earlier in the survey that they were not in higher education). Furthermore, the results are robust to other specifications. The models were reestimated limiting the sample to individuals without a college degree, and no enrollment effect was found. Likewise, when the sample is limited to 1995 to 2000 so that estimation is based on three years prior to the policy change and three years after, the results remain statistically insignificant.

Rather than affecting access, the tax credits may encourage individuals to buy more education. To test this proposition, table 3.12 tests how the likelihood of attending a four-year institution, conditional on attending any college, is affected by the policy change. If the tax credits encouraged students to attend more expensive colleges, then one would expect for the proportion of students at four-year colleges to increase. However, similar to the foregoing results, none of the estimates are statistically significant.[36] The same is true when testing whether the HTC and LLTC affected whether a person attended college full-time rather than part-time. Although one would expect a positive effect if the credits encouraged individuals to spend more on college, no statistically significant effect is found after the introduction of the credits as shown in table 3.13.

3.4.6   Conclusions on the Enrollment Effect

In summary, although the tax credits were promoted as a means of increasing college access, this analysis found no enrollment response. During the three years after policy enactment, general enrollment did not appear to increase, nor did the proportion of students that attended four-year

---

36. Similarly, a multinomial logistic model using three options (not enrolled in college; enrolled in a two-year college; and enrolled in a four-year college) finds no statistically significant change after the introduction of the higher education tax credits.

Table 3.11   The Likelihood of Attending Any College (odds ratios reported)

	Age of Traditional College Students		Traditional College Students (excluding full-tuition programs)		Nontraditional Students:	All Ages:
	Age 18–19 (1)	Age 18–24 (2)	Age 18–19 (no GA, FL, NM) (3)	Age 18–24 (no GA, FL, NM) (4)	Age 25–40 (5)	18–40 (6)
A. Variable of Interest: Eligibility for Any Higher Education Credit						
After	0.6889**	0.8720**	0.6601**	0.8748**	0.9535	0.9534
	(4.00)	(2.85)	(4.29)	(2.63)	(0.99)	(1.50)
Eligible for any credit?	1.1414**	1.1885**	1.1342*	1.1856**	0.9677	1.0778**
	(2.14)	(5.07)	(1.93)	(4.70)	(0.96)	(2.91)
After · any credit	0.9392	0.9342	1.0051	0.9390	1.0077	0.9825
	(0.63)	(1.38)	(0.05)	(1.19)	(0.21)	(0.56)
No. of observations	24,291	98,294	22,781	91,811	296,841	395,135
R^2	0.35	0.34	0.35	0.34	0.12	0.32
B. Variable of Interest: Monetary Amount of the Maximum Credit Eligible (thousands)						
After	0.6974**	0.8468**	0.6749**	0.8494**	0.9456	0.9467*
	(4.39)	(3.58)	(4.58)	(3.34)	(1.21)	(1.80)
Maximum credit	0.9846	1.1919**	0.9764	1.1871**	1.0049	1.2633**
	(0.36)	(5.74)	(0.53)	(5.29)	(0.14)	(10.20)
After · max credit	0.9421	0.9811	0.9844	0.9873	1.0170	0.9862
	(0.88)	(0.39)	(0.23)	(0.24)	(0.40)	(0.40)
No. of observations	24,291	98,294	22,781	91,811	296,841	395,135
R^2	0.35	0.34	0.35	0.34	0.12	0.32

C. Variable of Interest: Credit if Charged the State Mean Public Two-Year Tuition *(thousands)*

After	0.6800**	0.8539**	0.6626**	0.8580**	0.9604	0.9628
	(4.92)	(3.25)	(5.02)	(3.02)	(0.88)	(1.20)
Max credit at public 2-year	0.9977	1.1366**	0.9902	1.1302**	0.9935	1.1736**
	(0.04)	(3.87)	(0.18)	(3.52)	(0.20)	(7.28)
After · max 2-year credit	0.9651	0.9690	1.0093	0.9728	0.9895	0.9630
	(0.42)	(0.53)	(0.11)	(0.44)	(0.23)	(0.94)
No. of observations	24,291	98,294	22,781	91,811	296,841	395,135
R^2	0.35	0.34	0.35	0.34	0.12	0.32

Source: October CPS data 1990–2000.

Notes: Robust z statistics are reported in parentheses. Each model contains year fixed effects and controls for gender, race (dummy variables for black, Asian, and Hispanic), age, marital status, level of education, a dummy variable for being employed, family income (categorical), and the annual unemployment rate, per capita income, and percentage with a baccalaureate degree of the individual's state.

**Statistically significant at the 5 percent level.

*Statistically significant at the 10 percent level.

Table 3.12   The Likelihood of Attending a Four-Year College Conditional on Enrollment (odds ratios)

	Age of Traditional College Students		Traditional College Students (excluding full-tuition programs)		Nontraditional Students: Age 25–40	All Ages: 18–40
	Age 18–19 (1)	Age 18–24 (2)	Age 18–19 (no GA, FL, NM) (3)	Age 18–24 (no GA, FL, NM) (4)	(5)	(6)
	A. Variable of Interest: Eligible for Any Credit					
After	0.9691	0.7969**	0.9454	0.7977**	0.8588	0.8181**
	(0.24)	(2.91)	(0.41)	(2.86)	(1.47)	(2.94)
Eligible for any credit?	0.7314**	0.8295**	0.7549**	0.8447**	0.8457**	0.8435**
	(5.16)	(4.48)	(4.60)	(4.07)	(3.46)	(4.85)
After · any credit	0.8929	0.9251	0.9444	0.9155	1.0078	0.9462
	(1.00)	(1.18)	(0.51)	(1.33)	(0.09)	(0.99)
No. of observations	15,016	41,173	14,150	38,665	22,092	63,265
R^2	0.06	0.08	0.06	0.08	0.16	0.10
	B. Variable of Interest: Monetary Amount of the Maximum Credit Eligible (thousands)					
After	0.9005	0.7728**	0.8806	0.7656**	0.8597	0.8065**
	(0.86)	(3.48)	(0.97)	(3.46)	(1.45)	(3.24)
Maximum credit	0.7530**	0.7583**	0.7606**	0.7661**	0.8424**	0.7535**
	(6.51)	(7.90)	(5.84)	(7.12)	(3.97)	(9.83)
After · max credit	0.9885	0.9677	1.0384	0.9727	0.9966	0.9649
	(0.14)	(0.57)	(0.50)	(0.46)	(0.04)	(0.67)
No. of observations	15,016	41,173	14,150	38,665	22,092	63,265
R^2	0.06	0.08	0.06	0.08	0.16	0.10

Source: October CPS data 1990–2000.

Notes: See table 3.11.

**Statistically significant at the 5 percent level.

*Statistically significant at the 10 percent level.

Table 3.13   **The Likelihood of Attending Full-Time Conditional on Enrollment (odds ratios reported)**

	Age of Traditional College Students		Traditional College Students (excluding full-tuition programs)	
	Age 18–19 (1)	Age 18–24 (2)	Age 18–19 (no GA, FL, NM) (3)	Age 18–24 (no GA, FL, NM) (4)
A. Variable of Interest: Eligible for Any Credit				
After	1.1694	0.9345	1.1435	0.9061
	(1.01)	(0.95)	(0.81)	(1.35)
Eligible for any credit?	1.0219	0.9635	1.0395	0.9643
	(0.19)	(0.63)	(0.31)	(0.58)
After · any credit	0.8954	0.9908	0.9148	0.9989
	(0.83)	(0.12)	(0.63)	(0.01)
No. of observations	15,016	41,173	14,150	38,665
R^2	0.10	0.15	0.10	0.15
B. Variable of Interest: Monetary Amount of the Maximum Credit Eligible (thousands)				
After	1.0440	0.9320	1.0310	0.9032
	(0.30)	(1.07)	(0.19)	(1.52)
Maximum credit	0.8970	0.9215*	0.9084	0.9254*
	(1.50)	(1.88)	(1.23)	(1.67)
After · max credit	1.0420	0.9976	1.0535	1.0084
	(0.41)	(0.04)	(0.50)	(0.13)
No. of observations	15,016	41,173	14,150	38,665
R^2	0.10	0.15	0.10	0.15

Source: October CPS data 1990–2000.
Notes: See table 3.11.
*Statistically significant at the 10 percent level.

institutions or were full-time. The lack of finding a substantial response in student enrollment conforms to many of the forecasts by researchers and critics. The principal beneficiaries of the tax credits are not likely to be marginal students, and the disconnect between the aid and college attendance is likely to limit the effect of the credits on enrollment. Furthermore, if colleges raised tuition in response to the tax credits (this question is examined in the next section), this may help to explain why there was little enrollment effect. Finally, with the low take-up rates illustrated in table 3.8, not enough families may know about the benefit for it to have a discernible impact on enrollment.

However, the October CPS has several serious limitations for this type of analysis. Due to the categorical definitions of family income, particularly at the higher income levels, it is likely that some students were mislabeled since the data do not allow one to distinguish incomes above $75,000. Moreover, assumptions had to be made about dependent versus independent student status based on age and single versus joint filing status based on family type. For these reasons, eligibility is most certainly measured with error, and some individuals were probably labeled as eligible when in actuality they were not, and vice versa. As a result, the results suffer from attenuation bias. Furthermore, the CPS may not adequately capture college enrollment at two-year colleges or students who attend part-time. Therefore, if the credits had an effect on these groups, it may not be discernible from these data.

Further analysis of these issues using more detailed data sets is necessary before we can be more confident of the results. Beyond better income information, it would also be useful to have more data on college enrollment behavior. For example, knowing how many credit hours a person completed would help answer questions about the intensity of enrollment. Information on which institution the individual attended and the receipt of other financial aid would help researchers to understand how the tax credits influence college choices and the possible substitution of the credits for other types of aid. A panel data set would allow one to observe how these factors changed after the introduction of the credits for students already in college. In addition, longitudinal data would allow one to track how students' decisions change after transforming from being eligible for the HTC (the first two years of college) to instead qualifying for the LLTC. Additional questions exist on a possible consumption effect, but further information on family income and expenditures is necessary for this analysis. It is also worth noting that it may be too soon to witness an enrollment effect. As take-up rates for the tax credits increase, more individuals may be influenced by the support in ways discernible by quantitative research.

3.5   The Impact of the Tax Credits on College Pricing

While most of the literature on the impact of financial aid policy focuses on the reactions of individuals, researchers have long theorized that the policies may also affect the behavior of postsecondary institutions. Most notably, William Bennett surmised in a 1987 article in the *New York Times* that the rise in college tuition prices was due to increases in the availability of government financial aid.[37] With the creation of the higher education tax credits, the Department of Education seemed to be aware of this possibility in the form of reduced institutional aid. In a letter to college presidents, Secretary Richard Riley asked that the tax credits not serve as a "substitute for existing sources of financial assistance" (Riley 1998).

Researchers have tested the Bennett hypothesis by examining whether increases in aid translate into increases in tuition prices. McPherson and

---

37. From 1975–1976 to 1985–1986, the mean public four-year tuition increased 55.1 percent in real terms (after accounting for inflation). Private four-year tuition levels increased 37.3 percent (College Board 2001a).

Schapiro (1991) use annual institutional data to relate changes in the Pell Grant to institutional behavior. They find that increases in government aid are coupled with increases in institutional scholarship spending at private colleges, contrary to the predictions of Bennett. In contrast, Li (1999) finds some support for the Bennett hypothesis when she uses the master files of the Pell Grant Information System to track Pell recipients and the tuition levels of their respective colleges. One possible reason for these conflicting results stems from the difficulty in isolating the effect of government aid on tuition pricing from other factors. It is unclear whether changes in tuition are due to changes in aid or other general trends in higher education. Long (forthcoming-b) is able to circumvent the issue by examining the effect of the Georgia HOPE Scholarship on in-state institutions. She finds that most four-year colleges in Georgia did experience relative increases in net price. While public institutions increased room and board fees, private colleges raised list tuition price and reduced institutional aid. The net effect was to increase costs to students by as much as $0.30 for each dollar of aid. This highlights the importance of the design of a program in ensuring that students, rather than institutions, realize the full benefit and that students who do not receive the aid are not unintentionally negatively affected. This section exploits variation in the incentives created by the introduction of the tax credits to examine their effects on states and institutions.

3.5.1   How Might the Tax Credits Affect Postsecondary Institutions?

Due to the price and income effects created by the tax credits, colleges may have the incentive to increase their prices up to the amount of the aid. The strongest incentives are for colleges that charge tuition below $1,000. As described in the previous section, the marginal cost to a student of a college charging below this amount is zero. For example, if a school charges $500 in tuition, its first- and second-year students would be eligible for $500 in tax credits and therefore would be able to attend for free. However, the same would be true if the school increased its price to $1,000. With the HTC the marginal tuition subsidy is between 50 and 100 percent for institutions charging less than $2,000. It is an additional 20 percent for students past the second year at institutions charging less than $5,000 due to the LLTC.

Another possible institutional reaction to the tax credits could be to re-label room and board charges and other fees as tuition charges because the former do not constitute "qualified" expenses (Kane 1999a). For instance, a college with tuition of $1,000 and room and board charges of $4,000 might be induced to raise the tuition price to $2,000 and lower the room and board charge to $3,000.

Increases in college costs may ultimately stem from action taken by state governments. States are likely to view the increase in federal aid as an opportunity to reduce their support for higher education in the form of appropriations to public colleges, thereby increasing tuition prices. The incentives are strongest for states that heavily subsidize public tuition levels to below $2,000. As Kane (1999b) notes, "To not do so would mean forgoing rather generous new federal subsidies for state taxpayers" (148). While price increases might understandably affect a college's standing relative to competing institutions, state governments are best able to prevent a loss of students. This is because they are able to coordinate the price increases of a large set of colleges. Together with the fact that public colleges are already far less expensive than private schools, individual public colleges face little risk of losing students. However, such price increases may deter students from enrolling in college at all if the tax credits are not perceived by students to offset the additional costs. This is an especially troublesome prospect for students ineligible for the aid due to lack of tax liability.

The incentive to raise tuition prices is also strong for states with large financial aid programs. Since eligibility is based on tuition expenses net grants and scholarships, residents in states with generous programs may not qualify for the full tax credit due to receiving state support. In this case, the eligibility of residents would increase as tuition was increased. State and institutional aid would also be affected if colleges and states perceive the credits as substitutes for other types of aid. This reaction was found in an examination of the institutional impact of the Georgia HOPE Scholarship on institutional aid awards at private colleges in Georgia (Long, forthcoming-b).

In fact, many states did react to the introduction of the tax credits by considering ways to capture the federal resources available through the new tax credits. In a report from California's Legislative Analyst's Office, Turnage (1998) notes that the credits "create opportunities to increase the effective federal subsidy of California's higher education programs." He argues that due to California's low-cost community colleges, many other states will have higher per-student subsidies (estimated to be $360 in California but $1,250 in other states): "Due to interactions between the credits and recent state fee reductions, the state is unintentionally sending monies intended for students back to the federal government." Furthermore, by reducing the price differential between the state's community colleges, California State University system, and the UC system, Turnage suggests that HTC could "unintentionally shift enrollment away from our community colleges to the universities, at potentially great cost to the state and at cross purposes to the state's higher education master plan." For these reasons, Turnage suggests increasing fees at public colleges in California. He asserts that the tax credits would offset the increase for richer students while financial aid could be given to offset the effect for low-income students. According to his calculations, an increase from $360 to $1,000 at the community colleges would increase funding to these schools by over $100 million annually without affecting the California state budget.

Wolanin (2001) notes other states that responded to the introduction of the tax credits. Budget analysis by the Arkansas legislature recommended that the state reconsider its tuition policies in light of the tax credits. Minnesota, North Carolina, and Washington took similar actions to consider how to devise state financial aid programs while taking into account the HTC support. Another example is New York, which provides need-based aid through its Tuition Assistance Program. Under this program, New York families with a student in a four-year public college would not be eligible for the maximum HTC unless their taxable income is $45,000 or higher. In comparison, most families would be eligible for the full credit if their taxable income is at least $30,000. As a result, the New York State Higher Education Services Corporation recommended studying whether federal funds could be substituted for state funds (New York State Higher Education Services Corporation 1998).

If colleges do raise their prices in response to the policy, the tax credit could become a transfer from the federal government to schools and state governments rather than to families. However, some question whether postsecondary institutions would respond to the introduction of the tax credits. Since the strongest incentives to raise tuition prices are for community colleges (i.e., schools with lower tuition levels), and these schools predominantly serve low-income populations not eligible for the tax credit, some suggest that tuition inflation is an unlikely response to the credits (Kane 1999a; Cronin 1997).

The HTC and LLTC could affect postsecondary institutions in ways other than pricing. The tax credits may give institutions the incentive to find ways to grant half-time degree credit to middle-income taxpayers (Kane 1999a; Cronin 1997). One possibility is for colleges to create leisure-oriented courses for college credit that would attract taxpayers eligible for the tax credits. For example, colleges could offer $1,000 whale-watching tours with no cost to HTC-eligible students as long as participants receive half-time credit toward a degree (Kane 1999a). This potential abuse mirrors issues raised with the Pell Grant program; however, the risk may be greater given the larger number of eligible aid recipients.

Distributing aid through the tax system also creates a number of expensive regulatory requirements for colleges and universities. Higher education institutions must supply the Internal Revenue Service (IRS) with the names, addresses, and Social Security numbers of all of their students as well as indicating whether the students are enrolled at least half-time, a stipulation of eligibility for the HTC. Additional requirements may be imposed to include information on those who claim a student as a dependent for federal income tax purposes and who may claim HTC (Wolanin 2001). The National Association of College and University Business Officers (NACUBO) estimated that compliance with this full set of requirements would have cost institutions $137 million in 1999 (NACUBO 1998). Furthermore, the IRS estimates the current reporting burden on institutions to produce needed information is 2.4 million hours (IRS 2000). For tax year 1999, the UC system alone spent nearly $1 million to provide its 371,000 students with Form 1098, the tuition payment statement necessary to claim a tax credit (Hoblitzell and Smith 2001). These costs of compliance are an additional reason colleges might increase tuition prices.

3.5.2   Empirical Strategy

The incentives created by the introduction of the HTC and LLTC are predicted to affect states and colleges in three ways. First, based on the assumption that the intensity of the treatment should affect the magnitude of the response, one would expect to find that colleges with greater numbers of eligible students responded more dramatically to the introduction of the tax credits than colleges with fewer eligible students. Second, although all colleges may have incentives to raise prices due to the introduction of the tax credits, colleges with lower tuition rates should experience relatively larger increases in price due to the lower marginal cost to students. Table 3.14 displays how colleges with different tuition rates are distributed geographically since state support for higher education varies across region. It is important to note that a comparison of public colleges that charged less than $2,000 in 1997 to those that charged more reflects the differences in the state policies of colleges in the Southeast, far West, and Southwest regions from the policies of those in Mideast and Great Lakes regions.[38]

A third prediction is that public colleges in states with substantial aid programs should experience decreases in state support and larger increases in price. Table 3.15 separates colleges into two groups based on the amount of grant aid awarded by states during the 1997–1998 school year. States are considered to have large aid programs if they are in the top eight in terms of total money spent or the amount per student.[39] The states with large aid programs prior to the policy change were New York, Illinois, California, Pennsylvania, New Jersey, Ohio, Minnesota, Georgia, Florida, New Mexico, and Vermont. Table 3.15 also displays how colleges within these states are distributed by tuition level.

To test for these possible effects, I examine how state support for higher

38. The regions are New England (CT, ME, MA, NH, RI, VT), Mideast (DE, DC, MD, NJ, NY, PA), Great Lakes (IL, IN, MI, OH, WI), Plains (IA, KS, MN, MO, NE, ND, SD), Southeast (AL, AR, FL, GA, KY, LA, MS, NC, SC, TN, VA, WV), Southwest (AZ, NM, OK, TX), Rocky Mountains (CO, ID, MT, UT, WY), and far West (AK, CA, HI, NV, OR, WA).

39. The benchmark of "top eight" was chosen due to the natural break in the amounts of the next highest states. The next highest state in total amount was North Carolina, with $105 million (compared to Florida, which was $135 million). The next highest state in per-student expenditures was Indiana, with $292.50 (compare to $342 for Vermont). Georgia, Florida, and New Mexico are excluded because each has large aid programs that cover full tuition for a significant proportion of students. These states, therefore, do not have the incentive to raise tuition prices as they would have to pay for the increase out of their own aid programs.

Table 3.14   **The Distribution of Colleges by Region and Prepolicy List Tuition Level**

	Incentives Due to Price and Income Effects			Incentives Due to Income Effects	
	≤$1,000	$1,001–2,000	$2,001–5,000	$5,001–7,500	$7,500+
Public two-year colleges					
New England	—	6	20	1	—
Mideast	—	6	80	—	—
Great Lakes	—	11	85	9	—
Plains	1	37	27	—	—
Southeast	85	143	1	—	—
Southwest	34	52	9	—	—
Rocky Mountains	—	29	2	—	—
Far West	50	42	—	—	—
Total	170	326	224	10	—
Public four-year colleges					
New England	—	1	28	4	1
Mideast	—	—	65	25	1
Great Lakes	—	—	72	2	—
Plains	—	4	47	—	—
Southeast	—	32	107	3	—
Southwest	—	24	29	—	—
Rocky Mountains	—	8	19	—	—
Far West	—	18	31	—	—
Total	—	87	398	34	2
Private four-year colleges					
Total	—	—	44	90	735

Source: IPEDS data.

Notes: Tuition levels are for in-state students. The regions are New England (CT, ME, MA, NH, RI, VT), Mideast (DE, DC, MD, NJ, NY, PA), Great Lakes (IL, IN, MI, OH, WI), Plains (IA, KS, MN, MO, NE, ND, SD), Southeast (AL, AR, FL, GA, KY, LA, MS, NC, SC, TN, VA, WV), Southwest (AZ, NM, OK, TX), Rocky Mountains (CO, ID, MT, UT, WY), and far West (AK, CA, HI, NV, OR, WA). Dashes indicate that no colleges in the region meet criterion of column.

education and college tuition levels have evolved over time by noting the policy change between the 1997–1998 and 1998–1999 school years.[40] I analyze whether the introduction of the HTC and LLTC caused discontinuities among the states and colleges most affected by the policy or with the

40. Although the law was passed in 1997, it was not signed until August 1997, a time when tuition rates for the 1997–1998 school year were already set. This notion is supported by the timing of state reports in reaction to the credits (e.g., the New York State Higher Education Services Corporation preliminary report is dated March 1998). Furthermore, individuals were only able to claim the credits for higher education expenses incurred after January 1, 1998, for the HOPE and after July 1, 1998, for the LLTC.

Table 3.15   The Distribution of Colleges by Size of State Aid Program

	States with Large Aid Programs (have incentives to raise tuition)		States without Large Aid Programs	
	Public 4-Year	Public 2-Year	Public 4-Year	Public 2-Year
≤$1,000	0	40	0	130
$1,001–2,000	15	5	72	321
$2,001–5,000	111	138	287	86
$5,001–7,500	25	10	9	0
>$7,500	2	0	0	0
Total	153	193	368	537

Source: National Association of State Student Grant and Aid Programs (NASSGAP) Twenty-ninth Annual Survey, IPEDS data, and the National Center for Education Statistics.

Notes: High state aid is defined as being ranked as one of the top eight states in 1997–1998 in total grant aid or per student aid. However, Georgia, Florida, and New Mexico are excluded because they have large aid programs that cover full tuition for a significant proportion of their students (these states do not have incentives to raise tuition prices, as they would have to pay for them out of their own aid program). The states with large aid programs in terms of total expenditures are New York, Illinois, California, Pennsylvania, Georgia, New Jersey, Ohio, and Florida. The states with large aid programs in terms of per-student expenditures are Georgia, New York, New Jersey, Illinois, Pennsylvania, New Mexico, Minnesota, and Vermont. These benchmarks were chosen due to the natural break in the amounts of the next highest states.

strongest incentives to alter their behavior. To account for any general trends that have affected all states and universities, I use colleges in different tuition categories as a control group. The difference between the groups is considered the effect of the tax credits.[41] Using ordinary least squares estimation, this difference-in-differences calculation can be made:

$$(2) \quad y_i = \alpha + \delta_1(\text{After}_i) + \delta_2(\text{TargetGroup}_i) + \delta_3(\text{TargetGroup}_i \cdot \text{After}_i) + \varepsilon_i,$$

where i is the ith college and y is either state support for higher education or list college price. While the first two δs measure general differences in the dependent variable after the policy change and among the target group, the parameter δ_3 is the reduced-form effect of the tax credits: It measures whether colleges with greater incentives to lower state appropriations or raise tuition price acted differently from other schools after the introduction of the aid policy. The variable "TargetGroup" is a dummy variable equal to 1 if the college is part of a collection of schools with strong incentives to react to the tax credits. Three groups are examined to match the predictions I have outlined: (1) colleges with many credit-eligible students;

41. In order for the tax credits to be used as an appropriate natural experiment, it must be an exogenous policy. Stated another way, if the tax credits were created in response to the power and preferences of states or postsecondary institutions, the measured responses could reflect some endogenous effect. However, given the reaction of many states and institutions, there is little concern that the reactions of the colleges might be biased in some way.

(2) low-cost colleges for which tuition increases have a low marginal cost; and (3) colleges located in states with large financial aid programs. "After" is a dummy variable equal to 1 if the year is 1998 or after. Otherwise the dummy variables are equal to zero. Due to the fact that this paper relies on serially correlated outcomes, the standard errors are adjusted using clustering methods.[42] The following results are in logs so that the results may be interpreted as percentages.

While the models test whether colleges with a greater proportion of credit-eligible students experience larger responses, this variable can also be interacted with the other groups of interest. For example, when testing whether lower-cost colleges increased their tuition levels faster than more expensive colleges, it is also relevant to know if lower-cost colleges *with greater numbers* of credit-eligible students reacted more strongly than similarly priced colleges *with fewer potential recipients*. To test for this possibility, the analysis employs a differences-in-differences-in-differences (DDD) technique to distinguish the reactions of colleges by the intensity of the treatment. The DDD calculation is made:

$$(3) \quad y_i = \alpha + \delta_1(\text{After}_i) + \delta_2(\text{LowTuition}_i) + \delta_3(\text{LowTuition}_i \cdot \text{After}_i)$$

$$+ \delta_4(\text{ManyEligible}_i) + \delta_5(\text{ManyEligible}_i \cdot \text{After}_i)$$

$$+ \delta_6(\text{ManyEligible}_i \cdot \text{LowTuition}_i)$$

$$+ \delta_7(\text{LowTuition}_i \cdot \text{After}_i \cdot \text{ManyEligible}_i) + \varepsilon_i,$$

where "ManyEligible" is a dummy variable equal to 1 if the college has a large proportion of its student body eligible for a tax credit. The parameter δ_7 is the differential effect of the tax credits on low-cost colleges with and without many potential credit recipients.

Since institutions in the different target groups (i.e., ones with large and small proportions of credit-eligible students; colleges with high and low tuition levels) are likely to be different in ways that might affect tuition pricing and trends, other control variables are included. First, the market segment of the college and its likely competitors could affect its pricing and expenditures. The most selective colleges offer more institutional financial aid and spend more on instruction than less selective schools, and each group faces different competitive pressures from other institutions. For this reason, the models take into consideration the selectivity level of the college. Second, the preferences, wealth, and economic conditions of a particular state are likely to affect the general offerings and prices of colleges within the state. To account for these factors, the analysis controls for state characteristics such as annual per capita income, the percentage of the population with a bachelor's degree in 1999, and the annual unem-

---

42. See Bertrand, Duflo, and Mullainathan (2001) for a discussion of how serial correlation affects the standard errors of differences-in-differences estimation.

ployment rate. Controls for region are also included. Finally, the amount of state support awarded by the state legislature is highly influential in the pricing decisions of public colleges and universities, particularly in terms of tuition price.[43] Therefore, the models that examine tuition trends also control for the annual amount of state appropriations per student at each school.

The data for this analysis come from several sources. First, the Integrated Postsecondary Education Data System (IPEDS) provides the necessary institutional detail. This data set documents extensive information on postsecondary institutions within the United States including revenue sources (e.g., state appropriations), list tuition price, and enrollment figures. In order to capture the 1998 inception of the tax credits, I use IPEDS data from the 1993–1994 school year to the 1999–2000 school year (the most recent year institutional financial data are available).[44] All figures were inflated to 2000 dollars using the Consumer Price Index for All Urban Consumers (CPI-U). A second source, Barron's *Profiles of American Colleges,* provides selectivity groupings for institutions based on student body grades and test scores as well as admission policies. Data on state characteristics such as the annual unemployment rate, per capita income, and the percentage of the population with a bachelor's degree were taken from the U.S. Census Bureau and the Bureau of Labor Statistics. Considerable effort was made to have a complete and balanced panel of data. To avoid estimating results driven by yearly fluctuations in composition of the sample rather than a true effect, I imposed a restriction that at least six of the seven possible years of data had to be available for each institution.

To measure the proportion of credit-eligible students, I first determined the number of needy, ineligible students using information about the mean Pell Grant at each institution (total Pell Grant awards divided by full-time equivalent [FTE] enrollment). Since Pell Grant awards are partly determined by the cost of school attended, this mean was divided by the list tuition price of the institution, and therefore the measure should be considered as the percentage of college expenses covered by the mean Pell Grant. Using this measure, colleges with a larger percentage are assumed to have fewer credit-eligible students. Note, however, that a simple comparison of

43. The correlation between the mean tuition cost of four-year public colleges and the mean amount of state appropriations received by such schools was –0.7 from 1977 to 1997 (NCES data). In practice, schools are generally discouraged by legislatures from increasing the tuition above a certain percentage each year. However, substantial increases are allowed when state appropriations are reduced, thereby implicitly linking the subsidy and tuition level.

44. This time span is used for several reasons. First, other difference-in-differences studies have used similar series of data to study the effects of a financial aid policy. Both Hansen's (1983) and Kane's (1996) before-and-after Pell studies use three years of data before the policy change and four years after. Furthermore, this time span reflects the American economic expansion of the 1990s and is less likely to be tainted by nationwide business cycles than a longer series of data. Finally, using this time span maximizes the number of institutions that can be used as a constant sample.

colleges with and without many potential credit beneficiaries is really a comparison of public two-year colleges to four-year institutions due to enrollment patterns by income. Low-income students, who are not eligible for a tax credit, are more likely to attend public, two-year colleges, while middle-income students, who are eligible for a credit, often attend public or private four-year schools. Since these types of schools differ in important ways, a comparison of their pricing trends is not truly informative of the institutional effect of the tax credits. To avoid this complication, colleges were defined as having many eligible students if they were in the top half of the distribution (having a lower percentage of college expenses covered by the mean Pell Grant) for their type of school (public, two-year; public, four-year; or private, four-year).

3.5.3 The Effect on State Support for Higher Education

The introduction of the HTC and LLTC gave states the opportunity to reduce their support for higher education in order to capture some of the rents of the program. While all states had incentives to reduce appropriations because the credits increased student incomes, table 3.16 displays results that compare states with stronger incentives to change their behavior to those with weaker incentives. The coefficients of interest (δ_3) measure the percentage by which each group had either faster or slower relative growth after the tax credits were introduced. All models include controls for year fixed effects, college selectivity, state characteristics, and region.

The first model tests the notion that states had greater incentives to reduce appropriations at colleges with more credit-eligible students. However, the positive coefficient suggests this was not the case at public two-year colleges. In general, colleges with fewer Pell recipients (a proxy for many credit-eligible students) were no more likely to experience reductions in state appropriations and may have experienced increases in state support. However, the colleges with lower tuition prices did experience larger reductions in state appropriations after 1997 (specification 2). All else being equal, public two-year colleges that charged less than $1,000 experienced a 57 percent reduction in state appropriations per student relative to colleges that cost more than $2,000. The decrease was even larger for colleges that charged between $1,000 and $2,000 before the policy change. Among these schools, the reductions were largest at colleges with more credit-eligible students, conforming to the predictions of theory (specification 3). No similar pattern is found among public four-year colleges; the results are not statistically significant.

Given the geographic distribution of public colleges, these results reflect the actions of colleges in the Southeast and far West relative to colleges in the Mideast and Great Lakes regions. For this reason, these results may be partly driven by differences *across* regions, and it is therefore necessary to also examine trends *within* regions. Unfortunately, sample size precludes

Table 3.16   **The State Response to the Tax Credits by Tuition Price of Colleges**
(dependent variable: log of state support for higher education)

	Public Two-Year Colleges			Public Four-Year Colleges		
	(1)	(2)	(3)	(4)	(5)	(6)
After	−2.5596**	−1.8011**	−2.9293**	−0.0335	−0.0419	−0.0487
	(0.1292)	(0.1618)	(0.5829)	(0.0548)	(0.0459)	(0.0646)
Many Credit-Eligible Students (most affected by the introduction of the tax credits)						
Many credit-eligible	−0.3527**		−0.3843**	0.1466**		0.1423**
students	(0.0620)		(0.1397)	(0.0456)		(0.0492)
After · many credit-	0.4042**		1.3299**	−0.0685		−0.0570
eligible	(0.1599)		(0.5984)	(0.0608)		(0.0721)
Low-Tuition (incentives to reduce support due to student benefit)						
Tuition ≤$1,000		0.2848**	−0.1007			
		(0.1365)	(0.1852)			
After · tuition ≤$1,000		−0.5685**	0.5702			
		(0.2139)	(0.6019)			
Tuition $1,001–2,000		0.2307*	−0.0688		−0.0580	−0.0224
		(0.1189)	(0.1775)		(0.0550)	(0.0588)
After · tuition $1,001–		−0.9621**	0.2343		0.0655	0.0485
2,000		(0.1829)	(0.5971)		(0.0780)	(0.0979)
Differences-in-Differences-in-Differences (many credit-eligible and low-tuition)						
Tuition ≤$1,000 · many			0.1708			
eligible			(0.1505)			
After · ≤$1,000 · many			−1.5105**			
eligible			(0.6393)			
$1,001–2,000 · many			0.4038**			−0.0492
eligible			(0.1834)			(0.1397)
After · $1–2,000 · many			−2.6826**			0.1014
eligible			(0.8102)			(0.1102)
No. of colleges	705	730	705	513	521	513
No. of observations	4,935	5,110	4,935	3,591	3,647	3,591
R^2	0.1748	0.1805	0.1867	0.0594	0.0514	0.0596

Source: IPEDS data from 1993–1994 to 1999–2000.

Notes: Robust standard errors are shown in parentheses. Monetary amounts are in 2000 dollars. All models include year fixed effects and controls for college selectivity, the region of the college, and state characteristics (annual unemployment rate, annual per capita income, and 1990 percentage of the population with a bachelor's degree). State support for higher education is measured by state appropriations to a college divided by FTE enrollment. Tuition groups are defined based on tuition levels during 1997–1998.

**Statistically significant at the 5 percent level.

*Statistically significant at the 10 percent level.

repeating the analysis within most regions except for the Southeast, Southwest, and far West regions. Each has enough colleges distributed by tuition level, and table 3.17 presents the results. Because public two-year and four-year colleges are now being grouped together, the models also include a dummy variable that picks up general differences between the levels of

Table 3.17   **The State Response to the Tax Credits by Region**
(dependent variable: log of state support for higher education)

	Southeast Region		Southwest Region		Far West Region	
	(1)	(2)	(3)	(4)	(5)	(6)
After	−1.2577**	−0.2895**	−2.9170**	−1.4928**	−1.2591**	−0.4104**
	(0.1403)	(0.0995)	(0.2610)	(0.3029)	(0.2101)	(0.1400)
Many Credit-Eligible Students (most affected by the introduction of the tax credits)						
Many credit-eligible students		−0.0561		−0.1386		0.2066*
		(0.0649)		(0.1082)		(0.1129)
After · many credit-eligible		0.0591		−0.2909		−0.2469
		(0.2184)		(0.4157)		(0.2880)
Low-Tuition (incentives to raise tuition due to price and income effects)						
Tuition ≤$1,000		0.6796**		0.9250**		−0.3925*
		(0.1034)		(0.1496)		(0.2024)
After · tuition ≤$1,000		−1.3968**		−2.4325**		−1.3923**
		(0.2267)		(0.3751)		(0.2678)
Tuition $1,001–2,000		0.4024**		0.7820**		0.0641
		(0.0960)		(0.1362)		(0.1312)
After · tuition $1,001–2,000		−1.2669**		−1.6312**		−1.1585**
		(0.1659)		(0.3367)		(0.2248)
No. of colleges	365	371	139	148	133	141
No. of observations	2,555	2,597	973	1,036	931	987
R^2	0.1327	0.1567	0.3093	0.3391	0.2564	0.2874

Source: IPEDS data from 1993–1994 to 1999–2000.

Notes: Robust standard errors are shown in parentheses. Monetary amounts are in 2000 dollars. All models include year fixed effects and controls for college selectivity and state characteristics (annual unemployment rate, annual per capita income, and 1990 percentage of the population with a bachelor's degree). State support for higher education is measured by state appropriations to a college divided by FTE enrollment. Tuition groups are defined based on tuition levels during 1997–1998.

**Statistically significant at the 5 percent level.
*Statistically significant at the 10 percent level.

schools. No differences are found between schools with fewer or greater numbers of credit-eligible students. However, in each case, the models suggest that state appropriations did fall substantially at lower-cost colleges, with the steepest reductions in the Southwest. Moreover, the reductions were larger for the colleges priced less than $1,000 in comparison to colleges that cost between $1,000 and $2,000, in compliance with the predictions of theory. In summary, it appears that states did in fact lower state appropriations at colleges in which students faced the lowest marginal cost due to prepolicy tuition levels.

Table 3.18 investigates whether states with large financial aid programs also reduced their support for higher education in response to the introduction of the tax credits. In contrast to the previous results, state appropriations to public two-year colleges in high-aid states increased after 1997

Table 3.18   **The State Response to the Tax Credits by Size of State Aid Program (dependent variable: log of state support for higher education)**

	Public Two-Year Colleges		Public Four-Year Colleges	
	(1)	(2)	(3)	(4)
After	−2.7689**	−2.6876**	−0.0220	−0.0413
	(0.1131)	(0.1371)	(0.0529)	(0.0661)
States with Large Aid Programs (incentives to reduce support to capture federal funds)				
High aid state	−0.4049**	−0.5501**	−0.1014	0.0439
	(0.1079)	(0.1453)	(0.0617)	(0.0926)
After · high aid state	1.5564**	0.9681**	−0.0374	0.0381
	(0.1700)	(0.2999)	(0.0570)	(0.0867)
Many Credit-Eligible Students (most affected by the introduction of the tax credits)				
Many credit-eligible students		−0.2433**		0.2140**
		(0.0676)		(0.0538)
After · many credit-eligible		−0.2344		−0.0438
		(0.1793)		(0.0777)
Differences-in-Differences-in-Differences (many credit-eligible and higher state aid)				
High aid · many eligible		0.0970		−0.2160**
		(0.1469)		(0.1015)
After · high aid · many eligible		1.0460**		−0.0726
		(0.3654)		(0.1119)
No. of colleges	730	705	521	513
No. of observations	5,110	4,935	3,647	3,591
R^2	0.1925	0.1989	0.0528	0.0652

Source: IPEDS data from 1993–1994 to 1999–2000.

Notes: Robust standard errors are shown in parentheses. State support for higher education is measured by state appropriations to a college divided by FTE enrollment. Monetary amounts are in 2000 dollars. All models include year fixed effects and controls for college selectivity, the region of the college, and state characteristics (annual unemployment rate, annual per capita income, and 1990 percentage of the population with a bachelor's degree). High state aid is defined as being ranked as one of the top eight states in 1997–1998 in total grant aid or per-student aid. Georgia, Florida, and New Mexico are excluded because they have large aid programs that cover full tuition and therefore do not have the same incentive to raise tuition prices.

**Statistically significant at the 5 percent level.
*Statistically significant at the 10 percent level.

contrary to the incentives created (specification 1). These colleges experienced one and a half times the growth in appropriations of colleges in low-aid states. In fact, two-year public colleges with more credit-eligible students had larger increases than similar schools with fewer potential recipients (specification 2). This counterintuitive pattern illustrates the wide variance in state policies toward public postsecondary institutions. While some states seemed to have responded to the tax credits by shifting state appropriations at public two-year colleges in directions that would maximize the ability to capture federal funds, others that already had a proven record of supporting major aid programs for students continued to follow this mission and perhaps even bolstered it in the face of the federal policy. Although the results have the expected negative signs, the models provide no evidence that states altered their state support for public four-year colleges after the introduction of the tax credits.

3.5.4   The Effect on College Pricing

States were not the only actors to be affected by the new policy. Colleges also had incentives to increase their prices among the beneficiaries of the tax credits. Therefore, table 3.19 explores whether public colleges with many credit-eligible students and lower tuition costs increased their list prices faster than other schools after controlling for the aforementioned changes in state appropriations. The first two models suggest that differential trends were not evident among either of these groups. However, colleges that cost between $1,000 and $2,000 and had many credit-eligible students did experience 18 percent faster growth in tuition prices relative to schools with fewer potential recipients or a more expensive price. Dissimilar results are found for public four-year colleges. The less expensive colleges witnessed relative reductions in list price after the introduction of the credits and no difference between schools with fewer or greater numbers of credit-eligible students.[45]

Again, these results may be driven by comparisons of colleges in the Southeast and far West relative to colleges in the Mideast and Great Lakes regions. Therefore, table 3.20 breaks down the analysis within the three largest regions. In the Southeast, while colleges with more potential recipients experienced relative reductions in price, the opposite was true in the far West. As theory predicts, colleges with many credit-eligible students experienced a 25 percent relative increase in list price in comparison to schools with fewer potential recipients. The results are much clearer among low-cost colleges. Colleges in the Southeast that cost less than $1,000 prior to the tax credits experienced 32 percent faster growth in cost than colleges priced above $2,000. Likewise, colleges in the $1,000 to $2,000 range increased their prices by 11 percent after 1997. Similar results are found in the Southwest and far West regions among the less expensive colleges, suggesting that the incentives by price level were adequately strong for colleges to react to them.

Table 3.21 investigates the patterns of colleges in high-aid states. In this case, both public two-year and four-year schools in states with large aid programs raised their tuition prices faster than colleges in other states (by 4.8 and 17.1 percent, respectively). Furthermore, among the public two-year colleges, schools with many credit-eligible students experienced faster

---

45. Separate analysis was done on room and board trends, but no statistically significant results were found.

Table 3.19   **Impact of the Tax Credits on Public Colleges by Tuition Price**
(dependent variable: log of list in-state tuition price)

	Public Two-Year Colleges			Public Four-Year Colleges		
	(1)	(2)	(3)	(4)	(5)	(6)
After	−0.0968**	−0.0899**	−0.0854**	−0.1983**	−0.1916**	−0.1667**
	(0.0169)	(0.0194)	(0.0365)	(0.0190)	(0.0165)	(0.0210)
Many Credit-Eligible Students (most affected by the introduction of the tax credits)						
Many credit-eligible	0.4353**		0.1954**	0.2862**		0.2586**
students	(0.0366)		(0.0261)	(0.0207)		(0.0200)
After · many credit-	0.0016		0.0008	−0.0122		−0.0411
eligible	(0.0229)		(0.0418)	(0.0299)		(0.0312)
Low-Tuition (incentives to raise tuition due to price and income effects)						
Tuition ≤$1,000		−1.2201**	−1.0687**			
		(0.0400)	(0.0430)			
After · tuition		0.0556*	0.0415			
≤$1,000		(0.0314)	(0.0432)			
Tuition $1,001–2,000		−0.5067**	−0.4053**		−0.3018**	−0.1946**
		(0.0329)	(0.0388)		(0.0202)	(0.0196)
After · tuition $1,001–		−0.0401	−0.0477		−0.0976**	−0.1239**
2,000		(0.0285)	(0.0424)		(0.0388)	(0.0406)
Differences-in-Differences-in-Differences (many credit-eligible and low-tuition)						
Tuition ≤$1,000 · many			−0.0357			
eligible			(0.0345)			
After · ≤$1,000 · many			0.0193			
eligible			(0.0540)			
$1,001–2,000 · many			0.0856			−0.2480**
eligible			(0.0945)			(0.0423)
After · $1–2,000 · many			0.1790**			−0.0238
eligible			(0.0805)			(0.1627)
No. of colleges	705	730	705	513	521	513
No. of observations	4,902	5,067	4,902	3,523	3,574	3,523
R^2	0.6493	0.7815	0.7991	0.6074	0.5931	0.6519

Source: IPEDS data from 1993–1994 to 1999–2000.

Notes: Robust standard errors are shown in parentheses. Monetary amounts are in 2000 dollars. All models include year fixed effects and controls for state appropriations per FTE student, college selectivity, the region of the college, and state characteristics (annual unemployment rate, annual per capita income, and 1990 percentage of the population with a bachelor's degree). Tuition groups are defined based on tuition levels during 1997–1998.

**Statistically significant at the 5 percent level.
*Statistically significant at the 10 percent level.

tuition growth than others. This provides further evidence that colleges did react to the credits by raising prices at the schools with the greatest incentives. Given the composition of the states in this high-aid group, it is possible that the variable is really detecting a differential response to the tax credits in large versus small states. To test this hypothesis, the sample was

Table 3.20   **The College Response to the Tax Credits by Region**
(dependent variable: log of list tuition price)

	Southeast Region		Southwest Region		Far West Region	
	(1)	(2)	(3)	(4)	(5)	(6)
After	−0.0252	−0.1922**	−0.3714**	−0.3751**	−0.0688	−0.1821**
	(0.0181)	(0.0471)	(0.0359)	(0.0414)	(0.0547)	(0.0624)
Many Credit-Eligible Students (most affected by the introduction of the tax credits)						
Many credit-eligible	0.3432**		0.3594**		0.5006**	
students	(0.0339)		(0.1046)		(0.0648)	
After · many credit-	−0.2328**		0.0078		0.2544**	
eligible	(0.0567)		(0.0908)		(0.0624)	
Low-Tuition (incentives to raise tuition due to price and income effects)						
Tuition ≤$1,000		−0.9967**		−1.0226**		−1.6389**
		(0.0496)		(0.0866)		(0.1424)
After · tuition ≤$1,000		0.3189**		0.1443**		−0.0132
		(0.0518)		(0.0728)		(0.0750)
Tuition $1,001–2,000		−0.3880**		−0.4976**		−0.4909**
		(0.0389)		(0.0664)		(0.0848)
After · tuition		0.1087**		−0.0028		0.2249**
$1,001–2,000		(0.0507)		(0.0777)		(0.0619)
No. of colleges	365	371	139	148	133	141
No. of observations	2,550	2,588	965	1,022	865	916
R^2	0.6340	0.7717	0.4772	0.5926	0.7782	0.8966

Source: IPEDS data from 1993–1994 to 1999–2000.
Notes: See table 3.19.
**Statistically significant at the 5 percent level.
*Statistically significant at the 10 percent level.

limited to the top fifteen states in population, and the models were reestimated. For this analysis the sample size dropped from 1,251 to 709 public
colleges. Even with this restriction, the aforementioned results remained
the same, suggesting that they are not due to the relative reactions of larger
states.

The pricing trends of private colleges are examined in table 3.22. Specification 1 compares colleges with and without many credit-eligible students. Contrary to theory, the schools with the larger treatment experienced a small relative reduction in price. The second two models instead
examine patterns by prepolicy tuition level. Unlike public institutions, no
colleges charge less than $2,000. However, the private colleges that charge
less than $5,000 have slightly stronger incentives to raise price due to the
LLTC (the marginal cost to students with the LLTC is 80 percent). These
models suggest that these colleges did not have statistically significant differential pricing trends even when the variables were interacted with the
proportion of potential recipients. Further analysis by type of state also

Table 3.21   **Impact of the Tax Credits on Colleges in High-Aid States (dependent variable: log of list in-state tuition price)**

	Public Two-Year Colleges		Public Four-Year Colleges	
	(1)	(2)	(3)	(4)
After	−0.1154**	−0.0977**	−0.2402**	−0.2190**
	(0.0159)	(0.0179)	(0.0193)	(0.0212)
Colleges in States with Large Aid Programs (incentives to raise tuition to capture federal funds)				
High aid state	−0.1911**	−0.6559**	0.0614*	0.0293
	(0.0512)	(0.0958)	(0.0360)	(0.0402)
After · high aid state	0.0478**	−0.1115**	0.1712**	0.1870**
	(0.0232)	(0.0341)	(0.0233)	(0.0338)
Many Credit-Eligible Students (most affected by the introduction of the tax credits)				
Many credit-eligible students		0.2750**		0.2780**
		(0.0396)		(0.0274)
After · many credit-eligible		−0.0654**		−0.0513
		(0.0293)		(0.0412)
Differences-in-Differences-in-Differences (many credit-eligible and higher state aid)				
High aid · many eligible		0.7392**		0.0697
		(0.1129)		(0.0427)
After · high aid · many eligible		0.2510**		−0.0234
		(0.0436)		(0.0518)
No. of colleges	730	705	521	513
No. of observations	5,067	4,902	3,574	3,523
R^2	0.5776	0.6967	0.5339	0.6228

Source: IPEDS data from 1993–1994 to 1999–2000.

Notes: Robust standard errors are shown in parentheses. Monetary amounts are in 2000 dollars. All models include year fixed effects and controls for state appropriations per FTE student, college selectivity, the region of the college, and state characteristics (annual unemployment rate, annual per capita income, and 1990 percentage of the population with a bachelor's degree). High state aid is defined as being ranked as one of the top eight states in 1997–1998 in total grant aid or per-student aid. Georgia, Florida, and New Mexico are excluded because they have large aid programs that cover full tuition and therefore do not have the same incentive to raise tuition prices.

**Statistically significant at the 5 percent level.
*Statistically significant at the 10 percent level.

does not suggest that colleges reacted to the tax credits. Therefore, any impact on colleges appears to have been concentrated within the public realm.

3.6   Conclusions

The 1997 passage of the HTC and LLTC significantly increased federal support for higher education. According to the Department of Education, the estimated cost of the policy could exceed the amount spent on other major programs like Title I, Head Start, and the School Lunch Program.

Table 3.22 **Impact of the Tax Credits on Private Four-Year Colleges (dependent variable: log of list in-state tuition price)**

	(1)	(2)	(3)	(4)	(5)
After	0.0421**	0.0338**	0.0403**	0.0447**	0.0447**
	(0.0112)	(0.0087)	(0.0120)	(0.0101)	(0.0114)
Many Credit-Eligible Students (most affected by the introduction of the tax credits)					
Many credit-eligible students	0.4369**		0.4107**		0.4592**
	(0.0251)		(0.0229)		(0.0319)
After · many credit-eligible	−0.0273**		−0.0277**		−0.0246*
	(0.0116)		(0.0122)		(0.0131)
Low-Tuition (incentives to raise tuition due to price and income effects)					
Tuition $2,001–5,000		−0.8881**	−0.7824**		
		(0.0392)	(0.0450)		
After · tuition $2,001–5,000		−0.0242	−0.0221		
		(0.0267)	(0.0316)		
Differences-in-Differences-in-Differences (many credit-eligible and low-tuition)					
$2,001–5,000 · many eligible			−0.2983**		
			(0.0614)		
After · $2–5,000 · many eligible			−0.0105		
			(0.0524)		
Colleges in States with Large Aid Programs (incentives to raise tuition to capture federal funds)					
High aid state				0.1253**	0.1269**
				(0.0409)	(0.0470)
After · high aid state				−0.0207	−0.0032
				(0.0154)	(0.0286)
Differences-in-Differences-in-Differences (many credit-eligible and higher state aid)					
High aid · many eligible					−0.0638
					(0.0521)
After · high aid · many eligible					−0.0076
					(0.0290)
No. of colleges	874	937	874	937	874
No. of observations	6,059	6,483	6,059	6,483	6,059
R^2	0.4456	0.3716	0.5974	0.2214	0.4505

Source: IPEDS data from 1993–1994 to 1999–2000.

Notes: Robust standard errors are shown in parentheses. Monetary amounts are in 2000 dollars. All models include year fixed effects and controls for college selectivity, the region of the college, and state characteristics (annual unemployment rate, annual per capita income, and 1990 percentage of the population with a bachelor's degree). Tuition groups are defined based on tuition levels during 1997–1998. High state aid is defined as being ranked as one of the top eight states in 1997–1998 in total grant aid or per-student aid. Georgia, Florida, and New Mexico are excluded because they have large aid programs that cover full tuition and therefore do not have the same incentive to raise tuition prices.

**Statistically significant at the 5 percent level.
*Statistically significant at the 10 percent level.

The introduction of the tax credits also marks a new direction for financial aid, as the distinctive features of the HTC and LLTC set them apart from other financial aid programs. First, eligibility requirements are broadly defined so that up to two-thirds of the population could qualify for a credit based on the income criteria. In addition, the timing of the support in relation to attendance differs greatly from aid that is awarded at the time when the individual enrolls. As a result, the distribution of the credits, their impact on enrollment, and their influence on the behavior of states and postsecondary institutions are unique compared to other federal initiatives.

What was intended to be a transfer to the middle class has indeed benefited middle-income families. Insufficient tax liability due to low income levels, competing tax credits and deductions, and the interaction with other aid programs prevents many low-income individuals from qualifying for the aid. Conversely, income ceilings prevent high-income families from benefiting. As shown by IRS data on individual tax returns, proportionately more of the tax credits were claimed by returns with an AGI above $30,000. For the 2000 tax year, nearly half of the credits claimed in 2000 were by returns with an AGI between $30,000 and $75,000, although this group makes up only 35 percent of the eligible returns. In a similar manner, although they make up only 13 percent of returns, families with AGIs between $50,000 and $75,000 claimed 22 percent of all education credits during tax year 2000 and realized the largest credit on average. However, when the amount in credits is compared to federal tax liability, the greatest beneficiaries of the tax credits were those with incomes between $10,000 and $30,000.

Although the maximum HTC and LLTC were $1,500 and $1,000, respectively, for the time period of this analysis, the actual mean benefits were far below these levels. According to IRS data, the average credit was $731 in 2000. Moreover, the substantial number of nontaxable returns, an approximation of the returns with insufficient tax liability to claim a credit, suggests that many families were unable to get the full benefit for which they were eligible.

While tax credits are a new and distinct form of financial aid, the delivery of support through the tax system suffers from some of the same information problems that plague other programs such as the Pell Grant. Usage during the first three years was far below projections. Moreover, among eligible college students according to income level, enrollment behavior, and net tuition expenses, only one-third claimed a credit during the second year of the program. However, participation continues to climb, and if the experience with the EITC is any indication, take-up rates could become greater than for other forms of college financial aid.

As with any financial aid program, one would hope that the HTC and LLTC positively affect the enrollment patterns of beneficiaries. First, the credits reduce the overall cost of college. Additionally, they may encourage students to invest in more higher education by altering the marginal cost for students to increase their expenditures. For example, the marginal cost to a HTC recipient who wants to buy $800 of education rather than $500 is zero since the credit would cover the entire expense up to $1,000. However, this study found no evidence that the policy affected attendance behavior. Using a large sample of individuals from 1990 to 2000, the analysis did not find increased postsecondary enrollment among credit-eligible students after the introduction of the HTC and LLTC. Additionally, the models tested whether college students increased their investments in higher education by being more likely to choose a four-year rather than two-year institution or attend full-time rather than part-time. Again, there was no discernable effect on the behavior of students affected by the tax credits.

Therefore, although the stated goal of the tax credits was to increase access to higher education, they do not appear to have encouraged additional postsecondary enrollment. It is not surprising that no enrollment effect was found, given the design of the program. Foremost, the main beneficiaries of the tax credits are unlikely to be students on the margin of attending college. The low take-up rate of the credits also suggests that not enough families may know about the benefit for it to have a discernible impact on enrollment. Additionally, the disconnect between the timing of the benefit and college enrollment is likely to limit the effect of the credits on college access and choice. Nonetheless, the limitations of the CPS data used in the analysis prompt the need for further research in this area.

On the other hand, states and institutions appear to have responded to the HTC and LLTC. The analysis suggests that many states reacted by reducing appropriations to public two-year colleges at which students faced a lower marginal cost due to lower tuition levels. These results are robust to analysis within region. Moreover, there is some evidence to support that public two-year colleges responded to incentives created by the tax credits by raising tuition price beyond what can be explained by fluctuations in state support, and the responses were stronger for schools with a greater proportion of credit-eligible students. However, some of the model estimates did not conform to the predictions of theory. Most notably, states with large aid programs (although not the colleges within them) seemed to have continued their efforts to support higher education even after the introduction of HTC and LLTC. Additionally, public four-year colleges often were found not to have the expected differential trends after the policy change or had ones that were in the opposite direction. As with any analysis of this kind, other trends during the late 1990s may be driving the results, although numerous controls attempt to account for differences in college selectivity, region, and state economic trends.

It is important to note that all colleges had incentives to raise price since the credits increased student incomes. Since these results only highlight the relative differences in trends for low-tuition colleges rather than the price trends of all schools, it is possible that the true effect of the credits on institutions has been much larger. Furthermore, if colleges raised tuition in response to the tax credits, this may help to explain why little enrollment effect was found. These results document the importance of considering how a federal program affects the behavior of states and institutions in ways that might undermine the original policy.

References

Allingham, M., and Agar Sandmo. 1972. Income tax evasion: A theoretical analysis. *Journal of Public Economics* 1 (3/4): 323–338.

Applebome, Peter. 1996. Aid plan that inspired Clinton is a success. *New York Times,* June 6, 1996.

Bertrand, Marianne, Ester Duflo, and Sendhil Mullainathan. 2001. How much should we trust differences-in-differences estimates? Department of Economics Working Paper no. 01-34. Cambridge: MIT.

Binder, Melissa, and Philip T. Ganderton. 2001. Who benefits from a lottery-funded college subsidy? Evidence from the New Mexico Success Scholarship. University of New Mexico, Department of Economics. Manuscript.

Cameron, Stephen, and James Heckman. 1999. Can tuition policy combat rising wage inequality? In *Financing college tuition: Government policies and educational priorities,* ed. Marvin H. Kosters, 76–124. Washington, D.C.: The American Enterprise Institute Press.

Campbell, David, and Michael Parisi. 2001. *Individual income tax returns, 1999.* Washington, D.C.: Internal Revenue Service.

Campbell, David, Michael Parisi, and Brian Balkovic. 2000. *Individual income tax returns, 1998.* Washington, D.C.: Internal Revenue Service.

College Board. 2001a. *Trends in college pricing.* Washington, D.C.: College Entrance Exam Board.

———. 2001b. *Trends in student aid.* Washington, D.C.: College Entrance Exam Board.

Conklin, Kristin, and Joni Finney. 1999. State policy response to the Taxpayer Relief Act of 1997. In *Financing a college education: How it works, how it's changing,* ed. Jacqueline King, 151–164. Phoenix, Ariz.: American Council on Education, Oryx Press.

Cornwell, Christopher, David Mustard, and Deepa Sridhar. 2001. The enrollment effects of merit-based financial aid: Evidence from Georgia's HOPE scholarship. University of Georgia, Terry College of Business, Department of Economics. Manuscript.

Crenshaw, Albert. 1997. Now you see it, now you don't: Tax law to make benefits disappear. *The Washington Post (Business),* September 17, 1997.

Cronin, Julie-Anne. 1997. The economic effects and beneficiaries of the administration's proposed higher education tax subsidies. *National Tax Journal* 50 (September): 519–540.

Dynarski, Susan. 2000. Hope for whom? Financial aid for the middle class and its impact on college attendance. *National Tax Journal* 53 (3): 629–661.

————. 2003. Does aid matter? Measuring the effects of student aid on college attendance and completion. *American Economic Review* 93 (1): 279–288.

Gray, Jerry. 1997. Bills to balance the budget and cut taxes pass Senate. *New York Times,* August 1, 1997.

Greenwood, Kathryn. 1996. Commencement '96. *Princeton Alumni Weekly,* July 3, 1996.

Hansen, W. L. 1983. Impact of student financial aid on access. In *The crisis in higher education,* ed. J. Froomkin. New York: Academy of Political Science.

Hauptman, Art, and Lois Rice. 1997. Coordinating financial aid with tuition tax benefits. Brookings Policy Brief no. 28. Washington, D.C.: The Brookings Institution, December.

Hoblitzell, Barbara, and Tiffany Smith. 2001. Hope works: Student use of education tax credits. *Lumina Foundation New Agenda Series* 4 (November).

Holtzblatt, Janet. 1991. Administering refundable tax credits: Lessons from the Earned Income Tax Credit experience. *Proceedings of the Eighty-Fourth Annual Conference on Taxation, National Tax Association* 84:180–186.

Hoxby, Caroline. 1998. Tax incentives for higher education. In *Tax policy and the economy,* ed. James Poterba, 49–81. Cambridge, Mass.: National Bureau of Economic Research.

Internal Revenue Service (IRS). 1998a. Form 1040 U.S. individual income tax return instructions. Washington, D.C.: U.S. Department of Treasury.

————. 1998b. 1998 tax tables. Washington, D.C.: U.S. Department of Treasury.

————. 1998c. *Publication 970: Tax benefits for higher education.* Washington, D.C.: U.S. Department of Treasury.

————. 2000. Information reporting for payments of qualified tuition and payments of interest on qualified education loans. *The Federal Register,* June 16, 2000.

Jamieson, A., Andrea Curry, and G. Martinez. 2001. *School enrollment in the United States: Social and economic characteristics of students.* Current Population Reports P20-533. Washington, D.C.: U.S. Census Bureau.

Juhn, Chinhui, Kevin M. Murphy, and Brooks Pierce. 1993. Wage inequality and the rise in the returns to skill. *Journal of Political Economy* 101 (3): 410–442.

Kane, Thomas. 1995. Rising public college tuition and college entry: How well do public subsidies promote access to college? NBER Working Paper no. 5164. Cambridge, Mass.: National Bureau of Economic Research.

————. 1996. Lessons from the largest school voucher program ever. In *Who chooses? Who loses? Culture, institutions and the unequal effects of school choice,* ed. Bruce Fuller and Richard Elmore with Gary Orfield, 173–185. New York: Teachers College Press.

————. 1997. Beyond tax relief: Long-term challenges in financing higher education. *National Tax Journal* 50 (June): 335–349.

————. 1998. Saving incentives for higher education. *National Tax Journal* 51 (3): 609–620.

————. 1999a. *The price of admission.* Washington, D.C.: Brookings Institution Press.

————. 1999b. Student aid after tax reform: Risks and opportunities. In *Financing a college education: How it works, how it's changing,* ed. Jacqueline King, 137–150. Phoenix, Ariz.: American Council on Education, Oryx Press.

————. 2003. A quasi-experimental estimate of the impact of financial aid on college-going. NBER Working Paper no. 9703. Cambridge, Mass.: National Bureau of Economic Research.

Knight, Shahira. October 1997. College affordability: Tuition tax credits vs. saving incentives. Joint Economic Committee study for the U.S. Congress. Available at [http://www.house.gov/jec/fiscal/tx-grwth/college/college.pdf].

Leslie, Larry, and Paul Brinkman. 1989. *The economic value of higher education.* New York: Macmillan.

Li, Judith. 1999. Estimating the effect of federal financial aid on college tuitions: A study of Pell grants. Harvard University, Department of Economics. Manuscript.

Long, Bridget Terry. Forthcoming-a. Does the format of an aid program matter? The effect of state in-kind tuition subsides. *Review of Economics and Statistics.*

———. Forthcoming-b. The institutional impact of the Georgia HOPE. *Journal of Human Resources.*

Martinez, Gladys, and Jennifer Day. 1999. *School enrollment in the United States: Social and economic characteristics of students.* Current Population Reports P20–516. Washington, D.C.: U.S. Census Bureau.

McCubbin, Janet. 1999. Earned Income Tax Credit noncompliance: The misreporting of children and the size of the EITC. Washington, D.C.: U.S. Department of Treasury.

McPherson, Michael, and Morton O. Schapiro. 1991. Does student aid affect college enrollment? New evidence on a persistent controversy. *American Economic Review* 81 (1): 309–318.

———. 1997. Financing undergraduate education: Designing national policies. *National Tax Journal* 50 (September): 557–571.

Mortenson, Thomas. 1999. Hope and lifetime learning tax credits by state. *Postsecondary Education Opportunity* 83 (May).

Murphy, Kevin, and Finis Welch. 1990. Empirical age-earnings profiles. *Journal of Labor Economics* 8 (2): 202–229.

———. 1993. Industrial change and the rising importance of skill. In *Uneven tides: Rising inequality in America,* ed. Sheldon Danziger and Peter Gottschalk, 101–132. New York: Russell Sage Foundation.

National Association of College and University Business Officers (NACUBO). 1998. The Taxpayer Relief Act of 1997 reporting task force: Highlight of activities. Prepared for the 1998 National Association of Student Financial Aid Administrators Conference. 15–18 July, Chicago.

National Center for Education Statistics (NCES). 1998. *Digest of education statistics.* Washington, D.C.: U.S. Department of Education, Office of Educational Research and Improvement.

———. 2000. *Digest of education statistics.* Washington, D.C.: U.S. Department of Education, Office of Educational Research and Improvement.

New York State Higher Education Services Corporation. 1998. Preliminary report on the restructuring of New York's grant and scholarship programs, including the Tuition Assistance Program. Albany: New York State Higher Education Services Corporation.

Office of Postsecondary Education. 1997. Families' Guide to the 1997 Tax Cuts for Education. Washington, D.C.: U.S. Department of Education.

Orfield, Gary. 1992. Money, equity, and college access. *Harvard Educational Review* 72 (Fall): 337–372.

Purdum, Todd. 1996. Clinton proposes U.S. tax credits for college aid. *New York Times,* June 5, 1996.

Riley, Richard. 1998. Department of Education letter ANN-98-16. Washington, D.C.: U.S. Department of Education, December.

———. 2000. Department of Education press briefing. Washington, D.C.: Department of Education, January 20.

Scholz, John Karl. 1994. The Earned Income Tax Credit: Participation, compliance, and antipoverty effectiveness. *National Tax Journal* 47 (March): 59–81.

Seftor, Neil, and Sarah Turner. 2002. Back to school: Federal student aid policy and adult college enrollment. *Journal of Human Resources* 37 (2): 336–352.

Selingo, Jeffrey. 1999. In New Mexico, too many scholarships, too few lottery funds. *Chronicle of Higher Education,* November 5, 1999.

Stoll, Adam, and James B. Stedman. 2001. Higher education tax credits and deduction: An overview of the benefits and their relationships to traditional student aid. Washington, D.C.: Congressional Research Service.

Turnage, Robert. 1998. Taking advantage of new federal higher education tax credits [online]. Available at [http://www.lao.ca.gov/0298_highered_tax_credits.html]. Retrieved 10 June 2002.

U.S. Census Bureau. 1999. Current Population Reports, P60-200. Washington, D.C.: U.S. Department of Commerce, Economics and Statistics Administration, Bureau of the Census.

———. 2000. *Statistical abstract of the United States.* 120th ed. Washington, D.C.: U.S. Dept. of Commerce, Economics and Statistics Administration, Bureau of the Census.

U.S. Department of Education (DOE). 2000. *Learning without limits: An agenda for the Office of Postsecondary Education.* Washington, D.C.: U.S. Department of Education.

Wolanin, Thomas R. 2001. Rhetoric and reality: Effects and consequences of the HOPE scholarship. The New Millennium Project on Higher Education Costs, Pricing, and Productivity Working Paper. Washington, D.C.: Institute for Higher Education Policy, April.

Comment   Michael McPherson

This is an informative and inventive paper on an important topic. Good evidence on the incidence and effects of federal tax credits for college is hard to come by, in part because the programs are still pretty new and in part because it is hard to get adequate evidence about the characteristics of recipients of the tax credits. I will organize my comments around three elements of Long's paper: the incidence (or distributional impact) of the tax credits; their effects on students; and their effects on institutions.

Incidence of the Federal Higher Education Tax Credits

Long finds that the two tax credits are an effective mechanism for delivering benefits to middle-class families, which was presumably a major goal of the programs. At least for now, the take-up rate on the credits is rather low but will probably rise as people (including tax advisors) get a better handle on the opportunities offered by the credits. The addition in the Bush tax cuts of 2001 of a deduction for college costs as an alternative to the Hope or Lifetime Learning Credits will certainly extend the learning curve

Michael McPherson is president of the Spencer Foundation.

for families figuring out how best to take advantage of these tax opportunities.

It's frustrating that, so far at least, available data make it difficult to sort out the income profile of families with dependent students who receive the credits from the income profile of independent students. It is clearly very different for a middle-aged family with children of college age to receive a credit than it is for, say, two married thirty-year-old graduate students. Unfortunately at this point the distributional data available from the Internal Revenue Service (IRS) combine these two groups of recipients.

Presumably the IRS microdata that will become available will help sort out the income profiles of these two groups. The National Postsecondary Student Aid Study, whose 1999–2000 data have recently become available, may be helpful on this question as well.

Of course, beyond recognizing that the tax credit programs do indeed reach middle-income families, it is also of interest to track who within these populations benefits. Among middle-aged families, clearly these credits favor families with children and with children who attend college. Among younger, independent students, benefits accrue to those who pursue college education and particularly (for the Lifetime Learning Credit) those who pursue graduate or professional education.

Effects on Students

Long rightly points out that one publicly declared purpose of the tax credits was to raise college enrollments. It's not clear, though, how serious an aim this was. The legislative history indicates that the Clinton administration's main purpose was to offer an alternative to capital gains tax cuts that would be more favorable to the middle class. It is instructive that the early estimates by the Treasury Department of the cost of the tax credits assumed there would be no enrollment effects.

Long indeed offers several good reasons for expecting the credits to have at best a small effect on enrollments. In addition to the points she makes, it may be worth adding that since postsecondary attendance is already pretty high for young high school graduates from middle-income families, there isn't much room for increases in attendance among that population.

If one tries to think about who has the strongest incentive to change behavior in response to the credits, it may well be those adults who have HOPE eligibility and the right income levels to qualify for the benefit, plus the ability to go more than half-time in order to qualify. Empirically, however, as Turner shows in her piece in this volume, it is rare for adults who have never started college to begin after the age of twenty—and only people in their first or second year of college are eligible for the HOPE Credit.

The other place to look for behavioral effects, then, might be among adults who attend part-time and who qualify for the Lifetime Learning

Credit. The partial federal subsidy for additional credits might induce adults to take more courses than they would otherwise. Detecting these effects would require very good data.

Effects on Institutions

It is in a sense reassuring to see Long's evidence that state institutions respond rationally to the incentives to raise prices created by the tax credits. When the federal government introduced what are now called Pell Grants, it was obvious that public institutions with zero tuition could gain revenue by introducing tuition—a point that was made, controversially, in 1972 when the Keppel Task Force recommended introducing tuition at the City University of New York. The Task Force observed the following:

> New York state students and institutions will fail to some degree to qualify for Federal funds under the new statutes unless the public institutions charge higher tuitions than they do at present. . . . [We] consider it extremely important that the State take maximum advantage of Federal funding in order to reduce the burden on State taxpayers. (Task Force on Financing Higher Education 1972, 5, 15)

The same logic plainly applies in states with tuition low enough that students can gain additional tax credit dollars from higher tuition.

Long's evidence that states respond to tax credits reminds us that her estimates of the effects of the tax credits on students are reduced-form estimates. To the extent that schools raise prices in response to the credits, the observed enrollment response will be attenuated, compared to an analysis that focused on the impact of the credits holding tuition constant. In principle, some kind of multiple-equation structural analysis of these relationships would be desirable, but to attempt this with available data would be a huge stretch.

There is a second kind of institutional effect that might be anticipated from the tax credits. To the extent that colleges award financial aid to students in the form of price discounts, the availability of the tax credits gives institutions an incentive to reduce those discounts. Indeed, schools employing standard need analysis normally recognize that the receipt of tax credits expands a family's ability to pay and therefore reduces their need for student aid. There is heavy political pressure on colleges not to "capture" gains from the college tuition tax credits through this device (and indeed it is illegal to reduce eligibility for federal student aid grant awards on the basis of such an analysis.) Nonetheless, dollars going to student aid are fairly fungible, and financial aid officers have significant discretion in determining need, so it is quite possible that substitution of tax credits for institution-based student aid occurs. It would be interesting to try to estimate such effects.

Concluding Comments

I will conclude with two broader comments, one on theoretical public finance and a second on political economy.

Ted Schultz, an architect of human capital theory, observed long ago that, to the degree that spending on education is an investment in future earnings, there is an argument for making the spending tax deductible. Analytically, it is certainly interesting to ask what would be the optimal tax treatment of higher education investments in a general equilibrium framework. Under conditions of perfect competition, without externalities, and assuming that college is strictly an investment in future earning power, it is plausible on efficiency grounds that such investments should be fully tax deductible (a point I have heard Bill Gale make in conversation). Clearly, in practice, higher education is a mix of consumption and investment activity and is subsidized in a variety of ways, so it is far from obvious what practical consequences might flow from this theoretical point.

Finally, regarding political economy, it is of interest to note that during the 1990s the share of state government expenditures going to higher education fell, and in many states the real level of state appropriations to higher education fell. This came about because of tax limitation movements in many states and the ascendance of other budget priorities, including Medicaid, elementary and secondary education, and prisons. Many states permitted tuitions in public higher education to rise pretty rapidly in percentage terms to offset the falloff in state support. Not surprisingly, these tuition increases produced unhappiness among middle-class voters, and surely that unhappiness was one significant motivation for President Clinton's enthusiasm for tuition tax credits. Viewed in that light, this entire episode can be viewed as a kind of weird reverse federalism, with tax credits for college tuition helping to offset increases in public tuition occasioned by state budget pressures. Unfortunately, though not surprisingly, the losers in this shifting fiscal picture are poor families, who get hit with the tuition increases but who, as Long shows, do not receive the full benefit of the tax credits.

References

McPherson, Michael, and Morton Owen Schapiro. 1991. *Keeping college affordable: Government and educational opportunity.* Washington, D.C.: Brookings Institution.

Task Force on Financing Higher Education. 1972. *Higher education in New York State. A report to Governor Nelson A. Rockefeller.* Albany, N.Y.: Task Force on Financing Higher Education. Quoted in McPherson and Schapiro 1991, 198.

Education Savings Incentives and Household Saving
Evidence from the 2000 TIAA-CREF Survey of Participant Finances

Jennifer Ma

4.1 Introduction

College tuition inflation in the past thirty years has averaged 2 to 3 percentage points higher than the general price inflation and is showing no sign of slowing down. For the 2002–2003 academic year, the average in-state tuition and fees at four-year public colleges and universities was $4,081, a 9.6 percent increase from the previous year. For the same academic year, the average tuition and fees at four-year private colleges and universities was $18,273, a 5.8 percent increase from the previous year (College Board 2002).

As the cost of college continues to rise at a fast pace, how to finance a college education has become a growing concern for many families. In order to help families save for college, the federal government has introduced two tax-favored education savings programs in recent years: the 529 plan and the Education Individual Retirement Account ([IRA] recently renamed the Coverdell Education Savings Account). These savings programs can be considered Roth IRAs for education expenses. Contributions to these programs are not deductible for federal income tax purposes, but earnings on qualified withdrawals are exempt from federal income tax.[1] These education savings programs, the 529 plan in particular, have grown

Jennifer Ma is a senior research fellow of the Teachers Insurance Annuity Association-College Retirement Equity Fund (TIAA-CREF) Institute.

I would like to thank John Ameriks, Douglas Fore, Caroline Hoxby, Kathleen McGarry, Harvey Rosen, Mark Warshawsky, and participants at the National Bureau of Economic Research (NBER) conference on college decisions for their helpful comments and suggestions. I would also like to thank Jacob Rugh for excellent research assistance. The views expressed in this paper are those of the author and not necessarily those of TIAA-CREF.

1. Note that the tax law that provides federal tax exemption on earnings on qualified 529 plan withdrawals is scheduled to expire on December 31, 2010. Congress may or may not extend the law beyond this date.

rapidly since their inception and will likely grow even more quickly under the tax law passed in 2001.

The introduction of education savings programs is only one of the government's interventions in the capital market for higher education investments. However, it is an important one. The introduction of these savings programs represents a redirection of state and federal efforts toward saving and away from two major forms of public subsidy to higher education—direct state appropriations to public institutions and federal needs-based financial aid. For example, while state and local appropriations accounted for 47.4 percent of the total current-fund revenue for public degree-granting institutions in the 1980–1981 academic year, they accounted for only 35.6 percent in the 1999–2000 academic year (U.S. Department of Education 2003).

Enthusiasm for the tax-favored education savings programs was partly spurred by the idea that they would raise households' saving rate by targeting a segment of the population that is not targeted already by IRAs and 401(k)s. Moreover, by offering tax incentives, these programs may encourage marginal families to save and plan for college, which may have a positive influence on students' college experience.[2]

As in the case of other tax-favored savings programs, whether saving in education savings programs represents new saving is an empirical issue. In the last two decades, a large and contentious literature has developed over the impact of IRAs and 401(k)s on private and national saving. Some researchers (for example, Poterba, Venti, and Wise) have found evidence that suggests the majority of saving in tax-favored retirement accounts represents new saving, while other researchers (for example, Engen, Gale, and Scholz) have found evidence that suggests just the opposite.

While the debate on the impact of retirement savings programs has continued for years, little is known about how education savings programs affect household saving. One explanation for this gap in the literature is that because education savings programs are relatively new, data on education saving are not readily available. Using wealth data from a survey of TIAA-CREF participants, this paper attempts a first check on whether education savings programs offset other household saving, controlling for saver heterogeneity. Results suggest that, in general, education saving does not seem to offset other forms of household saving. For households with a high likelihood of using education savings accounts, education saving seems to be positively correlated with other household assets.

2. Despite the fact that loans are available and can be made the responsibility of the student himself, anecdotal evidence suggests that many families with a record of successful college attendance make considerable use of internal family financing (i.e., parental savings). Although the greater college success of savers may be due to their greater incomes or superior planning, it is also possible that savings and loans do not have parallel effects on students' college experience. Perhaps piling up debt worries students and causes them to disengage from college in order to earn money. It is also possible that the act of saving for college causes a family to think more concretely about college and prepare for it better.

The remainder of the paper is structured as follows. Section 4.2 describes the 529 plan and the recently renamed Coverdell Education Savings Account. Section 4.3 describes the data and presents some summary statistics. Section 4.4 provides a brief summary of the IRA and 401(k) literature and discusses the empirical strategies used in this paper to identify savers from nonsavers. Section 4.5 presents the regression results. Section 4.6 provides some concluding remarks.

4.2   The 529 Plan and the Coverdell Education Savings Account

4.2.1   The 529 Plan

Named after the section of the Internal Revenue Code (IRC) that created them, 529 plans are qualified tuition plans designed to help families save for college expenses. Two types of 529 plans are available: savings and prepaid. Savings plans are investment programs that typically offer a variable rate of return. Prepaid plans usually allow plan purchasers to prepay future tuition credits at current prices. As of August 2003, all of the existing 529 savings and prepaid plans were sponsored by individual states. However, a consortium of private colleges and universities is scheduled to launch an independent 529 plan in fall 2003. The independent 529 plan will allow investors to lock in the cost of future tuition at any of the consortium's participating colleges and universities.

Although the first prepaid plan (Michigan Education Trust) was introduced in 1988, it was not until 1996 that Section 529 was added to the IRC to clarify the federal tax treatment of state-sponsored plans. Under Section 529, earnings in state-sponsored plans grow federal and state tax-free until withdrawal. Contributions to 529 plans are not deductible for federal income tax purposes. However, they are deductible (usually subject to an annual maximum) in some states for state income tax purposes.

Before 2002, when withdrawals from a 529 plan were made to pay for qualified higher education expenses, the earnings portion was subject to federal income tax at the beneficiary's rate. The Economic Growth and Tax Reconciliation Act of 2001 (the 2001 Tax Act) provided more favorable tax treatment for 529 plans, as the earnings on qualified withdrawals from state-sponsored plans were made exempt from federal income tax, starting in 2002.[3] Most states exempt earnings on qualified withdrawals from state tax as well. Starting in 2004, independent prepaid plans established by private colleges and universities will also be eligible for the same benefits as state-sponsored plans.

The 529 plan is also more flexible than most tax-favored savings vehicles.

---

3. Note that the provisions of the 2001 Tax Act regarding Section 529 of the IRC are scheduled to expire on December 31, 2010. Congress may or may not extend the tax benefits beyond this date. If the law is not extended, the federal tax treatment of 529 plans will revert to its status prior to January 1, 2002.

There is no income restriction on participation or tax benefits. Anyone, regardless of income, can contribute to a 529 plan. Withdrawals may be used to pay for tuition, fees, room and board, books, supplies, and equipment required for enrollment or attendance at an eligible undergraduate, graduate, or professional institution of higher education, or any approved vocation/technical school. Eligible postsecondary institutions include those that are accredited and are eligible to participate in student aid programs administered by the U.S. Department of Education.

While most state-sponsored prepaid plans are open to state residents only, most savings plans allow anyone from any state to open an account. There is generally no annual contribution limit for 529 plans. Most plans impose a lifetime limit per beneficiary on account balances (the sum of contributions and earnings, less fees and expenses); a few plans impose a lifetime limit on gross contributions. Lifetime limits vary widely across states and are usually adjusted once a year to reflect inflation. Table 4A.1 shows that as of August 2003 the lowest lifetime limit on account balances was $187,000 (Arizona), and the highest was over $305,000 (New Jersey and South Dakota).[4] Table 4A.1 also shows that minimum contribution requirements are generally low.

Awareness of and interest in 529 plans have increased considerably after the 2001 Tax Act made the earnings on qualified withdrawals exempt from federal income tax. As of March 2003, there were approximately 4.9 million accounts with a total asset value of $29.4 billion across all 529 savings and prepaid plans, an increase of 53 percent in assets compared with March 2002. As of August 2003, forty-nine states and the District of Columbia had 529 savings plans in operation. The state of Washington was the only state that had not yet established a 529 savings plan. Nineteen states had 529 prepaid plans in operation.[5]

With increased interest in 529 plans, more and more employers are offering 529 plan automatic payroll deductions for their employees. To take things one step further, it would be interesting to see whether employers will make 529 plan enrollment a default for some employees (for example, those with young children) and whether automatic 529 enrollment would lead to a higher participation rate. There is some evidence in the 401(k) literature that suggests automatic 401(k) enrollment leads to a higher participation rate among employees (Madrian and Shea 2001).

Earnings on nonqualified withdrawals from a 529 plan are subject to

4. See Ma et al. (2001) for a study of using an economic approach to set the contribution limits for 529 plans. In practice, limits are set by states according to broad considerations set forth in the IRC and regulations. In states with lifetime limits on account balances, once the combined balance for a designated beneficiary reaches the maximum limit, the program will stop taking new contributions.

5. The sources of this information are the Investment Company Institute and the College Savings Plan Network.

federal and state income taxes at the distributee's rate in addition to a 10 percent penalty tax. However, the account owner may make a penalty-free, tax-free rollover by designating another "member of the family" as the new beneficiary. The 10 percent penalty does not apply in the event there is a withdrawal due to the beneficiary's death or disability. If the beneficiary receives a tax-free scholarship, educational assistance allowance, or other tax-free educational benefits, then the distribution from a 529 plan is not subject to the 10 percent penalty to the extent that the distribution is not more than the amount of the scholarship, educational allowance, or other similar benefits.

4.2.2   The Coverdell Education Savings Account

The recently renamed Coverdell Education Savings Account was introduced as part of the Taxpayer Relief Act of 1997. Contributions to the Coverdell are not tax deductible. However, earnings are exempt from federal and state income taxes if withdrawals are used to pay for qualified education expenses. Before 2002, qualified expenses included higher education expenses only. The 2001 Tax Act provided that, starting in 2002, qualified expenses would also include elementary and secondary school expenses at public, private, or religious schools.[6]

There is an income restriction on participation in the Coverdell. For 2003, the phaseout range was between $95,000 and $110,000 for single tax filers and between $190,000 and $220,000 for joint tax filers. Before 2002, the annual contribution limit for the Coverdell was $500 per beneficiary. The 2001 Tax Act raised the annual contribution limit to $2,000 per beneficiary, starting in 2002.

Earnings on nonqualified withdrawals from Coverdells are subject to federal and state income taxes at the distributee's rate in addition to a 10 percent penalty (with similar exceptions as those for 529 plans). Before the tax law changes in 2001, an excise tax was imposed if individuals contributed to both a 529 plan and a Coverdell on behalf of the same beneficiary in the same year. The new law provided that, starting in 2002, the excise tax would no longer apply. However, the federal law prohibits the use of same education expenses to support tax-free distributions from both a 529 plan and a Coverdell. Furthermore, the education expenses used to support tax-free distributions from a 529 plan or a Coverdell may not be used to claim a Hope or Lifetime Learning Credit.

Table 4.1 summarizes some key features of the 529 plan and the Coverdell. Because the 529 plan and the Coverdell have very similar tax treatment on earnings and contributions, a comparison of the attractiveness of

---

6. Allowable higher education expenses are the same as those for 529 plans. Allowable elementary and secondary school expenses include tuition, fees, academic tutoring, books, supplies, other equipment, "special needs services," room and board, uniforms, transportation and "supplementary items and services."

Table 4.1   Key Features of the 529 Plan and Coverdell Education Savings Account

	529 Plan (1)	Coverdell Education Savings Account (2)
Tax benefits	Earnings federal and state income tax deferred and federal income tax free, if withdrawals are used for qualified higher education expenses. Most states exempt earnings on qualified withdrawals from state tax. Some states also allow contributions to be deducted from state income tax (usually subject to an annual limit).	Earnings federal and state income tax free, if used for qualified elementary, secondary, and higher education expenses
Is the value of the account *excluded* from the owner's taxable estate?	Yes	Yes
How much can be invested?	Varies by state. Currently, the highest account balance limit is $305,000 per beneficiary.	Up to $2,000 per year
Qualified education expenses	Tuition, fees, books, supplies, room and board, and equipment at an eligible postsecondary education institution	Same as (1) for higher education expenses. Elementary and secondary education expenses also qualify.
Financial aid treatment	Savings plans: parents' assets if the account is under a parent's name; prepaid plans may reduce aid dollar for dollar.	Student's assets
Who makes investment decisions?	State sponsor with input from program money manager	Account owner
Income restriction	No	Yes
Impact on Hope and Lifetime Tax Credits	Education expenses used to support tax-free distributions from a 529 plan may not be used to claim a Hope or Lifetime Learning credit.	Education expenses used to support tax-free distributions from a Coverdell may not be used to claim a Hope or Lifetime Learning credit.
Flexibility	Earnings on nonqualified withdrawals taxed at the distributee's income tax rate plus an additional 10 percent tax	Earnings on nonqualified withdrawals taxed at the distributee's income tax rate plus an additional 10 percent tax

the two programs reduces to a comparison of fees (Ma and Fore 2002). Assuming both programs have the same rate of return, the one with lower fees will result in a higher level of asset accumulation. Another difference between the two savings programs is that 529 investors may not make direct investment decisions, while Coverdell investors may. Finally, when it comes to calculating a student's Expected Family Contribution (EFC) for financial aid purposes, assets in a Coverdell account will be considered as the student's assets and assessed at a 35 percent rate, while assets in a 529 account will be considered as the parents' assets (if the owner is a parent) and assessed at a 5.6 percent rate. Because a higher level of EFC means a lower level of financial needs, assets in a Coverdell account will reduce a student's financial aid more than assets in a 529 plan will.

Table 4.2 illustrates how families may use the 529 plan and the Coverdell to save for future college expenses. Column (1) of table 4.2 indicates that assuming a 5 percent annual increase in the college cost and a 6 percent annual rate of return on saving, monthly contributions of $22 over an eighteen-year investment horizon would be sufficient to fund the average cost of a two-year education at a public two-year college. Columns (2) and (3) indicate that monthly contributions of $257 and $668 over an eighteen-year investment horizon would be sufficient to fund the average cost of a four-

Table 4.2   **Examples of Saving for a College Education with the 529 Plan and the Coverdell**

	Public Two-Year College	Public Four-Year College	Private Four-Year College
Current annual cost (2002–2003 average total charges including tuition, fees, and room and board)[a]	$1,735	$9,663	$25,052
Projected cost (savings goal)[b] (average cost of a four-year education—or a two-year education for public two-year colleges—for a student enrolling in 2020)	$8,560	$100,233	$259,860
Investment period (years)	18	18	18
Monthly saving needed to meet the goal[c]	$22	$257	$668
Savings programs may be used	Coverdell or 529 plan	529 plan or combination of 529 plan and Coverdell	529 plan or combination of 529 plan and Coverdell

Source: Trends in College Pricing 2002, the College Board.
[a]Tuition and fees only for public two-year colleges.
[b]Assuming the average college costs increase by 5 percent per year into the future.
[c]Assuming a 6 percent annual nominal rate of return on saving.

year education at a public four-year and private four-year college, respectively.

It is also worth noting that the Registered Education Savings Plans (RESPs) in Canada are similar to the 529 plan and the Coverdell. Contributions to the RESPs are not tax deductible. However, earnings grow tax-free until withdrawal. When withdrawals are used to pay for qualified higher education expenses, earnings are taxed as the beneficiary's income. Earnings on nonqualified withdrawals (withdrawals not used for higher education) are taxable as the account subscriber's (owner's) income. As of August 2003, the annual contribution limit per beneficiary was $4,000 Canadian (CAD), and the lifetime limit was CAD $42,000.

4.3   The 2000 TIAA-CREF Survey of Participant Finances

To examine the impact of education savings programs on other household saving, information on contributions or accumulations in education saving, other saving, and demographics is required. At the time of this study, there was no publicly available wealth data that contained information on contributions or accumulations in education savings programs.[7]

The data used in this study are drawn from the 2000 TIAA-CREF Survey of Participant Finances (SPF) conducted by TIAA-CREF. TIAA-CREF is a nonprofit organization that provides retirement plans at about 12,000 colleges, universities, research centers, medical organizations, and other nonprofit institutions throughout the United States. The 2000 SPF sample consists mostly of employees of colleges and universities. A small portion of the sample consists of employees of research and other nonprofit organizations.

The 2000 SPF was conducted among members of the TIAA-CREF research panel. The research panel was established in 1993 when 60,000 participants were randomly selected to participate in the research panel project. The purpose of the research panel project was to select a sample of participants for future studies of participant financial decisions. A brief questionnaire was mailed to these 60,000 randomly selected participants asking information about themselves and their families. Of these 60,000 individuals selected, 9,847 responded to the 1993 research panel questionnaire and formed the initial research panel. In the subsequent years, some members were dropped from the research panel due to death, change of participant status, or change of address. Several sample replenishment efforts were made in 1995, 1997, and 1999.

The 2000 SPF is a comprehensive survey of household finances. It was

---

7. The 2001 SCF conducted by the Federal Reserve Board included questions on education savings programs such as the 529 plans. However, the 2001 SCF data was not yet available when the analysis for this study was conducted.

designed to examine in detail the types and amounts of financial assets owned by participants and apply this information to the study of household asset allocation and other financial decisions. Survey packets containing a cover letter and an eight-page questionnaire were mailed in January 2000 to a total of 9,234 research panel members. A total of 2,835 completed questionnaires (2,793 usable) were received, representing an overall response rate of 31 percent.

The 2000 SPF gathered a wide range of information on household finances and demographics. The demographic information gathered includes the respondent's age, gender, education, employment status, occupation, marital status, and the number of children for whom the respondent's household is financially responsible. The financial information gathered includes the amount and sources of the respondent's income, the types of retirement investments, nonretirement financial accounts, real estate holdings in the household, and the estimates of the current value for each of those investments. Information on household mortgages and other types of financial commitments was also gathered. For married respondents, information on the spouse's employment status, income, and retirement assets was also collected. Most importantly, respondents were asked whether anyone in his or her household had a Coverdell, a 529 savings account, or a 529 prepaid contract. Respondents were asked to provide a value if they answered "yes" to any of these questions. Respondents were also asked to measure on a scale of 1 to 10 how important it was for them to leave a bequest.

4.3.1   A Comparison of the 2000 SPF with the 1998 Survey of Consumer Finances

Table 4.3 shows the summary statistics of households from the 1998 Survey of Consumer Finances (SCF) and the 2000 SPF. Clearly, households from the two surveys are quite different in terms of both demographic and financial characteristics. As table 4.3 shows, respondents in the 2000 SPF are much older than those in the 1998 SCF—the median age of the 2000 SPF respondents was fifty-nine, compared with forty-six for the 1998 SCF. Moreover, respondents in the 2000 SPF are much more educated than those in the 1998 SCF. For example, while only 33.2 percent of the 1998 SCF respondents have a college degree, 87.5 percent of the SPF respondents have at least a college degree, and 33.4 percent have a PhD degree. This is not surprising given that the majority of SPF respondents are faculty members.

Table 4.3 also shows that households from the 2000 SPF, on average, earned much higher incomes than those from the 1998 SCF. The median 1999 household income from the 2000 SPF was more than twice as much as the median 1997 household income from the 1998 SCF ($75,000 versus $33,000). Even when the median household income from the 1998 SCF is inflated by 10 percent to the 1999 level, it is still less than half of that from

Table 4.3   **Summary Statistics of Households from the 1998 SCF and the 2000 TIAA-CREF SPF**

	Median	25th percentile	75th percentile	Mean
1998 SCF				
Financial characteristics				
Household income	$33,000	$17,000	$60,000	$52,296
Total financial assets	$17,320	$1,500	$85,000	$134,234
Total personal debt	$1,530	$0	$11,000	$9,920
Total real estate assets	$70,000	$0	$140,000	$109,063
Total mortgage debt	$0	$0	$55,000	$37,621
Total net worth	$71,700	$9,920	$208,850	$282,592
Percent own primary residence				66.3
Demographics				
Respondent's age	46.0	35.0	61.0	48.7
Respondent's education level				
Less than high school (%)				16.5
High school or GED (%)				31.9
Some college (%)				18.5
College and above (%)				33.2
2000 TIAA-CREF SPF[a]				
Financial characteristics				
Household income	$75,000	$48,000	$111,000	$94,550
Total financial assets	$336,750	$119,117	$859,000	$665,330
Total personal debt	$0	$0	$5,000	$9,221
Total real estate assets	$160,000	$95,000	$300,000	$257,469
Total mortgage debt	$15,000	$0	$89,000	$62,943
Total net worth	$467,728	$187,375	$1,108,500	$837,333
Percent own primary residence				85.7
Demographics				
Respondent's age	59.0	48.0	69.0	57.9
Respondent's education level				
High school or less (%)				3.2
Some college (%)				9.1
College graduate (%)				18.9
Master's or first professional (%)				35.2
PhD (%)				33.4

Source: Author's calculations based on the 1998 SCF and the 2000 TIAA-CREF SPF.
[a]For 2000 TIAA-CREF SPF, financial assets and demographic information was as of December 31, 1999.

the 2000 SPF. (The March Current Population Survey data suggest that for households with householders twenty-five years and older, the median income in current dollars rose by 10.1 percent between 1997 and 1999, while the mean income in current dollars rose by 10.6 percent.) Moreover, households from the 2000 SPF are much wealthier than those from the 1998 SCF. The median net worth for households from the 1998 SCF is only $71,700, compared with $467,728 for those from the 2000 SPF.

The above comparisons suggest that the sample in the 2000 SPF is quite different from the general population. The respondents in the 2000 SPF are older, much more educated, and wealthier than the general population. These unique characteristics make the 2000 SPF particularly well suited to the task of assessing the effectiveness of education savings programs for two main reasons. First, the SPF sample is more likely to be saving prone and more likely to plan for college. Thus, they are more likely to use the new education savings programs than the typical American household, especially when the programs are new and unfamiliar to most people. In fact, as of December 1999 (when the SPF was conducted), while 2.4 percent of the SPF households reported owning a 529 savings or prepaid plan, less than 1.2 percent of the U.S. households owned a 529 plan.[8] This confirms the SPF sample is much more likely to use education savings programs than the general population. The proneness of the SPF sample to use savings programs allows one to find a sufficient number of users in a small sample.

Second, estimates from the SPF sample will likely overstate the extent to which education saving crowds out other saving. Research on retirement saving suggests that reshuffling of assets is more likely to occur for high-income households (Engen and Gale 2000). Moreover, not only is the SPF sample wealthier and has accumulated higher levels of saving (and more saving to crowd out), it also consists largely of education-sector workers who are very consciously dedicated to ensuring their children's college opportunities. These individuals are far more likely to have been saving explicitly for college even in the absence of tax-favored programs, which also raises the likelihood of crowding out. Therefore, one can confidently predict that there would be much less crowding out in the overall population than in the SPF sample.

While the SPF has many advantages in examining the impact of education savings programs on household saving, it also has some limitations. One limitation is that the sample is representative of neither the U.S. population nor the TIAA-CREF participant population.[9] Therefore, results from this study should be interpreted accordingly.

8. These comparisons are for 529 plans only because data on the aggregate number of Coverdell accounts are not readily available. The source of this information comes from the author's calculations. The percentage of U.S. households owning a 529 plan was calculated by dividing the total number of 529 accounts in the United States by the total number of households, as of December 1999. Data on the total number of 529 accounts are from the College Savings Plans Network and data on the total number of households are from the U.S. Census Bureau. It is worth noting that to the extent that some households may have multiple 529 accounts, the actual percentage of *households* owning 529 plans may be slightly lower than the calculated 1.2 percent.

9. Because not much information is available on the characteristics of those individuals who did not respond to the SPF, it is not clear whether there are any systematic differences between those who did respond and those who did not respond to the survey and how the estimates would be affected.

4.3.2   Nonresponses in the Survey and Sample Selection

Although missing data are common for many wealth surveys, the item response rates in the 2000 SPF are quite high. Table 4.4 presents the proportions of nonresponses to financial asset questions in the 2000 SPF survey. As table 4.4 shows, the item response rates for the 2000 SPF are over 90 percent for most nonretirement financial assets (column [4]).

Missing data could arise as a result of nonresponse to ownership questions, value questions, or sometimes both. Column (1) in table 4.4 indicates that between 2.0 and 16.3 percent of respondents did not provide an answer to the ownership question for various types of financial assets. Column (3) suggests that among those who answered "yes" to the ownership questions, between 6.2 and 20.6 percent did not provide a value. As a result, between 5.9 and 23.2 percent of respondents had missing data for various assets (column [4]).

Of all of the assets listed in table 4.4, TIAA-CREF retirement assets (row one) seem to have a much higher nonresponse rate (23.2 percent) than other assets. One reason for this is that a third of the sample consists of annuitant respondents who were already receiving life-annuity income from TIAA-CREF. For these respondents, it was difficult for them to report the value of their TIAA-CREF retirement assets. In other words, since they had already annuitized part or all of their TIAA-CREF retirement assets, they would need to calculate the present value of their future annuity income in order to figure out the total value of their TIAA-CREF retirement assets. Fortunately, for annuitants, the value of their total TIAA-CREF retirement assets can be calculated by adding together their nonannuitized assets and an annuity reserve calculated based on TIAA-CREF accounting data.[10]

Nonresponses become more of an issue when one calculates aggregate wealth levels, even though the nonresponse rates for individual assets are rather low. For example, when one calculates households' self-reported noneducation net worth (the sum of net noneducation financial assets and real estate equity), 54.9 percent of the respondents have missing data due to nonresponses to the ownership and/or value questions for at least one of the assets. In order to reduce the number of observations with missing net worth, the respondent's self-reported data on TIAA-CREF retirement assets were replaced with TIAA-CREF accounting data for the analysis. As a result, the proportion of respondents with missing data for net worth dropped to 51.1 percent. It is worth noting that the net worth calculated

10. The annuity reserve for an annuitant is the amount of reserve set aside to fund the annuitant's life-annuity income. The value of an annuitant's annuity reserve can be considered as the present value of the annuitant's life-annuity income, using the TIAA-CREF guaranteed interest rate as the discount rate.

Table 4.4   Nonresponses to Financial Asset Questions in the 2000 TIAA-CREF SPF

Type of Asset	Nonresponse to Ownership Questions (%) (1)	"Yes" to Ownership Questions (%) (2)	Of Those Who Answered "Yes" to Ownership, Did Not Provide a Value (%) (3)	Observations with Missing Information (%) (4)
Respondent's retirement assets				
1. TIAA-CREF employer-sponsored retirement accounts	7.2	77.8	20.6	23.2
2. Non-TIAA-CREF employer-sponsored retirement accounts	7.7	31.2	17.3	13.1
3. IRA or KEOGH account	7.7	44.3	10.9	12.5
4. Other tax-deferred annuities	10.2	17.8	19.8	13.7
Other financial assets				
5. Stock mutual funds	5.8	46.8	10.6	10.7
6. Publicly traded stock	4.1	48.2	11.5	9.6
7. Tax-free bond mutual funds	5.8	16.0	17.9	8.7
8. Other bond mutual funds	6.3	11.7	17.7	8.4
9. U.S. government savings bonds	5.4	24.3	11.6	8.3
10. Corporate bonds or foreign bonds	6.4	5.7	20.3	7.6
11. Savings accounts	2.0	71.0	6.2	6.4
12. Checking accounts	2.1	94.9	6.3	8.1
13. Certificates and deposit	3.3	29.9	8.9	5.9
14. Money market mutual funds	5.2	41.9	11.2	9.9
Education saving				
15. Coverdell (former Education IRA)	16.3	3.9	11.9	16.8
16. 529 savings plan	16.0	2.0	7.0	16.2
17. 529 prepaid contract	16.0	0.5	15.4	16.0

Source: Author's calculations based on the 2000 TIAA-CREF SPF data.
Note: Total number of respondents 2,793.

from TIAA-CREF accounting data is highly correlated with that from self-reported data, with a correlation coefficient of 0.96.

Also of special attention are the nonresponses for the three questions on education saving. At first glance, the nonresponse rates for these questions seem much higher than those for other financial assets. Further investigation of the data reveals that the majority of these nonresponses represent nonresponses to all three questions on education saving (440 cases). Of these 440 cases, household's noneducation net worth is available for 184 cases. This indicates that these 184 respondents filled out all the necessary information needed for the calculation of household noneducation net worth but left the questions on education saving blank. Because the 529 plan and the Coverdell were rather new at the time of the survey (approximately two years after their introduction), it is likely that many respondents were not familiar with these savings programs and did not understand the questions. However, those respondents who did report having a 529 or a Coverdell account seemed to understand the questions and most of them provided a valid and positive answer for the value question. Therefore, it is reasonable to assume that these 184 respondents did not have such accounts. Under such an assumption, the nonresponse rate for the education ownership questions dropped to around 10 percent.

Of the 2,793 respondents, 171 reported having at least one education savings account. The number of respondents reported having a Coverdell, a 529 savings account, and a 529 prepaid contract was 109, 57, and 13, respectively. Moreover, 96, 53, and 11 provided a nonzero account balance. The reported median balance for the three types of accounts was $2,000, $10,000, and $5,000, respectively. Due to the small number of respondents who reported having these accounts, it is difficult to empirically distinguish the impact of each of these education incentives on household wealth. Therefore, all three education savings accounts are treated equally in the empirical analysis. In other words, the balances of all education savings accounts are aggregated to create a variable that measures a household's total education saving.

Observations with missing values for explanatory variables in the regressions are excluded from the analysis. Also excluded from the regression analysis are observations with extreme values of net worth (over $10 million, 1 case) and observations with missing values for net worth. The final regression sample includes 1,265 cases.

4.4 Empirical Strategy—How to Control for Saver Heterogeneity

As mentioned earlier, one important public policy question for tax-favored savings programs is whether saving in these tax-favored programs represents new saving. In other words, does saving in education savings programs offset other household saving? The answer to this question in large part depends on the source of contributions to these programs. If the source of contributions is reduced consumption or tax saving, then saving in these programs represents new household saving. However, if the source of contributions is borrowing, existing assets, or the portion of wealth that would have been saved anyway even in the absence of these programs, then tax-favored savings programs do not stimulate new private saving.

In empirically estimating the saving effects of tax-favored retirement or education savings programs, a challenging issue is how to deal with saver heterogeneity. Individuals' saving behaviors may be different due to unobservable individual-specific preferences, such as their propensities to save. For example, participants in tax-favored savings programs may have stronger tastes for saving than others and may tend to save more in all forms. Therefore, models that do not control for saver heterogeneity are likely to overestimate the saving effects of tax incentives.

In the retirement saving literature, a substantial amount of research has been devoted to estimate the impact of IRAs and 401(k) plans on household wealth. This section provides a summary of some selected studies in the retirement saving literature.

4.4.1   A Summary of Selected Studies in
the Retirement Saving Literature

Two major retirement savings programs—the IRA and the 401(k)—have been the subject of substantial public discussion and economic analysis. When first introduced in 1974, IRAs were only available to individuals not covered by an employer pension plan. There was no income restriction. Contributions were tax deductible and capped at $1,500 per year. The entire proceeds were subject to income taxes upon withdrawals. There was a 10 percent penalty on withdrawals made before the owner turned age fifty-nine and a half.

The IRAs grew rapidly after the Economic Recovery Act of 1981 raised the annual contribution limit to $2,000 and made all wage earners and their spouses eligible. However, the Tax Reform Act of 1986 reduced the tax benefits so that contributions were no longer deductible for higher-income individuals covered by a pension plan. Consequently, contributions to IRAs dropped sharply.

The 401(k) plan became popular in the 1980s and is one of the most important retirement savings programs. Sponsored by employers, only employees of firms that offer such plans are eligible to participate in a 401(k) plan. The 401(k) plan features pretax contributions, tax-free growth on earnings, and very often, employer matching contributions. The entire proceeds are subject to income taxes upon withdrawal. There is a 10 percent penalty on withdrawals made before the owner turns fifty-nine and a half. Before 1987, participants were allowed to contribute up to $30,000 per year. The Tax Reform Act of 1986 reduced the annual contribution limit to $7,000. The limit is adjusted annually to reflect inflation. The contribution limit for the 2003 tax year was $12,000.

Since the introduction of the IRA and 401(k), there has been a growing literature on the saving effects of these tax-favored retirement savings programs. The focus has been whether and to what extent IRA and 401(k) saving represents new saving. A central theme of this body of research is how to deal with saver heterogeneity. In dealing with saver heterogeneity, various methods have been used to identify savers from nonsavers, some of which are described in the following. For more detailed reviews of this literature, see Bernheim (1999), Poterba, Venti, and Wise (1996), and Engen and Gale (2000).

Comparing the Same Individuals or Similar Individuals Using Multiple Waves of Data

When panel data are available, one method to control for saver heterogeneity is to follow the same households and compare the retirement and nonretirement assets of the same households over time. This method relies on the assumption that any unobserved individual-specific preferences in tastes for saving can be "differenced out" when one calculates the change in wealth levels of the same individuals over a certain time period. Studies that have used this identification strategy include Venti and Wise (1992, 1995) and Gale and Scholz (1994). For example, Venti and Wise (1995) estimate whether IRA contributions reduce other non-IRA financial assets, using two waves of the Survey of Income and Program Participation (SIPP) data. They find that whether households contributed to IRAs had little impact on their non-IRA financial assets.

Another strategy to identify savers is to compare households with similar characteristics, using multiple waves of cross-sectional data. Using data from the 1984, 1987, and 1991 waves of the SIPP, Poterba, Venti, and Wise (1995) estimate the saving effects of retirement programs. They group households by whether households participated in IRA or 401(k) savings programs. They find that after controlling for age, income, education, and marital status, a family's IRA or 401(k) ownership or contribution status does not affect other non-IRA non-401(k) financial assets. Therefore, they conclude that contributions to IRAs or 401(k)s do not reduce other saving.

Engen and Gale (1995) use the 1987 and 1991 waves of the SIPP data and compare the wealth accumulations of the same comparison groups as Poterba, Venti, and Wise (1995). They find that, controlling for some demographics and income, 401(k)-eligible households accumulated more financial assets than other households. However, when they use a broad measure of wealth that includes net financial assets and home equity, 401(k)-eligible households did not accumulate more wealth than other households. They find similar results when comparing the wealth accumulations of IRA owners and nonowners. They argue that between 1987 and 1991, the housing value of 401(k)-eligible households rose compared with noneligible households, but the mortgage debt level of those households rose even more. As a result, the home equity of 401(k)-eligible households fell during that period. Their results suggest that 401(k)-eligible households substitute 401(k) assets for home equity.

The Eligibility Experiment

Another identification strategy, employed by Poterba, Venti, and Wise (1995) and Engelhardt (2000), relies on the assumption that the determination of 401(k) eligibility status is exogenous and uncorrelated with the observed or unobserved household characteristics.

Poterba, Venti, and Wise (1995) estimate whether 401(k) contributions offset other conventional personal financial asset saving and IRA saving, assuming the 401(k) eligibility status is independent of households' preferences for saving, given income. Using data from the 1984, 1987, and 1991 waves of SIPP, they find little substitution between 401(k) saving and other conventional personal financial asset saving. They also find very little substitution between 401(k) saving and IRA saving. They conclude that most 401(k) contributions represent net new saving.

Using the 1992 Health and Retirement Study, Engelhardt (2001) finds results that are similar to those in Poterba, Venti, and Wise (1995), when non-401(k) pension wealth is not taken into account. However, when non-401(k) pension wealth is included in the wealth measure, he finds that the total wealth levels of eligible and noneligible families are similar. Thus, his results suggest that families tend to substitute 401(k) pension wealth for non-401(k) pension wealth.

In an effort to reconcile the discrepancies in findings of different studies, Engen and Gale (2000) estimate the effects of 401(k) plans on household wealth. Their new econometric specification allows the impact of 401(k) to vary over both time and earning groups. Using data from the 1987 and 1991 waves of the SIPP, they find that 401(k) contributions by low-earning groups are more likely to represent new saving than those by high-earning groups. Because high-earning groups hold the majority of 401(k) balances, they estimate that only between 0 and 30 percent of 401(k) balances represent net additions to private saving between 1987 and 1991.

Given the wide range of estimates of the impact of retirement savings programs on household saving, which studies' results are closer to the "truth"? In a review of several studies, Hubbard and Skinner (1996) argue that the saving effects of retirement programs are likely to lie somewhere between the extremes of "no new saving" and "all new saving." Their conservative estimate is that twenty-six cents per dollar of IRA contribution represent new saving.

4.4.2 The Empirical Strategy to Control for Saver Heterogeneity in This Study

To examine the issue of saver heterogeneity in this study, table 4.5 presents some summary statistics of the respondents to the 2000 SPF by the ownership status of education savings accounts. Clearly, households who

Table 4.5   **Summary Statistics of Respondents to the 2000 TIAA-CREF SPF by Ownership of Education Saving**

	Own at Least One Education Savings Account (171 cases)	Do Not Own Any Education Savings Account (2,347 cases)
Median		
Respondent's age (years)	52.0	59.0**
Household 1999 income	$100,000	$73,000***
Household net noneducation financial assets	$346,493	$332,500
Household noneducation net worth	$473,000	$465,000
Number of children the household is financially responsible for	1	0***
Age of oldest child in the household	8.0	13.0***
Mean		
Respondent's age (years)	55.3	57.6**
Household 1999 income	$119,390	$93,995**
Household net noneducation financial assets	$680,093	$664,998
Household noneducation net worth	$892,684	$832,778
Number of children the household is financially responsible for	1.00	0.45***
Age of oldest child in the household	7.6	12.5***
Percent with a PhD degree	38.2	34.4
Percent own home	92.9	85.2***
Percent with IRA or Keogh	63.4	54.1***
Percent with supplemental pension	46.0	43.4
Percent married	82.5	65.0***

Source: Author's calculations based on the 2000 TIAA-CREF SPF data.

***Medians (means) of the two groups are statistically different at the 1 percent level.

**Medians (means) of the two groups are statistically different at the 5 percent level.

own education savings accounts have quite different economic and demographic characteristics than those who do not own. Those who own education savings accounts tend to be slightly more educated, earn higher incomes, be more likely to own a home, be married, and have an IRA or Keogh. For example, the median 1999 household income for those who own education savings accounts was $100,000, compared with $73,000 for those who do not own. The difference is statistically significant at the 1 percent level. Not surprisingly, households who own education savings accounts on average have more and younger children than those who do not own.

Table 4.5 also shows that households with education savings accounts have slightly more net worth than those without. But this does not necessarily mean that education savings programs stimulate new saving. It is possible that there may be systematic differences between households who own and do not own education saving. Therefore, analyses that do not take into account these fundamental differences are likely to attribute higher levels of wealth of the participant group to participation in education savings programs and thus lead to an upward bias in the estimates of the effectiveness of education savings programs.

Generally, panel data or multiple waves of cross-sectional data are better suited to assessing the impact of savings programs than a single wave of cross-sectional data in that they allow one to compare changes in household assets over time. However, because only one wave of the survey data is available for this study, any longitudinal "over time" comparisons are not feasible for this paper.[11] Furthermore, unlike 401(k) plans, almost anyone is eligible for 529 plans and Coverdells.[12] Therefore, there is no eligibility experiment here, either.

However, whether households have an IRA or Supplemental Retirement Annuities/Group Supplemental Retirement Annuities (SRA/GSRA) may be used to identify savers.[13] The SRAs or GSRAs are offered by TIAA-CREF and are available through employers. The SRAs or GSRAs provide tax benefits similar to those of 401(k)s. Contributions are voluntary and made with pretax dollars. Earnings grow tax-free, and the entire proceeds are subject to income taxes upon withdrawal. The annual contribution limit for an SRA or GSRA account was $12,000 in 2003.

Because participation in an IRA or an SRA/GSRA is entirely voluntary, it may be considered a reasonable signal for taste for saving. For example, Poterba, Venti, and Wise (1994, 1995) use whether households participated in an IRA or a 401(k) as a signal for taste for saving. In addition, participation in an IRA or an SRA/GSRA is also a good signal for households' familiarity with tax-favored savings vehicles. As table 4.5 shows, 63.4 percent of the households who owned education savings accounts also reported owning an IRA, compared with only 54.1 percent for households who did not own education savings accounts.

To the extent that the ownership status of an IRA or an SRA/GSRA only distinguishes savers from nonsavers to a certain degree, heterogeneity in individuals' propensities to save may still exist within the owner or nonowner group. Therefore, the propensity score approach is used to better control for unobserved saver heterogeneity. The propensity score approach is a recently developed technique often used to estimate the average

---

11. Although a previous wealth survey was conducted among the research panel members in 1996, less than 400 members responded to both the 1996 and the 2000 surveys, not enough to conduct a longitudinal comparison. See Bodie and Crane (1997) for a paper that used data from the 1996 Survey to analyze household asset allocation decisions.

12. Because there is no income requirement for 529 plans, almost anyone over eighteen can open a 529 account. For Coverdells, even though there is an income requirement, the income limit is high enough that more than 95 percent of U.S. households would be eligible.

13. For annuitants who had already annuitized part or all of their TIAA-CREF retirement assets, many of them no longer had existing contracts (including SRAs or GSRAs) with TIAA-CREF at the time of the survey. Therefore, the ownership status of SRA/GSRA for annuitants is determined by whether they ever owned a SRA or GSRA account before they annuitized their assets.

treatment effects of program participation. The propensity score approach has successfully reduced the selection bias in many studies where random experiments are not available. For example, Dehejia and Wahba (1999) use the propensity score approach to estimate the treatment effects in observational studies. Using LaLonde's (1986) composite data set of experimental treatment units and nonexperimental comparison units, they find that the propensity score approach succeeds in replicating the treatment effects of a random experimental study presented in LaLonde (1986). A detailed discussion of how the propensity score approach is applied in this study is included in section 4.5.3.

4.4.3   Empirical Model and Specifications

The empirical model to be estimated is as follows:

$$(1) \qquad W = \alpha + \beta \cdot \mathbf{X} + \gamma \cdot \text{Edsave\_balance} + \varepsilon,$$

where W is a wealth measure, and Edsave_balance is the aggregate balance of a household's education saving. $\mathbf{X}$ is a vector of household demographic variables, including the respondent's age, gender, education, marital status, household income, number of children, bequest motive, whether the respondent is an annuitant, and whether the household is covered by a defined benefit (DB) pension plan. For married respondents, the household income is the sum of the respondent's and the spouse's income. For other respondents, household income is set equal to the respondent's income. The income measure includes labor income, pension and social security income, rental income, interests, and dividends.

In the regression analysis, two wealth measures are employed as the dependent variable. The first measure is net noneducation financial assets, which is the total of noneducation retirement and nonretirement assets, including stock mutual funds, bond mutual funds, money market mutual funds, individual stocks, bonds, savings accounts, checking accounts, and certificates of deposit less personal loans, educational loans, and credit card balances. The second wealth measure is noneducation net worth, which is the sum of net noneducation financial assets and real estate equity. Real estate equity is defined as the difference between the total value of the household's primary home and other properties the household owns and the mortgage debt against these real estate properties.

4.5   Results

4.5.1   Using IRA Ownership to Identify Savers

This section presents results from estimating the model described in section 4.3. The model is estimated separately for households who own and do not own an IRA. Table 4.6 presents the summary statistics for the full re-

Table 4.6   **Summary Statistics of Dependent and Explanatory Variables**

Variable	Own IRA		Do Not Own IRA		Full Regression Sample	
	Mean	Standard Deviation	Mean	Standard Deviation	Mean	Standard Deviation
Noneducation net worth (in $000s)	1,044.482	1,063.457	543.162	839.841	803.928	994.371
Net noneducation financial assets (in $000s)	850.548	939.772	406.805	679.972	637.621	854.347
Education saving (in $000s)	1.230	9.822	0.231	1.660	0.751	7.191
Respondent's age[a]						
45–54	0.243	0.429	0.242	0.429	0.243	0.429
55–64	0.237	0.426	0.181	0.386	0.210	0.408
65 and older	0.274	0.446	0.252	0.435	0.263	0.441
Respondent is male	0.576	0.495	0.557	0.497	0.567	0.496
Household income (in $000s)	108.802	112.936	77.532	78.905	93.798	99.291
Respondent's education[b]						
Master's degree	0.388	0.488	0.329	0.470	0.360	0.480
Doctorate degree	0.340	0.474	0.316	0.465	0.329	0.470
Respondent is an annuitant	0.229	0.421	0.249	0.433	0.239	0.426
Other household variables						
Has an SRA/GSRA	0.447	0.498	0.379	0.486	0.414	0.493
Covered by a DB plan	0.348	0.476	0.298	0.458	0.324	0.468
Number of children	0.448	0.852	0.623	1.020	0.532	0.940
Bequest motive	4.711	3.269	4.890	3.330	4.797	3.298
Respondent's marital status[c]						
Single	0.157	0.364	0.201	0.401	0.178	0.383
Divorced	0.099	0.299	0.125	0.331	0.111	0.315
Widowed	0.043	0.202	0.051	0.220	0.047	0.211
Percent owning a Coverdell, a 529 savings, or a 529 prepaid account	0.071	0.258	0.046	0.210	0.059	0.236
No. of observations	658		607		1,265	

[a]The reference group consists of those respondents who are younger than forty-five.
[b]The reference group consists of those respondents with a college degree or less.
[c]The reference group consists of those respondents who are married.

gression sample and by IRA ownership. Table 4.6 indicates there are some significant differences between IRA owners and nonowners. For example, the average noneducation net worth of IRA owners is almost twice as much as that of nonowners ($1,044,482 versus $543,162), the average household income of IRA owners is much higher than that of nonowners ($108,802 versus $77,532), and a higher proportion of IRA owners have education savings accounts than nonowners (7.1 percent versus 4.6 percent).

Because wealth distribution is skewed, mean regressions are often driven by outliers. Therefore, median regressions are used instead. Heteroskedasticity in the error term is corrected by estimating the standard errors using bootstrap estimation with 200 iterations.

Using Net Noneducation Financial Assets as the Dependent Variable

Table 4.7 presents results from using net noneducation financial assets as the dependent variable. The coefficient estimates of most explanatory variables have the expected signs. Not surprisingly, net noneducation financial assets increase with household income and age for both IRA owner and nonowner groups. For example, a $1,000 increase in 1999 household income is associated with more than $3,000 increase in net noneducation financial assets. For both groups, having an SRA/GSRA account has a positive and significant impact on net noneducation financial assets. For the IRA owner group, those who also own an SRA/GSRA account have $135,517 more in assets than those who do not own an SRA/GSRA ac-

Table 4.7   **Median Regression Estimates by IRA Ownership Status (dependent variable: net noneducation financial assets)**

	Own IRA			Do Not Own IRA		
Explanatory Variable	Coefficient	Standard Error	$Pr > |t|$	Coefficient	Standard Error	$Pr > |t|$
Total education saving	5.553	2.721	0.042	10.859	10.808	0.315
Respondent's age						
45–54	198.766	58.879	0.001	103.189	26.457	0.000
55–64	422.272	67.675	0.000	311.243	61.304	0.000
65 and older	548.297	90.015	0.000	475.196	66.590	0.000
Respondent is male	129.881	43.938	0.003	18.817	20.758	0.365
Household income	3.471	0.912	0.000	3.349	0.989	0.001
Respondent's education						
Master's degree	74.682	50.279	0.138	−6.428	20.332	0.752
Doctorate degree	155.424	70.704	0.028	34.968	31.145	0.262
Respondent is an annuitant	−82.818	73.102	0.258	−141.594	60.170	0.019
Other household variables						
Has an SRA/GSRA	135.517	41.603	0.001	57.015	24.088	0.018
Covered by a DB plan	−98.677	41.094	0.017	−64.311	23.796	0.007
Number of children	3.391	33.515	0.919	7.986	11.315	0.481
Bequest motive	11.582	7.236	0.110	3.166	2.448	0.196
Respondent's marital status						
Single	53.758	64.898	0.408	57.465	33.338	0.085
Divorced	−125.311	63.726	0.050	−2.679	42.346	0.950
Widowed	87.716	107.929	0.417	−57.123	58.336	0.328
Constant	−258.595	73.870	0.000	−189.379	61.329	0.002
Pseudo R^2		0.248			0.255	
No. of observations		658			607	

Note: Standard errors are bootstrapped with 200 iterations.

count. For the IRA nonowner group, those who own a SRA/GSRA account have $57,015 more in total assets than those who do not own an SRA/GSRA account.

The coefficient estimate on the education saving variable is positive for both groups, and the estimate is statistically significant for the IRA owner group at the 5 percent level. This suggests that education saving does not crowd out other household financial assets. Specifically, for IRA owners, a $1,000 increase in education saving is associated with a $5,553 increase in net noneducation financial assets. This suggests that for IRA owners, saving with tax-favored education savings accounts seems to have a positive impact on other household financial assets.

Not surprisingly, a household's bequest motive (measured on a scale of 1 to 10) seems to be positively associated with net noneducation financial assets for both groups, and the estimate is somewhat significant for IRA owners. Moreover, households who are covered by a DB retirement plan tend to have less other financial assets than those who are not covered by a DB plan. This confirms that households who are covered by a DB plan save less in other forms. For example, among IRA owners, households who are covered by a DB plan have almost $99,000 less in noneducation financial assets than those who are not covered. Among IRA nonowners, the difference is slightly over $64,000.

Using Noneducation Net Worth as the Dependent Variable

Because there is a penalty on nonqualified withdrawals from tax-favored education savings accounts, education saving may be considered illiquid. Furthermore, education saving may be considered a long-term investment because many households are saving for their young children's future college expenses, which very often will occur many years later. To the extent that both housing and education saving may be considered illiquid and a long-term investment, households may increase education saving by taking out more home mortgage debt. Therefore, models that use wealth measures that do not include home equity may overestimate the impact of saving incentives.

To address this issue, the model is estimated using noneducation net worth (the sum of net noneducation financial assets and real estate equity) as the dependent variable. Results are presented in table 4.8. Most parameter estimates are similar to those presented in table 4.7. For both groups, a household's noneducation net worth increases with household income and age. Moreover, households who own an SRA/GSRA account have a higher level of net worth than those who do not own, while households covered by a DB plan have less net worth than those not covered by a DB plan.

The estimates of the education saving variable for both groups are still positive, yet statistically insignificant. This indicates that after real estate

Table 4.8   Median Regression Estimates by IRA Ownership Status (dependent variable: noneducation net worth)

	Own IRA			Do Not Own IRA		
Explanatory Variable	Coefficient	Standard Error	Pr > |t|	Coefficient	Standard Error	Pr > |t|
Total education saving	6.480	5.269	0.219	10.859	11.422	0.342
Respondent's age						
45–54	316.490	66.325	0.000	103.189	27.820	0.000
55–64	566.248	83.876	0.000	311.243	57.901	0.000
65 and older	731.023	90.442	0.000	475.196	69.941	0.000
Respondent is male	141.981	52.787	0.007	18.817	17.625	0.286
Household income	4.119	1.127	0.000	3.349	0.860	0.000
Respondent's education						
Master's degree	111.187	56.957	0.051	−6.428	19.727	0.745
Doctorate degree	162.612	78.517	0.039	34.968	28.265	0.217
Respondent is an annuitant	−19.477	83.469	0.816	−141.594	59.597	0.018
Other household variables						
Has an SRA/GSRA	178.298	54.753	0.001	57.015	24.482	0.020
Covered by a DB plan	−116.012	50.519	0.022	−64.311	24.223	0.008
Number of children	4.087	35.706	0.909	7.986	10.296	0.438
Bequest motive	18.604	8.809	0.035	3.166	2.588	0.222
Respondent's marital status						
Single	30.548	71.989	0.671	57.465	34.433	0.096
Divorced	−149.417	83.689	0.075	−2.679	41.091	0.948
Widowed	34.226	140.933	0.808	−57.123	58.533	0.330
Constant	−331.607	103.815	0.001	−189.379	54.773	0.001
Pseudo R^2		0.270			0.255	
No. of observations		658			607	

Note: Standard errors are bootstrapped with 200 iterations.

equity is taken into account, education saving has a negligible impact on households' noneducation net worth, that is, education saving does not seem to offset other household assets.

4.5.2   Using the Ownership Status of SRA/GSRA to Identify Savers

This section presents results from estimating the model separately for SRA/GSRA owners and nonowners. Again, two wealth measures are used as the dependent variable. Table 4.9 presents the summary statistics for the full regression sample and by SRA/GSRA ownership. Interestingly, the proportions of SRA/GSRA owners and nonowners who have education savings accounts are almost identical (5.9 percent). Moreover, the mean value of total education saving is higher for SRA nonowners than for owners ($949 versus $471). This indicates that the saver and nonsaver groups defined by the ownership status of SRA/GSRAs are somewhat different from those defined by the ownership status of IRAs.

Table 4.9   **Summary Statistics of Dependent and Explanatory Variables**

Variable	Own SRA/GSRA		Do Not Own SRA/GSRA		Full Regression Sample	
	Mean	Standard Deviation	Mean	Standard Deviation	Mean	Standard Deviation
Noneducation net worth (in $000s)	924.168	1,092.158	718.900	910.182	803.928	994.371
Net noneducation financial assets (in $000s)	743.893	939.874	562.471	780.249	637.621	854.347
Education saving (in $000s)	0.471	3.623	0.949	8.885	0.751	7.191
Respondent's age[a]						
45–54	0.250	0.433	0.238	0.426	0.243	0.429
55–64	0.198	0.399	0.219	0.414	0.210	0.408
65 and older	0.225	0.418	0.290	0.454	0.263	0.441
Respondent is male	0.544	0.499	0.583	0.493	0.567	0.496
Household income (in $000s)	100.456	99.463	89.089	98.966	93.798	99.291
Respondent's education[b]						
Master's degree	0.355	0.479	0.363	0.481	0.360	0.480
Doctorate degree	0.336	0.473	0.324	0.468	0.329	0.470
Respondent is an annuitant	0.158	0.365	0.296	0.457	0.239	0.426
Other household variables						
Has an IRA	0.561	0.497	0.491	0.500	0.520	0.500
Covered by a DB plan	0.323	0.468	0.325	0.469	0.324	0.468
Number of children	0.529	0.938	0.534	0.942	0.532	0.940
Bequest motive	4.908	3.281	4.748	3.310	4.797	3.298
Respondent's marital status[c]						
Single	0.179	0.384	0.177	0.382	0.178	0.383
Divorced	0.105	0.307	0.116	0.321	0.111	0.315
Widowed	0.038	4.821	0.053	0.223	0.047	0.211
Percent owning a Coverdell, a 529 savings, or a 529 prepaid account	0.0592	0.2361	0.0594	0.2365	0.0593	0.2363
No. of observations	524		741		1,265	

[a]The reference group consists of those respondents who are younger than forty-five.
[b]The reference group consists of those respondents with a college degree or less.
[c]The reference group consists of those respondents who are married.

Table 4.10 presents results from using net noneducation financial assets as the dependent variable. The coefficient estimates of many explanatory variables are similar to those presented in table 4.7. For both SRA/GSRA owner and nonowner groups, net noneducation financial assets increase with income and age. A $1,000 increase in 1999 household income is associated with a $4,049 increase in net noneducation financial assets for the owner group, and a $2,860 increase in net noneducation financial assets for the nonowner group.

Among SRA/GSRA owners, households who own an IRA have $141,057

Table 4.10   **Median Regression Estimates by SRA/GSRA Ownership Status (dependent variable: net noneducation financial assets)**

Explanatory Variable	Own SRA/GSRA			Do Not Own SRA/GSRA		
	Coefficient	Standard Error	Pr > $\lvert t \rvert$	Coefficient	Standard Error	Pr > $\lvert t \rvert$
Total education saving	19.461	12.759	0.128	5.704	2.586	0.028
Respondent's age						
45–54	174.266	50.506	0.001	119.547	28.422	0.000
55–64	526.887	91.981	0.000	298.150	51.675	0.000
65 and older	808.783	154.705	0.000	449.203	60.519	0.000
Respondent is male	97.545	38.312	0.011	23.441	18.987	0.217
Household income	4.049	1.382	0.004	2.860	0.772	0.000
Respondent's education						
Master's degree	13.354	40.578	0.742	39.874	25.280	0.115
Doctorate degree	99.337	73.087	0.175	82.344	32.122	0.011
Respondent is an annuitant	−166.672	144.350	0.249	−102.114	50.565	0.044
Other household variables						
Has an IRA	141.057	39.432	0.000	133.961	25.738	0.000
Covered by a DB plan	−31.770	48.722	0.515	−85.668	24.119	0.000
Number of children	−6.450	22.351	0.773	0.899	13.962	0.949
Bequest motive	5.619	6.272	0.371	7.705	2.880	0.008
Respondent's marital status						
Single	80.574	60.783	0.186	36.832	39.108	0.347
Divorced	−26.046	88.076	0.768	−56.097	35.198	0.111
Widowed	−51.430	157.248	0.744	−38.469	57.526	0.504
Constant	−297.439	108.130	0.006	−185.444	48.093	0.000
Pseudo R^2	0.294			0.276		
No. of observations	524			741		

Note: Standard errors are bootstrapped with 200 iterations.

more in net noneducation financial assets than those who do not own an IRA. Among SRA/GSRA nonowners, households who own an IRA have $133,961 more in net noneducation financial assets than those who do not own an IRA.

For both SRA/GSRA owner and nonowner groups, having a DB pension plan is negatively associated with net noneducation financial assets, and the estimate is statistically significant for SRA nonowners.

Total education saving is positively associated with net noneducation financial assets, and the estimate is statistically significant for SRA nonowners and somewhat significant for SRA owners. This suggests that saving with education savings accounts seem to stimulate other household saving for both groups.

Table 4.11 presents results from using noneducation net worth as the dependent variable. Table 4.11 suggests that when real estate equity is taken into account, total education saving is positively associated with noneducation net worth, and the estimates are statistically significant for both

Table 4.11   Median Regression Estimates by SRA/GSRA Ownership Status (dependent variable: noneducation net worth)

Explanatory Variable	Own SRA/GSRA			Do Not Own SRA/GSRA		
	Coefficient	Standard Error	$Pr > \lvert t \rvert$	Coefficient	Standard Error	$Pr > \lvert t \rvert$
Total education saving	25.411	15.320	0.098	6.190	2.738	0.024
Respondent's age						
45–54	281.438	60.139	0.000	153.994	39.615	0.000
55–64	630.262	89.600	0.000	397.628	56.849	0.000
65 and older	942.358	149.970	0.000	574.394	63.820	0.000
Respondent is male	98.371	43.115	0.023	39.231	29.331	0.181
Household income	4.802	1.489	0.001	4.207	1.135	0.000
Respondent's education						
Master's degree	19.526	49.788	0.695	68.008	31.335	0.030
Doctorate degree	142.515	78.821	0.071	98.484	43.687	0.024
Respondent is an annuitant	–78.273	128.859	0.544	–96.857	57.587	0.093
Other household variables						
Has an IRA	180.751	51.217	0.000	172.117	34.098	0.000
Covered by a DB plan	–27.206	58.012	0.639	–116.607	30.960	0.000
Number of children	3.490	25.240	0.890	–7.758	18.330	0.672
Bequest motive	12.680	7.139	0.076	7.625	3.928	0.053
Respondent's marital status						
Single	118.639	72.100	0.100	6.973	51.340	0.892
Divorced	–61.597	88.419	0.486	–64.798	47.706	0.175
Widowed	–84.079	191.382	0.661	–115.048	68.197	0.092
Constant	–387.224	122.123	0.002	–227.520	68.632	0.001
Pseudo R^2		0.3239			0.2903	
No. of observations		524			741	

Note: Standard errors are bootstrapped with 200 iterations.

SRA owner and nonowner groups. For example, a $1,000 increase in education saving is associated with a $6,190 increase in noneducation net worth for the nonowner group.

4.5.3 Using the Propensity Score Method to Control for Saver Heterogeneity

As mentioned earlier, the saver and nonsaver groups defined by IRA ownership are somewhat different from those defined by the SRA/GSRA ownership. This suggests that the ownership status of IRA or SRA/GSRA controls for saver heterogeneity only to a certain degree, and potential unobserved heterogeneity in individuals' propensities to save might still exist within the owner or nonowner group.

One way to better control for unobserved saver heterogeneity is to use the propensity score approach. This section presents results from using the propensity score approach (as employed by Dehejia and Wahba 1999) to control for saver heterogeneity.

In this study, the propensity score approach is applied in the following steps: (1) a probit model is used to estimate the propensity of households owning an education savings account, conditional on their observed characteristics, including many of the explanatory variables described in section 4.4.3. The coefficient estimates of the model are then used to predict the likelihood of households using these accounts; (2) households are sorted from lowest to highest by their predicted likelihood of using education savings accounts; (3) households are stratified into several strata based on their predicted propensities to have an education savings account. The strata are chosen so that the covariates are "balanced" within each stratum, that is, there are no statistical differences (at the 5 percent level) in means of covariates between households who have and those who do not have an education savings account.[14] In order to estimate the impact of education saving on household net worth, a reasonable number of households with education savings accounts are needed for each stratum. Therefore, strata with too few numbers of observations (less than five) with education savings accounts are discarded. The discarded strata are those in the bottom 40 percent of the predicted propensity score distribution; and (4) within-stratum robust regressions are run to estimate the impact of education saving on other household assets.

The propensity score approach greatly reduces saver heterogeneity within each stratum in that, by design, households who do and those who do not have an education savings account have similar predicted propensities to use an education savings account and similar covariates. In other words, there is no systematic difference between those who have and those who do not have an education savings account within a stratum. Therefore, the propensity score approach should provide reliable estimates.

Table 4.12 presents results from robust regressions within each of the remaining five propensity score strata. Table 4.12 indicates total education saving has a positive and significant impact on other household net worth for the top two propensity score strata (strata 4 and 5). Moreover, the estimates are consistent with those obtained from using IRA or SRA/GSRA ownership to identify savers. For example, estimates for stratum 5 indicate that a $1,000 increase in education saving is associated with a $7,000 increase in noneducation net worth. Because stratum 5 has the highest proportion of households who own education savings accounts, estimates for stratum 5 may be most reliable. For propensity score strata 1–3, total

14. To ensure a reasonable number of households with education savings accounts in each stratum, households who do not own an education savings account and have a predicted propensity score (likelihood) higher than the maximum or lower than the minimum predicted propensity score for those who do own are discarded. The remaining households are divided into ten strata. For each stratum, *t*-tests are run to compare the means of covariates between households who have and those who do not have an education savings account. If there is "imbalance" in a stratum, that is, the means of one or more covariates are statistically different between the two groups, then the stratum is fine-tuned until "balance" is achieved.

Table 4.12   **Robust Regression Estimates Within Propensity Score Stratum (dependent variable: noneducation net worth)**

Explanatory Variable	Stratum 1	Stratum 2	Stratum 3	Stratum 4	Stratum 5
Total education saving	−0.800	33.378	−1.630	43.720	6.987
	(8.886)	(22.766)	(3.227)	(5.792)	(1.612)
Respondent's age					
45–54	137.424	284.086	131.981	514.630	117.176
	(116.349)	(147.428)	(128.090)	(120.373)	(61.603)
55–64	334.479	505.351	420.808	1,000.985	574.172
	(112.218)	(146.733)	(153.895)	(175.217)	(139.212)
65 and older	568.080	1,122.364	889.738	1,602.332	315.813
	(119.067)	(145.528)	(163.574)	(189.815)	(297.402)
Respondent is male	183.186	−94.846	214.522	166.300	97.101
	(65.856)	(90.872)	(111.123)	(84.128)	(59.423)
Household income	7.492	2.265	6.192	1.171	4.156
	(0.466)	(0.245)	(0.870)	(0.282)	(0.362)
Respondent's education					
Master's degree	−52.866	−27.975	−76.745	133.015	9.418
	(75.267)	(100.989)	(122.333)	(90.734)	(71.019)
Doctorate degree	90.631	145.729	−233.562	24.053	26.835
	(77.299)	(104.068)	(124.768)	(105.587)	(71.649)
Respondent is an annuitant	10.668	−359.587	−149.138	−812.914	1,172.186
	(88.019)	(118.841)	(144.527)	(184.435)	(369.222)
Other household variables					
Has an IRA	204.630	237.669	496.727	191.161	116.935
	(86.250)	(112.528)	(165.217)	(121.449)	(73.718)
Has an SRA/GSRA	171.909	184.538	168.087	77.488	117.145
	(62.528)	(76.265)	(92.100)	(76.583)	(54.699)
Covered by a DB plan	−132.100	22.728	−110.346	−87.377	−90.475
	(64.673)	(79.958)	(94.594)	(74.608)	(54.713)
Number of children	100.496	68.385	105.115	60.098	15.151
	(101.888)	(85.665)	(94.173)	(56.592)	(40.904)
Bequest motive	28.097	18.675	12.485	22.126	−4.947
	(19.915)	(23.369)	(19.704)	(18.070)	(10.231)
Respondent's marital status					
Single	−35.388	−89.058	dropped	157.695	dropped
	(144.566)	(214.701)		(353.224)	
Divorced	−85.597	−49.300	−241.135	dropped	315.586
	(154.525)	(235.296)	(376.450)		(304.061)
Widowed	48.988	133.810	dropped	dropped	dropped
	(185.194)	(536.131)			
Constant	−664.085	−264.749	−625.249	−365.156	−245.880
	(151.256)	(206.924)	(214.536)	(189.813)	(149.174)
F statistics	30.15	15.64	14.99	31.03	21.30
No. of observations	253	195	104	96	125
No. of observations with an education savings account	5	10	15	12	25

Notes: Standard errors are in parentheses. The first-stage probit model includes the following covariates: a dummy variable for household owning an IRA, age, age squared, the number of children in the household, bequest motive, a dummy variable indicating that the respondent is married, and an interaction term of the number of children and bequest motive. Results from the probit model are not sensitive to the addition of other covariates.

education saving does not seem to have a significant impact on other household net worth.

As a sensitivity analysis, the propensity score approach is applied to only households with children (365 cases, slightly less than one-third of the full regression sample). Households are sorted into four strata based on their estimated propensity to use an education savings account. The lowest stratum is discarded due to the low number of households with an education saving account (three cases).

Table 4.13 presents the results using the subsample of households with children. Table 4.13 reiterates the findings in table 4.12. That is, total education saving has a positive and significant impact on other household net worth for high-propensity score strata (strata 2 and 3). Moreover, the estimates are very similar to those in table 4.12. For example, estimates for stratum 3 suggest that a $1,000 increase in education saving is associated with a $6,666 increase in noneducation net worth. This further confirms that the propensity score approach provides reliable and robust estimates. The estimates are especially robust for high-propensity score strata.

4.6   Concluding Remarks

Whether savings incentives increase total private and public saving has been the subject of an ongoing debate. In the last two decades, a substantial amount of research has been devoted to address this issue, with a focus on the saving effects of retirement savings programs on total household saving.

In recent years, the federal government has introduced two education savings programs in support of saving for education expenses. As in the case of retirement savings programs, an important public policy issue is whether these education savings programs stimulate new saving. Because these education savings programs are relatively new, data are not readily available. The lack of data makes it difficult to empirically estimate the saving effects of these education savings programs.

Using wealth data from a survey of TIAA-CREF participants, this paper attempts to estimate the impact of education savings programs on other household assets. Two strategies are used to control for saver heterogeneity in the analysis. The first strategy uses the ownership status of an IRA or a SRA/GSRA as a signal for household's taste for saving. The second strategy uses the propensity score method to control for saver heterogeneity.

Using IRA or SRA/GSRA ownership to identify savers from nonsavers, median regression results suggest that education saving does not offset other household assets. In many cases, education saving seems to stimulate other household saving, and the estimates are significant. Results from the propensity score method confirm these findings. Specifically, education saving is positively associated with other household assets for households with higher propensities to use education savings accounts. These findings

Table 4.13 **Robust Regression Estimates Within Propensity Score Stratum Including Only Households with Children (dependent variable: non-education net worth)**

Explanatory Variable	Stratum 1	Stratum 2	Stratum 3
Total education saving	19.105	63.864	6.666
	(29.630)	(13.440)	(1.469)
Respondent's age			
45–54	120.958	182.047	144.011
	(133.670)	(133.913)	(72.945)
55–64	552.632	278.244	dropped
	(253.275)	(189.202)	
65 and older	1,211.519	dropped	dropped
	(357.479)		
Respondent is male	−83.223	135.956	51.762
	(93.673)	(74.563)	(68.098)
Household income	3.372	1.191	4.330
	(0.920)	(0.220)	(0.357)
Respondent's education			
Master's degree	44.676	185.003	−0.595
	(114.485)	(87.852)	(80.848)
Doctorate degree	39.580	87.583	18.004
	(112.901)	(95.765)	(77.512)
Respondent is an annuitant	dropped	1,412.520	dropped
		(369.338)	
Other household variables			
Has an IRA	355.351	406.870	117.019
	(205.025)	(141.415)	(88.270)
Has an SRA/GSRA	194.686	−22.755	99.548
	(99.469)	(65.994)	(58.624)
Covered by a DB plan	−54.315	−68.183	−107.001
	(103.928)	(72.293)	(56.576)
Number of children	−46.238	−59.692	57.746
	(65.245)	(44.004)	(40.719)
Bequest motive	12.757	−8.072	1.060
	(18.554)	(15.219)	(10.168)
Respondent's marital status			
Single	−419.492	289.475	dropped
	(298.516)	(360.191)	
Divorced	−75.292	dropped	dropped
	(261.743)		
Widowed	dropped	dropped	dropped
Constant	−41.174	114.553	−346.402
	(274.015)	(153.946)	(120.001)
F statistics	9.25	19.42	23.90
No. of observations	60	118	91
No. of observations with an education savings account	9	10	30

Notes: Standard errors are in parentheses. The first-stage probit model includes the following covariates: a dummy variable for household owning an IRA, age, age squared, household income, respondent's education, the number of children in the household, bequest motive, a dummy variable indicating the respondent is married, and an interaction term of the number of children and bequest motive. Results from the probit model are not sensitive to the addition of other covariates.

are consistent with those of some studies in the 401(k) literature (Poterba, Venti, and Wise 1995; Venti and Wise 1995) that suggest retirement programs stimulate new household saving.

It is not surprising that this study finds no evidence of households shifting assets from other accounts to tax-favored education savings accounts. Such shifting behavior may be deterred because if withdrawals for education savings accounts are not used for college expenses, a 10 percent penalty is imposed on earnings in addition to regular income tax. If an individual withdraws money from an education savings account for noneducation purposes, the after-tax after-penalty asset accumulation could be easily trumped by that from a tax efficient mutual fund, assuming the same rates of return for the mutual fund and the education savings account. Therefore, if an individual anticipates that there is a high probability that withdrawals will not be used for education purposes, he or she would be unlikely to use an education savings account.

It is worth noting that the data used in this study are drawn from a survey of a nonrepresentative sample of TIAA-CREF participants. The sample of this study is quite different from the general population. One difference is that the sample of this study is much wealthier than the general population. Therefore, this study does not address the question of whether these education savings programs encourage less affluent households to save for college. Nevertheless, this study provides a useful first look at the saving effects of education savings programs. As mentioned earlier, the sample of this study is particularly suited to examining whether education saving offsets other household assets because shuffling will more likely occur for wealthy households simply due to the fact that they have more assets to shift around.

Also of considerable interest are the potential institutional responses to tax-favored education savings programs. Some researchers argue that these savings programs may have a long-term impact on admission policies. For example, Olivas (2001) argues that some higher education institutions may predicate admissions on ability to pay. There is also concern that these programs may also present an opportunity for some institutions to raise tuition even more.

As 529 plans and Coverdells continue to grow, new data may become available. With new and hopefully better data, alternative and possibly more robust methods may be used to control for saver heterogeneity. Such methods may include using panel data to compare changes in household assets for those who own and those who do not own education savings accounts. State variation in 529 plans may be used to examine the impact of plan features on individuals' saving behaviors. Another area for future research is the impact of education savings programs on national saving, which this paper does not address.

Appendix

Table 4A.1   Minimum and Maximum Account Balance Limits in 529 Savings Plans (as of August 2003)

State	Program	Initial Year of Operation	Minimum Lump-Sum Contribution	Minimum Automatic Payment	Current Lifetime Account Balance Limit
Alabama	The Higher Education 529 Fund	2002	$250 per portfolio	$25 per month	$269,000
Alaska	University of Alaska College Savings Plan	1991, revised May 2001	$250	$50	$250,000
Arizona	Arizona Family College Savings Program	1999	$20 to $500 per mutual fund	$20 to $500 per mutual fund	$187,000
Arkansas	GIFT College Investing Plan	1999	$250 initial and $50 subsequent	$250 initial and $50 subsequent	$245,000
California	Golden State Scholar-Share Trust	1999	$25	$15 for payroll deductions	$267,580
Colorado	Scholars Choice	1999	$25 initial and $15 subsequent	None for payroll deductions	$235,000
Connecticut	Connecticut Higher Education Trust	1997	$25	$15 for payroll deductions	$235,000
Delaware	Delaware College Investment Plan	1998	$500 initial and $50 subsequent	$500 initial and $50 subsequent	$250,000
District of Columbia	DC College Savings Plan	2002	$100 initial and $25 subsequent	$15 for payroll deductions, $25 for bank transfers	$260,000
Florida	Florida College Investment Plan	2002	$25	$15	$283,000
Georgia	Georgia Higher Education Savings Plan	2002	$25	$15 for payroll deductions	$235,000
Hawaii	Tuition-EDGE	2002	$15 per investment option	$15 for investment option	$297,000
Idaho	Idaho College Savings Program	2001	$25	$15 for payroll deductions	$235,000
Illinois	Bright Start College Savings Program	2000	$25 initial and $15 subsequent	None for payroll deductions	$235,000
Indiana	College Choice 529 Plan	1997	$50 initial and $25 subsequent	$50 initial and $25 subsequent	$236,750
Iowa	College Savings Iowa	1998	$50 per year	$50 per year	$239,000
Kansas	Learning Quest Education Savings Program	2000	$500 for residents ($2,500 for nonresidents)	$25 per month for residents ($50 per month for nonresidents)	$235,000
Kentucky	Education Savings Plan Trust	1990	$25	$15 for payroll deductions	$235,000
Louisiana	Louisiana START	1997	$10 initial and $10 subsequent	$10 initial and $10 subsequent	$182,440 (contribution limit)

(continued)

Table 4A.1 (continued)

State	Program	Initial Year of Operation	Minimum Lump-Sum Contribution	Minimum Automatic Payment	Current Lifetime Account Balance Limit
Maine	NextGen College Investing Plan	1999	$250	$50 per month	$250,000
Maryland	Maryland College Investment Plan	2001	$250	$25 per month	$250,000
Massachusetts	U. Fund College Investing Plan	1999	$1,000	$50	$250,000
Michigan	Michigan Education Savings Program	2000	$25	$15	$235,000
Minnesota	Minnesota College Savings Plan	2001	$25	$15	$235,000
Mississippi	Mississippi Affordable College Savings (MACS) Program	2001	$25	$15	$235,000
Missouri	Missouri Saving for Tuition (MO$T) Program	1999	$25	$15	$235,000
Montana	Montana Family Education Savings Program	1998	$250	$25 for payroll deductions, $100/month or $250/quarter for bank transfers	$262,000
Nebraska	College Savings Plan of Nebraska	2001	None	None	$250,000
Nevada	American Skandia College Savings Plan	2001	$250	$50	$250,000
New Hampshire	UNIQUE College Investing Plan	1998	$1,000	$50 per month	$250,000
New Jersey	NJBEST Educational Savings Trust	1998	$25 per month and $300 per year, until account reaches $1,200	$25 per month and $300 per year, until account reaches $1,200	$305,000
New Mexico	Education Plan's College Saving Program of NM	2000	$250 initial and $100 subsequent	$25 per month	$294,000
New York	New York's College Savings Program	1998	$25	$15	$100,000 in total contributions or $235,000 in account balances, whichever is reached first

State	Plan	Year	Minimum Contribution	Minimum Contribution	Maximum
North Carolina	North Carolina's National College Savings Program	1998	$5	$5	$276,046
North Dakota	College SAVE	2001	$25 initial ($300 for the first year)	$25 per month	$269,000
Ohio	Ohio College Advantage Savings Plan	1989	$15	$15	$245,000
Oklahoma	Oklahoma College Savings Plan	2000	$25	$15 for payroll deductions	$235,000
Oregon	Oregon College Savings Plan	2001	$250 initial and $25 subsequent	$25	$250,000
Pennsylvania	TAP 529 Investment Plan	2002	$1,000 initial and $50 subsequent	$1,000 initial and $50 subsequent	$290,000
Rhode Island	CollegeBoundFund	1998	$1,000 initial and $50 subsequent	$1,000 initial and $50 subsequent	$301,550
South Carolina	Future Scholar 529 College Savings Plan	2002	$250 initial and $50 subsequent	$50 per month for payroll deductions	$265,000
South Dakota	CollegeAccess 529	2002	$250	$50 per month	$305,000
Tennessee	Tennessee BEST Savings Plan	2000	$25	$15 for payroll deductions	$235,000
Texas	Tomorrow's College Investment Plan	2002	$25 per portfolio	$25 per portfolio	$257,460
Utah	Utah Educational Savings Plan (UESP) Trust	1997	$25	$25	$280,000
Vermont	Vermont Higher Education Savings Plan	1999	$25	$15 for payroll deductions	$240,100
Virginia	Virginia Education Savings Trust (VEST)	1999	$25 ($250 minimum for first year)	$25 ($250 minimum for first year)	$250,000
West Virginia	Smart 529 Plan	2002	$100 initial and $15 subsequent	$15	$265,620
Wisconsin	EDVEST Wisconsin College Savings Program	1997	$250	$25 per month	$246,000
Wyoming	Wyoming College Achievement Plan	2000	$250 initial for residents ($1,000 for nonresidents) and $50 subsequent	$250 initial for residents ($1,000 for nonresidents) and $50 subsequent	$245,000

Sources: Information on the web sites www.collegesavings.org, www.savingforcollege.com, and program disclosure booklets.

References

Bernheim, B. Douglas. 1999. Taxation and saving. NBER Working Paper no. 7061. Cambridge, Mass.: National Bureau of Economic Research, March.

Bodie, Zvi, and Dwight Crane. 1997. Personal investing: Advice, theory, and evidence. *Financial Analysts Journal* 53:13–23.

College Board. 2002. *Trends in college pricing 2002.* New York: College Entrance Examination Board.

Dehejia, Rajeev H., and Sadek Wahba. 1999. Causal effects in non-experimental studies: Re-evaluating the evaluation of training programs. *Journal of the American Statistical Association* 94:1053–1062.

Engelhardt, Gary. 2001. Have 401(k)s raised household raving? Evidence from the Health and Retirement Study. Aging Studies Program Paper no. 24. Syracuse, N.Y.: Syracuse University, Maxwell School of Citizenship and Public Affairs, Center for Policy Research.

Engen, Eric M., and William G. Gale. 1995. Debt, taxes and the effects of 401(k) plans on household wealth accumulation. American Enterprise Institute and the Brookings Institute. Unpublished Manuscript.

———. 2000. The effects of 401(k) plans on household wealth: Differences across earnings groups. NBER Working Paper no. 8032. Cambridge, Mass.: National Bureau of Economic Research, December.

Engen, Eric M., William G. Gale, and John Karl Scholz. 1996. The illusory effects of saving incentives on saving. *Journal of Economic Perspectives* 10:113–138.

Gale, William G., and John Karl Scholz. 1994. IRAs and household saving. *American Economic Review* 84 (December): 1233–1260.

Hubbard, R. Glenn, and Jonathan S. Skinner. 1996. Assessing the effectiveness of saving incentives. *Journal of Economic Perspectives* 10 (Fall): 73–90.

LaLonde, Robert J. 1986. Evaluating the econometric evaluations of training programs. *American Economic Review* 76 (September): 604–620.

Ma, Jennifer, and Douglas Fore. 2002. Saving for college with 529 plans and other options: An update. *Research Dialogue* 70 (January): 1–20.

Ma, Jennifer, Mark Warshawsky, John Ameriks, and Julia Blohm. 2001. An economic approach to setting the contribution limits in qualified state-sponsored tuition savings programs. *Proceedings of the Ninety-Third Annual Conference on Taxation 2000,* 107–115. Washington, D.C.: National Tax Association.

Madrian, Brigitte C., and Dennis F. Shea. 2001. The power of suggestion: Inertia in 401(k) participation and savings behavior. *Quarterly Journal of Economics* 116 (November): 1149–1187.

Olivas, Michael A. 2001. College savings plans: Second generation progress and problems. *Proceedings of the Ninety-Third Annual Conference on Taxation 2000,* 90–95. Washington, D.C.: National Tax Association.

Poterba, James M., Steven F. Venti, and David A. Wise. 1994. 401(k) plans and tax-deferred saving. In *Studies in the economics of aging,* ed. David A. Wise, 105–142. Chicago: University of Chicago Press.

———. 1995. Do 401(k) contributions crowd out other personal saving? *Journal of Public Economics* 58 (September): 1–32.

———. 1996. How retirement saving programs increase saving? *Journal of Economic Perspectives* 10 (Fall): 91–112.

U.S. Department of Education. 2003. *Digest of education statistics 2002.* Washington, D.C.: GPO.

Venti, Steven F., and David A. Wise. 1992. Government policy and personal retire-

ment saving. In *Tax policy and the economy,* ed. James M. Poterba, 1–41. Cambridge, Mass.: MIT Press.
———. 1995. Individual response to a retirement saving program: Results from U.S. panel data. *Ricerche Economiche* 49 (September): 235–254.

Comment   Harvey S. Rosen

In this paper, Ma analyzes the savings effects of two programs for tax-favored saving to meet college expenses, the 529 plan and the Coverdell Education Savings Account. The details of the plans are quite complicated, including the criteria for allowable expenditures from the accounts, penalties for using the funds for nonapproved expenditures, eligibility requirements, and interactions with other programs for subsidizing higher education such as the Lifetime Learning Credit. (See Ma's table 4.1.) For purposes of thinking about their impact on saving, though, it probably makes sense to think of these programs simply as versions of the Roth IRA. The key attributes are that contributions into the accounts are nondeductible; the contributions grow at the before-tax rate of return; and neither the contributions nor the returns are taxed upon (qualified) withdrawal. Understanding that these accounts are basically Roth IRAs is important because we can then use the substantial literature on the savings effects of IRAs to help us think about the approach taken in this paper.

Ma notes that in trying to determine the impact of education IRAs (henceforth EIRAs) on saving, a challenging issue is how to deal with saver heterogeneity. It is challenging indeed! Much of the voluminous and sometimes contentious literature on IRAs and saving has focused on the difficulties involved in figuring out whether IRAs actually induce more saving, or whether households with IRAs save more only because they have particularly strong tastes for saving. To deal with this problem, Ma assumes that whether households have an IRA account can be used to identify people with strong preferences for saving. She estimates her econometric model separately for those with and without IRAs. In effect, then, she tries to find out whether EIRAs increase saving among those who are already high savers (as measured by having an IRA). The key result that emerges from the regression analysis is that education saving is positively correlated with noneducation financial assets, but the estimates are not statistically different from zero. This suggests that saving with education saving vehicles seems to have a negligible impact on other household financial assets.

Harvey S. Rosen is John L. Weinberg Professor of Economics at Princeton University, and a research associate of the National Bureau of Economic Research.

The use of IRA holdings to classify people as savers is critical to the research design. It is worth emphasizing the possible problem with this strategy that Ma herself notes—even within the set of IRA holders, there may be unobservable differences with respect to tastes for saving. Given that the data are from a single cross section, there simply isn't much to be done about it. But a special caution might be appropriate given that the data are from the year 2000. During the early 1980s, one could plausibly have made the case that IRAs were a good proxy for preferences for saving. But in recent years, some people have been using IRAs as repositories for pensions from previous jobs—when people change jobs, they may roll their pensions into IRA accounts. I do not have any figures on how important this phenomenon is, but it certainly exists. For this reason, I am inclined to put more weight on the use of SRA/GSRA ownership status as a classificatory variable than on IRA ownership status.

Another issue relates to how representative the sample is. Of course, members of TIAA-CREF are not typical of the population. But the analysis sample is probably not representative even of the members of TIAA-CREF. Sixty thousand randomly selected members were originally asked to participate in the survey in 1993. Originally 9,847 responded; by 2000 this figure was 9,234. Of these, 2,793 gave usable responses. Additional observations were lost due to the fact that certain components of wealth were missing from some observations. The basic regressions ended up including 917 cases. Now, my view is that this is a very interesting data set and that it is certainly worth exploiting. Still, one must be sensitive to the fact that the results might not generalize to the population as a whole. In this context, I found puzzling Ma's assertion that the sample was nonrepresentative in a useful way because its members were likely to be particularly focused on the costs of college. Why is this an advantage? After all, even after the program has been up and running for a number of years, information about it still won't be perfect.

To conclude, I think that Ma's self-assessment of this paper is right on target when she describes her study as an important first step in examining the impact of these saving programs. This leads naturally to the question of what the next steps should be. I would be particularly interested in seeing an estimate of the impact of EIRAs on social saving, that is, the sum of public and private saving. If Ma's conclusion is correct, then education IRAs increase private saving. But they also reduce tax revenues, which lowers public saving, other things being the same. What is the net effect? That is a key question for assessing the impact on capital formation.

5

How Financial Aid
Affects Persistence

Eric Bettinger

The Pell Grant program is the largest means-tested financial assistance available to postsecondary students across the United States. Students from all types of degree granting postsecondary institutions can apply for Pell Grants. In 2000–2001, the federal government awarded almost $8 billion in Pell Grants among more than 3.8 million students, roughly one-third of all college students (College Board 2001). President Bush's 2003 budget allocates over $10.9 billion dollars for an estimated 4.5 million Pell Grant recipients (U.S. Department of Education 2002), potentially representing a 32.4 percent increase in the number of students receiving Pell Grants since the 1990–1991 school year. Yet despite this continued expansion of the Pell Grant, researchers have only limited evidence on the causal effects of these grants.

Most Pell Grant-related research focuses on the effects of Pell Grants on enrollment decisions, specifically focusing on initial enrollment and choice amongst colleges (see Kane 1999; Ehrenberg and Sherman 1984; Leslie and Brinkman 1987; Seftor and Turner 2002). However, there is surprisingly little research measuring the causal effect of Pell Grants on student outcomes in college (e.g., persistence, graduation). Regardless of whether Pell Grants affect initial enrollment patterns, Pell Grants may independently affect student outcomes.

Moreover, studying the effects of need-based aid on student outcomes may also be important since Pell Grant-eligible students are more likely to

Eric Bettinger is assistant professor of economics at Case Western Reserve University, and a faculty research associate of the National Bureau of Economic Research.

Special thanks go to Rob Sheehan and Andy Lechler for helpful comments and for providing the data. I am also grateful for comments from David Cooper, Jim Rebitzer, Bridget Long, Jon Guryan, and especially Caroline Hoxby. All errors are my own.

be on the margin of "stopping out."[1] At Ohio four-year colleges in 1999–2000, 18 percent of full-time freshmen who were *not* eligible for Pell Grants withdrew from college by the next year, while 28 percent of students who were eligible for a Pell Grant did not enroll the following year. It is an open question whether Pell Grants and other need-based aid programs affect these margins. This paper attempts to resolve these questions. Using unique student data from Ohio, this paper measures the causal relationship between need-based aid and student retention.

A study of the effects of need-based aid on student retention may be of interest to both policymakers and educational researchers. As Sarah Turner argues in her chapter in this volume, policymakers have often paid more attention to improving student access to college rather than improving student retention once in college. However, as college enrollment rates continue to increase while completion rates do not, both policymakers and researchers have begun focusing more heavily on indicators of student retention (e.g., DesJardins, Ahlburg, and McCall 1999; St. John, Hu, and Tuttle 2000; St. John, Hu, and Weber 2000), and the relationship between financial need and persistence is central to many of these studies (e.g., DesJardins, Ahlburg, and McCall 2002; St. John, Musoba, and Simmons 2003).

There are a number of reasons why more research has not investigated the effects of Pell Grants on student collegiate outcomes. One reason is that researchers have difficulty distinguishing between the effects of family characteristics and the effects of Pell Grants. Pell Grants are a means-tested program. Comparisons between Pell Grant recipients and non-Pell Grant recipients (e.g., Wei and Carroll 2002) may be difficult to interpret since Pell Grant recipients are poorer and may be more likely to drop out, even in the absence of need-based aid. To correct for such bias, researchers must sufficiently control for family characteristics.

Additionally, identifying the effects of Pell Grants is difficult since much of the variation in the size of students' Pell Grants is correlated with students' college enrollment decisions. For example, college choice and the size of a student's Pell Grant are directly connected. Students who attend more expensive (and often higher-quality) schools are eligible for larger Pell Grants than students at other colleges or universities. Pell Grants are also more generous for full-time rather than part-time students. Even in the absence of Pell Grants, students who benefit most from college are more likely than other students to attend more expensive schools and to attend full-time. However, since Pell Grant awards are systematically higher for these same students, it may be difficult to identify the effects of the Pell

---

1. "Stopping out" refers to students who withdraw from school after their first year. These students are not "dropouts" because many of these students do not leave school permanently, and their undergraduate credit hours do not "expire." I use these terms interchangeably throughout the paper.

Grant separate from college enrollment effects. To avoid this bias, researchers must exploit variation in Pell Grants that is independent of college choice (e.g., discontinuities in the Pell Grant formula).

A final reason that researchers have been unable to identify the effects of Pell Grants on outcomes is the absence of accurate data, in particular, the absence of accurate persistence and detailed financial data. Some researchers have measured persistence at a particular university; however, in these data, researchers cannot distinguish between a student who transferred to another school and one who withdraws from college. Other survey-based data rely on students' self-reports of their college experience. These data may not be as reliable as administrative data since students may not recall or do not wish to report small periods of time when they withdrew from college.

Financial data are equally as difficult to obtain. Most of the students who receive Pell Grants do not attend elite, expensive institutions, nor do they have substantial family support. Pell Grant recipients (and much of the variation in their awards) typically come from less-expensive colleges and their family contributions are much smaller. Moreover, the variation in Pell Grants is typically small. Exact financial data are necessary both to identify the small variations in Pell Grants and to employ creative identification strategies. Survey data (e.g., High School and Beyond, National Educational Longitudinal Survey) do not offer the level of detail necessary to identify accurately the level of students' Pell Grants.

To examine the effects of the Pell Grant, this paper presents evidence from data gathered by the Ohio Board of Regents (OBR). These data do not have the shortcomings of other data sets and offer a level of detail on both persistence and financial variables that is not available in other data. Since 1998, OBR has collected comprehensive data on college enrollment in Ohio's public two- and four-year colleges. As a result, the OBR data tracks students within and across schools. With the data, researchers can distinguish between students who withdraw from school and students who transfer to other Ohio schools. Moreover, through collaborative agreements, OBR has expanded the data to include students' American College Test (ACT) scores and data from the Free Application for Federal Student Aid (FAFSA). The FAFSA data are the exact data used by institutions to determine the amount of students' Pell Grant eligibility.

The level of detail in the financial data also facilitates the use of statistical tools that are impractical using other data. In particular, the level of detail allows researchers to identify small discontinuities in the Pell Grant formula. These discontinuities may be exploited to identify the causal effects of the voucher. While this paper may not completely resolve biases from college choice and enrollment or family background, the discontinuity analysis may be the best available method for dealing with such biases.

The paper presents evidence on the effects of Pell Grants using both panel and cross-sectional variation.[2] The panel specifications suggest that need-based financial aid reduces students' stop-out behavior. In identifying this effect, the paper shows that students who receive Pell Grants after their first year are a unique subset of students who applied for financial aid in their first year. Failure to control for this selection may confound causal estimates of the Pell Grant program.

The paper also presents evidence relying on cross-sectional variation. The paper estimates the effects of Pell Grants close to existing discontinuities in family size. The results based on discontinuity approaches suggest that Pell Grants increase persistence; however, the results are not robust to alternative specifications.

Section 5.1 of this paper presents a simple economic model of student persistence under uncertainty. Section 5.2 of the paper explains the OBR data in greater detail. Section 5.3 of the paper presents the empirical strategies and results. Section 5.4 discusses policy implications of the results and concludes.

5.1   Economic Model

Economists often model educational attainment as investment in human capital. Even basic economics classes teach that students will choose an education level that maximizes the expected present discounted value (PDV) of future wage payments less the expected PDV of educational costs. There have been a number of permutations to this model—factoring in scholarship aid, allowing the returns to education to vary, and showing how predicted education levels vary with expectations (Manski 1993). This paper investigates the relationship between financial aid and outcomes. Rather than use a traditional human capital model, the paper models students' dropout behavior using a multistage investment model.

Multistage investment models are particularly useful in cases where the agent must reevaluate the project after an initial period of time. For example, Myers and Majd (1990) investigate optimal abandonment rules for firms. Dixit and Pindyck (1994) review other examples of multistage investments.

The phenomenon of interest—students' stop-out behavior—is similar to these multistage investments. In the initial period, students must decide whether to attend the first year of college. After completion of the first year, students must then reevaluate whether to complete the next year. About 20 percent of first-time freshmen withdraw from four-year colleges after the first year.

To formalize the model, let person i's wage at time t (w_{it}) be modeled as a

2. It is important to distinguish between the effects of Pell Grants in general and the effects of Pell Grants conditional on initial enrollment. This paper focuses on estimating the effect of persistence conditional on a student having enrolled. I discuss in the following the relationship between the conditional effects of Pell Grants and the unconditional effects.

function of years of college (s_t) and ability (a_i), which is not perfectly known to the student. Let the cost of education at time t (c_t) be the difference between announced tuition (T_t) and financial aid. Financial aid contains two components: the need-based component is a function of initial wealth (I_0) and the number of children attending college at time t (n_t); the merit-based component is a function of perceived ability at time t. Let $E_t[\ ]$ denote the expectation operator conditional on information at time t.

(1) $$w_{it} = f(s_{it}, a_i)$$

(2) $$c_t = T_t - g(I_0, n_t) - h(a_i)$$

A student will attend a first year of college if the expected value of increased lifetime earnings for that year exceeds the cost of attending college (including forgone earnings).

(3) $$E_0\left\{\sum_{t=2}^{T} R^{t-1}[f(s_{it} = 1, a_i) - f(s_{it} = 0, a_i)]\right\}$$

$$> E_0[f(s_{i1} = 0, a_i) + T_1 - g(I_0, n_1) - h(a_i)]$$

At the start of the first year, a student will indicate an intention to attend a second year as well so long as

(4) $$E_0\left\{\sum_{t=3}^{T} R^{t-2}[f(s_{it} = 2, a_i) - f(s_{it} = 1, a_i)]\right\}$$

$$> E_0[f(s_{i2} = 1, a_i) + T_2 - g(I_0, n_2) - h(a_i)].$$

We could solve the decision rules for the maximum tuition level that a student would be willing to pay. For simplicity, let's assume that tuition is fully known one year in advance.

(5) $E_0(T_1^*) = T_1^*$

$$= E_0\left\{g(I_0, n_1) + h(a_i) - f(s_{i1} = 0, a_i) + \sum_{t=2}^{T} R^{t-1}[f(s_{it} = 1, a_i) - f(s_{it} = 0, a_i)]\right\}$$

and

(6) $E_0(T_2^*)$

$$= E_0\left\{g(I_0, n_2) + h(a_i) - f(s_{i2} = 1, a_i) + \sum_{t=3}^{T} R^{t-2}[f(s_{it} = 2, a_i) - f(s_{it} = 1, a_i)]\right\}$$

These tuition levels are likely the formulae that students use to make any decisions about the second year of school that must be made during the first year. For example, a student wanting to transfer to another university must file that application during the first year. Also, students who want financial aid in their second year must file applications during their first year. With these types of decisions in mind, there are a few insights that come from comparing these two tuition values:

1. For a given level of ability, if the returns to schooling are linear (or even concave) in schooling and scholarship aid does not change, then the maximum tuition that a student will pay falls over time. Hence, many students may rationally choose to get only one year of school.

2. Even if the returns to schooling are convex and scholarship aid does not change, then the maximum tuition a student is willing to pay may still decrease over time, leading to more planned attrition.[3]

3. Even expected changes in financial aid can alter the maximum that students would be willing to pay, leading to students to plan on withdrawing or transferring.

4. Since students must apply for second-year financial aid during their first year, they will do so only if they perceive that their benefits exceed costs in both periods.[4]

There are also a number of decisions about the second year that can be made after the first year—for example, the decision to withdraw from college altogether. Students make these decisions after gaining another year of information on which to base their decisions. The student will choose to attend another year if the expected value of the increase in lifetime earnings for the second year exceeds the cost of attending college that year (including forgone earnings).

$$(7) \quad E_1 \left\{ \sum_{t=3}^{T} R^{t-2} [f(s_{it} = 2, a_i) - f(s_{it} = 1, a_i)] \right\}$$
$$> E_1 [f(s_{i2} = 1, a_i) + T_2 - g(I_0, n_2) - h(a_i)]$$

We could rewrite this decision rule solving for the maximum tuition levels that the student would be willing to pay in order to actually attend a given year of college:

$$(8) \quad T_2^*$$
$$= E_1 \left\{ g(I_0, n_2) + h(a_i) - f(s_{i2} = 1, a_i) + \sum_{t=3}^{T} R^{t-2} [f(s_{it} = 2, a_i) - f(s_{it} = 1, a_i)] \right\}$$

---

3. Holding scholarship aid constant and as $T \to \infty$, the maximum tuition rises only if the following inequality is satisfied:

$$(1 - r) E_0 [f(s_{it} = 2, a_i) - f(s_{it} = 1, a_i)] > E_0 [f(s_{it} = 1, a_i) - f(s_{it} = 0, a_i)]$$

If in the extreme case, there is a "sheepskin" effect of a degree (i.e., returns only to a two- or four-year degree), then the inequality is always satisfied. Typical models of sequential investment show that the willingness to pay increases over time. The key difference is the usability of capital. Students may be able to drop out of colleges and use a year of college in the labor market.

4. There may be a small group who apply for financial aid even though they expect not to attend the second year. There is an option value to applying for financial aid because ability is not known perfectly (see discussion by Sarah Turner in chapter 1 in this volume).

Notice that the difference between equations (8) and (6) is the information set. Students have a chance to update their expectations with information from their first year of school. As the model stands, the updating comes in terms of ability. Similar to the model in Manski (1993), students discover their ability by attending college. Knowing the ability then changes the willingness to pay.

We could have also changed this model by introducing uncertainty in the financial aid formula. Unexpected changes in financial aid might lower the maximum tuition price that students might be willing to pay. For example, if a student's expected financial aid offer falls, the maximum that a student would be willing to pay declines. The student may wish to transfer to a cheaper school or drop out altogether.

A simple insight of the model is that changes in financial aid matter. Previous work on the effects of financial aid has looked at relationships between student outcomes and both changes and levels of aid. Recent work by Wetzel, O'Toole, and Peterson (1999) look at changes in financial aid for students at Virginia Commonwealth University. They find that increases in need-based financial aid likely improved student retention. Other work by Singell (2001) looks at the effects of the level of financial aid in the first year. He finds that the higher the student's levels of need-based financial aid, the more likely the student is to graduate.

While the model in this paper suggests that decisions about enrollment in the second year rely on financial aid changes rather than levels, there may be reasons that the level of financial aid in the first year matters. If the level of financial aid in the first year creates some inertia or helps to shape expectations about the financial aid offer in the second period, the level may affect the student in the next year. One example of this type of effect is the application for second-year financial aid. The higher a student's Pell Grant in the first year, the more likely the student will apply for a second-year award. If students expect to get a low second-year award, they may never even apply for financial aid.

The level of financial aid may even have deleterious consequences on the student. The model implicitly assumes that financial aid does not change students' behavior in other ways. But for example, if a student receives financial aid, he or she may be more detached from college. The student may not fully engage and take college seriously since his or her money is not on the line. In this way, Pell Grants eliminate the "sunk cost fallacy" for the student.[5] Since Pell Grant recipients did not make this initial investment (the federal government did instead), they may not have as strong of an incentive to work hard in school as students who made this initial investment themselves. As a result, Pell Grant recipients may perform worse. The model may capture some of this through the updates on students' abilities.

---

5. The "sunk cost fallacy" suggests that people often devote greater resources and more effort in areas where they have already made an investment.

Controlling for students' performance in school gives a clear indicator of whether they are exerting effort. The empirical results will investigate this hypothesis more fully.

Although they are outside of the scope of this paper, there are other outcomes in which we might be interested that are related to either the level or change in financial aid. For example, we might be interested in how financial aid affects the number of credits that a student successfully attempts. Students without financial aid may be reluctant to take loans and may spend more time working on the side. On the other hand, students without financial aid may want to cram in more credits per semester to try to reduce the number of semesters they have to attend (and as a result the total cost of college). We might also be interested in knowing how grade point averages (GPAs) vary with financial aid. In particular, if the level of financial aid affects hours attempted, completed, or GPAs, it might also affect students' perception of their abilities and, in the context of the previous model, affect their likelihood of completing college.

5.2   Data

The data for this project come from the OBR. Through a collaborative agreement with the OBR, the OBR has allowed me to access anonymous student data from Ohio's public institutions. The data are provided by the respective institutions to the OBR and include information on student demographics, enrollment, credit hours completed, and GPAs.

The OBR has collaborative arrangements with other agencies that allow them to expand the data. For example, the OBR links the student records to ACT and Scholastic Aptitude Test (SAT) records. Most Ohio students take the ACT exam, and the ACT records include the highest test score of the student and the most recent responses to the ACT survey (which includes student-reported data on high school performance). The OBR also links students to their respective FAFSA. The FAFSA data include detailed information about the finances of both students and their families. From the FAFSA, the variable of most interest is the "Estimated Family Contribution" that colleges use to award grants based on financial need.

One important limitation of the data is that they only include information about need-based financial aid. From FAFSA data, we know students' eligibility for federal grants and loans. We also know students' eligibility for Ohio's Instructional Grant program, a state-run need-based financial aid award. The data do not include information about merit-based financial aid. Ohio institutions are reluctant to divulge merit-based awards since these rewards are central to their recruitment strategies. While I do not observe merit aid, I observe students' GPAs once in college, their ACT scores, and their (self-reported) high school GPAs. If these variables adequately control for student ability and if colleges determine need- and merit-based awards separately, then not knowing students' merit-based awards should not affect the estimated results.

Another limitation of the data is that they only include students attending Ohio public universities. Students from Ohio that attend universities in other states, including the nation's elite schools, and students that attend private schools in Ohio are excluded from the sample.[6] These exclusions are both a weakness and a strength of these data. Excluding elite students may make the results not generalizable to all college students; however, excluding elite students gives us the opportunity to describe how financial aid affects students at nonelite schools. These nonelite schools educate the majority of college students and may be places where financial constraints are more binding.

Another concern related to the inclusion of Ohio public institutions alone is the measurement of dropout behavior. Students who transfer from Ohio public institutions to institutions located in other states are indistinguishable in the data from students who withdraw from Ohio public universities. This potential bias, however, should be very small because the percentage of students who probably transferred makes up a small fraction of the total number of observed dropouts.[7]

I focus entirely on the incoming freshman class in the 1999–2000 school year. These are the first students for whom FAFSA data are available through the OBR. I include students who enrolled in any college, including community colleges, for the first time in 1999, and I track these students through the 2000–2001 school year.

Table 5.1 provides summary statistics for the sample. At four-year institutions, about 10 percent of incoming full-time freshmen are from other states, and students are much less likely to be commuter students than at two-year colleges. At two-year colleges, which include local and state-run community colleges and technical colleges, about 2 percent of all students live on campus. Similar to other national surveys, the average age of first-time freshmen at two-year colleges is considerably higher than at four-year colleges, and students complete fewer semester hours in their first year (thirteen at four-year colleges as compared to eleven at two-year colleges). Seventy-five percent of incoming freshmen at Ohio's four-year colleges

6. Ohio State University and Miami University are the top ranked public universities in Ohio. In the 2004 version of *U.S. News & World Report*'s college rankings, they rank 60th and 64th, respectively, among national universities with doctoral programs. Other high ranking institutions in Ohio (e.g., Oberlin) are private colleges.

7. The Integrated Postsecondary Education Data System (IPEDS) tracks the number of transfers at each institution but does not record the state of residence of transfer students although it does track the states of residence for incoming freshmen. Assuming that transfer students are geographically representative of the incoming freshman class, then one would expect around 650 Ohio students to transfer to the non-Ohio schools with substantial Ohio enrollments. If we further assume that *all* 650 transfer students just finished their first year of school, then about 4.3 percent of observed dropouts are actually transfer students.

Table 5.1   Average Student Characteristics

	4-Year College	2-Year College
Out-of-state student	.103	.032
Lives on campus	.557	.024
Age	18.8	21.0
	(2.5)	(6.2)
Nonwhite	.134	.173
Hours completed by fall 1999	13.4	11.2
	(4.7)	(6.3)
Left institution after 1 year	.278	.491
Left higher education after 1 year	.201	.431
Took ACT exam	.750	.446
ACT composite score (36 = max)	21.8	18.9
	(4.3)	
Filed FAFSA for fall 1999	.653	.628
Uncovered financial need ($)	423.0	24.1
	(716.1)	(172.4)
Uncovered financial need conditional	1,081.8	82.0
on being >0	(773.7)	(310.5)
Filed FAFSA for fall 2000	.490	.399
Uncovered financial need ($)	1,261.5	21.3
	(951.4)	(93.1)
Uncovered financial need conditional	1,400.2	41.3
on being >0	(900.2)	(126.5)
Change in Pell Grant (conditional on Pell	1,691	881
eligibility in 1999 or 2000)	(994)	(762)

Source: Author's calculations from unpublished data from the Ohio Board of Regents.

Notes: Standard deviations appear in parentheses for nonbinary variables. Data are for full-time students who first entered Ohio public colleges and/or universities in fall 1999. Uncovered financial need equals tuition less the estimated family contribution from the FAFSA less any Pell Grant for which the student was eligible.

took the ACT exam while only 45 percent of students at two-year colleges took the exam. The four-year college students performed better than the two-year college students. Throughout the paper, I will at times restrict the sample to students who took the ACT exam. Not only do I know these students test scores, but I also have additional (self-reported) data on these students' high school experiences.

Throughout the paper, I will also restrict the sample at times to those students who filed a FAFSA in both fall 1999 and fall 2000. About 65 percent of four-year students and 63 percent of two-year students submitted FAF-SAs in 1999; however, only 49 percent and 40 percent, respectively, filed FAFSAs in 2000. As explained below, not observing FAFSA data for many applicants leads to substantial biases in the results using panel identification. The average, uncovered financial need is small across all students, but conditional on it being positive, the uncovered financial need is slightly greater than $1,400 for students at four-year schools.

Table 5.2 shows some basic least squares regressions of student stop-out

Table 5.2   **Association between Financial Aid and Stop-Out Behavior (dependent variable: student stopped out)**

	All Students				Students Taking ACT Exam	
	(1)	(2)	(3)	(4)	(5)	(6)
Level of financial aid (000s)	.033	.006	.0002	−.005	.005	.002
	(.002)	(.003)	(.003)	(.003)	(.003)	(.003)
Log of parents' income		−.036	−.030	−.042	−.030	−.024
		(.005)	(.005)	(.005)	(.006)	(.005)
Out-of-state student		.072	.055	.041	.365	.165
		(.077)	(.073)	(.073)	(.152)	(.172)
Age		.022	.018	.020	.018	.016
		(.004)	(.004)	(.004)	(.005)	(.005)
Male		.029	.003	.003	.017	−.002
		(.005)	(.004)	(.004)	(.005)	(.005)
Lives on campus		−.082	−.057	−.112	−.079	−.062
		(.007)	(.007)	(.004)	(.007)	(.007)
Took the ACT		−.113	−.063	−.088		
		(.007)	(.007)	(.007)		
ACT score					−.0003	.004
					(.0007)	(.001)
Freshman grade point average			−.138	−.136		−.132
			(.003)	(.003)		(.003)
Includes high school GPA controls	No	No	No	No	Yes	Yes
Includes race fixed effects	No	Yes	Yes	No	Yes	Yes
Includes campus fixed effects	Yes	Yes	Yes	No	Yes	Yes
R^2	.108	.112	.204	.192	.091	.169
No. of observations	37,028	30,851	29,778	29,778	24,627	24,012

Source: Author's calculations from unpublished data from the Ohio Board of Regents

Notes: White standard errors are in parentheses. Data are for full-time students who first entered Ohio public colleges and/or universities in fall 1999. The sample varies across columns due to missing data on student characteristics or first-year GPA data.

behavior on the level of students' financial aid. These regressions are not meant to show the causal effect of Pell Grants but rather to demonstrate associations between the stop-out behavior, financial aid awards, and other covariates. These regressions are also useful in understanding the types of biases present in the data. Comparing the various specifications will help identify important biases.

Column (1) shows a regression of whether a student drops out or not regressed on the student's financial aid award. The regression includes fixed effects that control for the school that the student attends. The estimated coefficient is positive and significant, suggesting that larger awards are positively associated with dropout behavior. As mentioned before, however, these coefficients are significantly biased for a number of reasons. For example, when we include controls for an individual's socioeconomic background and personal characteristics in column (2), the estimated relationship drops significantly.[8] The estimated relationship drops dramatically (from 0.033 to 0.006) and is still significant. Column (5) is similar to column (2) except that I focus only on students who took the ACT exam, including controls for a student's high school performance and entrance exam scores. The estimated coefficient is similar to column (2) but is no longer significant. The other rows in columns (2) and (5) suggest that wealthier students are less likely to stop out; out-of-state students are more likely to drop out; older students and men are more likely to withdraw; and students living on campus and students who took the ACT (and performed well on it) are less likely to stop out.

In column (3), I add controls for students' grades during their freshman years of school. As previously mentioned, a Pell Grant may have had a negative effect since students with a Pell Grant may have had less of a financial commitment to schooling and may not have worked as hard. Including GPA should control for these students and may further weaken the estimated relationship between financial aid and stop-out behavior. As shown in table 5.2, the estimated relationship is smaller than in columns (1), (2), and (5). The result is also not statistically different from zero. In column (6), I estimate a similar regression for students who took the ACT exam. Again, the estimated relationship is indistinguishable from zero.

In column (4), I estimate the relationship, controlling for personal and family characteristics and grades during a student's first year. I exclude the fixed effects for students' campuses of attendance. These fixed effects also control for differences in quality, price, and other unobservable campus characteristics (e.g., the strength of a campuses freshman intervention programs). These fixed effects control for the fact that students attending lower-quality schools (who also receive smaller financial aid awards because tuition is smaller) are more likely to withdraw than students attending better schools (who receive higher financial aid awards for similar reasons). Without these fixed effects, we would expect the estimated relationship between financial aid and student stop-out behavior to be even smaller and maybe even negative. This is exactly what column (4) of table 5.2 shows. The estimated relationship suggests that higher financial aid awards are negatively associated with student stop-out behavior.

5.3   Estimating the Causal Effects

There are three sources of variation that economists can use to identify the effects of Pell Grants: time series, panel, and cross-sectional. In this sec-

8. The sample sizes fall across columns in table 5.2. The first column includes all students in the sample. The second column includes only those students for whom demographic data are available. Columns (3) and (4) further restrict the sample to students who had a freshman GPA reported to the OBR. Columns (5) and (6) are based on the subsample of students who took the ACT exam.

tion, I discuss the feasibility of each of these identification strategies using the OBR data. I also present the basic empirical results for each identification strategy.

Each strategy aims at identifying the effects of Pell Grants *conditional* on initial enrollment. However, Pell Grants may affect enrollment, and, as a consequence, some students who would not be enrolled without Pell Grants would be included in the analysis, making the parameter estimated in this paper more difficult to interpret. If a Pell Grant affects enrollments, then the parameter estimated in this paper would be a combination of two different effects: (1) the effect of Pell Grants on the persistence behavior of students who would have attended college in the absence of the Pell Grant; and (2) the effect of Pell Grants on the persistence behavior of students who would not have attended school without the Pell Grant.

Under some circumstances, the latter effect does not matter. For example, any potential bias depends on the degree to which Pell Grants affect enrollment. If the Pell Grant has no effect, then the parameter estimated in this paper represents only the effect of the Pell Grant on all students eligible for Pell Grants. If the Pell Grant has a small effect, then any bias in the estimated parameter is likely to be small. Most of the research on Pell Grants and enrollment suggest that the Pell Grant has had either no effect or a very small positive effect on enrollment (see Kane 1999; Leslie and Brinkman 1987).

Additionally, if the unobservable factors that can potentially bias any estimate of the effect of Pell Grants on persistence are similar for those people for whom Pell Grants influenced enrollment decisions and those people for whom they did not, then the effect of Pell Grants estimated in this paper should be the same for both groups. For example, suppose that unobservable family characteristics affect both the size of students' Pell Grants and their likelihood of dropping out. We typically think that these unobserved characteristics likely bias our estimate of the effects of Pell Grants downward. If the bias is the same for students for whom Pell Grants did and did not affect initial enrollments, then the bias should be symmetric across both groups, and, while the overall parameter may be biased by these unobservables, the overall parameter is not made up of two components. If we can control for these unobservables in our empirical design, we can estimate a single parameter that is easily interpreted. However, if the determinants of persistence are not constant across groups, then the parameter will remain a combination of the two aforementioned effects.

5.3.1 Time Series Identification

One way to identify the effects of Pell Grants is to compare changes in students' outcomes after systematic changes in Pell Grants occur. For example, the Pell Grant program began in 1973. Previous work by Kane (1995) compares low-income student enrollment rates before and after the Pell Grant program was established. Kane finds that college rates grew about 2.6 percentage points slower for low-income students than other groups, suggesting that the Pell Grant had little effect. Other systematic changes in Pell Grant formulae are described in Mortenson (1988). For the study at hand, I am presenting evidence for a single cohort, so time series variation will not be useful in identifying the effects of Pell Grants.

5.3.2   Panel Identification

Another way to identify the effects of Pell Grants is to look at changes in students' Pell Grants over time. While this seems like a promising strategy since the OBR data contain two years of data for a single cohort, there are a number of reasons why this strategy might be limited.

To see the limitations and possibilities of this identification strategy, we need to understand how variations over time are generated for a single individual. There are really three basic reasons that a student's Pell Grant would change from one year to the next. First, the generosity of the Pell Grant may change. This could be the result of systematic changes in the Pell Grant formula or by a change in college tuition. Such changes are likely to be exogenous, and if they generate enough variation, they may help researchers to accurately identify the effects of Pell Grants. Unfortunately, there is little variation over time in the period of time that the OBR data are available. From the 1999–2000 school year to the 2000–2001 school year, the maximum Pell Grant increased from $3,125 to $3,300, a 5.6 percent increase. Over the same time, tuition at Ohio schools increased by 5 percent across the board (OBR 2001).

Another source of variation comes from changes in students' college choices. Students may transfer to another school after the first year. The corresponding change in tuition will generate variation in students' Pell Grants. Unfortunately, this source of variation does not help identify the effects of Pell Grants. Students who transfer may have different abilities than those students who do not transfer. For example, a student with high ability may transfer from a two- to a four-year college to gain access to more opportunities. This student's Pell Grant would automatically increase. However, this increase is correlated with the student's ability and may confound causal estimates of the Pell Grant. Another reason why using variation from transfer behavior may be misleading is that the size of students' Pell Grants may affect transfer behavior, making it even more difficult to interpret and identify the effects of Pell Grants using variation caused by student transfer behavior. Thus, changes in Pell Grants resulting from transfer decisions will not generate variation in Pell Grants that can be legitimately used to identify the effect of Pell Grants alone.

A final reason that students' Pell Grants may change is due to changes in students' circumstances. Some changes may be legitimate sources of variation. For example, a family of four with one child in college may have a second child come of college age, causing the existing college student's Pell

Grant to increase. Similarly, a change in family size (e.g., birth of another child or separation) may increase a student's Pell Grant. Even the natural aging of parents should increase students' Pell Grants, although only slightly. However, there are other changes in family circumstances that may not be legitimate sources of variation. For example, changes in income due to unemployment or health shocks may reduce family income and consequently increase students' Pell Grants from year to year. These sources of variation may also affect the likelihood that a student persists in college.

For panel identification strategies to be successful, variation in the Pell Grants must come from sources that are exogenous from changes in students' stop-out behavior. As mentioned previously, the most legitimate changes come from changes in the Pell Grant formula, changes in tuition, and changes in family size or sibling attendance. I can use changes from these legitimate sources as instruments for actual changes in financial aid.

Constructing the instrument from changes in the Pell Grant formula and tuition is straightforward. I simply impute what students' Pell Grants would have been during the 2000–2001 school year, assuming that their financial and family information is unchanged from the 1999–2000 school year. The imputed 2000–2001 Pell Grant does not include variation from changes in students' (or their families') circumstances. It only includes variation arising from changes in the Pell Grant formula and tuition.

Imputing student data not only allows me to isolate exogenous variation, but it also allows me to estimate data for many students for whom financial data are missing. In the 1999–2000 school year, 35,233 students filed FAFSAs. However, 12,143 of these students did not file FAFSAs in the 2000–2001 school year (hereafter referred to as the "nonfilers"). These nonfilers are not a random subset of all students. These nonfilers include 2/3 of all students who withdrew from college after the 1999–2000 school year. For these individuals, I am missing financial data and information about changes in their siblings' college attendance for the 2000–2001 school year. Because the imputation assumes that students' financial information is unchanged from their first to second year of college, I can estimate data for these nonfilers.

If I had data for all nonfilers, I could estimate out the causal effect of Pell Grants by using the imputed grant as an instrument for the actual grant. The instrumental variable estimate would be an unbiased estimate of the effect. Unfortunately, because the actual data are not available for nonfilers, I can only estimate reduced-form regressions of stop-out behavior on the imputed Pell Grant. Because there is a significant, positive relationship between students' imputed Pell Grants and their actual Pell Grants, the reduced-form estimates of the relationship between imputed Pell Grants and stop-out behavior should give us a sense of the sign and significance of the effect of actual Pell Grants, but the reduced-form estimates will not give a precise estimate of the magnitude of such an effect.

Table 5.3   **Ordinary Least Squares Regressions of Stop-Out Behavior on Changes in Pell Grants: Results with Panel Data (dependent variable: student stopped out)**

	Full Sample: Students Filing FAFSA in 1999–2000			4-Year Students	Students Filing FAFSA Both Years
	(1)	(2)	(3)	(4)	(5)
Imputed increase in financial aid (000s)	–.086	–.092	–.092	–.064	.018
	(.002)	(.002)	(.002)	(.003)	(.008)
Level of financial aid in 1999–2000 (000s)		.025	.026	.020	.006
		(.002)	(.002)	(.002)	(.002)
Includes covariates	No	Yes	Yes	Yes	Yes
Includes campus fixed effects	Yes	No	Yes	Yes	Yes
No. of observations	35,233	35,233	35,233	21,506	24,116

Source: Author's calculations from unpublished data from the Ohio Board of Regents.

Notes: Standard errors are reported in parentheses. Samples in columns (1) to (3) include all students who filed FAFSAs in 1999–2000. Column (4) focuses only on students who attended a four-year college in 1999–2000. Column (5) includes only those students who applied for financial aid in both years. Covariates include the following: an indicator for whether the student was from out of state; age; gender; whether the student lives on campus; whether the student took the ACT exam; student's freshman GPA; and controls for race.

Table 5.3 contains the reduced-form regressions regressing student stop-out behavior against the imputed increase in a student's Pell Grant from one year to the next measured in thousands of dollars. For students who withdrew or transfer, I impute the Pell Grant that students would have received if they remained at the same institution as their initial enrollment. Column (1) shows the results with fixed effects for school of attendance but no covariates. Column (2) shows the results without fixed effects for college of enrollment but with covariates for gender, age, campus living conditions, whether the student took the ACT exam, and GPA in the student's first years. Column (3) includes both fixed effects and covariates.

As column (1) shows, students whose Pell Grants increase are less likely to drop out. Without covariates, the coefficient suggests that a $1,000 increase in a student's Pell Grant leads to an 8.6 percentage point decrease in the likelihood that the student withdraws. With covariates, the estimated coefficient implies that a $1,000 increase in a student's Pell Grant corresponds to a 9.2 percentage point decrease in the likelihood that the student withdraws. These estimates suggest strongly and consistently that increases in financial aid decrease the likelihood that students withdraw from school.

Column (4) repeats the analysis, focusing only on the students whose initial college enrollment was at a four-year campus. As before, the estimated coefficient is negative and significant. A $1,000 increase in students' imputed Pell Grants corresponds to a 6.4 percent reduction in the likelihood that students withdraw from college.

Column (5) reports estimates when nonfilers are excluded from the analysis. As mentioned before, the students who filed FAFSAs in both years are a nonrandom subset of all students. Now the estimate is positive and significant. A $1,000 increase in a student's financial aid corresponds to a 2 percentage point increase in the likelihood that a student withdraws. I include the estimate of column (5) to provide some hint of what the bias may be from excluding the nonfilers in the previous columns. When we include the nonfilers, we get significant, negative relationships between increases in students' Pell Grants and the likelihood that students drop out; however, when these students are omitted, the estimates are positive and significant.

One might be able to further refine the estimates of students' Pell Grants in the cases where data are missing by using information about students' siblings. If ages or graduation dates were known or could be approximated, I could include this information in the estimation of what students' Pell Grants would have been in the 2000–2001 school year. Unfortunately, little information is available about students' siblings for the nonfilers.[9]

What conclusion should be drawn from the panel identification specifications? First, panel identification has only limited power to actually identify the effects of Pell Grants. Much of the variation created over time in a student's Pell Grant comes from sources that may also affect the probability that the student withdraws from school. It would be inappropriate to use this type of variation to identify the effects of Pell Grants. Second, the fact that many students, especially those who plan to withdraw from school, do not file FAFSAs in both years makes it difficult to estimate the effect of financial aid. When we impute data for these people, we find estimates suggesting that increases in financial aid reduce the likelihood that students withdraw from college.

5.3.3 Cross-Sectional Identification

One might also identify the effects of need-based financial aid by comparing the need-based awards of different students at a single moment in time. There are a number of reasons why students may have different need-based awards. Students may differ from each other in terms of personal income and assets, family income and assets, family size, parental age, college of attendance, and enrollment status (full- versus part-time). All of these differences will lead to differences in students' need-based financial aid. Much of this variation will not be helpful in identifying the effects of

---

9. Some information about the family (parental age, family size in 1999–2000, number of children in college in 1999–2000, parental marital status) may help predict changes in the number of children attending college; however, their predictive power is limited. When I model changes in sibling attendance on these variables, I get a very low R^2. After rounding the predicted values to the nearest integer, the specification predicts that 0.05 percent of students who filed FAFSAs in both periods would have had a change in the number of siblings attending college. In reality, 20.5 percent of students had a change in the number of siblings attending college.

Pell Grants. These sources of variation will also likely affect students' dropout behavior, independent of need-based awards.

However, there is some variation across individuals that might be useful. In particular, differences in family size and the number of children in college may facilitate identification in a cross section. The Pell Grant formula contains a number of discontinuities, the largest of which is based on family size and the number of students attending college. Even these sources of variation may not be exogenous. For example, if a family can only afford to send one child to school, they may choose the student who has the most potential to benefit from college. This student's Pell Grant would likely be smaller than it would be for a comparable family that sent multiple children to school. However, in this example, comparing this solitary student to other families with multiple children attending would lead to a bias because the family with fewer children in college sent a child to college with a greater chance of succeeding. As a result of this potential bias, I will primarily focus on results that take advantage of discontinuities in family size. I will also briefly show estimates based on discontinuities in both family size and the number of children in college.

Table 5.4 shows the changes in Pell Grants that accompany changes in

Table 5.4   Pell Grant by Family Size and the Number of Children in College

Number in Family	Number of Children in College			
	1	2	3	4
Income = $40,000				
2	$2,175	$2,475	n.a.	n.a.
3	$2,875	$2,775	$2,775	n.a.
4	$3,125	$3,125	$2,975	$2,875
5	$3,125	$3,125	$3,125	$3,075
6	$3,125	$3,125	$3,125	$3,125
Income = $50,000				
2	$975	$1,775	n.a.	n.a.
3	$1,575	$2,175	$2,275	n.a.
4	$2,325	$2,425	$2,575	$2,575
5	$3,125	$2,825	$2,775	$2,775
6	$3,125	$3,125	$3,075	$2,975
Income = $60,000				
2	$0	$975	n.a.	n.a.
3	$400	$1,475	$1,775	n.a.
4	$1,075	$1,825	$2,175	$2,275
5	$1,875	$2,275	$2,375	$2,475
6	$2,675	$2,675	$2,675	$2,675

Source: Author's calculations.

Notes: Calculations assume that the families have zero assets and no student contribution in the computation of the estimated family contribution. Calculations also assume that students attend high-cost institutions. n.a. = not applicable.

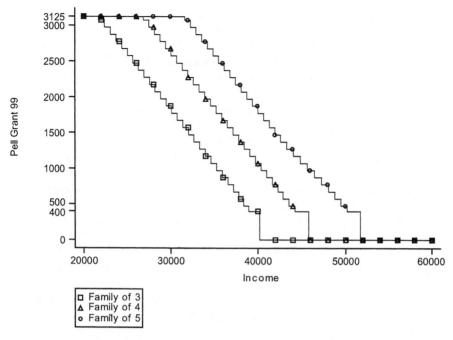

Fig. 5.1   Pell Grants by family size

Source: Author's calculations.

Notes: The estimated Pell Grants are formulated assuming no assets or student contribution. The Pell Grants further assume that only one person from the family is attending a high-cost institution.

family size. The table shows three different schedules linking family size and the number of children attending college.[10] Each schedule corresponds to a different income level ($40,000; $50,000; or $60,000). For example, among the families with $50,000 in income, a family of two with one in college would receive a Pell Grant of $975. If the family was actually a three-person family with one in college, then the Pell Grant would be $1,575 per person. Figure 5.1 shows similar comparisons for different family sizes. There are three lines corresponding to family sizes of three, four, and five. The Pell Grants shown in the figure assume that only one child is attending college. As seen, the differences in family size can lead to systematic differences in students' Pell Grants. These systematic differences create discontinuities that can be exploited to estimate the effect of Pell Grants on students.

Assuming that the differences between family size are unrelated to a stu-

10. The computations assume that the family has no assets and that the students do not contribute to the family's estimated family contribution.

dent's success in college, comparisons can be made between families of different sizes who have the same number of children in college. However, as table 5.4 shows, there is heterogeneity in income (and thus Pell Grant) within a given family size. For discontinuity analysis to work, the families on either side of the discontinuity should be similar except for the discontinuity. As a result, when making comparisons across family sizes, we need to stratify the groups so that comparisons are made across relatively homogeneous groups (e.g., people with similar income and assets).

Intuitively, the easiest way to estimate the effect of the Pell Grant while taking advantage of this discontinuity is to use a Wald estimator (Wald 1940). To find the Wald estimator, one must first isolate two groups that are fairly homogeneous. Across the groups, the Wald estimator is found by taking the ratio of the differences across groups of the dependent variable (stop-out behavior) and the independent variable (size of the Pell Grant). For example, suppose we could identify all people who have low income and few assets and have one child in college. Some of these families are two-person families, and some are three-person families. Assuming that family size is uncorrelated with an individual's success in college, we could estimate a Wald estimator across these groups. Let y_i be the average withdrawal rate for group i. Group i takes on a value of 1 for the group of students in two-person families with one in college and 2 for the group of students in three-person families with one in college. Let x_i be the average Pell Grant for group i. The Wald estimator between these groups would then be

$$\beta_{\text{Wald}} = \frac{y_2 - y_1}{x_2 - x_1}.$$

The denominator should be the expected change in the Pell Grant as a result of this discontinuity within this income-asset group. The numerator would be the difference in stop-out rates between these groups.

After computing the first Wald statistic, we could then create a Wald estimator between each income-asset grouping within the sets of two- and three-person families. If we had ten income-asset groupings, we would have ten Wald estimators. These Wald estimators can be combined by taking a weighted average of the estimators (weighted by the number of observations in each group 2). We could similarly create Wald estimators across adjacent groupings of family size. For example, we could compare three- and four-person families. Of course, in the estimation of each Wald statistic we would actually have multiple Wald statistics comparing income-asset groupings across each discontinuity.

While this approach seems straightforward, other discontinuities in the Pell Grant formula complicate the estimation of Wald statistics. For example, there are some income ranges where students would receive the maximum Pell Grant regardless of their family size or the number of children attending college. The Wald statistic would not be defined (or would be greatly inflated) over these ranges. Similarly, the Wald statistic will not be defined for families that would have received no Pell Grant regardless of their family size or the number of children in college. Because these groups will likely create additional noise in the estimation, we may want to exclude these groups at times.

Before estimating the Wald statistics, we need to create the income-asset groupings needed to create comparisons between homogeneous groups. To create groupings, I reestimate each student's Pell Grant, assuming that he or she belonged to a two-person family with only one person attending college. I then divide this group into six subgroups, based on the revised Pell Grant:

1. People whose Pell Grant in a two-person family with one in college would have been at the maximum of $3,125
2. People with revised Pell Grants between $3,124 and $2,001
3. People with revised Pell Grants between $2,000 and $1,001
4. People with revised Pell Grants between $1,000 and $401
5. People with revised Pell Grants at the Pell Grant minimum of $400
6. People with revised Pell Grants equal to zero

Having uniform groupings across cells makes it much easier to estimate the Wald statistics and their standard errors. Creating groupings around Pell Grant values also avoids the problem that wealthier families are more likely to apply if they have more children. These families are identified in subgroup 6. Also, I separate people who would have had the Pell Grant minimum ($400) because in the Pell Grant formula there is a discontinuity that allows families across a wider range of income to have this value of Pell Grant. I use these revised Pell Grants only for the purpose of creating homogeneous groups (i.e., identifying families with similar assets and incomes). When actually computing the Wald statistics, I use the actual Pell Grants.

Figure 5.2 shows an example of how the discontinuity works. The sample of students is from subgroup 3. These students would have had similar Pell Grants had their family size not been different. The left axis of figure 5.2 plots these students' actual Pell Grants across family size. The Pell Grant increases with the number of children. The right-side axis of figure 5.2 plots the stop-out rates for these students. The stop-out rate declines for students with larger families. Assuming that family size affects stop-out rates only through its effect on Pell Grant size, then stop-out rates are negatively related to Pell Grant size for these students. We could produce similar figures for each homogeneous group of students.

Table 5.5 shows the regression-based Wald estimates for the whole sample. Following Angrist (1991), the efficient combination of Wald estimators is just the instrumental variables estimate of y (stop-out behavior) on x (size of Pell Grant), where dummy variables for each homogeneous

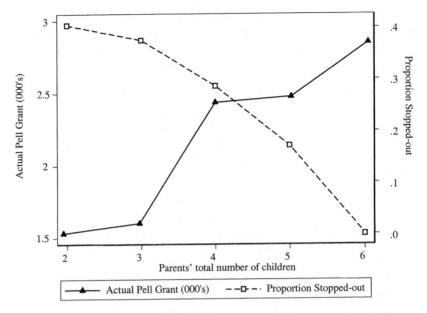

Fig. 5.2   Average Pell Grants and stop-out rates across family size discontinuity

Source: Author's calculations from unpublished data from the OBR.

Notes: Sample is restricted to families whose assets and income are such that their college-age children would have had a Pell Grant between one and two thousand dollars if they had only had one child.

Table 5.5   **Wald/Instrumental Variable (IV) Estimates of Effect of Financial Aid on Stop-Out Behavior**

	Wald (1)	Wald ACT Sample (2)	Wald Dependent Variable = ACT Score (3)	IV (4)	IV with Campus Fixed Effects (5)	Wald Family and Child Discount (6)
Level of Pell Grant in 1999–2000 (in 000s)	−.037 (.009)	−.012 (.010)	.100 (.099)	−.029 (.004)	.0004 (.004)	−.036 (.009)
No. of observations	6,114	4,470	4,470	29,936	29,936	6,398

Source: Author's calculations from unpublished data from the Ohio Board of Regents.

Notes: White standard errors are reported in parentheses. Columns (1)–(3) and (6) include only students with positive Pell Grants less than the maximum. In columns (4) and (5) the instrument for "Level of Pell Grant" is the residual from a regression of Pell Grant on a quartic of the key variables determining Pell Grants (family income, assets, family size, number of children in college). The IV columns exclude families with income greater than $115,000 or assets greater than $150,000. Campus fixed effects are included in the first stage of the specification in column (5) to control for the fact that different school costs will lead to different size Pell Grants.

group and family size combination are used as instruments for x. For example, if all families were two, three, or four people in size, then I would include eighteen dummy variables as instruments (i.e., for each of the six homogeneous income/asset subgroupings defined previously, I would include three dummy variables for the possible family sizes).

Column (1) of table 5.5 shows the instrumental variable estimate when I estimate the regression excluding those for whom there is no variation in Pell Grants.[11] The estimated effect is negative and significant. A $1,000 increase in Pell Grants stemming from differences in family size corresponds to a 4 percentage point decrease in likelihood that a student drops out. The result suggests that systematic differences in Pell Grants lead to differences in stop-out rates for students. Larger Pell Grants reduce students' probabilities of withdrawing.

In column (2) of table 5.5, I include only the students who took the ACT exam. The estimated effect suggests that a $1,000 increase in a student's Pell Grant leads to a 1.2 percentage point reduction in the probability that a student withdraws although the result is not statistically significant. In column (3), I provide a specification test. Rather than use stop-out behavior as the dependent variable, I use the ACT score. If the specification is correctly identified, there should be no significant differences between ACT scores between groups. Indeed, the estimated relationship is indistinguishable from zero.

Another way to estimate the effects of a Pell Grant is to use an instrumental variable approach where the "delinearized" Pell Grant is used as an instrument for the actual Pell Grant. To do this, I run a regression of the actual Pell Grant on a quartic in the key variables that determine the Pell Grant (family income, family assets, family size, and number of children in the family attending college). The residuals from this regression should be made up primarily of discontinuities in the Pell Grant formula along these dimensions. I then use the residual as an instrument for the actual Pell Grant in a simple regression of stop-out behavior on students' Pell Grants.[12] I restrict the sample to students whose families have less than $150,000 in assets or less than $115,000 in annual income. The results appear in columns (4) and (5) of table 5.5. Similar to column (3), I find that a $1,000 increase in a Pell Grant is associated with a 3 percentage point reduction in the likelihood that a student drops out.

In column (5), I use a similar procedure except that I put campus fixed effects in the regression that predicts students' Pell Grants. This is impor-

---

11. The maximum income in this group is $25,000.

12. This is identical to running a regression of stop-out behavior on the Pell Grant value and a quartic in the variables that determine the Pell Grant. These strategies estimate the same estimator with only a negligible change in standard errors. I report the standard errors from the "instrument" approach because it may be intuitively easier to identify what source of variation is behind the estimated effect.

tant because different campus costs can lead to differences in the size of students' Pell Grants. Again, I use the residuals from this first stage as an instrument in the next. The results drop in magnitude and are statistically indistinguishable from zero.

The final column of table 5.5 estimates the effects of Pell Grants using both the discontinuities from family size and the number of children in college. I use the same methodology except now I compare differences in Pell Grants resulting from differences in the number of children going to college as well. The results are similar to those in column (1). I find that a $1,000 increase in Pell Grants corresponds to a 4 percent reduction in the likelihood that students withdraw.

What conclusions should be drawn? First, while the estimates reinforce a negative relationship between the size of one's Pell Grant and stop-out behavior, they are not completely robust to specification. When I focus on the sample taking the ACT (column [2]) and when I include additional campus level controls (column [5]), the results are indistinguishable from zero. Additionally, there is substantial heterogeneity around the discontinuity, and efforts to create comparisons among homogeneous groups may not fully account for the heterogeneity. Overall the results seem supportive of those in the panel identification although the results are not robust to different subsamples.

5.4   Conclusion and Policy Implications

This paper set out to estimate the effects of Pell Grants on student retention. Using panel and cross-sectional variation as sources of identification, this paper attempts to estimate the relationship. The panel identification results suggest strongly that a Pell Grant reduces dropout rates. The regression-discontinuity results show similar results although they are more fragile. The regression-discontinuity results, however, are less likely to be biased by other factors than the specifications that use cross-sectional variation.

The finding that Pell Grants affect student persistence has several policy implications. Most importantly, it implies that federal and state need-based policies and aid matter and that they influence the likelihood that students continue from year to year in college. Even if these aid programs have no effect on enrollment (as Kane [1999] and Leslie and Brinkman [1987] show), need-based programs may impact educational attainment. The finding that aid increases persistence may suggest that front-loaded financial aid programs may improve student retention in the first years of college.[13]

---

13. DesJardins, Ahlburg, and McCall (2002) find that frontloaded aid programs have a "modest impact" on student retention.

The results in this paper may also support conclusions in Dynarski (2003) and Bound and Turner (2002). These papers focused on beneficiaries of the Social Security Student Benefit Program and the GI Bill, respectively. The papers found that need-based aid affected both enrollment and completion.

While many policymakers may view the finding that need-based aid improves retention as being "good" for society, it is not clear that this is so. As Jonathan Guryan points out in the comment that follows this chapter, more education may not be optimal for all students in society. There may be a number of students who do not have the skills and for whom a college degree may not improve earnings. If these students are the marginal students for whom the Pell Grant program influences college persistence, then the measured effect in this paper may reflect an inefficient use of societal resources.

In order to fully resolve the question of whether increased persistence is "good" for society, we would need to know how an additional year of education affects the earnings for these marginal students. In estimates of the returns of education for the entire population, Jaeger and Page (1996) argue that the returns to a second year of college have significant effects on earnings, particularly if students finish an associate's degree. These estimates suggest that persistence into the second year of college is a positive outcome; however, the estimated return in Jaeger and Page (1996) is for the whole population. It is not clear that this estimated return would be the same for the marginal students affected by Pell Grants. Evidence from Tobias (2003) suggests that the returns to education are concentrated at the highest-ability students and remain small for lower-ability students. Moreover, as Sarah Turner points out in chapter 1 of this volume, the marginal students are likely less prepared for college and more likely to hold a General Education Development certification (GED) than a high school diploma.[14] There is little empirical evidence on the returns to an additional year of college for these students.

Finally, there are two empirical points that should be considered in interpreting the results in this paper. First, the paper focuses solely on student persistence between the first and second year of college in adjacent years. Researchers have documented the growing trend of students to take breaks at various times during college (e.g., chap. 1 in this volume). Des-Jardins, Ahlburg, and McCall (2002) examine enrollment probabilities over a longer stretch of time. They find that need-based aid has no long-run effect on enrollment probabilities. They are using a sample in which students repeatedly enter and exit higher education. While the sample they use

---

14. Many of these students enroll in college remediation. Ongoing research by Bettinger and Long (2003) examines the effect of college remediation on college outcomes and student earnings.

focuses on students who initially enrolled at a four-year campus, their finding suggests that examining the effect of financial aid on retention over a longer stretch of time may be important.

Second, as states continue to gather more complete and expansive data on their students, economists and other researchers will be able to employ methods that exploit variation in Pell Grant formulae. However, even if better data are available, researchers should take care in how they deal with changes in Pell Grant eligibility and missing data. Students who leave school after their first year are less likely to file additional FAFSAs, making it difficult for researchers to measure their financial status. Research that fails to control for these missing data may be biased.

References

Angrist, Joshua. 1991. Grouped-data estimation and testing in simple labor-supply models. *Journal of Econometrics* 47 (2–3): 243–266.

Bettinger, Eric, and Bridget Long. 2003. The effect of remediation on student outcomes: The plight of underprepared students in higher education. Case Western University, Department of Economics. Mimeograph.

Bound, John, and Sarah Turner. 2002. Going to war and going to college: Did World War II and the G.I. Bill increase educational attainment for returning veterans? *Journal of Labor Economics* 20 (4): 784–815.

College Board. 2001. Trends in student aid 2001. Available at [http://www.collegeboard.com/press/cost01/html/TrendsSA01.pdf]. Retrieved 27 August 2003.

DesJardins, S. L., D. A. Ahlburg, and B. P. McCall. 1999. An event history model of student departure. *Economics of Education Review* 18:375–390.

———. 2002. Simulating the longitudinal effects of changes in financial aid on student departure from college. *Journal of Human Resources* 37 (3): 653–679.

Dixit, Avinash, and Robert Pindyck. 1994. *Investment under uncertainty.* Princeton, N.J.: Princeton University Press.

Dynarski, Susan. 2003. Does aid matter? Measuring the effect of student aid on college attendance and completion. *American Economic Review* 93 (1): 279–288.

Ehrenberg, Ron, and D. Sherman. 1984. Optimal financial aid policies for a selective university. *Journal of Human Resources* 19 (2): 202–230.

Jaeger, David A., and Marianne Page. 1996. Degrees matter: New evidence on sheepskin effects in the returns to education. *Review of Economics and Statistics* 78 (4): 733–741.

Kane, Thomas J. 1995. Rising public college tuition and college entry: How well do public subsidies promote access to college? NBER Working Paper no. 5164. Cambridge, Mass.: National Bureau of Economic Research, July.

Kane, Thomas J. 1999. *The price of admission: Rethinking how Americans pay for college.* Washington, D.C.: Brookings Institution.

Leslie, Larry L., and Paul T. Brinkman. 1988. *The economic value of higher education.* New York: MacMillan.

Manski, Charles F. 1993. Adolescent econometricians: How do youth infer the returns to schooling? In *Studies of supply and demand in higher education,* ed.

Charles Clotfelter and Michael Rothschild, 43–57. Cambridge, Mass.: National Bureau of Economic Research.

Mortenson, Thomas. 1988. Pell Grant program changes and their effects on applicant eligibility 1973–74 to 1988–89. American College Testing Program Research Series Report. Iowa City, Iowa: American College Testing Program.

Myers, S. C., and S. Majd. 1990. Abandonment value and project life. *Advances in Futures and Options Research* 4:1–21.

Ohio Board of Regents. 2001. State-supported Ohio college and university performance report: Student outcomes and experiences. Available at [http://www.regents.state.oh.us/perfrpt/2001index.html]. Retrieved 29 August 2003.

Seftor, Neil, and Sarah Turner. 2002. Back to school: Federal student aid policy and adult college age enrollment. *Journal of Human Resources* 37 (2): 336–352.

Singell, Larry. 2001. Come and stay a while: Does financial aid affect enrollment and retention at a large public university? University of Oregon, Department of Economics. Working Paper.

St. John, Edward P., Shouping Hu, and Tina Tuttle. 2000. Persistence by undergraduates in an urban public university: Understanding the effects of financial aid. *Journal of Student Financial Aid* 30 (2): 23–37.

St. John, Edward P., Shouping Hu, and Jeff Weber. 2000. Keeping public colleges affordable: A study of persistence in Indiana's public colleges and universities. *Journal of Student Financial Aid* 30 (1): 21–32.

St. John, Edward P., Glenda D. Musoba, and Ada B. Simmons. 2003. Keeping the promise: The impact of Indiana's 21st-Century Scholars program. Indiana Education Policy Center research report. Available at [http://www.indiana.edu/~iepc/hepolicy.html]. Retrieved 4 September 2003.

Tobias, Justin. 2003. Are returns to schooling concentrated among the most able? A semiparametric analysis of the ability-earnings relationships. *Oxford Bulletin of Economics and Statistics* 65 (1): 1–29.

U.S. Department of Education. 22 May 2002. Paige hails House for not leaving Pell Grant recipients behind. Available at [http://www.ed.gov/PressReleases/05-2002/15222002.html]. Retrieved 27 August 2003.

Wald, Abraham. 1940. The fitting of straight lines if both variables are subject to error. *The Annals of Mathematical Statistics* 11 (3): 284–300.

Wei, Christina, and C. Dennis Carroll. 2002. Persistence and attainment of beginning students with Pell Grants. NCES Publication 2002169. Washington, D.C.: National Center for Education Statistics.

Wetzel, James, Dennis O'Toole, and Steven Peterson. 1999. Factors affecting student retention probabilities: A case study. *Economics of Education Review* 23 (1): 45–55.

Comment   Jonathan Guryan

Eric Bettinger presents a careful analysis of an overlooked but important question. Economic researchers have noted the large sums of money the

Jonathan Guryan is assistant professor of economics at the University of Chicago Graduate School of Business, and a faculty research fellow of the National Bureau of Economic Research.

United States spends on subsidies for college costs annually and have responded with a number of studies on the effect of subsidies on college matriculation decisions. But few have investigated the impact of these subsidies on what Bettinger calls "stop-out" behavior, the choice to leave college after the first year. One might ask why stop-out behavior is an interesting outcome to examine. The answer is simple: A lot of college students do it. Twenty-eight percent of first-time full-time freshmen in Ohio do not return to school the next year. Depending on whether one considers stopping out an unambiguously negative outcome—a point I will discuss shortly—this number may be a signal of a large problem. What are the likely causes of stop-out decisions? Significant suspects include failing out, realization that the decision to attend college was wrong for the student, changes at home, cost concerns, or an inability or unwillingness to pay tuition. The latter factor is one that is easily manipulated by policy, so Bettinger asks whether subsidies affect stop-out decisions.

Bettinger has compiled a unique and detailed data set for this project. The data from the Ohio Board of Regents track every college student in the state of Ohio for the 1999–2000 and 2000–2001 school years and are merged to detailed financial aid data. The data allow Bettinger to measure stop-out behavior better than has been possible in the past. Previously, researchers could not distinguish students who left college to return home to work from students who transferred to a different school. Bettinger is able to track any student who transfers to another college in Ohio.

The linked detailed financial aid data allow Bettinger to employ two estimation strategies. In the first strategy, Bettinger estimates whether changes in Pell Grants for individual students from the first year of college to the second affect stop-out decisions. He isolates variation in Pell Grant changes that is otherwise unrelated to stop-out behavior. In the second strategy, Bettinger compares the stop-out behavior of students with slightly different characteristics that cause them to have significantly different Pell Grants. Both empirical strategies suggest that larger Pell Grants lead to a smaller propensity to leave college after one year.

I would like to make two points about this research agenda. First, it is important to understand the effect the Pell Grant has on college matriculation if we want to interpret the estimates of the effect of the Pell Grant on stop-out behavior. Because we do not have conclusive evidence on the former question, we must be careful when interpreting the evidence brought to bear on the latter. A simple empirical model will help to clarify this point. Bettinger estimates the effect of Pell Grants on stop-out behavior in two ways. Each method is intended to isolate the causal effect of a dollar of Pell Grant on the likelihood that an enrolled freshman will not return to school the following fall. Consider the following model of stop-out behavior for students currently enrolled as freshmen:

(1) $\text{stopout}_{it+1} = \beta_0 \text{Pell}_{it+1} + \beta_1 \text{Pell}_{it+1} \cdot I_{it} + \beta_2 I_{it} + \mathbf{X}_{it+1} \delta + \varepsilon_{it+1},$

where stopout_{it+1} indicates that the student does not return to school in year $t + 1$, Pell_{it+1} is the size of the Pell Grant for which the student is eligible in year $t + 1$, $\mathbf{X}_{it+1}$ is a vector of individual characteristics, ε_{it+1} is a random error term, and I_{it} is a variable that indicates whether the student was induced to attend college by the Pell Grant in year t.[1] Without a good estimate of which students were induced to begin college by the Pell Grant, we are forced to estimate the model excluding $\text{Pell}_{it+1} \cdot I_{it}$ and I_{it}.

For most policy questions, we are interested in knowing the magnitudes of β_0 and β_1. These parameters tell us how sensitive particular students are to changes in the price of college. However, because we are forced to estimate the model without information indicating which students matriculated because of the Pell Grant, we can only estimate the correlation between the Pell Grant and stop-out behavior among freshmen college students. For ease of exposition, allow me to partial out the variation in demographic characteristics $(\mathbf{X}_{it})$ and denote with asterisks the orthogonal variation in the remaining variables. The regression estimate of the effect of the Pell Grant on stop-out behavior is

$$(2) \quad \beta = \beta_0 + \beta_1 \cdot \frac{\text{cov}(\text{Pell}^*_{it+1}, \text{Pell}^*_{it+1} \cdot I^*_{it})}{\text{var}(\text{Pell}^*_{it+1})} + \beta_2 \cdot \frac{\text{cov}(\text{Pell}^*_{it+1}, I^*_{it})}{\text{var}(\text{Pell}^*_{it+1})}.$$

The first two terms confirm Bettinger's contention that the estimated effect combines the price sensitivity of both groups of students. There is reason to believe that students induced to matriculate by the Pell Grant are more price sensitive on the stop-out margin as well ($\beta_1 < 0$). If we are interested in how many students continue past their first year of college because of the Pell Grant program, then we need to know the magnitude of β_0. To the extent that $\beta_1 < 0$, Bettinger's estimate is an overestimate of the magnitude of β_0.

The final term highlights that there is an additional source of bias. It is likely that $\text{cov}(\text{Pell}^*_{it+1}, I^*_{it}) > 0$. All students induced to begin college by a Pell Grant received a Pell Grant, while most of the rest of the population received no Pell Grant. Additionally, a marginal increase in the Pell Grant may increase the likelihood that $I_{it} = 1$ but should not decrease that likelihood. It is also likely that students induced to begin college by the Pell Grant have an inherently larger propensity to leave college after the first year ($\beta_2 > 0$). If true, this combination of factors would induce a positive bias in the estimate of the causal effect of Pell Grants on stop-out behavior.

---

1. Note that the cross-sectional regressions presented in section 5.3.3 estimate β_1, while the panel estimates presented in section 5.3.2 estimate a similar model in which Pell_{it} is replaced with ΔPell_{it}.

The second point I would like to discuss is the idea that reducing stop-out behavior is not necessarily a good outcome. Like all goods, education comes at a cost. The economy as a whole bears the cost of allocating resources to provide education, and the individual investing in education bears a related cost, including both explicit tuition payments and forgone earnings. As economists, we usually assume that an individual weighs the potential benefits of attending college against the costs she must bear to do so. The Pell Grant, like any subsidy of higher education, lowers the net price of college. Viewed this way, it would be quite surprising if there were no resulting change in eligible students' propensity to stay in college. Anyone close enough to the margin between staying in college and dropping out should be significantly influenced by the change in price. The question at hand is how many students are close enough to that margin. Our evaluation of the Pell Grant program should also consider whether the subsidy helps the economy utilize resources more efficiently, by directing education resources to those who would benefit most or by directing the economy's resources to those who value them most.

Indeed, the increased education for the Pell Grant recipient comes at a cost. Resources in the form of teachers' time, library and computing facilities, and classroom space could have been used to educate someone else. The government funds could have been spent on welfare, on the Center for Disease Control, to buttress the Social Security trust fund, or to lower taxes. So we must ask two important questions. First, can students with the help of their parents effectively weigh the benefits of a college education against the costs they will have to bear? And second, are the costs that students must bear to attend college different from the total cost to the economy to provide the resources necessary to educate the student? These questions are addressed in multiple chapters of this book. It seems reasonable that many high school students, when making this decision, respond to incentives they probably should ignore and poorly estimate the costs and benefits of college. Risk-averse students who heavily discount the future may fear the uncertainty associated with the benefits of college that will not come for many years. All of these factors can cause students to drop out of school before they reach the level that would maximize their lifetime wealth.

If Pell Grants correct systematic mistakes made by students, as discussed in other chapters of this book, or if they compensate for higher borrowing costs that are due to discrimination or asymmetric information, then we should conclude such education price subsidies improve how education resources are allocated. If Pell Grants reduce stop-out behavior by students who are highly risk-averse or greatly discount the future, then supporters of college subsidies must justify the paternal nature of the federal government telling college-aged students what will be best for them when they "grow up." If Pell Grants increase the educational attainment of students solely because the price of college is lower, then it would seem easy to argue that there are better uses of government funds.

Bettinger has taken an important first step in recognizing the prevalence of stop-out behavior and in analyzing the effect of the Pell Grant on students' decisions to continue in college past the first year. He has comprised a unique data set, which is sure to produce additional important research going forward. The results indeed suggest that changes in individual Pell Grants affect year-to-year college attendance. The next important question in this research agenda is why.

Do and Should Financial Aid Packages Affect Students' College Choices?

Christopher Avery and Caroline M. Hoxby

6.1 How Scholarships and Aid Affect the College Choices of High-Aptitude Students

Every year, thousands of high school seniors who have high college aptitude are faced with complicated arrays of scholarships and aid packages that are intended to influence their college choices. Some of the scholarships and aid are meant purely to relieve liquidity constraints that might prevent needy students from attending the college they most prefer. Other scholarships and aid packages are designed to alter students' preference ranking of colleges—for instance, by attracting them to a college that might be unappealing in the absence of a scholarship. A student with high aptitude has complex financial supports for his college education: outside scholarships that are purely merit based; outside scholarships that are merit and need based; state scholarships that are usable only at in-state

Christopher Avery is professor of public policy at the John F. Kennedy School of Government, Harvard University, and a faculty research fellow of the National Bureau of Economic Research. Caroline M. Hoxby is professor of economics at Harvard University, and director of the Economics of Education program and a research associate of the National Bureau of Economic Research.

The authors are affiliated, respectively, with the John F. Kennedy School of Government and the Department of Economics, Harvard University. The authors gratefully thank Andrew Fairbanks and Jim Barker who helped to design and implement the College Admissions Project survey. They also thank Michael Behnke, Larry Momo, and Jay Mathews for help at initial stages. Five hundred ten high school counselors really made the survey happen; the authors wish they could thank them individually. The authors owe thanks to the research assistants who contacted high school counselors, coded data, programmed, and otherwise helped us greatly: Joshua Barro, Rohit Chandwani, Michael Cuthbert, Suzanne Ko, Ilyana Kuziemko, Michael McNabb, Kathryn Markham, Emily Oster, Chris Park, Jenna Robins, Aaron Roth, Jesse Shapiro, Maria Shim, Catherine So, Rania Succar, Michael Thakur, Kenneth Wang, and Jill Zitnik. Scott Resnick deserves special thanks.

public colleges; state scholarships that are usable at any in-state college; work-study programs; college scholarships that are purely merit based; college scholarships that are merit and need based; college grants (as opposed to named scholarships) that are merit and need based; subsidized and unsubsidized loans from their college, outside charitable organizations, and the government.

This fascinating array of scholarships, grants, loans, and work-study programs exists because many parties want to alter meritorious students' college choices. The parties' objectives are diverse—from a purely altruistic desire to relax constraints facing the needy to a college's self-interested desire to enroll high-aptitude students who raise its profile or improve education for other students on campus.

The students who face these complex choices are not a large group, but they are important. Many commentators would say that they are important because they will later account for a disproportionate share of the nation's leaders, scientists, and intellectuals. Their human capital and abilities are often thought to generate social spillovers. However, the behavior of high-aptitude students is also important purely for reasons of scientific inquiry. They are capable of the largest human capital investments in the nation: By the time these students complete their education, some of them will be "walking capital stocks" of considerable income-generating power. In this era in which the *human* capital stock of developed economies like America's is thought to be crucial to growth, it is important to know whether the biggest investors in human capital make their investments efficiently. It is not only the size of their investments that makes them interesting: Observing them allows us to witness the forces that affect human capital investments at their most highly charged because the stakes are high. Finally, high-aptitude students are likely to be the investors who most closely obey the model of the rational human capital investor: They are capable of complex analysis, they are the least risky for creditors, and they tend to be patient people who take future benefits seriously.

Despite the interest inherent in the question of how meritorious students respond to scholarships and aid, very little evidence exists. We believe that this is primarily because analysis is impossible with traditional sources of student survey data, which do not contain sufficiently large numbers of this relatively rare type of student. That is, one cannot hope to use survey data to understand such students' behavior unless the survey greatly oversamples them. For this paper, we created a survey directed specifically to high-aptitude students, with the result that we use the largest existing data set on this type of student.

Although almost no systematic evidence exists on how high-aptitude students respond to scholarships and aid, many selective colleges do perform internal analyses using data on the students they themselves admit. See, for instance, Ehrenberg and Sherman's (1984) study of students who were accepted by Cornell University in the spring of 1981. While we believe that college's internal analyses provide helpful evidence, they have flaws: They necessarily focus on a narrow set of students (the students accepted by one college); they are sometimes tacit about their empirical methods; and the studies are hard to compare because most are unpublished (distribution is often purely internal). Also, while colleges have complete information about their own aid offers and matriculation, they typically have poor information about their admittees' other college acceptances and aid offers.

Though there is a scarcity of systematic evidence on the college choice behavior of meritorious students who can attract complex offers of financial support, there is no similar scarcity about the effects of financial aid on the typical student or the poor student. We shall not attempt a survey here but instead direct readers to the chapters by Dynarski (chap. 2), Long (chap. 3), and Bettinger (chap. 5) in this volume.

6.2   How *Should* Students Respond to Scholarships and Aid?

6.2.1   A Swift Review of the Standard Model of Human Capital Investment

Throughout this paper, we are working from a model of human capital investment. It sets the standard we use in our attempt to determine whether students react too much or too little to scholarships and aid. Because it underlies our question, a quick review seems in order.

It may be useful to state the implication of the model in intuitive terms. In return for getting more aid, a student must generally accept a reduction in the human capital investment made in him at college or a reduction in the consumption he enjoys at college. Put more bluntly, a student must generally enjoy a less resource-rich college environment or a less rich peer environment in return for larger grants and other subsidies.

A simple version of the human capital investment problem will show why students generally face these trade-offs. Consider the problem facing a student who has very high college aptitude. In the United States, it is reasonable to assume that he knows that he is going to attend *some* four-year college and must only decide which college to attend among those that have admitted him.[1] If he acts as a "rational" investor, not bound by credit constraints (an issue we will consider in the following), then he need make only two calculations for each college in his choice set. Supposing that the

---

1. When he is applying to colleges, the student must form expectations of his probability of admission to each college and the scholarships or aid each college would likely offer him. That is, in order to avoid the inconvenience and cost of applying to all colleges, a student attempts to foresee the choices he will have and the actions he will take in the stage upon which we focus: the stage at which the student chooses among colleges that have accepted him. While we do not model the application stage because it is not necessary for our analysis, the extension of our model to the earlier stage requires only simple adaptations: Application must have a cost (at least an effort or psychic cost, if not a financial one); students must use expected probabilities of admission; and students must use expected grants, loans, et cetera.

student has figured out the cheapest way to attend each college, given the aid offered him, his first calculation is the present discounted cost of attending each college j:

$$(1) \qquad \sum_{t=1}^{t=4} \frac{(\text{TuitionFees}_{jt} + \text{RoomBoard}_{jt})}{(1+\delta)^{t-1}}$$

$$- \sum_{t=1}^{t=4} \frac{\text{ApplicableGrants}_{ijt} + \text{ApplicableLoans}_{ijt}^* + \text{WorkStudySubsidies}_{ijt}^*)}{(1+\delta)^{t-1}}$$

$$+ \sum_{t=1}^{t=T} \frac{\text{LoanRepayments}_{ijt}^*}{(1+\delta)^{t-1}}.$$

His second calculation is the present discounted value of the consumption he enjoys at college j plus the present discounted value of the stream of income generated by the human capital invested in him at college j:

$$(2) \qquad \sum_{t=1}^{t=4} \cdot$$

$$\frac{\text{FoodConsumption}_{ijt} + \text{HousingConsumption}_{ijt} + \text{OtherConsumption}_{ijt}}{(1+\delta)^{t-1}}$$

$$\cdot \sum_{t=5}^{t=T_i} \frac{r_{it}(\text{Resources}_{jt} + \text{PeerSpillovers}_{jt})}{(1+\delta)^{t-1}}.$$

In both equations (1) and (2), i indexes individual students, j indexes colleges, δ is the discount rate on future years, and t indexes years ($t = 1$ is the freshman year, $t = 5$ is the first postbaccalaureate year, and T_i is the end of working life.

In equation (1), the first term is the present discounted value of total potential costs of college: tuition, fees, room, and board. Notice that these costs apply only to the four years of college. The second term is the present discounted value of the potential costs that he does *not* (immediately) pay: the grants that apply to college j (college j's institutional grants and outside scholarships usable at college j), the loans that apply to college j (college j's institutional loans, subsidized loans from the federal government and outside charitable groups, and unsubsidized bank loans), and the subsidy value of the work-study program given the number of hours and job he works. The third term records the present discounted value of the payments the student makes (up to the end of his working life if necessary) in order to repay the college loans recorded in the second term. The variables that have asterisks require the student to choose them optimally.[2]

---

2. The optimal use of loans on offer should take into account each loan's interest rate, its repayment schedule, and its provisions (if any) in case of disability or other exogenous reason

In equation (2), the first term is the present discounted value of the consumption that the students enjoys at the college: food; housing; and other consumption, like recreational facilities, concerts, and so on. Of course, this consumption does not include consumption for which the student pays out of his own pocket, although it may include college-financed discounts at on-campus restaurants, concerts, et cetera. The second term is the present discounted value of the returns he enjoys on the human capital invested in him at college j. This human capital is assumed to come from two sources: resources invested in his learning (faculty time, college advisors' time, library resources, laboratories, etc.) and knowledge spillovers from his peers. Peer spillovers are only a *possible* source of human capital; though they are generally believed to exist, their form and even their existence is somewhat doubtful.[3] Notice that we allow the student's return on the stock of human capital he acquires in college to be specific to him (because of ability) and specific to each year (because human capital acquired at college interacts with human capital acquired through experience). The student's return on his stock of human capital need not be exclusively financial. Any return—psychic, social, et cetera—that the student values may be included in r_{it}. Of course, we will have difficulty quantifying nonfinancial returns.

The alert reader may notice that we have said nothing about the opportunity cost of college, which is the income and value of leisure the student sacrifices when he attends college. These opportunity costs are approximately the same for any college chosen by the meritorious student, so we do not need to consider them when we explain his college choice.

In order to choose which college to attend, the student has only to subtract equation (1) from equation (2) and consider the difference he obtains for each college. He should attend the college with the largest difference— that is, the college at which the present discounted benefits of college most exceed the present discounted costs.

---

why the student might fail to have sufficient income to repay. In practice, the optimal use of loans tends to be simple: Students exhaust more-subsidized loans, then exhaust less-subsidized loans, leaving their marginal loan an unsubsidized one. The choice of optimal work-study hours is a good deal more complicated. A student should take into account the per-hour subsidy implicit in the work-study program and the loss of human capital caused by using hours for work that might be used for study. Note the subsidy he needs is the *true* value of the subsidy, compared to the market wage for an equivalent job. In order to consider an equivalent job, he will generally need to think about the equalizing wage differential associated with the sort of job provided under the work-study program—is it menial, educational, or in a particularly convenient location? We can observe very little of the information that we would need to assess the true subsidy value of work study or to determine whether the student is choosing his work-study hours optimally. Therefore, we will have little to say about optimal work study after this.

3. Good peers may merely facilitate a student's absorbing the nonpeer resources invested in him; in this case the functional form, though not the spirit, of equation (2) should be altered. Specifically, the equation should include terms that interact with peer quality and resources, not the level of peer quality.

It should now be clear that it could not be an equilibrium for students *not* to face trade-offs between aid and the resources available at a college (including peers). For instance, suppose a group of students could be admitted to colleges A, B, and C, and that college C was preferable or at least as good as the others on the grounds of peers, the resources available for students, tuition (that is, lower tuition), campus life, location, and so on. Suppose also that college C systemically offered more aid (that is, systemically offered aid packages containing subsidies with a greater total value). Then, no trade-off would exist; the students would do better all around by matriculating at college C.

This no-trade-off situation could not be an equilibrium. If all students saw the clear advantages of college C and received more aid, college C would be so oversubscribed that it would automatically become more selective so that the typical student admitted to colleges A and B would no longer be admitted to college C. As a consequence, college C's peer quality would no longer be equivalent to that of colleges A and B. Of course, it is possible that an *individual* student will face no trade-off between two colleges in his choice set. However, such no-trade-off situations must necessarily be idiosyncratic to individual students. They cannot hold generally.

We will say that a student is acting like a rational human capital investor if he always chooses the college that maximizes the difference between equation (2) and equation (1) for him. That is, he will never be tempted by more aid to attend a college that offers such reduced consumption and human capital investment that he is worse off over his lifetime. Similarly, he will not refuse to attend colleges that offer aid packages that are so generous that they more than offset the reduction in consumption and human capital investment he experiences in college. Also, he will act in accordance with the present discounted value of various forms of aid—for instance, he will recognize that loans must be repaid and that only part of a work-study package is a subsidy. In this paper, when we test students against a standard of rational human capital investment, we are attempting to determine whether they act in accordance with the last few sentences. (The word "rational" can be loaded with meaning about mental processing. We are using it in a strictly limited way. In this chapter, "rational" means that a student obeys the standard model of human capital investment.)

There are three broad reasons why students might fail to respond to aid like the rational human capital investor. First, a student may be rational but credit constrained. In particular, his parents may be too well off to attract need-based aid *and* unwilling to pay for the optimal college themselves *and* unwilling to co-sign loans so that he can pay for the optimal college himself. Second, a student may be rational but systemically misinformed—for instance, he may be naive about colleges' different levels of resources and therefore choose a college at which he will accumulate much less human capital than he thought he would. Third, a student may simply not attempt to maximize his own lifetime utility when he chooses a college.

6.3   The College Admissions Project Survey Data

Our data come from the College Admissions Project, in which we surveyed high school seniors applying to college during the 1999–2000 academic year.[4] The survey was designed to gather data on an unusual group of students: students with very high college aptitude who are likely to gain admission to and attract merit scholarships from selective colleges. While such students are represented in surveys that attempt to be nationally representative, such as the National Educational Longitudinal Survey, they are a very small share of the population of American students. As a result, the number of such students is always so small in typical surveys that their behavior cannot be analyzed, even if the survey contains a large number of students. Yet questions of the type that motivate this paper apply acutely to students of high college aptitude, who can—if they wish—consider a wide variety of colleges, merit scholarships, and aid packages. By focusing on students with very strong academic credentials, we hope to learn how students who can attract interesting aid packages respond to them.

6.3.1   The Survey Design

In order to find students who were appropriate candidates for the survey, we worked with counselors from 510 high schools around the United States. The high schools that were selected had a record of sending several students to selective colleges each year, and they were identified using published sources (such as Peterson's guides to secondary schools) and the experience of admissions experts (Andrew Fairbanks, Michael Behnke, and Larry Momo). Each counselor selected ten students at random from the top of his senior class as measured by grade point average. Counselors at public schools selected students at random from the top 10 percent of the senior class, while counselors at private schools (which tend to be smaller and have higher mean college aptitude) selected students at random from the top 20 percent of the senior class.[5] The counselors distributed the surveys to students, collected the completed surveys, and returned them to us for coding.[6] Students were tracked using a randomly assigned number; we never learned the names of the students who participated.

Survey participants completed two questionnaires over the course of the

4. See Avery and Hoxby (2000) for additional detail.

5. The counselors were given detailed instructions for random sampling from the top twenty, thirty, forty, or fifty students in the senior class, depending on the size of the school. For example, a counselor from a public school with 200 students in a class was asked to select 10 students at random from the top 20 students in the senior class, with the suggestion that the counselor select students ranked 1, 3, 5, 7, 9, 11, 13, 15, 17, and 19.

6. The exception was the parent survey, which parents mailed directly to us in an addressed, postage-paid envelope so that they would not have to give possibly sensitive financial information to the high school counselor. Because counselors have access to the information on the students' surveys (and must, in order to support their applications competently), we were not as concerned about students' giving information to their counselors.

academic year. The first questionnaire was administered in January 2000. It asked for the same background, academic, and extracurricular information that college applications require. The majority of these questions were taken directly from the Common Application, which is accepted by many colleges in place of their specific application forms. In addition, each student listed (up to) his ten most preferred colleges regardless of whether he had applied to them yet. Each student also listed the colleges and graduate schools (if any) attended by each parent and the colleges (if any) attended by older siblings, along with their expected graduation dates.

The second questionnaire was administered in May 2000 and asked for information about the student's admission outcomes, financial aid offers, scholarship offers, and matriculation decision. Each student listed their financial aid packages with the amounts offered in three categories: grants, loans, and work study. Each student also listed institutional scholarships (scholarships offered by a specific college for exclusive use there) and outside scholarships (and their restrictions, if any).[7] The responses on merit-based scholarships, both institutional and outside, were accurate and clear, presumably because students were proud of them as accomplishments.[8] Finally, each student was asked an open-ended question: "Did finances play a role in your decision?"

A third questionnaire was distributed to a parent of each survey participant. The parent was asked to indicate whether either tuition or financial aid considerations (or both) would affect their child's choice of college. In addition, each parent was asked to check one of fifteen boxes to indicate their income range in 1999. (See table 6.1 for the income categories.)

We matched the College Admissions Project data to colleges' administrative data on tuition, room, board, comprehensive cost, enrollment, and expenditure. In all cases, the ultimate source for the administrative data was the college itself, and the data were for the 2000–2001 school year, which corresponds to the survey participants' freshman year.[9]

The College Admissions Project survey produced a response rate of approximately 65 percent, including information for 3,240 students from 396 high schools. So far as we could discern from the data we had on respon-

---

7. Students were offered the option of photocopying their financial aid offers, blacking out their names, and submitting the copy in place of answering the question. A minority of students did so.

8. In most cases, we were able to validate the terms of the scholarship because it is described on the college's website or in its publications. Our survey respondents' descriptions were very accurate; in no case did we fail to validate the key terms of a scholarship.

9. We collected the administrative data from the following sources in order: The United States Department of Education's Integrated Postsecondary Education Data System (IPEDS), the United States Department of Education's College Opportunities Online system (COOL; U.S. Department of Education 2001, 2002), the College Board's annual survey (ACS; 2002), the 2001 edition of *Peterson's Guide to Four-Year Colleges* (2002), and the colleges themselves. That is, we attempted to fill in each observation using the first source first; missing observations were filled in using one of the remaining sources, in order.

Table 6.1 **Description of the Students in the College Admission Project Data**

Variable	Mean	Standard Deviation	Minimum	Maximum
Male	0.4120	0.4923	0	1
White non-Hispanic	0.7321	0.4429	0	1
Black	0.0350	0.1837	0	1
Asian	0.1571	0.3640	0	1
Hispanic	0.0382	0.1918	0	1
Native American	0.0010	0.0313	0	1
Other race/ethnicity	0.0366	0.1878	0	1
Parents are married	0.8305	0.3752	0	1
Sibling(s) enrolled in college	0.2327	0.4226	0	1
Parents' income, estimated if necessary	119,929.0000	65,518.2100	9,186	240,000
Parents' income < $20k	0.0221	0.1469	0	1
Parents' income $20–30k	0.0379	0.1910	0	1
Parents' income $30–40k	0.0301	0.1710	0	1
Parents' income $40–50k	0.0398	0.1955	0	1
Parents' income $50–60k	0.0497	0.2174	0	1
Parents' income $60–70k	0.0594	0.2363	0	1
Parents' income $70–80k	0.0690	0.2535	0	1
Parents' income $80–90k	0.0522	0.2225	0	1
Parents' income $90–100k	0.0855	0.2796	0	1
Parents' income $100–120k	0.1495	0.3566	0	1
Parents' income $120–140k	0.0923	0.2895	0	1
Parents' income $140–160k	0.0771	0.2667	0	1
Parents' income $160–200k	0.0761	0.2653	0	1
Parents' income $200+k	0.1594	0.3661	0	1
Expected family contribution, estimated if necessary	27,653.4700	16,523.9200	0	120,000
Applied for financial aid?	0.5946	0.4910	0	1
Finances influenced college choice?	0.4114	0.4922	0	1
Amount of outside scholarships, applicable at *any* college	203.0781	799.9640	0	12,500
National Merit Scholarship winner	0.0494	0.2167	0	1
Student's SAT score, sum of math and verbal, converted from ACT score if necessary	1,356.9110	138.8193	780	1,600
Student's SAT score, expressed as national percentile	90.4013	12.3362	12	100
Median SAT score at *most* selective college to which student was admitted	86.4092	10.3836	34	98
Median SAT score at *least* selective college to which student was admitted	73.8469	14.5646	14	97
Number of colleges to which student was admitted	3.5250	2.1293	1	10
Student's high school was private	0.4534	0.4979	0	1
Student's high school in AL	0.0170	0.1292	0	1
Student's high school in AR	0.0028	0.0526	0	1

(*continued*)

Table 6.1 (continued)

Variable	Mean	Standard Deviation	Minimum	Maximum
Student's high school in AZ	0.0093	0.0958	0	1
Student's high school in CA	0.1222	0.3276	0	1
Student's high school in CO	0.0120	0.1091	0	1
Student's high school in CT	0.0327	0.1779	0	1
Student's high school in DC	0.0096	0.0974	0	1
Student's high school in FL	0.0287	0.1670	0	1
Student's high school in GA	0.0111	0.1048	0	1
Student's high school in HI	0.0201	0.1402	0	1
Student's high school in ID	0.0031	0.0555	0	1
Student's high school in IL	0.0633	0.2435	0	1
Student's high school in IN	0.0086	0.0926	0	1
Student's high school in KS	0.0046	0.0679	0	1
Student's high school in KY	0.0031	0.0555	0	1
Student's high school in LA	0.0105	0.1019	0	1
Student's high school in MA	0.0855	0.2797	0	1
Student's high school in MD	0.0327	0.1779	0	1
Student's high school in ME	0.0052	0.0723	0	1
Student's high school in MI	0.0198	0.1392	0	1
Student's high school in MN	0.0056	0.0743	0	1
Student's high school in MO	0.0198	0.1392	0	1
Student's high school in MT	0.0019	0.0430	0	1
Student's high school in NC	0.0219	0.1464	0	1
Student's high school in NE	0.0031	0.0555	0	1
Student's high school in NH	0.0167	0.1280	0	1
Student's high school in NJ	0.0522	0.2224	0	1
Student's high school in NM	0.0102	0.1004	0	1
Student's high school in NV	0.0031	0.0555	0	1
Student's high school in NY	0.1278	0.3339	0	1
Student's high school in OH	0.0309	0.1730	0	1
Student's high school in OK	0.0062	0.0783	0	1
Student's high school in OR	0.0105	0.1019	0	1
Student's high school in PA	0.0472	0.2121	0	1
Student's high school in RI	0.0086	0.0926	0	1
Student's high school in SC	0.0031	0.0555	0	1
Student's high school in TN	0.0201	0.1402	0	1
Student's high school in TX	0.0395	0.1948	0	1
Student's high school in UT	0.0071	0.0840	0	1
Student's high school in VA	0.0333	0.1795	0	1
Student's high school in VT	0.0031	0.0555	0	1
Student's high school in WA	0.0160	0.1257	0	1
Student's high school in WI	0.0077	0.0875	0	1
Student's high school in WU	0.0028	0.0526	0	1

Source: 3,240 students in College Admissions Project sample.

dents, partial respondents, and nonrespondents, lack of participation was uncorrelated with observable student and school characteristics. This was probably because counselor vagaries accounted for most of the partial responses and nonresponses.[10] The final sample contains students from forty-three states plus the District of Columbia.[11] Although the sample was constructed to include students from every region of the country, it is intentionally representative of students who apply to highly selective colleges and, therefore, nonrepresentative of American high school students as a whole. Regions and states that produce a disproportionate share of the students who apply to selective colleges are given a weight in the sample that is approximately proportionate to their weight at very selective colleges, not their weight in the population of American high school students. Of course, all of the students in the sample have very strong academic records. It is not surprising that the sample contains students whose parents have higher incomes and more education than typical American parents.

6.3.2   The Typical Student in the College Admissions Project

The summary statistics shown in tables 6.1 and 6.2 (and in tables 6A.2 and 6A.3) demonstrate that the sample is quite special. The average (combined verbal and math) Scholastic Aptitude Test (SAT) score among participants was 1357, which put the average student in the sample at the 90th percentile of all SAT takers. About 5 percent of the students won a National Merit Scholarship; 20 percent of them won an outside scholarship that was *fully* portable; and 46 percent of them won a scholarship from at least one college. Forty-five percent of the students attended private school, and their parents' income averaged $119,929 in 1999. However, 76 percent of the sample had incomes below the cutoff where a family is considered for aid by selective private colleges (the cutoff averaged $160,000 for 2000–2001, but the actual cutoff depended on family circumstances). Fifty-nine percent of the students applied for need-based financial aid, and 41 percent of the families reported that finances influenced their college choice.[12] Of course, a college may offer a student a scholarship or grant to persuade him to matriculate, regardless of whether he has applied for aid.

Eighty-three percent of the student's parents were currently married,

10. The most common reasons for failure to return the survey were changes in the job of the high school counselor (so that the survey would no longer be a natural part of his job), the counselor's becoming pregnant or ill, and other administrative problems that were unrelated to the college admissions outcomes of students who had been selected to participate. We tested whether respondents, partial respondents, and nonrespondents differed in school characteristics, January survey characteristics, and basic characteristics reported by counselors (sex, race, class rank). We did not find any statistically significant differences among respondents, partial respondents, and nonrespondents.

11. The states missing from the sample are Alaska, Delaware, Iowa, Mississippi, North Dakota, South Dakota, and West Virginia.

12. That is, either the parent, the student, or both claimed that finances influenced the college choice decision.

Table 6.2 **Description of the Colleges to Which Students Were Admitted, from the College Admission Project Data**

Variable	Mean	Standard Deviation	Minimum	Maximum
Matriculated at this college	0.2825	0.4502	0	1
Admitted to this college	1.0000	0.0000	1	1
Applied early to this college	0.1298	0.3405	0	2
Withdrew application from this college, usually after early decision elsewhere	0.0000	0.000	0	0
Grants specific to this college	2,719.8600	5,870.0240	0	36,000
Loans from this college	641.3459	2,282.1720	0	36,548
Work study amount from this college	172.1048	593.0736	0	15,000
Grant is called a "scholarship"	0.1958	0.3968	0	1
Grant is front-loaded (more in freshman year)	0.0212	0.1440	0	1
Grant is this share of tuition	0.1885	0.4369	0	7
Grant is this share of comprehensive cost	0.1109	0.2258	0	2
Student was a recruited athlete at this college	0.0275	0.1634	0	1
Father is an alumnus of this college	0.0401	0.1962	0	1
Mother is an alumna of this college	0.0283	0.1659	0	1
Sibling attended or attends this college	0.0484	0.2146	0	1
College is public	0.3325	0.4711	0	1
College is private not-for-profit	0.6628	0.4737	0	1
College is international, except for Canadian colleges, which are treated as U.S. colleges	0.0045	0.0672	0	1
College's median SAT score, in national percentiles	80.5947	12.5188	14	98
Student's SAT score is this many percentiles *above* college's median SAT score	11.2945	10.2160	0	82
Student's SAT score is this many percentiles *below* college's median SAT score	1.1006	4.3038	0	58
In-state tuition	16,435.1500	9,594.0020	0	27,472
Out-of-state tuition	19,293.5700	6,190.8330	0	27,472
Tuition that applies to this student	17,670.6000	8,491.8630	0	27,472
Room and board at this college	6,808.9370	1,322.2720	0	10,299
In-state comprehensive cost of this college	23,785.2000	10,368.3300	0	35,125
Out-of-state comprehensive cost of this college	26,641.5400	7,032.6210	0	35,125
Comprehensive cost that applies to this student	25,022.2000	9,219.1590	0	35,125
Per-pupil expenditure on students (instruction, student services, academic support, scholarships) of this college, in thousands	26.0321	15.5894	2	146
Instructional per-pupil expenditure of this college, in thousands	17.4502	11.8691	2	72
College is in-state	0.3270	0.4691	0	1
Distance between student's high school and this college, in miles	597.1856	808.9188	0	5,769
College is in AK	0.0000	0.0000	0	0

Table 6.2 (continued)

Variable	Mean	Standard Deviation	Minimum	Maximum
College is in AL	0.0053	0.0724	0	1
College is in AR	0.0004	0.0187	0	1
College is in AZ	0.0056	0.0748	0	1
College is in CA	0.1385	0.3454	0	1
College is in CO	0.0109	0.1038	0	1
College is in CT	0.0380	0.1913	0	1
College is in DC	0.0260	0.1591	0	1
College is in DE	0.0032	0.0561	0	1
College is in FL	0.0164	0.1271	0	1
College is in GA	0.0197	0.1389	0	1
College is in HI	0.0035	0.0592	0	1
College is in IA	0.0042	0.0648	0	1
College is in ID	0.0013	0.0363	0	1
College is in IL	0.0543	0.2265	0	1
College is in IN	0.0206	0.1422	0	1
College is in KS	0.0022	0.0468	0	1
College is in KY	0.0006	0.0248	0	1
College is in LA	0.0094	0.0965	0	1
College is in MA	0.1054	0.3070	0	1
College is in MD	0.0219	0.1462	0	1
College is in ME	0.0144	0.1191	0	1
College is in MI	0.0227	0.1488	0	1
College is in MN	0.0089	0.0938	0	1
College is in MO	0.0259	0.1589	0	1
College is in MS	0.0009	0.0296	0	1
College is in MT	0.0010	0.0311	0	1
College is in NC	0.0356	0.1852	0	1
College is in NE	0.0018	0.0419	0	1
College is in NH	0.0118	0.1078	0	1
College is in NJ	0.0217	0.1457	0	1
College is in NM	0.0017	0.0408	0	1
College is in NV	0.0008	0.0281	0	1
College is in NY	0.1212	0.3263	0	1
College is in OH	0.0273	0.1630	0	1
College is in OK	0.0018	0.0419	0	1
College is in OR	0.0087	0.0928	0	1
College is in PA	0.0713	0.2573	0	1
College is in RI	0.0193	0.1376	0	1
College is in SC	0.0049	0.0700	0	1
College is in TN	0.0139	0.1170	0	1
College is in TX	0.0222	0.1474	0	1
College is in UT	0.0045	0.0668	0	1
College is in VA	0.0391	0.1938	0	1
College is in VT	0.0104	0.1013	0	1
College is in WA	0.0122	0.1098	0	1
College is in WI	0.0090	0.0942	0	1
College is in WV	0.0000	0.0000	0	0
College is in WY	0.0003	0.0162	0	1

Source: 11,468 college admissions events for the 3,240 students in the College Admissions Project sample.

and 23 percent of the students had at least one sibling currently enrolled in college. The racial composition of the survey participants was 73 percent white non-Hispanic, 16 percent Asian, 3.5 percent black non-Hispanic, and 3.8 percent Hispanic. We found that the black and Hispanic subgroups were too small for separate analysis. We also found that the white and Asian subgroups behaved similarly, all else being equal. Thus, we will not discuss students' races further in this chapter.

Looking at table 6A.2, which shows descriptive statistics on the colleges where the students *applied,* we can see that the survey participants applied to a range of colleges that included "safety schools" (the mean college to which a student applied had a median SAT score 8.5 percentiles below the student's own). However, the participants also made ambitious applications: 47.5 percent of them applied to at least one Ivy League college.

Table 6.2 shows descriptive statistics for colleges to which the students were *admitted.* This is the set of observations on which we concentrate in our analysis of college choice—for the simple reason that students can choose only among those colleges to which they were admitted. Comparing table 6.2 to table 6A.2, we can see that the students made logical application decisions. The mean college to which they *applied* had a median SAT score at the 83rd percentile; the mean college to which they were *admitted* had a median SAT score at the 81st percentile. This small difference suggests that the students aimed a little high in their applications, a procedure that is optimal. Sixty-six percent of the colleges to which they were admitted were private, and their mean tuition was $17,671. Notice that we show the colleges' in-state tuition, out-of-state tuition, and the tuition that actually applies to the students in the sample (in-state or out-of-state as appropriate).

Finally, table 6A.3 shows descriptive statistics for the colleges at which the students matriculated. They are more selective, on average, than the colleges to which the students were admitted: their median SAT score is at the 83.4th percentile, as opposed to the 81st percentile median SAT score of the colleges to which students were admitted. This makes sense because it implies that students included "safety schools" in their choice sets but that they did not actually matriculate at their "safety schools" when they did not need to. One measure of the unusual college aptitude of the survey participants is the list of colleges at which the largest numbers of participants enrolled. Seventeen institutions enrolled at least fifty students from the sample: Harvard; Yale; University of Pennsylvania; Stanford; Brown; Cornell; University of Virginia; Columbia; University of California, Berkeley; Northwestern; Princeton; Duke; University of Illinois; New York University; University of Michigan; Dartmouth; and Georgetown.

6.3.3   Some Variables with Interesting Measurement Issues

Our measurement of most variables was perfectly straightforward, but a few exceptions are worth mentioning. We converted American College

Test (ACT) scores to SAT scores using the crosswalk provided by the College Board. We converted all college admissions scores into national percentile scores using the national distribution of SAT scores for the freshman class of 2000–2001.[13] We used longitude and latitude to compute the distance between a student's high school and each college to which he applied. We used parents' reports of their own incomes whenever available.

When a parent report of income was unavailable, we substituted an estimate of parents' income based on the Expected Family Contribution reported by the student. (The Expected Family Contribution is the standardized federal estimate of the amount that parents should be able to contribute toward the student's college education.) We can explain 88 percent of the variation in the Expected Family Contribution using just two variables: parents' income and likely current expenditures for the college education of older siblings. We know about siblings' enrollment and likely expenditures for their education. Therefore, our estimates of parents' income based on the Expected Family Contribution and siblings' college expenses are highly accurate. Later, readers will see that we only need to group parents into four income groups. For families that reported both parents' income and an Expected Family Contribution, our estimate of parents' income based on Expected Family Contribution placed families into the correct group 97 percent of the time.

A remaining 3.4 percent of families had neither a reported parents' income nor a reported Expected Family Contribution. For these families, we estimated parents' income by assigning parents the mean incomes for people with the same detailed occupation in the March 2000 Current Population Survey (which asks about a person's 1999 income from his occupation). For families for which we could check this method, we found that it assigned them to the correct income group 91 percent of the time.[14]

Finally, because the aid and scholarship variables are important, we hand-checked every observation to ensure that no scholarship was counted twice (as a grant and again as a scholarship), recorded incorrectly as a four-

---

13. This is an important, although often neglected, conversion. A given change in an SAT scale score (of, say, 100 points) corresponds to a differing number of percentiles, depending on where the scale score is in the distribution. For instance, the difference between a combined score of 1500 and 1600 is only a few percentiles, but the difference between a combined score of 1400 and 1500 is three to four times as many percentiles. The unconverted scale scores generate seriously biased estimates when used in regression equations where the scores enter linearly.

14. For the occupation-based estimate of parents' income, nearly all of the "mistakes" were caused by our assigning families to the medium-high-income group when they truly belonged in the high-income group. We suspect that our medium-high-income group probably contains about twelve families that should be assigned to the high-income group. The underassignment to the high-income group is caused by professional occupations' having income distributions with a right-hand skew. Think, for instance, of attorneys. Parents make it into the high-income group because they are, say, unusually highly paid lawyers, not because the mean income for a lawyer would put them there.

year total rather than an annual amount, or recorded with insufficient restrictions. In all cases where a student reported a named scholarship or grant with published parameters (for instance, Morehouse Scholars at the University of North Carolina), we validated the basic terms of the scholarship or grant.

6.4   Empirical Strategy

Our empirical strategy is straightforward. We are interested in discovering the factors that influence a student's choice among the colleges to which he is admitted. This is an estimation problem for which *conditional logit* (also known as McFadden's choice model) is ideally suited.

Intuitively, conditional logit groups together the colleges to which each student was admitted. This becomes a student's menu or college choice set. A binary outcome variable shows which college was actually picked—in our case, it is a dummy variable equal to 1 for the college at which the student matriculated and 0 for all of the other colleges in the student's choice set. Each college in the choice set has a number of attributes, some of which are the same for all students (such as whether the college is public or private) and some of which depend on the identity of the student (such as grants to the student from the college). Conditional logit estimation relates the binary outcome variable to the college attributes by maximizing the following log likelihood function:

$$(3) \qquad \ln L = \sum_{i=1}^{n} \sum_{j=1}^{J_i} \text{matric}_{ij} \ln \text{Prob(collegechoice}_i = j),$$

where

$$(4) \qquad \text{Prob(collegechoice}_i = j) = \frac{e^{\beta' x_{ij}}}{\sum_{j=1}^{J_i} e^{\beta' x_{ij}}}.$$

Examining equation (3), one sees that the conditional logit estimates are those that maximize the *similarity* of the estimated likelihoods and the actual matriculation decisions.

In equations (3) and (4), i indexes the student; j indexes the college; the indicator variable matric_{ij} is equal to 1 if student i chooses to matriculate at college j, and zero otherwise; and collegechoice_i is simply the student's college choice. The vector x_{ij} includes the attributes of choice j for student i—note that the subscripts indicate that the attributes may be match specific. β is the vector of effects that we are interested in estimating. One maximizes the log of the likelihood simply to make estimation easier.

The choice problem we are investigating is suitable for conditional logit estimation but unsuitable for multinomial logit estimation. Although multinomial logit is related to conditional logit and sometimes confused with it, it cannot be used to examine choice in a situation where choices have match-specific attributes, such as a scholarship that applies to one student accepted by a college but not to all students accepted by that college.

There are a number of empirical issues that deserve comment.

6.4.1   The Variation That Drives the Estimates

It is important to be explicit about the variation that drives our estimates. First, all of the variation used is *within* the choice set of a student. Second, within a given student's choice set, there is variation in the attributes of colleges because colleges vary for reasons that are effectively exogenous to the individual student. For instance, colleges differ in location, in whether they are publicly or privately controlled, in endowment, in the niche they fill in the market for college education, and so on. All of this and much more variation in their attributes is effectively exogenous or parametric to the individual student, who must accept the range of choices available to him given his characteristics and aptitude.

There is one possible worry about the endogeneity of the attributes of colleges, but it seems minor based on a priori grounds as well as empirical evidence. It is as follows. We might worry that a college's aid offer to a student is not only a function of his merit but also reflects effort on the student's part *that is observed by that college only* and that is a function of his desire to attend that particular college. Note our emphasis on the effort being observed by one college only. Any merit or effort that can be observed by all colleges is *not* a problem. For instance, if a student collects special letters or other evidence of merit that he sends only to his most preferred college, it could cause a problem (the aid package offered by his most preferred college might be a function of a match-specific liking). If he collects the special letters or evidence of merit with one college in mind but actually sends them with all his applications, there is no problem.

There are three reasons to think that this form of endogeneity is minor. First, even if a student gathers special information with only one college in mind, he is still best off sending it to all colleges. Second, colleges ask for information in a calculating way. Although a student who supplies unasked-for information may improve his aid package somewhat, he is unlikely to get it changed radically because most important achievements are revealed in the application materials. Third, in our survey data, there is little indication that students were able to make special efforts that convinced colleges to give them substantially different aid offers. The College Admissions Project survey asked students whether they had been able to get any aid offer revised. Revisions occurred in only 9 percent of possible college choices, and most of the revisions were very minor in character, based on the verbatim responses of students who described the revision they obtained. Only two students described a revision that would cost a college more than $1,000 over four years.

6.4.2   The Role of a Student's Own Attributes

People are sometimes surprised to find that there are no individual student attributes (such as the student's SAT score) included in the vector $\mathbf{x}_{ij}$ for conditional logit estimation. However, a little thought shows why this is so. The student's own characteristics are the same regardless of the choice he makes, so they cannot be a reason for choosing one college over another. It is only college attributes or *match-specific* attributes that can influence his choice. For instance, a student might care about whether his SAT score is much higher or lower than the average SAT score at a college. Thus, the difference between a student's SAT score and a college's average SAT score is a match-specific attribute included in the vector $\mathbf{x}_{ij}$. College attributes that differ across colleges but are constant across students within a college (such as whether the college is publicly or privately controlled) are also in the vector $\mathbf{x}_{ij}$ because they obviously can be reasons for choosing one college over another.

Individual student attributes may affect college choice even though they are constant across all of a student's choices. This is because they may affect the *way* that he responds to a particular college or match-specific attribute. For instance, a student from a low-income family may be more responsive to loans offered by a college than is a student from a high-income family (which presumably has many more alternatives to the college's loan, including regular bank or home equity loans). Thus, although we cannot include student attributes as $\mathbf{x}_{ij}$ variables that affect college choice, we do estimate our choice model separately for students with different attributes. For instance, we show tests for different responsiveness of students with different family income, of students whose parents attended more- and less-selective colleges, and of students from private and public secondary schools. In fact, we tested for different responsiveness along many other dimensions, such as region, gender, and race. We show every dimension for which the data even hinted at there being differential responsiveness.

6.4.3   The Consequences of Observing Only a Subset
         of a Student's Possible College Choices

We do not observe all of the colleges to which a student *could* have been admitted and all of the financial aid packages they would have offered him. We focus on the subset of colleges to which he was admitted, among those to which he applied. In the appendix, we offer more detail on this issue.[15] Here, we offer the logic of the situation.

Suppose that we *did* observe all of the colleges to which student could

---

15. Specifically, we address three issues: the independence of irrelevant alternatives, endogenous choice sets, and lack of balance in choice sets that arises naturally when choice sets are endogenous.

have been admitted and the financial aid packages he would have received at each college.[16] Then it would be the case that, given the student's preferences, some colleges were dominated by others. The dominated colleges would be irrelevant to the student's choice. For instance, many students apply to a "safety school" to which they know they will be admitted with near certainty. However, no student applies to numerous similar "safety schools." Some of the "safety schools" would be dominated and, therefore, irrelevant to his choice. When a student chooses to apply to a school, he is revealing that he expects the college to be a relevant alternative in some scenario. Put another way, when a student chooses not to apply to a college, he is revealing that the college will be dominated in all likely scenarios. Dominated colleges may be very similar to (but, nevertheless, less preferred than) other colleges in the student's choice set. By forming his choice set this way (called "endogenous choice set formation"), the student is helping to exclude irrelevant alternatives from his choice set. Irrelevant alternatives pose a problem for conditional logit estimation.

In addition, some readers may be comforted by the fact the data do not reject in the Hausman-type test of the independence of irrelevant alternatives (see appendix).

6.4.4 Early Decision Applicants

When a student applies early decision, he gets the admission benefits of an early decision application (a slight relaxation of the admissions standard) in return for giving up the right to use the knowledge conveyed by the regular admissions process (he cannot bargain with the early decision college using admissions and aid offers from other colleges). Essentially, he predicts what his other alternatives would have been and chooses to apply early decision based on those predictions, his preferences, and his beliefs about the relaxation in standards for early decision applicants.

Because our survey asks about the ten colleges most under consideration by a student, we know which colleges the student considered relevant even if he applies early decision. However, for some early decision applicants, we do not know what admissions and aid outcomes they would have received at the colleges to which they were applying through regular admission. We lack such information when a student is accepted early decision and, consequently, withdraws his regular applications. Some of our early decision applicants withdraw their applications before learning about their alternative admissions outcomes; other early decision applicants report admissions and aid outcomes from regular applications, which suggests that they got this information before withdrawing. (Early *action* applicants

---

16. We are simplifying for the purpose of exposition. We might actually want to estimate the probability distribution of aid packages for each college. For instance, the student might have only a 10 percent probability of receiving a special scholarship of $10,000 at college j but an 80 percent probability of receiving a small grant of $1,000 there.

rarely withdraw their regular applications, it being to their advantage to have as wide a menu as possible.) Out of 3,240 students, 338 (or 10.4 percent) are early decision applicants for whom we do not observe outcomes from regular college applications.

Our basic set of estimates does not use the behavior of these 338 students. (The estimation procedure automatically sets them aside because there is no variation in the outcome matric$_{ij}$; we do not have to purposely exclude them.) However, excluding the 338 students is not like excluding students at random—they might be an unusually risk-averse or sophisticated group of students.

We attempt to remedy the problem by showing a second set of results based on our predicting admissions and aid outcomes for the colleges in the 338 students' most preferred college lists that did not result in completed regular admissions processes. We have good conditions for forming these predictions because we nearly always observe outcomes for similarly qualified students *from the same school.* This is a useful consequence of our sample design. We use the following procedure to form the predictions for the "incomplete" colleges. In order to eliminate colleges to which the student would probably not have been admitted, we first eliminate incomplete colleges where the student's own SAT score would put him below the colleges' median SAT score. (We experimented with other percentile thresholds down to the 25th percentile, but we found that the results did not change much.) We now need to create reasonable aid packages for a student's incomplete colleges. Because aid tends to have a local character (a highly meritorious student from Detroit will systemically receive a different aid package at the University of Michigan than a highly meritorious student from Kansas City), we create an aid package for each student at each incomplete college by using the aid package of another student in his school who *was* admitted to that college. Because grants depend mainly on merit, each incomplete college's grant is filled by the grant actually received by the other student who (1) came from the student's own high school; (2) was accepted by the college; and (3) had the SAT score most similar to the student's own. Because loans and work study depend mainly on parental income, each incomplete college's loans and work study are filled by the loans and work study actually received by the other student who (1) came from the student's own high school; (2) was accepted by the college; and (3) had parental income most similar to the student's own.

We show the results based on these predicted choice sets, after presenting our basic results. So long as the two sets of results are similar, we can be reasonably confident that our evidence does not hinge on the exclusion of early applicants accepted by only one college. We are interested in whether the results are similar, not identical (or nearly identical). We do not expect the results to be identical because the estimates from the predicted choice sets are likely to be slightly inconsistent because they are based on explanatory variables that are measured with error for the incomplete colleges (attenuation bias).

6.4.5 The Specification of $\beta' \mathbf{x}_{ij}$

Except for reasons of parsimony, we have not attempted to restrict the set of variables that affect college choice. We have included all variables available to us that seemed at all likely to affect students' choices.

We have imposed only two restrictions that seem worth mentioning. First, we measure all the financial variables in thousands of annual dollars, not in the natural log of dollars or other transformation. This is because we wish explicitly to test whether students react similarly to the same dollar amount when it arises in two different but fundamentally similar forms. For instance, a student following the classic human capital investment model would be expected to react similarly to a reduction of $1,000 in the annual tuition of a college and an increase of $1,000 in the annual grant given him by the college. Also, we wish explicitly to test whether students react differently to the same dollar amount when it arises in two forms that cost the college very different amounts. For instance, the aforementioned rational student should not react similarly to $1,000 in grants and $1,000 in loans. The cost to the college of a loan may be anywhere from zero to about 15 percent of its face value, but it is rarely, if ever, close to 100 percent of its face value (as the grant is).

Second, we restrict most $\mathbf{x}_{ij}$ variables to having a linear effect because this choice facilitates interpretation. We have, however, allowed some variables, such as distance and a student's SAT "match" with a college, to have nonlinear effects.

6.4.6 The Interpretation of the Estimates We Show

We display the conditional logit results using odds ratios and Z statistics. An odds ratio gives us the ratio of the posterior odds of a college choice to the prior odds of a college choice *when only the variable in question is allowed to change*. For instance, we could compute the odds that college j is chosen, then raise its tuition by $1,000—holding all other variables equal—and recompute the odds. The former odds would effectively be the prior odds, and the latter odds would effectively be the posterior odds. In short, the odds ratio is α in the following expression:

$$\text{posterior odds} = \alpha \cdot \text{prior odds}$$

It is easy to compute the odds ratio from the estimated vector $\hat{\beta}$ because the odds ratio is just $e^{\hat{\beta}}$.

The way to interpret the odds ratio for a certain variable in $\mathbf{x}_{ij}$ is the proportional change in the odds of student i attending college j for a unit increase in the variable, holding all other variables constant. A simple example would be the indicator for whether a college is public. If the odds ratio is 1.1, then a one unit change in the variable (corresponding to a switch from private to public) would make the student's odds of attending the college 1.1 times whatever the odds were if the college had been private. Note that the change is proportional to the prior odds: If the student's prior odds of attending the college were 30 percent, the posterior odds would be 33 percent (30 times 1.1). If the student's prior odds of attending the college were 80 percent, the posterior odds would be 88 percent (80 times 1.1).

Naturally, an odds ratio greater than one means that an increase in the variable *raises* a student's probability of matriculating, all else being equal; an odds ratio less than one means that an increase in the variable *reduces* a student's probability of matriculating, all else being equal.

The Z statistics are easy to interpret. They are akin to familiar *t* statistics and have the same thresholds for statistical significance. Thus, an odds ratio with a Z statistic greater than 1.96 is statistically significantly different from 1 (the null hypothesis of no effect) with 95 percent confidence, and so on.

6.5   How Aid Affects College Choice

6.5.1   Basic Results on the Determinants of College Choice

In this section, we discuss our basic results on the determinants of college choice, which are presented in table 6.3. Recall that the outcome is matriculation, a binary variable equal to 1 for exactly one of the colleges to which a student was admitted.

If we examine table 6.3's overall pattern of signs and statistical significance, students' college choices appear to be very reasonable. Students are more likely to attend a college if, all else being equal, it offers them larger grants, offers them larger loans, offers them a larger amount of work study, is the most selective college to which they were admitted, is their father's alma mater, or is the same college that their sibling attended or attends. Students are less likely to attend a college if, all else being equal, its tuition is higher, its room and board is higher, its mean SAT score is below theirs, or it is the least selective college to which they were admitted. Several variables do not have a statistically significant effect on students in our survey: the amount by which the college's average SAT exceeds the student's, an indicator for the college being their mother's alma mater, the distance between the college and the student's high school, whether the college is public, and whether the college is in-state.

At the broad "sign and statistical significance" level, the results are close to our expectations. But are they so close to our expectations when we examine the odds ratios in detail?

The left-hand column of table 6.3 shows us that an additional thousand dollars in grants raises a student's probability of matriculating by 11 percent

	Estimated Odds Ratio
Table 6.3 **The Determinants of College Choice: Estimated Odds Ratios from Conditional Logic Regressions in Which the Binary Outcome Is Matriculation**	
Grant (in thousands), specific to the college	1.108*
	(14.81)*
Loan (in thousands) from the college	1.068*
	(4.03)*
Work study amount (in thousands) from the college	1.125*
	(1.64)*
College's tuition (in thousands), in-state or out-of-state as appropriate to the student	0.980*
	(−1.90)*
College's room and board (in thousands)	0.903*
	(−3.28)*
College's per-pupil instructional spending (in thousands)	1.020*
	(6.02)*
Student's SAT score is this number of percentiles *above* college's average SAT score	0.959*
	(−6.45)*
Student's SAT score is this number of percentiles *below* college's average SAT score	1.001
	(0.011)
College is *most* selective to which student was admitted	1.631*
	(7.41)*
College is *least* selective to which student was admitted	0.694*
	(−4.23)*
Father is alumnus of this college	1.703*
	(3.62)*
Mother is alumna of this college	1.001
	(0.189)
Sibling attended or attends this college	1.896*
	(5.04)*
Distance between college and student's high school, in hundreds of miles	1.000
	(0.06)
Square of distance between college and student's high school, in 10,000s of miles	1.000
	(1.03)
Cube of distance between college and student's high school, in 1,000,000s of miles	1.000
	(−1.01)
College is in-state for the student	1.162
	(1.59)
College is public	1.201
	(1.59)
No. of observations	9,112
Likelihood ratio (chi^2)	1,171.41
Prob > chi^2	0
Log-likelihood	−2,335.57
Pseudo R^2	0.201

Source: College Admissions Project.

Notes: The table shows results from conditional logit estimation of how a student chooses his matriculation college among the colleges to which he was admitted. The results are shown as odds ratios, with z statistics in parentheses.

*Statistically significantly different from zero at the 10 percent level.

of his prior probability; an extra thousand dollars in tuition lowers a student's probability of matriculating by 2 percent of his prior probability, and an extra thousand dollars in room and board lowers a student's probability of matriculating by 10 percent of his prior probability. These results hint at students' being more sensitive to grants and room and board than to reduced tuition. This is not altogether surprising. A student's reactions to a dollar of grants and tuition need not be *identical*. An increase in his grant affects the individual student's costs but leaves the college environment pretty much unchanged. In contrast, a reduction in tuition lowers the college's revenues, which may reduce the quality of the college environment.

What is more surprising is the response to loans and work study. Recall that an additional thousand dollars in grants raises a student's probability of matriculating by 11 percent. In comparison, an additional thousand dollars in loans raises a student's probability of matriculating by 7 percent of his prior probability, and an additional thousand dollars in work study raises a student's probability of matriculating by 13 percent of his prior probability. (Note that the work-study response is imprecise and is, therefore, not statistically significantly different from the response to grants.) These results suggest that students do not view loans and work study as much inferior to grants, despite the fact that they cost a college much less than a grant does. Loans and work study have substantial costs for students, even though the burden of loans is delayed, and the cost of work study is in the form of forgone leisure.

For every percentile that a student's SAT score *exceeds* the mean SAT score of a college, his probability of matriculating falls by 5 percent of his prior probability. Although the odds ratio on the percentile that a student's SAT score *falls short* of the mean SAT score of a college is not statistically different from one, its point estimate is greater than one, suggesting that students are not deterred by a college's having higher average SAT scores than their own. That is, the SAT match variables are not symmetric, but indicate that students only dislike a mismatch if their own SAT scores are "too high" for the college. Along similar lines, a student's probability of matriculating rises by 63 percent of the prior probability if the college is the most selective among the colleges to which he was admitted, and it falls by 31 percent of the prior probability if the college is the least selective among the colleges to which he was admitted. Overall, these results strongly suggest that students place substantial weight on a college's selectivity as a measure of its value. This is not necessarily because students value selectivity per se rather than a college's resources; it may simply be that selectivity is highly correlated with resources and that selectivity is easier for students to observe and econometricians to measure than resources are.

The overall resource measure in table 6.3 is the college's per pupil spending on student-related activities (instruction, academic support, student services, and scholarships). Each additional thousand dollars in spending raises a student's probability of matriculating by 2 percent of his prior probability. This may not sound like much, but it means that a 50 percent increase in spending would raise a student's probability of matriculating by about 31 percent. (The last estimate is for the average college in the sample.)

Finally, having a father or sibling who attended the college greatly increases a student's own probability of attending it. Having a father who attended raises the probability of matriculating by 70 percent of the prior probability; having a sibling who attended raises the probability by 90 percent. This strong family alumnus effect may be due to the student's familiarity with or allegiance to the college, but it might equally be match-specific attributes that are similar for the student and other members of his family (shared tastes, similar career plans, and so on).

6.6   Are Early Decision Students Different?

In table 6.4, we compare our basic results to results that include early applicants accepted by only one college. Specifically, the left-hand column of table 6.4 repeats our basic results from the left-hand column of table 6.3, and the right-hand column includes the early applicants accepted by only one college, substituting their predicted choice sets for their actual choice sets. We described the procedure for generating predicted choice sets in section 6.4.

The table shows that the results change very little when the early decision students are included with their predicted choice sets. The coefficients that change in an interesting way are those of the college's being the least or most selective college in the choice set. Consider the coefficient on the most selective college: The change in it suggests that early decision applicants are less apt than other students to matriculate at the most selective college to which they were admitted. The behavioral interpretation of this result is that early decision applicants are somewhat risk averse and also act strategically: They apply early decision knowing that they will face slightly less stringent admissions criteria. What they give up is the chance to apply to and matriculate at the college that would have been their "long shot."[17]

Now consider the coefficient on the least selective college. Its change suggests that early decision applicants are also less apt than other students to matriculate at the least selective college to which they were admitted. Again, this fits with postulated strategic behavior among early decision applicants: They aim for greater certainty at a college with moderately high selectivity on their list, not for certainty at the least selective college on their list.

---

17. Another interpretation of the change in the "most selective" coefficient is that we have mistakenly predicted admission to a college that the student himself knew would not admit him. It is unclear how the student would know such a thing if his admissions test scores were, indeed, above the median.

Table 6.4   **Including Early Decision Students in Estimates of College Choice, Estimated Odds Ratios from Conditional Logit Regressions in Which the Binary Outcome Is Matriculation**

	Actual Choice Sets	Predicted Choice Sets Used for Early Applicants
Grant (in thousands), specific to the college	1.108*	1.102*
	(14.81)*	(14.75)*
Loan (in thousands) from the college	1.068*	1.073*
	(4.03)*	(4.29)*
Work study amount (in thousands) from the college	1.125*	1.113
	(1.64)*	(1.47)
College's tuition (in thousands), in-state or out-of-state as appropriate to the student	0.980*	0.984*
	(−1.90)*	(−1.78)*
College's room and board (in thousands)	0.903*	0.893*
	(−3.28)*	(−3.76)*
College's per-pupil instructional spending (in thousands)	1.020*	1.020*
	(6.02)*	(5.35)*
Student's SAT score is this number of percentiles *above* college's average SAT score	0.959*	0.950*
	(−6.45)*	(−8.45)*
Student's SAT score is this number of percentiles *below* college's average SAT score	1.001	1.003
	(0.011)	(0.26)
College is *most* selective to which student was admitted	1.631*	1.313*
	(7.41)*	(6.57)*
College is *least* selective to which student was admitted	0.694*	0.886*
	(−4.23)*	(−3.49)*
Father is alumnus of this college	1.703*	1.650*
	(3.62)*	(3.54)*
Mother is alumna of this college	1.001	0.966
	(0.18)	(−0.19)
Sibling attended or attends this college	1.896*	1.854*
	(5.04)*	(5.03)*
Distance between college and student's high school, in hundreds of miles	1.000	1.000
	(0.06)	(−0.05)
Square of distance between college and student's high school, in 10,000s of miles	1.000	1.000
	(1.03)	(0.72)
Cube of distance between college and student's high school, in 1,000,000s of miles	1.000	1.000
	(−1.01)	(−0.70)
College is in-state for the student	1.162	1.196*
	(1.59)	(1.95)*
College is public	1.201	1.119
	(1.26)	(0.80)
No. of observations	9,112	10,227
Likelihood ratio (chi²)	1,171.41	1,447.94
Prob > chi²	0	0
Log-likelihood	−2,335.57	−2,516.18
Pseudo R^2	0.201	0.223

Notes: This table is the same as table 6.3, except that the right-hand column substitutes predicted choice sets for actual choice sets for early decision applicants. The prediction procedure is described in the text. All other notes from table 6.3 apply.

*Statistically significantly different from zero at the 10 percent level.

Because including the early applicants who have only one college in their choice set makes so little difference to our results, we do not show results for predicted choice sets from here onward.[18]

6.7 Do Students from Different Families Make College Choices Differently?

In this section, we investigate whether students from different family backgrounds make college choices differently. That is, do they respond differently to the same college and match-specific attributes? By design, the students in the College Admissions Project sample are similar in aptitude, but their backgrounds are much less similar along the dimensions of family income, parents' college experience, and so on. In tables 6.5 through 6.8, we show the results of reestimating our basic conditional logit specification (the specification in table 6.3) for different subsets of students.

6.7.1 Students with Different Family Income

One obvious hypothesis is that students with different family incomes will respond differently to aid, tuition, room and board, and other attributes of colleges. Because high-income families can more easily finance college out of savings or obtain cheap loans, we suspect that students from such families will be less sensitive to the variables that determine how much they will actually pay for college in any given year.

For table 6.5, we divided students into four groups based on family income: "low" being less than $40,000; "medium-low" being $40,000 to $80,000; "medium-high" being $80,000 to $140,000; and "high" being greater than or equal to $140,000. The right-hand column in the table contains the word "rejected" when the hypothesis that the odds ratios for the four income groups are equal is rejected with 90 percent confidence.

Students from families with low incomes respond to $1,000 in grants by raising their probability of matriculation by about 11 percent of their prior probability. Students with medium-low and medium-high family income respond, respectively, by raising the probability of matriculation by about 13 percent. Students from high-income families also respond but only by raising the probability of matriculation by 8 percent of their prior probability. We can reject the hypothesis that the effect is the same for all income groups with 90 percent confidence. Despite the statistically significant differences, we were somewhat surprised by the *similarity,* not the difference, in the response of meritorious students from different ends of the income spectrum.

We cannot reject the hypothesis that all income groups respond identi-

---

18. Readers may be interested to know that if we use predicted choice sets for *all* students (not just early applicants), we obtain estimates that suffer from attenuation bias. This is what we expect because the aid variables are only estimates for many observations.

Table 6.5 Are Students from Low- and High-Income Families Equally Sensitive to the Determinants of College Choice? Estimated Odds Ratios from Conditional Logit Regressions

	Parents' Income				Same effect for all groups?
	Low	Medium Low	Medium High	High	
Grant (in thousands), specific to the college	1.114*	1.128*	1.133*	1.075*	Rejected
	(5.15)*	(7.98)*	(10.68)*	(5.02)*	
Loan (in thousands) from the college	1.036	1.067*	1.072*	1.076*	
	(0.65)	(1.68)*	(2.55)*	(2.60)*	
Work study amount (in thousands) from the college	1.059	1.219	1.081	1.040	
	(1.32)	(1.45)	(0.66)	(1.66)	
College's tuition (in thousands), in-state or out-of-state as appropriate to the student	1.000	0.981	0.964*	0.980	
	(0.47)	(−0.40)	(−2.27)*	(−0.57)	
College's room and board (in thousands)	0.840*	0.945	0.911*	0.898*	
	(−1.67)*	(−0.85)	(−1.82)*	(−1.86)*	
College's per-pupil instructional spending (in thousands)	1.031*	1.016*	1.020*	1.021*	
	(2.56)*	(1.98)*	(3.69)*	(3.89)*	
Student's SAT score is this number of percentiles *above* college's average SAT score	0.986	0.946*	0.956*	0.957*	
	(−0.82)	(−3.86)*	(−4.33)*	(−3.36)*	
Student's SAT score is this number of percentiles *below* college's average SAT score	0.986	1.019	1.008	1.015	
	(−0.59)	(0.77)	(0.43)	(0.53)	
College is *most* selective to which student was admitted	1.430	1.612*	1.437*	1.899*	
	(1.57)	(3.27)*	(3.30)*	(5.41)*	
College is *least* selective to which student was admitted	0.986	0.798	0.625*	0.666*	
	(−0.05)	(−1.18)	(−3.39)*	(−2.46)*	

	Low	Medium low	Medium high	High	
Father is alumnus of this college	3.772	1.293	2.395*	1.256	
	(1.73)	(0.69)	(3.60)*	(0.94)	
Mother is alumna of this college	0.268	2.231*	0.510*	1.919*	Rejected
	(−1.02)	(1.79)*	(−2.13)*	(2.14)*	
Sibling attended or attends this college	2.559*	1.900*	2.268*	1.328	
	(2.04)*	(2.18)*	(4.17)*	(1.18)	
Distance between college and student's high school, in hundreds of miles	0.971	1.006	1.003	0.998	
	(−1.20)	(0.36)	(0.22)	(−0.13)	
Square of distance between college and student's high school, in 10,000s of miles	1.000*	1.000	1.000	1.000	
	(−2.00)*	(0.47)	(−0.08)	(1.17)	
Cube of distance between college and student's high school, in 1,000,000s of miles	1.003*	1.000	1.000	1.000	
	(2.00)*	(−0.47)	(0.09)	(−1.13)	
College is in-state for the student	0.967	1.079	1.379*	1.001	
	(−0.10)	(0.36)	(2.08)*	(0.01)	
College is public	1.602	1.909	1.128	1.062	
	(1.00)	(2.02)	(0.51)	(0.22)	
No. of observations	838	2,011	3,459	2,731	
Likelihood ratio (chi²)	151.91	348.23	456.62	314.11	
Prob > chi²	0	0	0	0	
Log-likelihood	−194.7	−468.1	−884.73	−715.03	
Pseudo R^2	0.28	0.27	0.21	0.18	

Source: College Admissions Project.

Notes: The table shows results from conditional logit estimation of how a student chooses his or her matriculation college among the colleges to which he or she was admitted. The results are shown as odds ratios, with z statistics in parentheses below the odds ratios. Parents are divided into four income groups: low (less than $40,000); medium low ($40,000 to $80,000); medium high ($80,000 to $140,000); and high (greater than or equal to $140,000). The right-hand column contains the word "rejected" when the hypothesis that the odds ratios for the four income groups are equal is rejected with 95 percent confidence.

*Statistically significantly different from 1 with at least 95 percent confidence.

cally to $1,000 of loans, although the point estimates hint that students from low-income families are less attracted by loans—perhaps because they foresee their families having trouble paying off loans. Also, we cannot reject the hypothesis that $1,000 in work study has the same effect on students from all income groups. Moreover, the pattern of estimates on work study is quite difficult to interpret. Students may respond to work study in a heterogeneous way that shows up as coefficients that bounce around. We suspect that this may be because work study has important attributes, contained in the job itself, that we do not observe. For instance, it may be that work study at one college is an academically valuable research job, while work study at another college is an onerous cleaning job.

The greatest negative response to tuition is among students from medium-high-income families. This is not surprising because medium-high-income families are well off enough to pay list tuition but not so well off that list tuition is small relative to their incomes. Low-income parents appear to be quite insensitive to tuition differences. This is probably because they rely on need-based aid and rarely pay the marginal tuition dollar anyway.

As family income rises, students become less willing to attend a college where their own SAT scores exceed the college's mean score. Conversely, students become more eager to attend a college where their own SAT scores fall below the college's mean score. For instance, the draw of the most selective college in a student's choice set rises from a 43 percent increase in the probability of matriculation for the low-income families to a 90 percent increase in probability for the high-income families. The repulsion of the least selective college in the choice set goes from a 1 percent decrease in the probability of matriculation for low-income families to a 33 percent decrease in probability of matriculation for high-income families.

Compared to other students, students from high-income families respond less to having a father or sibling who attended the college but respond to having a mother who attended the college. Only low-income students respond to a college's distance from their secondary school, and only medium-high-income students respond to a college's being in-state.

6.7.2 Students Whose Parents Attended More- and Less-Selective Colleges

It may be that college choice differs between families with more and less experience of selective colleges. We test this hypothesis in table 6.6, where parents are divided into groups based on the selectivity of their colleges (the maximum of the two parents' colleges selectivity).[19] Because the students themselves are solid applicants for *very* selective colleges, we were

---

19. There appear to be no students in the sample from families in which *neither* parent attended college. There are, however, a good many parents who have degrees from institutions that grant only the associate's degree or another degree below the baccalaureate.

Table 6.6   **Are Students Whose Parents Attended More and Less Selective Colleges Equally Sensitive to the Determinants of College Choice? Estimated Odds Ratios from Conditional Logit Regressions**

	Parents' College Selectivity			Same effect for all groups?
	Low	Medium	High	
Grant (in thousands), specific to the college	1.120*	1.100*	1.075*	
	(13.15)*	(6.41)*	(3.19)*	
Loan (in thousands) from the college	1.075*	1.096*	1.036	
	(3.48)*	(1.84)*	(0.93)	
Work study amount (in thousands) from the college	0.995	1.354*	2.534*	Rejected
	(−0.06)	(2.00)*	(2.62)*	
College's tuition (in thousands), in-state or out-of-state as appropriate to the student	0.980*	0.965*	1.029*	
	(−1.60)*	(−1.60)*	(0.90)*	
College's room and board (in thousands)	0.882*	1.021	0.834	Rejected
	(−3.17)*	(0.34)	(−1.89)	
College's per-pupil instructional spending (in thousands)	1.018*	1.023*	1.007	
	(4.68)*	(3.46)*	(0.88)	
Student's SAT score is this number of percentiles *above* college's average SAT score	0.962*	0.946*	0.952*	
	(−5.01)*	(−3.65)*	(−2.05)*	
Student's SAT score is this number of percentiles *below* college's average SAT score	1.022	1.176	1.496*	
	(0.71)	(1.96)	(4.74)*	
College is *most* selective to which student was admitted	1.496*	1.897*	1.635*	
	(4.74)*	(4.73)*	(2.60)*	
College is *least* selective to which student was admitted	0.699*	0.653*	0.722	
	(−3.32)*	(−2.31)*	(−1.26)	
Father is alumnus of this college	1.151	1.925*	1.493	
	(0.44)	(2.82)*	(1.45)	
Mother is alumna of this college	1.342	0.780	0.861	
	(0.84)	(−0.83)	(−0.37)	
Sibling attended or attends this college	1.936*	2.455*	0.841	
	(4.22)*	(3.43)*	(−0.39)	
Distance between college and student's high school, in hundreds of miles	1.010	0.878*	1.038	Rejected
	(1.12)	(−4.57)*	(1.66)	
Square of distance between college and student's high school, in 10,000s of miles	1.000	1.000	1.000	
	(0.53)	(2.18)	(−0.02)	
Cube of distance between college and student's high school, in 1,000,000s of miles	1.000	1.000	1.000	
	(−0.53)	(−1.43)	(−0.03)	
College is in-state for the student	1.191	0.688*	2.110*	Rejected
	(1.46)	(−1.87*)	(2.59)*	
College is public	1.206	1.587	0.789	
	(1.04)	(1.53)	(−0.48)	
No. of observations	5,673	2,280	1,159	
Likelihood ratio (chi²)	733.27	362.49	171.52	
Prob > chi²	0	0	0	
Log-likelihood	−1,447.93	−555.72	−283.98	
Pseudo R^2	0.2	0.25	0.23	

Source: College Admissions Project.

Notes: The table shows results from conditional logit estimation of how a student chooses his or her matriculation college among the colleges to which he or she was admitted. The results are shown as odds ratios, with z statistics in parentheses below the odds ratios. Parents are divided into college selectivity groups, based on the *maximum* selectivity of the two parents' colleges: low (college's median SAT is less than the 70th percentile); medium (college's median SAT is between the 70th and 90th percentile); and high (college's median SAT is greater than or equal to the 90th percentile). Note that selectivity is based on colleges' current selectivity, owing to the paucity of data on selectivity for the years parents attended college. The right-hand column contains the word "rejected" when the hypothesis that the odds ratios for the three selectivity groups are equal is rejected with 95 percent confidence.

*Statistically significant different from 1 with at least 95 percent confidence.

particularly interested in parents' experience with such colleges. Therefore, our high-selectivity group contains parents whose college has a median SAT score at or above the 90th percentile; our medium-selectivity group contains parents whose college has a median SAT score at or above the 70th percentile and below the 90th percentile; and our low-selectivity group contains all other parents.[20]

We find that students whose parents attended low-selectivity colleges are more responsive to grants and loans than students whose parents attended high-selectivity colleges. For instance, $1,000 in grants raises the probability of matriculation by 12 percent of the prior priority for a student with low-selectivity parents, but the corresponding number is only 8 percent for a student with high-selectivity parents. Also, $1,000 in loans raises the probability of matriculation by 8 percent of the prior priority for a student with low-selectivity parents, but the corresponding number is only 4 percent for a student with high-selectivity parents. It appears that students with high-selectivity parents are much more responsive to work study than other students, but we hesitate to interpret this result literally because of the variation in work-study jobs.

The difference in the response to tuition is interesting: While students with low- and medium-selectivity parents are repelled by higher tuition (each additional $1,000 in tuition reduces their probability of matriculating by 2 to 3 percent of their prior probability), higher tuition appears to attract students with high-selectivity parents (each additional $1,000 in tuition *raises* their probability of matriculating by 3 percent of their prior probability). It is unlikely that tuition itself is attractive to the high-selectivity parents, but it is quite probably correlated with measures of college resources that are not in the regression (for instance, the spending dedicated to undergraduates alone or nonlinear effects of per-pupil spending on students).

We also find that, compared to other students, students with high-selectivity parents are less attracted to their sibling's college. Students with medium-selectivity parents appear to be the most attracted by their father's and sibling's college.

6.7.3 Students from Public and Private Secondary Schools

In table 6.7, we investigate whether students from public and private high schools make college choices differently. We find that an extra $1,000

20. We were able to include Canadian colleges in the medium- and high-selectivity groups by approximating their selectivity. However, all other international colleges were included in the low-selectivity group, in part because we are trying to measure parents' experience with selective *American* colleges, which admit students, grant aid, and charge tuition in a manner that differs widely from other colleges around the world, including some colleges that are very selective in their own country. Only 1.1 percent of families have two parents who attended a non-Canadian international college.

Table 6.7 **Are Students from Private and Public High Schools Equally Sensitive to the Determinants of College Choice? Estimated Odds Ratios from Conditional Logit Regressions**

	Public High chool	Private High School	Same effect for all groups?
Grant (in thousands), specific to the college	1.112*	1.106*	
	(11.34)*	(9.49)*	
Loan (in thousands) from the college	1.084*	1.049*	
	(3.89)*	(1.76)*	
Work study amount (in thousands) from the college	1.187*	1.048	
	(1.84)*	(0.43)	
College's tuition (in thousands), in-state or out-of-state as appropriate to the student	0.977*	0.998	
	(−1.78)*	(−0.06)	
College's room and board (in thousands)	0.812*	0.955	Rejected
	(−4.77)*	(0.32)	
College's per-pupil instructional spending (in thousands)	1.020*	1.018*	
	(4.60)*	(3.99)*	
Student's SAT score is this number of percentiles *above* college's average SAT score	0.964*	0.952*	
	(−4.51)*	(−4.53)*	
Student's SAT score is this number of percentiles *below* college's average SAT score	0.992	1.015	
	(−0.51)	(0.83)	
College is *most* selective to which student was admitted	1.685*	1.583*	
	(5.70)*	(4.74)*	
College is *least* selective to which student was admitted	0.781*	0.555*	Rejected
	(−2.16)*	(−4.31)*	
Father is alumnus of this college	1.971*	1.470*	
	(3.43)*	(1.70)*	
Mother is alumna of this college	0.785	1.406	
	(−0.97)	(1.14)	
Sibling attended or attends this college	2.176*	1.388	Rejected
	(4.95)*	(1.48)	
Distance between college and student's high school, in hundreds of miles	1.004	0.987	
	(0.41)	(−1.10)	
Square of distance between college and student's high school, in 10,000s of miles	1.000	1.000	
	(0.13)	(1.15)	
Cube of distance between college and student's high school, in 1,000,000s of miles	1.000	1.000	
	(−0.13)	(−1.04)	
College is in-state for the student	1.301*	0.989	
	(2.02)*	(−0.07)	
College is public	0.967	1.96*	Rejected
	(−0.18)	(2.88)*	
No. of observations	4,817	4,295	
Likelihood ratio (chi²)	662.95	555.86	
Prob > chi²	0	0	
Log-likelihood	−1,232.24	−1,079.63	
Pseudo R^2	0.21	0.20	

Source: College Admissions Project.

Notes: The table shows results from conditional logit estimation of how a student chooses his or her matriculation college among the colleges to which he or she was admitted. The results are shown as odds ratios, with z statistics in parentheses below the odds ratios. Students are divided into two groups, based on the control (private or public) of their high schools. The right-hand column contains the word "rejected" when the hypothesis that the odds ratio for the two groups are equal is rejected with 95 percent confidence.

*Statistically significantly different from 1 with at least 95 percent confidence.

in room and board reduces the probability of matriculating by 19 percent of prior probability among public school students, but that it has a statistically insignificant effect of 5 percent on private school students. We find that private school students are more repelled than are public school students by a college's being the least selective that admitted them. For public school students, being the least selective college in the choice set reduces the probability of matriculation by 21 percent of the prior probability. For private school students, the corresponding number is a much larger—44 percent. Being an in-state college is an attraction for public school students, whose probability of matriculation rises by 30 percent of their prior probability. Being in-state has no such draw for private school students. Interestingly enough, a college's being public attracts private school students but has no such effect on public school students.

6.7.4   Summing up the Differences in College Choice among Students from Different Backgrounds

While students' choice behavior is affected by variables like parents' income, parents' college selectivity, and private high school attendance, many other background differences do *not* appear to affect students' college choices. We tried and failed to find significant differences in choice behavior along several other dimensions: gender; region of the country; recipiency of an outside scholarship, like the National Merit Scholarship; a record of leadership while in high school; size of the high school; and so on. There are no statistically significant differences by race either, but this may because there are insufficiently few nonwhites in the sample to extract distinct patterns from their choice behavior. We suspect that high aptitude students differ *systemically* in college choice behavior mainly when they face constraints that are not easily overcome—parents' income and parents' willingness to pay for private education (which is probably correlated with parents' own college selectivity and willingness to pay for private high school).

Overall, we find that students from high-income families, whose parents attended more-selective colleges and who themselves attended private high schools, are less deterred by college costs and less attracted by aid. They are also more attracted by a college's being selective, either because they are more attracted by the resources correlated with selectivity or because they are more attracted by high-aptitude peers. We might ask, however, whether the differences in responsiveness shown in tables 6.5 through 6.7 really add up to much. One way to answer this question is to investigate whether students would alter their college choices if we made them act in accordance with the estimated model for *another* group of students. To create table 6.8, we use the low-income students' coefficients with the high-income students' data and vice versa. We performed the same exchange for students with low- and high-selectivity parents and for students from private and public schools. We show the percentage of students who would be pre-

Table 6.8   **Share of Students Who Would Matriculate at Another College if They Were to Obey the College Choice Model of Students from a Different Background**

	Parent Income		Parents' College Selectivity		High School	
	Actually Low[a]	Actually High[b]	Actually Low[c]	Actually High[d]	Actually Public[e]	Actually Private[f]
Share who would matriculate at a different college in their choice set	0.315	0.417	0.244	0.238	0.167	0.172

Source: Predictions based on conditional logit regressions shown in tables 6.4 through 6.6.
[a]For students acting like high-income students.
[b]For students acting like low-income students.
[c]For students acting as though it had been high.
[d]For students acting as though it had been low.
[e]For students acting like private school students.
[f]For students acting like public school students.

dicted to change their college choice if they were to act in accordance with another group's model.

We find that a sizable minority of students *would* choose a different college within their choice set if they were to act like another type of student. Most notable are high-income students, 42 percent of whom would matriculate at a different college if they made choices the way that low-income students do. Similarly, 32 percent of low-income students would alter their college choice if they behaved as high-income students do. The corresponding numbers are in the range of 17 percent when we "exchange" the models of public and private high school students and are in the range of 24 percent when we exchange the models of students whose parents attended low- and high-selectivity colleges.

We might also ask *how* the characteristics of the students' colleges would change if they were to alter their choices. That is, would students merely choose another college that was indistinguishable from their initial college? It is not possible to answer this question satisfactorily given the limited exercise we are attempting at this point in this chapter. The reason we cannot give a satisfactory answer is that we are constraining students to rechoose within the set of colleges to which they applied and were admitted. Given our current purpose, which is merely to give readers a sense of the scale of the estimates in tables 6.4 through 6.6, this constraint is acceptable. Later, when we attempt more ambitious thought experiments, it will be important to relax this constraint. Students would apply to a different range of colleges if they were to foresee themselves acting differently when it came to choosing a college. For example, if a low-income student were to foresee that he would act like a high-income student when he chose a college, he might apply to some high-tuition colleges that he currently omits.

We can look at two outcomes in a satisfactory manner, however, because they are relative ones: the share of students who matriculate at the most and least selective colleges within their choice set. Here, we find that the altered choices are highly distinguishable. For instance, 95 percent of high-income students choose the most selective college in their choice set when they act like themselves, but only 57 percent would do so if they were to act like low-income students. Eighteen percent of low-income students choose the least selective college in their choice set when they act like themselves, but only 7 percent would do so if they were to act like high-income students.

6.8   Do Students Respond to Aid Variables They Should Ignore?

So far, we have had only one test of whether students are responding to aid variables as models of human capital investment suggest that they should: Our test was whether students responded as differently to grants, loans, and work study as they should, given the very different degree of subsidy incorporated in these three forms of aid. Students failed this test: They responded similarly to every additional $1,000, regardless of whether it was a grant or a loan. At this point in the paper, we have not made calculations that allow us to judge whether students respond too much or too little to grants, but *given* their responses to grants, their responses to loans and work study are too large.

Furthermore, tables 6.5 through 6.7 show that, while some students (high-income, high selectivity of parents' college, private high school) are less sensitive to aid, *all* students respond too much to loans and work study, in comparison to grants. For instance, high-income students treat grants and loans about equally.

6.8.1   Aid Variables That Students Should Ignore

In this section, we investigate whether students respond to aid variables they should largely, if not completely, ignore. Specifically, we look at three aspects of a grant. The first is whether the grant is called a scholarship. In other words, did the student merely report $4,000 in grants, or did he also report that the $4,000 was the, say, Jane Doe Scholarship for Merit? Based on the survey data, it appears that some colleges systemically name their grants, while others give similar amounts with no name attached. In fact, the correlation between the amount of a grant and its being called a scholarship is negative: -0.206.

We also examine whether a grant is front-loaded so that the student receives more in his freshman year than in later years. The students in our survey, all of whom have an extremely high probability of completing college, should largely ignore such front-loading and look at the total amount of grants. We characterize a grant as front-loaded if the (nominal dollar) amount for the freshman year is greater than the (nominal dollar) amount for later years.[21] As a rule, front-loaded grants are heavily weighted toward the freshman year (for instance, $10,000 for one year, and $2,000 thereafter), not steady declining over the college career (for instance, $5,500; $4,500; $3,500; and $2,500 for the four successive years). Keep in mind that we will be investigating the effect of front-loading, holding the amount of the grant constant. Thus, we ask whether students respond more to, say, $4,000 per year if it is front-loaded. As a matter of fact, the correlation between the amount of a grant and its being front-loaded is negative: –0.189.

The final aspects of grants that we examine is what *percentage* they are of tuition, comprehensive cost, and per-pupil spending on students. Obviously, if all colleges had similar tuition, comprehensive cost, and spending, larger grants would always represent a higher percentage of costs and expenditures. But colleges in our sample vary dramatically in tuition, comprehensive cost, and instructional spending. The standard deviation of in-state tuition is $9,594; the standard deviation of in-state comprehensive cost is $10,368; and the standard deviation of per-pupil spending on students is $15,489. Students in the sample applied to forty colleges at which per-pupil spending on students was less than $7,000, and they applied to about an equal number of colleges at which per-pupil spending on students was more than $28,000, which is *four times* $7,000. Students in the sample applied to 106 colleges that have in-state tuition below $2,500 and applied to 143 colleges that have in-state tuition above $20,000, which is *eight times* $2,500.[22] In short, we should not expect a very high correlation between the amount of a grant and the percentage of cost or expenditure that it represents. In fact, the correlation between the amount of a grant and the percentage of tuition that it represents is only 0.251, and the correlation between the amount of a grant and the percentage of comprehensive costs that it represents is 0.467.

If students behave according to a standard model of human capital in-

---

21. We do not assume that students understand discounting. That is, we do not characterize a grant as front-loaded if it offers the same nominal amount for each year of college, even though the present discounted value of the freshman year grant is greatest. Also, we do not characterize a grant as front-loaded if it merely has conditions for continued good performance. For instance, a grant might be $4,000 for the freshman year, which will be renewed thereafter so long as the student maintains a B average. Such conditions are clearly intended to maintain achievement, rather than exploit students' impatience or myopia. Many graduate and professional programs use front-loaded grants because students' ability to earn money or win outside grants rises steeply during a student's graduate career—think of law schools, business schools, or PhD programs. The same considerations do not apply to undergraduate programs.

22. These include many flagship public universities of the South, Southwest, West (Wyoming, Utah, Colorado), and the California State University system (not the University of California). However, most of the low-tuition group is made up of the least selective colleges to which students in the sample applied—branch campuses of public universities, non-flagship public colleges, and some low-selectivity private colleges (which had a mean SAT percentile of 53 as compared to the average of 84 among colleges in the sample).

vestment, they should care about the *amount* of a grant, not the share of cost or expenditure that it represents. The amount of the grant is a measure of the investment made freely *by others* in a student's human capital.[23] Given the amount of a grant, a student will care about the grant's *share* of tuition or costs only if he is an irrational investor (for instance, naively flattered by receiving a large *share* of tuition) or credit constrained (willing to give up others' large donations to his human capital investment in order to avoid having to make any cash contribution to that investment himself). Even if we suppose that colleges with high instructional spending are less efficient than others, it is unlikely their efficiency is so poor that 50 percent of a $28,000 expenditure truly represents a smaller investment than 100 percent of a $7,000 expenditure.

6.8.2   Evidence on How Students Respond to the Aid Variables They Should Ignore

Table 6.9 presents our estimates of how students make college choices when we allow them to respond to aid variables they should ignore. Column (1) of the table reproduces the estimates in table 6.3. Recall that the estimates suggest that each additional $1,000 of a grant is estimated to increase the probability of matriculation by 11 percent of the prior probability.

In column (2), we add the indicators for the grant's being called a scholarship and being front-loaded. We also add variables indicating the share of tuition and the share of comprehensive cost that the grant represents. The first thing to note about the results in column (2) is that students no longer respond to the *amount* of the grant. The estimated effect of each additional $1,000 of grants is statistically insignificant, and the point estimate is not even greater than one. Loans, work study, and other determinants of college choice have about the same effects that they had when we excluded the variables that should be ignored.

Column (2) also shows that, for a grant of a given amount, calling it a scholarship increases the probability of matriculation by 86 percent of the prior probability. This is a great effect for an essentially hollow feature of a grant that any college could replicate at no cost. It is implausible that the indicator for a named scholarship is picking up a nonlinear effect of the grant amount: Recall that the indicator is negatively correlated with the amount of the grant.

Front-loading also engenders a strong, positive matriculation response. For a grant of a given annual amount, its being front-loaded raises the probability of matriculation by 48 percent of the prior probability. Again,

---

23. There is another measure of the investment made *by others* in a student's human capital. It is the implicit grant created by the difference between a college's per-pupil expenditure and its list tuition. In practice, the size of a college's implicit grant increases with its selectivity.

Table 6.9   **Do Aid Variables That Should Not Matter Affect College Choice? Estimated Odds Ratios from Conditional Logit Regressions**

	(1)	(2)	(3)
Grant (in thousands), specific to the college	1.108*	0.968	0.968
	(14.81)*	(−1.46)	(−1.45)
Loan (in thousands) from the college	1.068*	1.062*	1.060*
	(4.03)*	(3.67)*	(3.54)*
Work study amount (in thousands) from the college	1.125*	1.207*	1.204*
	(1.64)*	(2.53)*	(2.48)*
College's tuition (in thousands), in-state or out-of- state	0.980*	0.998	0.998
as appropriate to the student	(−1.90)*	(−0.65)	(0.50)
College's room and board (in thousands)	0.903*	0.943*	0.946
	(−3.28)*	(−1.70)*	(−1.62)
College's per-pupil instructional spending	1.020*	1.020*	1.018*
(in thousands)	(6.02)*	(6.05)*	(5.64)*
Grant is this share of college's per-pupil instructional			1.121
spending			(0.50)
Grant is called a "scholarship"		1.860*	1.838*
		(6.15)*	(6.00)*
Grant is front-loaded (more in freshman year)		1.479*	1.475*
		(1.90)*	(1.88)*
Grant is this share of college's tuition		0.792	0.801
		(−0.98)	(−0.91)
Grant is this share of college's comprehensive cost		27.551*	23.511*
		(3.70)*	(3.30)*
Student's SAT score is this number of percentiles	0.959*	0.952*	0.951*
above college's average SAT score	(−6.45)*	(−7.31)*	(−7.36)*
Student's SAT score is this number of percentiles	1.001	0.998	0.997
below college's average SAT score	(0.11)	(−0.27)	(−0.18)
College is *most* selective to which student was	1.631*	1.641*	1.644*
admitted	(7.41)*	(7.38)*	(7.39)*
College is *least* selective to which student was	0.694*	0.676*	0.664*
admitted	(−4.23)*	(−4.43)*	(−4.60)*
Father is alumnus of this college	1.703*	1.629*	1.651*
	(3.62)*	(3.21)*	(3.26)*
Mother is alumna of this college	1.001	1.013	0.988
	(0.19)	(0.06)	(−0.06)
Sibling attended or attends this college	1.896*	1.907*	1.975*
	(5.04)*	(4.99)*	(5.21)*
Distance between college and student's high school,	1.000	1.003	1.003
in hundreds of miles	(0.06)	(0.36)	(0.42)
Square of distance between college and student's	1.000	1.000	1.000
high school, in 10,000s of miles	(1.03)	(1.20)	(1.20)
Cube of distance between college and student's high	1.000	1.000	1.000
school, in 1,000,000s of miles	(−1.01)	(−1.19)	(−1.19)
College is in-state for the student	1.162	1.191*	1.220*
	(1.59)	(1.80)*	(2.03)*
College is public	1.201	1.513*	1.536*
	(1.26)	(2.73)*	(2.80)*
No. of observations	9,112	9,112	9,112
Likelihood ratio (chi^2)	1,171.41	1,283.68	1,275.08
Prob > chi^2	0	0	0
Log-likelihood	−2,335.57	−2,255.89	−2,232.17
Pseudo R^2	0.2	0.22	0.22

Source: College Admissions Project.

Notes: The table shows results from conditional logit estimation of how a student chooses his or her matriculation college among the colleges to which he or she was admitted. The results are shown as odds ratios, with z statistics in parentheses below the odds ratios.

*Statistically significantly different from zero with at least 95 percent confidence.

this is a substantial effect for a feature that costs a college little for students who are very likely to stay enrolled for four years (as are all of the students in the sample). Because of discounting and inflation, front-loading does cost a college something but not much in comparison to the cost of inducing a student to attend by raising the amount of his grant. For instance, recall the annual grant of $4,000 and the front-loaded version mentioned previously ($10,000 for one year and $2,000 for three years). Discounting future years' spending at 6 percent, it costs the college an additional $654 to give the student the front-loaded version. However, in order to induce the same matriculation effect by raising the amount of the grant, the college would have had to raise the grant by $4,435 per year. While we should not take these numbers literally (because they are require a good deal of extrapolation and are based on different columns of table 6.9), it is fairly clear that students respond excessively to front-loading as compared to the amount of the grant.

The next two rows of column (2) show that students ignore the share of tuition that the grant represents but place a great deal of weight on the share of comprehensive cost that the grant represents. (If we were to exclude the share of comprehensive cost, the share of tuition would—for obvious reasons—pick up much of the same effect. However, the share of comprehensive cost consistently explains much more of college choice than the share of tuition.) For every increase of 10 percent (0.10) in its share of comprehensive cost, a grant induces a student to raise his probability of matriculation by 275.5 percent of his prior probability. At first glance, the odds ratio may be implausibly large, but let us interpret it. Suppose that a student's prior probability of matriculation was 10 percent. Then, his posterior probability would be 27.5 percent with a grant of 10 percent of comprehensive costs and 55.1 percent with a grant of 20 percent of comprehensive costs. What the high odds ratio is telling us is that students are offered grants that represent a large share of comprehensive costs only by colleges that they would have had low prior probabilities of attending in the absence of such grants.[24] Column (3) simply repeats the specification of column (2), adding the share of per-pupil spending that the grant represents. This additional variable does not have a statistically significant coefficient, but the magnitude of the odds ratio on the grant's share of comprehensive costs does fall somewhat (by about 15 percent).

Why is it that the grant's share of *comprehensive cost* matters, rather than its share of tuition or per-pupil spending on students? Previously, we argued that a student would care about the grant's *share* only if he were an irrational investor (flattery) or severely credit constrained (unwilling or un-

---

24. In addition, we should not really focus exclusively on the odds ratio attached to the share of comprehensive cost because the point estimate of the odds ratio on the share of tuition and the grant amount are below 1, and we know that the three variables are correlated.

able to pay cash). The grant's share of spending is only weakly related to either motive. Spending on students is difficult for students to observe, so the grant's share of spending is unlikely to be sufficiently salient to be flattering. Also, the grant's share of spending tells us little about a student's out-of-pocket payments because some colleges' spending substantially exceeds their "list" tuition and comprehensive cost. Students may respond to the grant's share of comprehensive cost rather than its share of tuition because comprehensive cost is both more salient and more relevant to the cash constrained. After all, there is a well-established term for getting a grant equal to 100 percent of comprehensive cost: "a free ride." There is no similarly accepted term for getting 100 percent of tuition. Also, the colleges that tend to offer grants that are large shares of comprehensive cost generally have low, even very low tuition ($1,500; $2,000; $2,500; etc.). At these colleges, the nontuition part of comprehensive cost is three to four times as large as tuition and makes up the lion's share of out-of-pocket expenses.

6.8.3 Do Students' Responses to Aid Variables That Should Not Matter Depend on Their Backgrounds?

In tables 6A.3 through 6A.5, we investigate whether a student's response to aid variables that should not matter depends on his background. We find some evidence that it does. To create the tables, we reestimate the regression shown in table 6.9 separately for students by parents' income group, parents' college selectivity group, and public versus private high school. Although we estimate odds ratios for all of the variables shown in table 6.9, tables 6A.3 through 6A.5 present only the coefficients relevant to our discussion of aid variables that should not matter.

We find that a grant being called a scholarship significantly attracts students in every group, *except* students whose parents have high incomes or whose parents attended highly selective colleges. Also, we find that the grant's share of comprehensive cost attracts students whose parents attended low- and medium-selectivity colleges but *not* students whose parents attended high-selectivity colleges. The latter students respond only to the amount of the grant.

Interestingly, when we investigate the very large average effect of the grant's share of comprehensive cost, we find that its significance depends crucially on medium-low-income students. Although the odds ratios for the other income groups are large also, the medium-low income group has by far the largest odds ratio and the only one that is statistically significant. This makes sense. Given their combination of merit and need, the low-income students in our survey are eligible for and attract need-based aid. Their out-of-pocket contributions are small, even at expensive private colleges. At the other extreme, medium-high and high-income students apply less often to colleges that offer grants that are a large share of a modest comprehensive cost. In contrast, consider students whose parents have medium-low incomes. They are sufficiently well off to be asked for out-of-pocket payments that are substantial (though not nearly as substantial as the payment asked of medium-high and high-income students). Yet medium-low income parents may be unwilling to pay out-of-pocket college expenses. In short, the circumstances of at least some medium-low-income students generate maximum susceptibility to small grants that represent a large share of comprehensive costs.

We find that students from private and public high schools respond quite similarly to aid variables that should be ignored.

6.9   Are Students Making Reasonable Trade-Offs?
Are They Too Attracted or Not Sufficiently Attracted by Aid?

We began with the project of determining whether students were behaving like rational investors in their own human capital. That is, are students making the best use of aid in order to maximize their lifetime economic well-being? Thus far, we have found two fairly obvious violations of rational human capital investment: students' responding excessively to loans and work study, given their response to grants; and students' responding to aspects of grants that should not matter, for a grant of a given amount. However, both of these tests are essentially *relative*. That is, we have tested whether, *given his response to grants,* the student responds excessively to loans and work study. We have tested whether, *given his response to the grant amount,* the student responds excessively to aspects of the grant that should not affect his human capital investment decision.

We have not yet addressed our principal question: whether the student's response to aid is too great or too small in an *absolute* sense. Before addressing this question, we should note that it presupposes that some trade-off exists—that is, that in order to get more aid, a student must give something up. Remember our example in which a student could be admitted to colleges A, B, and C, and where college C was as good as the others on the grounds of selectivity: the resources available for students, tuition (that is, lower tuition), campus life, location, and so on. If college C offered more aid, then no trade-off would exist: The student would do better all around by matriculating at college C. We argued that this no-trade-off situation cannot hold generally because it would not be an equilibrium: College C would be so oversubscribed that it would automatically become more selective so that the student admitted to A and B might no longer be admitted to C.

Although it is useful to demonstrate logically why the situation would not be an equilibrium, it is also useful to show empirically that the situation does not generally exist. In the College Admissions Project survey data, we find that if we look *within* students' choice sets (so that we are holding student merit constant), the correlation between the grant amount that a student receives from a college and the college's median SAT score is −0.32. The corresponding correlation between the grant amount and the college's spending on students is −0.36. These correlations suggest that, in general, a student must give up some college selectivity and/or some college resources in return for a larger grant. Put more bluntly, a student must generally allow the investment in his college education to be reduced in return for getting greater aid.

Of course, the fact that students are *generally* faced with a trade-off when they compare two colleges does not mean that students are *always* faced with one. For reasons that are idiosyncratic to the match between a particular student and college, a student may get the largest grant at the college at which he gets the most resources and which is the most selective. We have no difficulty with such idiosyncratic situations; we merely argue that such situations cannot be general as a logical matter and are not general as an empirical matter.

6.9.1   An Empirical Strategy for Determining Whether Students Respond Too Much or Too Little to Aid

Returning to our principal question (whether the student's response to aid is too great or too small in an absolute sense), recall that the student is responding as a rational human capital investor if he makes the trade-off according to a condition such as the following: (1) the subsidy value of the aid allows more consumption now, in return for an equally valuable decrease in future consumption, which will be caused by reduced human capital; and (2) the subsidy value of the aid allows the students to make less use of loans (thereby reducing future interest payments) in return for an equally valuable decrease in future earnings, which will be caused by reduced human capital.[25]

We need to measure the extent to which students reduce their human capital investment in return for increased aid. To make such a measurement, we use the estimated college choice model from the previous sections and perform some thought experiments. We take away all grants, loans, and other forms of aid (we zero out all of the aid variables), and we see how students' predicted college choices change. That is, we see how students' choices would predictably change in the absence of aid.[26]

Once we have measures of how students' predicted college choices change when we remove aid, we can estimate the losses associated with the

---

25. An additional possible trade-off, which we cannot observe in our data, works as follows. The grant might allow the student to work less and study more, thereby losing income in college but gaining income later in life because increased study is increased human capital investment.

26. Note that we look at how students' *predicted* college choices change when we zero out aid. Thus, we do not incorrectly attribute to aid the differences between students' actual and predicted behavior.

reductions in human capital and consumption that they accept in return for aid. We can then compare these losses to the value of the aid we removed.

6.9.2   Measuring Human Capital Investment at a College

We would like to measure the human capital investment made in students at various colleges. In principle, there are two ways to do this: we could measure the *inputs* available at each college or we could measure the *value added* of each college. If we wanted to measure the value added, we would need to compute the earnings associated with each college and then control for differences in earnings due to differences in students' incoming aptitudes. We would not want to attribute all of a student's earnings to his college; much of his earnings would be due to the abilities that got him admitted to the college in the first place.

Although—in theory—either the inputs or value added strategy could be pursued, we reject the value added strategy as impractical. There have been several attempts to measure the value added associated with colleges, but there are no commonly accepted estimates and some of the best-known estimates are deeply flawed.[27] However, we do not reject the value added strategy to avoid controversy. We reject the strategy because every researcher would agree that it is currently impossible to estimate value added for a *wide range* of *specific* colleges. Some might argue that we could estimate value added for a handful of specific colleges; some might argue that we could estimate value added for coarse groups of colleges (groups so coarse that some would include hundreds of colleges). No one would argue that we could estimate value added for many specific colleges. This is for a

---

27. For instance, Dale and Krueger (1999) attempted to estimate the return to attending specific colleges in the College and Beyond survey data. They assigned individual students to a "cell" based on the colleges to which they are admitted. *Within* a cell, they compared those who attend a more-selective college (the treatment group) to those who attended a less-selective college (the control group). If this procedure had gone as planned, all students within a cell would have had the same menu of colleges and would have been arguably equal in aptitude. The procedure did not work in practice because the number of students who reported more than one college in their menu was very small. Moreover, among the students who reported more than one college, there was a very strong tendency to report the college they attended plus one less-selective college. Thus, there was almost no variation within cells if the cells were based on actual colleges. Dale and Krueger (1999) were forced to merge colleges into crude "group colleges" to form the cells. However, the crude cells made it implausible that all students within a cell were equal in aptitude, and this implausibility eliminated the usefulness of their procedure. Because the procedure works best when students have large menus, and most students do not have such menus, the procedure essentially throws away much of the data. A procedure is not good if it throws away much of the data and still does not deliver "treatment" and "control" groups that are plausibly equal in aptitude. Put another way, it is not useful to discard good variation in data without a more than commensurate reduction in the problematic variation in the data. In the end, Dale and Krueger (1999) predictably generate statistically insignificant results, which have been unfortunately misinterpreted by commentators who do not have sufficient econometric knowledge to understand the study's methods.

simple reason. There is no source of data that includes earnings and college identifiers for a broad array of colleges *and* has more than a few observations for any one college.[28] We need measures of human capital investments for nearly all of the colleges in our study if we are to determine whether students are making decisions like rational investors. We must use college-specific measures, not measures for coarse college groups: Many of the students in our sample are choosing within a single coarse group.

Therefore, we use the inputs strategy for measuring human capital investment. Our approach to measuring inputs is conservative by design: We count instructional spending and *only* instructional spending as human capital investment. Instructional spending not only excludes spending on research, it also excludes some categories of spending on students: student services (such as health care), academic support, and scholarships. In other words, a good deal of spending at high-spending colleges is excluded, even though we believe that much of the excluded spending is complementary to instructional spending and produces greater human capital.[29] By focusing on instructional spending, we "bend over backward" in favor of finding that human capital investment is almost as great at low-spending colleges as it is at high-spending colleges. Empirically, instructional spending is a *much* larger share of total spending at low-spending colleges than it is at high-spending colleges. Among the colleges in our sample, the colleges with the highest per-pupil spending have instructional spending shares around 0.1; the colleges with the lowest per-pupil spending have instructional spending shares around 0.6.

It is evident from the students' own choice behavior that they prefer more-able peers, and it seems likely that peers should be regarded as inputs. That is, part of the human capital gained by a student is probably generated by peer spillovers or by the interaction of good peers and college re-

28. The longitudinal surveys and the one Current Population Survey supplement that includes college identifiers have too few people in each college (often 0, 1, or 2); the College and Beyond survey includes numerous people in each college but only includes a tiny group of colleges. The longitudinal surveys with college identifiers and a reasonably representative sample of the U.S. population are the Panel Survey of Income Dynamics, the National Longitudinal Surveys, and five surveys conducted by the United States Department of Education (the National Longitudinal Study of the High School Class of 1972, High School and Beyond, the National Education Longitudinal Study, the Beginning Postsecondary Student survey and follow-up, and Baccalaureate and Beyond). The Current Population Survey supplement with college identifiers is the Occupational Changes in a Generation study.

29. We wish to clear up a common confusion, embodied in the following question: "Does not instructional spending understate the resources at a public college that is subsidized by the state?" Instructional spending does *not* understate resources at public colleges. State governments subsidize tuition, and they often provide land and buildings below cost. The tuition subsidies are important for understanding the sources of *revenue* related to instruction, but they are irrelevant to instructional *spending*. We use instructional spending precisely because it is what it is, regardless of how the college's tuition is subsidized. Instructional spending excludes spending on buildings and land, so all colleges are treated equally with regard to these two spending categories.

sources. There is no simple way to quantify peer inputs and add them to instructional inputs. Nevertheless, we do not wish to ignore peer inputs and recognize only instructional inputs. We deal with this problem in a way that is at least transparent: We simply show changes in peers' SAT scores and remind readers that they should mentally add peer inputs with the weight they consider appropriate.

Although the students' choice behavior suggests that a student benefits from having more-able peers, there is an alternative theory. A high-aptitude student surrounded by significantly worse peers may be able to use much more than his share of a college's resources. While some attributes of a college must be shared relatively equally by all students, others (such as faculty time) can be disproportionately allocated to certain students. Logically, the disproportionality must be a function of the degree to which a high-aptitude student differs from his peers. If a high-aptitude student attends a very selective college where he is typical, he cannot expect to receive much more than an equal share of the college's per-pupil resources.

In short, we show how a student's peers change when he accepts a certain college's aid package, but we leave readers to judge for themselves whether more able peers are not generators or net destroyers of human capital, for a given level of instructional spending.

6.9.3 How Students' College Choices Would Differ in the Absence of Aid, Part 1: The Structure of Table 6.10

To create table 6.10, we first estimate the conditional logit model shown in the second column of table 6.9. We then use the coefficient estimates to predict which colleges the student would be most likely to attend (1) with the aid he was actually offered; and (2) in the absence of aid (that is, with all of the aid variables zeroed out).[30] For simplicity, we will call the former college the "with-aid college" and the latter college the "without-aid college." We then compute the present value of the aid we zeroed out, and we show this in column (2) of table 6.10.[31] That is, column (2) shows the benefit of taking aid. The succeeding columns show the costs of taking aid. Column (3) shows the difference in consumption between the with-aid and without-aid colleges. We measure the difference in consumption by sub-

30. We allow the student to rechoose among all of the colleges that appear in the College Admissions Project sample. It is reasonable to have the students choose just among the 755 colleges to which at least one surveyed student applied. This is because there are more than 3,000 other institutions of higher education in the United States that virtually never enroll a student like those in our sample. They include community colleges and other institutions that never or rarely grant the baccalaureate degree.

31. The vast majority of the variation in the value of aid comes from scholarships and other grants. Our results would not be noticeably affected by any reasonable procedure to estimate the subsidy value of loans and work-study commitments. In fact, we use federal estimates of the subsidy value of loans in the federal subsidized loan program. We do not attribute any subsidy value to loans with unsubsidized interest rates and repayment schedules. We assume that the subsidy value of a work-study commitment is one-third of its value.

Table 6.10   Students Who Gain and Lose Lifetime Present Value by Responding to Aid

	% of Students in Group (1)	Average Value of Aid ($) (2)	Average Change in College Consumption, Due to Student's Response to Aid ($) (3)	Average Change in Instructional Spending, Due to Student's Response to Aid ($) (4)	Average Change in Median Peer's SAT Percentile, Due to Student's Response to Aid (5)	Average Change in Lifetime Present Value, Due to Student's Response to Aid ($) (6)
Students who gain lifetime present value, due to their response to aid	30.8	11,534	−171	−26	−2.7	44,075
Students who lose lifetime present value, due to their response to aid	38.9	2,793	−960	−14,538	−8.5	−76,096

Source: Based on predictions from conditional logit equations like that estimated in column (2) of table 6.9. See text for details.

Notes: Top panel students may re-choose among all colleges when all aid is zeroed out. The remaining 30.3 percent of students would not change their college choice in response to aid being zeroed out, largely because they actually received little or no aid.

tracting the room and board at the without-aid college from the room and board at the with-aid college. If the difference in consumption is negative, students at the without-aid college enjoy greater food and housing consumption than students at the with-aid college.[32]

Column (4) shows the difference in instructional spending between the with-aid and the without-aid colleges. Column (5) shows the difference in the median SAT score, in percentiles, between the with-aid and the without-aid colleges. This difference indicates the change in a student's peer group.

In order to compute the change in a student's net present value from taking aid, we have to make a few assumptions to create the present values. We assume a *real* discount rate of 3 percent per year and an annual inflation rate of 3 percent. We assume a conservative 7 percent real rate of return on human capital investment, and we assume that human capital pays out for forty years.[33] In column (6), we show the change in a student's net present value, due to his response to aid. To get column (6), we first sum the instructional spending difference between the with-aid and without-aid colleges over four years of college. This gives us the human capital asset that pays out at 7 percent for forty years. We compute the present discounted value of this stream of payments and then add the present value of the change in aid and the present value of the change in consumption. Keep in mind that the calculation omits the benefits and costs of peers, which we cannot quantify accurately.

For display in table 6.10, we divide students into two groups. The top row contains students who, when we conducted our thought experiment, appeared to have made good use of the aid they were offered. Their with-aid choices have higher lifetime values than their without-aid choices. Keep in mind that, merely by sticking with the same college when aid is zeroed out, a student will be placed in this group; this is because his college variables will not change, and the student's lifetime value will mechanically be higher an amount exactly equal to the present value of the aid itself. If high achiev-

---

32. If all grants were tuition discounts, it might be appropriate to consider aid as one side of the trade-off and human capital investment (and only human capital investment) as the other side of the trade-off. But, many grants are greater than tuition and only make sense in comparison to comprehensive costs. It would obviously be incorrect to count such tuition-exceeding grants on one side of the trade-off yet exclude the consumption they finance from the other side of the trade-off.

33. Our assumption about the number of years over which human capital pays out is not crucial because the out years are so heavily discounted. Our assumption about the rate of return to human capital is more important, so we make a conservative assumption of 7 percent, which is near the bottom of the generally accepted range of estimates. It is probably especially conservative for the highly meritorious group of students whom we are studying. Indeed, the tendency of highly meritorious students to continue in school beyond the baccalaureate degree strongly suggests that they earn a supernormal rate of return during their baccalaureate years, which prompts them to continue enrolling until their rate of return is more in line with their discount rate.

ing peers make a student get more human capital from instructional spending, this group's size is overstated: Some students who appear to have made a rational human capital investment actually gave up too much in the way of peers. If high-achieving peers make a student get less human capital from instructional spending, this group's size is understated.

The bottom row contains students who, when we conducted our thought experiment, appeared to have been seduced by aid into making "irrational" human capital investments. That is, in return for aid, they accepted such large reductions in human capital investment and consumption that they lost lifetime value. If high-achieving peers make a student get more human capital from instructional spending, this group's size is understated. If high-achieving peers make a student get less human capital from instructional spending, this group's size is overstated.

Of course, there is a third group of students: students whose without-aid college was the same as their with-aid college because they actually received no aid. It is not interesting to show changes for them because zeroing out their aid changes nothing. Clearly, this group contains students who are not easily tempted by aid—if they were, they would presumably have attempted to get at least a few merit scholarships, which can be obtained by any student in our sample, no matter how rich he is, if he is willing to attend a less-selective college.

6.9.4 How Students' College Choices Would Differ in the Absence of Aid, Part 2: The Evidence in Table 6.10

Table 6.10 shows that 30.8 percent of students responded to aid in such a way that their lifetime value was increased. Some of these students simply accepted aid at the same college that they would have picked if no aid had been offered. More interestingly, some of these students accepted aid that was sufficiently generous that it swamped the reduction in college consumption and human capital investment that they generally faced. Notice that the average value of aid for students in this group was high: $11,534 per year. They attended a with-aid college that offered consumption that was, on average, $171 lower per year and instructional spending that was, on average, $26 lower per year. These losses are small. As a consequence, by responding like a rational investor to aid, the average student in this group gained lifetime present value of $44,075. This gain would be somewhat different if peers matter because we have not deducted or added any amount for the students' worse peers. The students probably lost some human capital investment because their peers were slightly worse (2.7 percentile points worse on the SAT, relative to the peers they would have had at their without-aid college). On the other hand, their slightly worse peers may have allowed them to enjoy more than their share of instructional spending.

The bottom row of table 6.10 shows that 38.9 percent of all students did *not* act like rational investors. These students accepted an aid package that was too small to make up for the losses in college consumption and human capital investment that they accepted. Notice that the average value of aid for students in this group was quite small: $2,793 per year. Compared to the without-aid college they would have attended, students in this group attended a with-aid college that offered consumption that was, on average, $960 lower per year and instructional spending that was, on average, $14,538 lower per year. On net, the average student in this group lost lifetime present value of $76,096. The loss would be somewhat different if peers matter because we have not deducted or added any amount for the student's worse peers. They probably also lost some human capital investment because their peers performed 8.5 percentile points worse on the SAT.

Readers may be initially surprised that such a nonnegligible share of students lose when they respond to aid, but the statistics in table 6.10 are really a straightforward implication of the behavior that we saw illustrated in table 6.9. The students who lose the most are precisely those students who accept aid that is actually quite modest in value but covers a large share of comprehensive cost at a college that spends very little on instruction. We know from tables 6A.3 and 6A.4 that not all students are equally likely to be losers of lifetime value: Students who have high-income parents or parents who are graduates of selective colleges themselves do not appear to be tempted by grants that are large shares of comprehensive cost at low-spending colleges. These students react only to the actual amount of a grant. We suspect that these students behave more like rational investors either because they are more sophisticated than other students or because they are less credit constrained than other students.

6.10   Interpreting the Evidence

Overall, we would describe the college choice behavior of the high-aptitude students in our sample as sensitive to college attributes in the expected direction. We find that high-aptitude students are nearly indifferent to a college's distance from their home, to whether it is in-state, and to whether it is public. However, they are sensitive to tuition, room, and board in the expected direction (lower is better). They also prefer to attend the most selective colleges in the set to which they are admitted. They are attracted by grants, loans, and work-study commitments. Although we find that students from different backgrounds do exhibit somewhat different college choice behavior, the differences are not dramatic and much college choice behavior is shared by the entire array of high-aptitude students. The main exceptions to this rule are students whose parents have high incomes or who themselves graduated from very selective colleges. Such students exhibit less sensitivity to variables that affect college costs.

This being said, the students in our sample exhibit some hard-to-justify responses to aid that they are offered. They are excessively attracted by loans and work study, given the value of these types of aid compared to grants. They are attracted by superficial aspects of a grant, like its being called a scholarship (with a name) and its being front-loaded. They are far more sensitive to a grant's share of the college's comprehensive costs than they are to the amount of the grant. All these behaviors are deviations from the expected behavior of a rational investor in human capital. We should note that these peculiar behaviors are generally *not* shared by the students whose parents have high incomes or who themselves attended very selective colleges.

When we quantify the effect of students' responses to aid, we find that 61.1 percent of students in our sample respond as rational investors would in the presence of aid. Of these rational types, about half do not get enough aid to measurably respond to it, and about half improve their lifetime present value by accepting an aid offer that is more than generous enough to offset the reductions in college consumption and instructional spending associated with the aid. However, about 38.9 percent of students in our sample respond to aid in such a way that they reduce their own lifetime present value. They accept an aid offer that is too small to offset the reductions in consumption and instructional spending that they experience. There are two major possible explanations for their behavior: a lack of sophistication and credit constraints.

A lack of sophistication accounts for at least some of the self-defeating responses to aid: Credit constraints cannot explain why a student would be strongly attracted by a grant's being called a scholarship (when it costs a college nothing to do it). A lack of sophistication probably also accounts for the attraction of front-loaded grants—an alternative explanation is impatience, but this seems unlikely in a population of students who so obviously do not exhibit impatience as a rule. They all have records that show that they can work hard now in return for gains in the distant future. Credit constraints are also not a good explanation for the attractiveness of front-loading, because a front-loaded grant does not reduce the credit needs of families who know that their child will be enrolled for four years.

Either a lack of sophistication or credit constraints could explain the great attractiveness of grants that are a large share of comprehensive cost, regardless of what that comprehensive cost is. It would probably be impossible to parse the effect into the share, due to naivete and the share due to credit constraints. However, we did examine the open-ended comments by parents whose children exhibited the most self-defeating responses to aid. The overwhelming impression is that a lack of sophistication, and not credit constraints, is the problem. Over and over, these parents complain that they are baffled by the aid process. They argue that the colleges do not explain their offers well. They complain that other families are more "in the know." Most of all, they worry about whether their children will benefit sufficiently from greater resources to justify the additional cost. Credit constraints do not receive nearly as much comment: Among parents who commented and whose children exhibited self-defeating responses to aid, only 6.9 percent stated that they were simply unable to pay the costs associated with their child's most preferred college. We do not want to overinterpret the anecdotal evidence from parents' comments because they may have been embarrassed to say that family circumstances prevented them from paying college costs. Nevertheless, we think that it is revealing that words like "bewildering" and "confusing" are the modal words in their comments.

We began this chapter by asking whether highly meritorious students, who are the big investors in the human capital market, act in a manner consistent with maximizing their returns—and thus, American economic growth, which is increasingly dependent on human capital investments. We come down with a very qualified yes: High-aptitude students understand the incentives that they face well enough to "get the sign right" when they react to any one factor. However, a substantial minority of them make trade-offs among factors that are wrong. About a third of the students are probably underinvesting and our conservative calculations suggest that a typical mistake is worth $76,096 in present value. Being the cost of mere error, $76,096 is a useful number to keep in mind when thinking about the magnitude of human capital investments and the consequent importance of getting them right.

Appendix

The conditional logit specification implies that the ratio of probabilities of any two alternatives j and j'

$$(A1) \qquad \frac{\text{Prob(collegechoice}_i = j)}{\text{Prob(collegechoice}_i = j')}$$

is independent of the probabilities of the remaining alternatives in the choice set. This property, the independence of irrelevant alternatives (IIA), is violated in certain applications. For our application, it is probably most useful to think about violations being likely to occur if is a natural nesting structure in students' choice sets. In this section, we first construct an example of a violation in order to elucidate the problem. We then construct an example in which IIA is unlikely to be violated; this example will help readers see how students' endogenous formation of their choice sets is actually helpful. We finally construct an example in which IIA is likely to be violated.

There is a specification test for IIA, but we have decided to explain the issue logically rather than merely present the results of the test because we believe that a logical understanding will better enable readers to judge our results. Nevertheless, knowing the results of the specification test is helpful. Hausman and McFadden (1984) and McFadden (1987) propose a typical Hausman-type test in which, under the null hypothesis that likelihood ratios are indeed independent of irrelevant alternatives, excluding some alternatives from the choice set will produce inefficient but consistent estimates. Under the alternative hypothesis, consistency and not merely efficiency will be lost. Our application never comes close to being rejected by this specification test: If we remove a random college from the choice sets, we get a test statistic that averages 0.43 (p-value 0.48, it is distributed at $\chi^2_{(1)}$). This test statistic is based on the specification in table 6.3.

Consider the following example in which IIA is violated. Suppose that Colgate University (a private liberal arts college) and Ohio State University (a public research university) are in a student's choice set and that we are considering the ratio of the probabilities associated with these institutions. Suppose also that the grant at the University of Michigan (another public research university) increases, raising the probability associated with it. The Colgate–Ohio State probability *ratio* need not change: Michigan becomes a more probable choice overall, both Colgate and Ohio State necessarily become less probable choices overall, but the *relative* probability of Colgate to Ohio State may remain unchanged. Let us say, however, that the student actually had a nested structure to his choice: He first chose his favorite public research university and his favorite private liberal arts college, and then he held a runoff between the top schools from each group. Say that the grant increase makes Michigan bump Ohio State from its place as the student's favorite public research university. Then, the grant not only raises the probability of Michigan overall, it dramatically changes the Colgate-Ohio State probability ratio. IIA is violated; the role that nesting plays becomes clear.

Now consider how students' endogenous selection of their choice sets is helpful. Suppose students use all of the information on colleges that can be observed or predicted at the time of application. Suppose, moreover, that students assume that *unpredictable* college attributes (for instance, the part of an aid package that cannot be predicted based on a college's policies and conventions) are pretty much the same within each of several nesting groups. For instance, a student might figure that if his application has special appeal for private liberal arts colleges, each of them will offer him an aid package that is 5 percent more generous than what they would otherwise offer someone with his characteristics. The student's suppositions produce a natural nesting structure. The student should examine all colleges, apply to the top institution in each nesting group, and wait for the unpredictable attributes to be resolved—as they will be, when he receives his admissions offers. The student can then conduct his runoff.

If the above assumptions and behavior are fulfilled, then the student is likely to satisfy IIA because his runoff menu of colleges will not contain any nesting structure. He has already taken the nesting structure into account when deciding where to apply; he has already eliminated less preferred alternatives from each nesting group. This leaves us with an endogenous choice set in which it is more plausible that IIA holds. In our example, Michigan's and Ohio State's attributes have already been fully considered and only one of the two institutions is still in the choice set. In the real world, students may not *strictly* obey the above assumptions and behavior, but students do act in accordance with them to a great extent. For instance, no student applies to all or even many public research universities: He applies his nesting structure and eliminates many of the choices within each nest group. We econometricians need not know what the nesting structure is. The student has already applied it; we econometricians need only observe how he makes choices in the runoff among nesting groups.

Let us consider how the previous example may fall afoul of IIA. We assumed that *unpredictable* college attributes are pretty much the same within each of several nesting groups. This assumption is most likely to be violated if, say, the student believes that admission is random within a nesting group. Such randomness is most likely to occur at the top handful of selective colleges, where admissions probabilities are so low that there is probably some arbitrariness in admissions even among institutions that have the same preferences about students. Thus, a student might apply to the top institution in each of his nesting groups, *except,* say, for the nesting group that contains the most selective private research universities. He might, in this one nesting group, figure that he has a 33 percent chance of getting into each of his five favorite institutions and figure that these chances are independent. The student might decide to apply to all five favorites: This would give him an 86.5 percent chance of getting into at least one institution, a 32.8 percent chance of getting into exactly two, and so on. If he gets into multiple institutions in the nesting group (as he will with some nonnegligible probability if he applies to all five), the student will face an endogenous choice set that has some nesting structure.

Overall, we believe that our data do not reject in the IIA specification test because endogenous formation of choice sets works for us. That is, we believe that our data fit the model's restrictions better than data would fit them if we knew nothing about students' endogenous choice sets and estimated a conditional logit with *all* colleges in every choice set. (Indeed, if we put all College Admissions Project colleges into each choice set, we get rejections in the IIA specification test.) We do not claim to have remedied the IIA issue that arises with conditional or multinomial logit estimation, but we believe that students' endogenous choice set formation is largely a help, not a hindrance.

Readers interested in endogenous choice sets where the choice is observed (as it is in our exercise) may wish to consult Peters, Adamowicz, and

Boxall (1995), Haab and Hicks (1997), Hicks and Strand (2000), and Parsons, Plantinga, and Boyle (2000). Manski (1977) considers the case in which endogenous choice sets are not observed so that the econometrician must jointly estimate the endogenous choice set and the choice within the set. Identification is theoretically possible but very difficult to achieve unless there is ancillary evidence with which to predict a person's endogenous choice set.

Finally, with endogenous choice sets, different students have choice sets that contain different numbers of colleges and arrays of colleges (that is, the choice sets are "unbalanced"). We have been asked whether this implies that students who have more colleges in their choice sets exercise disproportionate influence over the estimates. The answer is "no" on both counts. This becomes clear if we return to the conditional logit equations:

$$\ln L = \sum_{i=1}^{n} \left[\sum_{j=1}^{J_i} \text{matric}_{ij} \ln \text{Prob(collegechoice}_i = j) \right],$$

$$\text{Prob(collegechoice}_i = j) = \frac{e^{\beta' x_{ij}}}{\sum_{j=1}^{J_i} e^{\beta' x_{ij}}}.$$

Examine the log likelihood equation. It shows that each student contributes equally to the log likelihood because each student's college choice probabilities must sum to 1 (see second equation).

Table 6A.1   **Description of the Colleges to Which Students Applied, from the College Admission Project Data**

Variable	Mean	Standard Deviation	Minimum	Maximum
Matriculated at this college	0.1813	0.3853	0	1
Admitted to this college	0.6566	0.4748	0	1
Applied early to this college	0.1281	0.3389	0	2
Withdrew application from this college, usually after early decision elsewhere	0.0516	0.2212	0	1
Grants specific to this college	1,777.8140	4,933.3550	0	36,000
Loans from this college	413.4718	1,855.6370	0	36,548
Work study amount from this college	110.7380	482.5519	0	15,000
Grant is called a "scholarship"	0.1291	0.3354	0	1
Grant is front-loaded (more in freshman year)	0.0137	0.1161	0	1
Grant is this share of tuition	0.1229	0.3676	0	8
Grant is this share of comprehensive cost	0.0722	0.1902	0	2
Student was a recruited athlete at this college	0.0327	0.1779	0	1
Father is an alumnus of this college	0.0314	0.1744	0	1
Mother is an alumna of this college	0.0209	0.1431	0	1
Sibling attended or attends this college	0.0388	0.1932	0	1
College is public	0.2631	0.4403	0	1
College is private not-for-profit	0.7328	0.4436	0	1
College is international, except for Canadian colleges, which are treated as U.S. colleges	0.0040	0.0633	0	1
College's median SAT score, in national percentiles	83.8816	12.0390	14	98
Student's SAT score is this many percentiles *above* college's median SAT score	8.7393	9.5927	0	82
Student's SAT score is this many percentiles *below* college's median SAT score	1.7454	5.6654	0	68
In-state tuition	18,181.2300	9,198.9780	0	27,472
Out-of-state tuition	20,497.7600	5,890.7530	0	27,472
Tuition that applies to this student	19,276.9000	7,965.1400	0	27,472
Room and board at this college	6,975.7190	1,244.3320	0	10,299
In-state comprehensive cost of this college	25,745.7900	9,935.6770	0	35,125
Out-of-state comprehensive cost of this college	28,059.7200	6,681.4230	0	35,125
Comprehensive cost that applies to this student	26,841.9800	8,662.0230	0	35,125
Per-pupil expenditure on students (instruction, student services, academic support, scholarships) of this college, in thousands	29.9219	17.1009	2	146
Instructional per-pupil expenditure of this college, in thousands	19.8160	12.5401	2	72
College is in-state	0.2666	0.4422	0	1
Distance between student's high school and this college, in miles	673.2152	873.1788	0	5,774
College is in AK	0.001	0.0106	0	1
College is in AL	0.0038	0.0613	0	1
College is in AR	0.0003	0.0168	0	1
College is in AZ	0.0039	0.0622	0	1

Table 6A.1   (continued)

Variable	Mean	Standard Deviation	Minimum	Maximum
College is in CA	0.1388	0.3458	0	1
College is in CO	0.0078	0.0881	0	1
College is in CT	0.0533	0.2246	0	1
College is in DC	0.0260	0.1591	0	1
College is in DE	0.0025	0.0497	0	1
College is in FL	0.0111	0.1047	0	1
College is in GA	0.0169	0.1290	0	1
College is in HI	0.0024	0.0491	0	1
College is in IA	0.0032	0.0561	0	1
College is in ID	0.0009	0.0300	0	1
College is in IL	0.0458	0.2090	0	1
College is in IN	0.0166	0.1278	0	1
College is in KS	0.0014	0.0375	0	1
College is in KY	0.0005	0.0212	0	1
College is in LA	0.0070	0.0836	0	1
College is in MA	0.1339	0.3406	0	1
College is in MD	0.0199	0.1395	0	1
College is in ME	0.0159	0.1250	0	1
College is in MI	0.0173	0.1303	0	1
College is in MN	0.0075	0.0865	0	1
College is in MO	0.0217	0.1456	0	1
College is in MS	0.0007	0.0260	0	1
College is in MT	0.0006	0.0249	0	1
College is in NC	0.0411	0.1986	0	1
College is in NE	0.0012	0.0344	0	1
College is in NH	0.0170	0.1293	0	1
College is in NJ	0.0311	0.1735	0	1
College is in NM	0.0011	0.0327	0	1
College is in NV	0.0005	0.0225	0	1
College is in NY	0.1187	0.3235	0	1
College is in OH	0.0201	0.1405	0	1
College is in OK	0.0011	0.0335	0	1
College is in OR	0.0058	0.0759	0	1
College is in PA	0.0723	0.2589	0	1
College is in RI	0.0320	0.1761	0	1
College is in SC	0.0037	0.0604	0	1
College is in TN	0.0106	0.1023	0	1
College is in TX	0.0185	0.1346	0	1
College is in UT	0.0032	0.0565	0	1
College is in VA	0.0361	0.1866	0	1
College is in VT	0.0110	0.1042	0	1
College is in WA	0.0088	0.0936	0	1
College is in WI	0.0061	0.0781	0	1
College is in WV	0.0001	0.0075	0	1
College is in WY	0.0003	0.0168	0	1

Source: 17,871 college application events among the 3,240 students in the College Admissions Project sample.

Table 6A.2   **Description of the Colleges at Which Students Matriculated, from the College Admission Project Data**

Variable	Mean	Standard Deviation	Minimum	Maximum
Matriculated at this college	1.0000	0.0000	1	1
Admitted to this college	1.0000	0.0000	1	1
Applied early to this college	0.3142	0.4722	0	2
Withdrew application from this college, usually after early decision elsewhere	0.0000	0.0000	0	0
Grants specific to this college	4,029.0040	7,051.1670	0	36,000
Loans from this college	1,020.0040	2,721.6190	0	36,348
Work study amount from this college	296.3472	768.4207	0	15,000
Grant is called a "scholarship"	0.2692	0.4436	0	1
Grant is front-loaded (more in freshman year)	0.0343	0.1820	0	1
Grant is this share of tuition	0.2875	0.5517	0	7
Grant is this share of comprehensive cost	0.1665	0.2728	0	2
Student was a recruited athlete at this college	0.0402	0.1964	0	1
Father is an alumnus of this college	0.0664	0.291	0	1
Mother is an alumna of this college	0.0396	0.1949	0	1
Sibling attended or attends this college	0.0831	0.2761	0	1
College is public	0.2843	0.4512	0	1
College is private not-for-profit	0.7086	0.4562	0	1
College is international, except for Canadian colleges, which are treated as U.S. colleges	0.0068	0.0822	0	1
College's median SAT score, in national percentiles	83.4215	12.5494	32	98
Student's SAT score is this many percentiles *above* college's median SAT score	8.4548	9.1831	0	53
Student's SAT score is this many percentiles *below* college's median SAT score	1.4351	4.8994	0	50
In-state tuition	17,431.8300	9,512.6270	0	27,472
Out-of-state tuition	19,841.1300	6,370.6670	0	27,472
Tuition that applies to this student	18,340.3700	8,599.1560	0	27,472
Room and board at this college	6,821.8120	1,352.4620	0	10,299
In-state comprehensive cost of this college	24,881.0900	10,409.1500	0	35,125
Out-of-state comprehensive cost of this college	27,285.9500	7,335.3150	0	35,125
Comprehensive cost that applies to this student	25,792.1800	9,469.9140	0	35,125
Per-pupil expenditure on students (instruction, student services, academic support, scholarships) of this college, in thousands	29.6174	17.6089	2	78
Instructional per-pupil expenditure of this college, in thousands	19.4170	12.4205	2	72
College is in-state	0.3368	0.4727	0	1
Distance between student's high school and this college, in miles	575.6313	827.2526	0	5,769
College is in AK	0.0000	0.0000	0	0
College is in AL	0.0050	0.0705	0	1
College is in AR	0.0006	0.0250	0	1
College is in AZ	0.0053	0.0727	0	1
College is in CA	0.1199	0.3249	0	1

Variable	Mean	Standard Deviation	Minimum	Maximum
College is in CO	0.0094	0.0963	0	1
College is in CT	0.0537	0.2255	0	1
College is in DC	0.0265	0.1608	0	1
College is in DE	0.0022	0.0467	0	1
College is in FL	0.0203	0.1410	0	1
College is in GA	0.0131	0.1138	0	1
College is in HI	0.0044	0.0060	0	1
College is in IA	0.0025	0.0499	0	1
College is in ID	0.0022	0.0467	0	1
College is in IL	0.0571	0.2321	0	1
College is in IN	0.0190	0.1367	0	1
College is in KS	0.0025	0.0499	0	1
College is in KY	0.0006	0.0250	0	1
College is in LA	0.0050	0.0705	0	1
College is in MA	0.1218	0.3271	0	1
College is in MD	0.0187	0.1356	0	1
College is in ME	0.0140	0.1177	0	1
College is in MI	0.0194	0.1378	0	1
College is in MN	0.0053	0.0727	0	1
College is in MO	0.0212	0.1442	0	1
College is in MS	0.0012	0.0353	0	1
College is in MT	0.0012	0.0353	0	1
College is in NC	0.0390	0.1937	0	1
College is in NE	0.0022	0.0467	0	1
College is in NH	0.0172	0.1299	0	1
College is in NJ	0.0284	0.1662	0	1
College is in NM	0.0009	0.0306	0	1
College is in NV	0.0022	0.0467	0	1
College is in NY	0.1065	0.3085	0	1
College is in OH	0.0178	0.1322	0	1
College is in OK	0.0022	0.0467	0	1
College is in OR	0.0078	0.0880	0	1
College is in PA	0.0743	0.2623	0	1
College is in RI	0.0300	0.1705	0	1
College is in SC	0.0066	0.0807	0	1
College is in TN	0.0140	0.1177	0	1
College is in TX	0.0225	0.1483	0	1
College is in UT	0.0091	0.0947	0	1
College is in VA	0.0406	0.1974	0	1
College is in VT	0.0106	0.1025	0	1
College is in WA	0.0094	0.0963	0	1
College is in WI	0.0059	0.0768	0	1
College is in WV	0.0000	0.0000	0	1
College is in WY	0.0006	0.0250	0	1

Source: 3,240 college matriculation events among the students in the College Admissions Project sample.

Table 6A.3   **Are Students from Low- and High-Income Families Equally Sensitive to Aid Variables That Should Not Matter? Selected Estimated Odds Ratios from Conditional Logit Regressions**

		Parents' Income		
	Low	Medium Low	Medium High	High
Grant is called a "scholarship"	2.584	2.538	2.048	1.313
	(3.11)	(4.39)	(4.26)	(1.24)
Grant is front-loaded (more in freshman year)	1.004	0.971	1.989	1.687
	(0.01)	(−0.06)	(2.00)	(1.28)
Grant is this share of college's tuition	0.760	0.540	1.153	0.621
	(−0.42)	(−1.44)	(0.32)	(−0.75)
Grant is this share of college's comprehensive cost	10.789	24.333	16.695	6.585
	(0.97)	(2.84)	(1.24)	(1.85)

Note: Regressions include all other variables shown in table 6.9.

Table 6A.4   **Are Students Whose Parents Attended More and Less Selective Colleges Equally Sensitive to Aid Variables That Should Not Matter? Selected Estimated Odds Ratios from Conditional Logit Regressions**

	Parents' College		
	Low Selectivity	Medium Selectivity	High Selectivity
Grant is called a "scholarship"	1.927*	1.887*	1.236
	(5.32)	(2.88)*	(0.62)
Grant is front-loaded (more in freshman year)	1.277	1.671	2.599
	(1.00)	(1.00)	(1.44)
Grant is this share of college's tuition	0.789	0.718	2.227
	(−0.80)	(−0.74)	(0.59)
Grant is this share of college's comprehensive cost	27.988*	30.870*	1.315
	(3.08)	(1.87)*	(0.06)

Note: Regressions include all other variables shown in table 6.9
*Statistically significantly different from zero at the 10% level.

Table 6A.5   **Are Students from Public and Private Schools Equally Sensitive to Aid Variables That Should Not Matter? Selected Estimated Odds Ratios from Conditional Logit Regressions**

	Public High School	Private High School
Grant is called a "scholarship"	1.833	1.934
	(4.69)	(3.98)
Grant is front-loaded (more in freshman year)	1.519	1.130
	(1.74)	(0.29)
Grant is this share of college's tuition	0.782	0.826
	(−0.88)	(−0.37)
Grant is this share of college's comprehensive cost	25.484	20.827
	(2.93)	(1.88)

Note: Regressions include all other variables shown in table 6.9.

References

Avery, Christopher, and Caroline M. Hoxby. 2000. The college admissions project: Counselor report. National Bureau of Economic Research online publication. Available at [http://www.nber.org/~hoxby/collegeadmissions/pdf/counselorreport.pdf].

Brewer, Dominic J., Eric R. Eide, and Ronald G. Ehrenberg. 1999. Does it pay to attend an elite private college? Cross-cohort evidence on the effects of college type on earnings. *Journal of Human Resources* 34 (1): 104–23.

College Board. 2002. Standard research compilation: Undergraduate institutions. Electronic data.

Dale, Stacy, and Alan Krueger. 1999. Estimating the payoff to attending a more selective college: An application of selection on observables and unobservables. NBER Working Paper no. 7322. Cambridge, Mass.: National Bureau of Economic Research.

Ehrenberg, Ronald, and Daniel Sherman. 1984. Optimal financial aid policies for a selective university. *Journal of Human Resources* 19 (2): 202–230.

Haab, Timothy, and Robert Hicks. 1997. Accounting for choice set endogeneity in random utility models of recreation demand. *Journal of Environmental Economics and Management* 34:127–147.

Hausman, Jerry, and Daniel McFadden. 1984. A specification test for the multinomial logit model. *Econometrica* 52:1219–240.

Hicks, Robert, and Ivar Strand. 2000. The extent of information: Its relevance for random utility models. *Land Economics* 76 (3): 374–385.

Hoxby, Caroline M. 1998. The return to attending a more selective college: 1960 to the present. Harvard University. Unpublished manuscript.

Manski, Charles. 1977. The structure of random utility models. *Theory and Decision* 8:229–254.

McFadden, Daniel. 1987. Regression-based specification tests for the multinomial logit model. *Journal of Econometrics* 34:63–82.

Parsons, George, Andrew Plantinga, and Kevin Boyle. 2000. Narrow choice sets in a random utility model of recreation demand. *Land Economics* 76 (1): 86–99.

Peters, Thomas, Wiktor Adamowicz, and Peter Boxall. 1995. The influence of choice set consideration in modeling the benefits of improved water quality. *Water Resources Research* 613:1781–787.

Peterson's guide to four-year colleges. 2002. Princeton, N.J.: Peterson's.

U.S. Department of Education, National Center for Education Statistics. 2001. *Integrated postsecondary education data system, higher education finance data file.* Electronic data.

———. 2002. *College opportunities online.* Electronic data.

Comment   Michael Rothschild

What a treasure trove this paper is! It is the debut of a new and fascinating data set constructed with skill and sweat. It demonstrates that skilled re-

Michael Rothschild is William Stuart Tod Professor of Economics and Public Affairs, and professor of economics and public affairs at the Woodrow Wilson School, Princeton University, and a research associate of the National Bureau of Economic Research.

searchers can use these data to pose and answer good new questions. Still, it is a discussants job to quibble, and quibble I shall. Simplifying drastically, Avery and Hoxby find the following.

1. Prospective students respond to prices when choosing colleges.
2. In general, the responses are reasonable, but errors are systematic, both in the kinds of errors made and the kind of people who make them.
3. Some students make bad choices.

The authors regard these errors as cause for concern because their sample is restricted to a scarce resource, America's most academically qualified students. A dog that does not bark is the question of what prices in higher education should do. Because their paper is an empirical one, this is no surprise. Still it is worth speculating about equity and efficiency in the allocation of resources in higher education. In the spirit of Avery and Hoxby, assume that each college produces human capital from inputs of student ability and other resources. To fix ideas, suppose that $y_i = R_i^a(G[x_{i1}, \ldots, x_{iN}]^{(1-a)}$, where y_i is output of human capital per capita, R_i is the amount of other resources used per capita, x_{in} is the ability of the nth student attending college i, and $0 < a < 1$. The efficiency problem is to allocate students and resources to colleges so as to maximize total output of human capital. I simplify by assuming both that exactly N students attend each college and that there are K colleges. This is an inessential simplification. The optimal allocation depends on the educational technology. Consider the following three cases:

$$G(x_1, \ldots x_N) = \mathrm{Min}(x_1, \ldots x_N) \quad \text{(MIN)}$$

$$G(x_1, \ldots x_N) = \sum x_n \quad \text{(SUM)}$$

$$G(x_1, \ldots x_N) = \mathrm{Max}(x_1, \ldots x_N) \quad \text{(MAX)}$$

In each case it is easy to characterize the optimal allocation. If the production function is MIN, then students should be allocated so that the most able N students go to the best college, the next N most able students go to the next best college, and so on. Resources are allocated so as to make the labels "best," "next best," and so on descriptive of the allocation of resources. The best college gets a lot of resources, the next best less, and so on. If the production function is MAX, the best student goes to the best college, the next best to the second best, and so on until the Kth best student goes to the worst college. It doesn't matter how the other $N(K-1)$ are allocated to colleges. Allocations of resources are qualitatively similar to the MIN case, but the differences in resources allocation are less pronounced. The SUM case is in between. Students should be allocated to most nearly equalize the sum of ability at each college. Because total ability is nearly equal at each college, other resources should be allocated almost equally at each college. This characterizes efficiency. It is natural to ask what kind of prices system will support the optimal allocation in each case. I do not think it is difficult to answer this question following the argument in Rothschild and White (1995). I am positive that the efficiency prices do not look anything like the current American price system for undergraduate education.

What about equity? This cannot be answered without specifying some kind of social welfare function. However, some simple observations are possible. Suppose we care about equality of income in the very general sense set out by Atkinson (1970), that is, that we agree that an increase in inequality is something all those who dislike inequality would disapprove of; in other words, an increase in inequality decreases the value of all quasi-concave social welfare functions. Assume that income is determined by human capital and that colleges distribute human capital on a per capita basis. It follows then that the MIN regime is the worst regime and SUM the best; MAX is in between.

Another natural question is what do we know about educational technology in the sense used here. The candid answer is "almost nothing." Surely the technology of the U.S. educational system is not remotely like the technology of any of these examples. However, the allocation of students and resources that we observe in the United States (Winston 1999) bears more than a casual resemblance to the solution to the optimal allocation problem for the MIN technology. Whether this observation justifies this allocation or gives us reason to worry when talented prospective students make the "mistakes" that Avery and Hoxby observe is not clear to me.

References

Atkinson, A. B. 1970. Measurement of inequality. *Journal of Economic Theory* 2 (3): 244–263.

Rothschild, M., and L. J. White. 1995. The analytics of the pricing of higher education and other services in which the customers are inputs. *Journal of Political Economy* 103 (3): 573–586.

Winston, G. C. 1999. Subsidies, hierarchy and peers: The awkward economics of higher education. *Journal of Economic Perspectives* 13 (1): 13–36.

7

Resident and Nonresident Tuition and Enrollment at Flagship State Universities

Michael J. Rizzo and Ronald G. Ehrenberg

7.1 Introduction

The recent economic downturn in the United States has led to severe current and projected budget deficits in most states. Sharp rises in health care costs and increased competition for state funds from other sources has concurrently led to a decrease in the shares of state budgets earmarked for the higher education sector.[1] Because universities are able to attract revenue from other sources (e.g., tuition, annual giving, and federal student aid) and they are a discretionary component of most state budgets, they are often the first to go under the knife during tough times. The resulting revenue shortages from these budget cuts will most certainly have deleterious effects on college accessibility and on the behavior of these higher education institutions. Inasmuch as 65 percent of the 9.2 million students enrolled in four-year institutions in 1999 were enrolled in public institutions and in most states the major public research universities are also the most selective in terms of admissions, it is important to understand institutional responses relating to tuition

Michael J. Rizzo is assistant professor of economics at Centre College and a research assistant at the Cornell Higher Education Research Institute (CHERI). Ronald G. Ehrenberg is the Irving M. Ives Professor of Industrial and Labor Relations and Economics at Cornell University, director of CHERI, and a research associate at the National Bureau of Economic Research (NBER). Without implicating them for what remains, we are grateful to the Andrew W. Mellon Foundation and the Atlantic Philanthropies (USA) Inc. for their support of CHERI and to Michelle White, Caroline Hoxby, participants at the NBER conference, and two referees for their comments on earlier versions.

1. From fiscal year (FY) 1992 to FY2002, the share of states' discretionary budgets allocated to higher education has fallen 0.8 percentage points, from 13.5 percent to 12.7 percent. Health care's share has risen from 12.1 percent to 16.0 percent during this time. See National Association of State Budget Officers (2002).

and enrollment policies, as well as the likely changes in state grant aid policies.

During the 1979 to 2000 period, the average state appropriation at the flagship public research institutions, as a share of total current fund revenues at the institution, fell from 42 percent to 31 percent. Only ten institutions saw increases in the share of their revenues coming from state appropriations over this period, and only three of these saw any increase in the share during the 1988 to 2000 period.

To make up for this revenue shortfall, public institutions can increase their undergraduate tuition revenues in two ways.[2] First, they may increase the tuition level they charge in-state students; however, this is often a politically unpopular move. Second, because all public research institutions charge a higher tuition to out-of-state students than they do to in-state students, they can raise the tuition level they charge out-of-state students and/or adjust the composition of their student body by enrolling more out-of-state students.

Adjusting the share of students that come from out-of-state is at best a short-run solution and for political reasons may be much less easily adjusted than the out-of-state student tuition level. After some point, it may be politically very difficult to further expand the share of out-of-state students, while state officials may not be concerned about charging nonresident students increasingly higher rates of tuition. The political difficulties arise because enrolling more nonresidents may preclude qualified students from one's own state from attending the flagship public university in the state. On the flip side, it would be unwise for a state to totally exclude nonresidents from its universities' corridors because other states might then retaliate against students from the state in question.

The prospects for revenue augmentation from increasing nonresident enrollments are diminished by the presence of tuition reciprocity agreements. These are either bilateral or multilateral agreements between schools and/or states allowing nonresident students to attend a public university at less than the normal out-of-state tuition.[3] These agreements are often program specific, have a regional focus, and were created to encourage universities to achieve cost efficiencies in their program offerings.

An institution's ability to employ different tuition and enrollment strategies is dependent upon its degree of autonomy from state interests. Be-

2. There are, of course, other sources of revenue. Total educational and general current fund revenues include undergraduate and graduate student tuition and fees; federal, state, and local appropriations; government grants and contracts; private gifts; payouts from endowments; sales and services of educational activities; and other sources. Local revenues are typically directed to community colleges, while federal monies are focused on direct student support. The endowment levels at most public institutions are small, so increasing the payout rate is unlikely to have a large impact on annual revenues. Public institutions are actively seeking to increase their fund-raising revenues, but many are starting from very low bases.

3. In some cases, if the flow of students between states taking advantage of tuition reciprocity agreements is not roughly equal, the state that exported more students than it imported makes a payment to the importing state to compensate it for bearing more than its fair share of the costs. These payments go to the state treasury, however, not to the universities themselves.

cause elected state officials' interests diverge from those of university administrators and faculty members, we expect institutions in states where there is more legislative oversight in the form of a statewide coordinating board and/or fewer governing boards to find it more difficult to increase tuition and to adjust their enrollment margins.[4]

Some observers have expressed concern that direct student aid (both federal grant aid and state aid), which was designed to improve access, has instead given institutions the freedom to increase tuition. States' financing of higher education is increasingly being provided in the form of grant aid to students rather than in the form of appropriations to institutions. From 1979 to 2000, average (median) direct student aid as a share of total higher education aid has increased from 3.0 percent to 5.8 percent (1.8 percent to 4.8 percent). While the real value of the federal Basic Educational Opportunity Grant (Pell Grant) fell by 9 percent over this time period, access to federal subsidized loans was vastly expanded. In fact, by 1999, 45.4 percent of students receiving financial aid did so in the form of federal loan aid.

How tuition levels, or the availability of grant or loan aid, influence access are empirical questions that we will not address in this chapter. Rather, we will analyze how tuition and enrollment strategies at institutions react to changes in federal and state need-based student aid and to state appropriations to public higher education institutions. The former increases student mobility by expanding their choice set, while the latter does not travel with the student.

Institutions may also choose nonresident enrollment policies to satisfy different interests. Because many flagship publics are also high quality institutions, they typically experience an excess demand for seats and can enroll nonresidents to improve academic quality or to enhance the diversity of their student bodies.

Given differing state governance structures, political climates, institutional objectives, and the like, it is not surprising to see the dramatic disparity across states in their use of nonresidents as an enrollment strategy. Figure 7.1 shows that many of the larger, more populous states such as Ohio, Illinois, Texas, California, and New York, do not make great use of this strategy, enrolling less than 10 percent of their first-time freshmen from out-of-state in 1998.[5,6] However, other states that are smaller, older,

---

4. See Lowry (2001a,b). Lowry also points out that states (schools) where a high percentage of university trustees are appointed by elected officials or directly elected by the voting public also have lower tuition.

5. The categories were defined using a means-clustering analysis described by Everitt (1993). This is an exploratory data technique meant to find natural groups in the data. Multiple iterations suggest that the data be broken into four nonoverlapping groups. Multiple iterations suggest that the most natural partition was four groups. States near the average include Maine and Georgia, enrolling about 20 percent each.

6. Public Universities in Texas do not get to keep the extra tuition revenue they receive from enrolling out-of-state students; this revenue flows into the state government coffers. As such they have no financial incentive to enroll out-of-state students.

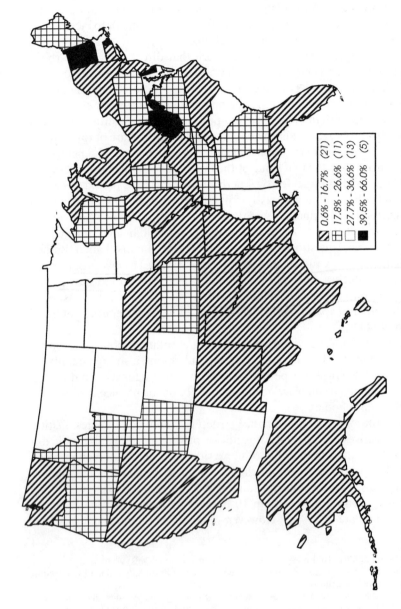

Fig. 7.1 1998 average share of first-time freshmen that are nonresidents at research institutions in the fifty United States (categories computed through means-clustering analysis)

Source: Integrated Postsecondary Education Data System residence and migration files.

Legend:

- 0.6% - 16.7% (21)
- 17.8% - 26.6% (11)
- 27.7% - 36.6% (13)
- 39.5% - 66.0% (5)

and/or have a history of private provision of higher education enroll nearly half of their entering classes as nonresidents. Vermont, Delaware, Rhode Island, and New Hampshire respectively enrolled 66 percent, 60 percent, 48 percent and 40 percent of their classes in 1998 in this manner.

Table 7.1 lists the ninety-one flagship public research institutions whose behavior is analyzed in our study.[7] They are primarily Research I and II institutions and were chosen because they are the most selective and largest public institutions in each state, and they enroll the largest shares of nonresidents, or out-of-state students. This chapter is motivated by our desire to understand the causes and consequences of nonresident enrollment. We seek to explain how the share of nonresidents among first-time freshmen varies at a point in time across these institutions and over time at any given institution. We employ panel data from a variety of sources and estimate a system of equations to explain the levels of state need-based grant aid per student, in-state tuition, out-of-state tuition, and the share of out-of-state students among first-time freshmen. The longitudinal nature of the data permits us to control for omitted variable bias.

In the next section, we briefly survey related literature. Section 7.3 presents information on trends in tuition, enrollment, and grant aid. In addition to summarizing the data we use to explain these trends, it also discusses the results of a survey we undertook to obtain information on the nature and prevalence of tuition reciprocity agreements. Section 7.4 describes our estimation strategy, presents empirical results, and conducts some policy simulations based upon these results. Section 7.5 briefly concludes.

7.2   Selective Literature Review

The literature on pricing and access in public higher education is replete with papers that analyze issues related to one or more of the following—state grant aid, in-state tuition, out-of-state tuition, and nonresident enrollment shares—but none has studied all of these issues simultaneously. Two papers have addressed the determinants of nonresident enrollments. Mixon and Hsing (1994) found, using cross-section data for a sample of public *and* private academic institutions, that higher nonresident tuition levels were associated with higher nonresident enrollment shares. Their findings lent credence to the notion that universities enroll nonresidents for revenue purposes. Siow (1997) found, after controlling for student body

7. There are eighty-four schools from forty-three states that were classified as Research I and II institutions in 1994 by the Carnegie Foundation for the Advancement of Teaching. To fully exploit state variation in tuition, enrollment, and grant aid policies, we added the flagship public institution from each state that did not have a Research I or II institution. These states were Alaska, Maine, Montana, Nevada, New Hampshire, North Dakota, and South Dakota.

Table 7.1   Flagship Public Research Institutions in the Sample

School	1994 Carnegie Classification	School	1994 Carnegie Classification
Arizona State University (AZ)	RI	University of Hawaii at Manoa (HI)	RI
Auburn University (AL)	RII	University of Houston (TX)	RII
Clemson University (SC)	RII	University of Idaho (ID)	RII
Colorado State University (CO)	RI	University of Illinois at Chicago (IL)	RI
Florida State University (FL)	RI	University of Illinois at Urbana-Champaign (IL)	RI
Georgia Institute of Technology (GA)	RI	University of Iowa (IA)	RI
Indiana University at Bloomington (IN)	RI	University of Kansas (KS)	RI
Iowa State University (IA)	RI	University of Kentucky (NY)	RI
Kansas State University (KS)	RII	University of Louisville (KY)	RII
Kent State University (OH)	RII	University of Maine (ME)	DII
Louisiana State University (LA)	RI	University of Maryland, College Park (MD)	RI
Michigan State University (MI)	RI	University of Massachusetts, Amherst (MA)	RI
Mississippi State University (MS)	RII	University of Michigan (MI)	RI
New Mexico State University (NM)	RI	University of Minnesota, Twin Cities (MN)	RI
North Carolina State University (NC)	RI	University of Mississippi (MS)	RII
Ohio State University (OH)	RI	University of Missouri, Columbia (MO)	RI
Ohio University (OH)	RII	University of Montana (MT)	DII
Oklahoma State University (OK)	RII	University of Nebraska at Lincoln (NE)	RI
Oregon State University (OR)	RI	University of Nevada, Reno (NV)	DII
Pennsylvania State University (PA)	RI	University of New Hampshire (NH)	DII
Purdue University (IN)	RI	University of New Mexico (NM)	RI
Rutgers University, New Brunswick (NJ)	RI	University of North Carolina, Chapel Hill (NC)	RI

Institution	Classification	Institution	Classification
Southern Illinois University, Carbondale (IL)	RII	University of North Dakota (ND)	DII
State University of New York at Albany (NY)	RII	University of Oklahoma, Norman Campus (OK)	RII
State University of New York at Buffalo (NY)	RII	University of Oregon (OR)	RII
Temple University (PA)	RI	University of Pittsburgh (PA)	RI
Texas A&M University (TX)	RI	University of Rhode Island (RI)	RII
Texas Tech University (TX)	RII	University of South Carolina at Columbia (SC)	RII
University of Alaska at Fairbanks (AK)	DII	University of South Dakota (SD)	DII
University of Alabama, Birmingham (AL)	RI	University of South Florida (FL)	RII
University of Arizona (AZ)	RI	University of Tennessee at Knoxville (TN)	RI
University of Arkansas (AR)	RII	University of Texas at Austin (TX)	RI
University of California, Berkeley (CA)	RI	University of Utah (UT)	RI
University of California, Davis (CA)	RI	University of Vermont (VT)	RII
University of California, Irvine (CA)	RI	University of Virginia (VA)	RI
University of California, Los Angeles (CA)	RI	University of Washington, Seattle (WA)	RI
University of California, Riverside (CA)	RII	University of Wisconsin, Madison (WI)	RI
University of California, San Diego (CA)	RI	University of Wisconsin, Milwaukee (WI)	RII
University of California, Santa Barbara (CA)	RI	University of Wyoming (WY)	RII
University of California, Santa Cruz (CA)	RII	Utah State University (UT)	RI
University of Cincinnati (OH)	RI	Virginia Commonwealth University (VA)	RI
University of Colorado at Boulder (CO)	RI	Virginia Polytechnic Institute (VA)	RI
University of Connecticut (CT)	RI	Washington State University (WA)	RII
University of Delaware (DE)	RII	Wayne State University (MI)	RI
University of Florida (FL)	RI	West Virginia University (WV)	RI
University of Georgia (GA)	RI		

Note: Carnegie Classification descriptions can be found at http://chronicle.com/stats/carnegie.

ability, that universities with more successful researchers were more likely to have larger shares of nonresident and foreign students.

Other studies have addressed the determinants of tuition levels for in-state students at public universities. Using cross-section data, Lowry (2001a,b) found that net tuition and fee revenues were higher at public universities that receive less state government funding per student and in states in which public universities have more financial autonomy. Quigley and Rubinfeld (1993) found that states with high private enrollments and many private colleges and universities charged higher tuition levels at their public universities.

Several studies have treated tuition levels at public higher education institutions and state appropriations to these institutions as being simultaneously determined. In the context of a model in which state appropriations were treated as endogenous, Koshal and Koshal (2000) found that lower state appropriations per student, higher median family income, and a higher share of students that came from out of state were all associated with higher in-state tuition levels. However, Lowry's (2001a,b) work suggests that state appropriations per student can be treated as exogenous in in-state tuition equations.

Greene's (1994) work is one of the few studies that addressed out-of-state tuition levels at public universities. Using cross-section data, he found that states with many private colleges, lower tax rates, poor labor markets, and strong in-migration of both population and students charged higher nonresident tuition. While he observed that higher regional tuition was associated with higher nonresident tuition levels, the association was not statistically significant.

Research relating to federal and state grant aid has addressed how grant aid affects tuition levels and access. Examples include Balderson (1997), Coopers and Lybrand (1997), Hauptman and Krop (1998), McPherson and Schapiro (1998), and the National Center for Education Statistics (2001). Of concern to many researchers and policymakers is whether academic institutions respond to increases in the Pell Grant program maximum-benefit level by increasing their tuition levels. Estimates of the size of this "Bennett hypothesis" at public institutions range from negligible to a $50 increase in tuition for every $100 increase in aid.[8] Little attention has been given to the determination of federal grant aid levels themselves, let alone to how states determine how much of their resources to devote to financial aid for students.

Most of the prior studies are cross-section analyses and are subject to the criticism that unobserved institution- or state-specific variables may lead to biased coefficient estimates. To avoid this problem, we employ a rich lon-

8. It is named for William Bennett, the secretary of education during the Reagan administration.

gitudinal institution-level data set that is derived primarily from the Higher Education General Information Survey (HEGIS) and its successor, the Integrated Postsecondary Education Data System (IPEDS), in the estimation reported below. The HEGIS and IPEDS data are supplemented with data from numerous other sources.

We report estimates of a system of four simultaneously determined equations for state need-based grant aid, in-state tuition, out-of-state tuition, and the share of undergraduate students that are nonresidents. The explanatory variables that are treated as exogenous in our models include federal financial aid parameters, institutional characteristics, state governance characteristics, tuition reciprocity agreement parameters, measures of higher education competition in the state and the institution's enrollment capacity, and other state- and regional-specific information. Our analyses should be viewed as reduced form in nature due to the difficulty of finding suitable supply-and-demand restrictions for each equation.

7.3 Data

Our study uses data on resident and nonresident enrollment and tuition levels for a sample of ninety-one American public research institutions representing all fifty states. The data come from a variety of sources including HEGIS, IPEDS, the National Association of State Student Grant and Aid Programs (NASSGAP), and the annual Current Population Surveys (CPS), as well as other sources. Our econometric analyses use data for eight years during the 1979 to 1998 period.[9]

Table 7.2 presents data on the shares of full-time first-time freshmen that were nonresidents at sample institutions during the 1979 to 1998 period. Overall, the enrollment share of nonresidents rose from 0.174 to 0.191 during the period. However, from 1981 through 1992, when states faced particularly difficult financial times, the average share increased from 0.166 to 0.205, an increase of almost 0.04, and then remained relatively constant as budget situations improved during the remainder of the period.

To illustrate the magnitude of a 4 percentage point increase in nonresident enrollment, consider a school with a freshman enrollment of 3,000 students and a nonresident tuition premium of $6,000. If this school decides to enroll 4 percent more of its class as nonresidents (120 students) over the course of four years, this would provide the institution with an additional $2.88 million of revenues that could be used to raise faculty salaries, invest in start-up costs for new scientists, hire additional faculty and staff, reduce class sizes, and offer more courses.

9. Table 7A.1 details the sources for all of our data. The specific years included in the study were dictated by the years in which information on resident and nonresident enrollments were collected as part of HEGIS or IPEDS. The 1998 academic year was the most recent year for which IPEDS Residence and Migration data was publicly available at the time of this writing.

Table 7.2 Proportion of First-Time Freshmen from Out of State (excluding foreign students): Flagship Public Research and Doctoral Institutions

Year	Unweighted Average	Standard Deviation	Weighted Average	Median	Minimum	Maximum
1979	0.174	0.120	0.168	0.136	0.011	0.550
1981	0.166	0.120	0.161	0.133	0.007	0.543
1984[a]	0.171	0.128	0.170	0.127	0.010	0.629
1988	0.203	0.136	0.205	0.158	0.012	0.602
1992	0.205	0.157	0.201	0.169	0.001	0.660
1994	0.202	0.152	0.196	0.172	0.005	0.674
1996	0.196	0.145	0.194	0.167	0.005	0.665
1998	0.191	0.139	0.185	0.179	0.006	0.660
%Δ	9.4	15.7	10.3	31.2	−47.8	19.9

Source: NCES Higher Education General Information Surveys (HEGIS) and Integrated Postsecondary Education Data System (IPEDS) via direct surveys and WebCASPAR.

Notes: For weighted averages, weights are full-time equivalent first-time freshman enrollments. Δ indicates change.

[a]Numbers of out-of-state freshmen imputed for the eight California schools in 1984.

Schools that exhibited the largest increases in nonresident enrollment shares during the period included Pittsburgh, Massachusetts, Minnesota, and Mississippi State, which all more than doubled their shares during the period. In contrast, the University of Illinois at Chicago, Texas Tech, Houston, South Florida, and the University of California schools reduced their nonresident enrollment shares by more than half. While the time series variation in nonresident enrollment shares exhibited in this table may not appear very striking, more dramatic cross-section variation exists and can be seen in figure 7.1.

The well-documented increases in resident and nonresident tuition that occurred during the period are shown in table 7.3. In real terms, both resident and nonresident tuition levels more than doubled between 1979 and 1998, with each growing at about 4 percent per year above the rate of inflation. This table veils the dramatic cross-section variation that exists in public higher education tuition levels. For instance, in 1998 Vermont charged its residents over $7,000 and Pittsburgh, Temple, Michigan, Penn State, and New Hampshire all charged over $6,000, while all of the Florida universities, Arizona universities, Idaho, Houston, Texas A&M, and the University of Nevada at Reno charged near $2,000. The public higher education institutions in California and Texas are among those that increased tuition at the fastest rates, while the Florida and Mississippi schools exhibited the smallest increases during the period.

Every public research institution charges a higher price to nonresidents, presumably because state taxpayers do not want to subsidize the schooling of nontaxpayers from other states. Moreover, the extent to which

Table 7.3   In-State and Out-of-State Tuition Levels (1996 dollars): Flagship Public Research and Doctoral Institutions

Year	In-State						Out-of-State					
	Average	% Increase	Weighted Average	Median	Minimum	Maximum	Average	% Increase	Weighted Average	Median	Minimum	Maximum
1979	1,552 (520)		1,582	1,509	676	3,435	4,250 (1,273)		4,246	4,097	2,068	8,182
1981	1,633 (615)	5.2	1,667	1,569	638	3,799	4,431 (1,401)	4.3	4,460	4,105	1,844	8,402
1984	1,943 (756)	19.0	2,006	1,861	557	5,126	5,203 (1,614)	17.4	5,334	5,047	1,755	9,799
1988	2,266 (859)	16.6	2,320	2,100	1,018	4,840	6,282 (1,833)	20.7	6,454	6,059	3,238	13,393
1992	2,833 (1,065)	25.0	2,887	2,656	1,315	6,724	8,055 (2,551)	28.2	8,243	7,604	4,139	16,103
1994	3,145 (1,189)	11.0	3,174	2,847	1,417	6,919	8,766 (2,768)	8.8	8,939	8,169	3,982	17,131
1996	3,348 (1,185)	6.5	3,397	3,102	1,568	7,726	9,459 (2,659)	7.9	9,689	9,030	5,100	17,916
1998	3,525 (1,181)	5.3	3,553	3,302	1,697	7,669	10,094 (2,687)	6.7	10,284	9,586	5,512	18,623
% Δ	127	125	119	151	123	137	142	134	167	128		
CAGR (%)	4.2		4.1	4.0	4.7	4.1	4.4		4.5	4.3	5.0	4.2

Source: NCES Higher Education General Information Surveys (HEGIS) and Integrated Postsecondary Education Data System (IPEDS) via WebCASPAR.
Notes: Standard deviations in parentheses. Weights are full-time equivalent first-time freshmen enrollments. CAGR = compound annual growth rate.

Table 7.4   In-State, Out-of-State Tuition Differentials (1996 dollars): Flagship Public
Research and Doctoral Institutions

Year	Out-of-State/ In-State Ratio (1)	Mean Differential (2)	% Increase in Differential (3)	Weighted Average (4)	Median (5)	Minimum (6)	Maximum (7)
1979	2.74	2,698		2,664	2,537	1,138	5,028
1981	2.71	2,798	3.7	2,793	2,517	1,077	5,321
1984	2.68	3,260	16.5	3,328	3,150	1,198	6,526
1988	2.77	4,016	23.2	4,133	3,878	1,469	8,968
1992	2.84	5,222	30.0	5,357	4,855	1,878	10,891
1994	2.79	5,620	7.6	5,765	5,471	1,770	11,439
1996	2.82	6,110	8.7	6,292	6,060	2,400	12,206
1998	2.86	6,569	7.5	6,731	6,471	2,537	12,695
% Δ	4.6	143		153	155	123	152
CAGR (%)	0.2	4.5		4.7	4.8	4.1	4.7

Source: NCES Higher Education General Information Surveys (HEGIS) and Integrated Postsecondary Education Data System (IPEDS) via direct surveys and WebCASPAR.
Notes: Weights are full-time equivalent first-time freshmen enrollment. CAGR = compound annual growth rate. Δ = change.

nonresidents pay more than residents increased during the period. While both in-state and nonresident tuition levels have experienced roughly equal percentage increases during the period and, thus, the ratio of nonresident to in-state tuition has remained nearly constant, the real difference in resident and nonresident tuition levels substantially increased during the period because nonresident tuition levels began at a higher base.

Table 7.3 shows that while in-state tuition increased by an average of less than $2,000 in real terms, nonresident tuition increased by an average of more than $5,000 in real terms. As a result, the average premium charged to nonresidents has increased in real terms from $2,700 in 1979 to over $6,500 in 1998 (see table 7.4). This change is significant because as the absolute difference between in-state and nonresident tuition widens, out-of-state enrollments become less desirable from the student-demand side.[10]

The lowest out-of-state tuition levels and smallest increases occurred largely in the southeastern region. Both the largest out-of-state tuition levels and tuition increases occurred at Michigan, the Virginia schools, North Carolina schools, and the California schools. As with the overall level of nonresident tuition, the smallest premia charged to nonresidents and the smallest increases tended to occur at southeastern public institutions. The strong regional patterns that we observe in tuition and enrollment trends

10. These raw data suggest that during the period institutions adjusted their out-of-state tuition levels to generate revenue.

suggest the importance of historical competitive and political economic factors.

Turning to trends in state support for public higher education, tables 7.5 and 7.6 outline the changes in state need-based grant aid to students attending public institutions and state appropriations to public higher education institutions that occurred during the period. Table 7.5 shows that average state-provided need-based grant aid per full-time-equivalent undergraduate enrolled in public higher education institutions in the state has

Table 7.5 Need-Based Grant Aid to In-State Undergraduate Public Students per Full-Time Equivalent Public Undergraduate in the State (1996 dollars): Flagship Public Research and Doctoral Institutions

Year	Unweighted Average	Standard Deviation	Median	Minimum	Maximum
1979	67.5	78.4	34.9	5.4	415.9
1981	77.2	89.9	45.2	4.5	410.9
1984	93.2	127.0	51.3	11.0	663.4
1988	117.0	134.2	60.9	10.3	594.8
1992	128.6	140.4	89.2	9.0	644.0
1994	139.1	162.4	92.0	10.8	881.1
1996	183.5	196.6	125.8	10.7	949.1
1998	284.7	322.0	180.2	6.8	1,585.6
% Δ	321.6	310.8	416.8	25.6	281.2
CAGR (%)	7.5	7.3	8.6	1.1	6.9

Source: NASSGAP Annual Reports, HEGIS, and IPEDS.
Notes: CAGR = compound annual growth rate. Δ = change.

Table 7.6 State Appropriations per FTE Undergraduate (1996 dollars): Flagship Public Research and Doctoral Institutions

Year	Unweighted Average	Weighted Average	Standard Deviation	Median	Minimum	Maximum
1979	9,446	8,932	4,355	8,430	3,200	25,297
1981	9,394	8,809	4,747	8,532	3,126	29,429
1984	9,977	9,544	4,495	9,162	3,180	26,045
1988	11,397	10,788	5,203	10,615	3,698	24,741
1992	11,227	10,934	4,769	10,549	3,300	26,736
1994	11,069	10,835	4,522	10,454	3,361	25,372
1996	11,204	10,922	4,429	10,666	3,180	24,421
1998	10,777	10,569	4,030	10,429	3,218	23,306
2000	11,402	11,173	4,364	11,032	3,328	24,073
% Δ	20.7	25.1	0.2	30.9	4.0	−4.8
CAGR (%)	0.9	1.0	0.0	1.2	0.2	−0.2

Source: HEGIS and IPEDS.
Notes: CAGR = compound annual growth rate. Δ = change.

more than quadrupled in real terms, growing from roughly $67 per student per year to $285 per student per year.[11] One recent study found that 68.5 percent of first-time full-time students enrolled in public higher education institutions received financial aid from any source and that 26.9 percent of these students received state grant aid averaging $1,742 per year.[12] Inasmuch as the average in-state tuition in 1998 was $3,525, state grant aid alone appears to cover over half of the tuition costs for *eligible* students.

Among the most generous states, in terms of state-provided grant aid per full-time-equivalent student enrolled in public higher education institutions are New York, Illinois, and Pennsylvania, while the least generous states include Wyoming, Utah, Montana, and Mississippi. New Mexico, Virginia, Washington, Maine, and Massachusetts are among those states that increased state aid per student the fastest during the period, while Utah, Wyoming, Montana, Alabama, and Mississippi actually decreased, in real terms, the amount of need-based grant aid they awarded per student enrolled in public institutions during the period. While direct student aid grew rapidly, real state appropriations per full-time-equivalent student to public higher education institutions saw very little growth during the period. Table 7.6 summarizes data on real average state government appropriations per full-time-equivalent undergraduate. Nationwide real state appropriations per student did not increase between 1988 and 2000 and only grew by 21 percent between 1979 and 2000, a 1 percent per annum annual growth rate. Again, dramatic cross-section variation existed in state funding per student.

A few states were able to generously increase support for selected institutions during the period. New Mexico, Maryland, Georgia Tech, Maine, and Oklahoma State all enjoyed a doubling of real state support, amounting to increases between $6,000 and $12,000 per student. However, of the ninety-one schools in our sample, twenty-two faced decreases in real state appropriations per student between 1979 and 2000. Among the hardest hit were many of the California and Virginia schools, each losing anywhere from 10 percent to 49 percent of its state support. These losses represented $1,000 to $12,000 per-student cuts in real state appropriations.

In the face of budget pressures and changing political attitudes, states may have an easier time funding direct student aid increases under the guise of promoting access. Legislators and their constituents may also prefer not to fund institutions directly because they may worry that the dol-

---

11. Although the annual percentage increases in real student grant aid (7.5 percent) outpaced the annual real increases in tuition (4.5 percent), the real dollar cost to students still rose during the period.

12. See National Center for Education Statistics (2001). In addition, 28.3 percent of aid recipients receive federal grants averaging $2,262, 30.9 percent of aid recipients received institutional grants averaging $2,576 per student, and 45.4 percent received loan aid averaging $3,490 per student in 1999.

lars will not go to the intended uses. Raw correlations, however, do not indicate that states that are more generous to students are less generous to institutions (the simple correlation coefficient is 0.14). In fact, it appears that there are states that are generous to higher education on both dimensions and states that are not.

Figure 7.2 depicts state preferences for direct student aid versus institutional aid in 1996, controlling for per capita tax revenues.[13] Controlling for per capita tax revenues accounts for the fact that states that have more money will be able to spend more on both grants and institutional appropriations. The axes represent U.S. averages. We see that New York, Michigan, Maryland, and California exert a great deal of effort to fund both student financial aid and state appropriations to public higher education, while Wyoming, Nebraska, Delaware, Idaho, Utah, and Montana fund neither very well. Some states do appear to prefer one form of aid to another. New Jersey, Minnesota, Pennsylvania, and Illinois are above average funders of public higher education institutions, while Alaska, Hawaii, North Dakota, and Mississippi are above average funders of aid to students.[14] Wealthier and larger states seem to support higher education on both fronts (northeast quadrant of figure 7.2) more greatly than the rural and poorer states (southwest quadrant of figure 7.2). It is somewhat of a surprise that no clear regional disparities emerge when comparing state preferences for direct student aid versus in-kind institutional aid.

During the 1990s, Arkansas, Florida, Georgia, Mississippi, and New Mexico each introduced direct student financial aid programs that were based on student performance rather than student need. In some cases these grant aid awards came at the expense of their need-based aid programs. The largest program was Georgia's Helping Outstanding Pupils Educationally (HOPE) Scholarship Program, which awarded $208 million of Georgia's total grant aid support of $209 million in academic year 1998. Florida and New Mexico's programs each comprised well over 50 percent of their states' total grant aid funding, while the programs in Mississippi and Arkansas were very small.

Tuition reciprocity agreements are agreements between a school or state and another state or consortium that allow a nonresident student from a neighboring state to attend the public institution at less than the normal out-of-state tuition. The magnitude of the discount may depend on the type of program in which a student is interested, the county in which a student resides, the availability of opportunities in the home state, whether the

13. Figure 7.2 plots normalized residuals from a regression of grant aid on per capita tax revenues in 1996 against residuals from a regression of state appropriations on per capita tax revenues in 1996. These are institution-level regressions, and each point on the graph represents enrollment weighted state averages for those states with multiple institutions.

14. This table shows results for need-based aid. Many states are now moving to merit-based aid programs (e.g., Georgia), and inclusion of this would alter this picture.

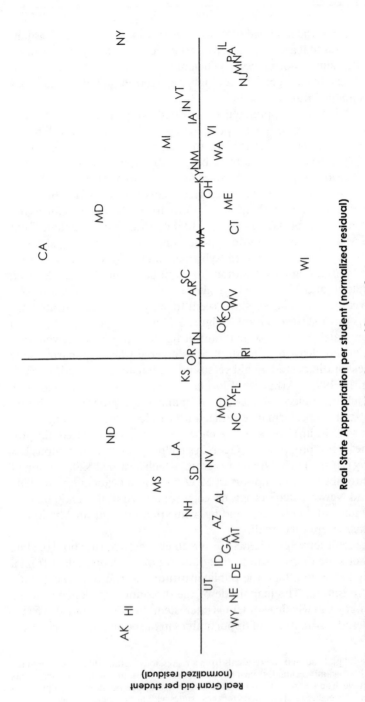

Fig. 7.2 1996 state appropriation per student versus need-based grant aid per student

Note: Plot of state averages of residuals from regression of state appropriations per student on per capita tax revenues versus residuals from regression of grant aid per student on per capita tax revenues.

student is an undergraduate or graduate, whether the student attends part- or full-time, and many other factors. While some schools negotiate agreements bilaterally with other states, many now choose to participate in consortium agreements in which a number of states in a geographical region are treated similarly under the agreement.

Tuition reciprocity agreements typically do *not* require that an institution accept a given number of students, or all students whose "quality" is above a specified level, from out-of-state. They only specify that if the out-of-state students are admitted, that the tuition charged to them be below the normal out-of-state student rate. Given that the political process has approved the agreement, at the margin, institutions will only accept students under a tuition reciprocity agreement if there is excess capacity at the institution for the programs in which the students are applying or if the accepted students yield more in prestige to the university than accepting more in-state students would yield the institution and if rejecting the marginal in-state students will not cause political problems for the institution.[15]

Under these circumstances, the marginal revenue received by the public university from accepting out-of-state students enrolled under tuition reciprocity agreements is always at least equal to the marginal revenue the institution would have received if it had not enrolled these students. While the marginal revenue the institution receives from a student admitted under a tuition reciprocity agreement may be less than the institution would have received if it *could* have enrolled more out-of-state students paying its normal out of state tuition, the latter would not always be possible. Moreover, the state as a whole is better off with the tuition reciprocity agreement because students from the state also have the opportunity to study in other states' public institutions. As we have indicated above, if the balance of students flowing between two states is not equal, often there are additional payments made directly to the coffers of the state that is receiving more students than it is sending.

In the spring of 2001, CHERI conducted a Tuition Reciprocity Agreements at Public Research and Doctoral Universities survey. The sample consisted of all 149 public institutions that were classified as Research or Doctoral institutions by the Carnegie Foundation in their 1994 classification scheme. Of the 128 universities that responded to the survey, 61 said that they participated in a tuition reciprocity program with schools in another state or as part of a consortium. Table 7.7 indicates that thirty-nine of the ninety-one institutions in our sample, a slightly smaller percentage than found in our reciprocity survey sample, participated in such an arrangement.

---

15. Because of these conditions, sometimes the flagship institutions in a state opt out of the program. So, for example, the University of California campuses are not part of the Western Interstate Commission on Higher Education (WICHE) undergraduate exchange consortium, but the California Maritime Academy at California State University is a participant.

Table 7.7   **Tuition Reciprocity Agreements**

Year	No. of Schools Reporting Reciprocal Enrollments (1)	Agreements That Don't Report Enrollment (2)	Mean Share of Undergrads That Are Reciprocal (%) (3)	Max. Share of Undergrads That Are Reciprocal (%) (4)	Mean Share of Enrollment That Are Nonresidents (%) (5)	Mean Share of Nonresidents That Are Reciprocal (%) (6)
1979	3	36				
1981	4	35				
1984	10	29	3.6	16.6	21.5	16.7
1988	15	24	3.1	22.4	23.8	13.0
1992	20	19	7.6	30.1	24.2	31.4
1994	24	15	6.7	30.1	25.4	26.4
1996	28	11	5.5	28.6	23.9	23.0

Source: HEGIS, IPEDS, and 2001 Annual Cornell Higher Education Research Institute Survey. For more information about this survey, please see http://www.ilr.cornell.edu/cheri and click on "Surveys."

Note: Column (5) reports results for those schools that report reciprocal enrollment.

Four consortia are represented among our survey responses: the Academic Common Market, the Midwest Student Exchange Program, the New England Regional Student Program, and the Western Interstate Commission for Higher Education. Some institutions in the survey also participate in student exchange programs (e.g., the National Student Exchange, the Consortium of Universities in the Washington Metropolitan Area, and the Tuition Exchange, Inc.). Student exchange programs differ from reciprocity agreements in that students participating in them are either visiting another school for a specified time period, or eligibility is limited to a narrowly defined group of students.[16]

While the number of schools participating in these agreements has not changed over our sample period, columns (4) and (5) suggest that students have been increasingly taking advantage of such programs. In addition, the schools that report reciprocal enrollments also enroll a larger share of nonresidents than the average school in our survey. In 1996, for example, an average of 23.9 percent of enrolled students were nonresidents in the twenty-eight schools reporting reciprocal enrollments, while an average of 19.6 percent of enrolled students were nonresidents in the entire sample.

Increasing nonresident enrollment shares under these programs does not translate into higher revenues for public higher education institutions given that these students often pay the in-state tuition level.[17] The final column of the table indicates that for these schools, nearly a quarter of their nonresident enrollments are covered under this plan. Returning to our example from earlier, a typical school would then forgo about $720,000 in additional tuition revenues due to the presence of these agreements.[18]

7.4   Estimation Strategy and Results

7.4.1   Model Specification

To achieve a fuller understanding of the causes and consequences of changing tuition and enrollments, we move to a multivariate analysis. We

---

16. A brief description of each of the consortia and exchange programs and the institutions participating in each is found at http://www.ilr.cornell.edu/cheri. Click on surveys and then click on tuition reciprocity.

17. Recall from the preceding that sometimes revenues flow from one state to another if the flow of students across the two states does not equalize. However, such revenues accrue to the state, not to the academic institution.

18. Of course, it is unlikely that anyone would leave cash on the table. The long-term cost savings from eliminating program duplication will very likely make up for the revenue losses. States might also gain politically from engaging in these agreements. States that send students likely save money because they do not have to establish and maintain costly programs. States and colleges that receive students can operate programs more efficiently because they gain quality students, and if the supply of students is elastic, they might be able to fill spaces that otherwise would have been vacant. Students benefit by not having to pay out-of-state tuition, which may have prevented many of them from earning degrees in the fields they had chosen.

estimate a system of four simultaneously determined equations using panel data, with the institution year as our unit of analysis in which the logarithm of state need-based grant aid per student, the logarithm of in-state tuition, the logarithm of out-of-state tuition, and the logarithm of the odds ratio of the share of first-time freshmen that are nonresidents are each specified to be functions of each other, a vector of exogenous variables and random uncorrelated (across equations) error terms.[19] Our model should be thought of as being only a "semistructural," rather than a structural model, because the variables found on the right-hand side of each equation likely capture both demand and supply factors and represent an equilibrium condition in the underlying structural model.

Table 7A.3 provides the reader a sense of from which side of the market each variable originates. The variables are grouped into six major categories: state demographic and institutional variables, variables reflecting the sources of institutional aid, variables reflecting the sources of student financial aid (including federal financial aid program variables), variables reflecting institutional enrollment pressures, variables reflecting quality measures and the competitive position of the institutions, and the endogenous variables.[20]

The table shows the variables that are excluded and included in each equation.[21] A blank indicates that the variable is excluded from that equation. For included variables, D indicates that the variable is assumed to influence the outcome through the demand side of the market, S indicates that it is assumed to influence the outcome through the supply side of the market, and B indicates that it is assumed to influence the outcome through both sides of the market. Similarly, + indicates that we expect that the net effect of the variable is to increase the outcome, – indicates that we expect that the net effect of the variable is to decrease the outcome, and ? indicates that the prediction is ambiguous. Our preferred specification for each of the four equations of interest is described in the following.

The state need-based grant aid equation is assumed to result from the interaction of students' demand for financial aid and the state's willingness to supply it. The in-state tuition equation is assumed to result from the interaction of in-state students' demand for seats at the institution and the institution's willingness to supply such seats. The institution's willingness

19. The first variable, average state need-based aid per student, is observed at the state, not institutional, level.

20. These categories are not mutually exclusive. Some variables might be considered to have an impact for multiple reasons. For example, institutions with larger per-student endowments have greater financial capabilities ("institutional financial aid"), but larger endowments are also indicative of an institution's "high quality." Further, it is not unreasonable to think that enrollment-pressure variables and school-quality variables also capture an institution's competitive position to the same extent as well.

21. There are obvious complications in estimating the system exactly as we have specified it here. The most glaring difficulty is our ability (or lack thereof) to properly identify the system of equations. We discuss the structural system here for expositional purposes and address the empirical relevance in detail in the next section.

to supply seats can be thought of as being derived from a utility-maximizing model of university behavior in which the objective of the university is to maximize its prestige, which in turn depends upon the average quality of the students that it enrolls, subject to a balanced budget constraint (Ehrenberg and Sherman 1984; Ehrenberg 2000; Garvin 1980; Winston 1999). A public university's behavior may also be constrained by its state government, which may have different objectives than the university does. For example, while the university may want to maximize student quality, the political process may want to keep in-state tuition as low as possible (Groen and White 2001). The out-of-state tuition and the share of nonresident students enrolled at an institution are similarly assumed to result from the interaction of out-of-state students' demand for seats at the institution and the institution's willingness to supply such seats, the latter constrained by the political process in the state.

The grant aid equation includes variables that relate to federal and other state and institutional sources of student financial aid. Federal loan and grant program variables included in the model are the size of the maximum Pell Grant (PELL), the percent cap on costs (CAP), and categorical variables that indicate the degree of access that students have to subsidized federal loans (1979, 1992).[22] The presence of state merit aid programs (MERIT) both reduces student demand for need-based aid and the state's pool of available resources from which it might fund need-based aid programs. Variables that relate to institutional sources of aid are the logarithm of real state appropriations per student (APP), the logarithm of real endowment per student (END), and the logarithm of in-state tuition (TUITI)—each of these variables generates income that the institution can use, in principle, for scholarship aid. State demographic and institutional structure variables that are included in this equation (to capture a state's financial capacity to provide need-based student aid) are its real tax revenues per capita (TAX), its unemployment rate (UNEMP), the share of its households with incomes below that necessary to be eligible for a Pell Grant (ELIG), and the share of its population that is college aged (AGE). Also included is the degree of political autonomy of each school, as measured by the number of governing boards in the state (GOV).[23]

22. The percent cap is a percentage of college costs that students were eligible to receive in Pell Grants. The cap was removed in 1992 so that students at low-tuition institutions that were eligible for the maximum Pell Grant could use any funds in excess of tuition costs to pay for living and other expenses. In 1981, student access to subsidized loans was dramatically reduced with the repeal of the Middle Income Student Assistance Act (MISAA) after a run-up in usage from its inception in 1978. Access was expanded again in 1992 with the removal of a portion of housing assets in the Expected Family Contribution formula.

23. Lowry (2001a,b) hypothesized that the greater the number of different independent governing boards in a state, the more decentralized state governance of higher education was and, thus, the less that political pressure from the state could be used to keep tuition levels down. He found evidence that this relationship held. It is not clear, however, whether state aid per student will be higher or lower in states with more political autonomy for their higher education institutions.

To control for the impact of enrollment pressure on grant aid, we include a measure of state seating capacity (SEAT), calculated as the ratio of a state's predicted enrollment in its public higher education institutions to its actual enrollment in these institutions in a year.[24] Additional measures of enrollment pressures that are included are the ratio of graduate enrollments to undergraduate enrollments in the state (GRAD); the share of new students in the state enrolled in private colleges (PRIV) and in two-year colleges (TWO); and the logarithm of real average tuition in the region excluding the state in which the institution is located (TUITR).[25] Also included are measures of overall quality in the state, as measured by the weighted average Barron's rating of public (BPUB) and private (BPRIV) institutions in the state.

Our in-state tuition equation is similarly specified. However, real state tax revenues per capita are excluded from this equation because the impact of state resources on tuition is captured by the inclusion of real state appropriations per student (APP). The latter is treated as exogenous in our model.[26] In addition, we include institutional measures of school quality—categorical variables that indicate the Barron's rank of each institution as well as the level of per-student grant aid (the dependent variable in the previous equation)—where higher levels would be expected to allow institutions to raise tuition.[27]

More generous student financial aid packages (e.g., federal financial aid programs) make it easier for a school to increase tuition for at least two reasons. First, federal financial aid may reduce barriers to entry for students

24. Predicted enrollments are calculated by dividing a state's full-time equivalent public four-year enrollment in 1970 by the size of the college-age population in the state in 1970 (ages eighteen–twenty-four) and then multiplying this ratio by a weighted cohort size in each year of our study. If both the share of students going to public institutions and college enrollment rates in a state remained constant over time, then the weight used to calculate predicted enrollments in year t would simply be the size of the college-age population in year t. Between 1970 and 1998, the share of students attending public institutions was stable (between 75 and 80 percent), but enrollment rates increased nationwide from 28.8 percent to 42 percent. To account for the enrollment rate expansion, we allow the population weight to grow as the enrollment rate grows in each year. We would prefer to have used the ratio of seats available in public colleges to the number of its high school graduates as a capacity measure, but we did not do so because of endogeneity concerns. Nonetheless, estimates that excluded this variable from the analysis were very similar to those that included it. Because this suggests that the endogeneity of capacity is not driving our results, this variable is included in all of the estimates that follow.

25. The grant aid per student equation is estimated using state-level data. As such, all institution-level variables, including real state appropriations per student, are excluded from this equation.

26. As noted previously, Lowry (2001a,b) found that it was permissible to treat state appropriations per student as exogenous in the in-state tuition equation.

27. For roughly three decades, Barrons Profiles of American Colleges has assigned categorical rankings to four-year institutions according to a subjective measure of quality. From best to worst, they rank institutions as *most competitive, highly competitive, very competitive, competitive, less competitive,* and *noncompetitive.* We created a categorical variable HIGHB for those institutions in the top two categories as well as LOWB for those in the bottom two. The coefficients on these variables are then relative to the omitted middle categories.

at the margin of attending college. Second, institutions can increase tuition, and for those students not at the grant or loan limits, each dollar of tuition increase will be covered by an additional dollar of aid, up until some maximum. Further, the availability of merit aid will increase the desirability of attending college for all students, putting upward pressure on tuition. Institutional sources of aid have a less obvious impact on tuition. While increased state appropriations per student may allow schools to keep tuition low, this increase in in-kind student aid may result in an increase in demand, forcing tuition upward. Larger endowments per student generate more income for an institution, but more importantly reflect higher institutional quality and permit higher tuition levels. Similarly, higher institutional quality in absolute (as measured by the Barron's ranking) and relative terms (as measured by the ranking of other schools in the state) measures as well as strong enrollment pressure allows institutions to charge high tuition levels.

The logarithm of real out-of-state tuition (TUITO) is specified to be a function of the logarithm of real in-state tuition (TUITI) and most of the variables included in the in-state tuition equation. Again, real state tax revenue per capita is excluded from the equation. A notable difference is that we replace the institution's Barron's ranking with measures of the shares of students in the state enrolled at other public (BSPUB) or private (BSPRIV) institutions in the state that are of equal or better Barron's rankings than the institution. These variables capture the institution's monopoly power within the state for students seeking to attend institutions of its quality or higher. Similarly, we include the share of students in the region enrolled in schools of equal or better quality that are enrolled in private schools (SPRIV); the greater this share, the higher the average tuition will be at institutions perceived as good alternatives to the institution. The logarithm of the share of first-time freshmen that are nonresidents (NON) is included to capture the financial benefits to the institution from increasing out-of-state enrollment. Finally, we include the logarithm of the share of undergraduates that are enrolled under reciprocity agreements (RECIP) whose a priori impact on nonresident tuition is unclear.

The final equation is the nonresident enrollment share equation. The dependent variable is specified as the logarithm of the odds ratio of the share of first-time freshmen that are nonresidents to allow the error term to be normally distributed. This equation is specified very similarly to the out-of-state tuition equation, with the logarithm of real out-of-state tuition (TUITO) included as an explanatory variable. We also include the logarithm of the mean Scholastic Aptitude Test (SAT) scores in the state in which the institution is located (SAT) to see if states with a low supply of "high-quality" high school graduates seek to recruit out-of-state students to attract top talent.[28]

---

28. Groen and White (forthcoming) discuss this issue in detail.

Starting with the Georgia HOPE program, which was established in 1993, a number of states have recently adopted merit-based grant aid programs for students who attend college within state. These programs increase the incentive that students from those states have to attend college within state (Dynarski, chap. 2 in this volume). During our sample period, only Georgia, Arkansas, Florida, New Mexico, and Mississippi instituted such programs (between 1994 and 1998), but seven more did so by 2002. Such programs should serve to increase the demand for in-state students to attend public institutions in the state, which may limit the public institution's ability to expand, or even maintain, its nonresident enrollment share. We include year/state interaction terms for those years in which an institution was in a state that had adopted one of these programs in the nonresident enrollment share equation to test if these programs do, in fact, reduce nonresident enrollment shares.[29]

We present two types of estimates for each equation. First, to understand why tuition, grant aid, and nonresident enrollment vary across states and institutions at a point in time, we present pooled cross-section time series estimates, using institutional level data for eight years between 1979 and 1998. Year dichotomous variables are included in these models to control for idiosyncratic time effects.

While the wide variation in the cross-section data makes this approach appealing, it is subject to possible omitted-variables bias. For example, institutions located in beautiful areas, other factors held constant, may be able to charge higher tuitions. In this example, omission of "beauty" as an explanatory variable might bias the estimates of other explanatory variables' parameters effects on tuition if these variables are correlated with "beauty." We have attempted to minimize this problem by including a carefully constructed, rich set of explanatory variables in our models.

An alternative way of controlling for omitted variables is to take advantage of the panel nature of the data and employ a fixed effects estimation strategy. The panel data results are useful in understanding how *changes* in explanatory variables affect *changes* in the dependent variables. In addition, the panel data results will be employed to simulate how changes in key explanatory variables will affect changes in the outcomes of interest to us.

Inasmuch as these four outcomes are determined simultaneously, we would prefer to estimate a jointly determined system of four equations using two-stage least squares (2SLS) to control for the endogeneity of these outcomes.[30] However, the success of this procedure is highly dependent on

29. For example, we include a dummy variable that takes on the value of 1 for Georgia institutions in our sample for 1994, 1996, and 1998 and is zero otherwise.

30. The 2SLS estimation is necessary to attempt to correct for the biases that result from the violation of the orthogonality conditions necessary for ordinary least squares (OLS) to be unbiased, though the signs of the potential biases here are ambiguous.

finding appropriate "instruments" for the endogenous variables in the system.[31] Determining a suitable vector of restrictions has proven to be a challenging endeavor, and to avoid debate over the restrictions we have chosen, we will report estimates from the reduced-form model for our system.

The reduced form is found by solving for the endogenous variables in the system. What one is left with is a system of four outcome equations, with each outcome being a function of purely exogenous variables. Without agreement on acceptable exclusion restrictions, we are unable to recover the underlying structural parameters from estimates of the reduced-form model. However, the only real cost of using this procedure is that we are unable to make direct assessments of the impacts that changes in each of the outcomes explicitly has on the other outcomes in the system.

We should caution that without a properly specified structural model, one cannot be sure that the estimated associations in our data are causal. However, we believe that our results are of interest and provide a guide to how a public university and prospective students react to state actions and other changes in environmental variables. Those estimates and those we tried using a variety of different sets of instruments proved to be very similar to the estimates of the reduced-form system that follows. Tables 7A.4 and 7A.5 present the 2SLS "structural" results for readers that are interested in these findings.[32]

7.4.2 Econometric Estimates: Cross-Section Findings

The odd-numbered columns of tables 7.8 and 7.9 present the estimated coefficients from the cross-section equations. We have suppressed the stan-

31. We tried to instrument using the following: In the grant aid equation, we instrument for in-state tuition using the institution's Barron's ranking because the quality of an institution's students likely affects tuition, but not a state's willingness to disperse financial aid to all students in the state. In the in-state tuition equation, we instrument for grant aid with state tax revenues per capita and the weighted ranking of public schools in the state. In the out-of-state tuition equation, we instrument for in-state tuition with state private enrollment share, state two-year enrollment share, weighted ranking of private schools in the state, state tax revenues per capita, and weighted rank of public schools in the state. Nonresident enrollment shares are instrumented with average SAT scores of high school seniors in the state. In the nonresident enrollment share equation, out-of-state tuition is instrumented with state private enrollment share, state two-year enrollment share, weighted ranking of private schools in the state, state tax revenues per capita, and weighted rank of public schools in the state.

32. Although finding suitable exclusion restrictions is a challenging endeavor for this system of equations, the estimates in tables 7A.4 and 7A.5 have proven to be robust to a variety of specification changes. The key exclusion restrictions that are necessary to identify the model are real state tax revenue per capita in the in-state and out-of-state tuition equations and average SAT scores of high school students in the state in the nonresident enrollment share equation. Many of the other exclusions are made to reduce multicollinearity. We suspect that the insensitivity of the 2SLS estimates and their similarity to reduced-form estimates is due to the instruments being either "too weak" or "too strong." By the former, we mean that there is not enough exogenous variation to produce a change in the outcome in question (with a corresponding large asymptotic variance matrix of the 2SLS estimator). By the latter, we mean that the instruments may also be correlated with the underlying model's disturbance term.

Table 7.8   State Need Based Grant Aid and Instate Tuition Equations Reduced Form Regression Results

	Grant Aid		In-State Tuition	
Variable	Cross Section (1)	Panel (2)	Cross Section (3)	Panel (4)
State demographics/institutional characteristics				
Log tax revenues per capita (TAX)	0.57*	0.20*	0.07	0.05
Log unemployment (UNEMP)	0.34*	0.04	0.20*	0.08*
Share of population aged 18–24 (AGE)	–23.38*	–13.49*	0.49	–9.31*
Share of population with incomes below maximum Pell allowable (ELIG)	–0.07	1.14*	–1.23*	0.40
Log number of governing boards (GOV)	0.01	n.a.	0.00	n.a.
Sources of institutional aid				
Log state appropriations per student (APP)	–0.27*	0.53*	–0.24*	–0.18*
Log endowment per student (END)	0.02	0.01	0.02*	0.01
Sources of student financial aid				
Log maximum Pell Grant award (PELL)	–10.70	1.32*	–1.89	0.48*
Percent cap on costs (CAP)	–3.50	0.70*	–0.72	0.34*
Post-1979 subsidized loan access (1979)	n.a.	0.57*	n.a.	0.15*
Post-1992 subsidized loan access (1992)	n.a.	0.73*	n.a.	0.38*
Arkansas Merit Program (MERIT)	1.01*	0.77*	0.05	0.24*
Florida Merit Program (MERIT)	–0.82	–0.30	–0.47*	–0.19*
Georgia Merit Program (MERIT)	–1.77*	–1.55*	–0.15	–0.10
Mississippi Merit Program (MERIT)	–1.90*	–1.01*	0.19	–0.09
New Mexico Merit Program (MERIT)	0.69	0.73*	–0.21	–0.07
Enrollment pressure				
Ratio of FTE grad to undergrad enrollments (GRAD)	0.14*	–0.09	0.05*	–0.02
Share of FTEFTF in state in privates (PRIV)	1.36*	–1.14*	0.86*	0.53*
Share of FTEFTF in state in 2 years (TWO)	0.63*	1.32*	–0.35*	–0.07
Seating capacity (predicted enroll/actual enroll) (SEAT)	–0.87*	0.31*	–0.23*	0.15*
Log composite regional tuition, ex-in-state (TUITR)	0.27*	–0.08	0.12*	0.06*
School quality/competitive position				
Weak Barron's rank (LOWB)	0.04	0.03	0.00	0.06*
Strong Barron's rank (HIGHB)	–0.01	–0.01	0.10*	0.06
Weighted Barron's rank of privates in state (BPRIV)	0.32*	0.02	0.00	0.04*
Weighted Barron's rank of publics in state (BPUB)	0.30*	0.00	0.05*	0.01
Adjusted R^2	0.595	0.618	0.722	0.866

Notes: FTE = full-time equivalent. FTEFTF = full-time equivalent first-time freshmen. n.a. = not applicable.

*Significant at the 95 percent level.

dard error reporting to make the tables more readable. Variables that have an asterisk (*) are significant at the 95 percent confidence level. Turning first to the average state need-based grant aid per-student equation (column [1]), it appears that differences across states in the level of per-student grant aid awards are best explained by differences in demographic charac-

Table 7.9   **Out-of-State Tuition and Nonresident Enrollment Share Equations Reduced Form Regression Results**

Variable	Out-of-State Tuition		Nonresident Share	
	Cross Section (1)	Panel (2)	Cross Section (3)	Panel (4)
State demographics/institutional characteristics				
Log tax revenues per capita (TAX)	0.00	0.08*	−0.25	−0.21*
Log unemployment (UNEMP)	0.13*	0.05*	−0.37*	−0.16*
Share of population aged 18–24 (AGE)	−1.26	−4.10*	10.16*	3.45
Share of population with incomes below maximum Pell allowable (ELIG)	−1.25*	0.59*	1.24*	−1.10
Log number of governing boards (GOV)	0.00	n.a.	−0.03*	n.a.
Sources of institutional aid				
Log state appropriations per student (APP)	−0.15*	−0.23*	−1.16*	0.07
Log endowment per student (END)	0.05*	0.01*	0.16*	0.04
Sources of student financial aid				
Log maximum Pell Grant award (PELL)	−0.35	0.16	5.11	0.00
Percent cap on costs (CAP)	−0.43	−0.17*	1.57	0.08*
Post-1979 subsidized loan access (1979)	n.a.	0.05*	n.a.	−0.52*
Post-1992 subsidized loan access (1992)	n.a.	0.46*	n.a.	−0.84*
Arkansas Merit Program (MERIT)	−0.08*	0.17*	0.17	−0.44
Florida Merit Program (MERIT)	−0.27	−0.02	−1.28*	−1.18*
Georgia Merit Program (MERIT)	−0.11*	−0.07	−0.29	−0.44*
Mississippi Merit Program (MERIT)	−0.27*	−0.03	0.48	0.24
New Mexico Merit Program (MERIT)	−0.02	0.03	0.31	0.18
Enrollment pressure				
Ratio of FTE grad to undergrad enrollments (GRAD)	−0.01	0.02	−0.04	−0.10
Share of FTEFTF in state in privates (PRIV)	0.20*	0.19	0.39	−0.67
Share of FTEFTF in state in 2 years (TWO)	−0.09	0.08	−0.37*	0.23
Seating capacity (predicted enroll/actual enroll) (SEAT)	0.04	0.16*	−0.26*	−0.28*
Log composite regional tuition, ex-in-state (TUITR)	0.15*	0.10*	0.08	0.35*
Log share of the undergrads in reciprocity agreements (RECIP)	0.00	0.00	−0.09*	0.06
School quality/competitive position				
Weak Barron's rank (LOWB)	n.a.	n.a.	n.a.	n.a.
Strong Barron's rank (HIGHB)	0.04	0.00	−0.20	0.11
Weighted Barron's rank of privates in state (BPRIV)	0.04*	0.05*	−0.31*	0.04
Weighted Barron's rank of publics in state (BPUB)	0.07*	0.03	0.28*	−0.03
Institution's share of quality public seats in the state (BSPUB)	−0.01	−0.04	1.29*	0.28*
Institution's share of qual. private seats in the state (BSPRIV)	0.00	0.00	0.01*	0.00
Share of quality seats in region that are private (SPRIV)	0.37*	−0.11	−0.03	−0.56*
Log SAT (SAT)	−0.01	2.11*	−1.07*	−0.15
Adjusted R^2	0.794	0.904	0.501	0.204

Notes: FTE = full-time equivalent. FTEFTF = full-time equivalent first-time freshmen. n.a. = not applicable.

*Significant at the 95 percent level.

teristics, enrollment pressures, and overall institutional quality in the states.[33]

With respect to demographic characteristics, wealthier states, as measured by per capita tax revenues (TAX), award more grant aid per student, but states in which a larger share of the population is of college age (AGE) award less aid per student. Further, states in which labor markets are loose award more grant aid per student. However, institutional autonomy (GOV) does not seem to be correlated with state grant aid generosity.

The entire vector of enrollment and state quality variables are strongly related to grant aid awards. Undergraduates in states with less competition for funds with more costly graduate students (GRAD) receive more grant aid. In addition, when private and community college enrollments (PRIV, TWO) are large relative to public four-year college enrollments, grant aid awards are larger—presumably due to the private colleges' subsidizing their own students and the large in-kind subsidy provided by the low-cost (and hence low state appropriations) community colleges.[34] Further, the average (excluding in-state) tuition in the region (TUITR) that the state is located in seems to be positively correlated with the level of grant aid that is awarded. Curiously, states with greater available seating capacity in their public institutions—that is, their predicted enrollments exceed what they actually enroll in a given year (SEAT)—award less grant aid per student, contrary to our a priori expectation. As expected, states with higher-quality public (BPUB) and private (BPRIV) academic institutions, and thus likely higher costs, offer more grant aid.

Do other sources of student financial aid affect state need-based grant aid awards? One might expect that growing state affinities for non-need-based aid programs would crowd out spending on need-based grant aid to students. The preliminary evidence varies by state. While it is not surprising to see that Georgia, Mississippi, and Florida have coupled increasing merit-based aid generosity with decreasing need-based aid support, it is surprising to see that Arkansas and New Mexico have responded by increasing their need-based aid generosity, ceteris parabis. However, as hinted at by figure 7.2, it appears that states prefer one type of aid to another. It appears that states awarding larger in-kind awards (state appropriation per student to four-year institutions [APP]) award significantly less grant aid per student than states where appropriations are lower.

Moving to the in-state tuition equation (column [3]), we find that sources of institutional aid and enrollment pressures go a long way in explaining

33. All of the results discussed in the paper are ceteris paribus, or other variables in the model held constant, findings.

34. However, this result may be picking up higher-order moments of the state income distribution as the share of two-year students from lower-income families is far greater than that for four-year students. Therefore, states with comparatively large two-year enrollments may have wider and lower income distributions than others.

differences across institutions in in-state tuition levels. Schools that receive higher state appropriations per student (APP) charge lower tuition, though the elasticity is far from unity. Taken together, the impacts of having a strong Barron's ranking (HIGHB) and having higher endowment per student (END) suggest that higher-quality schools are able to charge more for their product.

Once again, the entire enrollment-pressure vector is significant in explaining cross-institution variation in in-state tuition levels. When private competition in a state is important, as measured by the share of first-time freshmen in the state that are enrolled in private academic institutions (PRIV), public universities are able to charge higher tuition, as do institutions in states in which a smaller share of students attend two-year colleges (TWO). A striking result is that the cross-section evidence suggests that in-state undergraduate students are partially subsidizing the huge costs of graduate education at these research universities. Across institutions, the higher the ratio of graduate to undergraduate students (GRAD), the higher the in-state undergraduate tuition. However, this finding might merely reflect that universities with larger shares of their students enrolled as graduate students may be higher-quality institutions, which attract better faculty and thus can charge higher tuition levels to its residents. Not surprising, however, is that institutions with more seating capacity (SEAT) tend to charge a lower price for their product and that higher regional tuition (TUITR) allows institutions to charge a higher price.

There is little evidence that differences in student financial aid affect in-state tuition levels and mixed evidence on state demographic and institutional factors. Public universities in states in which the unemployment rate (UNEMP) is high, and hence the opportunity cost of enrolling in school is low, charge higher in-state tuition. Unlike Lowry (2001b), we find no evidence that public universities in states with more autonomous governance structures (GOV) charge higher tuition.

Column (5) of table 7.9 displays the results for the nonresident tuition equation. Contrary to our results for in-state tuition, we do not find that nonresident undergraduates are subsidizing graduate education. Also, given that nonresident enrollments can be viewed to either enhance revenues or school quality, it is not surprising that institutional aid and school-quality variables primarily drive the out-of-state tuition results.

Institutions receiving higher state appropriations per student (APP) charge less to nonresidents, though the elasticity is small, and institutions with larger endowments per student (END) charge a higher price to nonresidents. Further, schools charge nonresidents more in states in which the average quality of private colleges (BPRIV) and public colleges (BPUB) are higher. As alluded to previously, these quality measures are closely related to the broader concept of competitive position. In the case of nonresident tuition, regional competition clearly also matters, as schools located in regions in which a large share of students attend private schools (SPRIV) are able to charge more to out-of-state residents. Similarly, when the average tuition in the geographical region is higher (TUITR), schools also charge more to nonresidents.

While demographic characteristics in the state affect nonresident tuition the same way they affect in-state tuition, unlike in the in-state tuition equation, evidence of the impact of merit-aid programs (MERIT) on tuition is not mixed. These programs seem to have had a negative effect on nonresident tuition levels—likely deriving from the fact that the increasing prevalence of merit-based aid programs provides an incentive for students who otherwise would have attended more costly out-of-state or private institutions to remain in-state.

Column (7) presents the nonresident enrollment share equation. Taken as a whole, the entire vector of variables aside from the sources of student financial aid are strong predictors (across institutions) of nonresident enrollment share differences. The results seem to indicate that nonresident students are used both for the purposes of generating revenues and to augment institutional quality. Turning to the institutional aid variables, we see that states providing higher state appropriations per student (APP) tend to enroll fewer nonresidents. While one might expect nonresidents to prefer to attend institutions that receive more state support per student, sometimes state support per student is endogenous in the sense that institutions may receive greater state appropriations per student for each in-state student they enroll. Further, institutions that receive high levels of state support may not need to turn to nonresidents to generate needed revenues. We also find that schools with larger endowments per student (END) attract more nonresidents—further suggesting that this variable be included in the "quality" vector.

Flagship public institutions face political pressure to ensure access to the children of state residents. We do not find, however, that when seating capacity at all public institutions in a state is low (SEAT), that public institutions enroll smaller fractions of nonresidents. In fact, we find that institutions with a shortage of capacity enroll the largest nonresident enrollment shares.[35] Again, this might be a result of the higher-quality institutions being the ones with less excess capacity than lesser institutions. Another enrollment result that is somewhat surprising is that institutions that enroll a larger share of their undergraduates under tuition reciprocity agreements (RECIP) tend to enroll a smaller share of nonresidents than other institutions.

We do find that schools located in states where high school student qual-

---

35. Due to concerns that the enrollment constraints at the University of California may be heavily influencing our results, we reestimated all of our equations without these schools. These results were very similar (with larger standard errors) to those presented in the text.

ity is relatively poor (SAT) enroll a larger share of nonresidents—they need to look elsewhere to find high-quality students. Another variable relating to institutional quality is the institution's share of enrollments in a state at schools of equal or higher quality. Other variables held constant, institutions whose enrollment is large relative to the total of all public enrollments (BSPUB) or all private enrollments (BSPRIV) at institutions of equal or greater quality in the state have larger shares of nonresident enrollments.[36] It is also not surprising to see that institutions located in states where the average quality of public institutions is high (BPUB) tend to enroll more nonresidents, and those in states where average private school quality (BPRIV) is high enroll fewer nonresidents. Given the tuition premium paid by nonresidents at public institutions, the cost-per-quality unit of attending private schools in the state may be comparable to that for attending out-of-state public institutions.

Turning last to the demographic characteristics, the effect of unemployment rates and the proportion of households that are Pell Grant eligible are as expected. Contrary to our expectations, we find that once we control for other factors, schools in states with more governing boards (GOV), hence more autonomous institutions, enroll smaller shares of nonresidents. Further, the institutions located in states with larger college-aged population shares (AGE) enroll more nonresidents.

7.4.3   Econometric Estimates—Panel Data Results

The even-numbered columns of tables 7.8 and 7.9 present our fixed effects estimates. Because these parameters are estimated from within institution changes over time, they are useful for understanding the potential impacts of policy changes. One might expect that because most of the variation in our data occurs across institutions, fewer statistically significant coefficients would arise, but this is not what we observe. Our discussion focuses on results that significantly differ from those found in the cross section, and we make some brief comments on those that do not, which are noteworthy nonetheless.[37]

Turning first to the state need-based grant aid equation (column [2]), we find that changes in sources of student financial aid are the primary determinants of changes in state student need-based grant aid. As students have more access to federal grants (PELL, CAP) and loans (1979, 1992), states respond by awarding more grant aid. Three other results stand out. First,

36. For example, for the public schools, we simply take the ratio of full-time-equivalent first-time freshmen enrollments in the school under observation and divide it by the total number of full-time-equivalent first-time freshmen students in public institutions in the state that have at least as high a Barron's ranking as the school under observation.

37. If a so-called "fixed effect" result differs from a cross-sectional estimate, it is likely because the cross-sectional equations did not properly control for time-invariant, institution- (or state-) specific information that was also *correlated* with the other explanatory variables in the model.

we find that, controlling for other factors, increases in state appropriations per student (APP) lead to states' awarding more grant aid—indicating that in-kind aid and direct student aid are perhaps complementary. Second, the impact of enrollment pressures within states is very different than the impact across states. Most notably, we find that as the seating capacity in a state increases (SEAT), states respond by awarding more need-based grant aid per student. Third, we find that state grant aid responds to changes in the income distribution of a state's population. An increase in the share of households whose incomes fall below the maximum level that permits them to be eligible for Pell Grants (ELIG) leads to higher levels of state need-based grant aid per student. Note, too, that changes in institutional quality in the state are not good predictors of grant aid changes. In fact, since quality measures are unlikely to vary much within institutions over time, we do not expect to find statistical significance in many of these variables in any of the equations. As a result, we will ignore these variables in the discussion that follows.

We turn next to the in-state tuition equation (column [4]). While institutional aid and enrollment factors were largely responsible for explaining cross-institutional differences in the cross section, these results indicate that changes in the availability of student financial aid are also very important. In addition, the impact of enrollment pressures and demographic changes are felt somewhat differently.

We find that increased state appropriations per student (AID) are still associated with lower in-state tuition changes, but neither increases in endowment per student (END) nor changes in the share of students that are graduate students (GRAD) are statistically significantly associated with changes in in-state tuition in the panel. What may be of concern to policymakers is that it appears that institutions are attempting to capture the additional revenues that have been generated by federal financial aid programs. We find that an increase in the generosity of the Pell Grant (PELL) by 10 percent leads institutions to raise in-state tuition levels by 4.8 percent. We also find that tuition has also significantly increased as students have had more access to federal subsidized loans (19xx). The implementation of state merit-aid programs has produced mixed results, with tuition rising in the Arkansas institutions and falling in the Florida institutions.

Two additional results are of interest. Unlike in the cross section, as the share of the population that is college aged (AGE) increases, in-state tuition levels fall, but increases in seating capacity result in tuition increases. The latter result is difficult to explain and may reflect reverse causality in the data, despite our best efforts to control for this potential occurrence.

The nonresident tuition equation results in the panel (column [6]) are very similar to the cross-section results, with the most notable difference being that changes in nonresident tuition are largely explained by changes in state demographic characteristics. As tax revenues, unemployment rates, and the share of households with low incomes increase within a state, we find that nonresident tuition will increase. As the college-aged population increases in its size relative to the remainder of the population, we find that nonresident tuition will decrease. While we saw that institutions responded to federal grant aid increases by increasing in-state tuition, we do not see the same occurring with nonresident tuition. However, it appears that as students have more access to federal subsidized loans, institutions in-turn respond by increasing nonresident tuition. An interesting difference from the cross-section results is that as average SAT scores improve within a state, institutions will have less pressure to pursue nonresident enrollment strategies to improve quality, and we find this manifestation through nonresident tuition increases. Last, just as in the in-state tuition equation and similarly puzzling, we find that as seating capacity increases at an institution, it responds by increasing nonresident tuition.

Finally, turning to the nonresident enrollment share equation (column [8]), we see that the fixed effects results are starkly different from the cross-sectional results. No longer do institutional aid factors matter. This may be due to the finding that as state tax revenues increase (and hence the pool of funds available for institutional and student aid), nonresident enrollment shares decrease within an institution.

While sources of student financial aid were not able to explain cross-sectional differences in nonresident enrollments, taken as a whole they seem to do a better job of explaining within-institution changes. We find that as the cap on costs covered by the Pell Grant increases (CAP), more nonresidents would attend an institution, but surprisingly, as access to subsidized loans expands, fewer nonresidents would attend. The presence of merit-aid programs in Florida and Georgia have led institutions in each state to enroll far fewer nonresidents than they had before these programs were instituted.[38]

As a whole, changes in enrollment pressure are not able to explain changes in nonresident enrollment shares. However, we find that nonresident enrollment shares increase as regional tuition levels (TUITR) increase. Last, as more of the quality slots in institutions in a region are in private schools (SPRIV), the share of nonresidents at the public schools falls. Taken as a whole, these results indicate that nonresident student demand is primarily responsible for explaining within-institution changes in nonresident enrollment shares over time.

Before turning to some simple policy simulations in the next section, we address several important issues. First, inasmuch as we are estimating a reduced-form system, it is natural to run specifications with and without certain variables that might be problematic (e.g., seating capacity, state ap-

38. An unstated goal of each of these programs was to keep high-quality residents from attending universities out of state. This evidence suggests that this may have indeed occurred.

propriations per student, state need-based grant aid per student) to see how sensitive our other results are to those variables' inclusion or omission. Our estimates of the system when we exclude/include different permutations of the preceding three variables proved to be remarkably similar to the previously described results. Second, it would be interesting to determine the impact that per-student need-based grant aid awards have on tuition and enrollments. Because grant aid is a state-level, rather than an institutional-level, variable one can argue that it is reasonable to treat it as exogenous to the institution and include it as an explanatory variable in the other equations. We have done this, and the results are reported in tables 7A.6 and 7A.7.

When per-student grant aid is included as an explanatory variable, the estimated effects of the other variables in the model are qualitatively (and in most cases quantitatively) similar to the results presented in tables 7.8 and 7.9. What is interesting is that we find an impact of state need-based grant aid per student on tuition and enrollment only in the cross section. That is, institutions located in states that award more need-based student aid are those that charge the highest in-state and nonresident tuition, ceteris parabis, and are also the institutions that enroll the smallest share of nonresidents. However, *changes* in state need-based grant aid do not affect *changes* in in-state and nonresident tuition and nonresident enrollment.

7.4.4   Policy Simulations

Table 7.10 outlines the effects that selected policy changes have on the four outcomes, using the panel data estimates presented in tables 7.8 and 7.9.[39] The discussion below focuses only on those factors that are likely to vary substantially between years. Inspection of the grant aid results indicates that changes in grant aid are a result of a variety of factors in a state, not solely the result of economic factors. If a state at the average per-student grant aid level experienced an increase of $1,000 in per capita tax revenues, that state would only increase per-student grant aid by $12 over an average of $307. It appears that there are some spillover effects of increasing institutional and other student sources of financial aid. When the Pell Grant maximum is increased by $100, we see states respond by increasing per-student need-based grant aid by $14, and when states increase state appropriations per student by $1,000, they also increase support for students by $15.

Increases in state support for higher education institutions helps to curb

---

39. The table reports marginal effects from the presented regressions evaluated at the sample means in the data. When we calculated the marginal effects for individual institutions and then took their means, the impacts were nearly identical.

Table 7.10   **Effect of Selected Policy Changes on Outcomes: Fixed Effects Reduced-Form Regression Results, Evaluated at 1998 Level of Appropriate Variable**

Selected Policy Change	Grant Aid ($)	In-State Tuition ($)	Out-of-State Tuition ($)	Nonresident Share
Increase state tax revenues per capita by $1,000	12*	32	158*	–1.16*
Increase maximum real Pell Grant award by $100	14*	58*	56	–0.01
Increase real state appropriations per student by $1,000	15*	–60*	–222*	0.19
Increase real endowment per student by $1,000	0	2	7*	0.05
Increase ratio of grad students to first-time freshmen by 10 points	–3	–5	20	–0.30
Increasing seating capacity 10 percentage points	11*	63*	187*	–0.81*
Increases in average regional tuition by $1,000	–3	23*	145*	1.42*
Increase share of students enrolled in privates by 1 percentage point	–15*	80*	84	–0.82
Increase share of students enrolled in two-year schools by 1 percentage point	10*	–6	20	0.16
Having higher SAT scores by 10 points in your state			201*	–0.40
Increasing the share of students reciprocal by 10 percentage points			–24	0.003
Average 1998 value of dependent variable	307	3,525	10,094	19.1%

Notes: Nonresident share represents percentage point changes: for example, –2.0 would indicate that nonresident share falls from x percent to $(x-2)$ percent. For enrollment equation, numbers indicate percentage point change in share due to being in this category relative to average. Table reports marginal effects evaluated at mean.
*Significant at the 95 percent level.

in-state tuition increases, but the magnitude of this effect is quite small. For the average institution in our sample, it would take an increase of $1,000 in state appropriations per student to generate an in-state tuition reduction of only $60. The comparable reduction in out-of-state tuition would be larger, about $222. The small estimated elasticities of some of the other variables are misleading. For example, while the elasticity of in-state tuition with respect to the Pell Grant is only 0.48, this translates into institutions raising in-state tuition by $58 every time the Pell Grant maximum increases by $100 (while the magnitude of the effect is similar for nonresident tuition, the effect is not statistically significant). This result is particularly alarming when one considers that a majority of students receiving the Pell Grant do not receive the maximum award (and thus will experience a larger price increase than those at the margin) and that the Pell Grant program annually exceeds its program allocation from Congress.

Finally, our estimates suggest that most things within institutional or state control would fail to influence the share of nonresidents that public universities enroll. Even the statistical impact of reciprocity agreements is inconsequential. While increases in average tuition rates in the region tend to increase nonresident enrollment shares, clearly individual institutions have little or no control over these rates. About the only tool a state seems to have at its disposal (according to this model) to reduce the dependence on nonresidents is to raise tax revenues. Our estimates suggest that raising per capita tax revenues by $1,000 will result in the nonresident enrollment share falling by 1.2 percentage points—which would probably not be viewed favorably by state taxpayers.

7.5   Conclusion

In this chapter, we have analyzed why state need-based grant aid per student, in-state and out-of-state tuition levels, and nonresident enrollment shares differ across flagship public research universities at a point in time and how each changes over time. There are wide disparities across states in political persuasion, demographic characteristics, income, the availability of private college alternatives, historical factors, university governance, and funding priorities that lead to most of the cross-section differences that we observe in these outcomes. Exploiting the panel nature of the data enables us to control for unmeasured institutional heterogeneity and allows a look within specific institutions to determine which factors are most important in determining changes in these outcomes.

This paper was largely motivated by our interest in understanding why flagship public institutions make such varying use of nonresident enrollments. As such, the major insight that we draw is that these public institutions do not appear to use nonresident enrollments to supplement or replace revenues (as is the a priori belief of many observers). Rather, it appears that they enroll nonresidents to improve institutional quality or to serve other interests. This assessment can be reached after considering three major findings in this paper.

First, the flagship institutions appear to use nonresident enrollments to take advantage of cost efficiencies achieved through participation in tuition reciprocity agreements. Though the empirical evidence we present on the matter is scant, the increased usage of tuition reciprocity programs (as observed in our survey) suggests that institutions realize the revenue limitation in expanding nonresident enrollments. Further, these agreements also reflect the growing regionalization of these state schools. In fact, we find that institutions respond to higher regional tuition by charging high in-state and out-of-state tuition and we see that nonresident students tend to migrate more often when average tuition in their region of residence is higher.

Second, it does appear that institutions attempt to capture additional revenues by cannibalizing the monies provided by federal and state grant aid programs. Consistent with the Bennett hypothesis, we find substantial evidence that increases in the generosity of the federal Pell Grant program, access to subsidized loans, and state need-based grant aid awards lead to increases in in-state tuition levels. However, we find no evidence that nonresident tuition is increased as a result of these programs. This observation suggests that institutions look to nonresident enrollments not as a revenue source but rather as a quality source. In fact, our nonresident tuition results provide more support for this theory by showing that institutions decrease nonresident tuition substantially when the quality of the high school graduates in their own state falls ($200 for every fall in average SAT scores by 10 points). Further, there is little evidence that institutions in states where merit-based aid programs were initiated have made attempts to capture these additional monies in the form of higher tuition (with the exception of Arkansas). However, recent research suggests that institutions in other states attempt to capture rents through increases in other fees and charges (Long, forthcoming).

Third, while differences in state appropriations per student can partially explain cross-sectional differences in the use of nonresident enrollments, it does not appear that public institutions make up for losses in state institutional appropriations by adjusting the proportion of students they enroll from out of state. As expected, we find that institutions respond to state appropriations slowdowns by increasing both in-state and nonresident tuition. The lack of response to changes in state appropriations in the nonresident enrollment share suggests that the top flagship institutions may have already reached an equilibrium with regard to nonresident enrollments.

It should also be recognized that institutional and overall measures of state education quality and competitive position are very strong predictors of cross-sectional differences in tuition and enrollment. Clearly, these factors do not vary rapidly within institutions or states over time, so it is not surprising that we are unable to parse out any statistically significant relationship between these factors and the tuition and enrollment outcomes. This should not be taken to diminish the importance of these factors.

We must caution that the period our data span ends before the recession of the early years of the twenty-first century, the accompanying growing tightness in state government budgets, and thus the decline in the growth—and in some cases the decline in the level—of real state appropriations per student to public higher education institutions. Finding other sources of revenue became increasingly important to public higher education institutions, and a number increased their in-state tuition levels at double-digit rates for the 2002–2003 academic year. Time will tell if they will increasingly turn to out-of-state students' tuition revenues to fill the holes in their budgets.

Appendix

Table 7A.1   **Sources and Definitions of Variables**

Variable	Definition/Explanation	Source
1979	Dummy for years subsequent to repeal of Middle Income Student Assistant Act in 1979, which reinstated needs test for eligibility for subsidized federal loans	1.2
1992	Dummy for years subsequent to 1992, when the 5.64% of home equity that was taxable in the expected family contribution (EFC) calculation was removed from taxable assets	1.2
AGE	Share of population in a state between ages 18 and 24	3
AID	Logarithm of need-based state grant aid to in-state undergraduate students attending institutions in their own state per full-time equivalent four-year undergraduate in the state. Includes federal matching LEAP/SSIG monies	4
APP	Logarithm of state government appropriations in 1,000s per full-time equivalent undergraduate at the institution	5
BPRIV	Undergraduate enrollment weighted average Barron's ranking of all rated four-year private institutions in the state	6.5
BPUB	Undergraduate enrollment weighted average Barron's ranking of all rated four-year public institutions in the state	6.5
BSPRIV	Institution's undergraduate enrollment divided by the total undergraduate enrollment of all equally or higher-rated private (Barron's) institutions in the state	6.5
BSPUB	Institution's undergraduate enrollment divided by the total undergraduate enrollment of all equally or higher-rated public (Barron's) institutions in the state (including the institution of observation)	6.5
CAP	Maximum percentage of college costs covered by Pell Grants. Initially 50% of costs, raised to 60% in 1986 and eliminated in 1992.	7
ELIG	Share of state's households with incomes below the maximum allowable to be eligible to receive federal grant aid. Maximum income eligibility estimated from EFC calculation.	8.7
END	Logarithm of institutional endowment in 1,000s per full-time equivalent undergraduate at the institution	5
GOV	Number of governing boards in the state	9
GRAD	Ratio of full-time equivalent graduate students to full-time equivalent undergraduate students at the institution	5
HIGHB	Dummy variable equal to 1 if Barron's ranking is "Highly Competitive" or "Most Competitive"	6
LOWB	Dummy variable equal to 1 if Barron's ranking is "Not Competitive" or "Less Competitive"	6
MERIT	Dummy variable equal to 1 if state had a merit aid program in that year	4

Variable	Description	
NON	Logarithm of the share of first-time freshmen that are nonresident, nonforeign students. In nonresident share equation, we use the log-odds ratio. That is the share divided by one minus the share.	5.10
PELL	Logarithm of the maximum available Pell Grant award	7
PRIV	Share of FTEFTF in state in privates (PRIV)	
RECIP	Logarithm of the share of full-time equivalent undergraduates enrolled under tuition reciprocity programs	11
SAT	Average SAT score in the state (includes public and private high school students)	12
SEAT	Maximum number of full-time equivalent first-time freshman enrollment in the state historically at public schools of equal or greater Barron's rank divided by the current number of high school graduates in the state	5.12
SPRIV	In the census region, the share of full-time equivalent first-time freshmen in schools that are of equal or greater Barron's rank that are enrolled in private schools	5.6
TAX	Logarithm of total state tax revenues received per population in the state, excluding federal receipts, in 1,000s	13.3
TUITI	Logarithm of in-state tuition charged	5
TUITO	Logarithm of out-of-state tuition charged	5
TUITR (EQUN 1&2)	Logarithm of the enrollment weighted average of public out-of-state (for schools outside my state), public in-state (for schools in my state, excluding my school), and private tuition in the census region	5
TUITR (EQUN 3&4)	Logarithm of the enrollment weighted average of public in-state, public out-of-state, and private tuition in the census region, including schools in the state of observation	5
TWO	Share of public full-time equivalent first-time freshman enrollment in the state in two-year colleges	5
UNEMP	Logarithm of the state average unemployment rate	14

Sources: 1. United States Department of Education web site; 2. Michael Mumper, *Removing College Price Barriers*, SUNY Press, 1996; 3. U.S. Bureau of the Census, Population Estimates Program—Age distribution data on web site; 4. National Association of State Scholarship and Grant Programs. Annual Survey Reports; 5. Integrated Postsecondary Education Data System Surveys via WebCASPAR (see http://caspar.nsf.gov or www.nces.ed.gov/ipeds); 6. *Barron's Profiles of American Colleges, 1979–1996*; 7. American Council on Education Center for Policy Analysis, *2000 Status Report on the Pell Grant Program*; 8. Current Population Surveys, *Estimates of Income of Households by State 1979–1996*; 9. Education Commission of the States; 10. Older resident enrollment data from Higher Education General Information Surveys not available on WebCASPAR retrieved through original "Fall Residence and Migration Surveys;" 11. Cornell Higher Education Research Institute (CHERI), *Survey of Tuition Reciprocity Programs of Public Research Doctoral Institutions.* Summer 2001 (available on CHERI website at www.ilr.cornell.edu/cheri); 12. U.S. Department of Education, National Center for Education Statistics, *Digest of Education Statistics*; 13. U.S. Bureau of the Census, Census of Governments via the *Statistical Abstract of the United States*; 14. U.S. Department of Labor, Bureau of Labor Statistics, Employment and Earnings.

Notes: FTEFTF = full-time equivalent first-time freshmen. All data in real values using 1996 calendar year GDP impact price deflator.

Table 7A.2   Average Values of Selected Independent Variables

Variable	1979	1981	1988	1992	1994	1996	1998
State demographics/institutional characteristics							
Per capita real state tax revenues	2,279	1,865	3,070	2,535	2,669	4,720	5,185
Unemployment rate	5.78	6.91	6.43	6.51	6.36	5.38	4.80
Share of population aged 18–24 (%)	13.5	13.3	11.1	10.2	9.9	9.6	9.7
Share of population with incomes below Pell maximum (%)	63.9	57.5	53.5	49.3	45.0	44.9	49.8
Sources of institutional aid							
Endowment per student	957	1,401	4,466	7,726	9,809	13,977	19,337
Sources of student financial aid							
Pell Grant award (real)	3,416	2,663	2,734	2,617	2,392	2,470	2,917
Enrollment pressure							
No. of graduate students/first-time freshmen	1.20	1.24	1.27	1.59	1.58	1.49	1.10
Share of FTEFTF in state in privates (%)	30.3	30.7	30.0	31.1	30.7	30.2	23.3
Share of FTEFTF in state in two-years (%)	45.7	47.3	44.0	46.0	44.9	44.2	41.9
Seating capacity (predicted/actual)	1.34	1.31	0.99	0.82	0.82	0.81	0.86
Composite regional tuition	2,932	3,086	5,567	6,090	6,332	6,672	7,059
Composition regional tuition, ex-in-state	4,217	4,439	8,005	8,721	9,047	9,541	10,002
School and student quality/competitive position							
No. of schools strong Barron's rank	2	3	5	13	11	11	11
No. of schools weak Barron's rank	17	15	16	13	7	11	11
Weighted rank of privates in state	2.56	2.64	2.90	2.74	2.98	2.98	2.98
Weighted rank of publics in state	2.38	2.39	2.60	2.60	2.66	2.67	2.67
Institution's share of state's quality private seats (%)	251.0	299.3	262.0	267.7	273.9	191.6	191.6
Institution's share of state's quality public seats (%)	47.9	47.5	52.9	50.8	51.1	49.9	49.9
Share of quality regional seats, private (%)	37.8	37.3	39.4	40.9	40.0	39.5	39.5
Average SAT scores of high school graduates	936	939	1,042	966	1,043	1,057	1,062

Notes: Table contains values for those variables not in earlier tables. Also excludes categorical variables.
FTEFTF = full-time equivalent first-time freshmen.

Table 7A.3   Expected Impacts and Exclusion Restrictions in Estimated Equations

	Equation			
Variable	Grant Aid	In-State Tuition	Out-of-State Tuition	Nonresident Share
Endogenous variables				
Log need-based grant aid per public student (AID)		D+		
Log in-state tuition (TUITI)	B+		S+	
Lot out-of-state tuition (TUITO)				B?
Log nonresident enrollment share (NON)			B?	
State demographics/institutional characteristics				
Log state tax revenues per capita (TAX)	S+			
Log unemployment (UNEMP)	D?	D?	B?	B?
Share of population aged 18–24 (AGE)	S–	D+	D+	D+
Share of population with incomes below maximum Pell allowable (ELIG)	D+	D–	D–	D–
Log number of governing boards (GOV)	S?	S+	S+	S?
Sources of institutional aid				
Log state appropriations per student (APP)	B–	B?	B?	B?
Log endowment per student (END)	B–	B+	B+	B?
Sources of student financial aid				
Log maximum Pell Grant award (PELL)	B–	D+	D+	D+
Percent cap on costs (CAP)	D–	D+	D+	D+
Post-1979 subsidized loan access (1979)	D+	D–	D–	D–
Post-1992 subsidized loan access (1992)	D+	D–	D–	D–
State merit-based aid programs (MERIT)	B–	B+	S+	S–
Enrollment pressure				
Ratio of the grad to undergrad enrollments (GRAD)	D–	B?	B?	B?
Share of FTEFTF in state in privates (PRIV)	B?	S+		
Share of FTEFTF in state 2 years (TWO)	B?	S–		
Log seating capacity (SEAT)	S+	D–	B?	S+
Log composite regional tuition (TUITR)	B–	S+	D+	D+
Log share of the undergrads in reciprocity agreements (RECIP)			B?	B?
School and student quality/competitive position				
Weak Barron's rank (LOWB)		D–	D–	D–
Strong Barron's rank (HIGHB)		D+	D+	D+
Weighted Barron's rank of privates in state (BPRIV)	B+	D–		
Weighted Barron's rank publics in state (BPUB)	B?			
Institution's share of quality public seats in the state (BSPUB)			B+	D+
Institution's share of quality private seats in the state (BSPRIV)			B+	D+
Share of quality seats in region that are private (SPRIV)			D+	D+
Log SAT (SAT)				S–

Notes: D, S, or B refers to whether the variable would be included in a structural demand equation, a supply equation, or both, respectively. + or – refers to our a priori prediction on the direction of a variable's impact on the outcome under analysis. FTEFTF = full-time equivalent first-time freshmen.

Table 7A.4   **Structural Estimates: Two-Stage Least Squares Regression Results**

Variable	Grant Aid		In-State Tuition	
	Cross Section (1)	Panel (2)	Cross Section (3)	Panel (4)
A. State Need-Based Grant Aid and In-State Tuition Equations				
Endogenous variables				
Log need-based grant aid per public student (AID)			0.27*	0.18
Log in-state tuition (TUITI)	1.59*	0.30		
State demographics/institutional characteristics				
Log state tax revenues per capita (TAX)	0.48*	0.19*		
Log unemployment (UNEMP)	0.01	0.02	0.10*	0.06*
Share of population aged 18–24 (AGE)	−24.49*	−10.67	7.28*	−7.23*
Share of population with incomes below maximum Pell allowable (ELIG)	2.00*	1.03	−1.15*	0.14
Log number of governing boards (GOV)	0.01		0.00	
Sources of institutional aid				
Log state appropriations per student (APP)	0.10	0.59*	−0.25*	−0.32*
Log endowment per student (END)	−0.01	0.01	0.02*	0.01
Sources of student financial aid				
Log maximum Pell Grant award (PELL)	−7.95	1.17*	0.45	0.27
Percent cap on costs (CAP)	−2.40	0.59*	0.06	0.21
Post-1979 subsidized loan access (1979)	0.64	0.53*	−0.14	0.04
Post-1992 subsidized loan access (1992)	n.a.	0.61*	n.a.	0.23
Arkansas Merit Program (MERIT)	0.93*	0.69*	−0.17	0.11
Florida Merit Program (MERIT)	−0.10	−0.25	−0.26	−0.13
Georgia Merit Program (MERIT)	−1.58*	−1.52*	0.38*	0.19
Mississippi Merit Program (MERIT)	−2.18*	−0.99*	0.69*	0.10
New Mexico Merit Program (MERIT)	1.04	0.75*	−0.41*	−0.19
Enrollment pressure				
Ratio of FTE grad to undergrad enrollments (GRAD)	0.05	−0.08	0.02	0.01
Share of FTEFTF in state in privates (PRIV)	−0.06	−1.30*	0.51*	0.72*
Share of FTEFTF in state in 2 years (TWO)	1.20*	1.34*	−0.46*	−0.30
Seating capacity (predicted enroll/actual enroll) (SEAT)	−0.50*	0.26	−0.01	0.10
Log composite regional tuition, ex-in-state (TUITR)	0.08	−0.10	0.02	0.08*
School and student quality/competitive position				
Weak Barron's rank (LOWB)			0.01	0.05
Strong Barron's rank (HIGHB)			0.10*	0.06
Weighted Barron's rank of privates in state (BPRIV)	0.31*	0.01	−0.08*	0.04*
Weighted Barron's rank of publics in state (BPUB)	0.20*	−0.01		
Adjusted R^2	0.585	0.618	0.647	0.843

Table 7A.4 (continued)

	Out-of-State Tuition		Nonresident Share	
	Cross Section (5)	Panel 6)	Cross Section (7)	Panel (8)
B. Out-of-State Tuition and Nonresident Enrollment Share Equations				
Endogenous variables				
Log in-state tuition (TUITI)	0.49*	0.90*		
Log out-of-state tuition (TUITO)			−1.49*	−0.26
Log nonresident enrollment share (NON)	−0.03	−0.06		
State demographics/institutional characteristics				
Log unemployment (UNEMP)	0.01	−0.08*	−0.33*	−0.17*
Share of population aged 18–24 (AGE)	−1.25	1.13	3.12	4.57
Share of population with incomes below max Pell allowable (ELIG)	−0.69*	0.05	0.59	−0.54
Log number of governing boards (GOV)	0.00*		−0.02*	
Sources of institutional aid				
Log state appropriations per student (APP)	−0.05	0.00	−1.30*	−0.01
Log endowment per student (END)	0.04*	0.02*	0.21*	0.03
Sources of student financial aid				
Log maximum Pell Grant award (PELL)	−0.09	0.02	−0.12	−0.27
Percent cap on costs (CAP)	−0.18	−0.02	0.16	−0.02
Post-1979 subsidized loan access (1979)				
Post-1992 subsidized loan access (1992)				
Arkansas Merit Program (MERIT)	−0.14	−0.07	−0.11	−0.43
Florida Merit Program (MERIT)	−0.04	0.09	−1.34*	−1.16*
Georgia Merit Program (MERIT)	−0.06	0.05	−0.14	−0.44*
Mississippi Merit Program (MERIT)	−0.30*	0.04	0.06	0.19
New Mexico Merit Program (MERIT)	0.12	0.04	0.30	0.18
Enrollment pressure				
Ratio of FTE grad to undergrad enrollments (GRAD)	−0.04*	0.02	−0.08	−0.10
Seating capacity (predicted enroll/actual enroll) (SEAT)	0.14*	−0.02	−0.11	−0.29
Log regional composite tuition (TUITR)	0.11*	0.07*	0.34*	0.37*
Log share of FTE undergrads in reciprocity agreements (RECIP)			−0.07*	0.05
School and student quality/competitive position				
Poor Barron's rank (LOWB)	−0.10*	0.00	−0.41*	0.02
Strong Barron's rank (HIGHB)	0.07*	0.02	−0.08	0.11
Institution's share of quality public seats in the state (BSPUB)	−0.03	0.04	1.06*	0.29*
Institution's share of quality private seats in the state (BSPRIV)	0.00	0.00	0.02*	0.00
Share of quality seats in region that are private (SPRIV)	0.19*	−0.14*	0.72*	−0.59*
Lot SAT (SAT)			−1.21*	0.21
Adjusted R^2	0.865	0.933	0.374	0.203

Notes: The efficiency of a system such as ours can be improved if one accounts for the correlation among the error terms in each equation. 3SLS estimates were largely similar to the 2SLS estimates, but are not reported here due to concern that one or more of the equations in the system are misspecified, which can effect estimates in other equations (Johnston and DiNardo 1997). FTE = full-time equivalent. FTEFTF = full-time equivalent first-time freshmen.

*Significant at the 95 percent level.

Table 7A.5   Reduced-Form Regression Results Including Grant Aid as Explanatory Variable

	Grant Aid		In-State Tuition	
	Cross Section	Panel	Cross Section	Panel
Variable	(1)	(2)	(3)	(4)
A. State Need-Based Grant Aid and In-State Tuition Equations				
State demographics/institutional characteristics				
Log tax revenues per capita (TAX)	0.57*	0.20*	0.04	0.04
Log unemployment (UNEMP)	0.34*	0.04	0.16*	0.08*
Share of population aged 18–24 (AGE)	–23.38*	–13.49*	2.10	–9.04*
Share of population with incomes below maximum Pell allowable (ELIG)	–0.07	1.14*	–1.17*	0.37
Log number of governing boards (GOV)	0.01	n.a.	0.00	n.a.
Sources of institutional aid				
Log state appropriations per student (APP)	–0.27*	0.53*	–0.21*	–0.19*
Log endowment per student (END)	0.02	0.01	0.02*	0.01
Sources of student financial aid				
Log need-based grant aid per public student (AID)	n.a.	n.a.	0.08*	0.02
Log maximum Pell Grant award (PELL)	–10.70	1.32*	–1.18	0.44*
Percent cap in costs (CAP)	–3.50	0.70*	–0.47	0.32*
Post-1979 subsidized loan access (1979)	n.a.	0.57*	0.01	0.13*
Post-1992 subsidized loan access (1992)	n.a.	0.73*	n.a.	0.36*
Arkansas Merit Program (MERIT)	1.01*	0.77*	–0.04	0.22*
Florida Merit Program (MERIT)	–0.82	–0.30	–0.40	–0.18*
Georgia Merit Program (MERIT)	–1.77*	–1.55*	0.01	–0.07
Mississippi Merit Program (MERIT)	–1.90*	–1.01*	0.35*	–0.07
New Mexico Merit Program (MERIT)	0.69	0.73*	–0.27	–0.09
Enrollment pressure				
Ratio of FTE grad to undergrad enrollments (GRAD)	0.14*	–0.09	0.03*	–0.01
Share of FTEFTF in state in privates (PRIV)	1.36*	–1.14*	0.76*	0.55*
Share of FTEFTF in state in 2 years (TWO)	0.63*	1.32*	–0.39*	–0.10
Seating capacity (predicted enroll/actual enroll) (SEAT)	–0.87*	0.31*	–0.15*	0.15*
Log composite regional tuition, ex-in-state (TUITR)	0.27*	–0.08	0.10*	0.06*
School quality/competitive position				
Weak Barron's rank (LOWB)	0.04	0.03	–0.01	0.05*
Strong Barron's rank (HIGHB)	–0.01	–0.01	0.10*	0.06*
Weighted Barron's rank of privates in state (BPRIV)	0.32*	0.02	–0.02	0.04*
Weighted Barron's rank of publics in state (BPUB)	0.30*	0.00	0.03	0.01
Adjusted R^2	0.595	0.618	0.737	0.866

Table 7A.5 (continued)

	Out-of-State Tuition		Nonresident Share	
	Cross Section (5)	Panel (6)	Cross Section (7)	Panel (8)
B. Out-of-State Tuition and Nonresident Enrollment Share Equations				
State demographics/institutional characteristics				
Log tax revenues per capita (TAX)	−0.04	0.08*	−0.21	−0.21*
Log unemployment (UNEMP)	0.11*	0.05*	−0.30*	−0.16*
Share of population aged 18–24 (AGE)	−0.06	−4.06*	8.11	4.04
Share of population with incomes below maximum Pell allowable (ELIG)	−1.26*	0.58*	1.27	−1.13
Number of governing boards (GOV)	−0.01	n.a.	−0.16	n.a.
Sources of institutional aid				
Log state appropriations per student (APP)	−0.14*	−0.24*	−1.17*	0.07
Log endowment per student (END)	0.04*	0.01*	0.16*	0.03
Sources of student financial aid				
Log need-based grant aid per public student (AID)	0.06*	0.01	−0.09*	0.02
Log maximum Pell Grant award (PELL)	0.22	0.13	4.15	0.03
Percent cap on costs (CAP)	−0.25	−0.18*	1.25	0.08
Post-1979 subsidized loan access (1979)	−0.08	0.04	−0.02	−0.52*
Post-1992 subsidized loan access (1992)	n.a.	0.45*	n.a.	−0.83*
Arkansas Merit Program (MERIT)	−0.12	0.17	0.28	−0.46
Florida Merit Program (MERIT)	−0.24*	−0.02	−1.39*	−1.18*
Georgia Merit Program (MERIT)	−0.03	−0.05	−0.44	−0.42*
Mississippi Merit Program (MERIT)	−0.18	−0.02	0.23	0.25
New Mexico Merit Program (MERIT)	−0.06	0.02	0.40	0.15
Enrollment pressure				
Ratio of FTE grad to undergrad enrollments (GRAD)	−0.01	0.02	−0.02	−0.10
Share of FTEFTF in state in privates (PRIV)	0.11	0.20	0.40	−0.62
Share of FTEFTF in state in 2 years (TWO)	−0.13*	0.07	−0.38	0.20
Seating capacity (predicted enroll/actual enroll) (SEAT)	0.07*	0.16*	−0.35*	−0.29*
Log composite regional tuition (TUITR)	0.14*	0.10*	0.10	0.35*
Log share of FTE undergrads in reciprocity agreements (RECIP)	−0.01	0.00	−0.08*	0.06
School and student quality/competitive position				
Weak Barron's rank (LOWB)	n.a.	n.a.	n.a.	n.a.
Strong Barron's rank (HIGHB)	0.04	0.00	−0.20	0.11
Weighted Barron's rank of privates in state (BPRIV)	0.02	0.05*	−0.26*	0.04
Weighted Barron's rank of publics in state (BPUB)	0.06*	0.03	0.31*	−0.03
Institution's share of quality public seats in the state (BSPUB)	0.01	−0.04	1.27*	0.29*
Institution's share of quality private seats in the state (BSPRIV)	0.00	0.00	0.01	0.00
Share of quality seats in region that are private (SPRIV)	0.32*	−0.11	0.08	−0.57*
Lot SAT (SAT)	−0.12	2.12*	−0.86	−0.14
Adjusted R^2	0.802	0.904	0.508	0.205

Notes: FTE = full-time equivalent. FTEFTF = full-time equivalent first-time freshmen. n.a. = not applicable.

*Significant at the 95 percent level.

References

Balderston, Frederick. 1997. Tuition and financial aid in higher education. *Economics of Education Review* 16:337–343.

Barron's Educational Series—College Division. 1974–1996. *Barrons profiles of American colleges.* New York: Barron's.

Coopers & Lybrand, L.L.P. 1997. The impact of federal student assistance on college tuition levels. Washington, D.C.: Coopers & Lybrand, September.

Ehrenberg, Ronald G. 2000. *Tuition rising: Why college costs so much.* Cambridge, Mass.: Harvard University Press.

Ehrenberg, Ronald G., and Daniel R. Sherman. 1984. Optimal financial aid policies for a selective university. *Journal of Human Resources* 19:202–230.

Everitt, Brian S. 1993. *Cluster analysis.* 3rd ed. London: Edward Arnold.

Garvin, David. 1980. *The economics of university behavior.* New York: Academic Press.

Greene, Kenneth V. 1994. The public choice of non-resident college tuition levels. *Public Choice* 78:231–240.

Groen, Jeff, and Michelle J. White. 2001. In-state versus out-of-state students: The divergence of interest between public universities and state governments. Paper presented at the annual conference of the Cornell Higher Education Research Institute. 22–23 May. Ithaca, N.Y.

Hauptman, Arthur M., and Cathy Krop. 1998. Federal student aid and the growth in college costs and tuition: Examining the relationship. New York: Council for Aid to Education.

Johnston, Jack, and John DiNardo. 1997. *Econometric methods.* 4th ed. New York: McGraw-Hill.

Koshal, Rajindar K., and Manjulika Koshal. 2000. State appropriation and higher education tuition: What is the relationship? *Education Economics* 8:81–89.

Long, Bridget Terry. Forthcoming. How do financial aid policies affect colleges? The institutional impact of the Georgia HOPE Scholarship. *Journal of Human Resources.*

Lowry, Robert C. 2001a. The effects of state political interests and campus outputs on public university revenues. *Economics of Education Review* 20:105–119.

———. 2001b. Governmental structure, trustee selection and public universities and spending: Multiple means to similar ends. *American Journal of Political Science* 45:845–861.

McPherson, Michael, and Morton Owen Schapiro. 1991. *Keeping college affordable: Government and educational opportunity.* Washington, D.C.: Brookings Institution.

———. 1998. *The student aid game: Meeting need and rewarding talent in American higher education.* Princeton, N.J.: Princeton University Press.

Mixon, Franklin G., Jr., and Yu Hsing. 1994. The determinants of out-of-state enrollments in higher education: A tobit analysis. *Economics of Education Review* 13:329–335.

National Association of State Budget Officers. 2002. *State expenditure report 2001.* Washington, D.C.: National Association of State Budget Officers, November.

National Center for Education Statistics. 2001. *Study of college costs and prices, 1988–89 to 1997–98.* Available at [http://nces.ed.gov/pubs2002/2002157.pdf].

Quigley, John M., and Daniel L. Rubinfeld. 1993. Public choices in public higher education. In *Studies of supply and demand in higher education,* ed. Charles T. Clotfelter and Michael Rothschild, 243–278. Chicago: University of Chicago Press.

Siow, Aloysius. 1997. Some evidence on the signaling role of research in academia. *Economics Letters* 54:271–276.

Winston, Gordon. 1999. Subsidies, hierarchies and peers: The awkward economics of higher education. *Journal of Economic Perspectives* 13:13–36.

Comment   Michelle J. White

This is an interesting and ambitious paper. Researchers in the past have taken small bites from the problem of explaining how public universities behave, but Rizzo and Ehrenberg are the first to bite off the whole problem and attempt to understand simultaneously how in-state and out-of-state tuition levels, state grants to universities, and the number of out-of-state relative to in-state students at public universities are determined.

Because the paper is empirical, I will first discuss models of how public universities behave and then turn to Rizzo and Ehrenberg's empirical results.

Theoretical Considerations

The main problem in understanding how public universities behave is that economists don't really understand what public universities' goals are. We also don't understand how states want their public universities to behave or whether public universities actually do what their states want.

One possibility is that public universities' goal is to maximize average student ability—as measured by students' grades or standardized test scores or some combination—subject to a fixed-capacity constraint. If there are separate demand curves by in-state versus out-of-state students, then this approach implies that universities should admit both types of students in declining order of ability to the point where the marginal student admitted has the same ability level regardless of whether the student is from in-state or out-of-state. In this approach, universities don't care where students come from. Another possibility is that public universities maximize tuition revenue subject to the same capacity constraint. Because public universities charge out-of-state students higher tuition, this approach suggests that the marginal out-of-state student admitted to a public university will be of lower quality than the marginal in-state student admitted because the revenue collected from the out-of-state student is higher. Combining these two considerations suggests that some selective public universities can advance on both the quality and the revenue fronts simultaneously by admitting more out-of-state students, since marginal

Michelle J. White is professor of economics at the University of California, San Diego, and a research associate of the National Bureau of Economic Research.

out-of-state students may both be higher ability and pay higher tuition than marginal in-state students. In particular, high-quality public universities may attract and admit substantial numbers of out-of-state students.

The degree to which public universities can attract high-ability out-of-state applicants varies across institutions. As Hoxby (1997) has pointed out, over time students have tended to choose universities that are further from home. This has both increased the number of out-of-state applicants to public universities and also increased the extent of competition among universities of a given quality level. Public universities have the most market power and can charge the highest tuition if the number of students in the region is high, if there are few competing universities of the same or higher quality in the region, and if more of the competing universities are private rather than public and have high tuition.

Another important set of issues for public university behavior concerns state control. How do states want their public universities to behave, and do public universities actually behave in their states' interest? Again, it is unclear what states' goals are. State legislators often want public universities to set low admission standards for in-state students and to admit few out-of-state students so that constituents' children (deserving or not) will be admitted. States also want students from low-income families to be able to attend public universities, so they want low tuition levels for in-state students and grants in aid for in-state students from low-income families. Since state appropriations and tuition are alternative ways of financing public universities, states can keep tuition levels low by increasing state appropriations. But Rizzo and Ehrenberg present data suggesting that many state legislatures have allowed appropriation levels to stagnate so that low tuition levels reduce overall quality.

States also have long-term objectives for public universities. Attending university (whether public or private) increases students' human capital and productivity, meaning that in the future they will pay higher taxes and create new jobs (see Goldin and Katz [1998] for discussion). But whether the state benefits from graduates' higher productivity depends on whether graduates locate in the state as adults. Public universities are therefore a means by which states both retain high-ability students who grew up locally and attract high-ability students who grew up elsewhere; that is, public universities are recruiting devices as well as productivity-enhancement devices. (See Groen and White [2003] for discussion.) States thus want their public universities to have reasonably high quality so that high-ability high school graduates will stay at home. But they do not seem to want their public universities to be very high quality, because in-state students may be excluded, and the out-of-state students who replace them are likely to leave the state after graduation. These considerations suggest that states tend to prefer that their public universities have an intermediate quality level.[1] They also suggest that the largest states should prefer to have higher-quality public universities. Finally, states that have more migration have an incentive to spend less on their public universities. This is because in-migration allows states to obtain human capital without paying for it, while out-migration causes states to lose their investments in education (see Quigley and Rubinfeld 1993).

Tax considerations also affect how states finance public universities and indirectly affect the optimal quality level. If states use income taxes to raise revenue and if parents itemize on their federal taxes, then states and parents together can save money by using appropriations or direct grants to students to support public universities, while keeping tuition levels low. This is because state income tax payments are deductible from federal taxes, but tuition payments to public universities are not. However, this consideration does not apply to out-of-state tuition because the tax benefit goes to out-of-state parents. Thus tax considerations suggest another reason why states want low tuition levels for in-state students but high tuition levels for out-of-state students.

Finally, how do states induce their public universities to do what the state wants rather than what the universities want? How autonomous are public universities? These considerations seem to vary quite a bit across states. Some states' constitutions specify a high degree of autonomy for their public universities so that the state government has only indirect control. In Michigan, for example, public universities set their own tuition levels and can offset lower state appropriations by raising tuition. In other states, the state government engages in a high degree of micromanagement, including setting tuition levels and many other policies. As Rizzo and Ehrenberg point out, Texas does not even allow the University of Texas to keep the extra tuition that it collects from out-of-state students. My personal pet theory is that states tend to have more control over public universities when the university is located in the state capitol, due to the fishbowl effect.

Empirical Considerations

Now turn to the empirical work. To start with, Rizzo and Ehrenberg have constructed a very nice new panel data set of public universities. I hope that they will continue to expand the data set and that they will eventually expand it to include private universities because private universities are the natural group against which to compare the behavior of public universities. I also hope that they will expand the data set to cover the years since 1998, when economic conditions were much less favorable than dur-

1. However, Groen and White's (2003) results suggest that states, in fact, benefit when their public universities are high quality and admit many out-of-state students because the recruitment effect of public universities applies equally, regardless of students' ability and regardless of whether they are from in-state or out of state.

ing the 1990s, and many states had large budget deficits. The availability of the data set will hopefully encourage future research on the question of how universities behave.

The authors estimate four separate equations explaining in-state tuition, out-of-state tuition, grant aid per student, and the fraction of students from out of state. I was unclear why they included an equation explaining state grant aid to universities but did not explain state appropriations to universities, particularly because their evidence suggests that the two are closely related. Rizzo and Ehrenberg point out that their equations explaining in-state and out-of-state tuition are reduced forms that reflect both supply and demand considerations. On the demand side, it might be possible to measure demand directly by obtaining data on the number of in-state and out-of-state applicants to each university. It would also be of interest to include a measure of interstate migration flows.

The authors acknowledge that the various equations they estimate are likely to be subject to simultaneous equation bias, and they address the problem by using two-stage least squares. But simultaneity may be a larger problem than the authors have considered. For example, Rizzo and Ehrenberg treat the level of state appropriations to public universities as exogenous in the equation explaining in-state tuition levels. But at some public universities, such as the University of Michigan, legislators tend to cut the state appropriation if they think that the university has set in-state tuition too high. Thus causation can run in both directions. Student capacity (the SEATS variable) may also be endogenous because universities are more willing to expand when their tuition levels are higher, holding other factors such as state appropriations constant.

I'd also like to see Rizzo and Ehrenberg experiment more with proxy measures for how closely states control their public universities. Their only variable along these lines, the number of governing boards, was not significant in any of the estimated equations. Other possible variables might include whether individual public universities are located in the state capital and whether individual public universities are part of a multicampus university system. Another possible variable is whether the state constitution or other state legislation specifies an independent role for the university.

The results that I found the most interesting are those that tend to confirm the general hypothesis that higher education is a competitive industry and that public universities respond to competition in a similar way to firms in other industries. Thus higher-quality universities charge higher tuition, both to in-state and out-of-state students. Also, when competitor universities charge more, public universities respond by raising their own tuition. Finally, public universities that are large relative to their in-state student populations tend to adjust by providing more grants in aid (which increases demand) and by enrolling more out-of-state students (which also increases demand), rather than by lowering admission standards.

References

Goldin, Claudia, and Lawrence F. Katz. 1998. The origins of state-level differences in the public provision of higher education: 1890–1940. *American Economic Review* 88:303–308.

Groen, Jeffrey A., and Michelle J. White. Forthcoming. In-state versus out-of-state students: The divergence of interest between public universities and state governments. *Journal of Public Economics.*

Hoxby, Caroline M. 1997. How the changing market structure of U.S. higher education explains college tuition. NBER Working Paper no. 6323. Cambridge, Mass.: National Bureau of Economic Research, December.

Quigley, John M., and Daniel L. Rubinfeld. 1993. Public choices in public higher education. In *Studies of supply and demand in higher education,* ed. C. T. Clotfelter and M. Rothschild, 243–278. Chicago: University of Chicago Press.

8

Student Perceptions of College Opportunities
The Boston COACH Program

Christopher Avery and Thomas J. Kane

8.1 Introduction

Despite spending large sums to promote widespread access to college, we know surprisingly little about the impact of alternative public interventions on students' and parents' investment decisions. A large share of public subsidies to higher education come in the form of direct state appropriations to public postsecondary institutions, which totaled $63 billion annually in 2002 (see Grapevine database at http://www.coe.ilstu.edu/grapevine/50state.htm). In addition, the federal government provided more than $8 billion in means-tested grants to undergraduates during the 2000–2001 school year and guaranteed $37 billion in student loans (and paying the interest on roughly half of that loan volume while students are in school; College Board 2001). States added $5 billion in grant aid to students, much of it means-tested. Yet the gaps in college enrollment by family income did not close during the 1970s, when the main federal grant program for low-income students was initiated. Moreover, the gaps in college enrollment by race and by family income seem to have been widening since

Christopher Avery is professor of public policy at the John F. Kennedy School of Government, Harvard University, and a faculty research fellow of the National Bureau of Economic Research. Thomas J. Kane is professor of policy studies and economics at the University of California, Los Angeles, and a faculty research fellow of the National Bureau of Economic Research.

We acknowledge the generous support of the Andrew W. Mellon Foundation. We are also grateful to the School-to-Career Department of the Boston Public Schools for program support and assistance with data collection. Jonathan Vaupel collected much of the data and created the databases upon which most of this analysis is based. Rachel Garber, Rachel Deyette Werkema, Gavin Samms, and Jonathan Vaupel provided valuable comments on drafts of the survey instruments. Katherine Huyett provided invaluable research assistance. The Boston Public Schools also provided data.

1980, as the earnings differentials associated with college degree completion rose dramatically.

In this paper, we present evidence on student perceptions of the economic benefits of college and the college application and financial aid process. We then use our results to assess the likely effectiveness of several policy responses aimed at reducing the gap in educational attainment between high- and low-income youths.

The first hypothesis asserts that low-income students are relatively unlikely to attend college because they simply do not believe that it is profitable: They overestimate tuition, underestimate financial aid opportunities, and/or underestimate the market differential in wages for college versus high school graduates. We find limited support for this hypothesis. Students in the Boston public schools and in a comparison (affluent) suburban school tend to overestimate tuition, but they also tend to overestimate the wage benefits of going to college. Despite their obvious differences in background, the expectations of these two samples of youths are strikingly similar. Approximately 75 percent of the students in each group report estimates that indicate that the net present value of a BA degree is positive (using their expectations of tuition costs, forgone wages, and post-college wage expectations). For these students, the imputed present value of a college degree is not a strong predictor of enrolling in a two-year or a four-year college.

The second hypothesis asserts that low-income students are discouraged by the complexity of the process of applying for financial aid and college admissions, even if they are qualified and enthusiastic about going to college. We find somewhat more support for this hypothesis. More than 65 percent of the Boston public school students in the study reported at the start of their senior year in high school that they planned to attend a four-year college immediately after high school graduation, but less than 25 percent of them actually did so. Many of these students did not have the academic qualifications to gain admission to a four-year college. Still, among students with at least a 3.0 grade point average (meaning that they probably could be admitted to one of the public four-year colleges in Massachusetts), only 65 percent of those who originally intended to go to a four-year college did so. Most of these students were far behind their suburban counterparts in the college application process at the beginning of the senior year; some were sufficiently far behind that they never submitted an application to a four-year college.

An alternate, third hypothesis is that some Boston public school students reported that they wanted to go to college yet either believed that they were not qualified and/or never intended to pursue postgraduate education in the first place. This hypothesis is consistent with our findings that some Boston public school students who said that they wanted to go to a four-year college did not take the SAT exam, while others took the SAT but then never completed an application to a four-year college. The requirements of completing the SAT and an application essay are sufficiently costly that they would deter students with only a halfhearted interest in college. Taking our survey results at face value, however, we do find that a significant percentage of Boston public school students want to go to a four-year college and have sufficient academic qualifications to do so yet do not complete the application process successfully.

The implications of these findings are ambiguous. However, they do suggest that the low-income students in the study are not deterred from going to college because they are overly pessimistic about costs of college or about their own qualifications. If anything, the Boston public school students are overconfident about their prospects for admission to college and about their future wages at each possible level of educational attainment. Thus, an intervention that only provides information about tuition, financial aid, and likely wages is unlikely to be effective at changing the percentage of low-income students who go to college.

8.2   Persistent and Widening Gaps in College-Going by Income and Race

There are large gaps in college-going by family income. As reported in Ellwood and Kane (2000), 80 percent of the students from the top income quartile attended some type of postsecondary institution within twenty months of their high school graduation, as compared with 57 percent of those from the lowest income quartiles.[1] The gaps by family income were particularly large in four-year college entrance, with 55 percent of the highest-income youths attending a four-year college at some point and only 29 percent of the lowest-income youths.

Clearly, the gaps are not entirely due to the causal effect of family income differences. Higher-income parents may have stronger "tastes" for college; children of higher-income parents typically score higher on measures of academic achievement. However, although the evidence is somewhat more sparse, these gaps appear to be widening over time. After constructing similar measure of income for the High School and Beyond and National Education Longitudinal Study samples, Ellwood and Kane (2000) reported that, although college entry rates grew for all groups between the high school classes of 1980[2] and 1992, the increases were larger for middle- and higher-income families. For example, there was a 10 percentage point increase in the proportion of youths from the highest income quartile at-

1. These data rely upon the parent-reported family income data, rather than the less-reliable student responses. If students attended more than one type of postsecondary institution, they were categorized as four-year college students if they ever attended a four-year college and, if not, as two-year college entrants if they ever attended a two-year college.

2. The 1980 sample is actually a combined sample of the high school classes of 1980 and 1982.

tending some postsecondary institution between 1980/92 and 1992. Moreover, the increase in postsecondary schooling was largest for high-income youths attending four-year colleges, rising from 55 percent to 66 percent. In contrast, there was only a 3 percentage point rise in postsecondary entry for youths from the lowest income quartile and a 1 percentage point decline (albeit statistically insignificant) in the proportion of low-income youths attending a four-year college.

Racial differentials appear to be widening as well. While the Current Population Survey makes it difficult to track college-going rates by parental income level, it is possible to track college-going rates by race. Between 1980 and 1998, the proportion of white eighteen-to-twenty-four-year-olds enrolled in college increased from 27 percent to 41 percent. Enrollment rates for African American youths also increased over that period—from 19 to 29 percent. But the magnitude of the increase for African Americans (10 percent) was smaller than the magnitude of the increase for white non-Hispanics (14 percent).[3] It is important to note that, while gaps in college enrollment were widening between the late 1970s and late 1980s, racial gaps in high school graduation and achievement test scores in the National Assessment of Educational Progress were closing.

However, even if the gaps in college-going by family income and by race were not widening, the rising payoff to college since 1980 has magnified the consequences of the preexisting gap in college entry by family income. While the gap in postsecondary training between the highest and lowest income quartiles grew by one-third (from 23 percentage points to 30 percentage points), the earnings differentials between college entrants and high school graduates more than doubled between 1980 and 1992.

8.3   Conflicting Evidence on the Impact of Tuition and Financial Aid Subsidies

Over the years, a large literature has developed that studies the impact of various types of tuition and financial aid policies on college-going. In their review of the literature on student responsiveness to changes in college cost, Leslie and Brinkman (1988) report a consensus estimate that a $1,000 change in college costs (in 1990 dollars) is associated with an approximately 5 percentage point difference in college enrollment rates. Such estimates are quite large, particularly in light of the college-going response to the rise in the labor market payoff to schooling. (Between 1980/82 and 1992, Ellwood and Kane [2000] reported a 7 percentage point rise in college-going.)

Table 8.1 summarizes the results from three recent sets of studies, pub-

---

3. The increases over the time period were larger for women than for men. See table 139 in National Center for Education Statistics (1999).

Table 8.1   **Estimated Impact of a $1,000 Change in Direct Cost of College on College Entry Rates College (per $1,000 1990)**

Study	Estimate	Brief Description
Literature before 1987		
Leslie and Brinkman	−.05 (.005)	Literature review of 25 articles
Based on between-state differences in tuition		
Cameron and Heckman (1998)	−.07 (.02)	State differences in public tuition charges (NLSY)
Kane (1994)	−.05 (.01)	State differences in public tuition charges (October CPS)
Kane (1999)	−.05 (.01)	State differences in public tuition charges (NELS)
Based on nontraditional financial aid		
Dynarski (1999)	−.04 (.02)	End of Social Security Student Benefit Program
Dynarski (2000)	−.03 (.02)	Hope Scholarship Program in Georgia
Before-after the Pell program was established in 1973		
Hansen (1983)		No disproportionate growth by low income students (October CPS)
Kane (1994)		No disproportionate growth by low income students (October CPS)
Manski (1993)		No disproportionate growth in BA completion by low income students (NLS-72 and HSB)

Notes: NLSY = National Longitudinal Survey of Youth. NLS = National Longitudinal Study. HSB = High School and Beyond. Standard errors are in parentheses.

lished since the Leslie and Brinkman review: those that use differences in public tuition levels between states and over time, those that evaluate the impact of financial aid policies that operate outside the usual need-analysis system, and those evaluating changes in financial aid policy operating through the regular financial aid process.

The first three papers use between-state differences in state tuition policy and essentially compare the college entry rates of otherwise similar youths in high- and low-tuition states. The empirical strategy in this literature uses the assumption that the price that is relevant for marginal students is the tuition at public institutions in their state and evaluates the effect of tuition and college-going by comparing college-going rates in high- and low-tuition states. Such studies also assume that the supply of college slots is perfectly elastic: Given a change in price, it is solely student demand that determines enrollment and not the supply of college slots.

Two characteristics of these studies deserve comment. First, although they use three different data sets—the October Current Population Survey, the National Longitudinal Survey of Youth, and the High School and Beyond—each generates similar results. A $1,000 difference in tuition is associated with a 6 percentage point difference in college-going. Indeed, these estimates are quite consistent with the older literature summarized by Leslie and Brinkman.

Second, a weakness of these studies is that they rely on relatively fixed differences in tuition levels between states. For instance, California has been a relatively low-tuition state for the past forty years. California has also built a number of community colleges around the state. One may be attributing to tuition policy the effect of these other policy differences, such as the construction of community colleges. As a result, Kane (1999) used administrative data to look at what happens to enrollments within a state when it raises tuition. Interestingly, one sees effects of tuition changes within states over time comparable to those one would estimate by looking across states.

Despite strong evidence of student and parent responsiveness to tuition costs, the evidence for the impact of the Pell Grant program is much weaker. Lee Hansen (1983) first noted that there had been little evidence of a disproportionate rise in college enrollment by low-income youths during the 1970s, when the Pell Grant program was established. Although that paper was criticized for relying too heavily on two years of data and for including males, whose decisions may have also been affected by the end of the Vietnam War, later work (Kane 1994) confirmed that the result was not sensitive to the choice of annual end points or to the inclusion of males.[4] Manski (1993) also reported little evidence of a disproportionate growth in BA completion by low-income youths graduating from high school between 1972 and 1980.

One hypothesis to reconcile the estimates of tuition impacts with the failure to find an increase in enrollment by low-income youths following the establishment of the Pell Grant program is that students are expected to make a significant up-front investment to apply to college and to apply for financial aid, before they learn anything about the amount of aid available, whereas they can read about a tuition increase in the newspaper or see it in a college's application materials.

Also cited in table 8.1, Susan Dynarski has recently estimated the impact of two other programs that operated outside of the federal need-analysis framework: one looking at the impact of the cessation of tuition benefits for Social Security survivors, and the other evaluating the effect of the Helping Outstanding Pupils Educationally (HOPE) Scholarship program in Georgia. Dynarski (2003) found that after the discontinuation of the So-

---

4. McPherson and Schapiro (1991) also studied the time trend in college enrollment for high- and low-income youths. But their estimate of the effect of net tuition on college-going appears to be identified primarily by a rise in tuition in the early 1980s rather than the decline in net price due to the Pell Grant program in the mid-1970s.

cial Security Student Benefit program, college entry by students with deceased parents declined by 19.4 to 25.6 percentage points relative to other youths. To convert this estimate to a scale similar to that earlier reported, Dynarski calculated that the value of the benefit program had been roughly $5,300 (in $1990). This implies an impact of 3.7 to 4.8 percentage points per thousand-dollar change in price.

In another paper, Dynarski (2000) studied enrollment rates for youths in Georgia relative to other southern states, before and after the HOPE Scholarship program was initiated in that state. She estimates that the program increased college enrollment rates of eighteen-to-nineteen-year-olds by 7.0 to 7.9 percentage points. Given the value of the HOPE Scholarship, this estimate converts to an estimate of 3.1 to 3.5 percentage points per $1,000 difference in cost.

Interestingly, because both of the programs evaluated by Dynarski—tuition benefits for Social Security survivors and the HOPE Scholarship program in Georgia—operated outside the typical need analysis system, eligibility was known a priori and did not require students to submit a Free Application for Federal Student Aid (FAFSA) form and wait for an award letter to know whether or not one qualified for the aid. Thus, both financial aid programs operated similarly to a tuition increase, which is relatively costless to anticipate. In contrast, the Pell Grant program requires remarkable foresight. One has to fill out a FAFSA, be assigned an expected family contribution, and receive an award letter from a school simply to learn how much federal aid is on offer.

In other words, the way in which students learn about tuition benefits and the process by which they apply may play some role in determining the impact on student college enrollment decisions. Our goal in this paper is to provide some evidence on student perceptions of the economic benefits of college and the hurdles presented by the financial aid and college application processes.

8.4   Hurdles in the College Application Process for Low-Income Students: Results from the COACH Program

Funded by the Andrew W. Mellon Foundation, the College Opportunity and Career Help (COACH) program brings students from Harvard University into three public high schools in Boston to work as coaches to help high school seniors make future plans and submit college and financial aid applications. In 2001–2002, a total of thirty-four coaches worked with a total of 282 high school seniors in three schools, with each coach working with the same set of students throughout the academic year. During the 2000–2001 and 2001–2002 academic years, program researchers surveyed the high school seniors participating in the program as well as students in two additional schools in each year. These students completed a baseline survey in the fall of the senior year, providing information on their backgrounds and educational aspirations, and an exit survey in the spring of the senior year, providing information on their college applications and concrete plans for the following year. Here we report on the results for all COACH students in 2001–2002 in comparison to Concord-Carlisle students in 2000–2001; Concord-Carlisle was the only non-COACH school with a large enough response rate on both surveys to permit its use as a comparison school.[5]

The COACH program worked closely with three of the twelve nonexamination district high schools in Boston: Boston High School, Charlestown High School, and Dorchester High Schools.[6] These schools have typical graduating classes of 150 to 300, with approximately 30 percent of students going directly to a four-year college after graduation and approximately 30 percent going on to either a two-year college or a vocational school after graduation. On the 2001 Massachusetts Comprehensive Assessment Test (MCAS), tenth graders at the three COACH schools ranked 304th, 274th, and 306th in English score, respectively, and 305th, 243rd, and 301st in math score among 332 public high schools in Massachusetts.

Concord-Carlisle is a regional high school that encompasses two neighboring suburban towns near Boston. Its typical graduating class consists of 200 to 250 students, with approximately 90 percent of them going directly to a four-year college after graduation. On the 2001 MCAS, tenth graders at Concord-Carlisle ranked sixteenth of 332 Massachusetts high schools in average English score and eighth in average math score.

Table 8.2 shows the response rates to the baseline survey and exit survey for both subgroups. The COACH surveys were supplemented with additional information compiled by coaches and program researchers over the course of the year. The most critical information from the baseline survey is the student's plan at the start of the senior year for the year after graduation, and the most critical information from the exit survey is the student's actual plan for next year at the time of high school graduation.[7] With the addi-

---

5. Both surveys were also administered in Concord-Carlisle in 2001–2002 and East Boston High School in 2001–2002, but the exit survey response rates were less than 50 percent in each case. The initial, baseline survey was also administered at Wellesley High School in 2000–2001, but it was not possible to administer the second, exit survey at Wellesley High School that year.

6. Three public high schools in Boston are exam schools (Boston Latin, Boston Latin Academy, and the O'Bryant School for Math and Science), where the enrollment is based on the score on an entry exam. On the 2001 Massachusetts Comprehensive Assessment Test (MCAS), these three exam schools ranked 1st, 4th, and 49th of 332 public high schools in Massachusetts in average math score. (Scores and rankings are available on the Boston Globe website at www.boston.com/mcas.)

7. At present, we do not know with certainty whether students followed through on the future plans that they reported at high school graduation. The Boston Private Industry Council conducts a follow-up survey with recent Boston Public School graduates in the spring of the following year. In future analysis, we will use those survey results to refine our findings.

Table 8.2   **Survey Response Rates for COACH and Concord-Carlisle Students**

	COACH Students (Boston, Charlestown, Dorchester High School) 2001–2002	Suburban Students (Concord-Carlisle High School) 2000–2001
Completed baseline survey, fall 2001	239 (84.8%)/264 (93.6%)	175 (70.0%)
Completed exit survey, spring 2002	228 (80.9%)/270 (95.7%)	165 (66.0%)
Completed both surveys	197 (69.9%)/257 (91.1%)	96 (38.4%)
Sample size	282	250

Notes: The first number in the COACH column reports the number of students who completed the actual surveys. The second number reports the total number of students included in the sample after inclusion of supplemental information for initial plans for the year after high school (baseline survey) and for final plans for the year after high school (exit survey). The Concord-Carlisle class size is approximate, based on information from school reports.

tional information compiled by the program over the course of the year, we were able to identify the original plans for 93.6 percent of COACH students (264 of 282) and the final plans for 95.7 percent of them (270 of 282, including 22 who did not graduate) and to match these plans for 91.1 percent of the COACH students (257 of 282, including 18 who did not graduate).

The response rates for Concord-Carlisle students are lower than for COACH students. Still, we believe that the samples of Concord-Carlisle students for both the baseline and exit surveys are broadly representative of the school population as a whole. For example, the results from the exit survey are quite consistent with aggregate results reported by the Concord-Carlisle school committee.[8]

As is portrayed in table 8.3, the students in the COACH and Concord-Carlisle samples were very different in demographic characteristics. While 67.1 percent of the COACH students were Latino or Black non-Hispanic, only 10.6 percent of the Concord-Carlisle students were classified in these categories. Almost all of the Concord-Carlisle students were U.S. citizens, as opposed to two-thirds of the COACH students. Finally, while only 18.9 percent of the COACH students had a parent who was a college graduate, 83.1 percent of the Concord-Carlisle students had a parent who was a college graduate (indeed, 47 percent of the suburban youths had a parent with a graduate degree).

8. According to the 2001 Concord-Carlisle school report, 84.5 percent of graduates in 2000–2001 were attending four-year colleges, and 6.5 percent were attending two-year colleges. Further, although we were only able to match 38.4 percent of the baseline and exit surveys, the subset of matched applicants is broadly representative of the respondents to both the baseline and the exit surveys as well. Among students who completed both surveys, 95.8 percent (91 of 95) reported in the baseline survey that they planned to attend a four-year college in the year after graduation, while 89.6 percent (86 of 96) reported in the exit survey that they would attend a four-year college in the year after graduation. These figures are quite close to the aggregate figures for all Concord-Carlisle students completing the baseline and exit surveys, respectively.

Table 8.3   **Demographic Characteristics of COACH and Suburban Students (%)**

	COACH Students (Boston, Charlestown, Dorchester High School) 2001–2002	Suburban Students (Concord-Carlisle High School) 2000–2001
Race/ethnicity		
Hispanic	20.7	3.3
Black non-Hispanic	46.4	7.3
Asian or Pacific Islander	16.7	8.0
Native American/other	4.1	0.0
White non-Hispanic	12.2	81.3
Citizenship		
U.S. citizen	67.0	96.3
Parental education		
High school dropout	32.3	2.0
High school graduate	24.4	6.1
Some college	10.4	4.7
Vocational degree	13.9	4.1
BA degree	15.4	35.8
Graduate degree	3.5	47.3
Sample size	239	175

Source: Based on responses to baseline surveys administered in fall 2001 (COACH) and fall 2000 (Concord-Carlisle).

Note: The parental education calculations exclude ten COACH students and nine Concord-Carlisle students who reported that they did not know the educational attainment of their parents.

8.4.1   Similarities in Initial Educational Plans, Belied by Preparation and Actual Results

Despite the obvious differences in background between COACH and Concord-Carlisle students, these two groups of students maintained similar plans for postsecondary enrollment as late as the fall of the senior year in high school, as shown in table 8.4. In their responses to the baseline survey, virtually all of the Concord-Carlisle students reported that they planned to attend a four-year college in the fall after graduation. A similar proportion of COACH students reported that they planned to attend postsecondary institutions in the year after graduation, although not all were planning to attend four-year schools. A vast majority of both groups of students (91.1 percent of Concord-Carlisle students and 70.3 percent of COACH students) planned to eventually complete at least a BA degree.

Although the two groups were similar in educational aspirations, they differed dramatically in the extent to which they had taken concrete steps to prepare for the transition from high school to college. The results in table 8.5 are limited to those who reported that they planned to attend a four-year institution the following fall. While more than 97 percent of the Concord-Carlisle students had already taken the SAT by October of the senior year, less than one-third of COACH students had taken the test.

Table 8.4   **Postsecondary Plans for COACH and Concord-Carlisle Students at the
Beginning of Senior Year in High School**

	COACH Students (Boston, Charlestown, Dorchester High School) 2001–2002	Suburban Students (Concord-Carlisle High School) 2000–2001
Plans for the following year		
Not going to school (%)	8.3	3.5
Vocational/trade school (%)	4.9	0.6
Two-year college (%)	21.6	2.3
Four-year college (%)	65.2	93.6
Sample size	264	171
Plans for eventual attainment		
High school diploma (%)	9.6	2.9
Vocational degree (%)	7.9	2.9
Associate's degree (%)	12.2	2.3
BA degree (%)	40.2	24.0
Graduate degree (%)	30.1	57.1
Sample size	229	156

Source: Based on responses to baseline surveys administered in fall 2001 (COACH) and fall 2000 (Concord-Carlisle).

Note: The sample size is much larger for COACH students for "Plans for the following year" because we used supplemental information from coaches to code this variable for students who did not complete the baseline survey.

Table 8.5   **Specific Activities Completed by Fall of Senior Year: Students Planning to Attend a Four-Year College**

	COACH Students (Boston, Charlestown, Dorchester High School) 2001–2002	Suburban Students (Concord-Carlisle High School) 2000–2001
Had taken PSAT (%)	58.6	89.7
Had registered for SAT (%)	72.3	96.6
Had taken SAT/ACT (%)	31.8	97.5
Met with guidance counselor four or more times (%)	17.1	55.4
Had visited a college (%)	34.6	83.0
Had the application from institution "most likely" to attend (%)	53.7	90.7
Had applied to a college (%)	18.2	40.9
Sample size	239	175

Source: Based on responses to baseline surveys administered in fall 2001 (COACH) and fall 2000 (Concord-Carlisle).

While more than half of the Concord-Carlisle students had spoken with a guidance counselor four or more times over the past year, less than 20 percent of COACH students had done so. While 83 percent of Concord-Carlisle students had visited a college and 91 percent had the application for the institution they were "most likely to attend," only 35 percent of

Table 8.6   **Plans for COACH and Concord-Carlisle Students at Graduation**

	COACH Students (Boston, Charlestown, Dorchester High School) 2001–2002	Suburban Students (Concord-Carlisle High School) 2000–2001
Plans for the following year		
Did not graduate from high school (%)	7.8	0.0
Not going to school (%)	19.5	4.1
Vocational/trade school (%)	6.0	0.0
Two-year college (%)	32.6	3.5
Four-year college (%)	24.5	88.3
Postgraduate year or still selecting a college (%)	6.0	3.5
Plans were unknown (%)	3.5	0.6
Sample size	282	171
Plans for following year, students originally intending to go to a four-year college		
Did not graduate from high school (%)	4.1	0.0
Not going to school (%)	16.9	4.5
Vocational/trade school (%)	3.5	0.0
Two-year college (%)	32.0	2.3
Four-year college (%)	35.5	93.2
Postgraduate year or still selecting a college (%)	6.4	3.5
Plans were unknown (%)	1.7	0.0
Sample size	172	88

Source: Based on responses to baseline surveys and exit surveys administered in 2001–2002 (COACH) and 2000–2001 (Concord-Carlisle). "Plans for the following year" is based on the exit surveys for Concord-Carlisle and the exit surveys supplemented with information from coaches for the COACH students.

Note: Plans for the following year for those intending to go to a four-year college are tabulated only for Concord-Carlisle students who completed both surveys.

COACH students had visited a college, and just slightly more than half had the application for the institution they were most likely to attend.

Not surprisingly, the results for the COACH and Concord-Carlisle students diverged sharply by the end of the academic year, as shown in table 8.6. Though nearly two-thirds of the COACH students stated at the start of the academic year that they intended to enroll in a four-year college in 2002–2003, less than 25 percent of all COACH students did so.[9] Further, only 35.5 percent of COACH students who originally intended to go to a

9. We treat the college plans reported by COACH students at the time of high school graduation to represent their actual enrollment decisions in the fall of 2002. Past history and anecdotal evidence suggest that these numbers are overestimates. Some students may change plans over the summer, and it is more likely that students who planned to go to college would not ultimately enroll than that students who did not plan to do so would change their minds over the course of the summer and both apply to and enroll in college in the fall.

four-year college did so, while 21.0 percent of the COACH students who originally intended to go to a four-year college either did not graduate from high school or decided not to continue education at all in 2002–2003. In contrast, 93.2 percent of the Concord-Carlisle students who stated initially that they wanted to enroll in a four-year college did so.

8.4.2   Further Hurdles in the College Application Process for COACH Students

We tracked the progress of COACH students carefully during the course of 2001–2002 and identified five steps that are necessary for attending a four-year college. In order of priority, these hurdles are (1) graduating from high school, (2) attaining a grade point average (GPA) sufficient for admission to a four-year college, (3) registering for the SAT, (4) taking the SAT, and (5) completing and submitting an application (and gaining admission). A sixth step, the FAFSA, is clearly of considerable importance for COACH students, but it is not an absolute requirement in the same sense as the first five requirements listed.

Figures 8.1 and 8.2 depict these steps for COACH and Concord-Carlisle students in flow charts that include conditional probabilities of completing that step among those passing all earlier steps. At stage 1, a total of 94.2 percent of COACH students attended school regularly and graduated at the end of the year.[10] These graduation rates for COACH students are somewhat higher than the aggregate percentage for high school seniors in district high schools in Boston.[11] In contrast, we believe that more than 99 percent of Concord-Carlisle seniors graduate from high school.[12] We discuss each succeeding step in the college application process separately in the sections that follow.

The Importance of Grade Point Average

We divide students who originally intended to go to a four-year college into two groups based on self-reported grades from the baseline survey. Here, there is a striking difference between the COACH and Concord-

---

10. We combined "Not Graduating from high school" and "Unknown" plans at this stage. A small number of COACH students who originally planned to go to a four-year college, 1.7 percent, graduated from high school despite very limited participation in the program and (we believe) limited attendance in classes not associated with COACH. The college choices for these students were unknown to us at the end of the year; we suspect that these students were not going to continue their education in 2002–2003.

11. Our initial analysis of administrative data from the Boston Public Schools suggests that the dropout rate for high school seniors may be even higher than the 5.4 percent for COACH students in 2001–2002.

12. Our research assistant, Katherine Huyett, coincidentally a Concord-Carlisle graduate, indicated that a total of only two students failed to graduate from the school from the past three cohorts, the classes of 2000, 2001, and 2002. If one student per year in a class of 250 does not graduate, that produces a graduation rate of 99.6 percent, the figure given in table 8.10 for Concord-Carlisle students.

	Graduated	GPA	REG SAT	TK SAT	APP 4 YR	GO 4 YR
	Y	3.0+	Y	Y	Y	Y
	94.70%	38.83%	91.90%	85.90%	85.70%	88.10%
	162/172	62/162	57/62	49/57	42/49	37/42
				N	N	N
				14.10%	14.30%	11.90%
				8/57	7/49	5/42
			N			
			8.10%			
			5/62			
	N	<3.0	Y	Y	Y	Y
	5.30%	61.70%	87.00%	76.00%	48.00%	55.60%
	10/172	100/162	87/100	76/100	36/75	20/36
			N	N	N	N
			13.00%	24.00%	52.00%	44.40%
			13/100	24/100	39/75	16/36

Fig. 8.1 Conditional probability flow chart: COACH students intending to go to four-year colleges

		GPA	REG SAT	TK SAT	APP 4 YR	GO 4 YR
Graduated	Y	3.0+	Y	Y	Y	Y
	99.60%	81.30%	100.00%	100.00%	100.00%	95.90%
		74/91	74/74	74/74	74/74	71/74
			N	N	N	N
			0.00%	0.00%	0.00%	4.10%
			0/74	0/74	0/74	3/74
	N	<3.0	Y	Y	Y	Y
	0.40%	18.70%	100.00%	94.10%	81.30%	92.30%
		17/91	17/17	16/17	13/16	12/13
			N	N	N	N
			0.00%	5.90%	18.70%	7.70%
			0/17	1/17	3/16	1/13

Fig. 8.2 Conditional probability flow chart: Concord-Carlisle students intending to go to four-year colleges

Carlisle students. Among those students who intended to go to a four-year college, the students at Concord-Carlisle were more than twice as likely to have a GPA of 3.0 or better than were COACH students (81.3 percent vs. 38.3 percent).[13] A 3.0 GPA is an important milestone for these students because that is the cutoff for consideration for admission to four-year public universities in Massachusetts. The Massachusetts Board of Higher Education allows students with GPAs between 2.5 to 3.0 to qualify for admission to four-year public universities if they have sufficient SAT scores, but Boston public school students very seldom meet these SAT score requirements. In plain terms, very few COACH students with GPAs less than 3.0 can qualify for admission to public four-year universities in Massachusetts.[14]

Among COACH students who originally intended to attend a four-year college in the year after graduation, only 21 percent of those with self-reported grades of 3.0 or less (21 of 100) actually did so.[15] None of the COACH students reporting a GPA less than 2.0 attended a four-year college in 2002–2003. By contrast, 53.3 percent of the COACH students who originally intended to attend a four-year college and had self-reported GPAs of 3.0 or better attended four-year colleges in 2002–2003. A 3.0 GPA is something of an important hurdle for Concord-Carlisle students as well, but not as much as for COACH students: 70.6 percent of Concord-Carlisle students who intended to go to a four-year college and had GPAs below 3.0 went to a four-year college immediately after graduation.

One possibility is that the grading standards are not the same at these two schools. The best, albeit limited, evidence for assessing the relative difficulty of these grading standards is to match grades to standardized test scores. For example, 86 percent of tenth graders at Concord-Carlisle scored at the "Advanced" or "Proficient" level on the 2001 MCAS English test (the lower levels are "Needs Improvement" or "Fail"), and 81 percent scored at the "Advanced" or "Proficient" level on the 2001 MCAS math test. By contrast, only 10.6 percent of tenth graders at COACH schools scored at "Advanced" or "Proficient" on the 2001 MCAS English test, and only 12.6 percent did so on the 2001 MCAS math test.[16]

---

13. Our analysis of grades for COACH and Concord-Carlisle students is based entirely on self-reported grades on our baseline survey. Subsequent results about college choices and college admissions outcomes for these students suggest that these self-reported grades are quite accurate. In subsequent analysis, we expect to be able to identify the true grades for all of the COACH students.

14. For students with GPAs between 2.5 and 3.0, the SAT score cutoff for consideration for admission to a public university in Massachusetts ranges from 920 to 1,150, with higher SAT scores required to compensate for lower grades in this range.

15. These calculations assume that students in both schools followed through on the plans that they reported in exit surveys at high school graduation.

16. These figures are taken from the following website: http://www.boston.com/mcas/scores2001. Percentages for COACH schools are weighted by enrollment and aggregated across the three COACH schools.

Thus, on the MCAS scoring scale, the borderline between "Proficient" and "Needs Improvement" corresponds to the 14th percentile for Concord-Carlisle students and the 89th percentile for COACH schools in English, and at the 19th percentile for Concord-Carlisle students and the 87th percentile for COACH students. A slightly higher percentage of Concord-Carlisle students are "Proficient or Better" on the MCAS than are "3.0 GPA or better," while a conspicuously lower percentage of COACH students are "Proficient or Better" on the MCAS than are "3.0 GPA or better." If test scores translate directly into grades, then a 3.0 GPA represents a somewhat higher level of academic achievement at Concord-Carlisle than in the COACH schools.[17] In summary, although a much higher proportion of Concord-Carlisle than COACH students meet the 3.0 GPA standard that is frequently necessary for admission to public four-year universities in Massachusetts, we certainly cannot conclude that this standard favors Concord-Carlisle students over COACH students with similar academic qualifications.

Registering for and Taking the SAT

At Concord-Carlisle, registering for and completing the SAT is simply taken for granted. The district website highlights the fact that 100 percent of its recent graduates completed the SAT; our baseline survey in the fall of 2001 found that all but four of the Concord-Carlisle students who intended to go to a four-year college had completed the SAT by October of the senior year. The College Board database indicates similar numbers for Boston Latin, a public examination school in Boston: Almost all Boston Latin students register for the SAT, and 99.2 percent of Boston Latin students from the class of 2000 who registered for the SAT completed the test. But at Dorchester High School, one of the three Boston district public schools that participated in the COACH program, only 71 percent of those students who register for the SAT complete the test.[18]

Most of the COACH students who wanted to go to a four-year college and who had GPAs of at least 3.0 both registered for and took the SATs. Even so, nearly 10 percent of these students did not register for the exam, and nearly 15 percent of those who registered for the exam did not com-

---

17. It is possible to criticize the MCAS exam as a measure of a student's academic attainment, particularly since so many COACH students are not U.S. citizens. We steer clear of this issue as much as possible, since we have no obvious way to quantify this possible objection. For students at the Boston Latin School, a selective magnet school in Boston with college-going rates similar to those at Concord-Carlisle, the senior-year students' GPA was roughly a quarter of a point (on a four-point scale) higher than the GPA of students in the COACH schools. However, differences in standardized test scores accounted for more than 100 percent of the difference. Among those with the same standardized test scores, Latin School students' senior year GPAs were a third of a point lower than those of the COACH school students.

18. Meri Escandon of the College Board provided us with these figures.

plete it. Thus, the seemingly innocuous requirement of completing the SAT as part of an application to a four-year college eliminated more than 20 percent of the COACH students with the highest GPAs. (Interestingly, the COACH students with lower GPAs registered for and completed the SAT at nearly the same rates as the students with the higher GPAs.)

Anecdotally, we observed several related factors that contributed to the difficulty of completing the SAT. First, COACH students were relatively unfamiliar with registration forms. Less than half of them had taken the PSATs, and it often took a full class period for a student to complete an SAT registration form. Some students began the registration form but never completed or never mailed it, even with assistance from their coaches.

Second, in a related development, COACH students frequently registered close to the deadline and routinely found themselves assigned to unfamiliar suburban test locations as much as thirty minutes away by car.[19] A number of them were discouraged by the travel time, others got lost on the way to the test site, and still others arrived at the correct test site only to be turned away for lack of a registration slip or picture ID.

Finally, some COACH students simply decided at the last minute to stay home. We surmise that most had concluded, correctly or incorrectly, that they would do so poorly that their scores would cause them to be rejected by the four-year colleges that they wanted to attend.[20] This fear is probably reasonably founded, for Boston public school students do notoriously poorly on average on standardized tests. Of course, all of these impediments are surmountable. Most COACH students who registered for the SAT completed the test, and most of those with relatively high grades did well enough on the SAT to gain admission to a four-year college.

Writing Essays and Applying to a Four-Year College

At some point in the application process, one would expect COACH students with low grades to become discouraged, recognizing that their options are limited and that they may not be admitted to any four-year college. Figure 8.1 suggests that discouragement takes hold at the point of completing an application. At this point, it may become undeniably obvious for a student with low grades and SAT scores that a four-year college is out of reach. In addition, coaches reported that their students had con-

---

19. Almost all of these students were able to obtain fee waivers for the SAT, but this often slowed down the registration process as they had to submit an additional form signed by a school counselor. (Until 2001–2002, it was not possible for students to register on-line if they were submitting a fee waiver.) There were only two or three test locations in the city of Boston for most administrations of the SAT in 2001–2002, and these locations were generally oversubscribed well in advance of the registration deadline.

20. This surmise is difficult to confirm. In the cases when we were able to talk to students after the fact, few or none of them cited performance anxiety or pessimism as the reason that they did not take the test.

siderable difficulty writing an application essay. A considerable percentage, more than one-quarter of those with high grades and more than half of those with low grades, completed the SAT but never submitted an application to a four-year college. By contrast, 100 percent of the Concord-Carlisle students with high grades who intended to go to a four-year college went on to submit an application to a four-year college. In addition, more than 80 percent of the Concord-Carlisle students who intended to go to a four-year college but who had low grades submitted an application to a four-year college.

Almost all of the COACH students with high grades who completed an application were admitted to and enrolled in a four-year college. Their success in gaining admission is not surprising since, up to a point, four-year colleges are anxious to recruit promising students from the city of Boston. In addition, coaches worked carefully with students to ensure that those with sufficient credentials applied to at least one four-year college where they were very likely to be admitted.

Among the COACH students with lower grades, the majority (64.5 percent) who completed an application were still admitted to and enrolled in a four-year college. This level of success reflects careful selection of colleges on the part of these applicants and their coaches. More than half of these students were admitted to private colleges known for relatively low admission requirements, and at least two were admitted in part because of their athletic ability. Within the set of COACH students with GPAs below 3.0, it also appears that the earlier stages of the application process selectively weeded out the students who had the lowest grades and the least chance of admission. It is unlikely that such a high percentage of the others with low grades would have been admitted had they applied to four-year colleges.

8.4.3 Similarities in Educational Plans between COACH and Suburban Students at Graduation

Table 8.4 showed that COACH students and Concord-Carlisle students had broadly similar plans for long-term educational attainment at the start of the senior year. Table 8.7 shows that the similarities in expectations for eventual education attainment remained at graduation, even though a large percentage of COACH students had changed their immediate plans after high school. Although less than one-third of the COACH students who completed exit surveys were going to a four-year college,[21] more than two-thirds of them stated that they planned to eventually complete a BA degree.

Table 8.8 compares the educational attainment plans reported by

---

21. Of the 218 COACH students who completed an exit survey, 66 (30.8 percent) were going to a four-year college.

Table 8.7   **Plans for Educational Attainment for COACH and Concord-Carlisle Students at Graduation**

	COACH Students (Boston, Charlestown, Dorchester High School) 2001–2002	Suburban Students (Concord-Carlisle High School) 2000–2001
High school diploma (%)	6.4	0.0
Vocational degree (%)	6.0	0.0
Associates degree (%)	20.6	1.9
BA degree (%)	37.2	32.3
Graduate degree (%)	29.8	65.8
Sample size	218	158

Source: Based on responses to exit surveys administered in 2001–2002 (COACH) and 2000–2001 (Concord-Carlisle).

Table 8.8   **Educational Aspirations for COACH Students over the Senior Year**

	COACH Students, Fall 2001	COACH Students, Spring 2002
All COACH students		
High school diploma (%)	9.9	6.6
Vocational degree (%)	7.1	5.0
Associate's degree (%)	13.2	20.3
BA degree (%)	38.5	38.5
Graduate degree (%)	31.3	31.3
Sample size	182	
Chi-squared test value	4.78 (*p*-value of .32)	
COACH students not going to 4-year college		
High school diploma (%)	13.8	8.1
Vocational degree (%)	8.1	6.5
Associate's degree (%)	19.5	28.5
BA degree (%)	34.2	39.0
Graduate degree (%)	24.4	17.9
Sample size	123	
Chi-squared test value	5.72 (*p*-value of .22)	
COACH students who intended to go to a 4-year college, not going to a 4-year college		
High school diploma (%)	8.3	9.7
Vocational degree (%)	4.2	2.8
Associate's degree (%)	5.6	19.4
BA degree (%)	52.8	48.6
Graduate degree (%)	29.2	19.4
Sample size	72	
Chi-squared test value	7.36 (*p*-value of .12)	

Source: Based on responses to baseline and exit surveys administered in 2001–2002 (COACH).

Notes: Tabulations are restricted to those students who reported their long-term plans for educational attainment on both the baseline and exit surveys. The chi-squared values are for a test for a difference in the distribution between the baseline and exit responses in each case. None of the chi-squared statistics are significant at the .10 level for four degrees of freedom.

COACH students in the baseline and exit surveys. These tabulations are restricted to those students who provided information on both surveys. Across all COACH students there was almost no change in the percentage of students expected to complete at least a BA degree (69.8 percent on the baseline survey and 68.2 percent on the exit survey).

Table 8.8 proceeds to restrict the analysis to COACH students not going to a four-year college and then to COACH students who planned to go to a four-year college but are not doing so. The results in the first of these two analyses are striking in two ways. First, more than half of the students (56.9 percent) who are not going to a four-year college immediately after graduation still expect to complete a BA degree eventually. Second, the expectations of COACH students who are not going to four-year colleges diminished very little during the senior year. The final section of the table lists the results for the seventy-two COACH students who did not fulfill their original plans to go to a four-year college (and who completed both surveys): 68.1 percent of those students still expected to complete a BA degree eventually, down from a figure of 82.0 percent on the baseline survey.[22] While these results reflect some reduction in aspirations as many COACH students learned that they would not be going to a four-year college immediately after graduation, the magnitude of this change is relatively small. While twenty-three students in this group reduced their long-term plans for educational attainment, eleven actually *increased* their plans. A chi-squared test for a difference in the distributions between baseline and exit survey is not significant at the 10 percent level for any of the three cases listed in table 8.8.[23]

Clearly, many COACH students had expectations for their future educational attainment that did not accord with their immediate educational prospects. This finding is consistent with the results from other national surveys. During the spring of their senior year in high school, student respondents in the National Educational Longitudinal Study (NELS) were asked to respond to the question "As things stand now, how far in school do you think you will get?" Table 8.9 presents a cross-tabulation of student responses to that question along with their subsequent postsecondary enrollment over the two years following graduation.[24] It is striking that 42 percent of those who expected to complete "some college" and 64 percent of those who expected to attend a vocational, trade, or business school had not enrolled in a postsecondary institution twenty months after high

22. We note that it seems contradictory that 18 percent of the students in this group reported on the baseline survey that they intended to go directly to a four-year college and yet did not expect to receive at least a BA degree.

23. Comparing the percentages of students expecting to receive at least a BA degree, the difference between the baseline and exit survey results for COACH students is insignificant in the first two cases and on the borderline of statistical significance (t-statistic of 1.95) for students who intended to go directly to a four-year college but are not doing so.

24. Rosenbaum (2001) reports similar results.

Table 8.9   Postsecondary Enrollment within Twenty Months of High School Graduation by Student Expectations as High School Seniors

"As things stand now, how far in school do you think you will get?"	None	Private <4-Year, Public <2-Year	Public 2-Year	4-Year (Public or Private)	Percent of Seniors
High school only	.904	.015	.069	.011	6.5
Vocational, trade or business school	.640	.103	.216	.040	11.0
Some college	.417	.080	.366	.138	14.0
4- or 5-year degree	.156	.028	.248	.568	35.4
Graduate school	.100	.013	.171	.717	33.1
Total	.276	.038	.224	.462	

The header spans: Enrollment within 20 Months of High School (%)

Source: Based upon authors' tabulation of the NELS second and third follow-up.

school. Moreover, only 57 percent of those who expected to finish a bachelor's degree and 72 percent of those who expect to finish a graduate degree had ever attended a four-year college within that time. Indeed, 16 percent of those expecting a bachelor's degree and 10 percent of those expecting a graduate degree did not attend any postsecondary institution twenty months after high school.

8.4.4   Alternate Explanations of Our Findings

We consider two alternate interpretations that might also explain our main finding that there is a large discrepancy between the percentage of COACH students who want to go to college and believe that it is economically advantageous to do so and the percentage of COACH students who enroll in college.

The first alternate explanation of this finding is that our survey induces biased responses to the questions about future educational plans. For instance, it is possible that some COACH students who had no intention of pursuing higher education beyond high school graduation nevertheless reported that they wanted to go to college to avoid the possibility of disappointing their teachers or those giving the survey. It is also possible that some COACH students are deceiving both themselves and others—perhaps they know subconsciously that they cannot or will not go to college and yet refuse to admit this openly.

Table 8.10 assesses this possibility by comparing the plans reported by COACH students on baseline surveys in October 2001 to the plans of those students in January 2002, as reported by their coaches after three months of program work. Only 5.1 percent of the students reported on the baseline survey that they did not plan to enroll in further education the following year, but their coaches reported that 11.6 percent of them would not do so.

Table 8.10   Plans for COACH Students on the Baseline Survey and in January

	Plan Reported by Student, Baseline Survey, October 2001	Plan Reported by COACH, January 2002
Will not enroll	11 (5.1%)	25 (11.6%)
Vocational program	11 (5.1%)	7 (3.3%)
Two-year college	42 (19.5%)	76 (35.4%)
Four-year college	151 (70.2%)	107 (49.8%)
Total	215 (100%)	215 (100%)

This suggests that some of the students who stated that they would pursue further education had little or no commitment to that plan. In addition, the percentage of students planning to attend four-year colleges dropped by more than 20 percentage points from the baseline survey to the January assessment, while the percentage planning to attend a two-year college increased by more than 15 percentage points. This suggests that these students either exaggerated their educational plans, or that their coaches helped them to realize that they did not have the qualifications to be admitted to a four-year college.[25]

While table 8.10 indicates that the baseline survey may not be a wholly accurate assessment of student plans, there is ample evidence to indicate that a substantial number of COACH students plan and want to go to college and yet do not do so. For instance, table 8.20 (described later) indicates that even among COACH students who have sufficient grades, who have completed at least three milestones in the application process, and who attended at least sixteen COACH sessions, more than 20 percent will not attend four-year colleges. These students appear to have invested in their plans to attend four-year colleges, yet they were unable to complete the process and bring those plans to fruition.

The second alternate explanation for our findings is that college is not actually in the economic interest of low-income students who do not currently pursue higher education beyond high school. One possibility is that the wage differentials observed in practice between those with a BA degree (or "some college") and those with only a high school diploma are not relevant "out of sample"—that is, for those who are not currently attending college. If the wage benefits of attending college are substantially smaller for those who do not attend college than for those who do, it may not be in the economic interest of many students from low-income families to attend college. But the students' own assessments of the costs and wage benefits to attending college impute a positive present value to attending college for

25. Among the students who reported on the baseline survey that they planned to attend a four-year college, 81.0 percent who had GPAs of 3.0 or higher still planned to attend a four-year college as of January 2002 (as reported by their coaches), while only 51.1 percent of those with GPAs of 3.0 or less still planned to attend a four-year college as of January.

the majority of them (including many COACH students who will not be enrolled in school in the fall of 2002). Assuming a 6 percent discount rate, approximately 75 percent of both COACH and Concord-Carlisle students would gain financially by completing a BA degree according to their estimates for tuition and future wages. Another possibility is that COACH and Concord-Carlisle students might have different discount rates so that, despite similar estimates of tuition and wages, it is in the economic interest of a higher percentage of Concord-Carlisle students to invest in four years of education to complete a BA degree.[26] But most students estimate quite large wage gains for completing a BA degree: The yearly discount rate would have to rise to 20 percent for COACH students for the present value of college to be positive for only 30 percent of COACH students—the percentage who are actually attending a four-year college.

8.5   Assessing Possible Interventions to Reduce the Gap in College Enrollment

We now use the results for the COACH students for a preliminary analysis of three possible policy interventions: (1) educating students on tuition levels, the financial aid process, and the college wage differential; (2) introducing class requirements that encourage students to get an early start on the application process (e.g., requiring all students to take the SAT, having a regimented set of meetings with a counselor to discuss college options, scheduling a college visit as a class field trip); and (3) creating outside programs such as COACH that provide regular individualized assistance with the application process.

8.5.1   Providing Accurate Information on Tuition, Financial Aid, and Wages

As we reported earlier, 65 percent of parents reported in a 1998 survey that the cost of a college education was one of their top five worries about their children's welfare. Yet, in that survey, the public greatly overestimated the costs of college tuition. Their estimated cost of in-state tuition at a community college ($4,026) and a four-year college ($9,694) was roughly triple the actual average cost of tuition at such institutions ($1,501 at community colleges and $3,111 at four year colleges).

The COACH program in Boston found similar results when it surveyed students regarding the estimates of tuition at several local institutions: The survey asked, "About how much do you think it costs to attend the following colleges *full-time* per year? (Think of the cost of full tuition. Do not ad-

---

26. COACH students may also have to enroll for more than four years to complete a BA degree, particularly if they have to spend the first year at college completing preliminary or bilingual courses before enrolling in regular freshman-level courses for credit.

Table 8.11   **Student Estimates of Tuition at Various Institutions**

	Bunker Hill Community College		University of Massachusetts, Boston	
	COACH	Concord-Carlisle	COACH	Concord-Carlisle
$0–499	5.2%	3.3%	1.8%	0.0%
$500–999	7.5%	2.6%	3.2%	0.0%
$1,000–1,999	16.0%	8.5%	4.6%	1.9%
$2,000–2,999	16.9%	17.0%	4.1%	3.2%
$3,000–3,999	10.3%	9.2%	6.5%	3.2%
$4,000–4,999	7.0%	13.7%	12.0%	6.5%
$5,000–7,499	10.8%	14.4%	11.1%	12.3%
$7,500–9,999	7.0%	14.4%	11.1%	18.8%
$10,000–14,999	8.0%	7.8%	8.8%	29.9%
$15,000–19,999	6.6%	7.2%	10.6%	19.5%
$20,000+	4.7%	2.0%	25.4%	4.6%
Implied mean using midpoints of categories	$5,941	$6,055	$11,525	$11,255
Implied standard deviation using midpoints of categories	$6,056	$5,244	$8,300	$5,512
Actual		$2,040		$4,681

Source: Based on responses to baseline surveys administered in 2001–2002 (COACH) and 2000–2001 (Concord-Carlisle).

Notes: Table based on responses to the question "About how much do you think it costs to attend the following colleges *full-time* per year? Think of the cost of full tuition. Do not adjust for financial aid. Do not include housing, dormitory fee or food." The tuition listed for Bunker Hill Community College and University of Massachusetts, Boston, is for 2001–2002. Concord-Carlisle students were presented with the eleven categories listed here. COACH students were presented with the first ten categories plus $20,000–$24,999" and "$25,000+." We combine responses in the top two categories for the COACH students for ease of comparison.

just for financial aid. Do not include housing dormitory fees or food.)" Students were then asked to check one of a number of categories of tuition amounts, reported in table 8.11. The actual tuition at Bunker Hill Community College in the fall of 2001 was $2,040. Yet roughly 40 percent of the COACH students and 60 percent of the Concord-Carlisle students estimated that the tuition at Bunker Hill was more than $4,000. The actual tuition at the University of Massachusetts-Boston in the fall of 2001 was $4,681, yet roughly 45 percent of the COACH students and 55 percent of the Concord-Carlisle students estimated that this tuition was more than $10,000. Using the midpoints of each of the categories and a value of $25,000 for those estimating the costs to be above $20,000, the mean response for both groups was between two and three times the actual tuition for each of these two schools. (As shown in table 8.12, COACH students reported slightly higher estimates of grants and aid for attending each of these colleges than did Concord-Carlisle students.)

Table 8.12   Student Estimates of Aid at Various Institutions

	COACH Students, 2001–2002	Concord-Carlisle Students, 2000–2001
Percentage of students reporting a positive value for aid		
Bunker Hill Community College	47.8	26.9
University of Massachusetts, Boston	52.1	36.0
Northeastern University	52.8	37.7
Average aid reported for those reporting a positive value for aid ($)		
Bunker Hill Community College	3,608	2,567
University of Massachusetts, Boston	6,291	3,542
Northeastern University	9,489	5,695
Average net cost (estimated tuition – estimated aid, in $)		
Bunker Hill Community College	4,994	5,787
University of Massachusetts, Boston	9,445	10,082
Northeastern University	13,478	16,812

Source: Based on responses to baseline surveys administered in 2001–2002 (COACH) and 2000–2001 (Concord-Carlisle).

Notes: Table based on responses to the question "About how much aid (grants, loans, and scholarships) do you think you and your family would receive to go to the following colleges next year?" The first section divides the number of positive responses by the number of surveys—effectively treating missing responses as $0. The second section is restricted to students who reported a positive value for aid for the given college and also excludes one outlying response for Concord-Carlisle students and up to three outlying responses for COACH students that estimated more than $50,000 in aid. The third section includes all students who completed the baseline survey except for those who reported an estimated aid value that exceeded the midpoint of the range they selected for tuition for that college. Students who did not estimate an aid level for a given college were assumed to have an estimated aid level of $0 for the purposes of estimating the net cost for attending that college.

Perceptions of the Payoff to College

As part of the COACH survey, students were also asked to report how much they thought they would earn with and without a college degree. Specifically, students were asked to respond to the following questions: "About how much money do you think you would earn per year (or per hour) if you did not go to a vocational/trade school or college and worked full-time? (next year and at age 25)" and "About how much money do you think you would earn per year (or per hour) if you graduated from a 4-year college/university? (at age 25)."

The responses of both groups of students are reported in table 8.13, which also reports the actual wages of such workers working full-time, full-year in the Boston metropolitan area in the Current Population Survey from 1996 to 1999. Three facts reported in table 8.13 stand out. First, despite their dramatically different backgrounds, the two groups of students had remarkably similar expectations of future wages, producing almost

Table 8.13   **Student Estimates of Earnings of High School and College Graduates**

	As High School Graduate Next Year			As High School Graduate at Age 25			As College Graduate at Age 25		
	BPS	Suburb	CPS	BPS	Suburb	CPS	BPS	Suburb	CPS
10th	$15,000	$12,000	$9,826	$20,000	$18,000	$15,186	$30,000	$30,000	$17,485
25th	17,000	16,000	12,817	24,000	22,000	18,478	40,000	40,000	24,931
50th	20,000	18,000	16,341	30,000	30,000	23,430	50,00	50,000	33,843
75th	24,000	22,000	21,161	40,000	40,000	29,830	80,000	70,000	45,124
90th	32,000	30,000	26,702	60,000	60,000	38,770	145,000	150,000	62,655
Mean (%)	22,851	21,109		37,702	33,464		69,848	55,892	
SD	11,461	10,676		33,912	15,697		56,076	28,856	

Source: Based on responses to baseline and exit surveys administered in 2001–2002 (COACH) and 2000–2001 (Concord-Carlisle).

Notes: Table based on responses to questions "About how much money do you think you would earn per year (or per hour) if you did not go to a vocational/trade school or college and worked full time?" (next year and at age 25) and "About how much money do you think you would earn per year (or per hour) if you graduated from a four-year college/university?" (at age 25). CPS data are for full-time workers in the Boston CMSA in the Merged Outgoing Rotation Group data. They were assumed to be working fifty-two weeks per year. Calculated means and standard deviations exclude responses below the 1st percentile or above the 99th percentile in each group of responses. SD = standard deviation.

identical estimates at each of the 10th, 25th, 50th, 75th, and 90th percentiles in response to each question. (The means and standard deviations for each question tend to be higher for the COACH students than for the Concord-Carlisle students, indicating that the extreme responses, particularly those beyond the 90th percentile, were higher for COACH than for Concord-Carlisle students.) Second, the wage expectations of both groups as high school graduates working full-time immediately out of high school were reasonably similar to the actual results for workers in the Current Population Survey. The wage expectations of the suburban youths were generally within $3,500 of the actual earnings of high school graduates at the 10th, 25th, 50th, 75th, and 90th percentiles. This need not mean that individual students are accurately anticipating the distribution of their expected earnings. Recall that we asked each student to report the central tendency of their expected earnings distribution. It just so happens that the distribution of these central tendencies matches fairly well the actual distribution of earnings.

Third, both groups entertained inflated expectations of their earnings at age twenty-five, particularly as college graduates. The median expectation of both groups is that they would earn $30,000 per year as high school graduates at age twenty-five—roughly $7,000 more than the actual earnings for high school graduates in the Boston area at that age. Their expectations were even more out of line for college graduates, with both groups expecting to earn $50,000 working full-time per year as college graduates at age twenty-five—considerably more than the median value of $33,843 in the Current Population Survey. Thus, both groups seem to overstate the payoff to educational attainment as well as to experience on the job. In addition, when we performed several (unreported) regressions using estimated wages as the dependent variable, we found that obvious factors that one might associate with higher wages, such as grades and sex, were not statistically significant and often had negative coefficients. This indicates a certain level of confusion among the students and, quite likely, overconfidence among those in the categories that would generally indicate lower future wages (e.g., women with low GPAs).

Tables 8.14 and 8.15 report the distribution of the present value of a college degree implicit in students' responses to the questions about tuition

Table 8.14   Implied Estimates of Present Value (PV) of College Degree

| | Implied PV of College Degree (Assuming constant absolute earnings gap after age 25, no financial aid, and 6 percent discount rate.) | |
	COACH Students ($)	Concord-Carlisle Students ($)
10th percentile	−193,416	−109,598
25th percentile	−4,250	−10,761
Median	111,201	145,670
75th percentile	311,027	319,453
90th percentile	883,278	750,237
% > 0	74.4	73.8
Sample size	156	111

Source: Based on responses to baseline surveys administered in 2001–2002 (COACH) and 2000–2001 (Concord-Carlisle).

Table 8.15   Cross-Tabulation of Implied Present Value (PV) and Educational Plans

| | COACH | | | Concord-Carlisle | | |
	Plan BA	Don't Plan BA	Total	Plan BA	Don't Plan BA	Total
PV < 0	26	14	40	28	1	29
PV > 0	85	30	115	90	1	91
Total	111	44	155	99	2	110
p-value for test of independence		.299			n.a.	

Source: Based on responses to baseline surveys administered in 2001–2002 (COACH) and 2000–200 (Concord-Carlisle).

Notes: Present value for going to college was calculated based on four years of college costs and forgon wages (at student's assessed level of wage at eighteen) followed by forty years of constant differenti wages (assessed wage at age twenty-five with college degree minus assessed wage at age twenty-five with out college degree), discounted yearly at a 6 percent rate. BA = bachelor's degree; n.a. = not applicabl and expected earnings.[27] (The data are portrayed graphically in figure 8.3.) Approximately three-quarters of the students in each group reported values that imply a positive present value for a college degree. Table 8.15 reports the cross-tabulation of students' stated educational plans with an indicator of whether their answers implied a positive or negative payoff to college. There was only a weak connection between students' plans and their implicit expectations regarding the payoffs. A total of 73.9 percent of COACH students with an implied positive present value for a college degree reported that they planned to get at least a BA degree, as opposed to 65.0 percent of the COACH students with an implied negative present value for a college degree. But it is possible that the relationship between perceived economic gain from a college degree and the decision to go to college is muted by outside factors—in particular, the ability to pay for college now.[28]

Given the importance of subjective earnings expectations in economic models of the decision to enroll in school, such data on earning expectations are remarkably scarce. For example, Betts (1994) asked youths to report mean earnings in different fields, but youths were not expected to report what they would have expected themselves to earn in those occupations. Smith and Powell (1990) and Blau and Ferber (1991) collected data on youths' own expected earnings in the future—but not conditional on educational attainment. Dominitz and Manski (1996) collected data on students' beliefs about the distribution of earnings, conditional on educational attainment, for a sample of high school seniors and college freshmen in Madison, Wisconsin. Rather than asking students to report the central tendency of their earnings beliefs under different scenarios, as we have done, Dominitz and Manski collected information on the distribution of earnings. Nevertheless, there are several important similarities in our findings. First, while they found a considerable amount of within-group variation in earnings expectations as we did, they found no difference in mean earnings expectations between groups of women and men. Recall that we found little difference in the distributions for youths from the high-income suburban and low-income urban schools. Students may have a difficult time conditioning on their own background variables in formulating expectations. Second, similar to our finding of high earnings

27. Several assumptions were necessary to do so: that all students were using a discount rate of 6 percent, that students were not expecting any financial aid from colleges or from their parents, and that the absolute value of the earnings gap between high school and college remains constant for the remainder of their careers.

28. Another possibility, suggested by Derek Neal, is that COACH students have lower discount factors and thus place less relative value on the future relative to the present than Concord-Carlisle students. If this is the case, then both sets of students could provide the same estimates of tuition and future wages and yet have systematically different net present values for attending college.

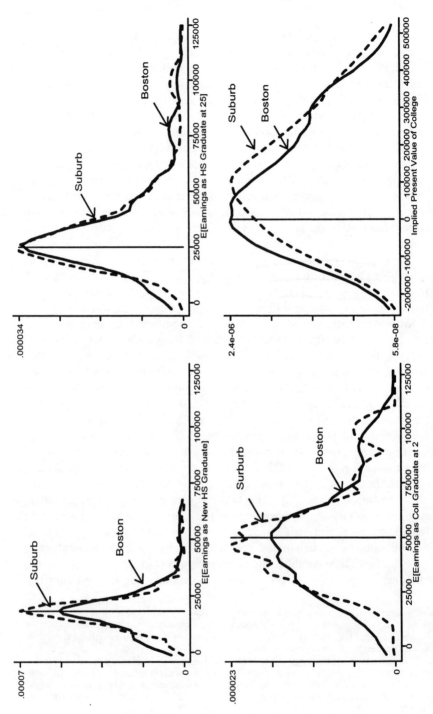

Fig. 8.3   Distributions of expected earnings in Boston public schools and suburban schools from COACH survey

expectations as college graduates, the medians of students' earnings expectations at age thirty with a bachelor's degree were considerably higher than the current actual earnings of bachelor degree holders at that age. Third, Dominitz and Manski found similar earnings expectations for high school seniors (some of whom will presumably not attend college) and college freshmen (who had already self-selected into college). This is consistent with our finding that subjective beliefs about the payoffs to college are only weakly related to students' plans for college.

Ability to Afford College

One question on the baseline survey asked students if they believed that they could find a way to pay to attend a public four-year college in Massachusetts if they applied and were accepted. As shown in table 8.16 more than half of the COACH students who responded to this question checked the box for "Maybe," and 11.4 percent checked the box for "No." Clearly, costs are a crucial consideration for these students. By contrast, more than three-quarters of the Concord-Carlisle students checked the box for "Yes," and only slightly more than 1 percent checked the box for "No."

Tables 8.17 and 8.18 show that COACH students who said that they could afford to go to college were roughly 10 percentage points more likely than others to report on the baseline survey that they planned to get at least a bachelor's degree and 10 percentage points more likely to enroll in a four-year college program for 2002–2003 than other COACH students. These 10 percentage point differences between those who believed that they could find a way to pay for a four-year college and others lie right on the boundary of statistical significance at the 5 percent level (grouping the "Maybe" and "No" categories together and comparing them to the "Yes" group).

Table 8.16   **Student Perceptions of Ability to Pay for College and Educational Plans**

	COACH Students	Concord-Carlisle Students
Yes (%)	37.0	76.3
Maybe (%)	51.7	22.4
No (%)	11.4	1.3
Sample size	211	156

Source: Based on responses to baseline and exit surveys administered in 2001–2002 (COACH), and 2000–2001 (Concord-Carlisle).

Notes: Table based on responses to question "Suppose you did want to attend a public four-year college in Massachusetts (for example, the University of Massachusetts, Boston) and imagine that you applied and were accepted. Do you think that you could find a way to pay for it?" Options for response were the following: (1) "Yes, I could definitely get the money from somewhere (for example: a job, family, scholarships, grants, loans, etc.);" (2) "Maybe. It would be hard to get the money, but I might get it from somewhere (for example: a job, family, scholarships, grants, loans, etc.);" and (3) "No. I don't think I could afford it." Students who listed multiple responses are coded in the category with the least certainty of being able to pay for college.

Table 8.17   Educational Plans as a Function of Postsecondary Plans and Assessments of the Cost of College: Student Responses and College Choices, COACH Students, 2001–2002

	Responses	Plan Bachelor's Degree as of Fall 2001	Going to 4-Year College	Estimation Tuition University of Massachusetts, Boston	Present Value of College > 0
Yes	78 (37.0%)	76.9%	34.6%	$12,143	77.6%
Maybe	109 (51.7%)	63.3%	22.0%	$11,439	77.3%
No	24 (11.4%)	66.7%	25.0%	$10,238	64.3%

Source: Based on the baseline survey response for COACH students in fall 2001. The percentage of students going to four-year colleges was compiled from the exit survey supplemented with additional information from coaches.

Notes: Table based on responses to question "Suppose you did want to attend a public four-year college in Massachusetts (for example, the University of Massachusetts, Boston) and imagine that you applied and were accepted. Do you think that you could find a way to pay for it?"

Table 8.18   Student Perceptions of Ability to Pay for College and Assessed Tuition for College

Estimation Tuition, University of Massachusetts, Boston	Can Pay for College?			Number of Students
	Yes	Maybe	No	
$4,999 or less	20 (31.3%)	37 (57.8%)	7 (10.9%)	64
$5,000–$9,999	19 (43.2%)	20 (45.5%)	5 (11.4%)	44
$10,000–$19,999	18 (42.9%)	18 (42.9%)	6 (14.3%)	42
$20,000 or more	18 (37.5%)	28 (58.3%)	2 (4.2%)	48

Source: Based on the baseline survey response for COACH students in fall 2001.

Interestingly, students with the highest estimates for the tuition for University of Massachusetts, Boston, were among the most sanguine about their ability to afford to go to a public four-year college. Only two of the forty-eight (4.2 percent) COACH students who estimated a tuition of $20,000 or more for University of Massachusetts, Boston, thought that they would not be able to afford to attend it, whereas more than 10 percent of the students with each lower tuition estimate said that they would not be able to do so. Furthermore, the students who had the most accurate perceptions of tuition—those who said that it would be $4,999 or less—were the least likely to say that they were certain that they could afford to go.[29] We found very similar results when we repeated the same analysis using

29. We estimated several (unreported) probit specifications to identify the factors that predict college attendance among COACH students. Correcting for GPA and other factors, the responses to the question about the affordability of college were not significant in any of these specifications.

perceptions of net cost (estimated tuition minus estimated aid) in place of perceptions of tuition.[30]

Summary

We found a slight correlation between the perception of COACH students about the affordability of a public four-year college and their actual college choices. Further, we found that both the COACH and the Concord-Carlisle students are overly pessimistic in their expectations for the tuition at public community and four-year colleges. But syllogistic reasoning breaks down at this second stage because there is little, if any, connection between the tuition level estimated by a student for a four-year college and that same student's perception that he or she would be able to pay to attend that college. In other words, while it would be nice in principle to educate students about the actual tuition for a public four-year college, it is not clear that this knowledge would have much effect in terms of college choices of these students. Further, it is hardly necessary to convince COACH students that it is in their economic interest to go to college, for most of them already believe that.

8.5.2   Giving Students a Head Start on the Application Process

One possible explanation of the difference in the results between Concord-Carlisle and COACH students is that Concord-Carlisle students had a large head start on the college application process. As shown in table 8.5, the Concord-Carlisle students had achieved most of the milestones toward enrollment at a four-year college early on in the senior year, whereas the COACH students were just starting the application process at that point.

How important are those milestones? How much could a program or a high school improve the college enrollment rates of its students simply by encouraging them to take these steps by the end of the junior year? Table 8.19 lists the percentage of COACH students in each category who went on to a four-year college, again restricting analysis to those students who planned to go to a four-year college at the start of the senior year. Four separate activities, including all three related to the SAT, are statistically significant in predicting attendance at a four-year college. In each of these cases, the conditional probability for attending a four-year college is at least 20 percentage points higher for COACH students who had completed a particular milestone than for COACH students who had not done so.

---

30. Among the COACH students whose answers indicated a net cost of $10,000 or less per year for attending a four-year public college, 35.1 percent said that they could definitely afford it, 53.9 percent said that they might be able to afford it, and 10.9 percent said that they could not afford it. These percentages were very similar for the COACH students whose answers indicated a net cost of more than $10,000 or less per year for attending a four-year public college: 40.0 percent said that they could definitely afford it, 47.5 percent said that they might be able to afford it, and 12.5 percent said that they could not afford it.

Table 8.19   Importance of Milestones for Attending Four-Year College, COACH
                    Students, 2001–2002

	Percentage to 4-Year College	T-Statistic for % Difference
Took PSAT**		
Yes	46.7% (43 of 92)	2.97
No	24.6% (16 of 65)	
Registered for SAT**		
Yes	46.4% (52 of 112)	4.11
No	16.3% (7 of 43)	
Took SAT**		
Yes	62.5% (30 of 48)	4.68
No	24.3% (25 of 103)	
Met with counselor 4+ times		
Yes	50.0% (13 of 26)	1.34
No	35.7% (45 of 126)	
Already applied to a college		
Yes	32.1% (9 of 28)	–0.61
No	38.1% (48 of 126)	
Visited a college		
Yes	49.1% (26 of 53)	1.93
No	33.0% (33 of 100)	
Have application, school most likely to attend**		
Yes	53.7% (29 of 54)	2.90
No	28.9% (22 of 76)	

Source: All milestone information based on baseline survey responses for COACH students, October 2001.

Notes: Test statistics are reported for a two-sample comparison of (conditional) probabilities for attending a four-year college. Missing values (where the student skipped the question or did not complete the baseline survey) are excluded from the calculation.

**Significant at the 5 percent level.

Table 8.20 classifies COACH students according to the number of milestones completed by the beginning of the senior year and the number of COACH sessions that they attended during the year.[31] The number of COACH sessions offered overall varied from twenty to twenty-three across the three participating high schools. Among those students who wanted to attend a four-year college and who had at least a 3.0 GPA, more than two-thirds of those who had completed at least three milestones by the start of senior year and/or attended at least sixteen COACH sessions will attend a four-year college.[32] By contrast, only 22.7 percent of those who had not completed at least three milestones by the start of senior year and did not attend at least sixteen COACH sessions will attend a four-year college. As

31. The variable "Already Applied to a College" is excluded from the number of milestones completed by the start of the year because table 8.16 suggests that completing this milestone does not increase the probability of going to a four-year college.

32. Among these students, the average number of COACH sessions was 15.6, with 59.7 percent of them attending at least 16 COACH sessions.

Table 8.20   **Importance of Prior Actions for Attending a Four-Year College**

	Percentage of COACH Students Attending a Four-Year College	
	0 to 15 Days of COACH	16+ Days of COACH
0–2 milestones completed at the start of senior year	22.7	66.7
3+ milestones completed at the start of senior year	71.4	77.3

Source: All milestone information based on Baseline survey responses for COACH students, October 2001.

Notes: Milestones include taking the PSAT, registering for the SAT, taking the SAT, possessing an application for the college that the student says he or she is most likely to attend, and meeting four times or more with a guidance counselor. The table is restricted to students in the COACH program who report at least a 3.0 GPA and who also reported at the start of the year that they wanted to go to college.

long as a student has sufficient academic qualifications and motivation (as indicated by the number of days of participation in COACH sessions), these results suggest that an early start on the application process is not a prerequisite for attending a four-year college.

Summary

The results in table 8.20 provide support for the common belief that programs that help students to start the application process early can have tremendous positive effect. For instance, Harvard has run an "early awareness program" for many years for students in Cambridge. Most, if not all, seventh grade classes in Cambridge public schools take a field trip to Harvard, meet with an admissions officer, take a campus tour, and eat lunch in a college dining hall. The college does not offer formal services to Cambridge students beyond the seventh grade, but it is thought by the Cambridge teachers that these visits have an important and lasting effect on their students.

At the same time that our results support the value of such early awareness programs, they also show that it is not necessary to have a head start in order to be successful in the college admissions process. For students who attended at least the average number of COACH sessions, the milestone variables were of only minor importance in predicting attendance at a four-year college. The conclusion is that it is still possible for the students in the COACH program (with sufficient academic qualifications) to catch up on the college process during the course of the senior year.

8.6   Conclusion

The U.S. system for financing higher education is at least as misunderstood today as the health care finance system was twenty years ago. Not only are parents paying for their child's college education in more ways than they realize—through direct subsidies to institutions, through financial aid programs to college, through generous new tax benefits for college—but the impact of each of those subsidies on the decisions of various groups of youths is not well understood by policymakers. In 2003, it will have been three decades since the Pell Grant program was established, yet differences in college-going by family income remain wide and, according to some recent evidence, appear to be widening. The higher education policy debate has become so bogged down with incremental questions involving issues such as changes in the need analysis formula to notice the bigger questions: Why is it that there was no apparent impact of the Pell Grant program's establishment on college enrollment rates of low-income youths? What is the bang for the buck achieved with different types of public subsidies—across-the-board subsidies to keep tuition low, Pell Grants, loan subsidies? Why do so few parents save for college, and how are their decisions influenced by state and federal policies? We will not make progress in closing the gaps in college enrollment by family income unless we have some of the answers to such questions.

Our experience with the COACH program in Boston provides a window into the decision making of low-income, mainly first-generation college students and allows us to compare their decision making to the decisions of suburban youth. First, we are struck by the similarity of youths' plans and the similarity in perceptions of college costs and payoffs, despite the very large differences in economic prospects for urban and suburban youths. Second, many youths have unrealistically ambitious plans for eventual educational attainment, which they maintain throughout their senior year, even if considerable obstacles exist to the achievement of those aspirations—such as low GPAs, low test scores, or even the failure to submit a college application! Third, we were impressed by the loose connection between students' financial valuations of a college degree implicit in their responses to our queries about expected earnings and their stated plans. In light of such a finding, clarifying youths' expectations about the cost of college (which tend to be overblown) or raising their awareness of the labor market value of a college degree (which also seems to be exaggeratedly high in their estimation) would seem to have little effect on behavior.

At the same time, we see considerable evidence of low-income youths with high aspirations and high implicit valuations of college failing to clear seemingly minor hurdles in the process of applying for college and applying for financial aid. A large share of youths register for the SAT but fail to take it or fail to complete a four-year college application out of an aversion to writing essays. When data become available for tracking the enrollment behavior of the high school classes of 2001 and 2002, we hope to learn more about the impact of our efforts to help youths in several Boston high schools clear these hurdles.

References

Betts, Julian. 1994. What do students know about wages? Evidence from a survey of undergraduates. *Journal of Human Resources* 31 (1): 27–56.

Blau, Francine, and M. Ferber. 1991. Career plans and expectations of young women and men. *Journal of Human Resources* 26:581–607.

Cameron, Stephen V., and James J. Heckman. 1998. Life cycle schooling and dynamic selection bias: Models and evidence for five cohorts of American males. *Journal of Political Economy* 106 (2): 262–333.

College Board. 2001. *Trends in student aid 2001*. Washington, D.C.: College Board.

Dominitz, Jeff, and Charles F. Manski. 1996. Eliciting student expectations of the returns to schooling. *Journal of Human Resources* 31 (1): 1–26.

Dynarski, Susan. 2000. Hope for whom? Financial aid for the middle class and its impact on college attendance. *National Tax Journal* 53 (3): 629–661.

———. 2003. Does aid matter? Measuring the effect of student aid on college attendance and completion. *American Economic Review* 93 (1): 279–288.

Ellwood, David, and Thomas J. Kane. 2000. Who is getting a college education: Family background and the growing gaps in enrollment. In *Securing the future,* ed. Sheldon Danziger and Jane Waldfogel, 283–324. New York: Russell Sage Foundation.

Hansen, W. Lee. 1983. Impact of student financial aid on access. In *The crisis in higher education,* ed. Joseph Froomkin. New York: Academy of Political Science.

Kane, Thomas J. 1994. College attendance by blacks since 1970: The role of college cost, family background and the returns to education. *Journal of Political Economy* 102 (5): 878–911.

———. 1999. *The price of admission: Rethinking how Americans pay for college.* Washington, D.C.: Brookings Institution and Russell Sage.

Leslie, Larry, and Paul T. Brinkman. 1987. Student price response in higher education: The student demand studies. *Journal of Higher Education* 58 (2): 181–204.

———. 1988. *Economic value of higher education.* New York: Macmillan.

Manski, Charles F. 1993. Income and higher education. *Focus* 14 (3): 14–19.

McPherson, Michael S., and Morton Owen Schapiro. 1991. Does student aid affect college enrollment? New evidence on a persistent controversy. *American Economic Review* 81:309–318.

National Center for Education Statistics. 1999. *Digest of education statistics 1999.* Washington, D.C.: National Center for Education Statistics.

Rosenbaum, James. 2001. *Beyond college for all.* New York: Russell Sage Foundation.

Smith, Herbert L., and Brian Powell. 1990. Great expectations: Variations in income expectations among college seniors. *Sociology of Education* 63 (3): 194–207.

Comment   Bruce Sacerdote

Chris Avery and Tom Kane have produced a very useful and interesting paper that measures (1) high school students' perceptions of their own likeli-

Bruce Sacerdote is associate professor of economics at Dartmouth College, and a faculty research fellow of the National Bureau of Economic Research.

hood of attending college; (2) concrete steps that the students have taken to gain admission; and (3) the perceived costs and benefits of college attendance. The paper contains survey data for both inner-city (Boston, Charlestown, Dorchester) and suburban (Concord-Carlisle) students. The inner city students appear to vastly overestimate the probability of college attendance and to significantly lag their suburban counterparts in completing the steps in the admissions process, for example, registering for the SAT. Both groups of students overestimate tuition costs but, on average, have reasonable expectations about the wages of high school and college graduates. The authors also note the fact that students appear to be less responsive to returns to college attendance than to tuition costs.

These findings raise a number of interesting puzzles, and I discuss possible causes of each puzzle in the following. I argue that the findings provide some strong motivation for the COACH experiment currently being run by the authors and which generated these data. The COACH experiment uses Harvard graduate students to mentor high school seniors in Boston public schools. This is an effort to help the high school students navigate the college admission process.

The authors highlight the COACH students' very high expectations of college attendance. For example, when asked in the fall of their senior year, 65 percent of COACH students planned to attend a four-year college in the next year, and 70 percent planned to obtain a BA or higher degree. However, at graduation, only 25 percent of these students actually had plans to attend a four-year school.

How is it possible for student expectations to be so far off? One answer may be that the COACH students do not reveal their true expectation of college attendance because they feel there is a "right" answer to questions about future college plans. The potentially good news is that at least the students have gotten the message that college attendance is something to which they should aspire.

The paper does a very nice job of identifying the success rate of COACH students at each point in the college application process. The initial hurdle for students is to maintain a 3.0 GPA in high school. This is an important cutoff because students with below a 3.0 are unlikely to gain admission to any of the four-year campuses of the University of Massachusetts (Amherst, Boston, Dartmouth, Lowell, Worcester). Sixty-two percent of the students do not clear this hurdle. Because the COACH intervention takes place during senior year, it is not intended to help students clear the GPA hurdle. The COACH program may be very valuable for students who meet the GPA cutoff, but in the absence of the program, students might fail to register for and take the SAT and to submit a college application.

Even with the help of a COACH mentor, five of sixty-two students failed to register for the SAT, and eight of the remaining fifty-seven did not take the test even after they registered. In contrast, none of Concord-Carlisle students dropped out at the SAT registration stage, SAT-taking stage, or the application-filing stage. Thus there is great scope for the COACH program to aid the students in the Boston schools by making sure that these students clear the SAT and application hurdles. As the authors noted during their presentation, the mentor may serve the role of a parent in nagging the student to make sure that the paperwork gets done properly and on time.

The current paper does not make any attempt to evaluate the treatment effects from COACH, but undoubtedly the forthcoming program evaluation will be quite interesting and widely read. One issue with the current program is that there are no randomized controls, so I predict that there will be future COACH-like studies that have some form of randomized control group.

Both the COACH students and the Concord-Carlisle students vastly overestimate tuition at University of Massachusetts, Boston by a factor of more than two. For both groups, the mean estimate of tuition is about $11,500, versus the actual tuition of $4,700. I can think of two explanations for this systematic error. Some of the students may have in mind the widely publicized, and much higher tuition, at selective private institutions. And students may also be erroneously including room and board costs in their estimates of tuition. The relevant question for the paper is whether or not students actually respond to their inflated tuition estimates. The answer might be no, given that there is little correlation between the tuition estimates and students' perceived ability to pay for college (table 8.15).

On average, the students in both groups do a good job of estimating the wages for recent high school graduates and recent college graduates. Most of the students report wage estimates that imply a large net present value gain from college attendance. Oddly, there are large numbers of students who perceive a large payoff to a BA but do not plan on attaining a BA. One possible explanation may be that such students are reporting average wages for college graduates but believe that they themselves would do significantly worse. Or maybe these students anticipate large psychic costs to future school attendance.

For future studies, it would be worth asking such students a series of follow-on questions to try to distinguish between these explanations. When confronted with the contradiction of large perceived payoffs but no expected college attendance, do students change their estimated wages? Do they change their actual college preparation behavior? I would also be very interested in calculations of imputed future wages for these students based on each student's characteristics. For how many of the students would the authors estimate a large payoff to college?

The bottom line is that COACH students have "gotten the message" that there are large returns to college. And their educational aspirations show a widespread desire to obtain college and graduate degrees. Assuming that the policy goal is to increase college attendance among able students, the low-hanging fruit for the COACH program may be the group of students who have the necessary high school grades for college admission but fail to both take the SATs and file college applications. Of course, if these students have difficulty completing the steps needed to apply to college, then they may not succeed once they are in college. The full evaluation of the COACH program would require following students for at least several years. The future evaluations and implementations of this program may have a huge effect on how high school students are counseled and may close some of the large urban-suburban gap in college attendance of high school seniors.

Peer Effects in Higher Education

Gordon C. Winston and David J. Zimmerman

9.1 Introduction

The existence and nature of peer effects are fundamental to understanding a variety of crucial issues facing both higher and lower education. Peer effects have played an important role in studies of primary and secondary education beginning when the prominent Coleman Report of 1966 claimed their centrality in the determination of childrens' schooling outcomes (Coleman, Campbell, Hobson, McPartland, Mood, Weinfeld, and York 1966). Arguments based on peer effects have been used to justify busing and have entered the debates on educational costs, on tracking, on distance learning, affirmative action, and on the effects of voucher systems (U.S. Supreme Court 1971; Summers and Wolfe 1977; Hanushek 1986; Robertson and Symons 1996; Epple and Romano 1998; Lazear 1999; Hoxby 2000). The relevance of peer effects to the economics of higher education has only recently been acknowledged (Rothschild and White 1995; Winston and Yen 1995; Winston 1999; Epple, Romano, and Sieg 2001) and has only a small, if growing, empirical basis (Zimmerman 1999; Stinebrickner

Gordon C. Winston is Orrin Sage Professor of Political Economy at Williams College. David J. Zimmerman is professor of economics and department chair at Williams College, and a research associate of the National Bureau of Economic Research (NBER).

We want to thank Atlantic Philanthropic Services and especially the Andrew W. Mellon Foundation for its continuing support of the Williams College Project on the Economics of Higher Education and for making their unique College and Beyond data set available for this study. Al Goethals, Georgi Zhelev, and Adam Sischy contributed a good deal to the chapter, while Caroline Hoxby went way beyond the usual volume editor in her interest in and contribution to the work. Finally, the participants in the NBER seminar at Bretton Woods—especially Tom Dee—were very helpful in spotting ambiguities and dubious assertions in an earlier draft.

and Stinebrickner 2000; Goethals 2001; Sacerdote 2001). In this chapter we will describe the importance of peer effects in some detail and will then offer new empirical evidence on their existence.

Estimating peer effects is difficult. First, we must decide on the appropriate set of educational outcomes believed to be sensitive to peer attributes. Second, we must specify the relevant peer attributes. Third, and perhaps most difficult, we must contend with the fact that *selection bias* is rampant in the estimation of peer effects. In a laboratory setting, we might randomly assign a set of subjects to different peer environments and gauge any resulting effects.[1] In the world of nonexperimentally derived observations, however, we must recognize that people choose their peers. And if people tend to associate with others with similar traits (many of which are likely to be unobservable to the researcher), then it is exceedingly difficult to determine whether we are observing peer effects or simply observing similar people behaving similarly. In this paper we use a unique data set that combines data for three schools from the Andrew W. Mellon Foundation's College and Beyond data for the entering class of 1989, along with phonebook data identifying roommates, to implement a quasi-experimental empirical strategy aimed at measuring peer effects in academic outcomes. In particular, we use data on individual student's grades, Scholastic Aptitude Test (SAT) scores, and the SAT scores of their roommates to estimate the effect of roommates' academic characteristics on an individual's grades. The schools selected for the analysis were chosen because their housing assignment protocols appear (near) random for first-year students. The results suggest that, for two of the three schools used, students in the middle of the SAT distribution may do somewhat worse in terms of grades if they share a room with a student who is in the bottom 15 percent of the SAT distribution. Students in the top of the SAT distribution are typically not affected by the SAT scores of their roommates.

Sections 9.2 through 9.4 of this chapter define peer effects and indicate the importance of peer effects in understanding several fundamental characteristics of higher education. Sections 9.6 through 9.9 review the existing empirical evidence and provide new evidence. Section 9.10 concludes.

9.2   Peer Effects in the Economics of Higher Education

Peer effects *exist* when a person's behavior is affected by his or her interaction with peers—"equals"—so in higher education peer effects result from interactions between students.[2] While peer quality is often included

---

1. For an interesting strategy to estimate peers in an experimental context, see Goethals (2001).

2. Peer effects among faculty (and administrators) can be important, too, of course, to recruiting, teaching, and scholarly productivity, but they are not the issue here (Rosovsky 1990; Kennedy 1997).

as an argument in an educational production function, it is useful to put it more directly as an interaction between two (for simplicity) students,

$$(1) \qquad\qquad B_1 = f(B_2, C_2, \mathbf{X}),$$

where B_i is behavior, C_i is characteristics for students $i = 1, 2$, and $\mathbf{X}$ is a vector of other things relevant to 1's behavior. Peer effects *exist* if the partial derivatives of equation (1) are not zero and they are asymmetric (or nonlinear) if those partials differ at different levels of B and C.

Peer effects, we will argue, are relevant to the economics of higher education in several important ways:

1. They eliminate awkward anomalies in the institutional behavior of colleges and universities and in the economic structure of higher education as an industry if they exist.

2. They might justify, as economically efficient, the observed segmentation of student quality and resources if peer effects are appropriately nonlinear.

3. They lead to trade in peer quality in an input market inextricably linked with that for educational services. Both of those markets and their interaction appear essential to understanding pricing, admissions, and competition in higher education (Rothschild and White 1995; Winston 2003).

We will focus on the first of these claims. We will examine the second but express our frustration because, while they are potentially important, the empirical evidence gives only hints about their nature. And we will do little more than note the third—the blended markets for educational services and peer quality—because its discussion would require a chapter to itself.

9.3   Peer Effects and Economic Anomalies in Higher Education

9.3.1   Anomalies

Higher education looks much like a normal industry that makes a product (educational services) using purchased inputs that it sells to customers for a price in a quite competitive market. There are, however, some fundamental differences:

- Colleges always charge a price that fails—significantly—to cover their production costs.
- They turn away a majority of potential customers who are willing and able to buy their product if they can.
- They don't expand output to meet persistent excess demand.
- They lower the price to attract one customer, replacing another who would pay a higher price.

- They judge institutional quality by how many customers they can turn away, and they may manipulate sales-admission policies to increase that number.[3]
- They require elaborate application procedures before one is allowed to make a purchase.
- They practice extensive price discrimination not only to increase sales revenues but often to redistribute income among their customers.

9.3.2 Economic Characteristics

Those anomalies disappear and higher education becomes an economically coherent industry if four economic characteristics are, in fact, typical of colleges, universities, and higher education:

1. If charitable donations significantly augment schools' commercial (sales, tuition) revenues (Hansmann 1980)

2. If those donated resources are unevenly distributed, supporting a hierarchy of schools based on their independence from sales revenues

3. If colleges and universities are less interested in profits than in a "mission" and in "achieving excellence or prestige"

4. If students provide an input critical to the production of higher education and if peer effects are important to educational output

9.3.3 Evidence of Those Characteristics

Donations—Noncommercial Resources

It is well established that colleges and universities charge prices that are less than the costs of production. National Integrated Postsecondary Education Data System (IPEDS) data for more than 2,800 U.S. colleges and universities support the data in table 9.1. Averaged over colleges and universities in both public and private sectors in 1995–1996, tuition revenues support only a fraction of the cost of producing a student's education; the rest was covered by donations (past and present, public and private). The price-cost ratio averaged 0.32 and ranged from an average of 0.13 in the public sector to 0.45 among private schools. In a more complete analysis of IPEDS data that also recognized collegiate saving, it appeared that 75 percent of the economic resources used in higher education came from charitable contributions—only 25 percent came from commercial sales (Winston, Carbone, forthcoming).

The Uneven Distribution of Donations

The bottom part of table 9.1 indicates how unevenly those donations, and hence the student subsidies they support, are distributed among

---

3. On early decision, see Avery, Fairbanks et al. 2001; Fallows 2001.

Table 9.1   The Distribution of Average Cost, Price, and Student Subsidies, 1996

	Subsidy per Student ($)	Average Educational Cost ($)	Average Net Tuition ($)
All college and universities	8,423	12,413	3,989
Public	8,590	9,896	1,305
Private	8,253	14,986	6,734
Schools ranked by student subsidies			
Decile 1	20,991	27,054	6,063
Decile 2	11,865	15,801	3,936
Decile 3	10,009	13,310	3,301
Decile 4	8,752	11,831	3,080
Decile 5	7,855	10,565	2,710
Decile 6	7,020	9,820	2,799
Decile 7	6,250	9,464	3,214
Decile 8	5,447	8,848	3,401
Decile 9	4,262	9,297	5,035
Decile 10	1,736	8,084	6,348

Source: Based on U.S. Department of Education IPEDS data. Includes 2,791 institutions, of which 1,411 are public and 1,380 are private. All dollar amounts are per full-time equivalent student averaged over institutions. See Winston (forthcoming) and Winston and Yen (1995) for details on the derivation of these data from the IPEDS Finance Survey (medical schools are omitted here).

schools. The average student at a school in the top decile got a subsidy of $21,000 a year—paying $6,063 for a $27,054 education—while a typical student in a bottom-decile school got $1,700—paying $6,348 for an $8,084 education.

A Nonprofit Objective Function

The third economic characteristic—institutional objective function—can't be supported by data, of course. However, the existence of nonprofit behavior like need-blind admissions with need-based financial aid, along with policies like Berea College's zero tuition combined with its family income cap, strongly imply it. And economists—including Hansmann, James (1990), Clotfelter (James 1978; Hansmann 1980; Clotfelter 1996), and others—have described the objective function for a college in terms of excellence (or prestige) and mission.

9.4   The Existence of Peer Effects

The fourth characteristic—that peer effects are important to educational output—is central. If peer effects exist, they could motivate the stratification of students and resulting concentration of student quality in those schools with the most noncommercial resources per student. Stratification, if peer effects exist, is the result of an efficiency wage (Akerlof and Yellen 1986; Winston forthcoming) in the form of a student subsidy paid to generate a queue of applicants from which the best, in terms of peer quality, are selected. All schools may value the educational quality that is provided by good students through peer effects, but peer quality is scarce, and those schools that are able to pay the most for it get the most of it. The uneven distribution of noncommercial resources evident in table 9.1 creates a hierarchy that supports the stratification of student quality and motivates the long-run supply restrictions on which that selectivity rests. So the existence of peer effects—in a world of unevenly distributed noncommercial revenues and an institutional devotion to excellence—would produce the industry structure we see.

It is worth noting that there are other production externalities of student quality, aside from the peer interactions on which we are concentrating— like an instructor's ability to assign more advanced readings to better students, to give more intense and efficient lectures, or to have more productive seminars. These might also be thought of as "peer effects" and may have the same sort of effect of making educational production a function of student quality and hence motivate segmentation as efficient. Our focus, however, is not on these types of production externalities but, rather, as previously mentioned, on the direct impact that peer behavior or characteristics have on academic outcomes.

9.5   Efficiency and the Asymmetry of Peer Effects

Hoxby (2000) noted that the existence, per se, of peer effects may leave any regrouping of students as a largely distributional matter. Resorting students creates winners and losers to the same extent under strictly symmetric peer effects. But if those peer effects are asymmetric so that students at different levels of behavior or characteristics are influenced differently by their interaction with others, then peer effects introduce an issue of economic efficiency, too. How students are grouped will affect the total amount of learning produced in given participants from given resources.

If weak students gain more from proximity to strong peers than the strong students lose from that association, overall learning would be increased by reducing stratification—a point made by McPherson and Schapiro (1990) in suggesting random assignment of students to colleges. But if asymmetries in peer effects run the other way so that strong students interacting with other strong students are also more sensitive to peer influence—gaining more in learning than would weak students in those circumstances—then stratification and segmentation could increase, not decrease, aggregate learning. In the extreme, stratification would be supported on grounds of efficiency if strong students were sensitive to peer quality at all levels while weak students were unaffected by peers at any level.

Yet framing the issue as one of "strong students" and "weak students," while it fits the empirical work that's been possible so far, masks a potentially important question of peer "distance"—how far apart the peers are in their behavior and characteristics. Are peer responses very different outside a "neighborhood" of proximity so that a slightly different peer is influential but someone very different is not?[4] It's certainly a question at the center of the stratification question—a strong student might typically inspire somewhat weaker peers, while intimidating those more distant from his or her abilities. For the strong student, moderately weaker peers might represent a challenge and a chance to learn by teaching, while much weaker peers would overwhelm the strong student. And numbers would play a role not captured in either our framing or our evidence; given differences and distances among peers, a student would likely respond differently to one such peer than to a whole school of them. So the shape of nonlinearities in peer effect responses would depend on both peer distance and numbers.

Finally, whatever the efficiency or inefficiency of higher education's existing stratification in producing aggregate learning, social policy would have to address the question recently raised with some force by Nicholas Lemann (1999a,b) about whether those high-ability students, after learning more from their expensive educations with strong and sensitive peers, *use* all that learning to do anything useful for society and whether their social marginal product justifies that selectivity. He argued that it doesn't.

9.6   The Evidence

9.6.1   The Ideal Data

As a transition from the potentially central economic role we have suggested—that student peer effects might play in higher education to the more modest empirical results we are able to report on next and add to—it's useful to describe the ideal data whose analysis would persuasively support that role. Inevitably, of course, the actual evidence must fall far short of perfection, but it is useful to see how and where.

The empirical test of the existence and shape of peer effects in colleges would ideally, in terms of equation (1), deal with the following:

- Student behavior, B_1, that is centrally relevant to the purposes of higher education, broadly defined to include, inter alia, the development of intellectual curiosity, persistence, acquisition of facts, humane values, aesthetic sensitivities, analytical and technical sophistication, social responsibility, and so on.

---

4. This, of course, is in keeping with the Manski and Wise observation that students "preferred to enroll in colleges where the average academic ability of the enrolled students was slightly higher than their own. Schools where the average SAT scores of entering freshmen were either too low or too high were relatively disfavored" (Manski and Wise 1983, 159).

- His or her behavior, B_1, and the characteristics and behavior of peers, B_2 and C_2, that were unambiguously measurable in order to investigate not only the sign of peer differences and response but also their magnitudes
- A large population of students that generated a good deal of variation in B_1, B_2, and C_2 and their interaction, describing different distances between peers to reveal neighborhood asymmetries and nonlinearities
- Truly random assignment of associations between students that eliminated preferences in peer association
- Variations in peer characteristics of communities to reveal any social critical mass in conditioning peer interactions

Data meeting these conditions would allow an effective test of the existence of peer effects and their nonlinearities or asymmetries. And they would eliminate misgivings about the importance of the peer behaviors and characteristics studied so far to higher education.

Inevitably, of course, the studies described in the rest of the chapter fall short of the ideal. Although selection bias has largely been avoided through the use of randomly assigned roommates and experimental groups, and the results consistently show the existence of peer influences on behaviors that are relevant to education, it remains that in measuring a student's grade point average (GPA) response (or test scores or retention or fraternity membership) to his roommate's SATs (or income or fraternity membership), we're looking at a fairly thin slice of student behaviors and characteristics that leaves out a whole lot of what is happening to shape higher education.

But we find optimism in that thinness. If evidence of student peer effects can be found in so narrow a range of academic characteristics and behaviors, it's hard not to believe that with a wider and more appropriate range they would appear with a good deal more strength. Indeed, in having to use such limited evidence for so broad an influence (and so sweeping a hypothesis), we didn't initially expect peer effects to be significantly evident. But we could neither conjure up more appropriate data nor convince ourselves that we could adequately account for selection effects in a more general population with broader behaviors.[5] We were trying to see if we could find an iceberg and feel confident that we've located the tip.

But clearly, it's been easier to find evidence of the existence of peer effects than to learn much about their nonlinearities. So these results do more to support the idea that peer effects help to *explain* industry structure and selectivity in higher education—their positive role—than to support the more demanding idea that asymmetries in peer effects can *justify* that structure on efficiency grounds—their normative role.

5. This makes it very difficult to document peer effects within athletic teams, for instance (Shulman and Bowen 2001).

9.6.2   What We Have Learned So Far

In an earlier study, one of us (Zimmerman 1999) investigated peer effects associated with a student's own GPA and the academic strength (as measured by SAT scores) of his peers. That study attempted to overcome the selection bias issue by assembling a unique set of data comprised of twelve classes of students at Williams College containing information on their grades, major, gender, race, and so on, along with information on where and *with whom* they were housed in their freshman year.[6] In that paper, Zimmerman argued that freshman housing at Williams College closely resembled random assignment. That being the case, it was meaningful to contrast students with high, medium, and low SAT scores who, by chance, had roommates with high, medium, or low SAT scores. This allowed, for example, comparisons between the grades of low-SAT students who roomed with other low-SAT roommates to the grades of low-SAT students who roomed with high-SAT roommates. Any differences in the outcomes could, because of the quasi-random assignment, be attributed to peer effects. The basic findings of that effort suggested that students in the middle of the SAT distribution did somewhat worse in terms of grades if they shared a room with a student who was in the bottom 15 percent of the verbal SAT distribution. Interestingly, students in the top and the bottom of the SAT distribution were not affected by the SAT scores of their peers. The effects for the middle group weren't large but were statistically significant in many models. Furthermore, peer effects were almost always linked more strongly with verbal SAT scores than with math SAT scores.

These results, however, were estimated in the context of a highly selective liberal arts college. In that study, the low-SAT students would, on average, still rank at about the top 15th percentile of the national SAT score distribution. The results could also have been idiosyncratic to Williams College.

Recent research has given additional support to the claim that peer effects exist in higher education (cf. Stinebrickner and Stinebrickner 2000; Goethals 2001; Sacerdote 2001). All of these studies have examined the influence the characteristics or behavior of one student has on the behavior of another. The peer characteristics observed were, for the most part, variants on academic ability—SAT or American College Test (ACT) scores or more nuanced evaluations of academic promise generated in the admission process—while the influenced behavior was largely grades or performance on a written test. These characteristics were broadened to include gender and income, and behaviors were broadened to include dropout behavior, choice of major, and fraternity membership.

Sacerdote (2001), using data from Dartmouth and also using a room-

---

6. See Zimmerman (forthcoming). This paper contains a broad overview of the academic literature considering peer effects.

mate-based strategy, found evidence of a peer impact of a student on his roommate's GPA as well as on his participation in fraternities. Sacerdote's results suggest a nonlinear relationship with both weaker and stronger students performing better when their roommate was in the top 25 percent of the academic index distribution. In addition, Sacerdote found evidence of peer effects in fraternity participation but no evidence of peer effects in choice of college major.

Stinebrickner and Stinebrickner (2000) employed a data set from Berea College. Like Zimmerman (1999) and Sacerdote (2001), they used the random assignment of roommates to identify the peer effect. Berea College targets low-income students (capping family income at about $65,000) and so provides a useful complement to the highly selective schools used in the other studies. Stinebrickner and Stinebrickner found no evidence at Berea College that either first-semester grades or retention are associated with roommates' ACT scores. They did, however, find evidence that roommate income had a positive impact on both grades and retention, holding ACT scores constant, but only for women.

Goethals (2001) employed a unique and innovative experimental framework to measure peer effects. The study explored whether students would perform better writing about newspaper articles they read and discussed in academically homogenous or heterogeneous groups of three. He found that students' performance was not linked to their own academic rating but was affected by whether they were placed with academically homogeneous or heterogeneous peers. He found that groups composed of students who all had a low academic rating and groups composed of students who all had a high academic rating perform similarly—with both groups of these types out performing groups in which some students had high ratings and some low ratings.[7] These results were stronger for men than for women. So he found that peers' academic characteristics influenced others' behavior but not with straightforward nonlinearities.

In sum, there is a growing—though still small—body of evidence suggesting that peer effects exist in higher education. The evidence is not clear on the nature of any nonlinearities or interactions based on gender. It also suggests that nonacademic peer characteristics may be important.

In this chapter we next add to the empirical evidence by employing data from the College and Beyond (C&B) database—created by the Andrew W. Mellon Foundation—along with matched housing data for three schools in the C&B data. This allows us to apply the same empirical roommate-based approach to measure the peer effects previously described. In so doing, this work adds further evidence on the impact of peer characteristics in higher education.

---

7. Should these results hold up on further study, they have clear implications for sorting, stratification, and hierarchy among colleges.

9.7   Empirical Strategy: New Evidence

To estimate academic peer effects from the College and Beyond data in terms of equation (1), we follow the now traditional path of relating the cumulative GPA of a student (B_1) to his own SAT scores and to the SAT scores of his first-year roommate (C_2). More formally, we estimate regression models specified as

$$(2) \qquad \text{GPA}_i = \alpha + \beta_1\text{SAT}_i + \beta_2\text{SAT}_i^{\text{RM}} + \beta_3\mathbf{X}_i + \varepsilon_{ic},$$

where GPA is the student's grade point average measured cumulatively to graduation,[8] SAT is the student's own SAT score (sometimes entered separately for math and verbal scores), SAT^{RM} is the student's freshman roommate's SAT score (sometimes entered separately for math and verbal scores), and $\mathbf{X}$ is a vector of other characteristics (such as race and gender) of the student.[9] If students are randomly assigned their roommates, then the estimated peer effect (β_2) will be unbiased. More generally, the estimate will be unbiased if it is plausible that the error term is uncorrelated with the explanatory variables.

In addition, we estimate models that allow for nonlinearities in the peer effect. In particular, we allow the peer effect to vary based on whether the student or his roommate is in the lowest 15 percent, the middle 70 percent, or the top 15 percent of the SAT distribution. Formally, we estimate

$$(3) \qquad \text{GPA}_{ij} = \alpha + \beta_1\text{SAT}_i + \sum_{g=1}^{3}\beta_g\text{SAT}_{ig}^{\text{DRM}} + \beta_3\mathbf{X}_i + \varepsilon_{ic}; \quad j = 1, 2, 3,$$

where $\text{SAT}_{ig}^{\text{DRM}}$ are dummy variables for each SAT score range (indexed by g) and β_g is the peer effect associated with that range.

As previously discussed, if a school's objective is to maximize learning (which we proxy with GPA), then the relative magnitude of β_g for the various ability groupings of students and their peers will be important in efficiently allocating roommates. And, by analogy, they would be suggestive in how students would be sorted across colleges of differing quality. Suppose, for example, that strong students enhance the academic performance of weaker students. Further, suppose stronger students' grades are not affected by having a weak roommate. Then, mixing students may yield higher aggregate learning than would grouping weak students with weak students and strong students with strong students. The weaker students' grades would increase as a result of mixed ability groupings while the

---

8. Grade performance for the first year alone was not available in C&B data, but analysis of the Williams College data where both cumulative and freshman-year GPA could be used showed that they yielded the same results (Zimmerman 1999).

9. An appealing alternative strategy would be to include the roommate's GPA in the regression. Such a variable might better measure actual rather than potential performance. The problem with including such a variable is that it is simultaneously determined within the roommate context. Using such a measure would introduce simultaneous equation bias.

stronger students grades would not suffer. If, on the other hand, stronger students' grades did suffer we would have to ask whether their decline was sufficient to offset gains to the weaker students. Thus, the coefficients on the β_g parameters for the various groups (along with the relative numbers of students in the different ability categories) are critical in thinking about optimal groupings. The evidence, as we will see, is still mixed on this important issue.

9.8   Data

The C&B data used in this study were created and made available to us by the Andrew Mellon foundation. The C&B data contain both institutional and survey data for over 90,000 students enrolled in thirty-four mostly selective colleges and universities in the United States for the entering classes of 1951, 1976, and 1989. The present study uses data from three of the schools in the C&B population for the entering class of 1989—the graduating class of 1993. Institutional data in College and Beyond provide information on the students' grades, major, race, gender, and so on. These data were combined with housing information extracted from college phonebooks to form a unique data set that allowed us to identify college roommates.

The schools selected for our subsample were chosen because (1) they house their first year students together, and (2) the assignment mechanism of students to rooms (as indicated by their housing descriptions on the World Wide Web and conversations with their housing offices) seems roughly random. It was necessary to use schools that group first-year students together because the C&B data do not provide information on other classes. If, for example, a school allowed first- and second-year students to live together, we would have no information on the second-year students given C&B's restriction to the three cohorts. Selection bias, as previously noted, can be serious when students are allowed to choose their roommates or if the housing office groups students in such a way that under- or overperformers are more likely to be housed together. In this case, the requirement that the error term be uncorrelated with the explanatory variables would be violated. In Zimmerman's earlier study (1999) of Williams College's freshmen, he was able to utilize data from the housing application forms to conduct some relatively simple analyses to check whether the assumption of random assignment was plausible, and it was.[10] The schools in this sample employed a similar protocol to that used by Williams College in using housing forms indicating sleep preferences, smoking behavior, and so on in assigning students to rooms

---

10. Similarly, estimates in Sacerdote (2001) were unaffected by the inclusion of housing preference variables.

and roommates—though the underlying housing-form data were not obtained.[11]

9.9   Empirical Results

Table 9.2 provides summary statistics for the sample. The number of observations for the samples from each of the three schools ranged from 1,458 to 2,116. Individual SAT scores ranged from a low of 360 on the verbal test and 420 on the math test to a maximum of 800 on both tests. The average combined SAT score ranged from 1,344 to 1,409. These scores are high, putting the average student in the top 10 percent of the population of test takers. Each school had between 7 percent and 9 percent African-American students and 2 percent and 5 percent Hispanic students.

Table 9.3 presents estimates of equation (2). The results for each school are reported in a separate column where a student's cumulative GPA is regressed on his own SAT score (divided by 100), race, gender, major, and roommate's SAT score. The model includes controls for a student's major (which is selected in his or her junior year) to provide some control for grade differentials arising from students' taking different courses (Sabot 1991).

The effect of a student's own SAT score is large and statistically significant, with each 100 point increase resulting in between a 0.116 and a 0.132 increase in GPA. After controlling for SAT scores, black and Hispanic students score between one-quarter and one-third of a grade point below white students. Female students score between 0.082 and 0.127 grade points higher than male students. Finally, a roommate's SAT score is found to have a positive and statistically significant effect only for school 2—where a 100 point increase in a student's roommate's combined SAT score translates into a 0.02 increase in the student's own GPA. This effect is about 17 percent as large as that of a 100 point increment in the student's own SAT score.[12]

Tables 9.4 through 9.6 report estimates of equation (3), allowing the peer effect to depend on the student's own position in the SAT distribution. The top sections of tables 9.4 through 9.6 allow us to see whether weak, average, or strong students (as measured by their SAT scores) are more or less

11. See Zimmerman (forthcoming) for a mathematical model that illustrates the possibility of bias in the estimated peer effects flowing from the use of housing forms in assigning students to rooms. Chi-squared tests indicate that we cannot reject independence between the SAT scores of roommates for schools 1 and 3 in the sample. For school 2, independence is rejected. The rejection is driven by a somewhat high fraction of low-SAT students living together and a somewhat low fraction of low-SAT students living with high-SAT students. The distribution of low, medium, and high students is as expected under independence for the middle-SAT students. In total, there are about 100 of the 2,116 students that show signs of selection.

12. It is worth noting here that models allowing for differential effects for math and verbal SAT scores were also estimated, but standard F-tests indicated no measurable difference in their impact. Accordingly, only models using combined SAT scores are reported.

Table 9.2   Descriptive Statistics

	Mean	Standard Deviation	Minimum	Maximum
School 1				
Sample size	1,863	0	1,863	1,863
Own SAT score—verbal	714	66	420	800
Own SAT score—math	695	69	480	800
Own SAT score—combined	1409	112	1090	1600
Black	.079	.270	0	1
Hispanic	.052	.223	0	1
Native American	.004	.069	0	1
Asian	.151	.358	0	1
Not a citizen of the United States	.03	.169	0	1
Female	.432	.495	0	1
School 2	.430	.494	0	1
Sample size	2,116	0	2,116	2,116
Own SAT score—verbal	668	68	360	800
Own SAT score—math	676	68	450	800
Own SAT score—combined	1344	110	950	1600
Black	.086	.282	0	1
Hispanic	.044	.206	0	1
Native American	n.a.	n.a.	n.a.	n.a.
Asian	.160	.367	0	1
Not a citizen of the United States	.095	.292	0	1
Female	.430	.494	0	1
School 3				
Sample size	1,458	0	1,458	1,458
Own SAT score—verbal	687	61	450	800
Own SAT score—math	681	68	420	800
Own SAT score—combined	1368	106	880	1600
Black	.072	.258	0	1
Hispanic	.022	.148	0	1
Native American	.001	.036	0	1
Asian	.079	.270	0	1
Not a citizen of the United States	.03	.148	0	1
Female	.466	.499	0	1

Note: n.a. = not available.

affected by roommates. The results in these panels suggest that strong students at all three schools are unaffected by the SAT scores of their roommates. Students in the bottom 15 percent of the SAT distribution benefit from higher SAT scoring roommates at school 1—though not at schools 2 and 3. Students in the middle 70 percent of the distribution are unaffected by the SAT scores of their roommates at schools 1 and 3—though they benefit from higher-scoring roommates at school 2. Students in the middle 70 percent of the SAT distribution at school 2 experience, on average, a 0.02 increase in their cumulative GPA when their roommates' SAT scores increase by 100 points.

The bottom sections of tables 9.4 through 9.6 allow the peer effect to be

Table 9.3   **Your Grades and Your Roommate's SAT Scores**

	Cumulative GPA (School 1)	Cumulative GPA (School 2)	Cumulative GPA (School 3)
Own SAT score/100	0.131*	.116*	.132*
	(0.01)*	(.013)*	(.012)*
Black	−.264	−.306	−.380
	(.068)	(.060)	(.054)
Hispanic	−.172	−.080	.005
	(.085)	(.055)	(.046)
Native American	−.268	n.a.	.145
	(.157)		(.071)
Not a citizen of the United States	n.a.	−.047	n.a.
		(.065)	
Asian	−.011	−.071	−.033
	(.031)	(.031)	(.042)
Female	.127	.082	.112
	(.028)	(.024)	(.024)
Major dummy variables	Yes	Yes	Yes
Roommate's SAT score/100	0.013	0.020*	.013
	(0.007)	(0.008)*	(.009)
Sample size	1,863	2,116	1,458
R^2	.303	0.215	0.2475

Note: Standard errors (in parentheses) are corrected for correlation within roommate cluster.
n.a. = not available.
*Significant at the 10 percent level.

nonlinear. That is, it allows us to see whether weak, average, or strong students (as measured by their SAT scores) are more or less affected by having roommates who are weak, average, or strong in terms of their combined SAT scores. For this model, at school 1 we find low-SAT students performing somewhat worse when roomed with a similarly weak peer. The coefficient shows grades for this group would increase by 0.156 points if they had a high-SAT roommate. The coefficient is significant at the 10 percent level. At school 2, neither the strongest nor the weakest students are affected by the SAT scores of their roommates. Students in the middle 70 percent of the SAT distribution, however, perform somewhat worse when their roommates are in the bottom 15 percent of the SAT distribution. The estimates suggest that a student with a bottom 15 percent roommate in this part of the SAT distribution would, on average, have a cumulative GPA that is lower by 0.086 points than that of a similar student whose roommate was in the top 15 percent of the SAT distribution. Similar results are found at school 3 where, in addition, there is evidence that the strongest students perform better when their roommates are academically stronger. It is worth noting that these results are robust to moderate variations in the percentile cutoffs used to define the groups.

Tables 9.7 through 9.9 report estimates of equation (3) separately for

Table 9.4   **Your Grades and Your Roommate's SAT Scores by SAT Group: School 1 (dependent variable is cumulative GPA)**

	Combined SAT Score (lowest 15%)	Combined SAT Score (middle 70%)	Combined SAT Score (top 15%)
A. Linearity in Roommate's Scores			
Own SAT score—verbal/100	.065	.223*	.036
	(.087)	(.029)*	(.124)
Own SAT score—math/100	.024	.172*	.124
	(.127)	(.033)	(.148)
Black	−.174	−.297	−.758
	(.186)	(.079)	(.165)
Hispanic	.0402	−.311	−.024
	(.086)	(.142)	(.116)
Native American	−.045	−.356	(dropped)
	(.160)	(.251)	
Not a citizen of the United States	n.a.	n.a.	n.a.
Asian	.226	−.004	−.040
	(.230)	(.039)	(.052)
Female	.233	.138	.012
	(.110)	(.032)	(.056)
Major dummy variables	Yes	Yes	Yes
Roommate's SAT score/100	.032*	.011	−.009
	(.010)*	(.008)	(.014)
Sample size	269	1,281	313
R^2	.0288	0.295	0.154
B. Nonlinearity in Roommate's Scores			
Own SAT score—verbal/100	.060	.223*	.021
	(.089)	(.02856)*	(.125)
Own SAT score—math/100	.021	.172*	.100
	(.128)	(.033)*	(.151)
Black	−.175	−.297	−.805
	(.183)	(.079)	(.163)
Hispanic	.043	−.312	−.022
	(.086)	(.141)	(.114)
Native American	−.075	−.352	(dropped)
	(.169)	(.251)	
Not a citizen of the United States	n.a.	n.a.	n.a.
Asian	.233	−.004	−.039
	(.231)	(.039)	(.051)
Female	.220	.137	.022
	(.110)	(.032)	(.051)
Major dummy variables	Yes	Yes	Yes
Roommate's SAT score—lowest 15%	−.156*	−.044	−.002
	(.086)	(.032)	(.050)
Roommate's SAT score—middle 70%	−.131	−.023	−.038
	(.086)	(.025)	(.043)
Sample size	269	1,281	313
R^2	0.295	0.295	0.154

Note: Standard errors (in parentheses) are corrected for correlation within roommate cluster. n.a. = not available.

*Significant at the 10 percent level.

Table 9.5 **Your Grades and Your Roommate's SAT Scores by SAT Group: School 2**
(dependent variable is cumulative GPA)

	Combined SAT Score (lowest 15%)	Combined SAT Score (middle 70%)	Combined SAT Score (top 15%)
A. Linearity in Roommate's Scores			
Own SAT score—verbal/100	.162	.142*	−.109
	(.088)	(.025)*	(.098)
Own SAT score—math/100	.077	.166*	.063
	(.101)	(.027)*	(.112)
Black	−.235	−.341	−.117
	(.079)	(.085)	(.160)
Hispanic	−.036	−.060	−.071
	(.127)	(.070)	(.095)
Native American	n.a.	n.a.	n.a.
Not a citizen of the United States	−.204	−.016	.026
	(.243)	(.079)	(.065)
Asian	.102	−.083	−.111
	(.145)	(.033)	(.081)
Female	.067	.099	−.109
	(.077)	(.026)	(.129)
Major dummy variables	Yes	Yes	Yes
Roommate's SAT score/100	.017	.020*	.0438
	(.021)	(.009)*	(.026)
Sample size	280	1,500	336
R^2	0.286	0.181	0.178
B. Nonlinearity in Roommate's Scores			
Own SAT score—verbal/100	.167	.143*	−.110
	(.088)	(.025)*	(.098)
Own SAT score—math/100	.088	.166*	.059
	(.100)	(.027)*	(.111)
Black	−.238	−.340	−.086
	(.079)	(.085)	(.168)
Hispanic	−.035	−.050	−0.05
	(.127)	(.069)	(.102)
Native American	n.a.	n.a.	n.a.
Not a citizen of the United States	−.174	−.009	−.109
	(.242)	(.078)	(.128)
Asian	.108	−.082	−.110
	(.142)	(.033)	(.081)
Female	.061	.102	.015
	(.077)	(.026)	(.064)
Major dummy variables	Yes	Yes	Yes
Roommate's SAT score—lowest 15%	−.042	−.086*	−.099
	(.088)	(.034)*	(.102)
Roommate's SAT score—middle 70%	−.066	−.022	−.079
	(.072)	(.023)	(.057)
Sample size	282	1,505	337
R^2	0.286	0.181	0.172

Note: Standard errors (in parentheses) are corrected for correlation within roommate cluster.
Significant at the 10 percent level.

Table 9.6   **Your Grades and Your Roommate's SAT Scores by SAT Group: School 3 (dependent variable is cumulative GPA)**

	Combined SAT Score (lowest 15%)	Combined SAT Score (middle 70%)	Combined SAT Score (top 15%)
A. Linearity in Roommate's Scores			
Own SAT score—verbal/100	.214*	.114*	.183
	(.061)*	(.032)*	(.085)
Own SAT score—math/100	.146*	.101*	.236
	(.065)*	(.031)*	(.106)
Black	−.309	−.498	−.186
	(.082)	(.112)	(.076)
Hispanic	.028	−.021	.191
	(.086)	(.064)	(.131)
Native American	(dropped)	.120	(dropped)
		(.087)	
Not a citizen of the United States	n.a.	n.a.	n.a.
Asian	.310	−.097	.045
	(.164)	(.049)	(.090)
Female	.108	.088	.122
	(.078)	(.030)	(.068)
Major dummy variables	Yes	Yes	Yes
Roommate's SAT score/100	−.016	.019	.036
	(.025)	(.011)	(.026)
Sample size	221	975	262
R^2	0.3560	(0.1151)	0.1215
B. Nonlinearity in Roommate's Scores			
Own SAT score—verbal/100	.207*	.114*	.186*
	(.056)*	(.032)*	(.083)*
Own SAT score—math/100	.148*	.100*	.238*
	(.065)*	(.031)*	(.102)*
Black	−.303	−.498	−.145
	(.078)	(.111)	(.079)
Hispanic	.031	−.014	.193
	(.082)	(.059)	(.116)
Native American	(dropped)	.110	(dropped)
		(.085)	
Not a citizen of the United States	n.a.	n.a.	n.a.
Asian	.314	−.094	.058
	(.165)	(.049)	(.090)
Female	.110	.090	.139
	(.078)	(.030)	(.066)
Major dummy variables	Yes	Yes	Yes
Roommate's SAT score—lowest 15%	.069	−.092*	−.175*
	(.096)	(.041)*	(.077)*
Roommate's SAT score—middle 70%	.004	−.038	−.127*
	(.081)	(.031)	(.061)*
Sample size	223	981	263
R^2	0.3585	0.1173	0.1377

Note: Standard errors (in parentheses) are corrected for correlation within roommate cluster.
*Significant at the 10 percent level.

Table 9.7   **Your Grades and Your Roommate's SAT Scores by SAT Group and Gender: School 1 (dependent variable is cumulative GPA)**

	Combined SAT Score (lowest 15%)	Combined SAT Score (middle 70%)	Combined SAT Score (top 15%)
	A. Men		
Own SAT score—verbal/100	.048	.266*	−.006
	(.108)	(.034)*	(.172)
Own SAT score—math/100	.113	.163*	−.002
	(.122)	(.043)*	(.002)
Black	.041	−.438	−.817
	(.124)	(.132)	(.206)
Hispanic	.067	−.128	.006
	(.096)	(.134)	(.091)
Native American	(dropped)	−.717	(dropped)
		(.254)	
Not a citizen of the United States	n.a.	n.a.	n.a.
Asian	.926	.039	−.075
	(.220)	(.056)	(.112)
Major dummy variables	Yes	Yes	Yes
Roommate's SAT score—lowest 15%	−.167	−.054	.078
	(.117)	(.046)	(.060)
Roommate's SAT score—middle 70%	−.108	−.042	−.022
	(.088)	(.035)	(.033)
Sample size	137	739	187
R^2	0.637	0.323	0.309
	B. Women		
Own SAT score—verbal/100	.117	.187*	−.101
	(.166)	(.057)*	(.182)
Own SAT score—math/100	−.062	.192*	.095
	(.200)	(.046)*	(.227)
Black	−.436	−.228	(dropped)
	(.347)	(.085)	
Hispanic	−.057	−.474	(dropped)
	(.161)	(.251)	
Native American	−.242	−.064	(dropped)
	(.185)	(.130)	
Not a citizen of the United States	n.a.	n.a.	n.a.
Asian	.105	−.073	−.040
	(.149)	(.052)	(.086)
Major dummy variables	Yes	Yes	Yes
Roommate's SAT score—lowest 15%	−.104	−.026	−.020
	(.124)	(.040)	(.084)
Roommate's SAT score—middle 70%	−.143	−.006	.028
	(.124)	(.034)	(.101)
Sample size	132	543	128
R^2	0.279	0.325	0.441

Note: Standard errors (in parentheses) are corrected for correlation within roommate cluster.
*Significant at the 10 percent level.

Table 9.8 **Your Grades and Your Roommate's SAT Scores by SAT Group and Gender: School 2 (dependent variable is cumulative GPA)**

	Combined SAT Score (lowest 15%)	Combined SAT Score (middle 70%)	Combined SAT Score (top 15%)
A. Men			
Own SAT score—verbal/100	.230	.194*	−.164
	(.166)	(.034)*	(.114)
Own SAT score—math/100	.105	.212*	.038
	(.165)	(.038)*	(.127)
Black	−.239	−.281	(dropped)
	(.187)	(.131)	
Hispanic	−.134	.055	−.087
	(.233)	(.077)	(.112)
Native American	n.a.	n.a.	n.a.
Not a citizen of the United States	−.068	.027	−.163
	(.377)	(.093)	(.141)
Asian	.188	−.053	−.166
	(.270)	(.048)	(.112)
Major dummy variables	Yes	Yes	Yes
Roommate's SAT score—lowest 15%	−.132	−.132*	−.092
	(.194)	(.056)*	(.121)
Roommate's SAT score—middle 70%	−.093	−.036	−.082
	(.109)	(.029)	(.068)
Sample size	110	839	245
R^2	0.258	0.209	0.238
B. Women			
Own SAT score—verbal/100	.126	.074	.093
	(.094)	(.041)	(.179)
Own SAT score—math/100	.165	.118*	.119
	(.123)	(.040)*	(.269)
Black	−.226	−.375	−.477
	(.083)	(.113)	(.166)
Hispanic	.046	−.273	(dropped)
	(.124)	(.116)	
Native American	n.a.	n.a.	n.a.
Not a citizen of the United States	−.358	−.087	(dropped)
	(.403)	(.070)	
Asian	.030	−.102	−.065
	(.133)	(.048)	(.145)
Major dummy variables	Yes	Yes	Yes
Roommate's SAT score—lowest 15%	.102	−.014	.139
	(.112)	(.043)	(.129)
Roommate's SAT score—middle 70%	.072	.022	−.018
	(.095)	(.036)	(.080)
Sample size	172	666	92
R^2	0.439	0.204	0.209

Note: Standard errors (in parentheses) are corrected for correlation within roommate cluster.
*Significant at the 10 percent level.

Table 9.9   **Your Grades and Your Roommate's SAT Scores by SAT Group and Gender: School 3 (dependent variable is cumulative GPA)**

	Combined SAT Score (lowest 15%)	Combined SAT Score (middle 70%)	Combined SAT Score (top 15%)
	A. Men		
Own SAT score—verbal/100	.079	.136*	.154
	(.073)	(.048)*	(.099)
Own SAT score—math/100	.255*	.174*	.176
	(.105)*	(.049)*	(.134)
Black	−.261	−.632	−.077
	(.151)	(.159)	(.077)
Hispanic	.006	−.170	.112
	(.124)	(.087)	(.170)
Native American	(dropped)	.043	(dropped)
		(.088)	
Not a citizen of the United States	n.a.	n.a.	n.a.
Asian	.236	−.158	−.008
	(.219)	(.071)	(.105)
Major dummy variables	Yes	Yes	Yes
Roommate's SAT score—lowest 15%	.161	−.085	−.107
	(.120)	(.069)	(.093)
Roommate's SAT score—middle 70%	.105	−.063	−.107
	(.112)	(.045)	(.063)
Sample size	104	464	204
R^2	0.4625	0.1634	0.1396
	B. Women		
Own SAT score—verbal/100	.292*	.110*	.460*
	(.081)*	(.044)*	(.127)*
Own SAT score—math/100	.200*	.031	.350*
	(.098)*	(.039)	(.123)*
Black	−.192	−.377	−.335
	(.107)	(.135)	(.055)
Hispanic	.0190	.070	.429
	(.145)	(.073)	(.233)
Native American	(dropped)	(dropped)	(dropped)
Not a citizen of the United States	n.a.	n.a.	n.a.
Asian	.128	−.050	.212
	(.150)	(.072)	(.084)
Major dummy variables	Yes	Yes	Yes
Roommate's SAT score—lowest 15%	.018	−.059	−.266*
	(.179)	(.048)	(.133)*
Roommate's SAT score—middle 70%	−.124	.003	−.149*
	(.114)	(.039)	(.076)*
Sample size	119	517	59
R^2	0.4546	0.1172	0.6660

Note: Standard errors (in parentheses) are corrected for correlation within roommate cluster.
*Significant at the 10 percent level.

Table 9.10   Peer Coefficients from Stacked Data for All Three Schools (dependent variable is cumulative GPA)

	Combined SAT Score (lowest 15%)	Combined SAT Score (middle 70%)	Combined SAT Score (top 15%)
Men and women			
Roommate's SAT score—lowest 15%	−.070	−.067*	−.063
	(.057)	(.021)*	(.044)
Roommate's SAT score—middle 70%	−.073	−.029*	−.066*
	(.050)	(.015)*	(.030)*
Men			
Roommate's SAT score—lowest 15%	−.004	−.077*	−.029
	(.088)	(.031)*	(.062)
Roommate's SAT score—middle 70%	−.042	−.044*	−.067*
	(.068)	(.020)*	(.035)*
Women			
Roommate's SAT score—lowest 15%	−.091	−.036	−.062
	(.075)	(.027)	(.057)
Roommate's SAT score—middle 70%	−.101	.006	−.021
	(.078)	(.022)	(.055)

Notes: Other controls are own SAT scores, gender, ethnicity, major, and school fixed effect. Standard errors are in parentheses.
*Significant at the 10 percent level.

men and women. Perhaps due to smaller sample sizes, peer effects are not statistically significant for most groups. Exceptions are found at schools 2 and 3. At school 2, male students in the middle of the SAT distribution are found to perform worse when their roommate is in the lowest 15 percent of the SAT distribution; at school 3, academically strong women perform better when given academically strong peers.

Table 9.10 presents estimates using data stacked for the three schools. School fixed effects are included in these models. The main advantage of stacking the data is that there are larger cell sizes—giving us more precise estimates—with which to gauge any nonlinearities. These results are presented pooled by gender and also separately for male and female students. The results mirror the foregoing ones with students in the middle showing lower grades if their roommate is in the bottom 15 percent of the SAT distribution. The estimates suggest that this result is driven by the male sample as the coefficients for women are not significant for any of the SAT groups. There is also some evidence—again particularly for men—that strong students perform somewhat worse if their roommate is in the middle of the SAT distribution rather than in the top.

To put the myriad results in context it is useful to summarize the existing research more succinctly. The research to date, including the evidence re-

Table 9.11   **Recent Students of Academic Peer Effects**

Study	Peer Characteristic	Coefficient on Grades	Comments
Zimmerman (1999)	Roommate's verbal SAT in bottom 15%	−.077 (.027)	Impact on middle 70% of SAT distribution, Williams College.
Zimmerman (as reported in this chapter)	Roommate's verbal SAT in bottom 15%	−.086 (.034)	Impact on middle 70% of SAT distribution, three schools from College and Beyond.
Sacerdote (2001)	Roommate in top 25% of Academic Rating Index	.060 (.028)	Dartmouth. Controls for housing questions. Also peer effect on fraternity membership but none on major.
Steinbrickner and Stinebrickner (2001)	ACT score	.001 (.004)	Controls for roommate's family income. Roommate income is significant with grades, rising .052 per $10,000 income, for women.
Goethals (2000)	Admissions office academic rating	n.a.	Finds performance increases with group homogeneity in academic rating.

Notes: Coefficient on grades data taken from table 4 in Zimmerman (1999), table 3 in Sacerdote (2001), table 3 in Stinebrickner and Stinebrickner (2000), and tables 9.5 and 9.10 in this chapter. Standard errors are in parentheses. n.a. = not available.

ported in this paper, on the effect of peer academic characteristics on a "grade type" outcome is summarized in table 9.11.

These studies differ in a variety of ways: the selectivity of the school surveyed, the measurement and detection of nonlinearities, the outcome considered, the existence of differences by gender, and so on. The evidence found thus far suggests that the existence of peer effects at the most basic level has been confirmed in each of the studies. Sacerdote (2001) finds that grades are higher when students have unusually academically strong roommates. Zimmerman (1999, 2003) finds that weak peers might reduce the grades of middling or strong students. Stinebrickner finds that peer ACT scores are insignificant after controlling for roommate's family income, which is significant. Goethals (2001) finds that homogeneity per se matters—students perform better when grouped with others of like ability.

Additional studies using data closer to the ideal described previously would certainly be useful. Most of the results, thus far, pertain to highly selective institutions. Data from multiple, more diverse, and more representative schools would provide greater variation in the variety of differing academic peer environments we observe and, thus, a chance to better evaluate the impact of peers across the spectrum of student abilities. In short, such data would enable us to better estimate the functional form relating outcomes, peer characteristics and behaviors, and their interactions.

9.10   Conclusion and Implications

Evidence on peer effects in higher education now exists at the most basic level for six colleges and universities—covering some 12,000 students (across published studies)—with interactions measured for randomly assigned roommates and participants in psych lab experiments. It seems clear that peer effects exist—students' characteristics and behavior do, indeed, influence other students' behavior with conventionally measured academic characteristics (like SAT) influencing conventionally measured academic performance (like GPA). New evidence presented in this chapter adds to our confidence that peer effects exist and that the signs of those effects are in the direction that would motivate institutional selectivity—strong students tend to increase peers' academic performance, and weak students tend to reduce it. Combined with a sharply skewed distribution of resources across colleges, the broad question "Can peer effects in educational production help explain the unusual economic structure and behavior of higher education?" is answered "Yes." The models of Winston (1999) and Epple, Romano, and Sieg (2001)—data-driven and formally derived, respectively—fit both the data and the peer effect evidence.[13]

But beyond that key question, the facts become less clear, and the agenda for investigation of peer effects becomes larger. So there are often different results by gender, as in Hoxby's (2000) K–12 results, even in these data that rest on individual interactions rather than on those between groups. On nonlinearities—whether peer influences operate equally and symmetrically across characteristics and behaviors—the evidence is puzzling, with strong or weak homogeneous groupings sometimes performing significantly better than those with peers of different abilities. Students of middling ability are usually more susceptible to peer influence than those at either end of the ability distribution (keeping in mind that the student populations reported on here represent very narrow ability ranges). And because our data are based on pairwise interactions, a similar analysis might well be extended to those interactions that are electronically mediated to see if a "distance learning" environment generates any evidence of peer effects.

---

13. Note that there is no evidence of a "teaching effect" in which strong students gain from association with weaker students whom they can teach (as implied by Zajonc's [1976] analysis of older siblings) nor is there strong evidence of an "intimidation effect," though that might help explain Goethals' (2001) finding that weak students do better when grouped with other weak students.

The range of peer characteristics and behaviors should be extended, too, wherever possible. The work reported here sticks, by and large, to the most measurable and obvious aspects of education—grade performance and academic ability—with occasional departure into fraternity membership, family income, and dropout behavior. But while these are clearly the right place to start, they capture a small part of the behaviors influenced by higher education and of interest to colleges in their selection of student peer quality—it may be possible to get closer to our "ideal data" with other measurable academic behaviors among randomly associated peers. Like Heckman (1999), Bowles, Gintis, and Osborn (2001) point out that a small part of the variance in wages attributable to education is explained by the cognitive skills we measure with tests and GPAs—the rest is attributable to behaviors learned before, after, in, and outside of school that may escape cognitive measurement but influence job performance, nonetheless, like reliability, attitude, discipline, fatalism, impatience, and so on. To the extent that these characteristics and behaviors can be identified and measured, they need to be included in studies of peer effects in higher education.[14]

So we conclude that evidence on the existence of peer effects in higher education is strong, consistent with an understanding of its economic structure—selectivity, skewed resources, and the resulting stratification—that relies on them, but that there remains a rich set of questions on how and how broadly peer effects operate among students in colleges[15] and especially on the shape of the nonlinearities that would help us evaluate that structure.

References

Akerlof, G. A., and J. L. Yellen. 1986. Introduction. *Efficiency wage models of the labor market.* Cambridge: Cambridge University Press.

Avery, C., A. Fairbanks, and R. Zeckhauser. 2001. What worms for the early bird? Early admissions at selective colleges. Faculty Research Working Paper Series no. RWP 01-049. Harvard University, Kennedy School of Government.

Bowles, S., H. Gintis, and M. Osborn. 2001. The determinants of earnings: A behavioral approach. *Journal of Economic Literature* 39 (4): 1137–176.

14. On the basis of evidence that a student's impatience (his time-discount behavior) influences his own academic performance (students with lower discount rates get better grades, holding SATs constant (Kirby, Winston et al. 2002), we tried, in a very small sample, to find evidence of peer influence such that one roommate's discount rate affected the other's academic performance. But while the sign of the relationship was right, it was decidedly insignificant.

15. Our discussion has not even touched on negative peer effects like binge drinking and date rape.

Clotfelter, C. T. 1996. *Buying the best: Cost escalation in elite higher education.* Princeton, N.J.: Princeton University Press.

Coleman, J. S., E. Q. Campbell, C. F. Hobson, J. McPartland, A. M. Mood, F. D. Weinfeld, and R. L. York. 1966. *Equality of educational opportunity.* Washington, D.C.: Office of Education, U.S. Department of Health, Education, and Welfare.

Epple, D., and R. E. Romano. 1998. Competition between private and public schools, vouchers, and peer-group effects. *American Economic Review* 88 (1): 33–62.

Epple, D., R. E. Romano, and H. Sieg. 2001. Peer effects, financial aid, and selection of students into colleges and universities: An empirical analysis. Working Paper no. 00-02. Duke University, Department of Economics.

Fallows, J. 2001. The early-decision racket. *The Atlantic Monthly* 288 (2): 37–52.

Goethals, G. R. 2001. Peer effects, gender and intellectual performance among students at a highly selective college: A social comparison of abilities analysis. Williamstown, Mass.: The Williams Project on the Economics of Higher Education.

Hansmann, H. 1980. The role of nonprofit enterprise. *The Yale Law Journal* 89 (5): 835–901.

Hanushek, E. 1986. The economics of schooling: Production and efficiency in public schools. *Journal of Economic Literature* 24 (3): 1141–1177.

Heckman, J. J. 1999. Doing it right: Job training and education. *Public Interest* (Spring): 86–109.

Hoxby, C. M. 2000. Peer effects in the classroom: Learning from gender and race variation. NBER Working Paper no. 7867. Cambridge, Mass.: National Bureau of Economic Research.

James, E. 1978. Product mix and cost disaggregation: A reinterpretation of the economics of higher education. *Journal of Human Resources* 12 (2): 157–186.

———. 1990. Decision processes and priorities in higher education. *The Economics of American Universities,* ed. S. A. Hoenack and E. L. Collins, 77–106. Buffalo: State University of New York Press.

Kennedy, D. 1997. *Academic duty.* Cambridge, Mass.: Harvard University Press.

Kirby, K. N., G. C. Winston, and M. Santiesteban. 2002. Impatience and grades: Delay-discount rates correlate negatively with college GPA. Williamstown, Mass.: The Williams Project on the Economics of Higher Education.

Lazear, E. P. 1999. Educational production. NBER Working Paper no. 7349. Cambridge, Mass.: National Bureau of Economic Research.

Lemann, N. 1999a. *The big test: The secret history of the American meritocracy.* New York: Ferrar, Straus & Giroux.

———. 1999b. The kids in the conference room: How McKinsey & Company became the next big step. *The New Yorker,* October 18 and 25, 209–216.

Manski, C. F., and D. A. Wise. 1983. *College choice in America.* Cambridge, Mass.: Harvard University Press.

McPherson, M. S., and M. O. Schapiro. 1990. Selective admission and the public interest. New York: The College Board Press.

Robertson, D., and J. Symons. 1996. Do peer groups matter? Peer group versus schooling effects on academic attainment. London School of Economics Centre for Economic Performance Discussion Paper.

Rosovsky, H. 1990. *The university: An owner's manual.* New York: W. W. Norton.

Rothschild, M., and L. J. White. 1995. The analytics of pricing in higher education and other services in which customers are inputs. *Journal of Political Economy* 103 (3): 573–586.

Sabot, R., and J. Wakeman-Linn. 1991. The implications of grading policies for student course choice. *Journal of Economic Perspectives* 5 (1): 159–170.

Sacerdote, B. 2001. Peer effects with random assignment: Results for Dartmouth roommates. *Quarterly Journal of Economics* 116 (2): 681–704.

Shulman, J. L., and William G. Bowen. 2001. *The game of life: College sports and educational values.* Princeton, N.J.: Princeton University Press.

Stinebrickner, T. R., and R. Stinebrickner. 2000. Peer effects among students from disadvantaged backgrounds. Working Paper Series no. 2001-3. University of Western Ontario, Department of Economics.

Summers, A. A., and B. L. Wolfe. 1977. Do schools make a difference? *American Economic Review* 67 (4): 639–652.

Swann v. Charlotte-Mecklenburg Board of Education, 402 U.S. 1, U.S. Supreme Court (1971).

United States v. Brown University, F.3d 658:1993 U.S. App. LEXIS 23895, United States Court of Appeals for the Third District (1993).

Winston, G. C. 1999. Subsidies, hierarchy, and peers: The awkward economics of higher education. *Journal of Economic Perspectives* 13 (1): 13–36.

———. 2002. College prices, peer wages, and competition. Williamstown, Mass.: The Williams Project on the Economics of Higher Education.

———. 2003. Differentiation among U.S. colleges and universities. *Review of Industrial Organization.*

Winston, G. C., and Ivan C. Yen. 1995. Costs, prices, subsidies, and aid in U.S. higher education. Williamstown, Mass.: The Williams Project on the Economics of Higher Education.

Zajonc, R. B. 1976. Family configuration and intelligence. *Science* 192:227–236.

Zimmerman, D. J. 1999. Peer effects in academic outcomes: Evidence from a natural experiment. Williamstown, Mass.: The Williams Project on the Economics of Higher Education.

———. 2003. Peer effects in academic outcomes: Evidence from a natural experiment. *Review of Economics and Statistics* 85 (1): 9–23.

Comment   Thomas S. Dee

Gordon Winston and David Zimmerman motivate their chapter with a provocative outline of how several "awkward" features of higher education are difficult to understand from a conventional economic perspective on firm behavior (e.g., the screening and rebuking of customers, subsidizing accepted customers, requiring that customers live together). They go on to discuss how the existence of peer effects and other traits (i.e., nonprofit objectives and the role of donative resources) provide a coherent framework for understanding these institutional behaviors. In particular, the possibility that the quality of peers influences student achievement could help to explain both the sharp concentration of student ability in relatively few

Thomas S. Dee is assistant professor of economics at Swarthmore College, and a faculty research fellow at the National Bureau of Economic Research.

schools as well as the receipt of larger, implicit subsidies among those students. However, they acknowledge that establishing the existence and possibly heterogeneous pattern of peer effects is a notoriously difficult empirical problem. First and foremost, identifying the mere existence of peer effects with conventional data sets is complicated by the fact that students often choose their peers in response to their own unobserved determinants of achievement. Second, the policy implications of peer effects depend in large measure on the pattern of response heterogeneity (e.g., how peer effects vary for students of different backgrounds and for sharp changes in peer quality). The central focus of this chapter is on extending and discussing the recent developments with regard to both of these empirical issues.

Specifically, Winston and Zimmerman use student-level data from three schools in the College and Beyond (C&B) data to evaluate the effect of peer quality (as measured by the SAT scores of freshman roommates) on cumulative GPA. The central contribution of this approach, which has also been adopted in other recent studies (Sacerdote 2001; Zimmerman 2003), is both novel and important. By relying on the putatively random assignment of freshman roommates, this research design may eliminate the confounding biases in estimated peer effects. Like the related studies, their results suggest the existence of peer effects, at least for students who did not have low SAT scores themselves. However, there are at least two reasons to interpret these new estimates with some degree of caution. First, the case for roommate assignments at these schools being completely random is not as clear as in the earlier studies. Second, the sizes of the estimated effects seem suspiciously large given that the dependent variable is cumulative, not freshman, GPA. Sacerdote (2001) found that freshman roommates had similarly sized effects only on freshman, not senior, GPA. Some lack of persistence in these effects seems reasonable since student interaction with freshman roommates is often limited and relatively short term.

Nonetheless, in conjunction with the studies by Sacerdote (2001) and Zimmerman (2003), the new empirical results presented here constitute a compelling case for the existence of some peer group effects in higher education. But, while that is a meaningful statement, it is not clear that the available evidence supports any further conclusions. For example, Winston and Zimmerman note that the weak statistical power implied by the available data make it difficult to ascertain how peer effects might vary across students and peers of different backgrounds. Furthermore, even if these data did indicate certain response heterogeneities, their external validity would be unclear at best. The segmentation of students across colleges and universities implies that the students at these three elite schools have a relatively narrow range of ability. This clearly implies that these estimates may not speak to the policy-relevant question of how sharp changes in peer quality would influence student achievement.

There is also little evidence that the peer effects associated with freshman roommates extend to other peer environments (most notably, classrooms). While we might be tempted to assume that the existence of roommate effects implies the existence of peer effects in other settings, there are two reasons to proceed more cautiously. First, Sacerdote (2001) found that peers' effects on GPA occurred only at the roommate level, not at the dormitory or floor level. Second, the broader existence of peer effects, combined with the sharp segmentation of students across colleges by ability, would clearly imply that there is a substantial return to attending elite schools. However, the evidence on the returns to college selectivity is decidedly mixed (e.g., Hoxby 1998; Dale and Krueger 2002).

Given these limitations, Winston and Zimmerman are correct to stress that many important questions about peer effects remain unanswered. In particular, despite important recent additions to the available research, we do not yet have evidence that could be used to justify existing educational policies or advocate policy changes. Additionally, it is also not entirely clear that peer effects explain the segmented structure of higher education. Even if peer effects exist, parents, students, and college administrators may still respond more to perceptions of prestige. Instead, a major contribution of recent evidence like that in this chapter is to motivate and direct further research in this area. For example, one possibly fruitful direction would be to test for peer effects in other settings (e.g., college classrooms). This could be done in a convincing manner by exploiting institutional mechanisms that may generate plausibly exogenous assignments. Other useful evidence about the scope of peer effects should also come from applying similar research designs to less elite schools that are more integrated by prior student ability.

References

Dale, S. B., and A. B. Krueger. 2002. Estimating the payoff to attending a more selective college: An application of selection on observables and unobservables. *Quarterly Journal of Economics* 117 (4): 1491–527.

Hoxby, C. M. 1998. The return to attending a more selective college: 1960 to the present. Harvard University. Unpublished Manuscript. Available at [http://post.economics.harvard.edu/faculty/hoxby/papers/whole.pdf].

Sacerdote, B. 2001. Peer effects with random assignment: Results for Dartmouth roommates. *Quarterly Journal of Economics* 116 (2): 681–704.

Zimmerman, D. J. 2003. Peer effects in academic outcomes: Evidence from a natural experiment. *Review of Economics and Statistics* 85 (1): 9–23.

Contributors

Christopher Avery
Harvard University
John F. Kennedy School of
  Government
79 John F. Kennedy Street
Cambridge, MA 02138

Eric Bettinger
Weatherhead School of
  Management
Peter B. Lewis Building, RM 266
Case Western Reserve University
Cleveland, OH 44106-7235

Charles Clotfelter
Sanford Institute of Public Policy
Duke University
Durham, NC 27708-0245

Thomas S. Dee
Department of Economics
Swarthmore College
Swarthmore, PA 19081

Susan Dynarski
Kennedy School of Government
Harvard University
79 John F. Kennedy Street
Cambridge, MA 02138

Ronald G. Ehrenberg
ILR-Cornell University
Cornell Higher Education Research
  Institute
256 Ives Hall
Ithaca, NY 14853-3901

Jonathan Guryan
University of Chicago
Graduate School of Business
1101 East 58th Street
Chicago, IL 60637

Caroline M. Hoxby
Department of Economics
Harvard University
Cambridge, MA 02138

Thomas J. Kane
School of Public Policy and Social
  Research
University of California, Los Angeles
Los Angeles, CA 90095-1656

Bridget Terry Long
Graduate School of Education
Harvard University
Appian Way
Cambridge, MA 02138

Jennifer Ma
TIAA-CREF Institute
730 Third Avenue, 24th Floor
New York, NY 10017-3206

Michael McPherson
The Spencer Foundation
875 North Michigan Avenue
Suite 3930
Chicago, IL 60611-1803

Michael J. Rizzo
Cornell Higher Education Research
    Institute
270 Ives Hall
Ithaca, NY 14853

Harvey S. Rosen
Department of Economics
Fisher Hall
Princeton University
Princeton, NJ 08544-1021

Michael Rothschild
Woodrow Wilson School of Public and
    International Affairs
Princeton University
Princeton, NJ 08544-1013

Bruce Sacerdote
6106 Rockefeller Hall
Department of Economics
Dartmouth College
Hanover, NH 03755-3514

Christopher Taber
Department of Economics
Northwestern University
2003 Sheridan Road
Evanston, IL 60208

Sarah E. Turner
Department of Economics
University of Virginia
Charlottesville, VA 22904-4182

Michelle J. White
Department of Economics
University of California, San Diego
La Jolla, CA 92093-0508

Gordon C. Winston
Department of Economics
Fernald House
Williams College
Williamstown, MA 01267

David J. Zimmerman
Department of Economics
Fernald House
Williams College
Williamstown, MA 01267

Author Index

Subject Index